HUMAN RESOURCE DEVELOPMENT

(Text and Cases)

For MBA, PGDBA, MHRM, and Other Management Programmes

Dr. Ram Kumar Balyan

B.E., M.B.A., M.P.M., P.G.D.B.A., P.G.D.A.M., M.A., L.L.B., D.C.A., M.A.I.M.A., & Ph.D.

Director

Advent Institute of Management Studies, Udaipur,
Affiliated to Rajasthan Technical University.

Former Director & Dean

Institute of Business Management and Research,
Ahmedabad - 380054.

Former Director GIMS, Rajkot, Gujarat.

&

President

National HRD Network, Ahmedabad Chapter

Suman Balyan

B.Sc. MBA (HR Specialization), Ph.D. (Pursuing)
KSV, University, Gandhinagar, Gujarat.
HR Professional & Visiting Faculty.

Himalaya Publishing House

ISO 9001:2015 CERTIFIED

First Edition : 2012
Edition : 2016
Edition : 2024
Edition : 2025

Published by : Mrs. Meena Pandey
for **HIMALAYA PUBLISHING HOUSE PVT. LTD.,**
Vishal Industrial Estate, 1st Floor, Office No. 63/64,
Bhandup Village Road, Subhash Nagar (Opp. CEAT Tyres),
Nahur (W), Mumbai - 400 078. **Phone:** 022-35131464/65/66/67
E-mail: himpub@bharatmail.co.in; **Website:** www.himpub.com

Branch Offices :

New Delhi : "Pooja Apartments", 4-B, Murari Lal Street, Ansari Road, Darya Ganj, New Delhi - 110 002. Phone: 011-23270392, 23278631; Fax: 011-23256286

Nagpur : Kundanlal Chandak Industrial Estate, Ghat Road, Nagpur - 440 018. Mobile: 09325409992, 09325908881

Bengaluru : Plot No. 91-33, 2nd Main Road, Seshadripuram, Behind Nataraja Theatre, Bengaluru - 560 020. Phone: 080-41138821; Mobile: 09379847017, 09379847005

Hyderabad : No. 3-4-184, Lingampally, Besides Raghavendra Swamy Matham, Kachiguda, Hyderabad - 500 027. Phone: 040-27560041, 27550139

Chennai : No. 34/44, Motilal Street, T. Nagar, Chennai - 600 017. Mobile: 09380460419

Pune : "Laksha" Apartment, First Floor, No. 527, Mehunpura, Shaniwarpeth (Near Prabhat Theatre), Pune - 411 030. Phone: 020-24496323, 24496333; Mobile: 09370579333

Cuttack : Plot No. 5F-755/4, Sector-9, CDA Markat Nagar, Cuttack - 753 014, Odisha. Mobile: 09338746007

Kolkata : 3, S.M. Bose Road, Near Gate No. 5, Agarpara Railway Station, North 24 Parganas, West Bengal - 700 109. Mobile: 09674536325

DTP by : HPH, Editorial Office, Bhandup. (Shilpa S)

Printed at : Geetanjali Press Pvt. Ltd., Nagpur. On behalf of HPH (P).

DEDICATION

This book is dedicated to the dearest person on this earth Smt. Harbai Devi Balyan, our beloved mother and grandmother respectively for her inspiration in life.

PREFACE

Every organization is established with certain objectives in present and past time. The efforts are put in different activities to achieve the predecided objectives. The objectives were not difficult to achieve in past due to stable business environment. In last few decades the global business has undergone drastic changes in social, cultural, legal, political, economy, physical, technological and competition areas. Management proposes and situation disposes in achieving the objectives. Organization performs its task with the help of resources as men, machine, materials and money. All are important in their places. Manpower is a live resource and others are non-living resources. It is manpower that uses other resources and generates them further. Manpower utilizes other resources and gives output. If manpower is not available or in short supply then other resources are underutilized or are useless and cannot produce as desired. Out of all the factors of production manpower has the highest priority and ignorance of human resource can prove to be disastrous. The human resource is critical and difficult to manage. It is because human behaviour is highly unpredictable. It differs not only from individual to individual but often on the part of some individual at different points of time. In spite of biological and cultural similarities, human beings not only differ in their appearance but also in their capabilities based on their background, training and experience. Human resource or a person at work is the most important component of the undertaking. Management cannot afford to ignore human resource at any cost. If done so, then management is inviting problems of its own for the organization.

According to nature of the business of the organization, various activities are performed. A marketing company would not be involved in production activities but would be involved in trading activities, The company involved in backward and forward integrated activities then it would be involved in production, marketing, finance, distribution, logistic, human resource and research activities. A large number of activities are performed by employees in such organizations depending upon the nature of the organization. All the different jobs are interrelated to achieve the targets. These are to be performed by the employees. They are supposed to give their best output so that they can contribute in achieving overall objectives of the organization. Their performance have great impact on the total production, sales, profit, progress and market shares, customers satisfaction and reputation of the organization in the global markets. Various factors like skills, training, motivation, dedication, welfare, management policies, fringe benefits, salary and packages, promotion, communication etc., are responsible to encourage the people to work sincerely and give their best output. The importance of employees' performance must be understood by the management and sincere efforts must be put in that direction. The management of the company taking timely steps in that direction will be in position to develop and motivate the people to do so. Finally the company may take the lead in the market and grab the opportunities available in the market.

Over and above, since last two decades, business environment is undergoing drastic changes and has become very uncertain and risky. It is very difficult to understand and predict about future. It has created a lot of challenges and opportunities for the company. The situation is beyond understanding and mistakes are likely to take place. If proper care is not taken then there are chances for risk and losses to the group. The organization may lose market shares, market position and lower profits or suffer losses. Further, the situation has become more critical due to high level of competition and rapidly changing technology. Organizations find difficulty in understanding the situation, nature of jobs, effects of situation and working on new technology. The employees raise their hand to handle such jobs in critical situation. There is requirement to understand the situation and handle new machines, and jobs. It has been observed that the existing competencies of employees are not in position to deal with the new situation. There is big gap between required and existing levels of competencies. This situation has given a warning to all organizations to wake up to improve the existing level of competencies and do the business. It is not possible to do the business the way organization wants. A high degree of competency is needed at levels of management and employees. The need for highly talented and motivated human resource is felt. If the employees are highly talented and motivated then they would definitely give high level of commitment, performance and productivity. So the importance of talented and motivated manpower or human resources has been realized by management. They are interested to hire, educate train, motivate and maintain the manpower in such a way that they are in position to achieve the performance standards and objectives of the organization properly.

In present situation there is question of survival, grow, stabilize, and excel in the business activities and that has become difficult. Every business unit is tried to improve the performance of employees, products, services to provide high level of satisfaction to the clients and customers. It has been realized to perform the tasks better and before others. There is strong drive towards productivity improvement across the organization. The organizations with competent, motivated and committed employees are in position to meet the objectives in stiff competitive situation. With improved performance of employees and organization as a whole the production quantity and quality, profits, customers' number and satisfaction level, Therefore, the focus of management is more on human resource. There is change in attitude of management towards the workforce. Now, they are considered as very valuable assets and partners in the business. Management is interested to develop the skills of existing manpower to meet the increasing needs of present time. A lot of efforts are needed in this direction to procure, develop employees and managers and maintain them satisfied at workplace. This is a challenging task. The organization with such manpower can make the show successful.

The major advantages of human resource development activities are to employees, management, organization and society as a whole. Due to this the main advantages are improvement in competencies, attitude, satisfaction level of employees, management and customers, easy to adjust in organization, level of attachment, commitment, trust, confidence, team spirit, cooperation, productivity, performance, profits, customers base, attracting talented employees in future, and overall reputation of the company. Keeping in view, the increasing importance of human resource development functions, it inspired us in giving insight into the topics related to human resource development related concepts to the academicians, practitioners, research scholars and students undergoing management programmes at postgraduation levels mainly. Special care has been taken to research in emerging trends and rapidly changing business environment. It highly expected that it would be in position to meet the study related requirements of all concerned.

Authors

ACKNOWLEDGEMENT

Gankar, Nadler and Wiggs, Bishwajeet Patnayak, KK Verma, SJ Abraham, MN Rudrabasavraj, Warner John, David Harris **Acknowledgement**

First of all we are highly grateful to the Almighty God, who gave us the ability and capability to take the challenge to author a book on human resource development topic. We have been lucky enough with the blessing of Almighty that we maintain good health and stable status of mind to concentrate on the topic despite our very busy schedule. We would like to express our gratitude towards our senior colleagues specially Dr JB Thakore, Dr. YP Hathi, faculty members, staff and members of NHRD Network, Ahmedabad chapter who inspired us to take the challenge to author this book. We do not take a chance or miss to acknowledge the contribution of Mr. Lakshdeep Raval, System engineer for his help in editing and formatting of text of the book. We got a continuous source of inspiration from them without this it was not possible to take responsibility to write about human resource development topic.

We would like to thank the experts from different universities and industries as they motivated and demanded a suitable book on the topic of human resource development that was the need of the hour. Next, we thank our senior and present students of MBA, PGDBA, PGPM, MHRM who contributed constructively towards the development of concepts through discussion, debate and presentations. We are thankful to various distinguished authors whose published works have been referred for development of concepts relating to human resource development especially to Udai Pareek, TV Rao, Edwin Flippo, Gary Dessler, Ashwathappa, H Aguinis, RL Cardy, RK Sahu, PP Arya, RP Gupta, Tandon BB, Bhatia SK, Nirmal Singh, RP Billimoria, NK Singh, Dale Neef, Ishwar Dayal, RS Dwivedi, Mager RF, Maheshwari, CB Memoria, SB, and others. Their published works have provided a lot of insight in development of concepts without which we may not have moved in the right direction. Special thanks to all of them again.

Next, we are highly indebted to our respected parents and grandparents for unending motivation and support provided by them during this work. We found them the source of inspiration to boost our morale high. They have taken a lot of interest in study and research work for motivational aspects. They have shown great patience over a long period, while we were closely working on the preparation of this book. They have also provided us a source of motivation, encouragement and morale support. We got a very peaceful family environment in our home for the study on this topic. We hope this acknowledgement will offset the sacrifices they have made towards this edition of book. Finally, we are thankful to our publishers for their keen cooperation and deep interest in the publication of this book of good quality and quite in time.

Dr. R. K. Balyan

Suman Balyan

CONTENTS

Part I: Introduction to HRD

Part II: HRD Process, Mechanisms and Practices

PART III: HRD Applications

Part IV: HRD Cases

DETAILED CONTENTS

Part I: Introduction to HRD

Part II: HRD Process, Mechanisms and Practices

PART III: HRD Applications

Part IV: HRD Cases

PART — 1
INTRODUCTION TO HRD

Chapter

HRD Environment

1. INTRODUCTION

An organization is a human grouping in which the jobs are preformed for attainment of specific objectives. Every organization has its objectives to be fulfilled. Organizations may be of different types and with different objectives. An organization may be a manufacturing firm, insurance company, a governmental agency, hospital, university and a religious trust. It may be small or large, simple or complex, objectives of the organization differ from organization to organization but remain relatively constant. These are likely to be modified over a period of time with the changing environment. Organizational goals may be more than one and organization tries to achieve these goals. In order to achieve these goals effectively and efficiently a set of rules and regulations is required. These rules and regulations will assist its members in accomplishment of the organizational goal. Large organizations in public and private sectors are operating their business from different locations scattered in different parts of the country and performing different types of activities. These organizations are incorporated either by Act of Parliament/Act of Legislature or under Company Act, 1956. In the corporate sector for attainment of objectives, variety of functions are performed by utilizing the available resources. We include men, machines, money and materials. These words are starting with letter M so these are called 4Ms.

These resources are being used by the management in the organization. Management is the art of getting the work done by others, by utilizing the available resources effectively and efficiently to achieve the predetermined goals of an organization. All the above-mentioned resources are important for attainment of objectives. Without these the task cannot be performed. Materials are used for manufacturing and other tasks. Different types of materials like raw materials, semi-finished and finished goods, inflammables, explosives, electrical and electronic items, gasses, chemicals, fuels, cleaning materials, consumables, etc., are used as per the need of the organizations. Without these the required functions cannot be performed. Second, resource is finance. Finance is life blood of the business. It works in business like blood in human body. If blood quality and quantity are not proper in our body then many problems are likely to be faced. In shortage of finance the routine, development, payment of workers, payment of bonus, welfare of employees, payment of suppliers, refund of loans, research and development, replacement of old machines and equipment related activities will be hampered. It may lead to make the profit making unit a sick unit. It means **paise sub kuchh to nahi but bahut kuchh hai.** Mr. Duleep Judev, Ex-central minister in government of India during government of BJP perfectly remarked that **paise khuda to nahi per khuda ki kasam khuda se kum bhi nahi.** Importance of finance cannot be overlooked. Third, machines or technology play very important role in accomplishment of tasks of the unit as per planning. Without technology the work is done manually. The speed at which the work is done is slow. The output per worker goes down and simultaneously the quality also goes down. The costs of production and operation increase. The organization cannot have competitive edge over the competitors using advance technology. With technology the performance increases. The productivity, efficiency and profitability of business unit increase. So use of technology cannot be ignored at any cost in present time. Out of these, human resource is the most important resource because through the combined efforts of men, other resources are utilized for accomplishment of the goals. Without human being other resources will be unproductive. Hence, human resource is the most importance resource that is to be managed properly.

Human resource is the most important component of an organization. Human resource has been defined from national point of view, as the total of knowledge, skills, creative abilities, talents and aptitudes obtained in the population. Whereas from an individual enterprise point of view, they represent the total of inherent abilities, acquired knowledge, skills and aptitudes contained in employees of the enterprise. The human resource is given increasing significance in modern organization. Obviously, a majority of the problems in organizational setting are human and social rather than physical, technical and economic. The failure to recognize this fact causes great loss to the nation, enterprise and the individual. People at work comprise a large number of individuals of different sex, age, education standards and groups. These people at work exhibit not only similar behaviour patterns and characteristics to a certain degree, but they also show many dissimilarities. Each individual who works has his own set of needs, drives, goals and experiences. Management, therefore, must be aware not only of the organizational needs but also needs and goals of employees.

The human resources assume importance from an economic standpoint at national, enterprise and individual levels of analysis. Ginzberg pointed out, human resource is the key to economic development. However, they are being wasted through unemployment, disguised unemployment, outdated skills, lack of job opportunities, poor personnel policies and practices and problems of adjusting to changes. There exists a wide scope to increase productivity through their proper development. The physical resources will not give output unless the human resources are applied to them. However, the human resource also has negative aspects. Over population and poorly trained workforce may prove disastrous to the national economy. If the national output does not increase faster than its population, the standard of living will decline. At enterprise level, there is also an urgent need for effective utilization of the human resource to attain organizational goals. This can be done by understanding their nature, potentials and limitations of human resource, developing and utilizing it to the optimal ability, maintaining its quality and coordinating it with other resources. From individual point of view, development of employees will get them a source of economic advantage, improves the economic status and living standards.

In a business organization different types of activities are performed as per the nature of business. All jobs cannot be performed by one person or team. So the jobs are divided and clubbed together as per area of specialization. Responsibility to perform tasks is given to a particular person or team and this way the management is divided in different groups and tasks are assigned accordingly.

Management is divided into different branches. The main branches of management are:

(a) Personnel Management/Human Resource Management

(b) Finance Management

(c) Production Management

(d) Material Management

(e) Marketing Management

Each branch of management is made responsible for one department. Hence, personnel management is made responsible to manage human resources. Personnel management has been defined by EFL Breach as "it is that part of management process which is primarily concerned with the human constituents of an organization." Personnel Management is that area of management which has to do with the planning, organizing and controlling various operative activities of procuring, developing, maintaining and utilizing labour force in order that the objectives and interests for which a company is established are attained as effectively and economically as possible and interests of labour itself are served to the highest degree. It is concerned with scientific procurement, effective utilization, development, motivation and maintaining good industrial relations.

The scope of Personnel Management/HRM would include the following:

Manpower planning, recruitment and selection, training and development, job design, compensation of employees, industrial relations, discipline, promotion, transfer and separation. The concept of personnel management developed somewhere at the end of 19th century. The growth of personnel management passed through the stages of needs of better industrial relations, efficiency and productivity movement, welfare, industrial psychology, human relations and strategic and goal-oriented approach. In the last quarter of the 20th century personnel management was recognized as a profession and concept of Human Resources Management. The two concepts are interchangeable and many organizations are using the concept of personnel management or human resource management.

Environment affects the function of the organization. Environment means the surrounding or atmosphere in which business activities are performed. There are two sets of factors those affect the environment. These are internal or controllable factors and external or uncontrollable factors. To carry out the business effectively the organization has to adjust its internal factors in such a way that the firm can do the business successfully. Business environment is dynamic. Many elements in the environment undergo changes. These changes are having effect on the health of the business. For that purpose management must have the dynamic policy so that the business operations can be adjusted successfully with changing environment. For example, with the changes in technology, it becomes necessary for the management to develop the knowledge and skills of employee to operate and maintain the new machines. Policies of personnel management will also undergo changes to adjust the human resources as per need of business. To get best contribution from employees, it becomes mandatory to develop the available human resources in corporate sector.

Human Resource Development is a subject of national importance, much more of great relevance in a developing and most populous country like India. There is a need to mobilize the human resource with the purpose to enable them to participate effectively in the task of nation-building and organizational development. Mobilization would include the need to develop resources, their skills, attitudes and aptitudes so that they can competently achieve the pre-determined goals. HRD, thus, constitutes a most complex and challenging problem. Human resource development at micro-level or organizational level is a process by which employees of an organization are helped in systematic and continuous way to:

(a) Acquire, sharpen or mould capabilities required to perform various functions relating to their present and future jobs and rates.

(b) Developing or moulding an organizational culture in which superior-subordinate relationships, teamwork and collaboration among sub-units are strong and contribute to the professional well-being, motivation and pride of employees.

(c) Develop and mould their general capabilities and discover and exploit their inner potentials for their own and organizational development process.

Human resource development is a function for personnel or human resource management. Unless the human resource is adequately trained and developed up to the required levels of proficiency and requirement, it cannot be said that they are managed effectively. Human resource development makes possible the effective management of human resource. In other words "Management through development" applies correctly to the human resource in any type of organization. In corporate sector, where a large number of business units are operated, manufacturing number of products or providing services, serving different markets and located in different parts of the country. These are managed from the central office or branch offices

With the changing environment, it becomes necessary to update the knowledge and skills of employees so that objectives of organization are fulfilled. The function of human resource development is performed by personnel or human resource management in the corporate sector. Human resource development is a continuous process and a comprehensive system by itself. To perform the function of human resource development, personnel management performs the activities of job-description and analysis, manpower planning, recruitment and selection, training and development, performance appraisal, promotion and transfer, employees' welfare and rewards. By performing the aforesaid activities Human Resource Management has developed the human resource effectively in multi-national organizations like Hindustan Lever Limited, Suzuki, Honda and Whirlpool could achieve the predetermined goals effectively and efficiently.

2. QUESTIONS FOR REVIEW

(a) How do you evaluate the present global business environment and discuss the challenges faced due to this in Indian markets?

(b) Do you feel the human resource is the most important resource in an organization in present scenario? Give your Comments.

Chapter

2

Human Resource Management

1. INTRODUCTION

Every organization performs its task with the help of resources as men, machine, materials and money. Except manpower other resources are non-living but manpower is a live and generating resource. Manpower utilizes other resources and gives output. If manpower is not available then other resources are useless and cannot produce any thing. Out of all the factors of production manpower has the highest priority and is the most significant factor of production and plays a pivotal role in areas of productivity and quality. In case, lack of attention to the other factors those that are non-living may result in reduction of profitability to some extent. But ignoring the human resource can prove to be disastrous. In a country where human resource is abundant, it is a pity that they remain underutilized. In words of Oliver Sheldon "No industry can be rendered efficient so long as the basic fact remains unrecognized that is human." The people at work comprise a large number of individuals of different sex, age, socio-religious group and different educational or literacy standards. These individuals in the work place exhibit not only similar behaviour patterns and characteristics to a certain degree but also they show much dissimilarity. Technology alone, however, cannot bring about desired change in economic performance of the country unless human potential is fully utilized for production. The management must therefore, be aware not only of the organization but also employees and their needs.

The human resource is critical and difficult to manage. It is because human behaviour is highly unpredictable. It differs not only from individual to individual but often on the part of same individual at different points of time. In spite of biological and cultural similarities, human beings not only differ in their appearance but also in their capabilities based on their background, training and experience. Human resource or a person at work is the most important component of the undertaking. Management cannot afford to ignore human resource at any cost. Management is the process of efficiently getting activities completed with and that other people. The management process includes planning. organizing, leading and controlling activities that takes place to accomplish objectives. Being a branch of management, personnel management also performs the same functions towards the achievement of objectives. Different terms are used for personnel management. The different terms are labour management, labour administration, labour management relations, employee-employer relations, personnel administration, human assets management, human resources management etc. In simple sense, human resource management means employing people, developing them, utilizing, compensating and maintaining their services in tune with the job and organizational requirements.

2. DEFINITIONS OF PERSONNEL MANAGEMENT/ HUMAN RESOURCE MANAGEMENT

Human resource management is concerned with the people dimension in an organization. Since every organization is made up of people acquiring their services, developing their skills, motivating them to high level of performance and ensuring that they continue to maintain their commitment to the organization are essential to achieving organizational objectives. This is true regardless of the type of organization like government, business, education, health, recreation or social group. Acquiring good people is difficult but retaining good people for longer period is more difficult in present time. Those organizations that are able to acquire, develop, stimulate and keep outstanding workers will be both efficient and effective. Survival of a unit requires competent managers and workers and coordinating their efforts toward an ultimate goal. Alone coordination also cannot be successful.

The look of Human Resource Management is more specifically a process consisting of functions of acquisition, development, motivation and maintenance of human resource. In academic term these might be described as four functions of getting people, preparing, activating and keeping them. Personnel management/HRM is that field of management which has to do with the planning, organizing and controlling various operative activities of procuring, developing, maintaining and utilizing labour force in order that the objectives and interests for which a company is established are attained as effectively and economically as possible and the objectives and interests of labour itself are served to the highest degree. It has been defined by the various experts as follows:

"Personnel management is that part of management function which is primarily concerned with human relationship in an organization. Its objective is the maintenance of those relationships which enable all those engaged in the undertaking to make their maximum contribution to the effective working of the undertaking." (Indian Institute of Personnel Management)

(a) "Personnel administration is the art of acquiring, developing and maintaining a competent workforce in such a manner as to accomplish with maximum efficiency and economy in the functions and objectives of the organization." (Society for Personnel Administration of America)

(b) "Personnel management is a method of developing potentialities of employees so that they get maximum satisfaction out of their work and give their best efforts to the organization." Pigors, Paul and Myres.

(c) "The personnel function is concerned with the procurement, development, compensation, integration and maintenance of the personnel of an organization for the purpose of contributing towards the accomplishment of the major goals or objectives of that organizing, directing and controlling of performance of those operative functions." E.B. Flippo.

(d) "Personnel management is the recruitment, selection, development, utilization of and accommodation to human resources by organizations. The human resources of an organization consist of all individuals regardless of their role who are engaged in any of the organizational activities." French.

(e) "Personnel management is that phase of management which deals with the effective control and use of manpower as distinguished from other sources of power." Dale Yoder.

(f) "Personnel management is an extension of general management, that of prompting and stimulating every employee to make his fullest contribution to the purpose of a business." Northcott C.H.

(g) "Personnel management is that part of management process which is primarily concerned with the human constituents of an organization." E.F.L. Breach.

In brief, it can be said that human resource management means employing people, developing their resources, utilising, maintaining and compensating their services in tune with the job and organisational requirements. Personnel management and HRM are two concepts interchangeable. These are performing the same functions but different names are used by different companies. In recent period HRM concept is more preferred in comparison with past. The difference between these two is of approach only and both deal with human resource only.

3. CHARACTERISTICS OF PERSONNEL MANAGEMENT

From the study of the above given definitions it is clear that personnel management is a branch of management which deals with the human resource of an organization. It has the following characteristics:

(a) It manages the human resource of the organization.

(b) It is mainly concerned with the effective utilization of human resource.

(c) Personnel management follows the principles and performs the functions of general management.

(d) It is concerned with the achievement of organizational goal as well as integration of individual efforts with common goals.

(e) To perform functions of personnel management, it requires specialization in human psychology, law and industrial relations etc.

In general, we can say that personnel management is a branch of management that is concerned with the human element of an organization. Its main objectives are to procure, develop, compensate and maintain the workforce to enable them to contribute maximum to the effective working of an organization.

4. EVOLUTION OF PERSONNEL MANAGEMENT/HRM

It is very difficult to trace out the exact time of the evolution of personnel management. Even though the stages of the development of personnel management can be easily determined, its development was marked towards the end of 19th century. Prior to this it was somewhat a slow process. Ordinarily, the growth and history of personnel management is divided into these five periods:

(a) Early Philosophy (before 1900)

(b) Efficiency and Productivity Movement (1900-1920)

(c) Period of Welfare and Industrial Psychology (1920-30)

(d) Period of Human Relations in Industry (from 1930-50)

(e) Modern Period (1950 onwards)

Now we shall study them one by one:

(a) Early Philosophy of Personnel Management

The history of modern personnel management begins with the name of Robert Owen. He is called the founder of Personnel Management. In year 1813, he wrote a book, '*A New View of Society*', wherein he has propounded the need of better industrial relations and improvements in the service conditions. His attitude towards workers was very cordial and liberal. He got good houses constructed for his workers by the side of his factory, eliminated child labour and provided healthy conditions. J.S. Mill and Charles Babbage were also contemporary of Robert Owen. They all maintained Personnel Management as a science and supported the idea of wage incentives, profit sharing and labour welfare, etc.

(b) Efficiency and Productivity Movement

During the last year of 19th century came the age of efficiency and productivity movement. The two decades of (1900-1920) were the years of scientific management movement. During this period, Taylor's Scientific Management thought was greatly accepted. The main contributions of these two decades have been the increase in the size of units, introduction of scientific thinking into actions, job analysis, standard costing, scientific selection and training of workers, and the idea of mental revolution. Taylor opposed the idea of trade unionism and workers' organisations.

(c) Period of Welfare and Industrial Psychology

Second stage is the period of welfare and industrial psychology. Up to 1925, the personnel management had taken a definite form and then line and staff organisation became the basis of personnel management. The opposition of scientific management movement by workers introduced the need of industrial psychology. The concept of industrial psychology developed many new techniques like psychological testing, interviewing, workers training and non-financial incentives. Industrial psychologists helped to give a professional form to personnel management. The personnel management began to be realised as a profession and a specialists function.

(d) Period of Human Relations

Since 1930, began the period of human relations in industry. Through Hawthorn experiments, Prof. Elton Mayo and his companions made the beginning of human relations in industries. Hawthorn experiments proved that human resources have greater influence on production than that of other physical resources. A worker must be treated as a human being. Social, psychological and moral instincts should be fully recognized by management. Due to these experiments the commodity concept of labour changed to social concept. The decade of 1940-50, is very important from the development of personnel management point of view. During this decade many new techniques were developed for selection, training and induction of workers. The personnel philosophy became people-oriented. Trade unions flourished and provision of fringe benefits for workers became common.

(e) Modern Times

The history of personnel management from 1950 up to 1980, is the age of modern development. It may be called as the period of the citizenship concept of labour where the workers have full right to be consulted in determining the rules and regulations under which they work. The concept of industrial democracy has imposed new responsibilities upon the personnel managers of various organisations. In modern times the personnel management is a behavioural science and personnel management is an open social system. After 1960, the personnel management began to be realised as a behavioural science which completely centered on human elements. The study of organisational behaviour became its main crux. After 1970s, the belief of 'open social and industrial system' became very popular for business organisations. During modern times personnel management is fully recognised as a profession dealing with the management of human resources. Some authors call it as 'Manpower Management' also. These development are making the scope of personnel management wider and wider.

The concept of HRM emerged from the writings of American academics associated with Human Resource Management School. These academics visualised HRM as a strategic and coherent management oriented approach to manage people and accomplishing their commitment to promote organizations interests. The HRM stage appeared when personnel specialists attempted to cope up with the enterprise culture and market economy. HR and business strategy were integrated to evolve strategic HRM approaches. Performance related pay emerged as a motivational device. Finally in the current stage there is focus on teamwork. Empowerment and learning organisations, specifically the role of HR in the total quality has become imperative. There is increasing stress on process such as culture management. Personnel directors are engaged in efforts such as downsizing and management of aftermath of a business process reengineering study. Their approach is strategic and aimed at evolving cohesive personnel policies.

5. NEED FOR HRM IN INDIA

During 1990s, there was emergence of a new human resource management, especially as a result of the globalisation and liberalisation of the economy. The economy and the policy of India has changed fast in the wake of the liberalistion policies mooted by Rajiv Gandhi Government and formalised by the Narasimha Rao Government. Consequently the form and the content of capitalist relations between the various factors of production are undergoing a change. What has emerged is a new era in human resource management. As a result of liberalisation, industrial relations and human resource management (HRM) have acquired strategic importance. The success of new policies depends to a large extent in the introduction of new industrial relations and human resources policies at the national and enterprise levels. Some pressure for change has already been witnessed in the IR and HRM areas. The actors of the system now realise that neither the economy nor industrial enterprise can survive by clinging to their rigid postures.

Indian industrial scenario is passing through a turbulent phase at present. The liberalisation of economy is beginning to make wide ranging and far-reaching impact on how we manage our resources, technology and people. As we enter into the age of stiff competition from global giants, quality of product and customer satisfaction become prime factors in organisational success. To get the best performance from the people, one needs to recruit well, place appropriately, train and develop consistently, compensate adequately, and create and maintain an organisational culture which motivates innovation and enterprise. Truly speaking in the coming years the human resource specialist will be at a premium.

6. SCOPE OF HRM

In recent years there has been relative agreement among HRM specialists as to what constitutes the field of HRM. The model that provides the focus was developed by the American Society for Training and Development (ASTD). In this study, ASTD identified nine human resource areas and these are:

(a) Training and Development.

(b) Organisation and Development

(c) Organisation and Job Design

(d) Human Resource Planning.

(e) Selection and Staffing.

(f) Personnel Research and Human Resource Information System.

(g) Compensation and Benefits.

(h) Employee Assistance.

(i) Union Labour Relationship.

The above mentioned areas of HRM have been termed spokes of the wheel and each area impacts on the human resource outputs, quality of work life, productivity and readiness for change. The scope of HRM even includes the functions beyond entry to exit of human resource from organization. The scope is very wide. A special care and professionalism is required to perform functions of a HRM manager in present rapidly changing business environment.

7. FUNCTIONS OF PERSONNEL MANAGEMENT/HRM

The functions of personnel management are very wide. An agreement over them is rare. Broadly, the functions of personnel management can be divided into two parts as follows:

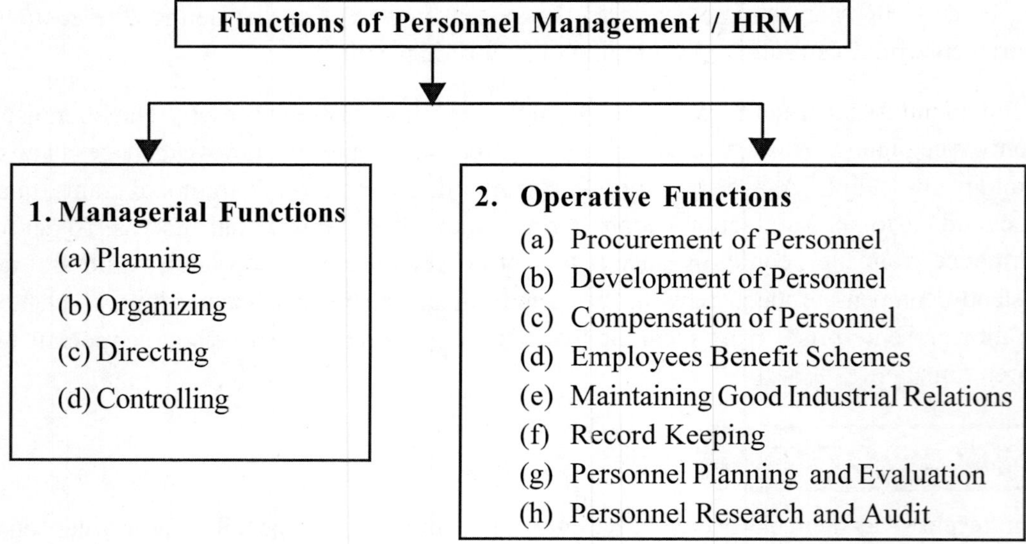

Diagram 2.1: Functions of Personnel Management/HRM

The above- mentioned functions are explained as follows:

(a) Managerial Functions

(i) Planning: It is the main function of the management. In case of personnel management, it is concerned with manpower planning, studying turnover rate, forecasting the future requirement of personnel, planning for selection and training procedures etc. According to objectives of the organisation manpower planning is done. To achieve corporate goals planning for human resource is done by head of HR department. This ensures timely availability of required manpower of right type and in number.

(ii) Organizing: Organizing involves the establishment of inter-relationships within the organization. It provides a structure for the company by identifying the various sub-groups created by individuals in managerial jobs as well as operative jobs.

(iii) Directing: Personnel management is directly concerned with direction function also. It includes issuing instructions and orders to the workers developing formal communication network, interpreting various labour laws and integrating workers.

(iv) Controlling: Personnel department helps in controlling too. It provides basic data for establishing standards, makes job analysis and performance appraisal etc. All techniques assist in effective control of qualities, time and efforts of workers.

(b) Operative Functions

These are services or routine functions of personnel management. They are as under:

(i) Procurement of personnel: The first operative function of personnel management is concerned with the obtaining of the proper kind and number of personnel necessary to accomplish organizational goals. It deals specifically with such subjects as the determination of manpower and their requirements, selection, placement and orientation etc. As required for existing vacancies advertisement is given and applications are shortlisted. Out of shortlisted candidates suitable candidates are selected on the basis of test and interview. This function involves HR managers and staff members.

(ii) Development of personnel: After personnel have been obtained they must to some degree be developed before going to work. Development has to do with the increase of skill through training. Different training methods are used in the process in order to develop the employees. Framing a sound promotion policy, determination of the basis of promotion and making performance appraisal are the basis of personnel development functions.

(iii) Compensation of personnel: Compensation means determination of adequate and equitable remuneration of personnel for their contribution to organizational objectives. It is one of the most difficult and important functions of the personnel management to determine the monetary compensation for various jobs. For choosing a suitable compensatory policy a number of decision are taken into the function, *viz.,* job evaluation, remuneration policy, incentive and premium plans, bonus policy and co-partnership etc. In addition to this, it assists the organization for adopting suitable wage and salary policy and payment of wages and salaries at right time.

(iv) Maintaining good industrial relations: It is one of the most essential functions of the personnel manager to create the harmonious relations between management and labour. It covers a wide field and intended to reduce strikes, promote industrial peace, provide fair deal to workers and establish industrial democracy. If the personnel manager is unable to make harmonious relation between the two, it will be very harmful to the organization. The industrial unrest will take place and millions of man-days will be lost. The moral and physical conditions of the employee will suffer if labour management relations are not good. It is the duty of personnel manager to make harmonious relations with the help of efficient communication system and co-partnership.

(v) Record keeping: Record keeping is also an important function of personnel manager. In this system, personnel manager collects and maintains data relating to the staff of the organization. Recording is essential for every organization because it assists the management in decision making. Records are maintained regarding requirement of manpower, manpower inventory, recruitment and selection, placement, transfer and promotion, wages and salary, bonus, leave and overtimes, workers benefits, accidents, strikes and lockouts, legal matters, absenteeism, discipline, grievances, performance appraisal, training, compensations, layoff and retrenchment, voluntary retirement schemes, welfare facility and many other related activities in the organisation.

(vi) Personnel planning and evaluation: Under this system different type of activities are evaluated such as evaluation of performance of the organization as a whole, personal policy of an organization and its practices, personnel audit, moral survey and performance appraisal etc.

(vii) Personnel research and audit: It is also an important function of personnel management. This function is concerned with the research in newer motivational techniques and auditing its effect on the workers of the organization etc. Personnel research helps in identification and solution of personnel problems. With the help of research expert a systematic study of the problem faced is carried out. On the basis of data collected analysis is carried out. Efforts are put to find the causes of the problem and suggestions are given by experts. As per recommendation remedial actions are taken by HR manager. This way the problems are solved easily. Further personnel audit studies the existing manpower and finds out whether the manpower is as per the requirement. It may be more or less than requirement. On the basis of finding the corrective actions are taken to match the existing manpower with the present and future requirement. These functions are getting importance day by day in present time.

8. PRINCIPLES OF PERSONNEL MANAGEMENT

Principles are those fundamental rules which guide the management in formulation of policies. Principles of personnel management are also the rules which help the personnel managers to conduct and direct the personnel policies in a proper way. Sound principles help them in developing good human relations. C.H. North Colt has given 4 principles of personnel management. According to George D. Nells, they are seven in number, while Labour Management Institute of England has put forth nine principles. But we are not going into controversy of number and we shall discuss main principles:

(a) Principle of Scientific Selection

For proper coordination between work and workers it is necessary to have a right person for the job so that the question on inability of person will not arise and he will be able to get to complete his assigned work. Candidates must be selected as per the merit and not as per favour. Unfair criteria for selection should not be considered. On the basis of unfair criteria if a candidate is selected then quality and quantity of the performance will be affected and in future that candidate will become burden for the organisation. Scientific selection will ensure right types of persons are selected for the job and gives proper match between job and the candidates. HRM must keep in mind this principle for selection of candidates in an organisation.

(b) Principle of Effective Communication

Communication means that orders of higher authorities are conveyed in a proper way. Management assigns various tasks to the subordinates and it is possible through proper communication. So there must be proper medium of communication between management and workers. Lack of proper medium and communication policy confusions are likely to take place. This ultimately defeats the purpose of the organisation. If there is no proper arrangement for communication and communication is incomplete, not relevant to the purpose, not in time and it is incorrect the complex problems are likely to take place. This may crease confusion, ambiguity, distrust, ill-will etc. In the long run the performance of individuals and organisation will be affected. So management must keep in mind that communication must be to the right person in right time, in right manner and right way. This will contribute in proper coordination and effectiveness of communication will improve.

(c) Principle of Maximum Individual Development

At present the business environment is changing very fast and to keep pace with the changing conditions it become necessary to update knowledge and skills of employees. So this principle stresses on the personnel development of every person working in an organisation to a possible extent. If employees are motivated and provided opportunity to develop they will be in a position to improve their knowledge and skill. This will contribute to achieve the objectives of the organisations.

(d) Principle of High Morale

Morale is the internal feeling of the individual at work. For good performance an employees should feel strong then only hard work and sincere efforts can be put. It is essential to have a high morale of workers towards organisation and work. It should be kept in mind while performing function by HR manager. Employees should be trerated like human beings. They should be compensated adequately, provided with good welfare facilities and better development opportunity. These will help to improve morale of employees. In leading organisation HR managers pay special attention to maintain high morale of employees. This ultimately contributes in maintaining good relationship in the organisation.

(e) Principle of Team Spirit

Management should understanding importance of collective working. One individual no doubt can perform better but it is very difficult to give more effective output. Team spirit develops in atmosphere of openness, mutual understanding, trust and cooperation. While performing HR functions managers must keep this principle in mind. When people work in a team they can work better and they feel secured. If people work in group they stand in market and in competition. Team spirit is essential for progress in every field of life.

(f) Principle of Dignity of Labour

Dignity of human being must be given utmost importance while dealing with employees. Employees should be treated like human being and should not be treated like machines. They should be provided all facilities required for human being. At work place they should feel proud. The feeling like "work is worship" should be developed among people. Their work should be recognised and appreciated where it is required. Favourable attitude and good behaviour of managers towards employees is necessary for this purpose. This should be kept in mind while performing various related functions.

(g) Principle of Joint Management Decisions

The principle of democracy should be introduced in industry. Participation in management decision is a vehicle for industrial democracy. Importance of workers is realised under this and they are assigned the tasks to participate in decision making at various levels in organisation. This helps in motivation of employees and they willingly take the responsibility. This creates sense of responsibility among employees with increasing mutual faith and friendship. Under this scheme decisions are taken jointly and question of opposition from workers and union does not arise. It contributes in developing and maintaining good industrial relations. Hr managers must have good feeling for this principle if they want to take the employees together to achieve objectives of organisation effectively and efficiently.

(h) Principle of Contribution towards National Prosperity

Human resource is very important in an organisation and nation. It is human resource that utilises money, machines and material to give production. Without manpower all other resources are unutilised and nothing can be produced. Human resource is a live and generating resource. The output of workers is the output of an organisation. If people work sincerely the performance and output will be more. The total production of the company will go high. If this way all companies produce and give higher output the gross domestic product will increase. This will lead to national prosperity in long run. It is possible when management maintain and motivate the people at work. The success of an individual organisation is ultimately contributing in developing economy of the nation. Therefore, contribution of individual worker should not be ignored by HR and other managers.

(i) Principle of Fair Reward

Reward means something in return that is earned. Employees are the people those who render their services and get remuneration in return. They do not want their service in return. For their service they should be compensated. The compensation should be adequate and timely. This creates sense of satisfaction and avoids labour problems like absenteeism, labour turnover, strikes, lockout and unrest. Work recognition must be there and those who perform better than others should be rewarded accordingly. The will cultivate habit of competition among workers. When doing so HR manager must deal the issue honestly and must be impartial.

9. OBJECTIVES OF PERSONNEL MANAGEMENT

The major objective of personnel management is the effective utilization of manpower working in the organization so that the organization may continue to survive and achieve its goals. A business organization is started with a long-term point of view. Its main objective is survival and growth. The various employees of the organization put their best efforts in order to achieve these objectives. But with the passage of time the organization is deprived of the service of the employees because of the various reasons such as death, retirement, dismissal, disablement, turnover etc. So they are to be achieved by new hands. Due to the growth of the organization more manpower is required. Their experience and quality characteristics also vary. The personnel management department objectives can be laid down as follows:

(a) To Attract and Secure Appropriate Hands

First objective of HRM is to procure suitable candidates for the jobs so that they can perform as per requirement. They should be retained also. This gives a positive signal in the market and in future more and better employees can be attracted.

(b) To Utilize the Manpower Effectively

Manpower is an important resource and further it depends upon its utilisation. If management can procure right number of then they must be utilised properly and must give their best at work. Otherwise, human resource that is an important resource may become a liability on the organisation.

(c) To Help Maximum Individual Development

HRM must help employees in their development. Business environment varies rapidly and to keep pace with this is very difficult. To deal effectively in the competitive situation skills of employees must be developed. This will improve quality and quantity of the performance. This is possible when HRM provides opportunities for development to employees. Management must stick to this objective to be effective in business.

(d) To Establish and Maintain an Adequate Organizational Structure and a Desirable Working Relationship

The objectives of organisation can be achieved with required structure. This organisational structure is to be decided by HRM to suit the requirement. This will help in maintaining reasonable working relationship.

(e) To Secure the Integration of the Individuals and Groups within an Organization

HRM performs its function with the objective to develop good working environment of openness, mutual trust, understanding, cooperation and team spirit. This enables to keep group and individual together and integrated.

(f) To Maintain a High Morale and Better Human Relations inside an Organization

At work people must be treated properly and motivated. They must feel well secured and must have strong internal feeling. In this situation they will be in position to give better output. This objective is bit difficult to achieve.

10. HRM AND PERSONNEL MANAGEMENT

The term 'human resources' at the macro level spells out the total sum of all the components possessed by all the people, whereas the term 'personnel' even at the macro level is limited to only employees of all organizations. HR even at the organizational level include all the component resources of all employees from rank and file to top management level all the employees like managing director, board of directors, person who work on honorary basis, expert drawn from various organizations and those people influencing the human resources of the former group. In short, it also includes the resources of all the people who contribute their services in the attainment of organizational goals. Thus the term human resources is wider than the term personnel either at the components level or in coverage or even at the macro level. As such human resources management at organizational level does mean management of dynamic components of all the people at all levels in the organizational hierarchy round the clock and throughout the year.

Table 2.1: HRM and Personnel Management

Personnel Management	HRM
1. Employee are treated as a cost centre and therefore management controls the cost of labour	Employees are treated as a profit centre and therefore it invests capital for human resource development and future utility.
2. Employees are used mostly for organizational benefits,	Employees are used for the multiple mutual benefits of the organization, employees and their family members.

The clear analysis of both the terms is presented in the following lines:

(a) The personnel approach tends to be tactical in its approach to activities. The focus of the human resource management approach is more strategic.

(b) The personnel approach tends to be short-term and responsive to others demands; the HRM approach is to think of the long-term and institutes policies on major new initiative.

(c) Personnel management tends to rely on traditional forms of communication. HRM tends to use a variety of communication channels.

(d) Personnel management tends to use traditional pay systems; Human resource management tends to encourage change and increased flexibility in ways of working.

(e) Personnel management tends to use traditional pay systems; human resource management emphasizes the need to manage performance and motivate people by the use of various payment systems.

(f) Personnel Management focus therefore on getting the same condition for groups; HRM focus is on individual contract payment and reward system.

(g) Personnel managers may sometimes need to help individual with their problems; HR Managers feel individuals should be prepared to be responsible for their own decision and actions.

(h) Personnel managers want a system that is fair for all and are keen to have rules and procedures to encourage this; human resource managers tend to say that people have a right of proper treatment at work and efficient management will achieve this.

(i) Personnel management is a special activity because of the difficulties of working with people; HRM management says that managing people is same as managing any other resource.

11. QUALITIES OF A HRM/ PERSONNEL MANAGER

Personnel manager is treated as a member of the top management team of the organization. It is evident that the personnel manager is first of all an executive requiring essentially the same executive qualities as other executives. Like other executives the personnel manager or director needs technical competence in the areas of his specialization. He needs not be a specialist in all the areas of the personnel division yet he should have a high degree of skill and competence in at least one of the areas. The chief officer of the personnel department should have keen sense of social justice and be fully appreciative of the rights and interest of the men and women as well as of the economic necessities of management. His philosophy of social justice should include two fundamental concepts.

(a) Industry is a partnership between management, men and owners whose objective is profits through services.

(b) Industry can make profit greatly by developing and coordinating the capacities, interests and the opportunities of each worker and of each member of the management. He should take interest in people. He must possess a wealth of common sense that will protect him from sentimentality on one side and from coldness on the other. He must be a man qualified to advise management on matters of personnel and capable of talking without fear or favour with any executive in the organization. He should possess legal, social, human and managerial qualities of head and heart as well. HRM manager should possess the following qualities in brief:

  (i) Physical strength.

  (ii) Intelligence.

  (iii) Education qualification.

  (iv) Maturity in judgment.

  (v) Communication skills.

  (vi) Experience and training.

(vii) Specialization in HRM.

(viii) Leadership.

(ix) Initiative and decision making.

(x) Ability to inspire and motivate employees.

12. CONCLUSION

Different resources are being used in an organization and out of these; human resource is very critical and difficult to manage. It is because human behaviour is highly unpredictable. It differs not only from individual to individual but often on the part of same individual at different points of time. In spite of biological and cultural similarities, human beings not only differ in their appearance but also in their capabilities based on their background, training and experience. Human resource or a person at work is the most important component of the undertaking. Management cannot afford to ignore human resource at any cost. Personnel management is a branch of management that takes care of human resource. The different terms are used for it and these are labour management, labour administration, labour management relations, employee-employer relations, personnel administration, human assets management, human resources management etc. In simple sense, human resource management means employing people, developing them, utilizing, compensating and maintaining their services in tune with the job and organizational requirements.

It has been defined by the various experts at different point of time. Personnel management and HRM are two concepts interchangeable. These are performing the same functions but different names are used by different companies. In recent period HRM concept is more preferred in comparison with past. The difference between these two is of approach and both deal with human resource only. To perform functions of personnel management, it requires specialization in human psychology, law and industrial relations, etc. Its main objectives are to procure, develop, compensate and maintain the workforce to enable them to contribute maximum to the effective working of an organization.

It is very difficult to trace out the exact time of the evolution of personnel management. Even though the stages of the development of personnel management can be easily determined, its development was marked towards the end of 19th century. Prior to this it was somewhat a slow process. Ordinarily, the growth and history of personnel management is divided into these five periods:

(a) Early Philosophy (before 1900)

(b) Efficiency and Productivity Movement (1900-1920)

(c) Period of Welfare and Industrial Psychology (1920-30)

(d) Period of Human Relations in Industry (from 1930-50)

(e) Modern Period (1950 onwards)

The scope of HRM even includes the functions beyond entry to exit of human resource from organization. The scope is very wide. A special care and professionalism is required to perform functions of a HRM manager in present rapidly changing business environment The functions of personnel management are very wide. An agreement over them is rare. Broadly, the functions of personnel management can be divided into managerial and routine functions. While performing functions HR manager follows principles of scientific selection, effective communication, maximum individual development, high morale,, team spirit, dignity of labour, joint management decisions, contribution towards national prosperity, fair reward, effective utilization of human resource etc.

The personnel management department objectives can be summarised as to attract and secure appropriate hands, utilize the manpower effectively, help maximum individual development, establish and maintain an adequate organizational structure and a desirable working relationship, secure the integration of the individuals and groups within an organization, maintain a high morale and better human relations inside an organization. The term 'human resources' at the macro level spells out the total sum of all the components possessed by all the people, whereas the term 'personnel' even at the macro level is limited to only employees of all organizations. Thus the term human resource is wider than the term personnel either at the components level, in coverage or even at the macro level. As such human resource management at organizational level does mean management of dynamic components of all the people at all levels in the organizational hierarchy round the clock and throughout the year. To carry out the tasks effectively personnel or HR manager should possess legal, social, human and managerial qualities of head and heart as well. HRM manager should possess the qualities of physical strength, intelligence, educational qualification, maturity in judgment, communication skills, experience and training, specialization in HRM, leadership, initiative and decision making and ability to inspire and motivate employees.

13. QUESTIONS FOR REVIEW

1. Define Human Resource Management and discuss its main characteristics.
2. Trace evolution of Human Resource Management in detail.
3. In present time what are the functions being performed in a modern organization. Illustrate this with an example from market.
4. Human Resource Management has evolved with certain objectives, highlight these objectives.
5. Being an HRM manager what qualities would you like to possess for effective working in your organization. Discuss.
6. HRM and personnel management are two different concepts but interchangeable, how would you differentiate between these two.
7. With rapid changing business environment the scope of HRM is becoming wider. Do you agree with this or not?

8. For effective working and to achieve objectives of organization what principles should HR manager should keep in mind.
9. How would you assess future of HRM in present scenario of globalization and liberalization?

14. OBJECTIVE QUESTIONS

1. "Personnel management is that phase of management which deals with the effective control and use of manpower as distinguished from other sources of power." The definition was advocated by:
   (a) E.B. Flippo
   (b) Dale Yoder
   (c) E.F.L Breach
   (d) J.S. Mill
   (e) None of the Above
2. The branch of management deals with human resource in an organisation is known as:
   (a) Production Management
   (b) Marketing Management
   (c) Financial Management
   (d) Human Resource Management
   (e) All the above
3. Resources that uses other resources in an organisation for further generation of them is called:
   (a) Machine
   (b) Money
   (c) Materials
   (d) Manpower
   (e) None of the above
4. Scope of HRM covers the activities are:
   (a) Requirement and selection
   (b) Orientation and placement
   (c) Training and development
   (d) Promotion and compensation
   (e) All the above
5. The evolution of Personnel Management started mainly in the:
   (a) 19th Century
   (b) 20th Century
   (c) 21th Century
   (d) 15th Century
   (e) None of the above
6. Scientific Management movement was advocated by:
   (a) Robert Owen
   (b) Henry Fayol
   (c) Taylor
   (d) J.S. Mill
   (e) None of the above

7. Howthorne experiments carried out to know the importance of manpower at work by:
   (a) Elton Mayo
   (b) Peter Duruker
   (c) Charles Babbage
   (d) E.B. Flippo
   (e) All the above
8. Operative functions of HRM/Personnel management covers:
   (a) Procurement of manpower
   (b) Development of manpower
   (c) Maintaining Industrial Relations
   (d) HR Research
   (e) All the above
9. Objectives of HRM does not include:
   (a) To attract talent people
   (b) To develop competency of employees
   (c) To utilize manpower optimum
   (d) To earn more profits
   (e) To motivate and retain employees
10. Principles adopted by HRM does not including the principle of:
    (a) Scientific principle of:
    (b) Effective communication
    (c) High morale
    (d) Dignity of labour
    (e) Hire and fire
11. Industry can make profit greatly by developing and coordinating the capacities, interests and the opportunities of each worker and of each member of the management. The role of HR manager is very important. He should possess the qualities of:
    (a) Physical strength, intelligence, education qualification.
    (b) Maturity in judgment, communication skills.
    (c) Experience and training specialization in HRM.
    (d) Leadership, initiative and decision - making. Ability to motivate employees
    (e) All the above

Answer Keys:

Question No.	Answer	Question No.	Answer
1	b	7	c
2	d	8	a
3	d	9	e
4	e	10	d
5	a	11	e
6	e		

Chapter

Human Resource Development

1. INTRODUCTION

Out of all factors of production, man has the highest priority and is the most significant factor of production and plays a pivotal role in areas of productivity and quality. In case, lack of attention to the other factors those are non-living may result in reduction of profitability to some extent. But ignoring the human resource can prove to be disastrous. In a country where human resource is abundant, it is a pity that they remain underutilized. Technology alone, however, cannot bring about desired change in economic performance of the country unless human potential is fully utilized for production purposes.

Rapid development in technology in the field of telecommunication, electronics and computer is taking place in advanced countries and also having corresponding effect in the technological base in our country. These technological changes are the fruits of innovative mind and entrepreneurship. Out of all the resources of an organization, human resource is probably the most critical resource. This is the only active resource and uses of other resources depend on efficient utilization of human resource. In the field of management, 1980s can be called as a decade of human resource development and computer. Last decade is called the decade of new technologies in every field including human resource. It is well recognized everywhere that human competency development is an essential prerequisite for any growth or development effort.

The human resource is critical and difficult to manage. It is because human behaviour is highly unpredictable. It differs not only from individual to individual but often on the part of some individual at different points of time. In spite of biological and cultural similarities, human beings not only differ in their appearance but also in their capabilities based on their background, training and experience. Management recognizes the importance of human resource competency development. Personnel management/ human resource management is doing remarkable work in attempting to find out new ways of developing competencies. The well-known mechanisms used for this purpose are training, performance and potential appraisals, feed back, counselling, job-rotation, career development systems etc. Human resource development is certainly a very fascinating subject but at the same time it is confusing also because it is inter-disciplinary in nature. It crosses the limit of management and enters into the field of psychology rather than keeping itself confined to the field of management.

2. HUMAN RESOURCE DEVELOPMENT (HRD)

With increasing global competition, it has become difficult for organizations to start, survive, grow, stabilize and excel their performance in business. They are under tremendous pressure to improve their performance quantitatively and qualitatively with cost effectiveness. The business environment is rapidly changing. It has become necessity to keep pace with the changing environment otherwise they will be thrown out of business by market forces. In the modern times, management has grown very complex and it has acquired new dimensions. The new challenges are faced by the management. The challenges faced by business organizations are how to improve profitability, tune products and services as per changing need of customers and organizational development to stay in competitive race of business. To tackle this situation the different experts suggested different activities and management has recognized the development of competency of people, coordination between people at different levels, minimizing production cost and improving productivity. The priority in personnel management has changed vastly. Now the tasks of framing rules, regulations and standing orders have been changed to promote the motivation generating factors and minimize the de-motivating factors for maximum capacity utilization. All these activities were clubbed together under umbrella of Human Resource Development.

Human Resource Development can be defined as a set of systematic and planned activities designed by an organization to provide its members with the opportunities and facilities to learn necessary skills and develop competencies to perform the current jobs and prepare them for further jobs also. Learning process is main for development activities and HRD activities is a continuous process. It should start with the entry into organization and continue throughout the career of employees. It is required for all people working at different levels and performing different tasks. HRD programs must meet the changing requirement of jobs and must be must be aligned with the long-term strategies of the company to ensure effective utilization of resources.

Human Resource Development concept has been defined by different Human Resource Management experts as follows:

In the opinion of Nadler and Wiggs, the ultimate purpose of HRD activities is "to make a difference" in the real world of costs, quality, quantity, accuracy and timeliness. HRD activities, as such, do not reduce costs, improve quality or quantity, or benefit the enterprise in any way. It is the on-the job applications of learning that ultimately can reduce costs, improve quality, and so forth.

It has been rightly observed by Billimoria and Singh that "each human being is born as something new, something that never existed before. Each is born with the capacity to win in his life, has his own unique potentials, capabilities and limitations."

According to Ishwar Dayal, "HRD is an approach founded on the belief that people are capable of growth given an environment that facilitates individual growth. Growth is, therefore, important for organizational growth. It is to make a person, a total person in terms of skill, maturity, competence, self-awareness, adjustment to the environment, and confidence. HRD can be seen as a philosophy rather than as a programme. HRD is for both which prevents growth and which leads to growth".

In opinion of Khan, "HRD is the process of increasing knowledge, skills, capabilities and positive work attitude and value of all people working at all levels in a business undertaking".

According to Rao, Verma, Khandelwal and Abraham, "HRD is a process by which people in various groups are helped to acquire new competence continuously so as to make them more self-reliant and simultaneously developing a sense of pride in them. HRD is an approach to the systematic expansion of people's work related abilities, focused on the attainment of both organizational and personal goals."

Nadler defined, "HRD means an organised learning experience, within a time frame, with an objective of producing the possibility of performance change".

According to Rao, in the organizational context, HRD is a process in which the employees of an organization are continuously helped in a planned manner to:

(a) Acquire or sharpen their capabilities that are required to perform various functions associated with their present or expected future roles.

(b) Develop their general capabilities as individuals, so as to discover and exploit their inner potentials for their own or organizational development purposes;

(c) Develop organization culture in which superior-subordinate relationships, teamwork and, collaboration among sub-units is strong and contributes to the professional well-being, motivation and pride of employees.

Further, Rao defined (HRD) as essentially consisting of these three Cs: competencies, commitment, and culture. All three are needed to make an organization function well. Without competencies many tasks of the organization may not be completed cost effectively or with maximum efficiency. Without commitment, they may not be done at all or are done at such a slow pace that they lose relevance. Without an appropriate culture, organizations cannot last long.

From the study of above mentioned definitions given by experts it can be said that that HRD is the process of helping people to acquire competencies. In an organizational context, HRD is a process by which the employees of an organization are helped in a continuous and systematic way to:

(a) Acquire or develop capabilities required to perform various functions relating to their present and future roles.

(b) Improve their general capabilities as individuals, discover and exploit their available potential for their own and organizational development purpose.

(c) Improve supervisor–subordinate relationship, teamwork and collaboration among different departments in an organizational culture and to contribute to the welfare, motivation and pride of employees. Human resource development therefore is defined as the total knowledge, skills, creative abilities, talents and aptitudes of an organization's workforce as well as the values, attitudes and beliefs of the individuals involved.

Human resource development process is facilitated by mechanisms or subsystems like performance appraisal, training, organizational development, potential development, job rotation, welfare and reward. People are helped to acquire new competencies through the various systems continuously. Personnel management has to deal with the interactive policies, techniques and procedures which together can help to develop the human resource of an organization. In present time Personnel managers are designated as HRD managers or along with routine functions they take care to HRD functions too. Line managers and staff personnel can cooperate to make sure that all these activities are planned and administered with the aim of development in mind. Since every achievement in every activity is related to human resource, it is important that a department is created within the organization to serve continuously the areas of human resource development.

3. NEED FOR HUMAN RESOURCE DEVELOPMENT

Employees feel the need of knowledge, skills attitudes and values to perform the task efficiently. We call these competencies. Higher degree of competencies is required for higher degree and quality of job performance. Hence to achieve the goals in the changing situation, it is necessary to develop competencies continuously in an organization. In the present competitive situation to survive, grow and excel, the competent and motivated employees are essential. To maintain the growth level over a period of time, competencies of employees need to be sharpened or developed as organization operates in the changing environment. The organizations are interested to develop their business though products or services. They want to bring effectiveness in the organization through cost reduction, delay reduction, better customer satisfaction, service promptness and better quality. Hence for these, the organization needs to develop its human resource competencies to perform better.

For example, a university, bank, hospital, profit making company etc., are interested to improve their services and want to give better satisfaction to customers, HRD activities may be needed to be undertaken to equip the employees with better competencies. Thus, the need for HRD is felt by every organization that is interested in the following **objectives** to be achieved:

(a) To stabilize itself

(b) To grow

(c) To diversify the products or services

(d) To renew itself to become more effective

(e) To improve its systems, products and services

(f) To change and become more dynamic

(g) To play the role of a leader.

Organizations need to be developed to make it dynamic and growth-oriented to stay in the race in the competitive environment. This is possible only through the updated competencies of the human resources. To meet the critical requirements of fast changing environment, organizations need to review their HRD activities continuously. HRD is an approach that applies various personnel functions according to need and urgency of the organization.

The need for HRD is felt due to following reasons:

(a) HRD is Required for Developing Competencies

No organization can work better without competent manpower. The employees must be capable and competent in terms of knowledge, skills and attitudes. Talented and motivated manpower is an assets of the organization whether it is profit or non-profit making organization. Every organisation needs competent employees for performing different tasks effectively and to make it successful in its business operations. A profit organization interested in growing, stabilizing, excelling and surviving by improving its performance in cost reduction, process time reduction, improved quality of products, services and behaviour of people. All these are possible only through competent manpower. Similarly, non-profit organizations like bank, university or a hospital interested in improving its quality of service, promptness in operation work culture, attitude of employees and goodwill of the organization in the market.

(b) HRD is Needed to Improve Quality of Work Life

In past, in factory system the workers were asked to work for long hours and were paid very less salary. It can be said that they were exploited to a good extent. The working conditions, attitude of employers, job security were very poor. Further, the rules, regulation and personnel policies were not favourable to employees. It can be said in brief the quality of work life was very poor. To mitigate the effect of these under HRD, systematic adequate facilities and support are provided to employees to learn and develop their individual skills and develop organization as a whole. HRD contributes in development of skills, knowledge, attitudes and provides career planning, self-respect and opportunity for self-growth. Under career development planning they know their career path in future and it is assured also. Further with the help of other HRD mechanisms like counseling, guiding, monitoring, etc., the quality of work life is improved which is not possible under old factory system working.

(c) HRD is for Organizational Changes

It is a new approach adopted by management to tackle the drastic changes taking place in business environment. Traditional approaches no doubt are relevant but it is not possible to bring major changes to tackle the current situation. To bring changes in procedures, systems, attitude and skills the need for HRD is felt. Through this the working procedures, attitude of top level management, skill of employees and performance is different areas have been changed. It is only possible through HRD approach. It gradually enriches the whole organization.

(d) HRD for Improving Organizational Climate

Unfavourable organizational atmosphere includes the feelings of fear, misunderstanding, non-cooperation, threat and jealousy. There the top executives are more authoritative and do not give due importance to human being. They are not aware of problems faced by people at work. They are ignored. In this working climate the sense of belongingness, attachment and initiatives are generally found missing. This is not suitable with the present rapidly changing working environment. To tackle the present situation the need for HRD approach is strongly felt to develop a new and better climate in the organisation. Here the importance of human being at work, human values, human problems and human relations is accepted. It replaces the old values by new ones. People become more open, independent, cooperative, friendly, creative and believe in teamwork.

4. NEED FOR HRD IN INDIAN CONTEXT

The rapid export growth, direct investment in foreign countries, joint ventures, mergers and acquisitions show the movement toward globalization. Foreign companies from USA, Europe, Japan and South Korea are presently focusing foreign markets through different modes of entry. It becomes necessary to manage activities relating to production, marketing, human resource, finance, research etc. Along with other branches of management the importance of Human Resource Management has also increased due to globalization, enactment of new or amendment of existing labour legislations, development of knowledge of employees and research activities relating to human resource, changing role of trade unions in present time, increasing expectation of employees from organization and competitive demands of employees.

In the present global competitive situation it has become very difficult to manage business of foreign subsidiaries. As it happened across the world, Indian economy was also liberalized. Due to this liberalization of licensing policy many changes have taken place in corporate sector in India. Now many public sector units are privatized or level of competition increased due to entry of MNCs. Government has stopped new recruitment and permits retrenchment and imposition of voluntary retirement schemes. This has increased the work load of employees. Further Tenth Five Year Plan recommended reduction in number of government employees. This has badly affected the working women. In this critical situation now there is pressure on Indian industry to improve quality of products and services with cost reduction. To stay in competitive race is possible only through upgraded working methods, technical and managerial skills and motivation of employees working at different levels. Therefore, the need for HRD is also felt, like other developed countries, in India.

5. IMPORTANCE OF HRD

In present rapidly changing and competitive environment it has become very difficult to survive, grow and excel in business. Further this has been exaggerated by entries of MNCs in Indian market. To tackle this situation it is only possible through development of human resource. Organisations who have developed their human resource have become successful in all competitive situations. The importance of HRD can be judged by observing the following points:

(a) HRD and Restructuring of Organizations

In past in most of the companies the organisation structure was very complicated. There were many hierarchy levels from top to bottom. The authority used to flow from boss to the person at lower levels in more time. It used to reduce the effectiveness of the structure. Now due to development of managerial skills the focus is on flat organization. Management is interested to increase the span of control and make organization flat and wide by reducing the number of layers of subordinates. This has proved successful in present time. Further, the departments are formed not on the basis of functional specialization but on the basis of products and services. HRD has made these structural changes possible.

(b) HRD and Global Competition

Due to liberalization of world economies many multinational corporations have entered in different countries through export, licensing, consultancy, collaboration, joint venture, merger and acquisition and foreign direct investment. These have increased the level of competition in almost every country. It has become difficult to carry out the business effectively. It has become a question of bread and butter for everybody in business. Now focus has been shifted towards development of competencies of employees. Organisations with competent and motivated manpower have proved themselves by giving better performance in quantity, quality for products and services. They are enjoying leader position in the market. Now importance of competent human resource has been realized to a great importance.

(c) Technological Changes and HRD

Due to development of science and technology industrialization started further improvement in these brought better machines and techniques. Due to globalization pressure the focus is on cost reduction, short production time, quality of products and services. In this situation unskilled person can not deliver the goods as per expectations. They will be facing a lot of difficulties to work on the latest technology. Unless a person is trained the quality and quantity of performance cannot be improved even the organization may have machines and equipment of latest technology. With the latest technologies people can work at distance or at home also. This has accepted outsourcing of functional areas. To survive in this critical situation again support of trained and motivated people is required. Without development of human resource it is not possible in present time to stay in competition with multinational corporations. This has increased the importance of competent human resource in the market across the world.

(d) HRD and Employee Empowerment

In present global markets the MNCs are operating a number of foreign subsidiaries located in different countries. For example, a company based in USA, having its foreign subsidiaries in China, India, Brazil and Australia and involves a long distance. It has become very difficult to manage these units from its corporate office located in New York. It has been felt that such type of business can be managed if company is having motivated, talented and dedicated manpower. This is not possible to get such type of manpower. For this management has to put sincere efforts to procure, develop and motivate employees. This dream can be converted into reality through human resource development process only. After this only the company can vest its employees with more authority, increase their accountability. This leads to empowerment of employees only through HRD.

(e) HRD and Outsourcing

In present time it has become a need of the business to provide goods and services with lower cost. This compelled many companies to outsource their non-core activities. This helped to develop the concepts of tele-working and flexible timing. Now focus has been shifted to physically handicapped workers, women and workers from rural and backward areas. They are forming a larger portion of working force and they can work at distance with flexible time. This contributes to cut down in house costs. Hence the need for training and development of such workers has been felt at micro and macro levels. Through proper training and development activities these worker can contribute to a good extent in cost reduction in operations.

(f) Compensation to Top Management

Top management compensation in U.S. firms is fixed as per shareholder value. If the value of shares of the firms increases then the compensation packages of top management will increase. This keeps the managers motivated and triggers them for good performance. To achieve good performance from employees and of organization as a whole the importance of higher level of skills and competencies is realized. Human resource development process contributes to achieve good performance from employees and of organization as a whole and helps to increase value of share of shareholders. This approach has not been adopted in India until now but in future it may be accepted.

(g) HRD Job Satisfaction

Organization where favourable climate for learning is created and facilities for training and development, Career development and proper guidance are provided the employees take initiative to learn more. This way they attempt to improve their skills, knowledge, aptitude and competencies. With higher degree of talents they are in position to perform their tasks without any difficulty. They get higher degree of job satisfaction. This provides solution to many labour problems and helps to maintain good industrial relations in that organization.

(h) HRD and Employee Turnover

Through HRD efforts the employees become competent and motivated. They work in a good organization climate. They are satisfied at their work and facilities provided to them. They know their career path and try to achieve through sincere efforts. They would like to stay with the organization for a longer period. In the present competitive environment it is difficult to procure good employees but it is more difficult to retain them. Through HRD process the firms retaining their employees get competitive advantage by cutting labour costs. Further the firms get rid of hardly working employees by motivating through HRD process. The level of commitment and sense of responsibility in employees develop. This gives long-term positive impact on the business of the firm.

(i) Bright future of HRD Research

To manage the business more effectively and better than their competitors the management of the firms has realized that HRD process can help them a lot. Further to find out more and better HRD methods and intervention, research in HRD areas is needed. It is possible when the top level management is having HRD oriented approach.

From the analysis of the above mentioned point it has been accepted that the HRD process is very important. In future its importance will increase further. It is very difficult to ignore HRD function in a multinational corporation operating in different foreign subsidiaries.

6. THE EVOLUTION OF HUMAN RESOURCE DEVELOPMENT

The human resource development has not developed within a short period. It took decades together for development of HRD concept to the present form. Evolution of it can be traced as way back to beginning of industrialization. It is necessary to trace history of it for understanding the modern concept of HRD. The evolution involves the following stages:

(a) Early Training Programs Arranged by Shopkeepers

In early stage of industrialization the skilled artisan used to produce household goods. With the increasing demand of their products, they started giving training to their workers and sometime they used to keep extra manpower. These people were trained some time with pay or without pay. They used to work with the owners because their resources were limited and they were not in a position to invest in machines and infrastructure facilities. They worked for longer period with the shopkeepers because they were unable to start their own shop. Later on this apprentice model was adopted for training of doctors, educationist and lawyers. The workers who acquired all skills of an efficient worker were called yeomen. Some of them left their masters and started their own shop but many of them could not start because they could not afford to buy tools and equipment for their craft shops. With growing number of skilled craftsman they formed their network to establish standards of product quality, wags of workers, working hours and apprentice testing procedure. This way the craft guilds were established and became powerful. It made difficult for yeomen to start their own independent craft shops. The yeomen too started their guilds and these started working to protect their interests in negotiating for higher wages, better working conditions and reasonable working hours. These yeomanry were the forerunners of present trade unions.

(b) Early Vocational Education Programs in USA

With the objective to provide vocation training to unskilled young and unemployed people, Mr. D. Clinton established a vocational school in New York City in USA in early beginning of nineteenth century. This was accepted and got popularity slowly. Further it provided training to unemployed with criminal records. This provided solution of the social problems in mid-eastern states in USA. This school was accepted as a model for vocational education and government passed The Smith-Hughes Act. Under this act the value of vocational education was recognized and funds were allocated for this purpose for state programs in agricultural trades, home economics, industry, and teacher training. Nowadays the vocation education is an important part of every state public education systems. This has been accepted in other countries including India.

(c) Early Factory Schools in Developed Countries

With the development of science and technology, new machines and equipment were introduced in manufacturing. This led to industrialization in developed countries first mainly. The manual workers were replaced by machines. Under scientific management principles advocated by Henry Fayol and F.W. Taylor, the importance of machines in production system for better and efficient performance was realized. The demand for skilled and semiskilled workers increased. The semiskilled workers were used for production and skilled workers were used for designing, repairing and assembly of machines. This way the factory system developed. The demand of skilled workers was not fulfilled due to short supply. Further rapid increase in number of factories this demand was increased more. In order to meet this demand, some of the companies established factory school. The training programmes were prepared and workers were trained to meet the increasing demand. First school of this type was established at Hoe & Company in New York and later on in the last quarter of nineteenth century other companies also established such school. The focus of these schools was to develop skills of workers for a particular job related to the factory work and not in general.

(d) Early Training Programs for Semiskilled and Unskilled Workers

In the beginning training was only given to skilled workers and not to unskilled or semiskilled workers. In 1913, a model of car for mass public known as model T was produced by Ford Company. It used an assembly line to produce this car with the help of semiskilled workers. The assembly line production technique reduced the production cost and it was possible to provide car at lower price. This became affordable to a larger segment of the public. With the increased demand it was required to design and operate more assembly lines. This increased opportunities for training. Other manufacturers of automobiles too started using assembly line. Next reason for demand of semiskilled workers was an historical event known as outbreak of World War 1. The demand of military weapons increased drastically. To produce more military weapons many new factories were established. Further the demand for semiskilled workers increased. To fulfil the demand of semiskilled workers training programmes were started to train the workers on the job. This was called job instructional training (JIT) and in present time it is known as on job training method.

(e) Human Relations Movement

Due to industrialization the production started on a large-scale. The demand of products increased due to two world wars and increased population. Workers were asked to work for longer hours, with very poor working conditions at meager salary and unfavourable attitude of the management. It can be said that they were exploited in the factory system. The deplorable condition of workers became reason of anti-factory campaign at national level. It was led by Mary Parker Follett and Lillian Gilberth and it was known as human relations movement. Under this movement it was advocated that the workers are human being and not a part of the machine. They must be treated like a human being and not a machine. At work place their requirements should be fulfilled to a satisfactory level.

The importance of human behaviour at work was accepted as an important factor for better performance. This was also supported by Chester Barnard, in 1938 and said that an organization is a social structure integrating principles of management and behavioural science at work. Abraham Maslow published his Motivation Theory based on human needs, stating that people can be motivated by different levels of needs. It was accepted by industrialists as a tool to motivate people by fulfilling their needs and increased their production. Further, Elton Mayo carried out Howthorne experiments and advocated the impact of human involvement in the job if they are cared properly. Other experts also expressed their views and advocated that human resource is an important resource and it must be looked after properly at work place. This may help to increase quality and quantity of performance and reduce production costs

(f) Establishment of New Training Programme

The demand of military weapons and equipment increased further due to outbreak of World War II. Industries were asked to support the war efforts by manufacturing military weapons. It was needed to rearrange the production facilities on a large-scale to meet the needs of the war. Demand of skilled workers increased further. The initiatives were taken to establish new training programmes with the larger organizations and unions. The federal government took lead and established the Training Within Industry (TWI) Service to coordinate training programs in industries where military war related goods were produced. Instructors of different industries were trained by TWI so to enable each manufacturing unit to start training at their plant itself. TWI trained nearly 25,000 instructors by the end of the war. The supervisors were issued certificates from many industrial units. With the trained instructors many companies designed, organized and arranged for training programme. Most of defense-related companies established their own training departments for training of their own workers. Due to this the demand of skilled workers was met and production of military related goods increased to meet the requirement of World War II. Further to improve the standard of training in 1942, the American Society for Training Directors (ASTD) was formed to establish standards of training in emerging profession in the country. To become members of ASTD qualification and experience criteria were fixed by ASTD.

(g) Emergence of Human Resource Development Concept

After world war the importance of human resource was realized more in comparison with the past. The trained instructors realize that their role is not limited to class room training. They can play an important role out side of class room also. They started coaching, couselling and problem solving activities. To perform this task the need for training and development skills including interpersonal skills, coaching, group facilitation and problem solving was strongly felt by the management. The focus on human resource development inspired ASTD to rename itself. It was renamed as American Society for Training and Development (ASTD). During seventies and eighties ASTD arranges many national conferences and discussion was mainly on training and development of employees. As a result, the ASTD approved and accepted the concept of human resource development and linked its support and contributed in accomplishment of the objectives of the organization. Further, it was advocated that through HRD efforts the performance and efficiency of employees and system can be improved. In this direction in 1990s, efforts were made to strengthen the strategic role of HRD.

(h) HRD Concept and Philosophy

With increasing global competition, it has become difficult for organizations to start, survive, grow, stabilize and excel in their performance in business. They are under tremendous pressure to improve their performance quantitatively and qualitatively with cost effectiveness. The new challenges are faced by the management. The challenges faced by business organizations are how to improve profitability, tune products and services as per changing need of customers and organizational development to stay in competitive race of business. To tackle this situation the different experts suggested different activities and management has recognized the development of competency of people, coordination between people at different levels, minimizing production costs and improving productivity. All these activities were clubbed together under umbrella of Human resource Development. Human Resource Development concept has been defined by different Human Resource Management experts like Nadler, Billimorea and Singh, Ishwar Dayal, TVS Rao and Udai Parikh.

From the study of above mentioned definitions given by experts it can be said that that HRD is the process of helping people to acquire competencies. In an organizational context, HRD is a process by which the employees of an organization are helped in a continuous and systematic way to:

(i) Acquire or develop capabilities required to perform various functions relating to their present and future roles.

(ii) Improve their general capabilities as individuals, discover and exploit their available potential for their own and organizational development purpose.

(iii) Improve supervisor–subordinate relationship, team work and collaboration among different departments in an organizational culture and to contribute to the welfare, motivation and pride of employees. Human resource development therefore is defined as the total knowledge, skills, creative abilities, talents and aptitudes of an organization's workforce as well as the values, attitudes and beliefs of the individuals involved.

Human resource development is a systematic and planned activities designed by an organization to provide its members with the opportunities and facilities to learn necessary skills and develop competencies to perform the current jobs and prepare them for further jobs also. Human resource development process is facilitated by mechanisms or subsystems like performance appraisal, training, organizational development, potential development, job rotation, welfare and reward. People are helped to acquire new competencies through the various systems continuously. This has been realized and accepted at macro, micro and individual levels. Under different universities and institutions degree and diploma coursed in HRD were introduced at graduation and post graduation levels in different countries including India also.

7. ESSENTIAL CONDITIONS FOR HRD

Human resource development is a systematic and planned activity that is managed by HRD executives. This contributes in development of skills, knowledge, ability, capability, attitude, aptitude and competencies of human resource of the organization. Through HRD functions efforts are put to bridge the gap between the existing and presently required competencies. It is a strategic move but it is very difficult to predict results in near future. It takes a long time to give its results to the organization. It can be ensured only when the person whose competencies are to be improved are ready and willing to learn. It cannot work out in isolation but many factors are responsible for effective working of HRD activities. Following are the essential conditions to plan and make HRD efforts successful:

(a) Positive Attitude

First of all to make HRD efforts it is necessary that whoever is involved must have position attitude. Without positive attitude the persons will not take interest in the jobs to teach and learn. It will become half hearted effort. It may prove a mere effort to waster time, efforts and money.

(b) Willingness to Learn

A person who is interested in learning more skills and acquire knowledge should be ready and willing to learn more. He may face difficulties during learning process. Whatever changes he wants to bring will be going to prove for his benefits in career development and success in working life.

(c) Favourable Working Conditions and Culture

These two conditions make the situation easier for the individuals and motivate them to go for learning. They are induced through conselling, better facilities, career development and other favourable policies. In a favourable environment a desire to learn more can be created because they know that this learning will be helpful for them. They are provided all relevant facilities to learn, develop and acquire more knowledge, skills and improve attitude. It is only possible in favourable working culture to give the desired standard of performance and behaviour.

(d) Support of Top Management

For planning and making HRD efforts successful the style and attitude of top level management should be favourable. If they are interested then only the resources can be allocated and facilities can be provided. Hence, involvement of top level of management is must without it the HRD efforts cannot be made successful.

(e) Support of Trade Unions

Trade unions are group of workers and they work to protect interests of workers. Trade union leaders must know that HRD efforts for the benefits of employees and organization both and not only for organization. They must convince the employees to get involved willingly in HRD activities. If unions support the decision of management then only the resistance from employees can be avoided.

(f) Skills of Trainer

Trainer is the person who trains the employees regarding rules, regulation, procedures of working and technology. If we have a well trained trainer with positive attitude, proper communication skills and knowledge of the jobs the effect of training will be more. It may contribute to make the efforts more successful.

(g) Evaluation

Evaluation of HRD efforts must be done periodically. Through evaluation the effectiveness of HRD efforts can be measured. Further remedial action can be taken to remove the deviation. If no evaluation is done then the weakness cannot be identified and system cannot be more effective and successful.

HRD efforts cannot work out in isolation. The essential conditions mentioned above are necessary for its success. If these conditions are fulfilled then we can expect the result to be good. HRD efforts cannot give result immediately. It gives impact in the long run so the favourable conditions are necessary. Otherwise it can be proved fruitless and it may be a mere wastage of efforts, time and money. Top level management must understand importance of essential conditions for making HRD programme successful.

8. TRENDS IN HRM/HRD FUNCTIONS

The term globalization can be understood as removing the national boundaries of different countries, entering and making the whole world as one market. In past, most of the economies were protected due to individual interests of the nations. As business environment is changing at a drastic speed, it has become very difficult in present time to live in isolation and meet all requirements from its own resources.

Most of the countries seek support from other countries in social, political, legal, technological and economic areas. Under needs of the present time and international community pressure, economies of various countries have been liberalised. India is also one of them. Companies from foreign countries are allowed to come and do business with or without conditions.

Further, development of transportation and communication technology has made it easier to start and manage business of a foreign subsidiary from a far away place. Distances between different continents and countries are reduced. These factors led to the concept of globalization of markets. In future the whole world will become one market and may be called global market. The concept of globalization is a debatable topic and it encompasses the widespread changes in politics, international relations, world economic systems, business strategies and management approaches. Examples of worldwide changes are foreign direct investments, political treaties and unifications and global financial markets.

Now it is a burning topic whether it is an opportunity or challenge for business organisations. The sociologist Anthony Giddens defines globalization as "the intensification of worldwide social relations which link distant localities in such a way that local happenings are shaped by events occurring many miles away and *vice versa.* Due to globalistion the national boundaries of political, economic, business and technological areas have been crossed. In future, the cultural diversity also will be reduced or removed. The removal of established physical boundaries and compression of distance and space may provide opportunities to some of the citizens and deny to poor people. Present existing cultural diversity has implication for Human Resource Management to manage culturally diversified workforce.

The rapid export growth, direct investment in foreign countries, joint ventures, mergers and acquisitions show the movement toward globalization. Foreign companies from USA, Europe Japan and South Korea are presently focusing foreign markets through different modes of entry. Huge global companies like Procter and Gamble, IBM and Citibank have long extensive overseas operations. But with European market unification that occurred in 1992, the opening of Eastern Europe and the rapid development of demand in the other areas of the world, more and more companies are finding their success depending on their ability to market and manage overseas.

As a result of this internationalization, companies must increasingly manage globally, but globalization confronts managers with some tough challenges of market, product, and production plans. These must be coordinated on a worldwide basis. For instances, organization structure capable of balancing centralized office control with adequate local autonomy must be created. We will see in this chapter that some of the most pressing challenges impact on an employer's HRM system and specifically the techniques used to recruit, select, train, compensate and maintain the quality of work life of employees who are based abroad.

9. INCREASING IMPORTANCE OF HRM/HRD MANAGER

Under globalization number of activities, areas, destinations and customers increased drastically. It has become bit difficult for management to manage the business activities effectively and efficiently in the present competitive scenario. If resources are managed properly by organisation then requirements of customers, employees and society as a whole can be met. This may give competitive advantage to a company over others. It becomes necessary to manage activities relating to production, marketing, human resource, finance, research etc. Like other branches of management the importance of Human Resource Management/HRD manager has also increased due to following reasons:

(a) Globalisation.

(b) Enactment of new or amendment of existing labour legislations.

(c) Development of knowledge of employees and research activities relating to human resource.

(d) Shortage of trained HRD managers at senior level to provide on job training.

(e) Rapidly changing technology creating skill gap among employees.

(f) Changing role of trade unions in present time.

(g) Increasing expectation of employees from organization.

(h) Competitive demands of employees.

(i) Educational at national and regional level are not in a position to meet the requirements of industries.

The above mentioned reasons increased importance of Human Resource Management in present time. These reasons are very critical and top level management cannot afford to ignore them. Hence, it has been realized that human resource management is a very important branch of management. Further, to carry out business in different countries the need for HRM has been felt strongly. Because of employees from diversified culture, sex, highly skilled employees, different labour laws in different countries, enlightened labour unions and leaders, high expectation of employees and competitive demands, management is not in position to do justice to the job. So a specialist in HR area is needed to handle the situation effectively worldwide.

10. CHALLENGES TO HRM/HRD MANAGER

Social, economic, technological conditions are changing. These changes have already affected business and will have an even greater impact in future. Human behaviour is also complex. The individuals rarely react exactly in an identical manner even in identical situations. These changes pose a major challenge to the human resource management. The human resource function has to make a pro-active and creative response to these challenges and the consequence they hold for human resource function. Some of these challenges are discussed under three broad groups are:

(a) Organisation Level
(b) Workplace Level
(c) Human Resource Department Level

(a) Challenges at Organisation Level are:

(i) Integration of human resource plans with corporate plans
(ii) Stay in global competitive business.
(iii) Task of motivating executives in view of reduced promotional opportunities.
(iv) Integration of change techniques.
(v) Task of keeping the organization young and productive.
(vi) Development of an organization culture.
(vii) Diversified working force.
(viii) Elimination of skill gap created due to rapid changes in technology.
(ix) Creation of suitable environment of learning in organization.

(b) Challenges at Workplace

Workers are working at the work place with different machines, equipment and facilities. Methods, system and technology are changing very fast and following challenges are faced:

(i) Adapting to technological changes
(ii) Challenges from hardly working workers
(iii) Challenge related to grievances
(iv) Focus on socio-psychological needs
(v) Improvement in managerial effectiveness

(c) Challenges at Human Resource Department Level

The following are challenges at HRM department level:

(i) There must be a focus on process orientation involving development of less formal processes that the line executives can use in managing people effectively.

(ii) There must be a concern to develop human resource strategies in line with organisational goals. The development of these strategies must be based on environmental scanning embracing emerging political issues, socio-cultural changes, economic factors, advancing technology and international events influencing domestic labour relations.

(iii) The challenge relating to research orientation involves audit of current practices and manpower utilisation, experimentation of innovative ideas, evaluation of personnel programmes and computerisation of manpower information system for enhancing the quality and efficiency.

(iv) There is a challenge for developing personnel policies. This may involve improvement of human resource systems to fulfill growth and development needs of people, formulation of policies to meet organisational internal requirements, long-term perspective and maintenance of consistency, and firmness in implementation and interpretation of these policies.

(v) There is a challenge relating to reinforcement of a matrix organisational personnel department at plant level. This challenge can be met by:

- Working closely with the executives.
- Seeking to handover the personnel function to the line executives through persuasion, education, and adopt a consultative role.
- Evolving a participative approach in developing personnel policies.

11. APPROACHES TO HRD

In last two decades due to rapidly changing business environment in social, economic, political, legal, technological areas it became very difficult to manage the business to survive, grow, excel and stabilize. To tackle this situation it was strongly felt that there should be talented and motivated manpower. Hence, HRD had emerged as a distinct area of concern in many organizations. This emerged first mainly in European and American countries mainly and later on in developing countries like India and other countries. A variety of HRD practices were adopted across the world and even in India also. The main approaches followed by Indian companies are identified as follows:

(a) People-oriented Approach

(b) Reciprocal Approach

(c) Selective Approach

Though these are the main approaches identified but there is no clear demarcation among these. Because, there is overlapping between these approaches. It is bit difficult to draw a clear cut line between these approaches. These are explained in the following paragraph in detail to understand the concept properly.

(a) People-oriented Approach

The focus of management was on development of ability, capability, skills, knowledge and competencies of employees. Development of employees became main motto with the objectives to tackle the stiff competitive business situation. Management took the responsibility for development of employees willingly by considering it their primary responsibility. A favourable working environment of openness, trust, mutual understanding, cooperation and team spirit was created in many Indian companies. Personnel polities regarding welfare, discipline, promotion, transfer, recruitment and selection, training, retirement etc., were prepared keeping in view the interest of the employees and their family members.

Management took initiatives to maintain good personal and industrial relationship within the company. This approach was adopted by public sector and private sector units. Welfare facilities were provided not under labour laws but beyond what was required by labour laws. Focus was on health, housing, transportation facility, education of employees and their children, canteen, entertainment, safety of employees. Management was interested and even today to maintain good living standard of employees. Top officials attend informal functions and develop good relations with their subordinates. This approach was followed and still prevailing in leading business houses like Tata, Birla, Ambani, Thapar etc., and public sectors like ONGC, SBI, BHEL, LIC and ITC.

This approach developed good faith of employees in their boss. He is considered as a care taker and fatherly treatment is given. In the above mentioned favourable environment the decisions taken by the top executives are accepted by employees willingly. Even during difficult time employees may accept to work for the company at lower salary to support the management in critical situation. Management also takes the moral responsibility to pay bonus to employees in poor financial condition due to their better relationship with employees. Management has utilized people-oriented approach for development of skills and knowledge and proved successful in tackling tough competitive situation. The main features of such organizations are:

(i) Top level executives develop their own team of loyalist and discuss the issues privately. They are treated like family members.

(ii) Leaders are actively involved in formal and informal functions. They actively take part in social functions of employees and develop informal relations too.

(iii) Top executives are given freedom to take decisions and they feel like owner and not as an employee. They enjoy higher degree of autonomy in management of the business of their organizations.

(iv) For well-being of employees and their family members the welfare facilities are being provided beyond legal requirements.

(v) HRD philosophy and practices and matching properly to meet the requirement of present business environment.

But these organizations are facing certain difficulties like changes in technology, leadership and aspiration of young and new employees. It becomes very difficult to adjust with the changes and HRD efforts get affected. These difficulties have been faced in many Indian companies time to time. But management could overcome these with sincere efforts. If these changes are accepted as inevitable then HRD functions can be performed properly with little difficulty.

(b) Reciprocal Approach

This approach is a mix of business and individual interests. Under present business environment management realized that it is difficult to stay in the competitive situation in business and sustain organizational performance without development of employees. The growth of organization is possible through growth of individuals and HRD is assumed important for growth of the organization. Therefore, it was in the interest of the business organization to develop human resource. Sincere

HRD efforts were put to tackle difficult situations of diversification, declining profits, falling market shares and speedy growth. HRD programmes were brought by leading companies in India relating to development of skills, role development, appraisal system, training, counseling etc. Focus of HRD programmes in Indian companies like ITC, Crompton Greaves, Larsen & Toubro, SBI and others was on development of managers and employees for new projects, assignment of new responsibility, overall organizational development, reorganization of structure, sustain growth and overall strategy for improving performance.

The practices of HRD were followed differently in various organizations to meet their needs and approaches followed were also unique. Some HRD practitioners developed a new HRD system including old traditional functions of well developed functions of Personnel Management. HRD programmes in organizations are different from traditional personnel management. The main aim of HRD programme is the growth of individual as a total human being. The business unit may be involved in any activity but the end result should be growth and development of individual who are performing that activity. Here HRD programmes focus on freedom in performing job, job design, risk taking in decisions, autonomy etc. The individual is taken as a total person and not only as a employee deployed on a particular job. It is aiming at development of total capability of person and not only skills required for a particular job. The HRD programme links individual and organization development together.

(c) Selective Approach

Under this approach the particular organization has taken up HRD programme for development of employees selectively for a particular job at a particular time. The main objectives of the programme can be selective. It depends upon situation to situation. Different types of practices have been followed by different companies. It is mainly to meet the need of the situation. This approach has been followed by a very less number of companies in past.

12. HRD MECHANISM, PROCESSES AND OUTCOMES

Human Resource Development must be continuous in an organization. The efforts and investment in development of human resource vary from organization to organization depending on its size, need and nature etc. It may also vary in the same organization depending upon the nature of changes the organization is going through. For developing competencies of employees there are numerous methods available for an organization. There are numerous HRD methods or instruments. When HRD instruments are used, these should lead to the HRD processes like role clarity, performance planning, development of climate, risk-taking, dynamism etc., in employees. Such HRD processes should result in more competent, satisfied and committed people that would make the organization grow by contributing their best to it. Ultimately such HRD outcomes influence the organizational effectiveness.

A model advocated by TV Rao in 1986, explains the linkages between HRD instruments, processes, outcomes and organizational effectiveness is presented below:

Diagram 3.1: A Schematic Presentation of Linkages between HRD Instruments, Processes, Outcomes and Organizational Effectiveness

HRD Mechanisms or Subsystem or Instruments	HRD Processes & HRD Climate Variables	HRD Outcome Variables	Organizational Effectiveness Dimensions
- HRD Department - Performance Appraisal - Review, Discussion, feedback, counselling - Role analysis, exercises - Potential development exercise - Training - Communication policies - Job rotation - OD Exercises - Rewards - Job-enrichment programmes - Other mechanisms	- Role clarity - Planning of development of every employee - Awareness of competencies required for job performance - Proactive orientation - More Trust - Collaboration and teamwork - Authenticity - Openness - Risk taking - Value generation - Clarification of norms and standards - Increased communication - More objective rewards - Generation of objectives, data on employees etc.	- More competent people - Better developed roles - Higher work commitment and job involvement. - More problem solving - Better utilization of human resources - Higher job satisfaction and work motivation - Better generation of internal resources - Better organizational health - More teamwork, synergy and respect in each other.	- Higher productivity - Growth and diversification - Cost reduction - More profit - Better image.
	Other Factors Personnel policies, Top management style and commitment, Investment on HRD, History, Culture etc.		Other Factors Environment, Technology, Resource availability, History, Nature of business etc.

Diagram: represents the relationship between HRD instruments, processes, outcomes and effectiveness of organization. HRD mechanisms like performance appraisal, training, OD interventions, counselling etc., are systematic interventions and an organization can make to set into motion or to develop the desired HRD processes and outcomes. However, mere introduction of HRD mechanisms and HRD departments do not automatically result in the development of HRD climate or HRD processes. There are organizations in our country today, who claim that they have been able to generate a good HRD climate and outcomes without having any formalized HRD mechanisms. It is possible to have a HRD culture without having a HRD department or without using any HRD systems that requires good leadership at the top, visions and building of HRD values from the inception of the organization. Other factors like management style and commitment, policies, previous culture and history affect the HRD processes and culture. Further, organizational effectiveness depends on a number of variables like environment, technology, competition, nature of business etc. The relationship between HRD mechanisms and HRD processes can be explained in the following lines:

(a) HRD mechanisms are useful instruments for initiating and strengthening development processes and culture and achieving HRD outcomes.

(b) HRD mechanisms and sub - systems should be designed keeping in view the HRD process and culture to be achieved.

(c) The review of HRD mechanisms should be carried out periodically to keep them updated to facilitate HRD processes and culture.

(d) It should be ensured that top management should have commitment to HRD and the same should be communicated to all employees.

(e) Sometimes HRD processes and culture remain a slow moving process and may take years to establish despite sincere efforts.

13. HUMAN RESOURCE DEVELOPMENT CLIMATE

HRD climate plays an important role in developing competencies of employees, motivation and teamwork. The climate can be created by the top management support and style by using the different HRD mechanisms. HRD climate helps to achieve the end and it is an end itself. Climate means the atmosphere in which different tasks are performed in an organization. Both the informal and formal structures of an organization contribute to create the organization culture.

Climate is the atmosphere in which persons work, support, decide, reward, restrict and find out about others. The term "Climate" represents internal environment that conditions the quality of cooperation, team spirit, dedication and commitment of employees to the job. It affects the efficiency with which the objectives are converted into goals. Climate influences the morale and attitudes of the people towards work and the organization as a whole.

Organization climate became popular in the last quarter of 20th century and this concept has been reviewed repeatedly. Climate has been defined as follows:

(a) Hellriegel and Slocum (1974) defined organizational climate as a "set of attributes which can be perceived about a particular organization and/or its sub-systems, and that may be induced in the way that organization and/or its sub-systems deal with their members and environment".

(b) "Organization climate is a relatively enduring quality of the internal environment that is experienced by the members influences their behaviour and can be described in terms of values of a particular set of characteristics of the organization." Renato Tagiuri.

(c) "Organization climate is the set of characteristics that describes an organization and distinguishes one organization from other organization, are relatively enduring overtime and influences the behaviour of the people in the organization," Forehand and Gilmer.

(d) From the above-mentioned definitions it can be said that if the organization climate is good and favourable then development of human resource is easy and effective. When climate is not favourable then HRD activities will be hampered.

14. ELEMENTS OF HRD CLIMATE

Elements of HRD climate can be divided into three groups – general climate, OCTAPAC culture and HRD mechanisms. General climate expresses how the top management supports and gives importance to human resource management. The OCTAPAC (Openness, Confrontation, Trust, Autonomy, Pro-activity, Authenticity and Collaboration) deals with, how the components are promoted and valued in an organization. The third element of HRD climate deals with the HRD mechanisms and up to which extent these are seriously implemented. Following are the assumptions regarding the elements of HRD climate:

(a) Favourable working environment is needed for effective HRD programme implementation. Top management must be committed toward HRD and must prepare good policies regarding HRD.

(b) For development purpose, HRD mechanism like performance appraisal, potential appraisal, career planning, welfare and rewards, feedback and counselling, training, job rotation must be used.

(c) OCTAPAC element of climate facilitates human resource development.

(d) Openness means employees discuss their feelings and ideas with each other.

(e) Confrontation brings the issues and problems forward for solution rather than hiding.

(f) Trust means the employees are believed what they say and do.

(g) Autonomy means the employees are given responsibility with freedom to work independently. Pro-activity means the employees are encouraged to take initiative, be creative and take calculated risks. Collaboration means the employees work in a team and help each other. They accept interdependencies in work. This concept of HRD climate was introduced by Rao and Abraham in 1986.

15. HRD CLIMATE AND ORGANIZATIONAL CLIMATE

Human resource development climate is a part of climate of an organization. HRD climate means the perception of the employees regarding atmosphere or environment for development of human resource in an organization.

Following are the features of HRD climate:

(a) Treating the people as the most valuable resource at all levels in an organization.

(b) Developing the competencies of employees is the job of every one in an organization.

(c) Employees are capable to change and acquire the competencies at any stage of life.

(d) Timely communication and free discussion rather than secretive.

(e) Inspiring to take initiative and risks.

(f) Top management support to employees to know their plus and minus points

(g) Climate of trust.

(h) Cooperation and team spirit.

(i) No favour and no fear tendency.

(j) Favourable personnel policies

(k) Healthy human resource development practices.

All organizations are not having the above-mentioned tendencies. HRD climate helps to develop individual competencies, team spirit and efficiency of the entire organization. For measurement of HRD climate, a questionnaire can be prepared relating to above-mentioned features and information can be collected and analyzed.

16. FACTORS CONTRIBUTING TO HRD CLIMATE

Following factors are considered as contributing to HRD climate:

Philosophy and style of top management: Open mind, welcome of suggestions from subordinates, belief in the ability of people and participative approach of management are contributing to develop positive HRD climate.

(a) **Personnel Policies:** Personnel policies favourable to employees will fulfil their needs as per their expectation and will not face resistance from employees. It will be possible to get support of employees and maintain good industrial relations. The problems like strikes, gheraoes, dharna, slow work practices etc., are avoided. Ultimately this would contribute to develop HRD climate.

(b) **HRD mechanisms:** In large organizations many mechanisms have been used to develop HRD climate. These mechanisms are counselling, feedback, welfare, appraisal, training and reward and career development.

(c) Attitude of personnel staff: The behaviour of the concerned staff dealing with development activities affects a lot. If the attitude is favourable, the person taking care of HRD functions will be in position to manage the development activities and people properly. The effect of this will be positive otherwise HRD climate will be spoiled or disturbed.

(d) Commitment of Line Managers: For development of employees the commitment of line managers is necessary. If the line manager spares his time for his subordinates willingly, it will give positive impact in the creation and development of HRD climate. Without support and commitment of line managers it is not possible to carry out HRD functions.

17. HRD, ORGANIZATION DEVELOPMENT AND INDUSTRIAL RELATIONS

Industrial Relations are equated in India with explanation of rules, industrial laws court judgments, collective bargaining, problems of indiscipline and grievances. The main terms used in industrial relations are like power, conflict, litigation and legislation. Industrial relations is a short-term approach and views relationship mainly from economic point of view. Management of men is very important and challenging job because of dynamic nature of the people. Human beings feel, think and act so they cannot be treated like a machine. Labour is no longer an article or a commodity that can be bought and disposed of at the desire of employers. They should be allowed to develop and keep their self-respect. Industrial relations pose delicate and complex problems to the modern society. Industrial relations is more or less seen as a business nuisance. Continuous neglect of industrial relations functions by corporate top management has only created problems for them. Problems of indiscipline, deteriorating work culture, distrust and disputes are related to industrial relations.

The problems of industrial relations relating to employees can be solved by human resource development through applied behavioural science interventions. Newly emerging functions of HRD and OD provides the solution of the individual and developmental aspects of organization. HRD and OD have been considered separate functions but these are relevant to the industrial relations. HRD, OD and cordial industrial relations are interrelated, interdependent and inseparable from each other. We cannot think of harmonious industrial relations without proper OD and HRD functions.

Human Resource Development is mainly concerned to develop competencies relating to technical, managerial and behavioural aspects of the people. Through HRD process the employees are supported in a planned way to acquire or sharpen their capabilities and to develop their competencies. This may exploit the potential of employees, create and develop favourable climate which will develop sense of cooperation and team-spirit.The main techniques or mechanisms of HRD generally used in organizations are manpower planning, recruitment and selection, training, performance and potential appraisals, welfare and rewards, promotion and transfers, quality of work life, communication, counselling, grievance handling and task forces.

18. ASSUMPTIONS OF IR AND HRD/OD

Differences between these topics can be brought out on the basis of following assumptions:

(a) Industrial Relations Assumptions

(i) It is economy, law and sociology oriented.

(ii) It is a reactive and short-term approach.

(iii) Its focus is on compliance.

(iv) Conflict is considered unhealthy in IR.

(v) It focuses on best use of available human resource.

(vi) Emphasis is on reward system to motivate people and develop sense of commitment.

(b) HRD/ OD Assumptions

(i) Psychology and organization behaviour are the bases.

(ii) Long-term and collaborative problem solving approach.

(iii) It focuses mainly in internal factors to manage changes.

(iv) Its main focus is on sense of commitment.

(v) Conflicts are likely to take place but must be managed effectively.

(vi) Creates environment of trust and mutual understanding.

(vii) Develops competencies of the people.

(viii) Emphasis is on internal motivation and intrinsic rewards and developing commitment.

19. ORGANIZATION DEVELOPMENT

Organization works as a system. It can be adjusted and improved to achieve its goal in the best possible way. The main goals of an organization are survival, growth, profitability, stability and better service to society. According to level of development of organization, its goals also differ. An organization is doing its business in the environment. External and internal environmental factors affect the performance of the business. External factors like social, political, economic, cultural, competition, changing needs of public and rapid change of technology threat the effectiveness of the business. External environmental factors are beyond the control of the organization. Management has to pay attention on internal factors which includes technology, manpower, materials and finance.

Management has to adjust or develop internal environmental factors with the external factors so that effectiveness of the organization can be achieved. This is called organizational development. It is a planned approach to respond effectively to the changes taken place in environment. OD may be defined as a systematic, integrated and planned approach to improve the performance of the organization. This approach is adopted to remove the problems faced by the organization in its performance. This approach is based on organizational dynamics and human behaviour. It focuses on integration of individual goals with organizational goals, team spirit and participative management. OD aims at development of conducive work culture of trust, openness, understanding and collaboration to help the individuals to interact more effectively to achieve goals. Thus through OD, organization is enabled to stand against the external environmental factors. The main objectives of OD are to improve organizational performance, better adaptability, create willingness and improvement in internal behaviour, personnel functions partly contribute to organizational development.

20. INDUSTRIAL RELATIONS

Industrial relations mean the relationship between different parties within an industrial unit in the day to day working of industry. The term industrial relations has been defined by different writers to suit their own needs and circumstances and the degree of industrialization in their country. It is commonly used to denote relations of all those associated in productive work including industry, agriculture, mining, trade, transport and other services. The concept of industrial relations has been extended to denote relations of the state with employers, workers and their organizations. This has been defined as follows:

(a) "The term industrial relations have been described as relationship between management and employees or among employees and their organizations that grows out of employment." Dale Yoder.

(b) "Industrial Relations is that part of management which is concerned with the manpower of the enterprise whether machine–operator, skilled worker or manager." Bethel and Smith.

International Labour Organization has used the term industrial relations in a wide sense to denote such matters as freedom of association and the right to organize. The application of the principle of the right to organize and right of collective bargaining, conciliation and arbitration proceedings and the machinery for cooperation between the authorities and the occupational organizations at various levels of the economy.

(c) "Industrial Societies necessarily create industrial relations defined as the complex of inter-relations among workers, managers and government." Prof. Dunlop.

Thus, the term industrial relations refers to "a set of relations arising out of the employer–employee relationship in the modern industrial society." Such a relationship is however, complex and multidimensional resting on economic, social, psychological, ethical, occupational, political and legal levels. State also plays a major role in shaping industrial relations in a country.

21. RELATIONS BETWEEN HRD–OD–IR

HRD focuses on developing human resource by developing their competencies like capabilities, attitude, knowledge and skills. Its emphasis is on motivational aspects of human being and organizational culture which help in development of competencies. Human resource development is needed to develop competencies for the growth and vitality of an organization. Organization development attempts to help the development in different ways using a variety of intervention including structural changes, technological changes, strategic changes, human process changes etc.

Industrial relations is a specialized function that evolved to protect the interests of the organization as well as of workers. There are many approaches to industrial relations like regulatory, descriptive, conflict and collaborative. A development approach has been adopted by few organizations to industrial relations.

They keep their employees in the forefront in preparation of their plan and their implementation. Focus of HRD is on employee's development and focus of organization development is on development of organization as a whole. Industrial relations are mainly concerned to maintain good relations between parties and to protect the interests of workers and management both in a balanced way. For HRD the focus is very individual, for OD the focus is on team and organization as a whole. For industrial relations the focus is on management, workers and their unions. Of the three concepts the focal point differs due to philosophy and purpose of the functions. But the dynamics of human processes are similar. HRD and OD can contribute a lot in the field of industrial relations.

22. NEED FOR COLLABORATION

Managers are dissatisfied with the industrial policies which are based on laws and management attitude. The conflict of interests between parties develops and this spoils the working atmosphere in the organization. This affects the progress of the business. Further, technological and environmental changes makes the things difficult to carry out the business under environment of conflicts, misunderstanding and distrust. Both management and unions are forced to review their relations in the interest of the business. Both parties adopt collaborative approach to solve the problem. Need for collaboration between different parties has been felt due to following reasons:

(a) Development of new technology and computerization.

(b) Workers are enlightened and they are creating anxiety to the union and management relating to their individual interest.

(c) Legal systems are causing delay in problem solution and increase the cost unnecessarily.

(d) Improvement in the business performance due to programme of quality of work life adopted by management of many organizations.

(e) Workers participation scheme and pressure from government.

Hence, development approaches to industrial relations to be adopted to create good industrial relations. This will create trust, mutual understanding and sense of cooperation. Both management and union should share common ideology. This development approach will solve many problems of industrial relation. So the need for collaborative approach is felt between them.

23. DEVELOPMENT APPROACH TO INDUSTRIAL RELATIONS

Development approach to IR will create the favourable environment of trust, understanding and openness. This development approach can be divided into two parts:

(a) Development of Competencies

(b) Development of Processes.

(a) Development of Competencies

The competencies can be developed at management, union and workers levels.

(i) At top-level management: Development of competencies of top level management is required because the objectives, style, tempo and atmosphere are set by them. The impact of style, knowledge and attitude of top management is considerable on the industrial relations. Due to development of competencies, top management has paid attention on human activities and the impact on the organization growth has been noticed. Development of top management will aim to create awareness in management to treat industrial relations as an important managerial function.

(ii) At middle level: Development of middle level is also needed because role of middle level is very important. Knowledge, skills and attitudes of middle level managers are to be developed. Knowledge regarding rules, regulations, legal framework, unions and environment are to be developed. Skills of managers regarding problem diagnosis, grievance redressal and inter-personal relations will help to perform better. Attitude of managers should be changed regarding problem solution, unions and participative management.

(iii) At workers level: Development of workers is needed because technology is changing very fast. To keep pace with the changing environment skills, knowledge and attitude of workers are to be developed. This will help to increase the performance of employees and organization as a whole. Better performance will help to achieve the goals of the organization and provide satisfaction to employees.

(iv) Development of union leaders: Development of union leaders at top and middle level is also vital. Top-level union leaders must develop their understanding regarding economy, industrial environment, legal and technological aspects. Their vision should be developed relating to issues of unemployment, poverty, workers' apathy, grievances and manpower crisis. Knowledge, skills and attitude of union leaders at middle level are also to be developed to improve union-management relationship.

(b) Development of Processes

In an organization many processes are used to perform the tasks. There should be a clear understanding at managerial level. Process means the 'How' aspect. Processes like decision making, problem solving, negotiation, sharing of information, goal setting and confrontation. Understanding of processes enables the managers to deal with industrial relations effectively. In development process the main tools used for development are bi-partite meetings, information sharing, joint research, special task forces, training, grievance redressal, participative forums, counselling and collaborative approach.

24. IMPACT OF LIBERALIZATION AND GLOBALIZATION ON HRD

Indian economy is a mixed economy, public and private sectors both co-exist. Indian economy was called a protected economy. Indian Government did not permit foreign investment in Indian economy. But since 1991, Indian industrial policy was liberalized and multinational companies entered the Indian market. Government accepted liberalization due to following reasons:

(a) Public sector was not in position to deliver the goods as per expectation.

(b) Private sector was performing well even better than public sector and could raise sufficient money from stock market.

(c) In communist countries the practice of free market was followed and it performed well.

(d) Globalization of financial market took place rapidly.

(e) To get loans from IMF and World Bank Indian Government followed the directions of these institutions to promote private sector.

(f) Better experience of development of private sector in countries like South Korea, Japan, Malaysia etc.

(g) Foreign-investors started investing in Indian capital market.

(h) Development and marketing of technological resources through multinational corporations.

Keeping in view the aforesaid points Indian Government took the following steps in the direction of liberalization, privatization and globalization:

(a) New industrial policy abolished all industrial licensing irrespective of the level of investment except for 18 industries related to security and safety concerns.

(b) Technological agreement and foreign direct-investments were not required to take permission from Government.

(c) Public-sector units were allowed to disinvest and raise funds through selling their shares to private sector.

(d) Competitiveness was increased in the Indian market by reducing import-duties and cover provided to domestic firms has been removed.

(e) For investment purpose non-resident Indians were permitted to invest in India.

(f) Removal of mandatory convertibility clause.

(g) MRTP Act and FERA act were amended.

25. CRITICISM OF THE NEW INDUSTRIAL POLICY

At present Indian population is nearly 125 crores. It is very difficult to provide employment to such a large number of people. Due to this new policy the job opportunities have been reduced. During the implementation of new policy a large number of workers have been retrenched. Sick units in the public sector have been closed. Government retrenched the workers and now Voluntary Retirement Scheme has been introduced. The fear of losing the job has created a great pressure on the minds of the workers. This is not good for the development of the human resource. VRS has been introduced in BHEL, Indian Tourism and Development Corporation, nationalized banks and in the private sector too. Government permission for shut down of units and retrenchment became more frequent. Management in the private sector adopted the policy of hiring and firing the workers. Hence, due to the aforesaid reasons this policy was criticized by the unions and employees.

Employees opposed the new policy of the government because of losing their jobs. It was a question of their bread and butter. They went on strikes to pressurize the Indian Government but in vain. The response of trade unions was very critical. Irrespective of their ideology the trade union joined together to fight against the new industrial policy. They gave calls for strikes in public sector units at state and central levels. This created a great loss of man working days. Trade unions opposed all moves of liberalization and globalization. They raised their issues both in the parliament and press. They opposed this policy on the basis of following reasons:

(a) It led to excessive layoff and retrenchment.

(b) Future job opportunities will be reduced.

(c) Hiring and firing policy creating a sense of job insecurity.

(d) Private sector will dominate the Indian economy.

(e) Wages of the workers are likely to be reduced.

(f) Social-injustice will prevail.

The new policy has been opposed by employers also. The new policy has permitted the foreign companies to enter in the Indian market. This will create a higher degree of competition. The domestic companies may not be in a position to compete with the MNCs, so they will be at disadvantage. The government mentioned that the new policy is implemented keeping the mind the workers' interests. But this policy has not been in position to follow the objectives of employment and growth with equity. This has increased the closure of units and more retrenchment of workers. It could not look after the interest of workers.

26. PRIVATIZATION

After independence Indian Government was interested to give a boost to the national economy. So public sector was established to develop infrastructure mainly road, transportation, communication, power etc., in the beginning the objective of public sector was to serve the public. But it changed with the time. As on today the objective of the public sector is to serve the society with higher profitability. This could not be achieved by the public sector. In public sector except a few units the performance of the organization is not appreciable. A huge investment was required in public sector but profit was not as per the investments. At present nearly 150 public sector units are sick. It is not possible for the government to finance every year. Further this situation has been worsened due to excessive job security to workers. In public sector job is considered baby of none. To make the show successful a large capital is required which is not available. To meet the need of the hour it was required to strengthen the working of the public sector undertakings. The resources to meet the need of PSUs can be increased through:

(a) Increasing production and prices of the products and services.

(b) Selling land and assets of PSUs.

(c) Ploughing back of profits.

(d) Loans

(e) Public Sector disinvestment.

Out of the above alternatives public sector disinvestment is the easiest and cheapest. Central government had raised a huge amount through disinvestment in the last decade. And in the recent past central government has sold BALCO and further Central Committee of Disinvestment (CCD) is planning disinvestment of Air-India, Maruti Udyog Ltd. etc. This disinvestment is done through disinvestment of up to 49% so the control of running of enterprise remains with the government. The main objective of disinvestment of the government is to increase the efficiency of PSUs.

27. CRITICISM OF PRIVATIZATION

The concept of privatization was advocated by the central government and it was favoured by industrialists also. But, it was opposed by the workers and their trade unions. Against privatization workers went on strike at national level. This created a loss of crores and man-hours. In late nineties against privatization, strike-call was given by employees and their unions in Department of Telecom. In December 1999, Insurance Regulatory and Development Authority (IRDA) Act was passed by the central Government. This was opposed strongly by workers and their Unions by declaring strikes in all PSUs in Insurance area. In 2002, over the issue of BALCO privatization the undertaking working was stopped due to strike call.

Disinvestment programme has been criticized by employees and their unions on the basis of the following points:

(a) This has diluted the role of public sector.

(b) There will be a shift in the control of the enterprises from public to private sector and it may not be in the interest of the public.

(c) Government can raise the fund once through disinvestment, but not again and again.

(d) Land assets of PSUs are sold out at very low prices to influential parties.

(e) Privatization is likely to create insecurity of job.

28. CHALLENGES FACED

The supporters of liberalization of Indian economy felt that it will increase the competitiveness of the Indian industry. The competitiveness from outside and inside of India would remove the cover of protection which was provided earlier to the Indian industry. Indian companies were now forced to survive on the basis of their own merits. It was expected to improve the efficiency of the Indian industry through the use of advanced technology. Indian government also tried to encourage the efficiency through various legal measures. However, due to liberalization and globalization following challenges have been faced:

(a) Unemployment rate increased.

(b) A large number of workers were shunted through retrenchment, layoff and closure.

(c) Percentage of industry sickness increased

(d) Slower growth rate of industry.

(e) Higher degree of competition in Indian market.

(f) Tremendous shortage of competent manpower to operate machines of advance technology.

29. HRD STRATEGIES TO DEAL WITH GLOBAL COMPETITION

To face global competition management, trade unions and government adopted different strategies:

(a) Management strategy towards new economic policy has been pro-reform. Management of private sector was under the fear of heavy competition from MNCs. So to fight with the MNCs equipped with advanced technology management tried to develop internal strength. There was shortage of trained and competent employees. Management tried to develop the competencies of their people through different methods. They adopted short-term strategy for this purpose. To fight management should adopt long-term strategy to develop human resource. HRD managers must develop an integrated approach. They should have knowledge of various departments, people, processes and performance. Management should create a favourable environment to support HR processes. The organizations which have followed these strategies are in position to meet the new challenges.

(b) The old approach of trade unions was of fault finding and oppose the policies of management. But due to liberalization and globalization the approach of trade unions should change. Trade unions should not pressurize management for unwanted demands. Trade unions should keep organizational success in mind and have to take up the responsibility of explaining to workers the present economic and industrial scenario. Changes are to be made in the strategy to meet the challenges thrown by liberalization. Unions have to make sincere painstaking efforts to convince the employees the topics like quality, total quality management, ISO- 9000. Trade unions must take initiative for development of employees if management has not started. If initiative has been taken by the management then trade unions must provide sincere support for development of human resource.

(c) Government strategy in this situation also needs to be updated. Government strategy has been to bring reforms with human-face. Government should monitor the present situation and bring suitable policies. To deal with the impact of liberalization and privatization government brought VRS (Voluntary Retirement Scheme) that satisfied the unions and workers to a good extent. Government, unions and management need to rethink their strategies jointly to raise the level of technology and productivity of workers and industry as a whole. Their motto should be first to raise the standard of competencies, performance and then become global.

30. CONCLUSION

Out of all the factors of production manpower has the highest priority and is the most significant factor of production and plays a pivotal role in areas of productivity and quality. In case, lack of attention to the other factors those are non-living may result in reduction of profitability to some extent. But ignoring the human resource can prove to be disastrous. Out of all the resources of an organization, human resource is probably the most critical resource. This is the only active resource and uses of other resources depend on efficient utilization of human resource. But this does not find place in balance sheet of the organization.

In the present competitive situation to survive, grow and excel and stabilize have become difficult. Different challenges like cost reduction, production volume, quality of products and services, higher expectations of customer and promptness in service delivery are faced. To tackle this situation the different experts suggested different activities and management has recognized the development of competency of people at work. All these activities were clubbed together under umbrella of Human Resource Development. The term "human resource development" has not developed within a short period. It took decades together for development of HRD concept to the present form, Evolution of it can be traced as way back to beginning of industrialization. It has taken almost a decade to come to the present form.

Human resource development can be defined as a set of systematic and planned activities designed by an organization to provide its members with the opportunities and facilities to learn necessary skills and develop competencies to perform the current jobs and prepare them for further jobs also Human resource development process is facilitated by mechanisms or subsystems like performance appraisal, training, organizational development, potential development, job rotation, welfare and reward. People are helped to acquire new competencies through the various systems continuously. Personnel management has to deal with the interactive policies, techniques and procedures which together can help to develop the human resource of an organization.

Organizations need to be developed to make it dynamic and growth-oriented to stay in race in the competitive environment. This is possible only through the updated competencies of the human resources. To meet the critical requirements of fast changing environment, organizations need to review their HRD activities continuously. HRD is an approach that applies various personnel functions according to need and urgency of the organization. In present rapidly changing and competitive environment it has become very difficult to survive, grow and excel in business. Further this has been exaggerated by entries of MNCs in Indian market. To tackle this situation it is only possible through development of human resource. Organisations who have developed their human resource have become successful in stiff competitive situation.

HRD plays very important role in restructuring of organization, global competition, technological changes, employee empowerment, strategic outsourcing, compensation to top level mangers, commitment, retention of employees and future of HRD research. From the above points it is felt that HRD efforts play very important role in present competitive environment for a organization. To make HRD efforts effective the essential conditions are positive attitude of parties involved, willingness to learn, favourable working conditions and culture, support of top management and trade unions, higher skills of trainer and evaluation of HRD efforts in the last. From the study of HRD topic it can be said the future of HRD efforts will be very bright.

31. QUESTIONS FOR REVIEW

1. Define Human Resource Development concept and explain its main characteristics in detail.
2. Why is the need for human resource development has been felt in industries across the world? Discuss.
3. Explain the need for human resource development arised in Indian industries also.
4. Highlight the importance of HRD in industries in present rapidly changing business environment.
5. Critically evaluate the role of HRD in development of employees and organization as a whole.
6. Trace and discuss the stages involved in evolution of HRD concept in detail.
7. What are the essential conditions for effective HRD activities? Discuss.
8. What are the problems faced in planning and implementation of human resource development activities? Explain.

9. Find out the challenges faced by HRD manager in present scenario.
10. What are the emerging trends in HRD functions? Discuss.
11. Explain the approaches of management towards HRD in highly competitive situation.
12. Define human resources development climate and explain its features.
13. Carry out the comparative study between HRD and OD climates.
14. Highlight the factors contributing to HRD climate.
15. Discuss the relationship between HRD, OD and industrial relations.
16. Critically evaluate the impact of liberalization and globalization on HRD.
17. Discuss the HRD strategy to deal with globalization.
18. Short notes on the following:
    (a) Increasing importance of HRD manager
    (b) Elements of HRD climate
    (c) Organization development
    (d) Industrial relations
    (e) Development approach to industrial relations
    (f) Privatization

32. OBJECTIVE QUESTIONS

1. It is a set of systematic and planned activities designed by an organization to provide its employees the opportunities and facilities to improve their competencies to perform the current jobs and prepare them for further jobs also. It is known as:
    (a) Human Resource Planning
    (b) Recruitment and Selection
    (c) Human Resource Development
    (d) Promotion and Transfer
    (e) All the Above
2. "HRD means an organised learning experience, within a time frame, with an objective of producing the possibility of performance change". This has been defined by:
    (a) Nadler
    (b) Rao and Abraham
    (c) Khan
    (d) Ishwar Dayal
    (e) None of the Above
3. The need for HRD is felt by every organization that is interested in the following objectives to be achieved:
    (a) To stabilize and grow
    (b) To improve competencies of employees

(c) To improve its systems, products and services
(d) To improve effectiveness of human resource and organization as a whole
(e) All the above

4. Organisations who have developed their human resource have become successful in stiff competitive situation. HRD has played its important role in:
   (a) Restructuring of organizations
   (b) Global competition
   (c) Technological changes and outsourcing
   (d) Job satisfaction
   (e) All the above

5. With the objective to provide vocation training to unskilled young and unemployed people Mr. D. Clinton established a vocational school in early beginning of nineteenth century in:
   (a) New York City in USA
   (b) London in UK
   (c) Berlin in Germany
   (d) Paris in France
   (e) None of the above

6. Abraham Maslow published his work based on human needs, stating that people can be motivated by different levels of needs. It was accepted by industrialists as a tool to motivate people by fulfilling their needs and increased their production. It was known as:
   (a) Theory of motivation
   (b) Leadership theory
   (c) Learning theory
   (d) Industrial relation theory
   (e) None of the above

7. To make HRD efforts more effective the essential conditions are positive attitude of parties involved, willingness to learn, favourable working conditions and culture, support of top management and trade unions, higher skills of trainer and evaluation of HRD efforts in the last. Do you agree with this statement?
   (a) Fully agree
   (b) Partially agree
   (c) Partially disagree
   (d) Fully disagree
   (e) Cannot say anything

8. The changes pose a major challenge to the human resource management. The human resource function has to make a pro-active and creative response to these challenges and the consequence they hold for human resource function. The major challenges faced are:
   (a) Organisation Level
   (b) Workplace Level
   (c) Human Resource Department Level
   (d) All the above
   (e) None of the above

9. A variety of HRD practices were adopted across the world and even in India also. The main approaches followed by Indian companies are identified as follows:

   (a) People–oriented approach
   (b) Reciprocal approach
   (c) Selective approach
   (d) All the above
   (e) None of the above

10. HRD and OD have been considered separate functions but these are relevant to the industrial relations. HRD, OD and cordial industrial relations are interrelated, inter-dependent and inseparable from each other. We cannot think of harmonious industrial relations without proper OD and HRD functions. Do you agree with this statement?

    (a) Fully agree
    (b) Partially agree
    (c) Partially disagree
    (d) Fully disagree
    (e) Cannot say anything

Answer Keys:

Question No.	Answer	Question No.	Answer
1	c	6	a
2	a	7	a
3	e	8	d
4	e	9	d
5	a	10	a

Chapter

Planning and Organisation for Human Resource Development

1. INTRODUCTION TO PLANNING OF HRD SYSTEM

Various resources like men, machines, materials and money are used by every organization. The organizations may be of any type like manufacturing unit, trading, school, education institute, bank or a government department and a hospital. Out of these resources, manpower is the most important because other resources are utilized my manpower. Further in present competitive situation it has been realized that without talented and motivated manpower the business cannot be carried out effectively and efficiently. It has become need of the hour to go for planning of HRD. Planning will ensure the HRD efforts are implementation properly. If the HRD systems are planned properly then implementation and effectiveness of HRD efforts will better. In addition to this HRD planning must be in line with the corporate planning. HRD planning must include the following elements:

(a) HRD Philosophy,

(b) HRD Subsystems,

(c) HRD Objectives,

(d) HRD Policies, and

(e) HRD Strategy.

(a) HRD Philosophy

The first element of HRD plan is its philosophy. It represents attitude, ideas, views and style of management regarding growth and development of its manpower. Practices adopted by middle level managers depend upon philosophy of management regarding human resource development. This gives a clear picture of goals of HR efforts. Without clear ideas regarding HRD activities, the manager cannot put their efforts in required direction. For any successful HRD programme following are the essential conditions:

(i) Manpower is the most important resource out of other resources because it is live, utilizing and generating other resources. Without talented and motivated manpower other resources will be idle and nothing can be produced. Hence, utmost care is to be taken of human resource.

(ii) Human resource is to be developed in total and not only relating to a particular job. Multidimensional development of human resources should be focused.

(iii) A sense of attachment or belongingness must be developed among employees towards the organization. This will bring feeling of commitment towards their jobs and organization. They will take care of their tasks as a mother cares for her child in even the worst situation also.

(iv) Adequate care must be taken by the management to provide welfare and other facilities to fulfil different level of needs of employees. An employee with satisfaction only can give commitment to the job. If the needs are not satisfied then he will be interested for his and his family need satisfaction.

(v) An opportunity for development and utilization of full potential motivates the employees. This creates interest among employees to learn and develop attitude, aptitude, skills and knowledge to perform the tasks properly.

(vi) Favourable working environment should be created by management for development and utilization of potentials of employees.

(vii) Top level management and other managers must support HRD functions to make them more effective and successful.

(viii) A healthy and motivating working climate of trust, openness, mutual understanding, cooperation and team spirit will be conducive for HRD programme.

In some of the Indian companies HRD philosophy was considered an important part of planning HRD programmes. TISCO a leading company from steel industry has given a good example of HRD Philosophy. The founder of it Jamshedji Tata accepted and included identification of needs and rights of employees, adequate wages, good working conditions, job security, proper redressal of grievances, opportunity for promotion and development, environment of trust and mutual understanding, cooperation and team spirit as main elements of HRD philosophy. Similarly Indian Tobacco Company in business of tobacco and cigarettes diversified its business in different areas launched HRD programme. Its HRD philosophy the main elements included are human resource as an important assets and need to be developed, good working conditions, adequate compensation, quality of work life, identification, development and utilization of potential, favourable environment to develop sense of commitment and shouldering responsibility and opportunity for self-actualization.

(b) HRD Subsystems

In HRD planning the next step is to specify HRD mechanisms or subsystems which are to be used in HRD functions after laying down the HRD philosophy. There are nearly 15 mechanisms for HRD purpose but uses of these depend upon requirement of each organization. These mechanisms are manpower planning, recruitment and selection, orientation, training, performance appraisal, potential appraisal, transfer and promotion, counseling, organization climate, welfare, etc. The contribution of every subsystem is that it more or less depends upon situation to situation. Out of these training is considered the most important. Some time the organizations consider training as synonymous for HRD. But training alone is not enough to improve skills and knowledge of human resource. The training subsystem is to be supported by other subsystem for effective HRD efforts. Top level management must select HRD systems as per the requirement. The following points must be kept in mind at the time of designing a new HRD system:

(i) HRD systems should aim at overall development of the whole organization.
(ii) Organization culture should be taken into account for designing systems.
(iii) Coordination should be made between different subsystems.
(iv) There should be provision for monitoring of HRD systems.
(v) HRD systems should be implemented in phases and not at once in the beginning.

If proper care is taken and abovementioned points are kept in mind while designing HRD systems, the designing of systems will be effective and may contribute to a good extent in achieving objective of HRD efforts in the organization.

(c) HRD Objectives

Having described the HRD subsystems, the next important third step is to determine objectives of HRD programme. The objectives are the end result that is to be planned and achieved. The objectives may be of job, department and organization related. The objectives at different levels should not be contradictory to each other. The objectives should be mutually supporting each other to achieve the main objective. The objectives at job levels may be to perform the task without difficulty and quality of job must be improved. The objectives of department may be to improve performance, achieve predetermined targets and contribute in profitability of the organization. The objectives of the organization may be to increase profit, improve product or service quality, meeting customer satisfaction and improving market share. Similarly the objectives of employees may be attractive salary, good welfare facilities, better working conditions, improved competencies, job security, timely opportunity for promotion and self-improvement. These objectives must be realistic and tangible and should not be beyond reach to achieve. If not, they may frustrate the concerned parties. The efforts will be directed in one direction to achieve the end objectives.

(d) HRD Policies

The next important step in HRD plan is formulation of policies. Policies are the statement relating to particular activity that guides thinking and action of concerned HRD manager and staff. Policy is considered as a sound base for practices. On the basis of policies the actions are taken and similarly the thinking is also changed. For sound HRD functions HRD policies are to be prepared and implemented. In absence of policies the decisions may be taken but the uniformity in decision making and action cannot be maintained. The action may be taken on situation base and they are likely to vary:

(i) **HRD policies can be formulated regarding the human resource development:** Decision regarding calculating manpower planning, existing manpower and net requirement of manpower and human resource planning integration with corporate planning can be taken.

(ii) **Recruitment and selection policy:** Should provide guideline regarding advertisement of vacancies, job analysis, reservation for reserved categories, selection process, reference check, medical checkup, issue of offer letter, probation period, selection process expenses etc.

(iii) **Orientation policy:** Should guide regarding orientation procedure, responsibility of manager for orientation, information to be shared and meeting with people working at different levels.

(iv) **Training policy**: Should provide guidelines regarding training need identification, selection of trainee, selection of trainer, selection of training methods, training facility and support materials, training schedules, training evaluation and review effectiveness of training.

(v) **Salary policies:** It should provide guidelines regarding wages and salary fixation, consideration for industry and market rates prevailing, revision of salary, salary for different jobs in company itself, provision of bonus, allowances and other benefits, increments in salary, settlement of disputes regarding salary, time and mode of payment of salary etc.

(vi) **Working policies:** Should provide guideline regarding pattern of working, working hours, weekly holiday, leave with or without wages, rest interval, lunch and tea interval, interval for working women to feed their children in crèches, vacations, working conditions, health and safety, discipline and grievance handling etc.

(vii) **Promotion and transfer policies:** Should provide guidelines regarding type of promotion, basis of promotion, compensation package on promotion, transfer, type of transfer and basis of transfer, duration of stay for promotion, transfer in normal and abnormal situations etc.

(viii) **Welfare policies:** Should give guideline regarding conditions for welfare facilities, facilities for different level of employees, procedure for availing welfare facilities, responsibility for providing welfare facilities, types of welfare facilities at working place and outside of unit for employees, welfare facilities for family, budgeting of facilities and review of welfare facilities.

(ix) **Industrial relations policies:** Should provide guidelines regarding standing orders, discipline, grievances, dispute prevention, disputes settlement, collective bargaining, negotiation, right of workers and their unions, intervention of police and court, workers participation, training of union leaders regarding improving industrial relations etc.

(x) **Miscellaneous polices:** Should provide guidelines regarding other matters those relating to human resource development like couselling, motivation of employees, working environment, involvement of management and trade unions, support of consultants etc.

(e) HRD Strategy

This is the game plan for HRD. Strategy serves the purpose of a weapon that helps to defend itself and defeat the other competitors. It is required to carry out HRD tasks effectively, better and before others. It contributes in providing competitive advantage to the organization over others. It will explain how to go for human resource development. For effective working on HRD a strategy is to be prepared. It is required for effective implementation. It will decide the responsibility of HRD, procedure, source of finance for HRD, evaluation of HRD efforts, time frame for particular activities for development etc.

2. HRD POLICIES AND CORPORATE POLICY

HRD policies are formulated for development of human resource whereas corporate polices is prepared not only for manpower but for other resources to achieve the organizational objectives, It is prepared by top level management and HRD head may be involved in this. Corporate policy is at corporate office and HRD polices are prepared at HRD department level. HRD polices are to be formulated in line with the requirement of corporate policy. The HRD policies cannot be contradictory to corporate policy. The main objective of HRD policies are to develop human resource and to contribute in accomplishment of corporate objectives effectively and efficiently. The two must be integrated properly by HRD manager or whoever is responsible for formulation of HRD policies. Now it is widely acknowledged that integration of HRD policies and corporate policy is necessary. For this HRD must play important role in parallel simultaneously. Formulation of HRD policies will be affected by size and life cycle of the organization, culture and style and support of management.

3. ORGANIZATION FOR HUMAN RESOURCE DEVELOPMENT

It is necessary is to assign responsibility of human resource development functions to any department. It may be in different form. HRD functions cannot be performed in isolation. Responsibility of human resource development can be assigned to the existing personnel department, an organization separately, committee or a different cell can be formed in an organization. Organization for HRD function can take many forms. The form of structuring depends upon the background of the organization, nature of the activities performed, the size of the organization and structure of the organization. It is not possible to have one form of organization in all the companies for HRD functions. Following can be different forms of organization for human resource development:

(a) Separate HRD Department

A dedicated and fully manned separate HRD department can be formed. A group of persons may be assigned HRD functions and create a separate department. This department may be a part of Personnel Department or an independent entity with required links with personnel department. The sizes of HRD department will be affected by nature of activities and organization size. There is no hard and fast rule regarding number of HRD staff. They may be called HRD managers or HRD Executives. The designation may be in tune with the culture of the organization. It depends upon the status of personnel department to make HRD department an independent or part of it. HRD staffs are to develop human resource and it involves inspiration and persuasion.

(b) HRD under Personnel Department

It is an administrative department ensures recruitment, selection, compensation, discipline, welfare, transfer and promotion etc., And a separate cell within the personnel department may be formed mainly responsible for development of employees. If management feels a separate independent department can be formed exclusively for human resource development functions. The decision regarding placing HRD department under personnel department needs to be taken after careful discussion. Whether it is a part of personnel department or a separate department, it should have strong link with the personnel decisions. HRD manager must understand the need of employees development through various committees and systems. Representatives of HRD department should be appointed in the committee on personnel policy formulation. HRD department should link with corporate planning, different departments or units or groups.

(c) Task Force or Committee form of Organization

This type of organization is mainly suitable for small or even in medium size organization. On the experiment basis large organizations also can try this form of organization. In this form of organization, persons from different departments, units, areas, regions may be selected to form a committee or task force. These persons are given the responsibility of HRD in addition to their main responsibility. They participate in formulation of policies, identification and development of HRD Systems, implementation, monitoring and review of HRD policies. This group may be known by different titles such as HRD committee or HRD group or HRD task force. The main job of HRD task force is not HRD activities. HRD job is the secondary job of this group. But for separate HRD department, the staff responsibility mainly is development of employees. The committee or task force will have a head, may be called chairman or president and assisted by HRD officer and other members representing different departments, units and areas. The task force may conduct meetings periodically to perform various functions relating to development of employees. The trained people with positive attitude must be appointed to the committee. This type of organization will be more effective if the members take the work of HRD seriously and devote more time in HRD functions.

(d) Chief Executive Officer Handling HRD

CEO may handle HRD functions himself. In this case he can take help of other cells like corporate planning cell or training cell. The personnel functions are separated and entrusted to personnel department. In small organizations where it is not possible to have separate formal HRD department, HRD functions are mainly looked after by the CEO. If he feels, he may appoint temporary working group or committee to look after the specific task or help him. CEO in an organization is having lot of jobs to decide. Due to his more workload, he may not be in position to devote more time towards HRD activities. Hence, it may become risky for the organization. This type of structure is generally found in small organizations like hospitals, schools and colleges, voluntary agencies, post offices etc. When CEO is looking after HRD activities, many non-HRD activities may keep coming to CEO as problems, threats, challenges and crisis. This situation will take the most of his time and giving no time to HRD activities. Hence, HRD functions face a high degree of risk. To avoid this risk, CEO may appoint one of his senior staff members to look after HRD activities directly under his supervision. To perform HRD functions, CEO may develop HRD activities related checklist and keep reviewing at a certain period of interval. This may be effective mainly in small organizations.

(e) Human Resource Development Through Other Departments

It is observed that in some of the organizations the HRD activities are performed through other departments. The departments which can perform this functions are training department, administrative department, strategic planning cell, management service department etc., out of different forms of organization structure, this is considered the least effective form. The main purposes or objectives of the other departments are different from HRD. The departments are established to achieve their main objectives. Hence, it is possible that HRD activities may interfere with the main tasks of the departments. People of the departments may not have the same level of commitment to departmental activities and HRD activities. Despite of this, in some of the organizations, this form of structure has performed well. This form of HRD organization may be cost effective and the simplest form of organizing activities of HRD. HRD activities are likely to be reduced to administrative activities when responsibility of HRD is given to personnel or administrative departments. To avoid this special care is to be exercised. In an organization if a separate Organization Development Cell (OD Cell) exists, it will be ideal to assign HRD task to it. Because HRD and OD are having similar concerns and staff of OD cell are well equipped to handle human resource development activities.

4. HRD RESPONSIBILITY

The responsibility of human resource development lies on shoulders of top level management, HRD managers mainly. But other managers also can be involved in development of their subordinates on jobs. The line managers are responsible for giving vision, direction, support to others, allocation of budget and review of HRD efforts. HRD manager must be made responsible for designing and development of HRD subsystems and provide for use to other managers in the organization. Other managers working in different departments must be made responsible for development of their subordinates on job where it is possible to provide then on job training and to solve their difficulties by guiding them on the spot. It can be said the responsibility of HRD is not of one manager but it is a joint responsibility. No doubt, the contribution of different managers will vary from organization to organization. Collective efforts can create a good environment for creating desire for learning, improve knowledge and skills, provide job satisfaction and enhance performance of people and organization as a whole. An initiative should be taken by top management to assign tasks relating to HRD to managers working at different levels and departments performing various tasks. There can no clear cut demarcation of HRD responsibility in the organization.

5. FUNCTIONS OF HRD/ PERSONNEL DEPARTMENT

The main purpose of concerned department is to create the favourable climate for learning and development. In the favourable environment the employees learn from the learning facilities provided in an organization and from their own experience also. The employees should be motivated by the department to utilize their potential. Due to continuous learning the employees will acquire new competencies (skills, knowledge, capability and attitude).The main objective of HRD department is to develop the competencies of the employees to meet the changing needs of the organization. To achieve this objective the concerned department should perform the following functions:

(a) Formulate the human resource policy in the organization and open support of top management.

(b) Create a constant desire to learn and develop by inspiring employees by line managers.

(c) Canalize all HRD efforts in one direction to achieve the goals of the organization.

(d) For creating and developing suitable climate, planning and designing of new systems and methods.

(e) Monitoring of implementation and performance of various human resource development mechanisms.

(f) Close contact with associations and unions and their inspiration.

(g) Conducting research periodically relating to various human aspects.

(h) Supply relevant information to the top management.

(i) Influencing formulation of personnel policies due to staff expertise.

To perform the above-mentioned functions, it is required that staff of the concerned department, must be well qualified and experienced. Otherwise these activities cannot be performed effectively. When it is found that HRD staff is not well qualified or experienced then they should be trained on their jobs so that effectiveness in handling HRD functions can be improved. If not done so then the efforts put for development will be fruitless or less effective.

6. QUALITIES OF A SUCCESSFUL HRD MANAGER

Manager for development of human resource is working for a special purpose. He is a man on mission. So he should have the qualities of a missionary. The special purpose of HRD manager is to create the favourable environment for learning and development. In the modern organization in present situation, the employees are busy in routine works like, power conflict, rewards, discipline, promotion, grievance handling, status solving problems, fire fighting operations, industrial relations, exercising authority etc. Under this situation self-examination is missing. The above-mentioned factors affect the quality of work life. For development of employees healthy environment and willingness to learn are needed. For satisfaction and motivation of employees the factors like growth of organization, its future, personnel policies etc., will have good effect. Next, the healthy environment of openness, mutual understanding and support, willingness to sacrifice individual interests, trust etc., must be created. If these two things are combined, the HRD manager can go a long way in building people and organization. HRD manager in the development climate can bring desired changes in thinking of employees. For the aforesaid reasons, HRD manager should possess the following qualities:

(a) Physical strength
(b) Intelligence.
(c) Education qualification.
(d) Decision making power.
(e) Communication skill.
(f) Training and experience.
(g) Positive thinking and positive attitude.
(h) A constant desire to learn and develop himself.
(i) Helping attitude.
(j) Initiative and creativity.
(k) Inspiring and interested in employees.
(l) Objectivity in approach.
(m) Discipline.
(n) Specialization in HRD.
(o) Respect for knowledge of others and their functions.
(p) Understanding of individuals and group behaviour.

7. DEVELOPMENT OF PROFESSIONAL KNOWLEDGE AND SKILLS IN HRD

To perform the tasks of human resource development some special skills are required. The professional skills and knowledge in HRD can be acquired in the following ways:

(a) Short-term Courses on HRD

Short-term courses on HRD are being offered by many professional institutions and consulting groups. Business schools, XLRI and Indian Institutes of Management offer short-term courses on HRD. These courses are for the beginner and line executives of different categories. These courses are offered on regular basis. National HRD network offered HRD programme and Indian Society for Applied Behaviour Science offers programme on OD. Diploma and certificate programmes are also provided by many institutions and universities.

It is suggested that every HRD staff member should join the professional courses and refer HRD study materials to develop the professional skills and knowledge.

(b) Understanding of Human Processes in Organization

In addition to professional knowledge, it is necessary for every HRD staff member to have understanding of human processes in organization. The main human processes in organization are personality, group and group dynamics, organizational behaviour, interpersonal dynamics etc. Human process competencies or understanding can be developed through specialized skill training. This type of training is being offered in India by Indian Society for Applied Behavioural Science (ISABS) and Indian Society for Individual and Social Development (ISISD). Specialized skill training are offered in the areas of personal growth, human process growth, human growth, Institution building etc. through laboratories and workshops. Such types of training is also being offered in UK and USA through professional bodies.

(c) Development of Individual Skill: Individual HRD Staff

It can be developed themselves by way of experimentation. HRD staff member may have new ideas and they can try these on the job. They may consult with the other managers, networking with fellow professionals, visiting other organizations, discussing with the line managers of other organizations and learning from their experiences. For further development, there are number of publications on HRD. These can be referred by the HRD staff.

8. ISSUES AND TRENDS IN STRUCTURING OF HRD FUNCTIONS IN INDIAN INDUSTRIES

The concept of HRD was recognized by some organizations in India in 1970, and further a large number of organizations started showing interest in HRD. Whereas some organizations renamed their personnel department as HRD department to keep up with the fashion of times. But some of the organization in-fact established a separate HRD department. The issues and trends in HRD functions were studied by Kaith D'Souza (1987). In addition to this, a study was conducted by National HRD Network, Centre for HRD and XLRI regarding the structure of HRD functions in Indian business organizations in 1987. 29 business organizations were studied from different parts of the country, public and private sectors and from different areas of manufacturing, trading, finance, construction etc. Out of 29 only 12 organizations (about 35%) had separate department for HRD functions. Many others renamed personnel department as HRD department or HRM department. The organizations which entered into business and diversified into different areas, to survive, grow and maintain viability in the competitive situation, induced the management to pay greater attention and invest more in the development of human resource.

Another factor responsible for setting up a separate HRD department mainly was philosophy of the top management of an organization. Organizations like L&T, SBI took the lead in this direction. The leading organizations are mainly from public sector in India. But some of the companies from private sector also took interest in HRD. Mainly the organizations from public sector are State Bank of India, Bank of Baroda, IOC, SAIL, BHEL and ITC. Some private sector companies launched HRD programmes are Tata Steel, Voltas, and Larsen & Toubro. Overall it can be said still the progress of HRD in Indian organizations is not satisfactory. In small organizations the concept of HRD is still missing but the future of HRD in Indian organizations will be bright due to liberalization and globalization. In the last three decade some progress has been done in big size of organizations. Still small organizations have not done remarkable progress in this direction. Yet the difference between HRD and personnel functions has not been clarified. Further difference between HRD and organization development is not cleared and whether they are to be linked or not, yet not clear. These two cannot work in isolation. For introduction of HRD programmes proper strategies have not be prepared. Due to all these factor the progress was slow. It was observed that the HRD was not effective in past in India due to various reasons. One factor is not responsible for this less effectiveness of HRD. Experts have given following suggestions to make HRD more effective in Indian organizations:

(a) There should be clear cut policies regarding human resource functions. This will provide clear and uniform guideline to HR manager to perform his functions properly and avoid problems relating to human resource.

(b) Top level management should take active part in HRD functions. He should provide full support to HRD manager in planning and budget allocation. He should review HRD programme progress time to time and supervise HRD manager too. He should understand importance of human resource and try to maintain them motivated and talented. He should contribute in creating good working culture in his organization.

(c) Time to time performance of people and organization both must be reviewed and try to find out the gap between existing and required level of competency of employees. If knowledge and skills gap is found then action should be taken to abridge this gap through HRD efforts.

(d) HRD department should be headed by a competent HRD manager and further HRD staff also should be trained in HRD activities. Unqualified person should not be given the charge of HRD department. Otherwise the image of HRD will go down in the organization. Top level management must be kept well informed by HRD manager timely.

(e) A good working climate should be developed with important features like openness, trust, mutual understanding, team spirit, cooperation must be developed. This may create a sense of attachment and commitment. A desire to learn more about jobs can be created in this climate. Problems can be solved through confrontation easily.

(f) Managers responsible for HRD functions in organizations should be encouraged to share their knowledge and experience with others so that learning within organization can be encouraged further.

(g) For development of knowledge and skills of employees help from external agencies like consultants, managers of other units, HRD network can be taken.

If the above mentioned suggestions are implemented sincerely then it can be said that HRD efforts can be initiated, developed and made more effective to abridge the gap of competency created due to rapidly changing business environment. It is expected that with the above mentioned suggestion the future of HRD in Indian organizations will be bright.

9. CONCLUSION

The organizations may be of any type like manufacturing unit, trading, school, education institute, bank or a government department and a hospital. In present competitive situation it has been realized that without talented and motivated manpower the business cannot be carried out effectively and efficiently. It has become need of the hour to go for planning of HRD. Planning will ensure the HRD efforts are implementation properly. If the HRD systems are planned properly then implementation and effectiveness of HRD efforts will better. In addition to this HRD planning must be in line with the corporate planning. HRD planning must include the elements of HRD philosophy, subsystems, objectives, policies, and strategy.

HRD policies are formulated for development of human resource whereas corporate polices is prepared not only for manpower but for other resources to achieve the organizational objectives. Corporate policy is at corporate office and HRD polices are prepared at HRD department level. HRD polices are to be formulated in line with the requirement of corporate policy. The HRD policies cannot be contradictory to corporate policy. It is necessary is to assign responsibility of human resource development functions to any department. It may be in different form. Responsibility of human resource development can be assigned to the existing personnel department, an organization separately, committee or a different cell can be formed in the organization. Organization for HRD function can take many forms. The form of structuring depends upon the background of the organization, nature of the activities performed, the size of the organization and structure of the organization.

It is not possible to have one form of organization in all the companies for HRD functions. Manager for development of human resource is working for a special purpose. He is a man on mission. So he should have the qualities of a missionary. The special purpose of HRD manager is to create the favourable environment for learning and development. To perform the tasks of human resource development some special skills are required. The professional skills and knowledge in HRD can be acquired through short-term courses on HRD, understanding of human processes in organization and development of individual skills The concept of HRD was recognized by some organizations in India in 1970, and further a large number of organizations started showing interest in HRD. Whereas some organizations renamed their personnel department as HRD department to keep up with the fashion of times. But some of the organization in-fact established a separate HRD department.

10. QUESTIONS FOR REVIEW

1. What do you know about planning of HRD system? Discuss its main elements.
2. Define planning of HRD system and explain the main steps involved in this process in detail.
3. Define HRD philosophy and discuss essential conditions for a successful HRD programme in an organization.

4. Explain HRD subsystems or mechanisms and which points should be kept in mind for designing a new HRD system.
5. Define HRD policies and explain the role of HRD policies in maintaining uniformity in decision making and implementation of HRD functions.
6. Discuss the different forms of organization for HRD and which is the best to perform HRD functions.
7. Do you feel the HRD policies should be in line with corporate policy? Discuss.
8. Who should take the responsibility of human resource development activities in an organization? Critically explain.
9. What are the functions an HRD manager performs in an organization? Discuss.
10. To carry out the functions of an HRD manager what qualities are needed. Describe.
11. How professional knowledge and skill in HRD can be developed? Discuss.
12. Write short note on the following concepts:
    (a) Separate HRD department.
    (b) HRD under personnel department
    (c) Taskforce or committee for HRD.
    (d) HRD through other departments.
    (e) Trends in structuring HRD functions in India.

11. OBJECTIVE QUESTIONS

1. HRD Planning will ensure the HRD efforts are implemented properly. HRD planning must be in line with the corporate planning. HRD planning must include the elements of:
   (a) HRD Philosophy and HRD Subsystems,
   (b) HRD Objectives
   (c) HRD Policies
   (d) HRD Strategy
   (e) All the above
2. An opportunity for development and utilization of full potential motivates the employees. This creates interest among employees to learn and develop attitude, aptitude, skills and knowledge to perform the tasks properly. Do you agree with this statement?
   (a) Fully agree
   (b) Partially agree
   (c) Partially disagree
   (d) Fully disagree
   (e) Cannot say anything
3. Top level management must select HRD systems as per the requirement. The following points must be kept in mind at the time of designing a new HRD system:

(a) HRD systems should aim at overall development of the whole organization.
(b) Organization culture should be taken into account for designing systems.
(c) Coordination should be made between different subsystems.
(d) There should be provision for monitoring of HRD systems.
(e) All the above

4. It is not possible to have one form of organization in all the companies for HRD functions. Different forms of organization for human resource development are:
   (a) Separate HRD Department and HRD under Personnel Department
   (b) Task Force or Committee Form of Organization
   (c) Chief Executive Officer Handling HRD
   (d) Human Resource Development through other Departments
   (e) All the above

5. HRD policies are formulated for development of:
   (a) Material resource
   (b) Human resource
   (c) Sales promotion
   (d) Marketing
   (e) Financial development

6. HRD programme are implemented by the management with the objectives:
   (a) To increase competencies of employees
   (b) To increase performance of employees and organization as a whole.
   (c) To improve profit, product or service quality,
   (d) All the above
   (e) None of the above

7. For effective working on HRD a strategy is to be prepared. It is required for effective implementation. It will decide the responsibility of HRD, procedure, source of finance for HRD, evaluation of HRD efforts, time frame for particular activities for development etc. Do you agree with these statements?
   (a) Fully agree
   (b) Partially agree
   (c) Partially disagree
   (d) Fully disagree
   (e) Cannot say anything

8. HRD manager in the development climate can bring desired changes in thinking of employees. For the aforesaid reasons, HRD manager should possess the qualities of:
   (a) Physical strength, intelligence and education qualification
   (b) Decision making power, communication skill, training and experience
   (c) Initiative and creativity, inspiring and interested in employees
   (d) Objectivity in approach, discipline and specialization in HRD
   (e) All the above

9. To perform the tasks of human resource development some special skills are required. The professional skills and knowledge in HRD can be acquired in the following ways:
   (a) Short-term Courses on HRD
   (b) Understanding of Human Processes in Organization
   (c) Development of Individual Skill: Individual HRD Staff
   (d) All the above
   (e) None of the above

10. Top level management should take active part in HRD functions. He should provide full support to HRD manager in planning and budget allocation. He should review HRD programme progress time to time and supervise HRD manager too. He should understand importance of human resource and try to maintain them motivated and talented. He should contribute in creating good working culture in his organization. Do you agree with this?
    (a) Fully agree
    (b) Partially agree
    (c) Partially disagree
    (d) Fully disagree
    (e) Cannot say anything

Answer Keys:

Question No.	Answer	Question No.	Answer
1	e	6	d
2	a	7	a
3	e	8	e
4	e	9	d
5	b	10	a

PART — 2

HRD PROCESS, MECHANISMS & PRACTICES

Chapter

5 HRD Process

1. INTRODUCTION

For development of human resource competencies management has to put sincere efforts. These efforts are to be put step by step. Like other activities in HRD also a set of activities are to be performed in proper sequence. The link of the activities cannot be disturbed. Therefore, HRD can be called a process. The set of activities like need assessment, designing HRD programme, introduction of HRD programme and evaluation are to be performed in chronological sequence without fail. The objectives of HRD process are to find out needs for HRD, create good organizational climate for learning, creating interest in workers to learn and to improve skills, knowledge, attitude, aptitude and competencies of workers to fill up the competency gap. The final objective is to improve performance of employees and organization as a whole to achieve competitive edge over other competitors in present scenario of globalization. If a company is not in position to achieve these then there are chances to exit from the business in cut-throat competition.

2. STEPS INVOLVED IN HRD PROCESS

For accomplishment of objectives of HRD the following steps are to be followed in HRD process:

(a) HRD needs identification or assessment.

(b) Designing of HRD programme.

(c) Delivery or implementation of HRD programme.

(d) Evaluation of HRD programme.

These steps are explained in the succeeding paragraph below.

(a) HRD Need Identification or Assessment

Before starting any activity its needs are to be identified or assessed. If the need exists then only that particular activity is to be undertaken. Otherwise it will be fruitless. Here also our purpose is to make HRD intervention more effective and fruitful. So the needs for HRD are to be identified. Needs assessment is a process by which needs of an organization are identified and articulated. A lot of efforts and information are required to go for need assessment. It is not an easy task. If it is done in time then it can avoid a lot of efforts later on. In identification of needs, examination of organization, its working environment, jobs, employees and organizational performance, and market share take place. These information can be used to identify the gap in knowledge, type of training required to fill up the gap and evaluation criteria for HRD efforts. In present rapidly changing business environment the environmental factors like demand, preference, and taste of customers, economy, legal systems, technology, and competition in market, social and cultural are changing. In this situation the skills and knowledge of higher degree are required. In a particular organization the employees may not have the required level of skills and knowledge to perform the tasks effectively. They are not in position to make the organization more effective in the race.

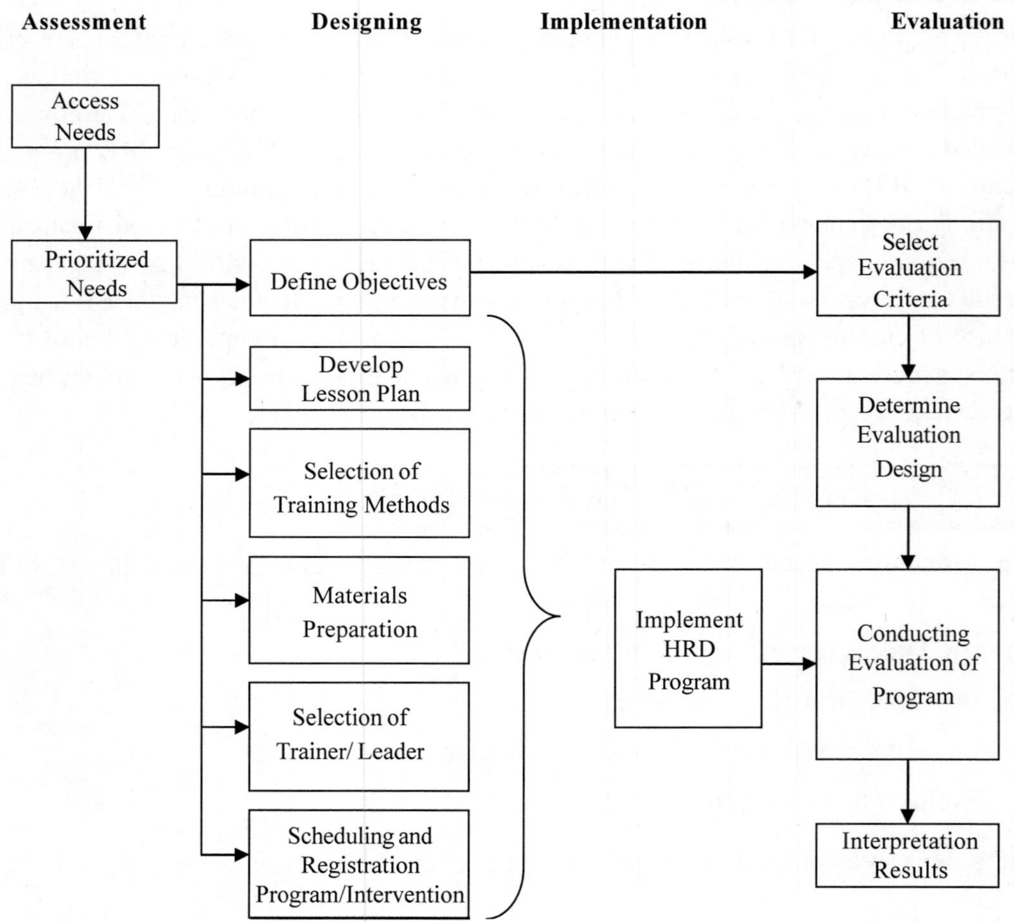

Diagram 5.1: HRD process

There might exist a gap between required and existing levels of knowledge and skills. This gap may be due to tough competition, advance technology, modified legal systems and policies or diversified nature of business. There may be a question of growth, survival, stability and excel in the performance of business. According to requirement of planning the performance is not given despite sincere efforts then deficiency of human resource knowledge and skills is felt. If it is felt then only further step should be taken for HRD. In this case it will be useful otherwise or not. During HRD needs identification, many organization felt the knowledge gap. Further these organizations in India took steps to launch HRD programme. Their efforts have proved fruitful for the organization and contributed in development of competencies of employees. This ultimately improved effectiveness of the organization in business and at present they are enjoying comfortable position in the market. These organizations are SBI, LIC, IOC, BoB, ITC and Tata Steel Ltd. HRD became effective in these organizations through need assessment.

(i) Types of needs: Robert Brinkerhoff argued that finding performance deficiency is restrictive. The need assessment should focus on other training needs like democratic, diagnostic, analytic, and compliance needs. Democratic needs are those needs preferred or opted by employees and managers or both. These needs are to be accepted to build support for HRD. Diagnostic needs mean focus on factors that prevent performance problems and contribute in giving better performance. Analytical needs mean a new and better way of doing the work more effectively. Though this type of need management is innovate in approach. Lastly, compliance needs are those needs which are to be fulfilled because these are required under law. These must be fulfilled as a legal requirement.

(ii) Needs assessment levels: Needs assessment can be carried out at following levels:

- **Individual level**

It is carried out to find out type of employees and determine the training needs for them. This analysis can be carried out with the help of performance evaluation, direct observation, interview and questionnaire, conducting tests, performance of critical incidents and personal log books of employees. Through performance appraisal system skills and knowledge, behaviour at work, attitude etc., can be assessed and discrepancies can be identified. Performance of individual employee is assessed and try to find out the weak areas and problems faced by individuals. Those who are not in a position to give better performance as per the standard pre decided they are identified for development of their skills and knowledge. The reasons of poor performance are analysed and if it is a temporary reason then remedial action are taken to sort out the problem. If performance of person is due to lack of knowledge or improper knowledge then for them HRD efforts can be initiated. It differentiates between successful and unsuccessful employees on jobs.

- **Task level analysis**

In it, data regarding different jobs are collected to find out what type of efforts are required for improving the performance of employees on the job. Data can be collected by using instruments like job descriptions, job analysis, standards of performance, by performing, observation, interview and questionnaire. The task analysis process will include preparing job details, identification of main jobs, method of doing the job and identification of areas that can improve task performance through

HRD. In this level tasks are analysed and efforts are put to find out the proper procedure of performing the tasks. For better result what should be done is identified. During analysis the method of doing the job, sequence of performing the job and relevance of each job is assessed. The problematic tasks are identified for remedial action with objective of achieving better performance.

- **Organisational level analysis**

In this analysis study of organization characteristics is carried out to understand the organization to decide whether training can be provided or not. If it can be provided, then where and what type of training can be provided. It can be provided by internal team or help of external expert is required. The organizational analysis is carried out by keeping in mind organizational goals, resources available, prevailing working environment and environmental trends and constraints. Organisational analysis will find out where HRD required position of organizational and environmental condition for HRD and aligns HRD policies with corporate policies. Organisation analysis can be carried out by measuring working climate, studying performance efficiency indices, going through skill inventories and HR inventories.

(iii) Prioritizing HRD needs: During needs assessment different types of needs are revealed. Management and HRD staff must look into these needs. All needs cannot be fulfilled. These are to be ranked on the basis of priority. In most of the organizations different resources are being used to carry out their functions. Further, limited resources are being spared for HRD functions. These functions are considered less important. So it must be decided what resources are required for HRD like facilities, machines and equipment, study materials, skilled trainers, consultants and accommodation. For effective use of these resources it should be decided that where these can be used more effectively. The priority must be decided on basis of return on investment and effect on individual and organizational performance. If priorities of needs are decided then first important needs will be fulfilled. This will ensure optimum utilization of available limited resources.

(iv) Employees' participation: Employees' participation should be encouraged while deciding priority of needs. Management is responsible for taking decisions regarding needs priority but these decisions should not be in isolation. This will make the need assessment less effective. Employees must be encouraged to participate in this decision. HRD programmes can be launched for employees of an area or areas of that organization. The employees of those areas must be encouraged to forward suggestions. These suggestions may provide relevant inputs in decision making. This will create more interest among people towards HRD and their support will be there for HRD programme. This may contribute further in creating favourable working climate for HRD.

(v) Advisory committee: In prioritizing needs there may be requirement of an advisory committee. This committee can be composed of representatives from various departments or areas. The main functions of advisory committee are to advise management in deciding priority of needs. This committee will chalk out its programme and will meet at regular interval as decided. This committee must review need assessment, data collected from different departments or areas, types and contents of HRD programme and effectiveness of HRD programme offered in the organization. The members of advisory committee must be selected on voluntary basis those who can devote their time without disturbing their routine tasks. Further, it should be recognized by the management. In return it will contribute to create good working environment for HRD.

(vi) Objectives of needs assessment: Main objectives of needs assessment are:

- To identify the areas and the knowledge and skills actually required for task performance effectively and efficiently to provide competitive edge to the organization in competitive situation prevailing in the market.
- To assess the knowledge and skills the employees are possessing while performing their tasks in the organization.
- To identify the gap between existing and actually required knowledge and skills for carrying out the tasks without any difficulty with efficiency.
- To identity the employees for whom HRD efforts are required to abridge the knowledge and skills gap existing.
- To find out the kind of HRD programmes required to fill up the knowledge and skills gap.
- To decide the criteria for evaluation of HRD programmes in practice.

(b) Designing of HRD Programme

Before going for designing HRD programme or intervention in HRD process through needs assessment the training needs, type of training required, people required, facilities and condition under which programme will be conducted are identified. The main objective of organination is to design a suitable HRD programe for people to improve their skills and knowledge so that they can perform better and provide competitive edge over competitors to the company. The designed programme should fulfil the objective of HRD process. Through needs prioritization, management and HRD managers are having clear ideas which issue requires attention and resources. Through needs assessment required data may be available which may help the concerned managers for designing HRD programme. If data available are insufficient then designing of programme may not be effective. Designing of HRD programme is not an easy task. A lot of discussion is required and many factors are to be considered. A proper designed programme can contribute in effectiveness of HRD efforts otherwise it may be fruitless. Special care is to be taken to serve the purpose of HRD efforts. Well equipped with information from needs assessment the management may design HRD programme and it can include the following activities:

(i) Setting objectives of programme.

(ii) Selection of source of trainer.

(iii) Development of lesson plan.

(iv) Selection of training methods.

(v) Materials preparation.

(vi) Preparation of schedule for programme.

(vii) Registration and enrollment for programme.

The aforesaid activities are explained in the succeeding paragraphs below.

(i) Setting objectives of programme: Every programme or activity is undertaken with certain objectives. Without objectives the efforts cannot be put in one direction. The objectives channelize all efforts and resources to achieve the end result. Here designing of HRD programme is also no exception. It also needs defining its objectives. It must be made clear that an HRD programme is prepared for what purpose. What management wants to get out of it. This objective will communicate the intention of the programme designer clearly to others. If not defined then many parties involved will be confused regarding the purpose of the programme. This is the first step to be taken in designing HRD programme also like other activities. A separate and well defined statement is to be prepared for each outcomes expected. Rober Mager defined an objective as a description of a performance you want learners to be able to exhibit before you consider them competent. HRD programme objectives describe the intention regarding the desired result from the programme. The main objectives of training programme may be to deliver training programme to employees to improve their knowledge and skill, improve in quality and quantity of performance, improve effectiveness of employees and organization as a whole and provide competitive edge over other competitors in the market. Finally it should help the organization to excel in business and develop its goodwill.

(ii) Selection of source of trainer: Management will decide about trainer from where to arrange. The trainer may be from the organization itself if available or outside. This decision can be taken after a detail analysis of many factors. For design and delivery of programme a series of decisions are to be taken. The programme can be designed and delivered by outsiders as consultants if it is cost effective. It may be designed internally if situation is favourable or partly in combination. The consultants can provide services like assisting in designing programme, guiding internal staff in designing, preparing and supplying training materials, presenting previously designed programme for others and conducting training for trainer or for all employees. What service is to be taken from consultants or outsiders depends upon decision of management:

- **Vendor selection:** There may be a number of vendors in market to help in this matter. Out of these one is to be selected based on the following factors:
- **Cost of programme:** The vendor who provides the required programme at lower cost will be better and should be selected out of many.
- **Vendor credentials:** On the basis of degrees, diplomas and other documents of vendors relating to his expertise must be considered. Further the projects undertaken by vendor in the past must be taken into account on the basis of reports of clients of vendor. Out of many select one who is the most recommended one.
- **Vendor background:** The success rate, number of years in business and experience are to be considered.
- **Philosophy:** Philosophy of vendor must match with philosophy of the organization which is interested to avail service. These two must be compared and if match is proper then it will work in a better way in the long run. Otherwise problems may arise at every stop and may lead to chaos.

- **Vendor experience:** The number of years of experience of vendor in this job must be considered. A newcomer might not be in position to deliver the goods as an experienced person can do.
- **Training Methods:** Training methods of vendor must be looked into and find out whether he is suitable to the requirement of the organization. If the training method is found suitable then vendor can be accepted.
- **Contents of materials:** Training programme and materials for training both are to be studied and find out whether these are suitable to the requirement of the organization. If matching the requirement of the organization then go for them otherwise not.
- **Definition of programme product:** Whatever programme is being offered by the vendor must be defined clearly to the client. If well defined then the objectives of it can be understood by the client. It should be taken into accout for selection of vendor too.
- **Results:** On the basis of results of past programmes it can be expected that the particular programme may give the desired result.
- **Support service:** With the main programme what type of other services are given by the client must be considered. Problem solving, follow up action and favourable attitude of clients are to be considered.
- **Request for proposal:** The request made by the client and the offer made by the vendor must be studied and try to find the match between these two. If these two match properly then there is green signal to go further.

By considering the aforesaid factors, out of available vendors, a merit list is to be prepared and on the basis of rating, the best is to be selected. Some time the requirement of the organization may not be fulfilled by one vendor then the service of others can be taken out of merit list, The final decision is to be taken by the management and HRD manager in selection of vendor.

- **In-house trainer:** When company is not interested to go for help of consultant then company can rely upon its own in-house trainer. If the situation is in favour of in-house facilities then it will be better and cost effective. In-house trainer will be in position to understand the requirements of the company, its employees and management. The training facilities can be arranged at required time for number of employees without any difficulty. For selection of in-house facilities and trainer the following points should be considered:
- **Expertise:** If the organization is having expert trainer then training can be conducted in house. They may utilize the available human resource.
- **Time of requirement:** The time of requirement of training is important factor to be considered. If it is required urgently then in-house facilities can be arranged within short period. The service of vendors cannot be arranged early. It takes a long time to decide.
- **Cost effectiveness:** Out of the two options, the cost effective must be considered. Further if the budget of the company permits then it may go for vendor services, if not the in-house facilities should be used.

- **Target group:** Size of target trainees must be discussed. It a large number of trainees are to be trained then in-house facilities will more suitable. In case the trainees are less then vendor services can be taken.
- **Nature of subject matter**: If the nature of subject matter of training is confidential the question of opting for vendor services does not arise. In-house trainer will be in position to serve the purpose in a better way.
- **Size of HRD department:** If HRD department is large enough and having number of expert managers with required competencies then in-house training can be arranged without any problem.
- **Other factors:** Any other factor that may be considered by management as important may be considered for selection of in-house training in the company.

Once the company has decided the source of trainer then a trainer must be selected. When it is decided that the HRD programme will be designed by internal expert then out of available experts a trainer is to be selected. A trainer should have good knowledge and skills of designing and implementing training programme. He should have good communication skills, knowledge about training methods and interpersonal skills. He must be in position to deliver the goods to the trainees effectively and must motivate then during training. Further a trainer must have thorough knowledge of the subject matter. Some experts having thorough knowledge of subject matter but are not in a position to deliver the programme effectively. They have poor communication skills. For a good trainer all above mentioned qualities must be there. This will serve the purpose of HRD programme. If a competent trainer is not available then help can be taken from outsiders. They can be supported by outside experts. Subject matter experts can be from in-house team. A trainer training programme can be arranged to train in-house expert to develop his training skills.

(iii) Development of lesson plan: For imparting training to employees a lesson plan is to be prepared. To accomplish the objectives of HRD programme there is need of lesson. Through a lesson plan the trainer can deliver the goods to the trainees effectively. Before planning lessons it is to be decided regarding contents to be covered during training period. According to nature and type of training the contents of lesson plan are to be decided. The contents of a lesson plan cannot be same for different types of trainees. Gilley and Eggland suggested the following points should be included in lesson plan:

- Contents to be covered during training.
- Logical sequence of activities to be performed
- Selection of medium of instructions.
- Selection and development of training exercises.
- Selection of training methods.
- Planning and scheduling of each training activity.
- Planning and development of evaluation process.

In designing the lesson plan the person having expertise can help a lot. Person having educational backgrounds in instructional design will serve the purpose properly. A standard lesson plan will be prepared by the experts and this will help the trainers and trainees during training programme. The lesson plan can be reviewed or modified if required in future to tune it in line with the requirement of the training.

(iv) Selection of training methods: After preparing a lesson plan the next important step in this direction is selection of training method. Through training method the knowledge and skills can be imparted to the trainees. There are many methods of training available. It entirely depends upon the management decision. Broadly the training methods can be classified as on-job and off-job training methods. In on-job methods, we can include the methods which provide training while working on the job under supervision of an expert person. Off-job training methods include classroom, lecture, conference, seminar, workshop, case study, role playing, games, simulations and vestibule methods. Each method is having its importance in a particular situation. Decision regarding selection of method will be taken by management and HRD manager. The following points must be kept in mind for selection of training method:

- **Objectives of training programme:** This is an important factor. By the selected training method the purpose of the programme must be served properly. To achieve objectives some of training methods may be better than others. For example, theoretical and practical training can be given better through vestibule method.
- **Time and budget:** For training purpose there will be requirement of time and money. This is to be decided by management that how much money can be spared and training is to be completed in how many days. Accordingly a training method can be selected. HRD manager has to compromise with the training method most suitable according to time and money spared by top management.
- **Availability of training facilities:** For training purpose different facilities like expert trainers, accommodation, training equipment, training materials etc. If these are available then training can be given effectively. Management has to decide training methods keeping in view the available facilities for training.
- **Types of trainees and their preferences:** It is to be decided for what type of trainees the training is going to be conducted. Trainees may be educated or highly educated. Further, they like reading and writing or not. These must be kept in mind and then final decision is to be taken. For example, computer based training programme can be selected for trainees having good computer literacy.

(v) Materials preparation: During training programme trainees are to be provided some supporting materials. The trainers deliver the lectures or give instructions to perform a task. But this must be supported by some written materials that can be referred by trainees when ever they want to study or refer to the topics. The study materials will help them to prepare their lesson and in future also these can be referred. The study materials can be in form of programme announcement, programme syllabus, notes printed or zeroxed, manuals, textbooks, blueprints or circuit diagrams, schematic diagrams of machines and equipment. These can in different form as per the requirement of training programme. These must be translated according to medium of instructions during training programme.

First, through programme announcement the target group will be informed about the training programme, objectives of programme, time and place of conducting training programme, procedure for qualifying to participate in the programme. This announcement must be given well in time so that the candidates can prepare for the programme properly. The programme announcement should be sent through newsletters, noticeboard, internet facility of organization, mail, union circulation and training bulletins. Programme schedule will provide information regarding topics covered in programme, objectives, materials required, requirement of each trainee and tentative schedule of the whole programme. This also gives information regarding attendance, discipline, work habits, class participation, teaching methodology, evaluation pattern etc.

The training material supplied by the organization is accepted by the trainees. They rely on training materials more than other materials. It may be in form of training manual, textbooks, instruction manual, reading notes, exercise books, and test exercises. Textbooks give information regarding the subject matter in depth whereas instruction manual provides information in brief and includes main points with a little explanation. Training materials can be prepared by utilizing the available resources in a cost effective way. If training material of other agency is being used for training purpose the written permission of that party must be obtained. If not done so it may attract the provision of Copyright Act relating to violation of copyright.

(vi) Preparation of schedule for programme: The last step in designing HRD programme is preparation of schedule for programme. It must be prepared according to requirements of production schedule, supervisors, managers and trainees. The objective of schedule preparation is to ensure participation of trainers and trainees. If participation is low then the purpose of scheduling will be defeated. The programme can be scheduled during or after working hours.

Scheduling during working hours can be opted if management thinks that learning is a part of the job. This may avoid conflicts from daily commuters, family and personal obligations. For scheduling programme during working hours certain points like day of the week, time of the day, peak work hours, staff meeting and traveling requirement must be kept in mind. Some of the employees at the weekend want to avail prefix and suffix on Friday and Monday. So these must be avoided. In beginning of the working day the employees may face more job workload and at lunch time they would like to take their lunch without any disturbance. Mid-afternoon time employees feel tired resulting in sluggishness. At the end of working hours some of employees would like to leave early for personal obligations. Peak working hours, end of month and year must be avoided because employees are with more work to perform. For scheduling the programme, managers and supervisors must be consulted. It will ensure best scheduling and maximum participation of trainers and trainees.

Scheduling training programme after working hours is second option. If done it can avoid many problems of the organization discussed above. But it can create other problems like hardship to employees, family obligations, and other personal commitment after working hours. If it is scheduled during weekend then it should be communicated well in advance to employees so that they can prepare them mentally. Still it will face opposition from many employees who are not interested to give up their holidays for training. In this case the employees must be provided overtime for training, compensatory leave, and training as a qualification for further promotion. All these may ensure proper participation from trainers and trainees and purpose of designing programme will be served in a better way.

(vii) Registration and enrollment for programme: Registration and enrollment is a practical problem faced by HRD managers. Issues relating to registration and enrollment must be made clear to the participants and HRD manager. It must highlight the procedure for registration, travel arrangements, lodging and boarding, cancellation and rescheduling procedure. In past, a lot of time was consumed in correspondence and things were not done at the time of requirement. Many complaints were received by HRD manager from participants. But today the situation has improved due to availability of information technology. The things can be communicated in time and timely actions can be taken. HRD managers too find it easier to manage registration and enrollment for different HRD programme.

(c) Delivery or Implementation HRD programme

After HRD needs identification or assessment and designing of HRD programme, the next step in HRD process is implementation of HRD programme. In this step whatever is designed and planned is put into action. This is an important function of HRD manager. If it is performed properly the whole process will prove effective.The responsibility lies on shoulder of trainer or HRD manager. This will include the following activities:

(i) Arrangement of facilities.

(ii) Arrangement of working conditions.

(iii) Coordination of training activities.

These activities are explained in detail below:

(i) Arrangement of facilities: According to the training methods planned under designing and planning of programme, the training facilities are to be planned. If it is on-job training method then the facilities required for training are to be arranged. These may include study and writing materials, noticeboards, communication facilities, computer facility if required, machines and equipment as per nature of requirement, instructions or machine manuals etc. If the training method is a classroom method then arrangement of space, furniture, training aid equipment like powerpoint projector, overhead projector, slide projector, notice and blackboards, wash and bathroom facilities, cafeteria, parking facilities, drinking water facilities etc. These facilities must be sufficient enough for the number of trainees and staff involved in conducting training programme.

(ii) Arrangement of working conditions: For conducting training, the physical environment must be good. The physical environment affects the comfort and output of the trainer and trainees. In a good working condition, they will be more comfortable and take good interest in learning. This may contribute in good learning and result of trainees and trainers. Under poor working conditions better comfort, interest in learning and results cannot be expected. Working conditions may include ambient temperature, ventilation, light arrangement, cleanliness, noise and interferences, facilities of wash and bathroom separately for gents and ladies, and seating arrangements. These are to be maintained up to a reasonable level. If not maintained these may create problems for trainers and trainees and the end result will be poor. The whole purpose of the training programme may be defeated. Good working conditions make the situation comfortable for concerned parties. They will take more interest in work and will not get tired very soon. The end result will be better. It must be kept in mind during implementation of training programme.

(iii) Coordination of training activities: In implementation of training programme the last step is very important. It will have direct impact on efficiency of the training programme. It may include the activities regarding collection of copies of designed programme, study materials, syllabus, announcement of programme, scheduling, informing trainers and trainees regarding date, time and place of training, distribution of required materials to trainees, and supervising when programme is conducted. If any change in any activity due to some unavoidable reason then it is to be informed to all concerned parties. In this stage, quick, proper and timely actions are required otherwise there may creep many problems during training programme. It should be ensured that there should not be any communication gap relating to training activities.

(d) Evaluation of HRD Programme

Evaluation is the process in which a particular activity, systems or a programme is assessed on the basis of its performance. It is being carried out to know its exact position whether it is doing its work as per planning or not. If doing then how much it is doing. This gives the clear picture of health of the work performed. During evaluation it may be found effective or not. Now Evaluation of HRD programme, information can be collected from concerned parties involved regarding its programme, syllabus, study materials, facilities made available, trainer skills and behaviour, interest of trainers, schedule of conducting training, interest of trainees, benefits to trainees and other relevant information. This will find out what has happened and what opinions of parties involved are. During evaluation if it is found the particular HRD programme is not working effectively then it can be stopped or modified as per requirement to make it successful. The evaluation may improve the image of HRD programme in organization and top level management will get information about benefits of HRD programme. During tough time or financial hardship it can be stopped if not effective.

Evaluation of HRD programme is very important and its importance can be judged from the following advantages:

(i) Information are collected about what is happening and it discloses the facts.

(ii) Identifies the problems faced during training programme.

(iii) Assesses the cost involved in conducting training programme.

(iv) Finds out who is benefited more or least from the programme.

(v) Finds out the participants' contribution in the programme.

(vi) Assesses the benefits to the organization as a whole and its effectiveness.

(vii) Tries to find out the discrepancies in programme and suggest remedial actions to make the programmes more effective for future.

There is no hard and fast rule when programme evaluation is to be carried out. It may be conducted during training programme or at the end of the programme. The main objective is to find out the benefits of it and reactions of the participants. Frequent evaluations also make the system less effective because in evaualtion a lot of time and efforts are required. It should be decided in advance the stage at that it should be conducted and then it should be conducted at regular intervals For conducting evaluation process, first research methodology must be decided. It should include the objectives of evaluation, types of research, sources of data, data collecting methods, responsibility of data collection, universe to be studies and respondents selection through sampling, data analysis techniques and limitations of the study. The research may be descriptive or exploratory. For conducting research source of data may be primary and secondary. Primary data can be collected from trainers and trainees and other parties involved. Primary data can be collected through interview, questionnaire and telephone. Secondary data may be collected from reports and results of training school, reports of supervisors, reports of organization published after training. On the basis of data collected the data analysis can be carried out and finding and suggestions are to be given If the procedure is followed then evaluation process will be more effective and purpose of evaluation will be served properly.

Kirkpatrick suggested that the information can be collected regarding reaction of participants, learning of trainees, behavour of trainers and trainees during training and on job after training and end results or benefits to organization to improve overall effectiveness. During training programme the reactions of trainees regarding their comfort, quality of teaching and study materials supplied, behaviour of trainers and supporting staff and physical environment can be studied. Next learning level of trainees can be studied. During training programme what they have learned and how much they have learned and effectiveness of learning in improving knowledge and skills of trainees can be studied. Further behaviour of trainees on job after training can be studied. The behaviour on job, performance on job, their satisfaction on job, cost reduction and solving customers' problems will provide relevant information regarding job behaviour after training. Lastly the results or benefits to employees and organization can be studied. Effects of training on knowledge and skills, job performance, cost reduction, productivity and total production, profits and overall effectiveness of organization due to training programme can be studied. The information regarding these four levels will provide relevant inputs for HRD programme evaluation.

3. CONCLUSION

In HRD process a set of activities like needs assessment, designing HRD programme, introduction of HRD programme and evaluation are to be performed in chronological sequence without fail. The objectives of HRD process are to find out needs for HRD, create good organizational climate for learning, creating interest in workers to learn and to improve skills, knowledge, attitude, aptitude and competencies of workers to fill up the competency gap. The final objective is to improve performance of employees and organization as a whole to achieve competitive edge over other competitors in present scenario of globalization. For accomplishment of objectives of HRD the following steps are to be followed in HRD process:

(a) HRD needs identification or assessment.

(b) Designing of HRD programme.

(c) Delivery or implementation of HRD programme.

(d) Evaluation of HRD programme.

Needs assessment is a process by which needs of an organization are identified and articulated. The needs assessment should focus on other training needs like democratic, diagnostic, analytic, and compliance needs. Needs assessment can be carried out at individual task and organization levels. For these needs priority must be decided on basis of return on investment and effects on individual and organizational performance. If priority of needs is decided then first important needs will be fulfilled. This will ensure optimum utilization of available limited resources. Second step is to design HRD programme. The designed programme should fulfil the objective of HRD process.

Well equipped with information from needs assessment the management may design HRD programme and it can include the following activities:

(a) Setting objectives of programme.

(b) Selection of source of trainer.

(c) Development of lesson plan.

(d) Selection of training methods.

(e) Materials preparation.

(f) Preparation of schedule for programme.

(g) Registration and enrollment for programme.

After HRD needs identification or assessment and designing of HRD programme the next step in HRD process is implementation of HRD programme. This will include the following activities:

(a) Arrangement of facilities.

(b) Arrangement of working conditions.

(c) Coordination of Training Activities.

In evaluation of HRD programme, information can be collected from concerned parties involved regarding its programme, syllabus, study materials, facilities made available, trainer skills and behaviour, interest of trainers, schedule of conducting training, interest of trainees, benefits to trainees and other relevant information. For conducting evaluation process first research methodology must be decided. It should include the objectives of evaluation, type of research, sources of data, data collected methods, responsibility of data collection, universe to be studies and respondents selection through sampling, data analysis techniques and limitations of the study. Kirkpatrick suggested that the information can be collected regarding reaction of participants, learning of trainees, behaviour of trainers and trainees during training and on job after training and end results or benefits to organization to improve overall effectiveness. On the basis of data analysis the discrepancies can be identified and remedial action can be taken to make programme more effective.

4. QUESTIONS FOR REVIEW

1. What do you know about needs assessment and discuss its main objectives?
2. In needs assessment discuss the different types of needs are to be considered.
3. Needs assessment is to be carried out at individual, tasks and organizational levels why and how?
4. Do you think identified needs are to be prioritized and how can these be prioritized? Discuss.
5. In planning and designing of HRD programme what activities should be involved? Explain.
6. For designing HRD programme do you feel there is requirement of defining objective of HRD programme?
7. For section of vendor for their services in HRD programme which factors should be kept in mind?
8. Under what condition would you go for in-house training programme. Discuss.
9. How would you go for selection of training method for HRD programme?
10. Programme announcement, syllabus and study materials like manuals and textbooks are important elements of preparation of training materials. Discuss.
11. Which factors would you keep in mind while scheduling training programme to make it more participative and effective?
12. Discuss the main elements of implementation of training programme.
13. Critically analyze the role of HRD programme evaluation and discuss the procedure for evaluation.
14. What information do you require for evaluating HRD intervention or programme? Discuss.

5. OBJECTIVE QUESTIONS

1. Which of the following are steps involved in HRD process?
   (a) HRD needs identification or assessment.
   (b) Designing of HRD programme.
   (c) Delivery or implementation of HRD programme.
   (d) Evaluation of HRD programme.
   (e) All of above.

2. Needs assessment can be carried out at the following level
   (a) An individual level analysis.
   (b) Task level analysis.
   (c) An organizational level analysis.
   (d) All of above.
   (e) None of these.

3. "Human Resource Development Programme provides the following advantages", select odd one.
   (a) Human Resource Appraisal.
   (b) Identifies the problems faced during training programme.
   (c) Assesses the cost involved in conducting training programme.
   (d) Finds out who is benefited more or less from the programme.
   (e) Finds out the participant's contribution in the programme.

4. Delivery or Implementation of HRD includes the following activities?
   (a) Arrangement of facilities.
   (b) Arrangement of working conditions.
   (c) Coordination of training activities.
   (d) All of above.
   (e) None of these.

5. Which of the following point will be not considered for vendor selection for training by management?
   (a) Vendor credentials.
   (b) Vendor experience.

   (c) Competitor's vendor
   (d) Philosophy.
   (e) Cost of programme.

6. Which of the following are the criteria for vendor selection?
   (a) Training methods.
   (b) Contents of material.
   (c) Results.
   (d) Support services.
   (e) All of above.

7. The HRD Evaluation comprises the following steps?
   (a) Select evaluation criteria.
   (b) Determine evaluation design.
   (c) Conducting evaluation programme.
   (d) Interpretation of results.
   (e) All of above.

8. During needs assessment different types of needs are revealed. Management and HRD staff must look into these needs. All needs cannot be fulfilled. These are to be ranked on the basis of priority. Do you agree with these statements?
   (a) Fully agree
   (b) Partially agree
   (c) Partially disagree
   (d) Fully disagree
   (e) Cannot say anything

9. For conducting training purpose different facilities are to be arranged by the management at the training centre. These facilities include:
   (a) Expert trainers,
   (b) Accommodation,
   (c) Training equipment,
   (d) Training materials
   (e) All the above

10. In coordination of the training programme the activities included are:
    (a) Collection of copies of designed programme, study materials, syllabus,
    (b) Announcement of programme, scheduling,
    (c) Informing trainer and trainees regarding date,
    (d) Time and place of training, distribution of required materials to trainees, and supervising
    (e) All the above

Answer Keys:

Question No.	Answer	Question No.	Answer
1	e	6	e
2	d	7	e
3	a	8	a
4	d	9	e
5	c	10	e

Chapter

Human Resource Development Mechanisms

1. INTRODUCTION

Interest of academicians and management seems to have taken place mainly in last two decades. The initiatives have been taken to communicate the values of HRD and to adopt HRD systems in public and private sector companies. The main focus of HRD published work was on use of HRD mechanisms like training, role analysis, performance appraisal, potential appraisal etc., for development of managerial resources. HRD for workers was in a limited way it took place in the recent past. In the recent past, the need for HRD of workers was felt by management and academicians. This need was felt at different levels but there was a little progress in this direction. The main reasons for slow HRD progress were:

(a) Any effort for development of workers brings trade unions into focus.

(b) Lack of cooperation between HRD and industrial relation in many organizations.

(c) Unfavourable working climate in organizations.

(d) Keeping HRD as an issue out of reach of workers.

Now, it has been felt that along with managers, workers constitute a major resource of an organization and development of workers cannot be neglected. Otherwise, it will produce counter-productive results. Earlier, management felt that workers were the property of trade unions. But now the thinking has been changed. In this situation, it is necessary for both employees and trade unions to change their attitudes towards development issues. HRD for managerial staff may be different from HRD of workers. Different instruments and programmes are used for workers and managers separately. This is due to existing level of knowledge, required level of knowledge and competencies, job requirements, number of persons to be covered etc.

2. HRD MECHANISMS

The main mechanisms of HRD for managerial staff are like training, role analysis, performance appraisal and potential appraisal. These mechanisms may be suitable for development of workers also. The mechanisms or instruments mainly used for HRD of workers are manpower planning, recruitment and selection, training and developments, promotion and transfer, performance appraisal, potential appraisal, welfare and reward, counselling, participation, quality circle, quality of work life, role analysis, grievance handling, job-redesign and managing changes.

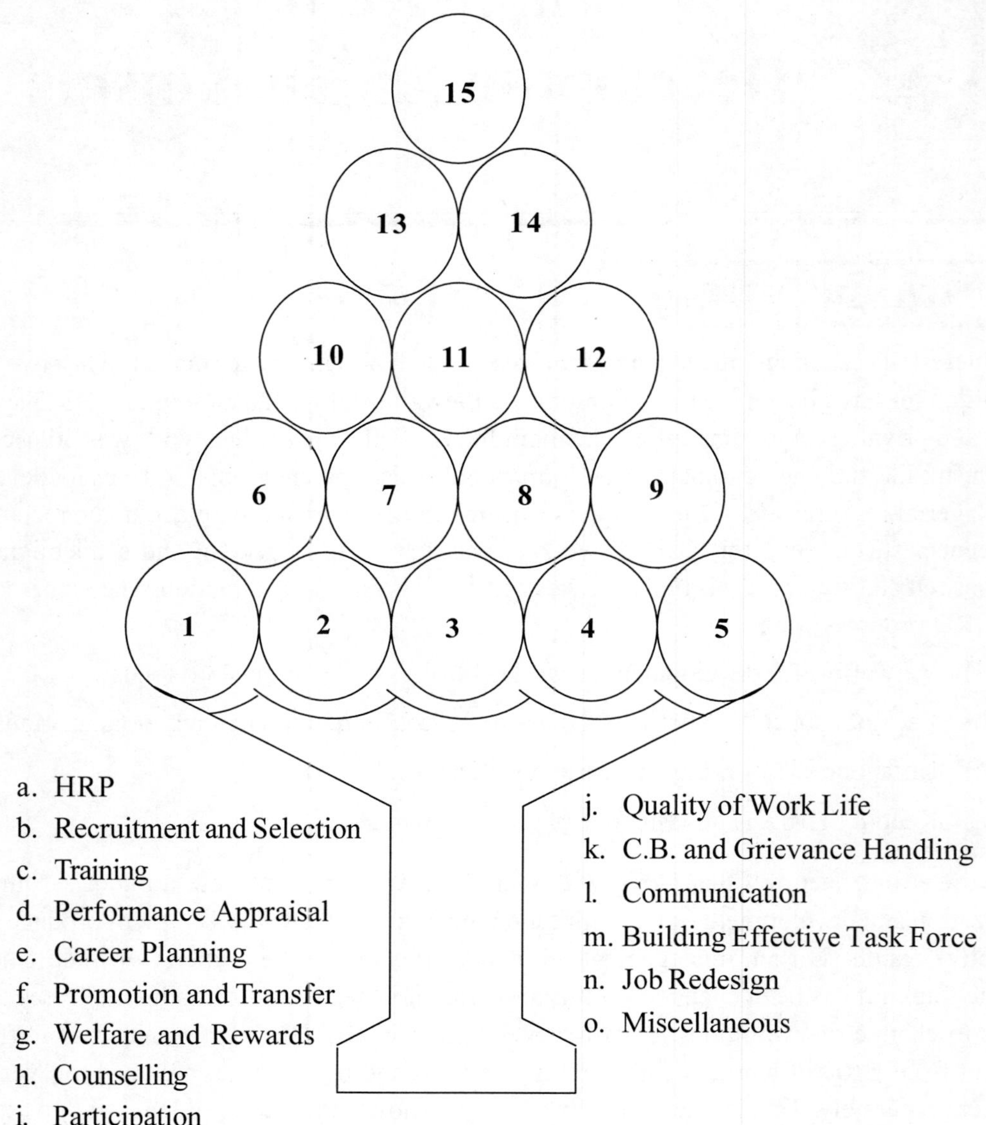

Diagram 6.1: Mechanisms of HRD

These mechanisms are not exhaustive and there may be many different ways to develop employees. All these instruments are linked with the personnel policy of the organization. The mechanisms used for development of people working at different levels in different capacities (i.e., workers, supervisors and managers) are explained below:

(a) Human Resource Planning

Environment is changing very fast. The rapid changes in environmental conditions are creating new challenges for Indian organizations. Organizations have started giving importance to human resource planning due to lower labour productivity and increasing production cost. Further, if the manpower is more or less than the requirement, it creates problem. It is very difficult to get rid of the excess manpower. Our legal system is not permitting to hire and fire the employees and does not give the guarantee of satisfactory performance of the employees. When the job security for employees is high they do not put their sincere efforts. But when job security is reduced employees start putting their sincere efforts, it is therefore, necessary to have a planned approach for optimizing the use of human resource. Organizations facing excess or shortage of manpower cannot think of growth in future. Organization due to lack of resources cannot think of expansion and diversification. The organization can determine its manpower requirement through human resource planning.

HRP is a mechanism by which an organization can ensure that it has the right number and types of people at the right place and the right time, capable of effectively and efficiently accomplishing the tasks which can assist organization to attain its objectives. If proper HRP is available the problems of excessive manpower, poor performance, improper development efforts, lack of motivation, and ineffective use of manpower will disappear. The management will be in position to develop and utilize the available human resource effectively. In large organizations attention has been paid on HRP nowadays. Comprehensive mechanism of human resource planning and development is the long-term alternative to deal with the quantitative and qualitative problem of human resource effectively.

HRP has been used for development of human resource. Its importance can be judged from the following points:

(i) Determines human resource requirement in terms of number, type and skill level.

(ii) Develops suitable standards and makes projections.

(iii) Makes efforts to develop internal sources.

(iv) Through planned efforts improves the utilizations and effectiveness of human resource.

(v) Forecasts the implications of various future decisions regarding products processes and technology.

(vi) Analyzes financial implications of human resource.

(vii) Provides basis for training and development.

(viii) Identify excessive manpower and plans for their proper utilization.

In brief, it is said the HRP provides the information for development of employees. Information regarding number and types of employees, skill levels, need to develop skill of number of employees. Many organizations have started using HRP as a mechanism of HRD and found it fruitful mainly in large organization.

(b) Recruitment and Selection

After determining the type and number of employees needed, the next task of HRM is the procurement of required employees. Procurement function involves recruitment, selection and placement of employees. The success or failure of an organization depends upon the extent to which efficient, experienced and competent people are procured. Recruitment is a mechanism of HRM to identify the prospective employees, stimulating and encouraging them to apply for a particular job in an organization. It is a positive action as it involves inviting people to apply. The purpose of this system is to have an inventory of eligible persons from whom selection can be made. Recruitment is the process by which organizations locate and attract individuals to fill up job vacancies. Most organizations have a continuing need to recruit new employees to replace those who leave or are promoted, and so it permits organizational growth. Recruitment follows human resource planning and goes hand in hand with the selection the suitability of candidates for various jobs. Selection is the second step in the process of procurement of people. It is the system or mechanism of choosing the individuals who possess the necessary skills, abilities and potential for the required jobs. Thus, in other words it matches the man with the job. It is a negative process as it seeks to eliminate the least promising candidates and discover those who appear most likely to succeed. Further, placement is viewed as a positive process involving filling up of positions with the most suitable candidates. Selection standards and personal qualities of a candidate determine whether he can be placed on a job or not. Proper placement will ensure better performance of employees.

Procedure for procurement can be designed to attract a suitable number of candidates who are qualified to meet established standard for work and for conduct. By applying selection procedure in the beginning of employment, management can do much to ensure that each new employee understands how he can best contribute to organizational goals and is willing to do his share as a participating member Proper selection of persons will procure competent person. Further, for development of competency of these people less effort will be needed. The recruitment and selection is being used as a mechanism which contributes in human resource development in public and private sectors in large and medium size organizations.

(c) Training

Training is one of the important mechanisms for development of executives and employees. The focus of training should be on development of competencies. This will include job skills, interpersonal skills, team building skills, problem solving skills and self-management skills. Routine training programme can upgrade only technical competencies but cannot contribute much in overall growth and personality development. This system is frequently used as HRD subsystem. In some of the companies HRD was equated with training. Even today also the training centre has been designated as HRD centre or training department as HRD department.

The main objectives of training systems are following:

(i) On the continuous basis the competencies of employees (technical, managerial, human and conceptual) are ensured to be developed so that employees and executives perform their tasks effectively.

(ii) To provide inputs to all concerned in scientific and cost effective manner to develop competencies.

(iii) To develop a culture of learning.

Training is a vital and necessary activity in all organizations. It plays a major role in determining the efficiency and effectiveness of the establishment. In this process the need for training is identified. Further, training programmes are designed and conducted. Finally, the training programmes are evaluated. Different methods of training are being used to impart training to managers and employees. The main methods of training are: coaching, understudy, job rotation, apprenticeship, vestibule training, simulation, lectures, case study, seminar brain storming, role playing and sensitive training. Training is mainly used in large and medium size organizations. This has been used to develop the attitude, knowledge and skills of employees in both public and private sectors. Due to this mechanism the improvements achieved are:

(i) Improved behaviour of employees.

(ii) Feeling of attachment developed.

(iii) Tendency of hiding own mistakes and highlighting the mistakes of others reduced.

(iv) Avoid deliberate confrontation and interest in suggestion scheme etc.

(v) More interest in family affairs.

(vi) Awareness of needs of wife and children increased.

(vii) Industrial relations improved.

With the main objective of developing a strong and more effective trade union through trained managers and enlightened employees, Government of India started a scheme of workers education in 1957. National Commission on Labour remarked that the main focus of this scheme was on the development of trade unions rather than development of employees. Institutional efforts should be there to provide training to managers and employees. Technical and behavioural training both are needed to balance development. Technical training will develop technical skills and behaviour training will develop attitude, interpersonal skills, sense of attachment and interest. Many Indian companies like SBI, Petrofils (Baroda), L&T are providing both types of training to their people.

(d) Performance and Potential Appraisals

Appraisal system is another important mechanism of HRD. Under appraisal system we can have two types of appraisal. These are:

(i) Performance appraisal.

(ii) Potential appraisal.

Uses of these two in HRD are explained below:

(i) Performance appraisal: It is the process of evaluating the performance of employees quantitatively relating to the job for which he is employed. Performance evaluation will point out the weaknesses and strengths of the employees. This will spot the areas where employees are weak and development efforts are needed. Performance appraisal is a tool for identification of deficiencies. It will differentiate between satisfactory and unsatisfactory performances of employees. The performance appraisal helps the management to perform functions relating to selection, development, salary administration, layoff and retrenchment. It provides guidelines for training and development of individuals. It encourages the employees at all levels to work hard since they are aware that their performance is being appraised and it can result into a reward also. It is also helpful for the development of organization, as objectives of company and development programmes can be matched with competencies of employees.

In the past it was considered as a simple and confidential method of rating the performance of individual employees by their supervisors. But now changes have taken place in the thinking of management. Rao and Abraham suggested that a good performance appraisal mechanism should have the following objectives:

- Administrative: Decisions for placement, transfer, promotion, rewards and salary increase.
- Motivation Appraisal interviews, self appraisal, participation in planning and counselling.
- Developmental: Training and development counselling and communication.
- Performance Development: Through MBO and other goal setting and work planning processes.

Different methods of performance appraisal are used in different organizations. These methods are rating scale, checklist method, forced choice method, critical incident method, 360 degree performance appraisal, self-appraisal and annual confidential reports (ACR).

Many organizations are going for annual assessment of performance on the basis of certain criteria like initiative, creativity, job knowledge, communication skill and leadership quality, behaviour with colleagues, superiors and subordinates etc. Different formats are being used for workers, supervisors and officers. Generally, the supervisors discuss the criteria and format of appraisal with employees. In some of the organizations, appraisal interviews are also conducted to discuss strengths and weaknesses of the employees. For effective performance appraisal the appraiser must have the ability to appraise the performance of his subordinates. Further, according to **Kathleen Guinn**, "Performance appraisal should not be a once-a-year event. For best results it should be a year round series of events". After performance appraisal, the need for training and development of employees, counselling or any follow up should always be conducted in order to make the system positive and objective.

(ii) Potential appraisal: Potential appraisal is also used for development of workers, supervisors and executives. Organizations where HRD is in practice, appraise the employees potentials periodically in order to find out their suitability to the changing requirement of the present job and future placement. Potential appraisal is important for the continuous development of the organization, diversification, entering into new markets, technological changes etc. So to take up the changing situations it becomes necessary for the organizations to develop the employees on continuous basis. The basic objective of potential appraisal is to find out the ability of employees and to discuss with them the ways and means through which he can realize his full capacity and continue to grow in the organization. It helps by providing the information for human resource planning and development programmes for employees. Further, it is very important to manage the high potential managers and it is possible through potential appraisal system. Surveys have been conducted by experts regarding potential appraisal.

Rao (1982) and Rao & Abraham (1986) have conducted the surveys and remarked that potential appraisal has not been conducted systematically in Indian organizations. Format used for performance appraisal is also used for potential appraisal. Potential appraisal is done along with the performance appraisal. At the time of evaluation the high potential managers are identified and interviewed. Accordingly future prospects are identified and action plan are made for future training and career. For potential appraisal generally the methods used are group discussion, simulation, case study, role-playing in depth personal discussion etc. Further, evaluation finds the difficulties in differentiating between performance and potential. Most of the times when these two appraisals are done together, appraisers ignore potential.

After potential appraisal, difficulties are faced in implementation of results of appraisal. Following are the difficulties faced:

- Managers are not willing to release their best man with high potentials. So implementation may not be possible.
- High potential people are not willing to accept the jobs located at different places.
- When technical and professional people cannot move into general management stream, they leave the organization.
- When high potential people move very fast from one job to another, then it becomes very difficult to account them for their jobs.
- Higher potential people leave the organization by getting better job opportunities. This is a tragic loss to the company.

In brief it can be said that potential appraisal is a very important mechanism for development of workers, supervisors and executives for their future role. It provides basis for utilization of present potential and development of existing potential for future needs by coordinating individual expectations and future requirements of the organizations.

(e) Career Planning

A person occupies a sequence of positions at different levels in an organization during the course of his life is called career. A person joins an organization with certain expectations and aspirations. These aspirations and expectations are the motivating factors for individuals. In turn organization provides the support to employees through conducive environment for their growth. In the favourable environment, the major thrust of HRD is to bring shift in the organization culture. The main areas will be honesty, openness, and personal development, career and growth aspirations of all members. These are matters of considerable interest to employees at all levels and will tend to become more openly talked about. Interaction between organization and individuals develops and this develops or builds the sense of commitment to the organization. At this crucial juncture, HRD through its subsystem creates the facilitative culture. Through the conducive culture, subsystems would ensure development of individual and development of sense of commitment. HRD using different subsystems and career planning is one of them which contribute for better development of people.

Pareek and Rao (1998) say "career development means the development of the general technical and managerial career in the organization. Career planning implies planning of specific career paths of the employees in the future in the organization with the help of reporting officer. As such planning flows from manpower planning and potential appraisal. Career planning gets closely linked with these components of human resource system."

Career planning is a slow and participative process. Both individuals and organization take part in the career planning. This career planning will help the employees to plan his career as per his capabilities within the organizational requirements. This whole process can be divided into two parts:

(i) Career planning
(ii) Career development

(i) Career planning: It will involve the following activities:

- Preparing of manpower inventory in the organization at different levels.
- Finding out the manpower requirement at different levels for future through human resource planning.
- Designing career path for different types of employees.
- Preparing plans for training and development of employees of different categories at different levels.
- Plan for promotion of employees.
- Review of the planning and to measure effectiveness of the plans.

(ii) Career development: Career development will include the following activities:

- Supporting the employees to assess their career needs in the organization, seminars, simulation, workshop, assessment centres, tests and interviews.

- Publishing the career path in the organization.
- Matching the career opportunities in the organization with needs, expectations and capabilities of employees through job rotation, job enlargement, coaching etc.

The career planning and development mechanism has been followed by a number of organizations. Many of them have designed the career path and it is liked with the promotion of employees. This way it has become a motivating factor for employees.

In the present time career planning and development is considered as a part of the career system and is linked with manpower planning, recruitment and potential appraisal.

(f) Promotion and Transfer

Promotion and transfer can be used for development of human resource. Opportunity for advancement is one of the best incentives an organization can provide to its employees. Promotion is the advancement of employee to a higher job, better in terms of greater responsibilities, more prestige or status, greater skill and this promotion can be given to persons having high potentials and seniority. Individual moves from lower level to higher level. This helps to improve the skill of the employees. Timely promotion shall build up sense of commitment among employees. Many organizations are aligning career path with promotion for development of the employees.

Transfer is the process in which employees are positioned where they are likely to be more effective or where they are likely to get more satisfaction. Through transfer manpower is adjusted as per the need of the organization or individuals. Individuals perform the different tasks at different places. This job rotation helps to develop the competencies of the person on different jobs. A number of organizations are using both promotion and transfer as a mechanism of human resource development.

(g) Welfare and Rewards

Employees' welfare is the effort of employer to establish within the existing working, living and cultural conditions of the employees beyond what is required by law, the customs of the industry and conditions of the market. ILO report speaks of "Welfare of employees as such services facilities and amenities which may be established outside or in the vicinity of undertakings, to enable the persons employed therein to perform their work in healthy and congenial surroundings and to provide them with amenities conducive to good health and high morale." **ILO Asian Regional Conference Report – II, 1947**.

In the highly inflationary economy like ours the salaries paid to the employees are not adequate to meet day to day requirements. At this crucial juncture it is required to support the employees by providing them various facilities like health, medical, education, transportation and house accommodation. This welfare programme shall create a sense of attachment to the organization. The organization will be benefited in the long run. The welfare measures started by employers can be divided in to two parts like:

(i) Statutory Welfare measures like drinking water, shelter or lunchroom, canteen, medical and storing under Factories Act, 1948.

(ii) Voluntary welfare measures like transport, housing, education, medical, credit, entertainment and uniform facilities.

These facilities will help the employees indirectly and their different needs will be satisfied. A satisfied group of employees will have a greater sense of belongingness to the organization. This will change the behaviour of the employees in the desirable manner. Tata group companies like TELCO and TISCO started providing welfare facilities to their employees much before the laws came into existence.

Reward is also used by the management as a tool for human resource development. Any HRD effort that wants to improve the performance of employees must consider the proper reward system. Better performance given by the employees must not go unnoticed. It must be recognized and rewarded by the management. Both employees and executives are having needs and motives. Further, attention should be paid for individual and team rewards. Proper reward system motivates the people and to utilize the existing skills. Further, it creates the interest to acquire new competencies. For reward system following can be considered:

(i) Appreciation letter.

(ii) Additional annual increments in salary.

(iii) Reward for good work.

(iv) Praising employees in functions orally.

(v) Cash rewards.

(vi) Incentives.

Proper reward system will give a drive to the employees to perform well. And well performers are given better opportunities. This would help in the utilization and development of human resource.

(h) Counselling

Counselling means listening the problems of employees and suggesting them the steps to be taken for solution of problems. Counselling is an important mechanism to provide them guidance and solve their problems. For guidance and problem solution, counselling session must be conducted at regular intervals. It will be better if an organization is having trained counsellors. If not, then counsellors must be trained on their job. Further, immediate supervisors must be given the responsibility of counselling. The concerned employees facing the problem can approach the counsellor and present their problems. At the earliest, counsellor must suggest the solution. This will help to solve the problems and will keep them free from tension and satisfied with the job. It is suggested that counselling sessions should be conducted more frequently at senior and junior levels. This counselling can help to avoid many conflicts and help the workers both in their jobs and personal life. In private sector companies like L&T and Voltas have taken initiatives in this direction. The counselling service can be extended to personal and family life of workers. Voltas conducted counselling session in its Thane Plant for drunkard employees to solve their problems. This achieved the success up to a good extent. Through counselling management can provide adequate guidance to workers and help them to learn more and more and even from their own mistakes.

(i) Participation

Government, businessmen, administrators and social workers all are interested to improve the functioning of industrial units. They wanted to bring the concept of democracy to the industry. Industrial democracy means management of a unit by the people and for the people. Here people mean all those concerned with a unit, i.e., owners, managers, workers, state and society. The purpose of industrial democracy is to give the workers a sense of belongingness to the organization and the sense of commitment to various decisions taken. In absence of it they will consider themselves just employees having no commitment to the objectives, policies and plans of the organization. Ultimately this will hinder the effective working of the organization. Industrial democracy is an ideal and an ultimate goal and should be approached for the benefit of the employees, the industry and the society as a whole, whereas workers participation is a process through which efforts are being put to reach to the goal.

Workers' participation is an essential step in the direction of industrial democracy. It is a vehicle with the help of it we can reach to the destination of industrial democracy. Workers' participation in management increases productivity, efficiency, brings harmony and better relations. In this workers' participates in decision making and take the decision jointly. It can only be described as a communication and consultation, either formal or informal, by which employees are kept informed regarding affairs of the organization and they are asked to express their opinion and contribute to decision making. Workers' participation in management is a very important mechanism for all round growth of employees and organization. There are different forms of participation. These are works committee, joint management council and board presentation. Steps taken by the government in this direction were considered as coercion from government. Research findings report that the worker director scheme in banks failed to create favourable climate in industrial relations. Some of the firms have experimented but in a limited manner. Steel Tubes of India, a small-scale company had made significant progress in this direction. It started the scheme through two participative institutions of joint committee and Jansabha, Free access and responsiveness developed through democratic institutions.

(j) Quality of Work Life and Quality Circle

Modern management has been aware of the fact that human factor is the most important factor of production. The effectiveness of the organization will be doubled if the management can tap the unrealized potential in their human resource. The management should have the basic knowledge about human behaviour and human inter-relationship. For development of the workers and organization good wages, incentives and better service conditions contribute. But the environment in which workers are working is also equally important. The environment mainly includes temperature, light, safety, welfare, behaviour, trust, mutual understanding and attitude of different parties. Management is interested to improve the quality of working at the work place through concept of quality of work life.

The focus of quality of work life is to improve the working life by paying attention on physical and motivational factors like flexibility in working hours, autonomy in job performance. This will help to improve the atmosphere of work. The environment of initiative, trust, mutual understanding and team spirit will enable the management to motivate the employees to learn more and utilize the human resource in the best way. But in this direction a little progress has been done. The slow progress is due to lack of understanding and inadequate support from management. Bharat Heavy Electrical Ltd. (BHEL) has taken initiative in this direction in the past. BHEL improved the environment through job redesign and very encouraging results were obtained. Due to this team spirit, self-esteem, job satisfaction and individual skills developed. Further, quality circle is used by HRD managers to get involved in the organizational matters to improve the quality by solving the problems. This mechanism has been coined in Japan. It gave very good result and more psychological satisfaction.

(k) Grievance Handling

When a person joins an organization he is having certain expectations. If these expectations are fulfilled he would be a satisfied person otherwise not. A dissatisfied person is likely to loose the interest in the job and organization. Further, if it continues it may create tension among workers. It will give adverse effect on the morale and productivity. The effect will be alarming. Management cannot afford to ignore the redressal of these grievances. In large organizations, the grievances are generally ignored and the workers are not allowed or encouraged to put-forth their grievances. In the later, stage, these grievances are put forward by the trade unions. This creates the sense of frustration and leads to conflicts in organization.

In this situation, management is interested to put development efforts but employees are aggrieved, the result will be counter-productive on employees. Hence, the grievances are to be redressed quickly to reduce the problem further, a quick grievance redressal system will help to develop employees. For this purpose conceptual understanding about grievance of workers, their sources and initiative to redress the grievances on the part of management is needed. TISCO adopted three-tier grievance procedure for its employees and it has the record of successful functioning. This helped to keep the employees away from frustrations and created sense of belongingness and commitment. This is essential for development of human resource.

(l) Communication

Communication is the process in which information are conveyed from one party to the other relating to the activities of organization. In an organization different jobs are performed by people working at different levels. Hence, a greater degree of coordination is required to achieve the objectives of the organization. Managers are spending a lot of their time on communication. Communication is the link between management and unions, workers and management and union and workers to utilize the human resource effectively. This is a very useful mechanism of human development. Management must communicate to the employees regarding rules, regulations, policies, objective etc. Through timely and proper communication it is expected to get the work done as per requirement. It will help to coordinate properly and improve efficiency of the men and organization.

It is not possible to work in vacuum of information. If management gives importance in sharing information in a straightforward manner to employees, it will get back much more than it gives. The well-informed employees are more effective employees in playing their role. Employees will show their positive attitude towards their jobs and organization. This will stop unfavourable messages and gossips. The effective communication, automatically do away with misunderstanding, frustration and distrust among employees. It will create the environment of better understanding, mutual trust and team spirit and it contributes in development of sense of commitment to learn more and develop skills of employees. Management and trade union both can use this mechanism for HRD. In most of the organizations importance of effective communication in HRD activities has been realized.

(m) Building Effective Task Force

Another mechanism of HRD is building of an effective task force. It is the responsibility of the HR manager to build effective team of employees. Strong task force influences the individual employees also. The strength of the work team and its culture can be improved by the concerned manager in different situations. The manager can set up a team for solutions of the problem instead of solving the problem himself. This type of task forces is very effective in dealing with special issues. Task forces are given the particular time to complete the task within the given time period. The concept of task force is used for urgent task to deal with the task on war footing. The task force working contributes to collaboration. If the organization is interested to develop the quality of service or products, it can do with the help of it.

For effective building of task force, management can use recognition of the task force and reward system. The most productive team must be rewarded. Competition must be introduced for selecting the most productive team or best task force contributing more in target achievements, cost reduction and quality improvement. Criteria of team selection and areas of competition are to be planned carefully. Some of the rewards may be of high prestige and of use to the group. The main objective of task force building is to confront the issues openly, developing system of proper and frank feedback to each other and to generate alternative solutions of the problems collectively. The team can be guided by the concerned manager and can improve the areas where needed. The building of task force contributes to the favourable environment to learn and put the best efforts. This results in development of employees and good performance. The mechanism of building task force is used mainly in ONGC, military, police and many other organizations in India.

(n) Job Redesign

A job that does not offer good quality of work life is a source of dissatisfaction and needs to be improved through job redesign. In order to make the job more meaningful and interesting it is required to improve the every character of the job. Hence, emphasis should be on redesigning the job itself. It is evident that jobs can be improved through redesign by making them more interesting and satisfying. This can be done by adding more activities, rotating jobs, extending boundaries of jobs and adding new responsibilities. Main techniques currently used for redesigning the jobs are job rotation, job enlargement and job enrichment.

(i) Job rotation: Under this technique the workers are asked to work on different jobs at different times. This is done where two or more jobs require the similar skills and are at the same level. Duration of the job rotation may vary as per the need of the organization. This technique is used primarily to remove monotony and boredom. It creates interest in the job so employee can learn more. This technique has been used successfully in banks, insurance companies etc.

(ii) Job enlargement: It is the other technique of job redesign. In this more activities are added with the original job and provide greater variety and requires more efforts and skills. It reduces monotony caused by doing the same job repeatedly. Job enlargement is a horizontal expansion of a job with an addition of more tasks. The job becomes more challenging and employees become better prepared for other similar assignment. It leads to higher wages and improves worker satisfaction. It provides satisfaction to the employees and creates willingness to learn and improve their skills.

(iii) Job enrichment: Job enrichment means addition of more responsibilities, autonomy and control of the job. It increases the responsibility of the employees vertically. The employees are asked to perform the task of next higher level with freedom of action. It motivates the employees and affects the performance. It provides opportunities for advancement growth and development. This satisfies the need of higher level. It creates interest in employees to learn more and more. This helps to increase the competencies of employees and their performance too. The job redesign techniques are used by the management in public and private sectors both, to make the jobs more interesting and to improve the competencies of the employee. These techniques can be used individually or in combination as per the requirement.

(o) Miscellaneous

Under miscellaneous techniques include like role analysis, goal clarity, discipline, managing changes, motivation and to retain and maintain health standard of employees. Role of top-level managers, middle level managers, supervisors and workers must be analyzed and clarified. Goal clarity means the objectives of the unit are to be highlighted to each employee so they can contribute in achievement of goals of organizations. Discipline means to perform the duty as per rules and regulations framed by the management. Change is a natural process. It is to be managed properly. It helps to improve the competencies of the employees. Motivation creates willingness and inspires to learn more. It becomes necessary to maintain the health standard of employees. Healthy workforce only takes interest in the work, improvement in their performance and competencies.

There are numerous methods of development of human resource. Whatever methods have been discussed here, are the major methods used by the management in public and private sectors. It depends upon the management which way they want to improve competencies of their people.

3. CONCLUSION

The main focus of HRD published work was on use of HRD mechanisms like training, role analysis, performance appraisal, potential appraisal etc., for development of managerial resources. HRD for workers was in a limited way it took place in the recent past. In the recent past, the need for HRD of workers was felt by management and academicians. This need was felt at different levels but there was a little progress in this direction. Earlier, management felt that workers were the property of trade unions. But now the thinking has been changed. In this situation, it is necessary for both employees and trade unions to change their attitudes towards development issues. HRD for managerial staff may be different from HRD of workers. Different instruments and programmes are used for workers and managers separately. This is due to existing level of knowledge, required level of knowledge and competencies, job requirements, number of persons to be covered etc.

The mechanisms or instruments mainly used for HRD of workers are manpower planning, recruitment and selection, training and developments, promotion and transfer, performance appraisal, potential appraisal welfare and reward, counselling, participation, quality circle, quality of work life, role analysis, grievance handling, job redesign and managing changes. These mechanisms are not exhaustive and there may be many different ways to develop employees. All these instruments are linked with the personnel policy of the organization. The mechanisms used for development of people working at different levels in different capacities (i.e., workers, supervisors and managers) are explained below: There is no hard and fast rule that these methods will be used by all organizations. Out of these any one or in combination may be used. It is entirely up to requirement and thinking of top level management.

4. QUESTIONS FOR REVIEW

1. What do you know about HRD mechanisms or methods? Discuss their significance.
2. Use of HRD methods depends upon requirement and thinking of management. Discuss.
3. Explain human resource planning as a technique of HRD in detail.
4. How would you explain recruitment and selection as a tool of HRD? Discuss.
5. Discuss significance of human resource planning as a method of human resource development.
6. Describe training as a method of HRD and further explain its objectives and contribution in improvement in different areas.
7. How would you relate performance and potential appraisals to HRD? Discuss their objectives in detail.
8. Define career planning and career development and explain their role in human resource development.
9. Discuss in brief the methods are being used for HRD in different organizations.

10. Select an organization you are familiar with or you are working with and find out the different methods being used for HRD in your organization.
11. Write short notes on the following:
    (a) Promotion and transfer.
    (b) Welfare and rewards.
    (c) Counselling and participation.
    (d) Quality of work life and quality circle.
    (e) Grievance handling.
    (f) Communication.
    (g) Building effective task forces and job redesign.

5. OBJECTIVE QUESTIONS

1. In the recent past, the need for HRD of workers was felt by management and academicians. This need was felt at different levels but there was a little progress in this direction. The main reasons for slow HRD progress were:
   (a) Any effort for development of workers brings trade unions into focus.
   (b) Lack of cooperation between HRD and industrial relation in many organizations.
   (c) Unfavourable working climate in organizations.
   (d) Keeping HRD as an issue out of reach of workers.
   (e) All the above
2. The mechanisms or instruments mainly used for HRD for development of employees competencies, motivation and level of commitments towards accomplishment of organizational objectives are:
   (a) Manpower planning, recruitment and selection,
   (b) Training and developments, promotion and transfer,
   (c) Performance appraisal, potential appraisal
   (d) Welfare and reward, counselling, participation, quality circle, quality of work life,
   (e) All the above
3. Human Resource Planning is a mechanism by which an organization can ensure that it has the right number and types of people at the right place and the right time, capable of effectively and efficiently accomplishing the tasks which can assist organization to attain its objectives. Do you agree this statement?
   (a) Fully agree
   (b) Partially agree
   (c) Partially disagree
   (d) Fully disagree
   (e) Cannot say anything

4. The focus of training should be on development of competencies. This includes:
   (a) Job skills
   (b) Interpersonal skills, team building skills
   (c) Problem solving skills and self-management skills
   (d) All the above
   (e) None of the above

5. Appraisal system is another important mechanism of HRD. Under appraisal system we can have different types of appraisal. These are:
   (a) Performance appraisal.
   (b) Potential appraisal.
   (c) Self-appraisal
   (d) All the above
   (e) Both (a) and (b)

6. It means listening the problems of employees and suggesting them the steps to be taken for solution of problems. It is an important mechanism to provide them guidance and solve their problems. This process is known as:
   (a) Human resource planning
   (b) Employees counselling
   (c) Potential appraisal
   (d) Participation and welfare
   (e) Role analysis

7. Organizations where HRD is in practice, appraise the employees potentials periodically in order to find out their suitability to the changing requirement of the present job and future placement for the continuous development of the organization, diversification, entering into new markets, technological changes etc. This mechanism is known as:
   (a) Potential appraisal
   (b) Performance appraisal
   (c) Job evaluation
   (d) Training and development
   (e) None of the above

8. Employees' welfare is the effort of employer for betterment of employees to establish within the existing working, living and cultural conditions of the employees beyond what is required by law, the customs of the industry and conditions of the market. Do you agree with this statement?
   (a) Fully agree
   (b) Partially agree
   (c) Partially disagree
   (d) Fully disagree
   (e) Cannot say anything

9. It is a horizontal expansion of a job with an addition of more tasks. The job becomes more challenging and employees become better prepared for other similar assignment. It provides satisfaction to the employees and creates willingness to learn and improve their skills. This process is:
   (a) Job enrichment
   (b) Job rotation
   (c) Job enlargement
   (d) All the above
   (e) None of the above

10. The managers can set up a team for solutions of the problem instead of solving the problem himself. This is very effective in dealing with special issues. It is given the particular time to complete the task within the given time period. The concept is used for urgent task to deal with the task on war footing. This statement is highlighting regarding:
    (a) Welfare officer
    (b) Training department
    (c) Appraisal supervisor
    (d) Establishing task force
    (e) None of the above

Answer Keys:

Question No.	Answer	Question No.	Answer
1	e	6	b
2	e	7	a
3	a	8	a
4	d	9	c
5	e	10	d

Chapter

Roles and Practices of HRD in Organisations

1. HUMAN RESOURCE DEVELOPMENT, MANAGEMENT AND UNIONS

HRD is a systematic activity and not only a set of mechanisms and techniques. This will have the mechanisms and instruments like training, counselling. Performance appraisal and organization development are used to initiate, facilitate and promote this process in a continuous way. The mechanisms may need to be examined periodically to see whether they are promoting or hindering the process. By proper planning the development process can be facilitated by the organization and by proper allocating the resources for development, it can be supported by the organization. In the concept of HRD there are three points to be focused. First, employees are to be considered as a valuable resource. Second, it is required to invest time and money in the development of employees. Third, along with individual employees, focus should be on human units and processes in the organization. Under human, we may include persons, roles, group resource consisting of persons and his boss (dyads), teams, inter-teams and the total organization. Personnel Management through HRD functions is interested to develop the employees so that they can contribute towards the fulfillment of the goal. They can be developed through self-management, competency development and their career advancement in the organization. Different roles are played by employees at different levels in an organization.

It becomes necessary to pay adequate attention on the roles independently. The roles can be developed by creating challenges within limit and creating optimum stress to meet the challenges developing link between roles and goals to be achieved and to play the roles, individual should be given autonomy to take initiative, solve the problems and to do creative work. The dyads or groups (an employee and supervisor) should be stronger to make the organization stronger. The dyad can be developed by developing trust, mutual understanding and communication among them. Strong team would help to achieve the target and will make the organization stronger. For development of teams, personnel management must focus on team cohesion and use of resources among team members to produce better results. Personnel management must focus on cooperation and coordination among different teams so they can work effectively and contribute maximum towards common objectives. This can be done by the teams working on their goals, linking them with the organization and their identity with the organization should be established. Further, the organization as a whole should be developed by increasing its size, operation and activities, by giving good impact on competitors and customers through self-renewal system of the organization. Time to time, corrective actions are required to meet the challenges and keep the organization fresh or young.

In addition to various targets of HRD function there are different HRD systems. These will give us HRD matrix. Many HRD practices have developed in India over a period of time. HRD activities should be concerned with developing system to make individual and the organization more effective.

Table 7.1: A Matrix View of HRD Systems

	Appraisal Systems	**Career Systems**	**Training Systems**	**Work Systems**	**Cultural Systems**	**Self-Renewal Systems**
Person	* Performance Analysis * Potential Appraisals	* Career Dev. * Career planning	* Identify Training Needs	* Role Efficacy	* Rewards Acculturation	* Involvement
Role	* Dev. of KPAs * Developing Critical Attributes	* Job Rotation	* Task Analysis	* Job Enrichment		* Stress Management
Dyad	* Performan. Review and Coaching * Feedback on HRD * Appraise Teamwork	* Mentoring	* Training in Performance		* Communication	
Team	* Counsel Teams * Team Appraisal * Team Counselling		* Identification of Training Needs	*Autonomous Work Groups	* Communication	* Team Building
Inter-team	* Common Procedures of Appraisal * Parity of Appraisal			* Productivity		* Collaboration
Org.	* Linkage of Appraisal with Goals and Values	*Succession Planning	* Develop Curricula	* Quality of Work *Quality of Work Life	* Climate * Rituals * Celebrations	* HRD Research * Organ. Learning

The systems which are related to individual employees are appraisal, promotion and training systems. For organization development, the systems are work, management of culture and renewal of the organization systems. Time to time, corrective actions are required to meet the challenges and keep the organization fresh or young.

In addition to various targets of HRD function there are different HRD systems. These will give us HRD matrix. Many HRD practices have developed in India over a period of time. HRD activities should be concerned with developing system to make individual and the organization more effective. The systems which are related to individual employees are appraisal, promotion and training systems. For organization development, the systems are work, management of culture and renewal of the organization systems.

2. LINE MANAGERS ROLE IN HRD

The role played by line managers in human resource development is very important. For development of human resource a large amount of money is needed to be invested. This should be provided by the top level management. Further, personnel management should provide the systems and mechanisms that can be used by the organization for the development of employees. First of all, line managers should realize responsibility to develop the competency that they have of the employees and utilize them. In development process the new competencies are developed or acquired and these will help the employees to improve their performance. In the competencies, things like concepts, ideas, attitude, values, skills, knowledge, team building and motivation can be included.

(a) Favourable Conditions

For development of human resource following favourable conditions are to be fulfilled:

(i) First of all the employee should understand that the new competency will help him in future.

(ii) Employees should be given opportunity for development.

(iii) Employees should know the needs to develop competency.

(iv) Relating to capability, employee should be in position to assess high growth rate on job. Employee should take active part in the process of development and enjoy. Personnel department provides the tools or mechanisms to use for the line managers to create the aforesaid conditions.

(b) Responsibilities to Fulfill

In performance appraisal system, line managers will play the role of appraiser and appraisee both. As an appraiser, he will fulfill the following responsibilities:

(i) Locating key performance areas (KPA) of employees.

(ii) Supporting employees to set goals.

(iii) Identify and provide the support needed by the employees.

(iv) Support the employees to achieve success.

(v) Enable the employees to analyze their weaknesses and strengths through periodical feedback.

(vi) Having regular appraisal and discussion over performance with employees.

(vii) Giving proper time to appraisal and review.

As an appraiser the line manager will fulfill the responsibilities such as setting goals, to carry out strengths-weaknesses analysis, identification of problems faced and their communication, and to prepare for performance review session. Line managers are having better understanding about the work and organization. So they can guide the subordinates to grow and build their career in the organization. Everyone would like to grow in the career in the organization. Line managers can play an important role in creating awareness about career opportunities; help to set the goals and work to achieve them. The support can be provided by identification of career opportunities, helping employees to assess their competencies, giving feedback to employees about their potential, providing opportunities to develop potentials and competencies.

Training is an instrument for development of competencies of employees. Top management has to fulfill certain responsibilities in this regard, Top management will outline the different competencies, i.e., managerial, technical and behavioural required for performing the jobs. Management will identify the needs for training; encourage the employees to develop their competencies by providing training facilities and getting feedback from subordinates returning from training. Further, the line managers can play an important role in developing the quality of work life. Working climate can be improved by framing favourable rules and regulation, trust on subordinates and participation in decision making.

Line managers play an important role in designing and introduction of the work system. Line managers evaluate the progress of the experiments done by employees. To make more effective the role of supervisor can be redesigned. With the help of HRD manager, line managers design quality circle and review their performance time to time.

Role of line managers is again important in creating and developing organization climate. Line managers pay attention on policies, rules and regulations, communication, technology and delegation of authority. These are giving very good effect on organizational climate. In favourable climate HRD activities can be undertaken effectively.

Line managers contribute in developing organization, organizational learning, dealing stress management and HRD related research. In nutshell it can be said the line manager is significant in HRD in an organization.

3. TRADE UNIONS AND HRD

Trade unions are considered opponent to the management. These are mainly confined to issues like wages, bonus and working conditions. But they had paid no attention towards the development of workers.In the recent past initiatives have been taken by the management for development of human resource.

(a) Reasons for Not Supporting

Trade unions have not supported the initiative taken by the management due to following reasons:

(i) Management communicate directly with the workers so role of trade union will be reduced.

(ii) Development of employees will enable them to participate effectively in union activities. This may not be in the interest of the union leaders.

(iii) This will involve the trade unions also and the bargaining power of trade unions will go down.

(iv) Progressive policies and HRD programmes keep unions out from companies.This may shift the loyalty of workers from union to management.

It is necessary to deal with the fears and doubts of trade union. Management should have continuous interaction with the trade unions regarding HRD activities. Trade unions must be taken into confidence and they must be involved in HRD activities. Working climate of trust and understanding must be developed. These efforts will develop involvement of unions in HRD programmes.

(b) Trade Union's Role in Development of Employees

(i) When the initiative for development of employees comes from management, trade unions must cooperate. If no initiative from management then trade unions must initiate for development of workers.

(ii) Trade union should not underestimate the capacity of workers. The employees should be informed on continuous basis regarding goals, diversification plans, marketing aspects etc. They must also know about union and its plans. This improved communication between union and employees can strengthen the role of trade unions.

(iii) Trade unions should provide counselling service to workers regarding excessive drinking, smoking, drug addiction, gambling etc. In absence of counselling the employees get involved in evils.

(iv) Trade union must help the employees to acquire knowledge and skills regarding work and human processes like team spirit, empathy, helping and attitude.

(v) Trade union must put continuous efforts to improve employees' living standard, social security and position in the organization. Trade unions should initiate for welfare programmes for overall development. Unions should extend the helps in creating a better family environment. They should guide the workers regarding education and career of their children. Trade unions should provide conciliation service in family quarrels also.

(vi) Trade unions should sponsor appropriate research projects to collect relevant data regarding various dimensions of workers needs, aspirations, development needs etc. They can seek involvement of experts, academicians by participating in research problems relevant to the trade unions.

For better and effective role in HRD, trade union should be professional. This means HRD within union. Trade unions had ignored development of union leadership. Trade unions must develop union leadership. The new developmental role will acquire new skills in the union leadership and the unions will play their roles more effectively.

4. HRD IN VARIOUS ORGANIZATIONS

In every economy different types of activities are being performed such as agriculture and allied activities, manufacturing, services, trading etc. According to the nature of the activities there exist different types of industries such as cement, textile, steel, automobiles, electronic, pharmaceutical telecom, transportation, entertainment, leather, rubber oil, construction and many others. In these industries different sizes of organizations are carrying out their business. These are of large, medium and small sizes. It is not possible to have all organizations of one size. The existence of organizations of different sizes is unavoidable. This situation is found in most of the economies across the world. Large sizes of organizations are those which are working in different areas, markets and employing a large number of employees. Different types of businesses are carried out by then in and out side of the country. They are having rich resources to meet their requirements. Medium sizes of organizations are with good position of resources and involved in many activities and market but their size is smaller than larger organizations. Small organizations are with limited resources, activities and employees. With the changing business scenario the need for development of human resources has been felt in all type of organizations more or less. It cannot be ignored by the management but it depends upon the situation of the organization to take initiatives for HRD or not. HRD practices followed by these organizations are explained in the following paragraphs.

5. HUMAN RESOURCE DEVELOPMENT IN LARGE ORGANIZATIONS

Large organizations are those organizations which are larger in size in terms of manpower, machinery, materials, finance, activities, markets, products and services. These exist in public and private sectors in India and other countries also. These are found in various industries. These are not limited to on market, activity or industry. Rapidly changing business environment has affected these organization the most. Examples of large organizations from Indian market are ONGC, LIC, SBI, Tata Group, Reliance Group etc. With the changing environment the need to develop the competencies of employees was felt. To handle the developed technology and to perform better in the stiff competitive situation, some of the large organizations started HRD activities in their organization. Top Management found their own way of developing competencies of employees. Many of them focused on developing and maintaining the motivation of people through welfare scheme, salary and incentives, promotions, workers participation in management and discipline. Those who started with the HRD activities, some of them developed employee's competencies faster than others. Now-adays top management realized that HRD cannot be limited to some of the employees. It must be a planned activity and not to be informal. In 1985, a survey was conducted by TV Rao and Abraham and found: Organizations did not have separate HRD department. = 32% and Organizations did not emphasize HRD on in their personnel policies =11%.

(a) Emerging Trends

Following **trends emerged** from a survey of HRD practices:

(i) Many organizations recognize today that training is a mechanism for initial development and development of competencies takes place on the job.

(ii) Mechanisms like training, performance appraisals, interpersonal feedback, potential development, job rotation, OD exercises and their utility are being recognized. Out of these many organizations are using these mechanisms.

(iii) Creating a healthy HRD culture in which employees feel free to express their opinions to others, mutual understanding exists, employees take initiative, mistakes are considered as opportunities for learning and problems are faced without fear and jointly.

(iv) In large size of organizations where thousands of employees are working, developing HRD climate is a difficult and challenging task. Failure rate is higher than the success rate. It takes a long time to change attitude, develop values, and change culture. However, the organizations are pursuing to do so.

(v) In HRD systems, public sector undertakings have taken a lead despite of many difficulties. The main difficulties faced by them are social responsibility to fulfill, change of top executives and large size of organizations.

(vi) Top-level management recognized the importance of human resource development and playing the role of a facilitator.

(vii) For workers and executives the HRD needs are different. To meet these needs new mechanisms are being explored.

(viii) With the changing needs their sharing of experience in HRD is becoming more popular. Large organizations started sharing willingly their HRD experience in the national forums like National HRD Network, NIPM, ISTD etc.

(b) Reasons for Slow Development

Despite sincere efforts of management the development of HRD competencies of employees had not developed as it was expected. The reasons for the slow development are:

(i) Development steps taken by top management are looked with doubt by some of the executives, office bearers of unions and union leaders.

(ii) In some of the organizations the development activities are criticized hence, here the changes have not given successes.

(iii) Trained and competent HRD staff is not in sufficient number. Hence, development in this field is not satisfactory.

(iv) Some organizations adopted HRD activities for namesake only. They are genuinely not concerned to develop their human resources.

(v) Top management willing support is not available for HRD. They give their cold shoulders. They only talk about HRD but not willing to allocate separate budget for HRD activities. Moreover, they blame HRD for every failure that takes place in the organization.

(c) Factors Affecting HRD Functions in Large Organizations

In large organizations the following factors affect HRD functions:

(i) Size: The size of the organization must be of adequate size. If it is of large size like State Bank of India, ONGC, and SAIL, it becomes very difficult to introduce and needs orientation of all employees. Circulars become ineffective and people do not have the culture to find time for reading booklets and manuals prepared for employees by the organization.

(ii) Geographical coverage: In large organizations the area covered is very wide. For example SBI, Indian Railways, and BSNL are very large organizations and cover entire territory of India. Hence introduction, implementation and monitoring of HRD subsystems become very difficult.

(iii) Improper communication: In large organizations there are chances for improper communication. Distortions and rumours are likely to creep in. Further, it is not possible to verify from where distortion and rumours have been added.

(iv) Frequent transfers of chief executives: Most of the large size organizations belong to the public sector. When the government changes in the Centre and the State, the chief executives of the PSUs are likely to be transferred. Even during normal routine also they are transferred from one PSU to another PSU. With the new executive the priorities of the organization also change. HRD manager has to wait and understand the philosophy of the CEO regarding HRD. Due to change of the top executive, a lot of time and enthusiasm gets lost in the transition time. This affects the HRD functions.

(d) Suggestion for Strengthening HRD Functions

Following points are suggested to strengthen HRD functions:

(i) Monitoring of implementation is must: HRD department develops new subsystems and are implemented by the other managers. Mere collection of data is not going to work out. HRD staff should be spending a large part of their time in contacting line managers, finding out the way they are implementing and the problems faced by them, guiding the line managers and ensuring good support from them.

(ii) Large number of HRD staff required: In large organizations, sufficient number of HRD staff is not available. For them, it is not possible to monitor implementation of HRD mechanisms. For the implementers, someone must be available in their proximity to guide, help and remind them their responsibilities. Hence in large organization more number of HRD facilitators are required. Their number is to be increased and developed.

(iii) Line managers must be made responsible for the job of HRD facilitators. They must be trained in this field and HRD facilitation must be part of their job and they should use their sufficient time (Nearly 1/5th of their time) on HRD facilitation. And HRD facilitations should be reviewed periodically.

(iv) Focus on HRD climate: In large organizations the focus must be on HRD climate development rather than HRD Mechanisms/Sub-systems. Mechanisms like training, performance appraisal, potential appraisal, and career planning, job rotation are being used to develop competencies of employees. These are meant for development of competencies which in turn is a means for organizational development. These mechanisms are to be kept in mind. The means should not become an end. The main focus should be to develop the HRD climate so that development activities can be performed effectively. Moreover, management should try many mechanisms for strengthening the HRD climate.

(v) Encourage line managers for innovations: In large organizations, many mechanisms are being used for development of competencies of employees. Management should not take it the end of mechanisms. There are ample chances to bring new and better mechanisms. There is a large scope for experimentation and develop new mechanisms. There is no single way to develop competencies. The top management must encourage the line managers to come up with as many as possible, new ways for helping employees development.

(vi) Establishment of HRD network: In large organizations managers are experimenting different ways for development of employees. HRD department must collect the new practices used by the different managers. Further, these must be communicated to the other employees so that they too can utilize these practices. These practices are to be shared. These can be shared through magazines, newsletters, circulars etc. Further HRD department must be in touch with the other organizations. Meeting with HRD professionals of other organization will help to share the experiences and practices. In addition to this, help of the professional bodies also can be taken.

(vii) More autonomy in HRD functions: All HRD functions should not be performed at the main office. At unit level, HRD cells must be established and should be allowed to work independently. Only the required restriction relating to HRD should be imposed at unit level. This will encourage the HRD staff to experiment in this field. Minimum interference should be there from the controlling office.

(viii) Meetings of HRD staff and facilitators: In large organizations decentralized system should be developed. HRD staff and facilitators should have get-together frequently to exchange their views on HRD. They should review their roles they are playing in HRD. This will help to improve their functioning and organizational development.

(ix) HRD surveys: Annually HRD survey must be carried out. This job must be given to the experts. They will collect the information regarding instruments, climate and achievements. The collected data can be disseminated to HRD staff and facilitators. The data can be collected within the organization (department basis) and from the other organizations on continuous basis by experts also.

(x) Knowledge of human process: Human resource development will be more effective in the climate of mutual understanding, trust, feel free to exchange views and cooperation. Further, employees are working in an organization to achieve the targets. Human processes are neglected. Human processes like work-motivation, grievances, team spirit, job satisfaction and conflicts must be known to the HRD staff and facilitators. HRD mechanism's implementation will be facilitated if the concerned people are having the knowledge of human process. Otherwise strong resistance will be faced.

6. HRD IN SMALL ORGANIZATIONS

Small sector units are established and managed by entrepreneurs. It is very easy to establish a small unit but very difficult to manage. Entrepreneurs are the people investing their money in their business and take a lot of risks. They are the people of hard working, self-respect, confidence and work independently. These people take responsibility personally and prefer to do most of the things themselves. These people are overloaded with the work and do not delegate their authority to the other employees. These organizations are with limited resources. They face shortage of funds, having old technology, a small size of manpower, untrained manpower and lack of competencies in the field of HRD, The major problem for them is shortage of financial resource, They are interested to bring changes as per the situation but the owners are helpless. A large percentage of small-scale units have been closed or suffering losses. It is a great tragedy for them. It is difficult for owners to revive them though they are putting their best efforts. In Indian economy, a large number of organizations are existing and doing their business. The situation for them regarding HRD is not very favourable. With the changing needs, they are not in position to develop their competencies. Hence, the business becomes failure. Employees are also dependent on the owner and do not develop their competencies.

(a) Suggestions for HRD

Following are the suggestions for HRD in small organizations:

(i) Entrepreneur should identify a few strategic employees to delegate his authority.

(ii) Entrepreneurs should perform the only the key functions as per his competencies.

(iii) Entrepreneurs should start trusting their subordinates.

(iv) Sharing of vision and plans of the organization with employees.

(v) Entrepreneur should individually interact with many employees.

(vi) Support of entrepreneurs to the employees through HRD budget and motivation is needed.

If the above suggestions are considered then we can expect positive outcomes from small organizations. In case of small organizations it seems that improvements in HRD activities will take a lot of time. The future of HRD in small organizations is unpredictable right now and difficult to say anything for long-term.

7. HRD ACTIVITIES IN SERVICE SECTOR

Under every economy across the world there are three sectors existing. These are primary, secondary and tertiary sectors. The primary sector includes agriculture and allied activities like forestry, piggery, poultry, fishery and animal husbandry. It was dominating pre-industrialization period. With development of science and technology the labour was replaced by new machines and industrialization tool place. The manufacturing started with the help of machines. This is called secondary activities, Further due to development and availability of more wealth the need for different types of services felt and tertiary activities developed. This is called service sector. At present it is dominating economy of every country whether it is a developing or developed country. Service sector plays an important role in economy and society. In service sector we can include activities and occupation which provide a large variety of facilities to users for exchange of money. The facilities are availed and money or price is paid by the customer. The service is different from manufactured good. It is intangible which cannot be seen, touched and carried but it can be availed. It cannot be stored like products so it is to be produced and delivered simultaneously. It is perishable therefore the consumers are an integral part of delivery system. It is necessary that presence of service provider is necessary for delivery of service. Therefore, the service of service provider cannot be separated from him. There is direct contact between users and service providers. There is requirement of human touch in the delivery system.

The main features of service are intangibility of service, heterogeneity, perish ability, non-transfer of ownership, high degree of public contact and specialized knowledge of staff required to deliver service. The development of service sector has brought social and economical changes in the society. Up to some extent the HRD activities have been started in industry. But in service sector HRD activities have been ignored. In the service sector the involvement of human resource is more than industry. The need for HRD activities is felt more in services like health, education. In these services very less number of mechanisms are used for development. Training is mainly used for development of employees. HRD is not considered important for the services. In the service organizations, no separate fund is allocated for HRD. At national level very less number of institutes are available to train people. Even these institutes do not have sufficient number of trainers. Central government also has not put sufficient efforts to train bureaucrats and politicians. Service sector must learn from industry and undertake HRD activities. No doubt, it needs more efforts and time. The need for HRD in services like banks, insurance companies, education, health, telecom and transportation has been felt strongly. But the progress is slow. In larger organizations the HRD activities have been undertaken whereas the progress in small size of organizations in service sector is still not satisfactory.

(a) Suggestions for Strengthening HRD in Service Sector:

To make HRD activities more effective and fruitful the following points are suggested:

(i) For HRD separate and sufficient funds must be allocated.

(ii) Every organization should be given autonomy to deal with development activities.

(iii) Every organization must be encouraged to plan for its own HRD activities.

(iv) For handling HRD activities effectively, the competencies of the concerned people at different levels must be developed.

(v) More number of mechanisms must be used for developing competencies.

8. EFFECTIVENESS OF HRD SYSTEMS IN ORGANIZATION

Different mechanisms have been used in different organizations. The mainly used mechanisms of HRD are training, performance appraisals, potential appraisal, counselling, task force, work teams, quality circles, rewards and career development plans. These mechanisms or systems are used to develop the competencies of the employees working at different levels. The development of the competencies is a continuous process and it is more fruitful on the job. It is assumed that the higher level competencies like leadership, team spirit development, managerial skills and initiative can be developed more on-the-job. If the HRD subsystems are implemented in a favourable climate that is conducive for learning, the effectiveness of the HRD system will be higher.

(a) Observation of Effectiveness

In conclusion, the effectiveness of HRD system can be judged by observing the following points:

(i) **Employees' initiative:** If employees take initiatives in their job then it can be said the HRD system is effective, otherwise not.

(ii) **Problems solution by employees at their own level:** Whenever the problems are taking place the employees take initiatives and solve the problems at their own level and not passing to others for solution. It is an indication of proper working of HRD activities.

(iii) **Team spirit and sense of cooperation:** At workplace if it is observed that they work properly with better understanding, cooperate with each other and work in team and not as an individual, it can be said that the efforts put for HRD are effective and good.

(iv) **Sense of attachment and commitment in employees towards organization:** When employees are working in good working climate, they feel satisfied and show a higher degree of attachment and commitment towards organization. It is only required for learning under HRD programme.

(v) **Innovative approach at various levels:** Under effective HRD system employees take initiative, think and act, innovative and give better ideas, products and services. It is to be observed to know the effect of HRD programme.

(vi) **Motivation of employees at work:** If people at work are satisfied then it can be said they are motivated and having interest to learn more. If not question of learning does not arise. It is to be observed to know effectiveness of HRD efforts already put in organization in this direction.

(vii) **Recognition and reward systems:** Recognition and reward systems are effective ways to create interest in learning. And learning is focal point in HRD. It is to be monitored.

(viii) **Willingness to accept the challenges and face crisis:** When employees feel they are part and parcel of the organization then they are committed to the cause of the organization. They will be willingly taking their responsibility and accountability. They will not avoid these even they may face hardship. If they avoid then it can be said the HRD is not working effectively.

(ix) **Willingness to learn more:** A desire to learning more and more in interests of individual and organization should be present for effective HRD programme.

(x) **Top management support:** To start HRD programme and make it effective the support of top management is must. Without it HRD cannot be thought.

(b) Reasons for Poor Performance

On the basis of the aforesaid points it was observed that the output of HRD systems in different organization was not satisfactory overall. In some of the organizations it failed but in other organizations it gave a little impact. But in a few it could perform well. The following reasons were made responsible for poor performance:

(i) Lack of knowledge of mechanisms.

(ii) Lack of HRD competencies in managers and HRD staff.

(iii) Lack of support from top-management.

(iv) No or insufficient funds for HRD activities.
(v) Unfavourable working environment.
(vi) Higher expectations from HRD.
(vii) Improper implementation of HRD mechanisms.
(viii) Insufficient number of HRD staff.
(ix) HRD is not considered as a line function.
(x) Improper monitoring of HRD mechanism implementation.

When the HRD systems are implemented properly in a good working environment the effectiveness of the HRD systems will improve. The organizations are likely to grow in size, profit, competencies etc. HRD systems are likely to take more time if the situation is not favourable. It may take 10-15 years to bring changes. If situation is favourable, it may take nearly five years to bring the change. It entirely depends upon HRD climate, management support and availability of trained and sufficient number of HRD staff mainly.

9. CONCLUSION

According to the nature of the activities there exist different types of industries such as cement, textile, steel, automobiles, electronic, pharmaceutical, telecom, transportation, entertainment, leather, rubber, oil, construction and many others. In these industries different sizes of organizations are carrying out their business. These are of large, medium and small sizes. It is not possible to have all organizations of one size. The existence of organizations of different sizes is unavoidable. Large organizations are having rich resources to meet their requirements. Medium organizations are with good position of resources and involved in many activities and market but their size is smaller than larger organizations. Small organizations are with limited resources, activities and employees. With the changing business scenario the need for development of human resources has been felt in all type of organizations more or less. It cannot be ignored by the management but it depends upon the situation of the organization to take initiatives for HRD or not.

Examples of large organizations from Indian market are ONGC, LIC, SBI, Tata Group, Reliance Group etc.

Top Management found their own way of developing competencies of employees. Many of them focused on developing and maintaining the motivation of people through welfare schemes, salary and incentives, promotions, workers participation in management and discipline. Those who started with the HRD activities some of them developed employee's competencies faster than others. In large organization the need for HRD has been felt and top level management provided support, maintaining good working environment, and sharing of experience is considered important in HRD. But still the progress is slow. To make it more effective it is suggested that the line managers must be encouraged for HRD, more autonomy must be given for HRD functions, a HRD network is to be established, competency of HRD staff is to be improved and a survey for HRD is to be conducted.

The progress of HRD in small organization is very slow because the entrepreneurs are over burdened with work and they are not in position to spare time for HRD. Their resources are also limited and they do not trust their subordinates much. Further they do not possess HRD skills also. A lot of work is to be done in this direction. If sincere efforts are put for HRD in small units then future of HRD can be bright. In service sector the need for HRD is strongly felt in present time due to direct contact of service providers with the customers. Some of the organizations in service sector have taken lead in HRD like SBI, LIC and BSNL. In India it can be said there is a lot of scope for HRD in manufacturing, service sector and trading whether it is a small, medium or a large organization. The future of HRD in Indian companies is bright if sincere efforts are put in this direction.

10. QUESTIONS FOR REVIEW

1. Human resource development is the need of the hour for small, medium and larger organizations. Discuss.
2. Discuss the major trends emerged in HRD practices across the world and in Indian industries.
3. Why is the progress of HRD activities slow in Indian organizations? Explain.
4. Which factors affect HRD functions in an organization? Discuss.
5. What would you suggest to strengthen or improve HRD functions in large organizations?
6. Progress of HRD function is very poor in small organizations. Suggest points to improve it.
7. Need for HRD function is critical in service sector due to direct contact between service providers and customers. Discuss.
8. What would you suggest to improve HRD functions in service sector in India?
9. Explain effectiveness of HRD functions and how it can be measured or judged in an organization.
10. Which factors are responsible for poor effectiveness of HRD functions? Discuss.
11. Discuss the relationship between HRD management and unions.
12. Explain the matrix view of HRD system in brief.
13. Role of line manager is very important in HRD. Explain.
14. Describe the role of trade unions in HRD in present time.
15. Write short notes on the following:
    (a) Lack of HRD competencies in managers and HRD staff.
    (b) Improper implementation of HRD mechanisms.
    (c) Reasons for trade unions not supporting HRD.
    (d) Emerging trends in HRD practices.
    (e) Future of HRD in small organizations.

11. OBJECTIVE QUESTIONS

1. HRD is a systematic activity and not only a set of mechanisms and techniques. Do you agree with this statement?
   (a) Fully agree (b) Partially agree
   (c) Partially disagree (d) Fully disagree
   (e) Cannot say anything
2. In the concept of HRD there are certain points to be focused. These points are:
   (a) Employees are to be considered as a valuable resource.
   (b) Required to invest time and money in the development of employees.
   (c) Human units and processes in the organization.
   (d) All the above
   (e) None of the above
3. HRD systems shown in the HRD matrix are used for their development. These include:
   (a) Persons and their roles (b) Boss (dyads),
   (c) Teams, inter-teams (d) And the total organization
   (e) All the above
4. They play an important role in designing and introduction of the work system. That group is known as:
   (a) Trade unions (b) Middle managers
   (c) Line managers (d) All the above
   (e) None of the above
5. It should sponsor appropriate research projects to collect relevant data regarding various dimensions of workers' needs, aspirations, development needs etc.
   (a) Government (b) Trade unions
   (c) Line managers (d) Employees
   (e) None of the above
6. It is not possible to have all organizations of one size. The existence of organizations of different sizes is ______________. This situation is found in most of the economies across the world:
   (a) Avoidable (b) Unavoidable
   (c) Both of these (d) None of these
   (e) Cannot say anything

7. In 1985 a survey was conducted and found: Organizations did not have separate HRD department. = 32% and Organizations did not emphasize HRD on in their personnel policies =11%. It was conducted by:

(a) TV Rao and Abraham
(b) TV Rao
(c) Abraham
(d) Ishwar Dayal
(e) None of the above

8. Management recognized the importance of human resource development and playing the role of a facilitator is at:

(a) Top level
(b) Middel level
(c) Lower level
(d) All levels
(e) None of the above

9. Factors affecting HRD functions in large organizations are:

1. Size
2. Frequent transfers of chief executives
3. Improper communication
4. Geographical coverage

(a) 1,3,4
(b) 2,3,4
(c) 3,4
(d) 1,2,3,4
(e) None of the above

10. Suggestions for strengthening HRD functions are:

1. Large number of HRD staff required.
2. Monitoring of implementation is must.
3. Line managers must be made responsible.
4. Frequent transfers of chief executives.

(a) 1,2,3
(b) 2,3,4
(c) 1,2,4
(d) 1,2,3,4
(e) None of the above

11. Suggestions for HRD

1. Entrepreneur should identify a few strategic employees to delegate his authority.
2. Entrepreneurs should perform the only the key functions as per his competencies.
3. Entrepreneurs should start trusting their subordinates.
4. Sharing of vision and plans of the organization with employees.
5. Entrepreneur should individually interact with many employees.

(a) 1,2,3 (b) 1,3,5
(c) 2,3,4,5 (d) 1,2,3,4,5
(e) None of the above

12. The effectiveness of HRD system can be judged by observing the points:
    1. Problems solution by employees at their own level.
    2. Team spirit and sense of cooperation.
    3. Sense of attachment and commitment in employees towards organization.
    4. Willingness to accept the challenges and face crisis.

    (a) 1,2,3 (b) 2,3,4
    (c) 1,2,4 (d) 1,2,3,4
    (e) None of the above

13. Reasons for Poor Performance of HRD in most of the organizations are:
    1. No or insufficient funds for HRD activities.
    2. Unfavourable working environment.
    3. Higher expectations from HRD.
    4. Improper implementation of HRD mechanisms.
    5. Top management support

    (a) 1,2,3,5 (b) 2,3,4,5
    (c) 1,3,4,5 (d) 1,2,3,4

Answer Keys:

Question No.	Answer	Question No.	Answer
1	a	8	a
2	d	9	d
3	e	10	a
4	c	11	d
5	b	12	d
6	b	13	d
7	a		

PART — 3
HRD APPLICATIONS

Chapter

Role Analysis and Competency in HRD

1. INTRODUCTION

At present, the business environment is changing rapidly. All environmental factors like social, cultural, legal, political, economic, technology and competition are undergoing changes. In this environment nothing is certain except changes. There are uncertainty and risks in the business. Now due to liberalisation and globalisation multinational companies are entering in markets of different countries with high degree of technology and with rich resources. Tough competition is being faced in domestic and international markets. It has become very difficult to grow, stabilize and excel in the business activities. It is needed to perform better and before other competitors. The need for higher degree of skills and knowledge is strongly felt. Talented and motivated human resource is needed at present. Sincere efforts must be put to develop human resource of the organisation. Through talented manpower competitive advantage can be achieved over other competitors. Human resource development is a systematic and planned activities designed by an organization to provide its members with the opportunities and facilities to learn necessary skills and develop competencies to perform the current jobs and prepare them for further jobs also. Human resource development process is facilitated by mechanisms or subsystems like role analysis, performance appraisal, training, organizational development, potential development, job rotation, welfare and reward. People are helped to acquire new competencies through the various systems continuously. This has been realized and accepted at macro, micro and individual levels. For development of competencies of human resources role analysis and competency mapping contribute to a good extent.

2. ROLE ANALYSIS

With the development of business and economy activities of organizations are becoming complex and more. At different levels different activities are being performed. In a corporate unit activities are performed at top, middle and lower levels. These activities include production, storage, logistics, marketing, operation, finance and accounting, human resource, research and development, communication, transportation, public relations etc. As per area of specialisation these activities are assigned to employees. To know the contribution of employees to the objectives of the organisation it is required to analyse the function being performed. This process is called role analysis. It is a function of HRM to understand these jobs. Detailed study of jobs is needed not only for planning, recruitment and selection, training, performance appraisal but also for development of people. For work different terms like tasks, jobs, roles and functions are used. These terms are explained as below:

(a) Task

To carry out a job many activities are performed. This may be called a part or an element of the job. It may be performed related to time limit.

(b) Job

To carry out a work many jobs are performed. To complete a work, specific jobs are to be performed. Job is called a component of work. A series of tasks is called a job. Jobs may not be time bound whereas task is time bound within a job.

(c) Work

An employee works at his job with other colleagues and uses various tools to perform his job. There a relationship with them develops and it is called work. It can be concisely said it is a wider concept than job. This relationship becomes complex with the increasing size of organisation. At work place, beyond individual the economic relationship develops. An environment of working develops due to social, cultural, psychological, technological and economic factors.

(d) Role

A person being in position in an organisation performs certain functions as per expectations of role setters is called role. A group of persons having certain expectations from role is called role set. Role is defined clearly by role analysis to avoid confusion in the organisation. A series of exercises was designed by Pareek in1974 to improve role effectiveness. These exercises help the role players to define his role clearly, prepare his role description and to avoid confusion in performance of his functions. In an exercise the role setters and occupant fill up job expectation forms, prepare a summary of expectations from these forms, occupant discusses expectations with role setters and express his reactions, finally role occupant prepares a description of role and sends a copy to every role set member.

Role analysis is the study of jobs or functions performed by persons in an organisation. Earlier it was done in relation to a job. This was done for personnel functions. Job analysis involves the study of job specification and job description. Job description is the process to study details of jobs like nature of job, place, level of responsibility, task to be performed, authority, facilities and reporting. To match a person for a job, process of job specifications is required. It explains details regarding qualification, age, experience, training and special skills required to perform the specific tasks. Job specifications explain what type of person is required for a particular job. The jobs at different levels are evaluation and compensation packages are decided. Mainly the job analysis is done to match the persons with the jobs. As per job details the characteristics of person should be matched. This will help in selection of suitable candidate for required job. This is helpful only for proper section and matching employee with the job. It does not contribute in human resource development activities much. If sincere efforts are put then role analysis can help in human resource activities.

3. ELEMENTS OF ROLE ANALYSIS

The main elements of role analysis are identification of important functions, critical attributes required, current status and experience. These are to be focused and explained below:

(a) Identification of Important Functions

In role analysis, identification of important functions or key performance areas are to be identified for performance appraisal, training and development both for jobs and people. Performance appraisal is one on the basis of certain functions performed and objectives for which a person works. When a person performs a job he performs some important and others are less important jobs. Before performing his job he must know what the important functions are and routine or less important functions. These can be decided on the basis of importance of the functions. Priority list of functions of his role must be prepared and performed accordingly. Important functions require more attention on top priority. A job description includes a big list of job function without identification of important and routine functions. Important or key functions are more critical for present and future. Identification of key performance areas helps the persons to focus more and first on critical functions without fail. This helps in performance of functions as per priority and can contributes to the objectives. This increases role effectiveness of the people at jobs. It provides role clarity and avoids ambiguity in expectations by different people. Identification of key performance areas is useful for performance appraisal and general development of people. For this purpose services of experts can be taken and tasks groups can be formed to prepare lists of important functions for various jobs.

(i) Identification of important and critical functions, process should include the following steps:

- Prepare a list of all the functions a job holder performs as a part of his role.
- This will include all important and less important functions irrespective of their significance.
- Divide these functions into different groups and label them. There should not be many categories of functions.
- Identify the functions that are more important and critical for his role. The critical functions are those if not performed timely will affect the end result to a great extent.

(ii) Guideline for preparation of critical functions

For effective work for preparation of critical functions or key performance areas the following guidelines are to be followed:

- There should not be many important or critical functions for a job. These should be limited in number.
- Key performance areas should clearly define the job and distinguish it from other jobs
- For important functions of the job, the job holder must be made responsible and not others.
- The important functions must differentiate between effective and non-effective job performance of job holders.
- For each important function the job holder must prepare its objectives time to time.
- Important functions must be reviewed periodically to make higher degree of role clarity.

In identifications of critical functions separate list of critical and routine functions must be prepared. It should explain the features of the job and distinguishes it from other jobs. This must be in position to attract attention of job holders for important functions more. Further on the basis of performance of critical functions role analysis can be done systematically.

(b) Critical Personal Qualities

In role analysis the critical functions indicate that these are important functions and contribute to the objectives of the organisation. Further in role analysis to perform critical functions certain critical personal qualities or characteristics are required. On the basis of critical qualities effective and not effective job holders can be identified. Critical qualities or attributes may include educational qualification, age, experience on job, skills and mental abilities, physical strength, attitude, personality and leadership. On the basis of these attributes differentiation between effective and less effective job occupants is possible. The critical qualifications can be used for effective recruitment and selection policy. On the basis on these attributes suitable candidates can be picked up out of applicants. Profile of candidates can be matched with the role requirements. This way recruitment policy of the company may be improved.

Further, critical attributes can be use for training programme also. We know the requirement of attributes for a role occupant; these attributes can be developed through designing various training programmes. By doing this effectiveness of the job holder in performing functions can be improved to a good extent.

For identification of attributes, different methods like observation, interview, questionnaire, checklists, critical incidents, techniques etc. In observation method a number of observers, observe the working of role occupants and from observation effective and non effective role occupants can be identified. A list of critical qualities or attributes can be prepared for effective role-playing. It is a bit expensive as a large number of observers will be required to observe different jobs and time consuming too. In interview method, role setters can conduct interviews of different role occupants. From the interview information can be gathered regarding attributes required for effective role occupants. Regarding this data collected can be used to summarize and prepare a list of critical attributes. In critical incidents method role occupants and role setters are requested to explain the incidents where they felt the critical attributes required for effective role-playing. A list of critical attributes can be prepared from the data collected through this method. Further through check list method also critical attributes can be identified. On the basis of experience and studies of books of various experts, a general list of qualities can be prepared. This list can be given to role occupants and role setters and requested to give their opinion regarding critical qualities out of the given list. On the basis of the response received a list of critical attributes can be finalised.

(c) Current Position and Experience Regarding Role Analysis

In recent past role analysis has been conducted by leading companies in India for development of human resources like ONGC, Indian Oil Corporation and Crompton Greaves Limited. As a result of role analysis exercise role directories have been prepared. It represents the details of the tasks expected from each job holder. On the basis of Indian experience, role analysis is considered as an important activity for human resource development. Once role analysis is carried out then other activities like recruitment and selection, performance appraisal, training, career planning, promotion and transfers, job rotation and enlargement and restructuring can be started. It can be concluded that role analysis is the base for aforesaid activities. Role analysis exercised can be carried out with participation of role occupants and their supervisors.

4. COMPETENCY

Any ability and capability required to perform a job or role effectively. It may be called competency. Competency may include knowledge, skills, attitude, aptitude and motives. Competency may be related for different areas like technical, managerial, behavioural and conceptual or theoretical. Technical competency is related to technology knowhow for operation and maintenance purpose. Managerial competency is related to managerial functions like planning, decision making, controlling monitoring and motivating. Behavioural competency relates to individual, group and interpersonal activities. Theoretical competency relates to models, concepts etc. For different jobs or roles different competencies are required. Competencies enable the persons to handle the task effectively and give expected results. Through required competencies the organisation can get competitive advantage over their competitors.

5. COMPETENCY MAPPING

The term competency mapping has become very popular in the last decade. Under globalisation the firms are facing very tough competition and have become very difficult to sustain the quality of performance of the unit as a whole. The need for competent manpower and development of their existing skills is strongly felt. Thus, competency mapping has become very important due to to following reasons:

(a) Increasing cost of manpower with increased demand of skilled people.

(b) Trained manpower is needed to perform critical functions.

(c) Cost reduction by downsizing manpower and shifting responsibility to fewer talented people.

(d) Right type of human resource can manage all type of functions in organisation effectively.

(e) Focus on job performance and time management is now more.

(f) Talented manpower provides strategic advantage to the organisation.

Competency mapping is the process of identification of competencies required to perform a given job or role within a given time period effectively. In this process the given job or role is broken into constituent elements and further competencies are identified which are needed to perform these elements successfully. The competencies may include operational, technical, financial, marketing, managerial, behavioural, concept knowledge, ability, capability, attitude etc. Further, through competency assessment the existing competencies of employees can be assessed. Whatever competencies they possess can be evaluated. Through these processes the competencies employees should possess and what actually they are possessing are studied. This way a gap between these two competencies can be identified. Further, through HRD policy efforts can be put to bridge this gap. This contributes to a good extent in human resource development of the organisation.

Competency mapping can be carried out by HR consultants, internal HR managers, job analysts, and psychologists in consultation with top-level managers, role setters, supervisors, review committee members, present and past role occupants. In recent past the leading organisations have conducted this exercise and used the following methods like observation, interviews, questionnaire, task force, task analysis workshops, Job description study, performance appraisal criteria, identification of critical functions and attributes. Out of these methods any one or in combination can be used for competency mapping.

6. COMPETENCY MAPPING PROCESS

Competency mapping is a very simple process and it involves the following steps:

(a) Appointment of experts or consultants for carrying out competency mapping.

(b) On the basis of their experience and literature review, prepare a general list of competencies required for job performance.

(c) Request the role occupants performing the roles to list the tasks performed by them and the competencies required to perform these tasks.

(d) Prepare a list of competencies required on the basis of response from role occupants.

(e) Consult with the experts and role setters appointed for this purpose.

(f) Prepare a final list of competencies required.

7. GUIDELINE FOR COMPETENCY MAPPING

To perform competency mapping successfully the following guidelines are to be followed:

(a) Pick up the jobs which are common, very simple and understood by all employees in the organisation.

(b) Prepare a list of competencies required for the selected job in consultants with experts, role setters and role occupants.

(c) Circulate this example to the other departments and ask them to do it on their own for their departments.

(d) Work done by others must be further circulated.

(e) Competencies like knowledge, skills and attitude must be illustrated.

(f) Select a sample work which is with more role clarity and competencies.

(g) Objective of competency mapping should be explained to all concerned properly.

(h) Interview of current and past job holders along with their seniors must be conducted.

(i) Final list is to be circulated to different role setters.

8. EVOLUTION OF COMPETENCY MAPPING

The concept of competency was first developed in USA in education field. Benjamin Bloom developed educational objectives and identified the knowledge, skills and attitude required in education service. Harvard school psychologist David McCelland pioneered competency movement across the world. He wrote books like *Talent and Society*, *Achievement and Motives* and *The Achieving Society on Competency*. The work done by David and Douglas Brey have laid the foundation of popularising competency movement. They developed Behaviour Event Interviewing (BEI) and advocated concept of assessment centre. The assessment centre was accepted in seventies and HRD plan prepared by a professor of IIM, Ahmedabad for L&T in India. Competency mapping was done by L&T but could not start assessment centre. This company prepared its appraisal system and identified a few competencies through competency mapping. Later on HLL, LIC and NDDB prepared their revised performance appraisal system and started focussing on assessment of competencies of employees. At present under global competitive situation it got momentum.

9. ADVANTAGES OF COMPETENCY MAPPING

This concept is very popular at present and picked up momentum in last decade only. The main advantages of it to the firms are following:

(a) Organisations gone for competency mapping have developed organisational structure.

(b) There is perfect role clarity for all employees without any ambiguity.

(c) For each role critical attributes have been mapped.

(d) For roles at different management levels competencies have been identified.

(e) This has been used by the organisation for recruitment and selection, promotion, transfers, training and performance appraisal systems.

Finally from the study it can be concluded that competency mapping is becoming more and more popular in present and future of it is very bright.

10. FINDINGS

From the study of different organisations selected from various industries, the findings are following:

(a) Business environment is changing very rapidly. External environmental factors like social, cultural, legal, political, economic, technology and competition are undergoing drastic changes. There is environment of uncertainty and risk prevailing at present.

(b) It has become very difficult to keep pace with the changing environment for organisations. To carry out business effectively it is needed to make suitable adjustments with internal environmental factors.

(c) For understanding of uncertainty high degree of skills are required. So the need for human resource development is strongly felt in almost every organisation.

(d) Human resource development has become an important function to develop skills, knowledge, ability, capability and competencies of human resource of the organisation. This is enabling the companies to meet its present and future requirements.

(e) Role analysis evaluates the roles of employees and assesses their effectiveness at work in the organisation. It contributes in human resource development function.

(f) Competency mapping is a process that helps in identification of competencies required for different tasks to perform properly.

(g) Current and expected competencies are identified through competency mapping and assessment. A gap between current and expected competencies can be found with these processes.

(h) At present large and medium size organisations are mainly involved in research related to human resource development functions for improvement in competencies of people.

(i) It is undoubtedly expected that research involvement will be more in human resource development functions in future.

11. SUGGESTIONS

On the basis of findings of this study the following points are suggested:

(a) Through training and participation the awareness of business environment of employees must be created and updated.

(b) Services of internal and external experts/consultants available must be availed without fail in role analysis, competency mapping and assessment.

(c) On the basis of competencies identified the HR functions like recruitment, selection, training, promotion, performance appraisal etc. must be performed.

(d) Human resource managers must be appointed through proper selection process and they must be trained in HR development functions if required.

(e) There is need for change in mindset of top level management and they must willingly support human resource development functions.

(f) Adequate funds are to be allocated for research so that timely manpower can be developed as per the need of the organisation.

12. CONCLUSION

The present business environment is unstable and uncertain and very risky for business. Nothing is certain except changes. It is very difficult to predict what will happen tomorrow. It is strongly felt that business environment awareness must be updated to understand and anticipate the opportunities and threats for the business. In tough competitive situation it is very difficult to grow, stabilize and excel in business performance. Only organisation with talented and motivated manpower can do the things better and before others. People of higher skills are needed. Organisation with talented manpower can get competitive advantage over other competitors. For this purpose, human resource development functions are becoming very important. Traditional process job analysis is suitable for matching the job and employees but does not contribute in human resource development. Role analysis helps to find out the effective of employees at work. Further, competency mapping and assessment identify the competencies required to perform various tasks and assess the existing competencies. These make human resource development functions more effectively. Research is very necessary in competency mapping and assessment for identification and assessment of competencies. At present in India leading organisations are more involved in research related human resource development functions. Undoubtedly it can be said the involvement of research in HRD will be more in future.

13. QUESTIONS FOR REVIEW

1. Explain the terms task, job, work and role in brief.
2. Define role analysis and explain main elements of it.
3. Define competency and discuss competency mapping in detail.
4. Why competency mapping is needed in an organisation in present time? Discuss.
5. Elaborate the steps involved in competency mapping process.
6. Discuss the guidelines that are to be followed in competency mapping performance.
7. Highlight the importance of competency mapping to a firm.
8. Write a short note on the following:
   (a) Evolution of competency mapping
   (b) Critical personal qualities required in role analysis
   (c) Guidelines for preparing critical functions
   (d) Identification of important functions
   (e) Contribution of role analysis in HRD
9. Explain current position and experience regarding role analysis in organisation in present time.

14. OBJECTIVE QUESTIONS

1. The contribution of employees to the objectives of the organization is required to analyze the function being performed. It is called:
   (a) Task analysis
   (b) Role analysis
   (c) Job analysis
   (d) Work analysis
   (e) None of the above
2. To carry out a job many activities are performed. This may be called a part or an element of the job. It may be performed related to time limit. It is known as:
   (a) Task
   (b) Job
   (c) Work
   (d) Role
   (e) None of the above
3. To carry out a work many jobs are performed. To complete a work, specific jobs are to be performed. Job is called:
   (a) A component of work.
   (b) A series of tasks
   (c) A component of role
   (d) All the above
   (e) None of the above

4. Role is defined clearly by the process to avoid confusion in the organisation while performing the jobs. This process is known as:
   (a) Task (b) Job
   (c) Role analysis (d) Work
   (e) None of the above
5. A series of exercises was designed by an expert to improve the effectiveness of employees in the organization. This was done by:
   (a) Robin in1974 (b) Khandelwal in 1975
   (c) Pareek in1977 (d) Pareek in 1974
   (e) TV Rao in 1999
6. Any ability and capability required to perform a job or role effectively. It may be called
   (a) Talent (b) Role
   (c) Performance (d) Competency
   (e) None of the bove
7. The process of identification of competencies required to perform a given job or role within a given time period effectively is called:
   (a) Task (b) Job specification
   (c) Competency (d) Competency mapping
   (e) Work
8. The activities involved in competency mapping process out of the following are:
   1. Prepare a list of all the functions a job holder performs as a part of his role.
   2. Increasing cost of manpower with increased demand of skilled people.
   3. Appointment of experts or consultants for carrying out competency mapping.
   4. Consult with the experts and role setters appointed for this purpose.
   5. Prepare a final list of competencies required.

   (a) 1,3,5 (b) 1,2,3,4,5
   (c) 2,3,4 (d) 3,4,5
   (e) 1 and 2
9. The main elements of role analysis are:
   (a) Identification of important functions, (b) Critical attributes required,
   (c) Current status and experience. (d) All the above
   (e) Preparing a list of competencies

10. Who developed educational objectives and identified the knowledge, skills and attitude required in education service?
    (a) David Mc Celland
    (b) McCelland
    (c) Benjamin Bloom
    (d) David and Douglas Brey
    (e) Abraham

Answer Keys:

Question No.	Answer	Question No.	Answer
1	b	6	d
2	a	7	d
3	a	8	d
4	c	9	d
5	d	10	c

Chapter

9 Performance Appraisal

1. INTRODUCTION

Organizations are set up to achieve certain objectives. Achievement of goals or targets depends upon the performance of individual employees. The objectives can be fulfilled when the tasks are assigned to the employees and they perform the tasks. Otherwise these cannot be fulfilled. Now the question arises how far the work has been done as per the planning. The responsibility, accountability and performance standards have been met or not. Hence, it is quite necessary to understand as to what extent employees have been successful at their jobs for achievement of their goals. This information will be available when the performances of employees have been evaluated at the end of the year. If it is not done then the management will not come to know the exact position about the targets achieved. They will be in the dark and there will be chances of planning failure.

The planning is done in the beginning of performance management process. The performance appraisal is an important stage in this process. It shows as per planning of objectives, performance standards and behaviour, communication, counseling, coaching, motivation and feedback have been given or not. Finally to see what is the impact of these planning and action on the performance of the employees. The performance standards regarding quality, quantity, cost and behaviour have been achieved or not. So it becomes necessary to carry out the performance appraisal of everyone for smooth working of the organisation. Thus performance appraisal forms an important part of HRM. This necessitates the study of the topic of performance appraisal.

Performance appraisal is mainly used for three purposes:

(a) As a basis of reward allocation such as salary increments, promotion and other rewards etc. In performance appraisal systems slow and fast working employees are identified. Under compensation, rewards and recognition plans the employees are given higher pay scales, higher incentives for better performance and appreciation for the work. Some time the cases of good performers are recommended for further promotion. It leads to development and motivation of employees.

(b) Performance appraisal will point out the weaknesses of employees and will spot the areas where development efforts are needed. The weaknesses in initiatives, leadership quality, problem solving approach, behaviour, discipline, difficulties faced during the work and competencies for performing the tasks. The deficiencies can be pinpointed. Performance appraisal is a tool for identification of deficiencies. On the basis of identification the remedial action can be taken to overcome the deficiencies. This way the performance of employees may improve to a good extent.

(c) It can be used for the selection and development programme. It will differentiate satisfactory performers from unsatisfactory ones. The performance appraisal will help the management to perform functions relating to selection, development, salary, promotion, penalties, lay-off and retrenchment.

2. IMPORTANCE AND USES OF PERFORMANCE APPRAISAL

Following are uses of performance appraisal:

It can be used for career advancement of an individual. On the basis of an individual's performance his promotion, training and development and career plans are formulated.

It can be used for transfer as it discloses various abilities of individuals which can form a basis to identify as to who is eligible for transfer in respect of different categories of jobs.

It provides guidelines for training and development of individuals. The training needs for individuals can be established on that basis. It encourages employees to work hard since they are aware that their performance is being appraised and it can result into a reward also.

Performance appraisal facilitates the determination of incentives, perquisites, fringe benefits and piece rate wages. It is also helpful for the development of organisation, as company's objectives and development programmes can be matched with employee's competence. By identification and correction action taken under performance appraisal the productivity of the employees, systems and of organization as whole can be increased. It gives clear picture into the work being done and the employees who have contributed in work achievement.

Through feedback from the managers and supervisors the employees get clear ideas about the competencies, difficulties faced and the performance achieved. On the basis of this the employees take the responsibility for their improvement. The performance appraisal is a regular opportunity to find out and deal with the important issues employees face while performing jobs.

3. DEFINITIONS OF PERFORMANCE APPRAISAL

A performance appraisal is known by other terms like employee appraisal, performance review. It is a method by which the *job performance* of an *employee* is measured in terms of quality, quantity, cost, behaviour and time. It is conducted by self, peers, seniors and junior. But generally in formal method it is conducted by the immediate manager or supervisor under whom the person is directly working. A performance appraisal is a part of measuring, comparing, finding, guiding, correcting and managing *career development* of the employees. It is the process of gathering, recording and critically analysing information about the relative importance of employees to the organization. Performance appraisal is study of present achievements, and failures, personal strengths and weaknesses, and suitability for incentives, rewards and recognition, increased pay scale, promotion or further training. Finally it shows the suitability of the person at present job to the organisation. Appraisal is the evaluation of worth, quality or merit. Appraisal should measure both performance in accomplishing goals, plans and performance as a manager. It is the evaluation of present performance and future capabilities. Different experts have defined this concept as follows:

(a) "It is the evaluation or appraisal of the relative worth to the company of a man's services on his job." (Alford and Beatty)

(b) "Performance appraisal is a systematic periodic and impartial rating of employee's excellence in matters pertaining to his present job and to his potentialities for a better job." (Flippo)

(c) "It is the process of evaluating the performance and qualifications of the employees in terms of the requirements of the job for which he is employed, for purposes of administration including placement, selection for promotions, providing financial rewards and other actions which require differential treatment among the members of a group as distinguished from actions affecting all members equally." (Heyel)

(d) "Performance appraisal is a method of acquiring and processing the information needed to improve an individual employee's performance and accomplishments." (Douglass)

(e) "It is the process of evaluating the performance of employees, sharing that information with them and searching for ways to improve their performance." (Newstrom)

(f) Performance Appraisal: A process in where an individual's performance is scored and feedback is given. A large component in psychology is trying to measure human behavior. Performance appraisals are often used in the work place to inform employees on their work progress. Promotions, bonuses and training needs are often based on the information provided by a performance appraisal.

(g) "Performance appraisal is a meeting between workers and their manager to discuss how well they are doing in their work." (Macmillan Dictionary)

(h) Process by which a manager or consultant (1) examines and evaluates an employee's work behavior by comparing it with preset standards, (2) documents the results of the comparison, and (3) uses the results to provide feedback to the employee to show where improvements are needed and why. Performance appraisals are employed to determine who needs what training, and who will be promoted, demoted, retained, or fired.

Some people confuse performance appraisal with merit rating. But both are basically different. In merit rating, employee's internal merits and qualities are studied like his nature, physical and mental merits and so on; while in performance appraisal, evaluation is made of quantitative factors based on production quantity, quantity of accepted and unaccepted jobs and strata of work, etc. Thus, in merit rating the stress is on what he is, while in performance appraisal the emphasis is on what he does and what potentiality does he possess.

4. APPROACHES TO PERFORMANCE APPRAISAL

The concept of performance appraisal came to light with the development of management. After industrialization when competition crept in the market, the need for effectiveness was felt. In past, the roots can be traced in the time and motion study. For effective working the need for capable and dedicated worker was felt. In time and motion study the efforts were there to save time and activities so that the performance output can be improved. This became more and more popular with the tough competition in the market. As on today the company get differential competitive advantage over their rivals whose employees are well trained, motivated, committed and achieving the performance standard. The formal use of performance appraisal procedure was used in the time of Second World War. The history of it is not very long. It is hardly a few decades old. The approach to performance appraisal can be explained as follows:

(a) Old Approach

In broader sense, the practice of appraisal is a very old technique or art. In short it can be claimed as one of the oldest profession. Performance appraisals are widely used in the society. The history of performance appraisal can be dated back to the 20th century and then to the second world war when the merit rating was used for the first time. An employer appraising their employees is a very old concept. Performance appraisals are an important part of performance measurement process. Dulewicz (1989), said that "performance appraisal is a basic human tendency to make judgement about those one is working with, as well as about oneself." Appraisal, it seems, is both inevitable and universal. In the absence of a carefully structured system of appraisal, people will tend to judge the work performance of others, including subordinates, naturally, informally and arbitrarily. The human inclination to judge can create serious motivational, ethical and legal problems in the workplace. Without a structured appraisal system, there are chances that the mistakes are likely to take place and these may be unlawful, biased and improper.

Performance appraisal systems was used in the past whether the payments have been made to the workers are justified or not. It can be said that is was a simple income justification. The process was firmly linked to material outcomes. The employees were paid as per the output. If the output was good the good salary was paid otherwise there was a cut in the salary. A pay increment was given when the performance was more the expected standard. There was no consideration for the human touch to the performance appraisal system. There was no scope for the development of employees. The motivational factors were only the wage cut or a rise to improve or continue to perform well. Sometimes this basic system could succeed in getting the results that were expected but most of the times it failed.

For example, early motivational researchers were aware that the employees with almost similar ability to work were paid same salary but with the different levels of motivation while performing the jobs. These observations were confirmed in empirical studies. There were many factors to influence to perform well. The factors were good salary, morale, self esteem and appreciation. But out of these the salary was a major factor to affect the performance of the workers. As a result, the traditional emphasis on reward outcomes was progressively rejected. In mid of twentieth century the performance appraisal was recognized as a tool for motivation and development of employees. The present form of performance appraisal started from that time onwards.

(b) Modern Approach

Performance appraisal may be defined as a structured formal appraisal system in which the subordinates' performance is appraised by his supervisor, that usually takes place in mid and end of the year assessments. In this the performance of employee is measured, compared and discussed with the objectives to find out the strengths, weaknesses, difficulties faced, and the deficiencies in competencies so that these things can be developed. The management is looking forward for improvement in individuals' performance and increase the effectiveness of human resource. This may leads to proper utilization of all resources and finally the company gets competitive advantage in the market over the rivals. In many organizations the appraisal system is used as base for deciding rewards, recognition, compensation, training, promotion, bonuses and many other opportunities for employees' development. On other side the poor performers are also identified who may need counseling, coaching, guidance or any other help for further problem solution and improvement in performance. Despite of sincere efforts of the management if the employee is not interested to improve them remedial action can be taken to correct him. Such action can include wage cut, dismissal, demotion and loosing seniority subject to provisions of law of the land prevailing. Now it is difficult to say that it is a good method for deciding the corrective and development action. Right now it is a matter for comprehensive discussion.

(c) Criticism of Performance Appraisal

Performance appraisal is a good method for improvement of performance of employees and increase effectiveness of organization in the business. Despite its advantages it has been criticized by some management experts, researchers and consultants. They argued that the reliability and validity of performance appraisal is uncertain. Due to its different types of errors it is impossible to say it is a perfect method for performance evaluation. Derven support this criticism in 1990. The appraisal of people is likely to be biased due to different factors. It creates confusion, frustration and employees reject the feedback given by the appraiser. Some time favour, nepotism, preference and other factors play their role in appraisal. In most of the cases the appraisal given by the appraiser are not uniform given at the different times of the same person or same person appraising the different persons. It leads to dissatisfaction. Further it is a time consuming and traditional method. It is not going to give any concrete decision for further action.

(d) In Favour of Performance Appraisal

On other side the experts give the extremely opposite view about performance appraisal. They are strong supporters of performance appraisal. Lawrie said that is the most crucial aspect of organizational life. The latest statement accepted worldwide by different organizations is– "get paid according to what you contribute" – the focus of the companies is toward performance management process and particularly to individual performance. Performance appraisal helps to evaluate the performance and contribution of employee towards the organizational goals. If the whole process formal and properly structured and implemented, it helps in giving the clear ideas to the employees regarding their, roles and responsibilities, targets achieved and difficulties faced while performing the jobs. It helps to align the individual performances with the organizational goals and also suggest how the effectiveness of employees and organization can be achieved further.

Further there are people of different opinions between the two extreme sides of performance appraisal. They have differences regarding the methods and time of application of performance appraisal. On group believe that performance appraisal is important to find out the strengths and weaknesses and development uses. But when it is related to rewards, pay rise or cut, promotion and demotion then it is taken as negative point. When it is related to these it eliminated the development part of the appraisal. They very objective of performance appraisal is hidden in punitive actions and not in development of employees. It is not providing the opportunity for development, encouragement but it is a deterrent approach of the management. When employee knows that his next pay rise is due, the employee is not going to disclose the difficulties faced by him. This may be taken as a weakness of the employee and wage rise may be denied.

Further, there may be difference of opinion of the appraiser and executioner. Supervisor in day to day working understand the employees in a better way. He may suggest for employee to brush up the certain skill for further improvement. But this may be taken by the executioner as a weakness and he may be denied further promotion. This may be taken in different way and can damage the morale, develop frustration and dissatisfaction. It may lead to bitter relationship, creates labour problems and productivity will go down. Ultimately the performance will be poorer further. These advocates say that the performance appraisal should not be linked with the reward and promotion. This should be considered separately on the basis of merit, results and efforts.

(e) The Link to Rewards

Bannister and Balkin said that the employees are more interested in accepting this. They feel that the appraisal system should be linked with the reward and compensation plans. They feel more satisfaction when it is related to the rewards in many organizations. On this point, the others argue that for reward purpose there should be clear communication in appraisal system. In present practice the reward issues are not discussed in appraisal of employees. It is the responsibility of the management to discuss with every employee over the issue of rewards. Consistency is not maintained in different organizations. This is further increased by conducting separate wage and salary review in which the rises, bonuses and other incentives are decided arbitrarily and often without disclosing the facts to the employees by manager and supervisor.

5. OBJECTIVES OF PERFORMANCE APPRAISAL

Every person differs in his abilities, attitude and aptitudes. There is always some difference in inputs, outputs and quality of outputs when two or more persons are working on the same job. It becomes very difficult to know who is more suitable to the job. Management is putting efforts for proper utilization of men, machines and materials. Except manpower other resources are non living resources. Once they are in use then full utilization is possible. But in case of manpower, when people are employed their full utilization may be possible sometime. The efforts will be to find out the weak element that contributes to the accomplishment of objectives. The need for contribution assessment of every person has been felt. This is only called performance appraisal. Performance appraisals of employees are necessary to understand each employee's abilities, competencies and relative merit and worth for the organization. Performance appraisal rates the employees in terms of their performance. Performance appraisal takes into account the performance of one year, looks critically into the strength, weaknesses and deficiencies in the performance given. The focus is on improvement in future performance of the employees. Performance appraisal shows relative worth of an employee. The focus of the performance appraisal is measuring, analyzing and improving the actual performance of the employee and also to find out the potentials of the employees for future assignments. It is a powerful tool to calibrate, refine and reward the performance of the employee. It helps to analyze his achievements and evaluate his contribution towards the achievements of the overall organizational goals.

By focusing the attention on performance, performance appraisal goes to the heart of human resource management and reflects the management's interest in the progress of the employees as well as organisation. It is the process of receiving, recording and critically studying information about the relative importance of employees to the organization. It finds out the present achievements, and failures, personal strengths and weaknesses, and suitability for incentives, rewards and recognition, increased pay scale, promotion or further training. Finally it shows the suitability of the person at present job to the organisation. The objectives of performance appraisal are summarised as follows:

(a) To review the performance of the employees and find out the impact of action plans on performance of employees over a given period of time.

(b) To gather, record and measure and analyse the information relating to the performance given in the current year.

(c) To find out the strengths, weaknesses, difficulties faced during work, performance standards achieved and the deficiencies available.

(d) To judge the gap between the actual and the expected performance standards, behaviour, leadership quality, competencies, initiatives for problem solutions.

(e) To help the management in planning and exercising organizational control.

(f) To support in improving communication process and relationship between people working at different levels.

(g) To identify the need and areas for further training and development of the employees on the basis of deficiencies in competencies of employees.

(h) To provide feedback to the employees relating to the performance they have given in the current year. Their plus and minus points may be communicated to them.

(i) To provide information to assist in the other personal decisions in the organization.

(j) To communicate to employees regarding the expectations from them and the functions they performed in the last year.

(k) To assist in determination of promotion and transfer policies.

(l) To reduce the grievances among the employees.

(m) To make the compensation plans more scientific and rational.

(n) To help in the proper placement of the workers after the completion of their training and probation.

(o) To judge the effectiveness of the other human resource functions of the organization such as recruitment, selection, training and development.

(p) To help the management in developing recognition, rewards, compensation plans and other corrective actions for improvement.

(q) Finally to improve the effective utilization of manpower to meet the desired goals and get the competitive advantages over their competitors in the markets.

6. PERFORMANCE APPRAISALS AS CAREER DEVELOPMENT

Performance appraisal is considered as a part of career development. "Get paid according to what you contribute" – worldwide this principle has been followed. Further this is expected by the employees also. The focus of the organizations is turning to performance management and specifically to organizational as well as individual performance. Performance appraisal helps to assess the competencies of employees, attitude at work, performance standards achieved to contribute to the objectives of organization, willingness to shoulder responsibility, initiatives to solve problems and leadership quality. Through performance appraisal the relative worth of employees to the organization is found out. It leads to the recognition of the work done by the employees, by rewarding, recognitions and higher compensation packages. Good performers are identified for promotion to the higher jobs. When employees take their own responsibility to work and overcome their weaknesses and improve performance. This opens the gate for further development in career. It plays the role of the link between the organization and the employees' personal career development goals.

Through Performance appraisal, the talents and potentials of the employees are identified. It helps the management to identify the individuals who can be assigned the new or higher responsibility in future. The performance appraisal process in itself is developmental in nature because the weaknesses, difficulties faced, deficiencies anywhere are identified and remedial actions are taken to overcome these. The objective is not to criticize or punish but to give opportunity to improve over the weak areas. Performance appraisal review opens gate for many other HR processes. It identifies the good performers and poor performers at work. For good performers the HR process like rewards, recognitions, incentives, higher packages, promotion, deputation, job enrichment etc., are initiated. For poor performers wage cuts, deprivation of welfare facilities, demotion, discharge or dismissal, lower rate of incentives etc., these HR processes would be applicable

During performance appraisal *feedback* is given to every employee relating to their performance with objective to explain the clear position of the performance of individual. It is with the positive approach to motivate the employees. The employee should take it as an opportunity to shoulder the responsibility to learn more to overcome the weak points so that he can improve the performance. In turn the improved performance would open the door for rewards, promotion, higher packages and other development opportunities. Based on the performance evaluation, employees can develop their competencies, performance, career goals, achieve and chart their career progression. *Performance appraisal* encourages employees to shoulder the responsibility willingly to learn more, increase their strengths and overcome their weaknesses. Finally the objective of performance appraisal is to develop individual performance, organization performance and career of employees.

7. FACTORS DISTORTING APPRAISAL

Performance appraisal is done by the managers or supervisors. They do this job under different situation, at different place and different state of mind and at different time. Their judgements are likely to be affected. They are human being. Their psychology, liking, disliking, preference, judgement etc., are likely to affect the appraisal of employees. There are chances that errors are likely to take place. But efforts should be there so that these can be minimized. Proper care should be taken to give fair and impartial assessment. Generally the following errors are likely to take place in assessment:

(a) General Bias Errors

It depends upon the attitude of the assessor. Some may be very strict and other may be very liberal during the assessment work. They may not consider the actual performance of the employees for assessment work. It affects everyone in general.

(b) Halo Effect

During assessment when the assessor considers or gives importance to one criterion of the assessment and ignoring the other factor, the error is likely to take place.. This is called halo effect. It gives wrong assessment of the employees.

(c) Relation Rating Error

When one task is related to another task then the assessor gives importance to that logical relationship more. It creates the error in the assessment of performance of employees. It should be avoided so that the report of appraisal is correct to a good extent.

(d) Central Tendency Errors

When the evaluator does not take the extreme steps for evaluation, he avoids the extreme two ends. He follows the central path and gives and average rating for the performance. The range of assessment is very narrow. It dissatisfies the excellent performers but protect the poor performers also.

(e) Contrast and Similarity Errors

The assessors assess the other employees based on their own assessment. The assessment may be similar or contrast to assessment of the employees. The assessment should not be on this basis. It should be individual to individual case so that appraisal is not biased.

(f) Proximity Errors

When raters assess one high side then he assesses others also on high side this is called proximity error. He wants to do justice with everyone but in the beginning he has done the assessment on wrong side and that affects the whole assessment.

(g) Rating Inflation

When supervisor's rating goes very high without any reason it is called inflated rating. The supervisor should make that the ratings are on fact basis and not based on emotions or feelings for individuals. This inflated rating can bring mistakes in proper appraisal of employees.

The aforesaid factors affect the performance appraisal individually or collectively. Hence, performance appraisal may not be correct or may be biased. There is no hard and fast rule that these errors will take place with every assessor. But these are like to affect the assessment work of the assessors. The assessors should keep these points in mind and review the rating errors on regular basis. If the proper care is taken then the assessment work will be adequate. Accountability can be rated as, does not meet standards, needs improvement, meets standards or exceeds standards. One each rating the assessor is supposed to give clear comments on the appraisal form.

For example if the person exceeds standard them comment should be, "very good, keep it up in future also". Similarly the other criteria like behaviour, leadership, quantity and quality of output, discipline, commitment to the work, level of competencies etc., are to be rated. Finally the overall performance of the employees is to be rated. It should be followed by the comments from the assessor. The assessor is to sign the assessment form and submit to the concerned cell in HR department.

8. ESSENTIAL CONDITIONS FOR EFFECTIVE APPRAISAL

The assessors should keep these points in mind and review the rating errors on regular basis. If the proper care is taken then the assessment work will be adequate. Accountability can be rated as, does not meet standards, needs improvement, meets standards or exceeds standards. One each rating the assessor is supposed to give clear comments on the appraisal form. For example if the person exceeds standard them comment should be," very good, keep it up in future also". Similarly the other criteria like behaviour, leadership, quantity and quality of output, discipline, commitment to the work, level of competencies etc., are to be rated. Finally the overall performance of the employees is to be rated. It should be followed by the comments from the assessor. The assessor is to sign the assessment form and submit to the concerned cell in HR department. Following are the essential conditions for effective performance appraisal.

(a) **Documentation:** It is an important activity of performance appraisal process. Special care should be taken to prepare documents and maintain them. The properly prepared and maintained documents provide documentary evidences. On the basis of that ratings will be decided. Further, it may be helpful in performance review. Corrective, development, rewards, incentives, compensation and training plans and programmes.

(b) **Objectives and Standards Clarity:** The overall objectives, individual objectives and performance standards expected from each employee should be decided and agreed with the managers, supervisors and employees. It makes the things clear to the job performers. They should not have any confusion regards their jobs and performance to be given by them. These should be clear, easy to understand, feasible to achieve, motivating, time bound and measurable. It should be SMART.

(c) **Simple Appraisal Format:** The appraisal format should not be very long and complicated otherwise it is likely to confuse the raters and further it takes a long time to complete it also. With the simple format the objective can be completed with minimum confusions, time consuming and efforts needed. The effectiveness of appraisal will improve.

(d) **Assessment Methods:** There are different methods of performance appraisal but at a particular time for a particular job the particular method may not be suitable. While selecting the evaluation method proper care should be taken. This job should be given to the trained managers to select the assessment methods. Otherwise the all efforts may be in vain. For selection of methods the criteria of performance standards should be considered.

(e) **Communication:** Communication is an important part of performance appraisal process. The objectives and standards of performance should be communicated to the supervisors and employees before they start their work. It is having clear understanding in their mind regarding their job, objectives of their jobs and expectation from them. They will perform accordingly to achieve the desired result. It is possible through proper and timely communication. Proper communication will overcome many problems in the beginning itself. After performance appraisal the feedback also should be communicated in proper language and tone so it works as a motivational tool for employees. The importance of it should not be underestimated by the managers and supervisors.

(f) **Training of Assessors:** The tasks of performance appraiser are very challenging. To perform this task a high degree of job knowledge, skills, competencies are needed. They should also have good knowledge of human behaviour at work. These traits can be developed with help of training only. Before starting the appraisal they should be trained. Further, with the new trends in appraisal methods in between short term training programmes on appraisal can be arranged. This may contribute in improving the appraisal system.

(g) **Feedback:** The purpose of the feedback should be to communicate, convince and develop the performance of employees rather than judgmental. To maintain its effectiveness, timely and correct feedback should be given to employees with positive approach. It should be in position to motivate the employees. This should be taken by them willingly and should take own responsibility for overcoming problems and development of performance. It should be totally interactive.

(h) **Personal Bias:** At work place the personal relations are likely to develop on the basis of blood, sex, caste, creed, language, religion, regions, lifestyle and friendship. The interpersonal relationships are likely to affect the evaluation and the decisions in the performance appraisal process, then personal bias is likely to take place. Therefore, the evaluators should be trained on the job of performance appraisal process. If we have already trained supervisor for that job then guidelines should be give so that in appraisal process the bias or mistakes can be avoided.

(i) **Ongoing Feedback:** The purpose of the feedback should be to communicate, convince and develop the performance of employees rather than judgmental. To maintain its effectiveness, timely and correct feedback should be given to employees with positive approach. It should be in position to motivate the employees. This should be taken by them willingly and should take own responsibility for overcoming problems and development of performance. It should be totally interactive.

(j) **Rewards to Accurate Appraisers:** The appraisal is being done in most of the organizations by the managers and supervisors. When they are doing the jobs they should be motivated to do the job in an effective way. For that purpose their work should be appreciated. Out of the appraisers whose work is proper should be rewarded. This will motivate them in their future assignments also. The effectiveness of appraisal can be improved with this technique also.

9. CHARACTERISTICS OF A SOUND APPRAISAL PLAN

The successful evaluation of any appraisal programme will be governed by the following factors:

(a) The line management must be in complete agreement as regards the need and the purposes.

(b) Complicated plans should be avoided.

(c) The supervisors' cooperation should be enlisted not only in preparing the appraisal form, but also in respect of the weights to be assigned to each factor.

(d) It is desirable that the appraisal plan is completely explained in advance to those who are likely to have an impact because of its implementation

(e) The supervisors must be provided necessary training for the same.

(f) There must be full cooperation of line and staff employees and also mutual checking of their performance appraisal.

(g) There must be provisions for challenges and review of performance appraisals, if so required by the union representative.

10. LIMITATIONS OF PERFORMANCE APPRAISAL

Though the performance appraisal is a very useful technique it does suffer from some of the following serious limitations:

(a) It is a useful technique of efficiency rating but there are certain personal characteristics which cannot be expressed either in figures or in any other measures.

(b) However systematic and objective a performance appraisal system may be used in the organisation, it is rather impossible to eliminate personal and subjective element from it.

(c) Normally there is the presence of 'a halo' effect. This leads to a tendency, to rate the same individual first who have once stood first.

(d) While assigning the factor points or number to the employees, there are some raters who are very strict while some are more liberal. They cannot keep a far distinction between two individuals. Such an approach also nullifies the utility of this system.

(e) Sometimes the outcomes of performance appraisals are not in conformity with the other techniques of motivation, incentive wages plans and so on. Factors are introduced in the managerial appraisal because of a fact possessed by the person concerned who conducts the appraisal.

11. OTHER ISSUES RELATED TO PERFORMANCE APPRAISAL

(a) Appraisal as Employee Motivation Mechanism

In present time the dissatisfaction and employees turnover rates are increasing. It is very difficult to retain the good employees. Keeping this thing in mind the HR professionals are much worried because a trained person dissatisfied at work or leaving the job adds to the costs to the organization. They have taken performance appraisal as a method for motivation of employees by connecting performance appraisal with rewards, recognition, incentives, pay rises and promotion. Further the needy persons are given chances for training and development. It has proved to a good extent as a motivational tool in the organisation. Performance appraisals and reviews can be used as a tool to reinforce the desired behaviour by coaching, guiding, communicating, correcting faulty performances and creating fear of wage cuts and punishments. A good appraisal is always accepted by the employees. Some of the employees willingly accept their good and bad performances. They take their weakness as a challenge to overcome and they willingly take the responsibility to improve both their skills and performance. When they achieve good performance their work should be appreciated and rewarded accordingly.

Errors in performance review can demotivate the employees, even if there has been an increase in the salary. Such errors can kill the team spirit and initiative in the employees. Similarly, inaccurate performance reviews with wrong decisions regarding rewards, recognition and incentives may increase the level of dissatisfaction and sometimes they may think to change the jobs also. The performance appraisal may work in both directions for motivation. If done properly the result will be positive otherwise it may affect the motivation of employees adversely. Employees' motivation goes high when they are given accurate performance review with adequate pay rise. Managers should take care for performance appraisal keeping in mind the motivational potential of it. It may be very beneficial for everyone if proper care is taken and it is properly reviewed.

(b) Challenges of Performance Appraisal

Every organization comes across various problems and challenges of performance appraisal in order to make a performance appraisal system effective and successful. The main challenges involved in the performance appraisal process are following:

(i) **Deciding the evaluation criteria:** Identification and decision regarding appraisal criteria is one of the biggest problems faced by the top management. In evaluation process the data are to be collected and evaluated very carefully. All data cannot be collected because these are not measurable. The data which are not quantified cannot be collected and measured. It is a great challenge to decide the performance criteria.

(ii) **Create a rating instrument:** The performance is to be rated so there is need for creating a rating instrument. It takes a lot of time and high degree of skill is need. That is not always possible. The focus of rater is on the performance appraisal and not appraisal of employees. It is bit difficult to overcome this challenge

(iii) **Lack of competencies:** Top management should go for careful selection of raters, managers and supervisors who are going to evaluate the performance of employees. Management should decide in advance the knowledge, skills and expertise required for this purpose. They should be well experienced and trained persons on the job. But generally very less number of persons possess these competencies. A lot of difficulties are faced in finding out such persons

(iv) **Errors in evaluation:** During performance appraisal different types of mistakes are being done by the appraiser. The reasons may be some errors or biased and due to these the appraisal is not proper. The mistakes can be due to halo effect, central tendency etc. These errors cannot be avoided totally. But the appraiser should take special care and objectivity and fairness is to be brought into appraisal.

(v) **Resistance:** When on the basis of performance appraisal the management takes the corrective action then it is opposed by trade unions and employees. Strong opposition is faced in the organization. The management should create awareness of employees regarding the appraisal process and its objectives. The performance standards expected from them be clearly agreed and communicated. Through proper communication the clarity should be maintained. If not done so the opposition is likely to take place.

(c) Global Trends in Performance Appraisal

The performance appraisal process has become very important function rather it is the heart of the human resource management system in the company. Performance appraisal system defines the objectives, performance standards to be achieved, collect and measure the performance, and analyse the performance of every individual and organization as a whole. It is the basis of corrective, development and planning function for future. It is a very important function of HRM for evaluation of performances. The major issues in it in present times are:

(i) Employees and career development is the major issue at present. Management is interested to develop the organization through development of employees. Efforts are being put to get success so that effectiveness of the group can be improved.

(ii) Improvement in performance appraisal system is again important. Management is interested to give proper appraisal of performance so the improvements are needed in measuring, rating and review systems. That is why the appraisal formats are well structured and in detail have become more detailed, structured and person specific than before.

(iii) Performance related compensation package is being parts of the strategic planning in major organizations. The management is interested to motivate the people through their compensation that is decided on the basis of performance.

(iv) Multiparty assessment is getting important at present. When the supervisor is doing the appraisal he is likely to commit mistakes. To overcome these mistakes, the assessment is being done by different concerned persons so that the mistakes can be overcome. That is why there is a trend towards a 360-degree feedback system.

(v) Proper implementation of performance appraisal is sought by all concerned parties. The supervisors are appraising the performance but the appraisal implementation is done by second party. There are chances of lapse in implementation and assessment of performance. The anticipated mistakes can be overcome.

(vi) Search of quantifiable indicators is on. The performance is measured on the basis of quantified data. The focus is changing towards the performance indicators which can be measured. The data which cannot be measured then these cannot be evaluated properly. So there is search of such performance indicators.

With the globalization of world markets the level of competition is increasing day by day. It is very difficult for everyone to survive, grow, stabilize and excel in the performance. Those who were leader in the market now their positions changed and they are laggard. Now focus has been shifted to the group performance. Those who are in position to give better performance than that of others they enjoy better positions in the market. For improvement in performances the focus has gone to performance appraisal methods. The modern methods of appraisal systems are becoming more popular. These methods are 360 degree method, team performance appraisal, assessment centers, MBO, rank and yank strategy. In rank and yank strategy the performances are identified from best to poor performers. The poor performers are asked to improve performance within the given period. If they do not improve their performance they are asked to exit. This strategy is being followed in leading companies like Microsoft, Sun micro-systems Ford etc. More companies are likely to follow in future to improve their competitive strengths in the global markets.

12. CONCLUSION

For achieving the objectives the responsibility, accountability and performance standards have fixed. It is required to see that what extent employees have been successful at their jobs for achievement of their goals. This information will be available when the performances of employees have been evaluated at the end of the year. If it is not done then the management will not come to know the exact position about the targets achieved. They will be in the dark and there will be chances of planning failure. The planning is done in the beginning of performance management process. The performance appraisal is an important stage in this process. It shows as per planning of objectives, performance standards and behaviour, communication, counseling, coaching, motivation and feedback have been given or not. Finally to see what is the impact of these planning and action on the performance of the employees. The performance standards regarding quality, quantity, cost and behaviour have been achieved or not. So it becomes necessary to carry out the performance appraisal of everyone for smooth working of the organisation.

Finally it shows the suitability of the person at present job to the organisation. The objectives of performance appraisal are summarised as follows:

(a) To review the performance of the employees and find out the impact of action plans on performance of employees over a given period of time.

(b) To gather, record and measure and analyse the information relating to the performance given in the current year.

(c) To find out the strengths, weaknesses, difficulties faced during work, performance standards achieved and the deficiencies available.

(d) To judge the gap between the actual and the expected performance standards, behaviour, leadership quality, competencies, initiatives for problem solutions.

(e) To help the management in planning and exercising organizational control.

The performance appraisal is done by the supervisors or managers at different time and different locations in different situations. They are likely to commit mistakes. The psychology of individual, liking and disliking, behaviour and judgement of assessors affect the appraisal. Proper care should be taken so that the mistakes can be minimised. For effective appraisal of employees the certain points are to be kept in mind are documentation, objects and standard clarity, simple assessment methods, proper communication, training of assessors, feedback, personal bias, ongoing feedback, rewards to accurate appraisers:

13. QUESTIONS FOR REVIEW

1. What do you mean by performance appraisal? Explain the importance of performance appraisal in organizations.
2. Define concept of performance appraisal and discuss its main characteristics in detail.
3. What are the approaches to performance appraisal? Elaborate them.
4. Performance appraisal is being used in most of the organization. What are the objectives behind it to use?
5. Discuss the role of performance appraisal in career development critically.
6. Performance appraisal is carried out very carefully. But still some errors take place. Discuss them.
7. Performance appraisal is distorted due to some errors. What are the essential conditions for effective performance appraisal?
8. What should be salient features of a sound appraisal plan? Highlight them.
9. Differentiate between performance appraisal and potential appraisal.

10. Write short notes on the following:
    (a) Limitation of performance appraisal
    (b) Issues related to performance appraisal
    (c) Training of assessors.
    (d) Documentation of appraisal.
    (e) Central tendency error
    (f) Criticism of appraisal
    (g) Old approach to performance appraisal

14. OBJECTIVE QUESTIONS

1. ____________ points out the weaknesses of employees and will spot the areas where development efforts are needed.
   (a) SWOT Analysis
   (b) Performance objective
   (c) Performance Appraisal
   (d) All the above
   (e) None of the above

2. Identify True/False out of the following:
   1. Performance Appraisal provides guidelines for training and development of individuals.
   2. Performance appraisal does not facilitate the determination of incentives, perquisites, fringe benefits and piece rate wages.
   3. Performance appraisal can be used for career advancement of an individual.
   4. The training needs for the individuals can be established on the basis of the guidelines provided after performance appraisal.
   (a) T/F/T/T
   (b) T/F/T/F
   (c) T/T/F/F
   (d) F/T/F/F
   (e) None of the above

3. It is a method by which the job performance of an employee is measured in terms of quality, quantity, cost, behavior and time. It is called:
   (a) Performance appraisal
   (b) Performance review
   (c) Employee appraisal
   (d) All of the above
   (e) None of the above

4. "Performance Appraisal is the evaluation or appraisal of the relative worth to the company of a man's services on his job." – is stated by:

(a) Flippo
(b) Alford and Beatty
(c) Heyel
(d) Macmillan Dictionary
(e) None of the above

5. "Performance appraisal is a meeting between workers and their manager to discuss how well they are doing in their work." It is defined by:
   (a) Flippo
   (b) Alford and Beatty
   (c) Heyel
   (d) Macmillan Dictionary
   (e) All the above

6. Identify True/False out of the following statements:
   1. Practice of appraisal is a very old technique or art.
   2. Performance appraisal systems was used in the past whether the payments have been made to the workers are justified or not.
   3. In the old approach, the wage cut or a rise to improve or continue to perform well were not the only motivational factors.
   4. In modern approach, performance appraisal may be defined as a structured formal appraisal system in which the subordinate' performance is appraised by his supervisor, that usually takes place in mid and end of the year assessments.

   (a) F/F/F/F
   (b) T/T/T/T
   (c) T/T/F/T
   (d) T/F/F/T
   (e) None of the above

7. The experts argued that the reliability and validity of performance appraisal is uncertain. Due to its different types of errors it is impossible to say it is a perfect method for performance evaluation. Further this criticism was supported by:
   (a) Derven in 1991
   (b) Derven in 1990
   (c) Ishwar Dayal in 1989
   (d) Pareek in 1992
   (e) None of the above

8. Performance appraisal helps to align the individual performances with the organizational goals and also suggest how the effectiveness of employees and organization can be achieved further. Do you agree with this statement?
   (a) Fully agree
   (b) Partially agree
   (c) Partially disagree
   (d) Fully disagree
   (e) Cannot say anything

9. Who felt that the appraisal system should be linked with the reward and compensation plans?

   (a) Bannister and Balkin
   (b) Alford and Beatty
   (c) Flippo
   (d) All the above
   (e) None of the above

10. Identify the objectives of performance appraisal out of the following statements

    1. To find out the strengths, weaknesses, difficulties faced during work, performance standards achieved and the deficiencies available.
    2. To judge the gap between the actual and the expected performance standards, behaviour, leadership quality, competencies, initiatives for problem solutions.
    3. To help the management in planning and exercising organizational control.
    4. To support in improving communication process and relationship between people working at different levels.

    (a) 1,2
    (b) 2,3
    (c) 1,3,4
    (d) 1,2,3,4
    (e) 3,4

11. Identify the factors distorting performance appraisal:

    1. Relation Rating Error
    2. Central Tendency Errors
    3. Contrast and Similarity Errors
    4. Deflation
    5. Rating Inflation
    6. Communication errors

    (a) 1,2,3,4
    (b) 1,.3.4.5.6
    (c) 1,2,3,5
    (d) 1,2,3,4,5,6
    (e) 1,4,5,6

12. The appraisal format should not be very long and complicated otherwise it is likely to confuse the raters and further it takes a long time to complete it also. Do you agree?

    (f) Fully agree
    (g) Partially agree
    (h) Partially disagree
    (i) Fully disagree
    (j) Cannot say anything

13. The main challenges faced during performance appraisal are:
    1. Errors in evaluation
    2. Lack of competencies
    3. Resistance
    4. Create a rating instrument
    5. Deciding the evaluation criteria

    (a) 1,2,3 *(b)* 2,3,4,5
    (c) 1,2,3,4,5 *(d)* 4,5
    (e) 1,5

Answer Keys:

Question No.	Answer	Question No.	Answer
1	c	8	a
2	a	9	a
3	d	10	d
4	b	11	c
5	d	12	a
6	c	13	c
7	b		

Chapter

10

Performance Appraisal Process and Methods

1. PERFORMANCE APPRAISAL PROCESS

The performance appraisal is the evaluation process in which the information is gathered, recorded, measured and analysed relating to the performance of the employees. A set of activities are arranged in a logical sequence to perform the task of evaluation It includes the steps as establishment of performance standards, communication of performance standards and expectations, measurement of performance, comparison, appraisal feedback, corrective, motivation and development action. These steps are explained below:

Step-1: Establishment of performance standards: These should have evolved out of job analysis and the job description. The performance standards should be clear to achieve the objectives. Further it is required that these should be understood and measured. Management identifies and prioritizes the goals of the organization. For accomplishment of the goals the jobs are to be performed. Now, what level of performance is expected from the employees is to be discussed. For fixing the performance standard the comprehensive discussion should be there among managers, supervisors, employees, experts in house and consultants.

The performance standard should be feasible to achieve. These should not be very low or high. The performance of slow, fast performer may not be suitable for everyone. That is why the average performance should be taken into account. Performance Standards are the statements that specify what constitutes good work. The all concerned persons involved in fixing performance standards develop the list of specific job tasks then they write statements that specify how the quality of the work will be determined. The performance standards should be specific, measurable, attainable, relevant and time-based. The performance standards should be decided regarding the quality of work, quantity of output, with reference to the time taken, manners of work performed, method of doing the tasks, behaviour and costs involved in performing the jobs. These will give a clear idea to the supervisors and performers regarding what are expected from them on job.

Step-2: Communication of performance standards and expectations: Once performance standards are established, it is necessary to communicate these expectations. It should not be a part of the employee's job to guess what is expected of them. Unfortunately, too many jobs have vague performance standards. The problem is compounded when these standards are not communicated to the employee. More transference of information from the manager to the subordinate regarding expectation is not communication. Timely and proper communication should be there between managers, supervisors and employees on jobs regarding the goals, expectation from employees, performance standards to be achieved, the jobs to be performed and methods of performing the jobs. It should clearly explain these things so the clarity should be maintained. Communication takes place, effectively only when the transference of information takes place, is received, clearly understood by the subordinate and he provides the 'feedback' to his superior.

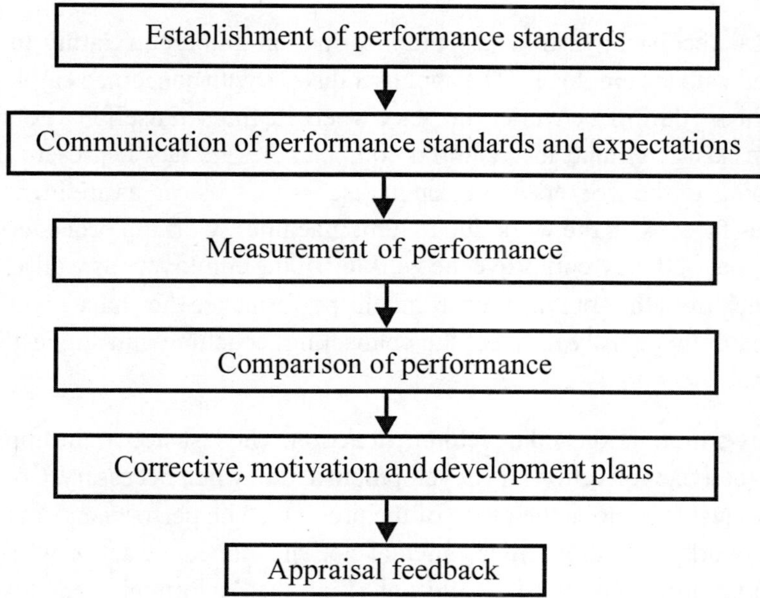

Diagram 10.1: Performance Appraisal Process

Step-3: Measurement of performance: The third step in the appraisal process is the measurement of performance. To ascertain what actual performance is, necessary information about it should be obtained. One is concerned with how he measures and what he measures. There are four common sources of information frequently used by managers to measure actual performance; personal observation, statistical reports, oral reports and written reports. Each has its strengths and weaknesses; however a combination of them increases both the number of input sources and the probability of receiving reliable information. It is the responsibility of the immediate manager or supervisor under whom the person is working. The performance can be measured in quality, quantity, time, cost, difficulties faced, competencies expressed during work and initiatives taken for problem solution. Only the trained person can perform this task effectively. Otherwise the objective of the performance appraisal may be defeated.

Step-4: Comparison: The fourth step in the appraisal process relates to the comparison of actual performance with standards. In first step the performance standards have been decided and in second stage the actual performance is measured. Now in this step the actual performance is compared with the prefixed standards. The attempt in this step is to locate variations between standard performance and actual performance so that one can proceed to the next step in the process. The deviations in quality, quantity, time, cost, competencies, behaviour, leadership, initiative etc., can be identified. The slow and fast working persons can be identified through this comparison. If the comparison is not carried out then the goals and performance cannot be aligned to meet the planning requirements.

Step-5: Appraisal feedback: In this step the information gathered relating to appraisal are analysed and discussed with the employee. The appraiser discuss with concerned employee regarding the strengths he has shown during the work. The place where he finds himself in a good position, the good performance he has given and the required competencies he has at present. Focus is also given on the weak points of the workers and through discussion these areas are identified. Further, discuss the difficulties faced with the work due to him, machines, working procedure of any other reason. The ultimate goal of this is to improve the working of the employees as well as organization. Employees get feedback from the appraiser regarding the performance they have given their positive and negative points. Simultaneously they get the counseling, coaching and suggestions for better working.

Step-6: Corrective, motivation and development action: The last step in the appraisal process is the initiation of corrective, motivation and development action when necessary. Corrective action can be taken at the earliest to remove the cause of the problem. The performance may be poor due to workers, machines, working method, environmental etc. The immediate action will be initiated so that the problem can be corrected and it should not affect the performance adversely. Next, the actions will be taken to motivate the persons by identifying rewards, recognition, incentives, compensation and promotion. This will motivate as well as correct the behaviour of employees, Finally, the management take action for further education, training, improvement in working procedure and replacement of old technology. The ultimate goal of this stage is to remove the problems so that in present as well as in future the performance should not be affected.

2. METHODS OF PERFORMANCE APPRAISAL

There are a number of methods that are used to evaluate employee's performance. It may be evaluated on the basis of his traits and attributes as well as on the basis of his work or results and objectives achieved by him. Thus his performance may be measured in terms of standards of his traits and general behaviour on the job or in terms of results and goals. Some of the common techniques are given below. Each method has its merits and demerits but one thing is clear that the technique employed has to evaluate mainly his job-related performance.

The appraisal methods can be classified as follows:

(a) Individual appraisal, group appraisal and other methods

(b) Traditional and modern methods

(a) Individual Appraisal Methods

Some of the methods which are widely used to evaluate an individual employee against the standard are as under:

(i) Rating Scale: This is the oldest and most popular method of evaluating individual's performance. In this technique the appraiser judges the employee's performance along a scale from low to high. The appraiser rates employee's work and traits such as output, dependability, loyalty, initiative, cooperation, attendance and the like as poor, average, good, very good, excellent etc. Rating is the subjective opinion of the appraiser about the individual work or particular trait. This is noted on the appraisal form against each criterion or trait. The ratings may be assigned numerical values or scores, so that an average can be calculated and a comparison be made. For example, poor standard may indicate no or zero score, fair, acceptable, good and excellent rates may have 1, 2, 3 and 4 scores respectively. Score for overall performance can be determined and compared in case of each employee. Sometimes grades A, B, C, D, E may be assigned as a rating measure. A-for excellent performance, B-for very good, C-for good, D- for average and E-for poor performance.

(ii) Check list method: The appraisal form in this technique is a checklist of statements or words which describes employee's performance or behaviour. The rater reads the same and rates the employee against that statement. It is in the form of yes-no response. The rater marks yes if he is in agreement with the statement or description. Marks no if employee does not agree with the statement. Finally the total of yes and no are taken into account. Sometimes, personnel department may assign weights to each item or statement of the check list according to its importance for evaluating performance. This is known as weighted check list rating method. Weighting helps in quantifying rating.

(iii) Forced choice method: In this case the appraisal form contains different sentences, each of them contains a pair of positive or negative statement relating to various classes of characteristics, such as learning ability, co-operation, leadership, dependability, loyalty, attendance, work performance etc. In each item, the appraiser or rater has to choose that statement out of the two, which fits the employee most. For example, if both the statements in an item benefit the employee performance, the rater has to discard any one. Hence this technique is known as forced choice method. For instance, take the item - has sound job knowledge. Works hard if both statements benefit an employee, in this method the rater has to choose only one of the two. The other is overlooked. The appraisal may be faulty on this account.

(iv) Critical incident method: In this technique, the rater records an extreme or extraordinary behaviour displayed by the employee when he works on the job. This will assist him to appraise his performance. The incidents that take place may indicate positive or good behaviour of the employee or his negative or bad behaviour. e.g. In case of a fire, the employee might have shown an exemplary courage. Without worrying about life risk he controls the fire. Another example, when there is an income tax department raid in the company office and the finance manager is not available in office. The dealing persons shows the initiative to handle the situation very effectively by explaining every points asked by the income tax inspector. The incidents are noted in a critical incident sheet. These are taken into account while evaluating employees' performance in critical situations.

(v) Field review method: In this method a specialist of the personnel department goes into the field and helps the supervisor in rating the employee. The work of the employees is observed actually in the field. The observer sees the nature of job, environment in which the job is performed, the climatic conditions, difficulties faced, working conditions, methods used for working, facilities available to the workers, risks involved in the jobs. The specialist prepares an evaluation based on the observation and information provided by the immediate supervisor about the performance of the employee. It is forwarded to the supervisor for review, modification or for discussion with the employee. The only difference is that a skilled specialist fills up the appraisal form.

(vi) Performance test and observation method: The purpose is to test the knowledge and skills of an employee. He is evaluated either by giving him a paper-pencil test or he is required to demonstrate his skill in a practical situation. For example, a baker may be asked to prepare a cake or a mechanical engineer may be required to locate a fault in a defective machine. It depends upon the type of the job. For a typist a letter can be given for typing. On the basis of work the assessment can be done. A programmer can be given a task to design a program for that task. Receptionist can be given a task to contact vendors or customers and simultaneously the conversation can be monitored.

(vii) Annual confidential reports (ACR): These reports relate to the performance of employees and they are kept quite confidential. They are prepared by superiors on the basis of their judgements, observations and intuitions. The subordinate is not permitted to see his report on performance. The whole process is conducted without disclosing any information of it to any concerned person. The employee does not get any feedback about his performance, shortfalls and strengths. They are kept in dark. The scope for self-development is very less in this. Generally it is being used in government organization.

(b) Group Appraisal Methods

There are a number of methods that are used to appraise the performance of groups of employees. Generally, these methods are used to rank various employees in a group or groups in accordance with their merits and hence they are, useful for deciding merit, promotion, pay increments, rewards etc.

(i) Factors and points method: In this method the factors affecting the performance of employees are identified. The factors may be performance standard achieved, behaviour, competencies, leadership quality, initiatives to solve the problems. There may be other less important factors may or may not be considered. Every factor is given points or marks as per their relating importance. Finally the total of all factors is taken. This has been explained with an example in the table given at the end of this method.

Table 10.1: IBMR - Performance Appraisal (2008-09)

SL No	Appraisal Criteria Total 100 Marks					Marks Obtained
	Perform. Achieved (20 Marks)	Behaviour (20 Marks)	Competency (20 Marks)	Leadership (20 Marks)	Initiatives (20 marks)	
Academic Deptt.						
1. Mrs V. Dahiya	18	18	17	17	18	88
2. Mrs Monika G	13	15	16	12	13	69
3. Mrs.Priyanka Gohil	13	12	13	16	13	67
4. Ms Poonam A	16	13	13	15	16	73
5. Ms.Karishma Singh	13	17	16	13	13	72
6. Mrs.Rajlakshmi	16	17	13	15	13	74
7. Mrs. Pragnya	13	16	13	13	13	68
8. Mrs. Kavita Sharma	16	12	13	12	13	66
Marketing Deptt.						
9. Mr Kiran R K	14	18	19	19	19	89
10. Mr Gaurav Gandhi	13	16	13	15	13	70
11. Mr Ram Yadav	12	10	13	13	13	61
12. Ms Jaya Ludhani	13	12	12	12	13	62
13. Mrs Usha Chettiar	13	13	13	13	13	65
Admin Department.						
14. Mrs. B. Vidhani	13	11	13	13	13	63
15. Mr. S. Shah	13	13	9	8	13	56
16. Mr. N. Vaishyak	13	13	13	13	12	64
18. Mr.R. Chauhan	12	13	12	11	12	60
19. Mr. Ashok	15	13	15	16	12	71
20. Mr. Bhadresh	12	16	15	18	17	78
21. Mr. Jagat Singh	17	13	15	16	15	76
22. Mr. Deepak	16	15	15	16	15	77
23. Mr. N. Parmar	18	16	15	13	13	75
24. Mr. R. Bhati	12	11	10	12	13	58
25. Mr. N. Bhati	16	18	15	15	16	80
26. Mr. Arvind Bhai	15	13	16	18	17	79
27. Mr Baccharam	16	15	18	15	18	82

Date: Signature of the Appraiser

Place:

(ii) Ranking method: It is very simple and easy method of judging the work of employees in a group. Ranks are assigned in order of their performances. In fact the workers on the basis of their performance can be ranked like first, second, third, fourth and so on. This method can be used independently or it can be used with factors and points method jointly. This is explained with the above method. In factors and points method the points are given to each employee on the basis of performance criteria. Further, the ranks of employees' performance are decided on obtained marks.

Table 10.2: IBMR - Performance Appraisal (2008-09)

Rank	Name	Department	Marks Obtained	Remarks
1	Mr Kiran R K	Marketing Department	89	
2	Mrs Vishal Dahiya	Academic Department	88	
3	Mr Baccharam	Administration Department	82	
4	Mr. Naresh Bhati	Administration Department	80	
5	Mr. Arvind Bhai	Administration Department	79	
6	Mr. Bhadresh	Administration Department	78	
7	Mr. Deepak	Administration Department	77	
8	Mr. Jagat Singh	Administration Department	76	
9	Mr. Natwar Parmar	Administration Department	75	
10	Mrs Rajlakshmi	Administration Department	74	
11	Ms Poonam Arora	Academic Department	73	
12	Ms Karishma Singh	Academic Department	72	
13	Mr. Ashok	Administration Department	71	
14	Mr Gaurav Gandhi	Marketing Department	70	
15	Mrs Monika Gahelawat	Academic Department	69	
16	Mrs Pragnya Kaul	Academic Department	68	
17	Mrs Priyanka Gohil	Academic Department	67	
18	Mrs Kavita Sharma	Academic Department	66	
19	Mrs Usha Chettiar	Marketing Department	65	
20	Mr. Nilesh Vaishyak	Administration Department	64	
21	Mrs. Bharti Vidhani	Administration Department	63	
22	Ms Jaya Ludhani	Marketing Department	62	
23	Mr Ram Yadav	Marketing Department	61	
24	Mr. Rajendra Chauhan	Administration Department	60	
25	Mr. Ramesh Bhati	Administration Department	58	
26	Mr. Suken Shah	Administration Department	56	
27	Mr. Laxdeep Raval	Administration Department	55	

Date:

Place: Signature of the Appraiser

Employees differ in their performances. The best performer is ranked first and the worst worker is ranked last. The ranks to others are assigned in between the two. Thus in a group of 10 employees, there are 10 ranks to be given to them in order of their evaluation. The best employee may be assigned rank 1, while the weakest rank 10. This method suffers from 'halo' effect. The evaluation is based on subjective opinion. Moreover it does not bring out the extent of difference between them. Sometimes there may not be much difference between the two, but human bias may play its role.

(iii) Paired comparison method: This is a slight variation of ranking method. In this method, performance of each employee is compared with the performance of each of the others and the rater has to select the better out of each pair, taking only one pair at a time. How many times an employee is better pair wise is computed and one who is considered the best is ranked 1. For example, if there are 10 employees in a group, they might comprise 45 pairs amongst them for comparison. The total number of comparison is computed by the formula n(n-1)/2. If the number of employees to be evaluated is 15, then the number of comparisons to be made will be 15 (15 - 1)/2 i.e. 105.

(iv) Forced distributions: In this method, the employees are rated and classified into categories such as best 10%, next 20%, middle 40%, next 20% and lowest 10% of employees. They are placed in their respective groups or they are categories as outstanding, above average, average or satisfactory, below average and poor respectively in view of the given percentages. The problem with method is that if the employee falls in one category more than specified percentage, they cannot be rated in that category. They will be shown lower or upper category.

(c) Other Methods Including MBO System

There are some methods which are future-oriented. They evaluate employee potential for future performance. They also aim at setting future performance objectives. The two important techniques that may have a bearing on future performance goals are self-appraisal, management by objectives approach, BARS, 360 degree appraisal method etc.

(i) Self-appraisal: A large number of enterprises use self-appraisal technique for further improvement of performance. Under this method, the employee has to evaluate himself against predetermined standard. Such self-evaluation assists the employee to understand his strengths and weaknesses. He can know the areas where he is lacking and hence requires improvement. Thus self-appraisal leads to self-improvement and self-development and is helpful to personal goals or objectives for future performance. The drawback of this method is that the employees appraise themselves very high. The appraisal is not realistic. Everyone is interested to show his aggravated rating. That misguides the management.

(ii) Appraisal by results or management by objectives (MBO) approach: In an enterprise the efforts of all the members of the organisation including management, supervisors and subordinates are directed towards realisation of enterprise objectives. These overall objectives are further split into sub-objectives, goals or end results to be achieved by various employees. In MBO approach, the performance of a subordinate occupier of a managerial position is assessed or evaluated on the basis of end results achieved or accomplished by him rather than on the basis of traits. The effectiveness or success of management is reflected in the accomplishment or achievement of objectives or end results set by the organisation. Thus the basis of appraisal by results is rooted in the concept "management by objectives".

(iii) 360° performance appraisal: The appraisal is done by any person with whom employee is in touch for performance of his job, i.e., his appraisal may be done by supervisor, manager, subordinates, employees themselves, customers, consultant etc. Performance can be evaluated on any day and from any angle of his work. Thus the appraisal can be done on all working days in a year, from all angles and by all parties who are connected with the employees. By this method, it is possible to notice all activities on all days and evaluate the same.

(iv) Behaviorally anchored rating scales (BARS): In this method, there is a combination of techniques used in the weighted check list, rating and critical incident method. Under BARS, effective and ineffective behaviours are described more objectively. This method takes services of a person who is quite familiar with a particular job to identify major components. He ranks the components and validates specific behaviour for each component of the job.

(v) Cost accounting method: In this method, for evaluation of performance of employee, cost is the base. Both the cost of employee and his output are considered and the relationship is established between cost and benefit. The time, efforts and expenditure are calculated in respect of each candidate. The output and cost in total are considered and then per unit cost can be calculated. This shows the relative worth of the candidate to the organization.

(d) Traditional and Modern Methods

The traditional methods are almost similar to individual and group appraisal methods. These methods have been explained under earlier topics other methods are similar to modern appraisal methods. The modern methods of performance methods are explained in detail under next topics. The classification of performance appraisal method as traditional and modern is depicted with the help of figure given below:

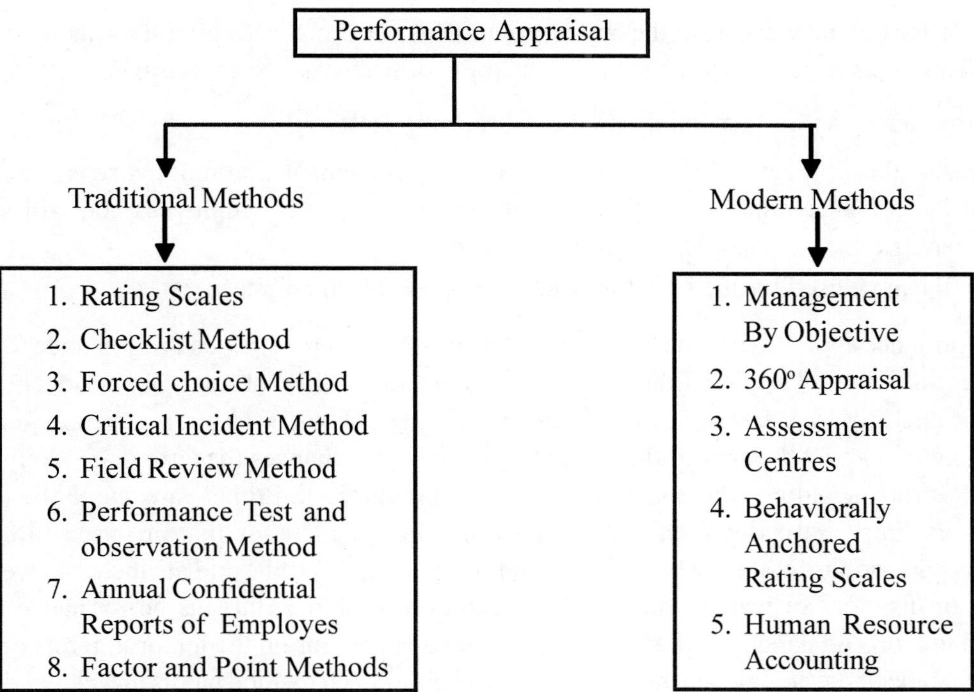

Diagram 10.2: Methods of Performance Appraisal

3. CONCLUSION

After depth study of various organisations, it is found that in every organisation different steps have been taken and there is no similarity in steps in performance management process. It entirely depends upon the requirement of the organisation and the management working pattern. Some organisations take help from the consultants and some are having their own internal experts for scanning the business the business environment, identifying and prioritizing the goals, fixing responsibility and accountability, expected performance standards and many more work related aspects. In large organisation many steps are followed but in small and further smaller organisations some of the steps may be or may not be followed. It is summarised that the steps involved in performance appraisal are planning for objectives and performance standards, communication and guidance, performance appraisal and review of it for development and planning action for future.

"Performance appraisal is a systematic periodic and impartial rating of employee's excellence in matters pertaining to his present job and to his potentialities for a better job." (Flippo) The performance appraisal is an important stage in this process. It shows as per planning of objectives, performance standards and behaviour the communication, counseling, coaching, motivation and feedback have been given or not. Finally to see what is the impact of these planning and action on the performance of the employees. The performance standards regarding quality, quantity, cost and behaviour have been achieved or not. So it becomes necessary to carry out the performance appraisal of everyone for smooth working of the organisation. Thus performance appraisal forms an important part of HRM. This necessitates the study of the topic of performance appraisal.

Performance appraisal is mainly used for three purposes:

(a) As a basis of reward allocation such as salary increments, promotion, rewards etc
(b) Performance appraisal will point out the weaknesses of employees and will spot the areas where development efforts are needed.
(c) It can be used for the selection and development programme.

Performance appraisal is done by the managers or supervisors. They do this job under different situation, at different place and different state of mind and at different time. Their judgements are likely to be affected. They are human being. Their psychology, liking, disliking, preference, judgement etc., are likely to affect the appraisal of employees. There are chances that errors are likely to take place. But efforts should be there so that these can be minimized. Proper care should be taken to give fair and impartial assessment. There are a number of methods that are used to evaluate employee's performance. It may be evaluated on the basis of his traits and attributes as well as on the basis of his work or results and objectives achieved by him. Thus his performance may be measured in terms of standards of his traits and general behaviour on the job or in terms of results and goals. Some of the common techniques are given below. Each method has its merits and demerits but one thing is clear that the technique employed has to evaluate mainly his job related performance. The appraisal methods can be classified as follows:

(a) Individual appraisal and group appraisal methods include rating scale, checklist method, forced choice method, critical incident method, field review method, performance test and observation method, annual confidential reports, factors and points method, ranking method, and paired comparison method.

(b) Other methods including MBO system, self-appraisal, 360° performance appraisal, behaviourally anchored rating scales,(BARS) and cost accounting method

4. QUESTIONS FOR REVIEW

1. What do you know by performance appraisal process? Explain the steps involved in it in detail.
2. Discuss the appraisal method for individual employee in an organisation.
3. What are the methods being used for appraisal of employees in group in a company? Elaborate.
4. Self-appraisal methods brings the appraisal from employees point of view which highlights the hidden talents of the employees. Discuss
5. What do you know about traditional and modern methods of appraisal? Highlight them in brief.

6. Do you know about traditional and modern methods of appraisal? Highlight them in brief.
7. You are an HR manager of a medium size of company, which methods for appraisal would you use for appraisal of your employees?
8. Write short notes on the following:
   (a) Establishment of performance standards.
   (b) Measurement of performance standards.
   (c) Appraisal feedback.
   (d) Check list method for appraisal.
   (e) Critical incident method.
   (f) Annual Confidential Reports. (ACR)
   (g) Rating scales for appraisal. (BARS)

5. OBJECTIVE QUESTIONS

1. The performance appraisal is the evaluation process, in which the information is gathered, recorded, measured and analyzed relating to the performance of the employees.

   (a) Fully agree
   (b) Partially agree
   (c) Partially disagree
   (d) Fully disagree
   (e) Cannot say anything

2. Arrange the steps involved in performance appraisal process:
   1. Measurement of performance
   2. Communication of performance standards and expectations
   3. Comparison of performance
   4. Establishment of performance standards
   5. Corrective, motivation and development plans
   6. Appraisal feedback

   (a) 1, 2, 3, 4, 5, 6
   (b) 2, 3, 4, 6, 5, 1
   (c) 4, 2, 1, 3, 5, 6
   (d) 3, 4, 6,5, 1, 2
   (e) None of the above

3. Which is the oldest and most popular method of evaluating individual's performance?

   (a) Check list method
   (b) Rating scale
   (c) Critical incident method
   (d) Forced choice method
   (e) None of the above

4. In this technique, the rater records an extreme or extraordinary behaviour displayed by the employee when he works on the job. It is known as:
   (a) Critical incident method
   (b) Forced choice method
   (c) Rating scale
   (d) Field review method
   (e) None of the above

5. In a method a specialist of the personnel department goes into the field and helps the supervisor in rating the employee. It is called:
   (a) Rating scale
   (b) Field review method
   (c) Check list method
   (d) Forced choice method
   (e) None of the above

6. In this method, the employees are rated and classified into categories such as best 10%, next 20%, middle 40%, next 20% and lowest 10% of employees. It is specified as:
   (a) Paired comparison method
   (b) Forced distribution method
   (c) Ranking method
   (d) Factors and point method
   (e) None of the above

7. In a method, there is a combination of techniques used in the weighted check list, rating and critical incident method. It is known as:
   (a) 360 degree performance appraisal method
   (b) Cost accounting
   (c) Behaviorally anchored rating scales (BARS)
   (d) Appraisal by results or management by objectives (MBO) approach
   (e) None of the above

8. The appraisal reports relate to the performance of employees are prepared by superiors on the basis of their judgements, observations and intuitions. and they are kept quite confidential. The employee does not get any feedback about his performance, shortfalls and strengths. This method of appraisal is known as:
   (a) Annual confidential report
   (b) Management by objectives
   (c) Assessment centre
   (d) 360 degree method
   (e) None of the above

9. Modern methods of performance appraisal include the following:
   1. Management by objective
   2. 360° appraisal method
   3. Assessment centres
   4. Behavioraly anchored rating scales
   5. Human resource accounting

(a) 1 and 2
(b) 1, 2 and 3
(c) 1,2,3 and 4
(d) All the above
(e) None of the above

10. The appraisal may be done by supervisor, manager, subordinates, employees themselves, customers, consultant etc. Performance can be evaluated on any day and from any angle of his work. Thus the appraisal can be done on all working days in a year, from all angles and by all parties who are connected with the employees. This is known as:

(a) Assessment centre
(b) Ranking method
(c) Grading method
(d) Management by objective
(e) 360 degree appraisal method

Answer Keys:

Question No.	Answer	Question No.	Answer
1	a	6	b
2	c	7	c
3	b	8	a
4	a	9	d
5	b	10	e

Chapter

Assessment Centre

1. INTRODUCTION

In present global business environment the external environment is changing over a short span of time. Due to this the situation has become very critical, uncertain and risky. Social, cultural, economic, political, competition and technology factors of business environment are undergoing turbulent changes. Worldwide economic reforms are constantly exposing business organizations to higher and tougher levels of competition. They face the competition from companies from outside as well as local companies. Two tier of competition is being faced and it is cut-throat competition. In order to meet competition, firms need to improve performance in various areas like technology, procedures, manufacturing or operation processes, management, finances, quality of products and services, costs, new market creation and development of existing, new product developments and modification of existing one etc.

This situation can be handled only by the competent and motivated employees only. Trained and motivated persons can give better performance and higher degree of productivity. All the competing organizations across the world are equally competent in technology, finance, systems and procedures, organizational structure and quality awareness. In present situation they have acquired better technology, cost effective finance, knowledge of markets and customers. To do all these things skilled, trained, motivated and committed persons are needed. This is the only difference in competing organizations. To get the competitive advantage the need for skilled, committed and motivated persons is strongly felt. Organisations with such manpower can capture the opportunities in the market. They may take the leading position in their areas. Under these conditions the competent employees are inevitable to play strategic role in every organization.

For effective working the rationalization of organizational structure is needed. The organizations are becoming less effective due to more layers in hierarchy. It causes delay in decisions and action so the profitability of the organization goes down. This frustrates the employees and increases inefficiency in operation. This structure is to be rationalized so that all these problems can be avoided. The culture of peers and performance must be developed. The importance should be given to the performance of the individual and not the position at which he is working. The need for identification of good performers in organization is strongly felt. It is possible through proper performance appraisal only.

To inspire the person for giving good performance is the current need of every job. The motivational tempo of employees is to be maintained. The appropriate mechanism of compensation is to be developed so that their motivation level can be maintained further. This is to be designed on the basis of performance criteria. It should not create frustration among employees. They should keep the aspiration of promotion low and limited. Further, those who perform good consistently then their case must be considered for promotion also. But it should be considered for those who are further willing to take the new and higher assignments. It should be accompanied with higher level of responsibility, status, higher pay scale and improved motivation of employees. It is all based on the performance analysis of the employees.

2. POTENTIAL APPRAISAL

In present scenario the strategic and important roles should be played by the competent persons. It can be said that all persons are not equally competent. Management has to identify the competent persons who can handle the new assignments in future. The need for potential appraisal is strongly felt worldwide. Managers should have the perfect knowledge of job analysis. It explains the types of jobs to be performed and the competencies required for performing the jobs. On the basis of this the competency requirement can be identified. For competency identification there should be some formal method for identification of competencies. Through this the given employee's competencies can be assessed for performing the new tasks in future. Through potential appraisal the competencies are assessed and potentials to perform the new or higher jobs are identified. The method of potential assessment can be very simple or bit difficult depending upon the nature of the jobs and requirement of organizations.

The current performance appraisal is the base for potential appraisal. It is carried out in a year and it identifies the potentials the employee possesses. It is suitable for the higher level in similar job. But it may not be suitable for altogether a new job to be performed in future. For new job the potential appraisal is possible by putting the person on job and then potential appraisal is done over a period of time. Again it may not be accepted because it can be risky and there may be many aspirants for that new job. The most probably new and best method of potential appraisal is creating the work like conditions or simulation and then observing the performance of employees. Before assigning the new job to the candidate the potential are identified through simulation exercises. Through simulation the critical competencies required can be identified. It may not be possible to identify all competencies required through simulation. Only the critical tasks can be studied and identified through it. Other remaining tasks may be handled on the basis of past experience. This potential appraisal may be used in deciding the future promotion. The employee is assigned the tasks of higher level, status and responsibility. It is to be assigned through a proper testing of competencies or potentials for holding the future assignments. For this reason the need for assessment centre is felt in many organizations. The objectives of this potential appraisal should be clearly communicated that the company is interested in performance and competency culture and not anything else.

3. ASSESSMENT CENTRE MEANING

Assessment centre is a modern method of performance appraisal. It is an improvement over other traditional methods. In assessment centre a comprehensive and standard procedure is used. For evaluation purpose different techniques have been used. These include job simulation, business games, situational exercises, group discussion, presentation, reports, role plays, case analysis etc. These techniques are applied for candidates for their performance appraisal to find out the potential for selection, special training, promotion and development activities. Assessment centre is a separate unit or section within the organization that has been established with the objective for performance appraisal and mainly to identify the potential of employees for future requirements. Generally it is centrally located in the organization or at the corporate or divisional office.

The aspirants apply to the centre as per the jobs time to time when the assessment centre inform them. The candidates may be internal as well as external. The candidates take part in different exercise for a definite period of time. The different techniques are applied to evaluate their performance. A team of assessors has been appointed on the basis of their expertise. It may include experts like psychologists, HR managers, job related experts etc. They are appointed on the basis of their skills, knowledge, areas of specialization and experience for a definite period of time. The candidates are assessed from different point of view by applying various techniques by team of experts. It can be said to be an assessment centre

360 degree performance appraisal is done by assessors. The angle of assessment of every assessor is different. An assessment centre consists of a standardized evaluation of behavior based on multiple inputs. Several trained observers and techniques are used. Judgements about behavior are made, in major part, from specifically developed assessment simulations. These judgements are pooled in a meeting among the assessors or by statistical integration process. In an integration discussion, comprehensive accounts of behavior, and often rating of it, are pooled. This result in evaluation of performance of the assessed on the dimensions of competencies or other variables for that purpose the assessment centre is established. Statistical combination methods should be validated in accordance with professionally accepted standards. — 'Guidelines and ethical considerations for assessment centre operations.' — 28th International Congress on Assessment Centre Methods

The performance feedback is communicated to the candidates as per planning of assessment centre. The assessment centre can be used for potential appraisal as well and for development purpose also. The potential of employees are identified for future new or higher jobs. On the basis of appraisal the deficiencies in competencies are identified and the programme for training and education are conducted. It serves the requirement of appraisal and development both.

4. DEFINITIONS OF ASSESSMENT CENTRE

Assessment centre has been defined by various experts, practitioners, consultants and academicians as follows:

(a) An assessment center is a comprehensive standardized procedure in which multiple assessment techniques such as situational exercises and job simulation (business games, discussions, reports & presentations) are used to evaluate individual employee for variety of manpower decisions. - Udai Parikh & TV Rao

(b) An assessment centre is a process in which individuals participate in a series of exercises, most of which approximate what they would be called upon to do in the future job. Assessors usually selected from higher management levels in the firm, are trained to observe the participants and evaluate their performance as fairly and impartially as possible. –'Can assessment centers be used to improve the salesperson selection process', E. James Randall, Ernest E. Cooke, Richard J. Jefferies, Journal of personal selling and sales management.

(c) Assessment centres are means of helping an organization to identify the strengths and potential development areas of its staff in relation to a particular job or role. – Beacon Consultants.

(d) The main feature of assessment centres is that they are a multiple assessment process. There are five main ways in which that is so. A group of participants takes part in a variety of exercises observed by a team of trained assessors who evaluate each participant against a number of predetermined job related behaviors. Decisions are then made by pooling shared data. – Iain Ballantyne and Nigel Povah

(e) Assessment centres are tools that involve assembling "recommended managerial candidates for specific purpose of assessing their potential and arriving at the decisions about their promo ability." Companies take a group of up to a dozen candidates away from work environment for several days, giving these candidates simulated management problems such as a case study, role plays and in-baskets. After a series of interviews and tests, observers (usually industrial psychologists or senior managers) collate the results to produce overall potential ratings for each candidate. Corporate Leadership Council.

(f) Assessment centre is a method of predicting future performance by using simulations and other techniques to measure a candidate's ability to handle future responsibilities. – Julie Hay, 'Assessment and Development Centre'.

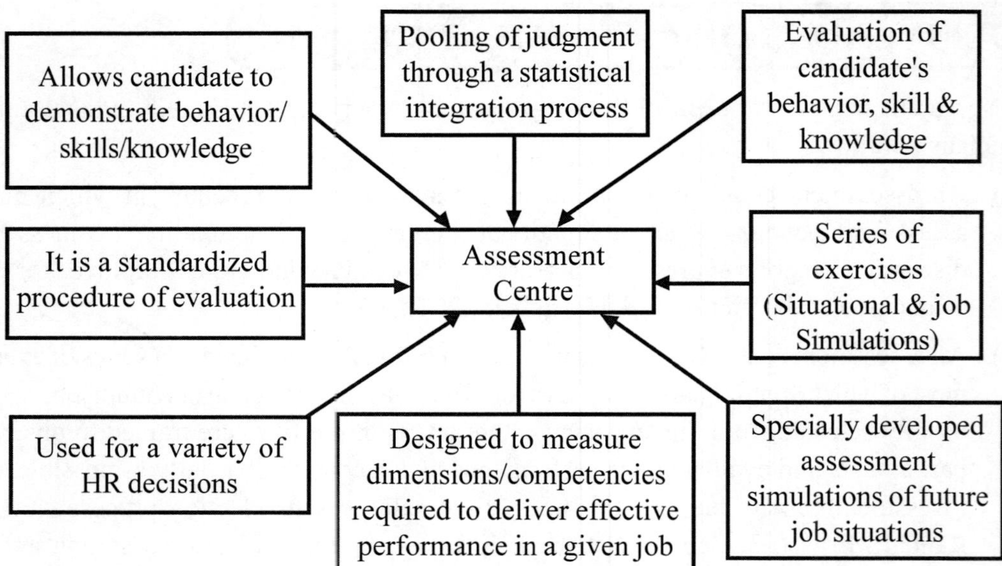

Figure 11.1: Summary of Assessment Centre of Various Definitions

(g) A typical assessment centre requires participants to complete several simulations that test two or more performance dimensions. Job analysis is used to develop both the simulations and the performance dimensions to ensure their job-relatedness. Assessors observe the behavior of the participants, and ultimately pool their observations, evaluate the behaviors, and provide a score for related performance dimensions. - 'Assessment Centre: Reducing inter assessor influence', Phillip E. Lowry, Public Personnel Management.

(h) An assessment centre is a multi-faceted and multi-dimensional approach designed to provide reliable and valid information about a range of competencies of an individual considered to be necessary for successful performance at a target level in a specific job. - '360 degree feedback, competency mapping and assessment centres', Radha R. Sharma.

(i) Assessment Centres are often described as the variety of testing techniques that allow the candidates to demonstrate, under standardized conditions, the skills and abilities most essential for success in a given job. - Dennis A. Joiner, 'Assessment centre in public sector: A practical approach', Public Personnel Management Journal.

5. ASSESSMENT CENTRE AS AN APPRAISAL METHOD

There are different methods of performance appraisal like traditional and modern methods. Out of modern methods assessment centre is one of them. The appraisal method can claim the status of assessment centre if the following multiple features exist:

(a) Multiple Competencies

In performance appraisal of employee multiple competencies are evaluated for in a candidate. The multiple competencies may include educational qualification, skills, knowledge, attitude, aptitude, ability, capability, leadership quality, initiatives for problem solving and team spirit. There may be more competencies also.

(b) Multiple Objectives

The assessment centre is established with a number of objectives. If it is used for one objective then the effectiveness of centre will go down and requirement of organizations may not be fulfilled. Nowadays the centre is being used for potential appraisal and development objectives.

(c) Multiple Observers

The performances of candidates are observed by number of observers at a time. Because the different techniques are used for assessment purpose and assessment is done from different angles. It is not possible for one assessor to evaluate on every part due to their area of expertise. The appointment of number of assessors is done from different fields. Further, to eliminate the subjectivity & increase objectivity in the performance appraisal, the multiple assessors are involved in assessment.

(d) Multiple Participants for Assessment

At assessment centre a number of candidates those who feel to be assessed should apply or to be appointed. They will be participating in number of exercises for a decided period of time. Their performance will be observed by the observers and then the feedback will be given. The number of participants may vary from organization to organization as per the planning.

(e) Multiple Techniques for Assessment

For assessment of performance a number of exercises or techniques are used at different times. These may include situational exercises, role playing, management games, group discussion, case study, and simulation and presentations exercises: Exercises like role plays, case analysis, presentations, group discussions etc.

(f) Multiple Simulations

There are different jobs to be performed by employees in an organization. Some are critical and important and some are not. For critical activities, the jobs are simulated. Less important jobs are not simulated. Their assessment is done on the basis of past experience. Different types of simulation may be used depending upon the situation of assessment.

(g) Multiple Observations

In every exercise the performance is observed repeatedly by number of observers. By repeated observations the mistakes or error may be avoided. The average of repeated observations can be taken as a score of those observations

The following cannot claim the status of assessment centre:

(a) Assessment procedures that do not require the participant to demonstrate competencies at simulated jobs. Without demonstration of competencies the potential appraisal is not possible, when assessment on the basis of one exercise. For assessment centre appraisal method a number of exercises are to be used. Panel interviews or a series of sequential interviews or group discussion or role playing as the sole technique cannot claim for status of assessment centre.

(b) Reliance on a single technique of assessment whether it is simulation or presentation cannot bring subjectivity in the assessment work. So it cannot claim the status of assessment centre. But it may be an exercise of assessment at assessment centre.

(c) Single-assessor evaluation gives subjectivity in appraisal system. This is the feature of a traditional method. To overcome the subjectivity in assessment work, numbers of assessors are appointed in an assessment centre. Assessment centre with one assessor cannot claim status of assessment centre.

(d) Using only a test battery composed of a number of paper-and-pencil measures, regardless of whether the judgments are made by a statistical or judgmental pooling of scores.

(e) The assessment is done by number of assessors with repeated observation but the data are not pooled. This assessment without pooling data is not accepted for assessment centre. Here the objective of assessment is defeated.

(f) Establishment of assessment centre that is labelled as assessment centre but does not meet the requirement then it cannot claim to be as assessment centre.

6. ESSENTIAL ELEMENTS OF AN ASSESSMENT CENTRE

The establishment of a centre for assessment of performance of employees is called as assessment centre. The functions of assessment centre may not be performed as required if the essential requirements are not fulfilled. For its effective working the following essential elements must be there so that it can be considered as assessment centre:

(a) Job Analysis

It is the study of job description and job specification. The knowledge of these two elements will give the knowledge about the jobs to be performed and determine the requirement of knowledge, skills, attitude, aptitude, qualities, ability, capability, motivation level, initiatives etc., that are required for effective working on the job and give good performance. These are to be evaluated in the performance appraisal. Without job analysis the assessors will not be in position to do the justice in appraisal work. It may be complex and different from the previous jobs studied. If the data pertaining to old and new jobs are available then the comparative study of these jobs becomes easier. If future anticipated job is not available then it can be done on the basis of projected tasks and skills.

(b) Predefine Competencies

For proper performance appraisal the competencies required for performance of tasks should be planned and agreed in advance in a meeting involving managers, supervisors and employees. If it is done the tasks will be performed as expected and the assessors will find comfortable in appraisal work.

(c) Behavioral Classification

Behaviors displayed by participants must be classified into meaningful and relevant categories such as dimensions, attributes, characteristics, aptitudes, qualities, skills, abilities, competencies, and knowledge. It may give clarity to the assessors regarding the appraisal work of employees.

(d) Assessment Techniques

These include a number of exercises to test the assessees of their potentials. The assessment techniques must be more. It should not be limited to one or two techniques. Various techniques like test, interview, questionnaire, group discussion, socio-metric devices, simulation, presentation, role playing etc., can be selected for assessment job. Each competency is to be tested through at least two exercises for gathering adequate evidence for the presence of particular competence.

(e) Simulations

Simulation is an exercise designed to create the artificial work like conditions similar to the actual jobs. The simulation techniques vary job to job. For all jobs the simulation cannot be used. It can be used for critical and important jobs only. The simulated exercise can be used for job related segments. The simulation exercise should be similar to actual work situation. The selection of simulation should be proper and should not favour a group of assessees. The exercises should simulate the job responsibilities as closely as possible to eliminate potential errors in selection.

(f) Repeated Observations

Through different assessment techniques the observations are taken by the assessors. Different assessors take observations relating to particular jobs and same observer also takes observation at least two times. The observations of different observers are pooled together and then the feedback is prepared. The efforts in repeated observations are to avoid subjectivity and bring objectivity in appraisal system. Accurate and unbiased observation is the most critical aspect of an assessment centre method.

(g) Multiple Observers

In traditional methods the assessment is done by one assessor. He is likely to commit mistakes or errors due to different reasons. To overcome the errors in assessment, more number of assessors are appointed for performance assessment. The assessment is done by them on different dimensions of the jobs. They are appointed or selected on the basis of age, sex, functional area work, experience etc. The number of assessors may vary from centre to centre depending upon the nature of job, involvement of assessor, technique used for assessment, availability of assessors and purpose of assessment centre. Generally an assessor takes care of two to three assessees.

(h) Trained Assessors

While making the appointment or selection of assessor special care should be taken. They should be well trained and experienced persons. A trained and experienced person is in position to understand the jobs properly. He does not face any difficulty during assessment. If any difficulty is faced then he knows the solution of the problem. This gives confidence to the assessor and finally the assessment work quality also improves. If they are not trained then before assigning the assessment tasks to them, they should be well trained. Otherwise there will be no justice with the job of assessor. The whole purpose of assessment centre will be defeated and many other problems might be invited. Management should take special care for selection and training of assessors.

(i) Systematic Recording System

A systematic procedure of recording must be used by the assessors for future reference. The assessors are taking repeated observation of different dimensions of the jobs when employees are performing their jobs. It is difficult to remember observations every time. Mistakes are likely to take place. To avoid these mistakes they should go for proper recording, The recording could be in the form of hand written note, behavioral check list, audio-video recording etc.

(j) Reports Preparation

After recording the observations the assessors should prepare a report out of the observation. If the report is not prepared then the meaning of observations cannot be conveyed properly. On the basis of notes, check lists, audio-video recording the final report is to be prepared or if required to be submitted. This report helps the observers in the final discussion regarding appraisal of employees.

(k) Data Pooling

The various assessors have recorded the observations on performance of employees. They have prepared their reports also. The final thing required is the integration of the information relating to performance of employees. In integration discussion the assessors meet and discuss their reports prepared on performance of employees. Through discussion or other techniques they arrive at consensus for performance of the candidates. The combined assessment report is to be prepared. It may take time but no doubt it will be better than the assessment done by one assessor. The subjectivity will be removed. The efforts are put to give accurate and reliable report. It may claim the objectivity in assessment work.

7. IMPORTANCE OF ASSESSMENT CENTRE AS A DEVELOPMENT CENTRE

Assessment centre is a modern method of performance appraisal and it is considered very useful for the organization. In traditional methods there are many errors taking place. To overcome these errors this method has been accepted by the management. Definitely it is an improvement over the old methods. This method is very important for the organizations because it is used for a variety of purposes. Due the various changeds in business environment the objectives and approach of assessment centre have changed drastically. Earlier the assessment centres were used for assessment purpose only. With changing requirement the existing assessment centre were found unsuitable to meet the emerging need of the organization. The needs for individual performance and organisational performance development were arisen. So the changes were made in approaches and objectives of assessment centre. Nowadays the assessment centres are being used for assessment as well as development purposes. Purely we cannot find any centre is working for assessment or development functions. Both the functions are being performed by assessment centres. Some are in more assessment work and less in development whereas some are more in assessment and less in development functions. The present assessment centres work between the two extremes of assessment and development. In nutshell it can be said the present assessment centre works as a development centre also. The objectives of assessment and development are fulfilled by the assessment centre are following: These are listed below:

(a) Selection

For recruitment and selection purpose the candidates apply to the assessment centre. At assessment centre a number of exercises are being conducted to assess the performance of the candidates during exercises. The potentials of the candidates are found out. On the basis os their performance and merit the candidates are selected for future role. The external as well as internal candidates are selected through this method. This method is used for selection of defense, administrative, police officers etc., in India. Candidates of different cadres are selected with the help of assessment centres. They are given the different exercises or tests to perform. On the basis of their performance they are selected or rejected. This is mainly for fresh and external candidates in leading organizations.

(b) Career Development

In performance appraisal the performance of the candidates are assessed. The strengths, weaknesses and difficulties faced by them are identified. To overcome the weaknesses and problems faced by them, the management takes care. The training and development programmes are designed for improvement. It helps a lot for improvement in performance of individuals and organization. Good performers are identified and assigned the new tasks. Some time they are given promotion also. This contributes in career development of employees. Further on the basis of identification of weaknesses and problems faced the employees take willing responsibility to improve their competencies and performance. They take it as an opportunity for further development in career.

(c) Identification of Potentials

On the basis of performance assessment the strengths, weaknesses, problems faced and behaviour of candidates are identified. These are part of potentials of employees. On the basis of present job performance it can considered suitable for future assignments. The potentials for higher jobs or future jobs are identified. On the basis of identification of potentials the new or higher assignments can be given to the candidates. Without proper identification the jobs can be assigned to the new candidates. Because it may be risky for management if the candidate is not performing at their new job. Allotment of higher or new assignment is possible through proper identification of potentials of the candidates.

(d) Motivation Plans

To get best contribution of employees to achievement of objectives the interest of the employees is to development and maintained further. If it is not done so the performance of all might fall below expectations. Through performance appraisal under this method the good and poor performers are identified. On the basis of assessment the rewards, recognition, incentives and compensation plans are prepared. This helps in motivation of employees. The motivation creates interest to do the work as desired and performance standards can be achieved. Different plans for motivation are designed on the basis of performance assessment. There may be positive as well as negative motivational plans for employees to get desired output.

(e) Succession Planning

Succession planning is very important in every organization. The existing manpower is to be replaced in future so for that purpose the planning is necessary. This assessment centre as a method of performance appraisal helps in identification of suitable candidates who will take the position if a particular post falls vacant. Identifying the right individual for critical positions such as CEO, CFO etc., is very important for the success of the organization. Assessment centre contributes a lot in reducing the risk of such wrong identification.

(f) Allocations of Challenging Assignments

The different types of jobs are performed in an organization. Some may be routine and some may be challenging one. If they are not performed properly it may affect the health of business of the company. Such jobs should be assigned to the committed and talented candidates. The necessity for identification of such candidates is felt. This requirement can be fulfilled by performance appraisal through assessment centre. In assessment centre the performance is assessed by multiple assessors from different angles. This helps the organization in deciding the candidates for allocation of challenging tasks. The candidates identified with necessary abilities to undertake the proposed challenging assignments are allocated the tasks.

(g) Management Development

In this method the observers assess the performance of other candidates. It provides ample opportunity to the observers and others to see the performance of candidates. It reflects on the performance of manager. They take it as opportunity and responsibility for improving their performance by observing when others perform.

(h) Identification of Training Needs

Through assessment method the performance of candidates are assessed. Their strengths, weaknesses, problems faced, behaviour, leadership quality and initiatives for problem solving are assessed. In performance review the weak areas of candidates are identified and management plans for improvement over these. The need for improvement is felt there. So the training and education programmes are prepared to overcome these problematic areas. This helps in development of competencies of employees, their performance and development of the organization as a whole.

(i) Identification of a Global Pool of Talented Managers

In present scenario the companies are entering in different markets worldwide. To handle the global assignments a talented and motivated persons are needed. There is critical requirement of some positions in the organization. In identification of such candidates the assessment centre helps organizations to identify such managers.

From the study of above functions performed by assessment centre it can be said the present assessment centre are less as a assessment centre but more as a development centre. The objectives, functions and approach of the assessment centre have undergone drastic changes as per the emerging need of the organization. Further in future it would be affected more and more. The future role of assessment centre in stiff competitive situation would be more significant. The future of assessment centre method would be bright definitely.

8. HISTORY OF ASSESSMENT CENTRE

In India the assessment centre were known or used in ancient time itself. Sawadekar (2002), indicated that the assessment centre methodology were use d by kings somewhere 1500 year ago. It is mentioned in Kautilya's Arthashastra. In Arthashastra, for assessment of candidates for ministerial post the different methods of assessing a candidate has been mentioned including observation, performance appraisal, assessment by those who know him, interviewing and other forms of testing etc. In present time the application of assessment centre can be traced way back to beginning of twentieth century. It was first used by Germany for selection of military officers. To find out the suitable candidates for filling up the vacancy in army this method of appraisal was used. Assessment Centre process was first used sometime between the two world wars. The Treaty of Versailles after world war restricted Germany from rearming and thus the traditional approach to the selection of officers was also denied. German psychologists then developed a new method which included a combination of tests, simulations and exercises to identify the potential of officer candidates. This method was further accepted by United Kingdom for selection of military officers during world wars. The British Army used this methodology in the early days of Second World War when they established the War Office Selection Boards (WOSBs) for the selection of officer candidates. Further it was used for appointment of British civil service officer also.

In the United Kingdom, assessment centres were developed in peacetime in which the civil service and other parts of the public sector were included. They followed the model of the WOSB and were sometimes labelled extended interviews. In the United States, the post-war development moved to the private sector. After world war second the industrial application of assessment centre was make in USA by pioneering company American Telephone and Telegraph Company (AT&T), which used assessment centres in its management progress study. After this it was first time used in private sector which began in 1956 onwards. It was accepted by other companies like (Bray, 1964), Standard Oil of Ohio took up the method in 1962, IBM, Sears, General Electric and J.C. Penney (Finkle, 1976).

For entrepreneurship development programme in Gujarat assessment centre was tried by Dr TV Rao in 1974. The details of this attempt are mentioned in article, Role Set Based Assessment Centre Approach to Personnel Selection, Journal of Management, 1975. Later on the efforts were made to introduce in Larsen & Toubro for identification of candidates for promotion purpose. But it was not used for assessment for potential despite of sincere efforts. For selection of candidate for post of General Manager from within this was used by Crompton Greaves also. It was only a one time effort and further they did not try for it. In 1986, Dr Anil Dixit with Behavioural Science Centre tried assessment centre in Ballarpur Industries but due to opposition from top level managers and change in HR head position.

Since 1990, mainly after globalization of world economies the concept of assessment centre has been getting high popularity in Indian organizations. In India this method has been used for selection of military, administrative and other officers in government services. Further, it is being used in leading organization in private sector too. Nearly a score of companies have tried to establish assessment centres and many are exploring the possibility to establish. The companies those who tries for assessment centre are Tisco, Aditya Birla Group, Siemens, Wipro, Mahindra and Mahindra, SAIL, Glaxo, Norton, Escorts, Eicher, Cadbury, ONGC, Castrol, Infosys, Philips, Global Trust Bank, Dr, Reddy Laboratories etc. They have been using the assessment centre for different reason such as recruitment and selection, promotion, placement performance appraisal, career development, identification of training needs, identification of higher potential managers, multifunctional managers, succession planning and other development purposes. Some of them have developed their full-fledged centres and some have taken help of outside agencies expert in assessment centre operation.

Day by day it is becoming more popular. In future the uses of assessment centre will increase further. In past the assessment centres were used mainly for selection purpose. But due to changing business scenario, advance research in field of assessment centre the roles of assessment centre have undergone drastic changes. In present time the assessment centre is being used for identification of talents for future requirements, motivation, promotion, adequate compensation plan and identification of training and development needs. The role of assessment centre in performance appraisal is very significant at present. It is performing the functions of assessment as well as development. The objectives and approach of assessment centre have changed with the changing business environment. It is in present time targeting at assessment and development of performance of individual as well as organization. The role of assessment centre in future is going to be more and more significant definitely.

During evaluation of progress of assessment centre across the world it is found that the progress was not very good. The assessment centre have been used for one or other purposes. Some of the companies have taken sincere interest and some not for establishment of assessment centre in their companies. In nutshell it can be said the progress done is not as per the expectation due to various reasons like difficulty in implementation, lack of clarity in description of competencies, shortage of qualified assessors, facility for assessors' training, adequacy of selection exercises, validity of exercises for selection, assessors' reliability, top management commitment, shortage of resources, improper or lack of feedback to assessees, proper documentation and data security. Due to these reasons one at a time or jointly made the progress of assessment centre below expectation of experts who tried to establish the assessment centre in different companies over a period of time.

9. DESIGNING, DEVELOPING AND MANAGING ASSESSMENT CENTRE

Assessment centre is one of the modern methods for performance appraisal. It overcomes the mistakes of traditional methods. But is a bit difficult and complicated to plan and implement. For this purpose trained persons are needed. Assessment centre designing, developing and managing process includes a set of activities. Designing and running an assessment centre is a complex project. It consists of a set of interlinked activities. For this purpose a lot of external factors are to be considered otherwise the design of the assessment centre may not be proper. The figure, below, shows the general process of designing a centre:

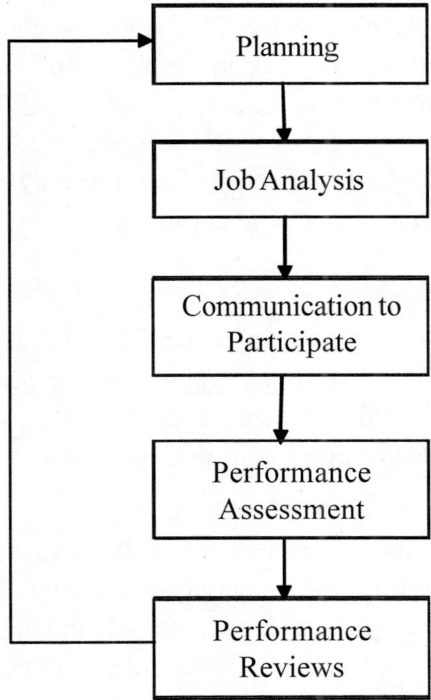

Figure 11.2: Designing, Developing & Managing Assessment Centre

10. PLANNING FOR ASSESSMENT CENTRE

Before going for planning of assessment centre the study of environment is to be carried out. It may include the business in which company is operating, level of competition, nature of the works are being performed, jobs are to be carried out for achieving the objectives and management thinking and support. After considering all these factors the planning work for assessment centre can be undertaken. For planning purpose the management should take the line managers into confidence regarding the present situation, difficulties faced and the objectives for which they want to establish assessment centre. The meetings are to be arranged when the participants agree to attend and contribute for planning purpose. The planning for assessment centre may include the following topics:

(a) Objectives

The objectives of assessment centre are to be finalized. The objectives may be long or short-term objectives. It may be used for a variety of purposes. These objectives may be for recruitment and selection, placement, transfer, promotion, early identification and evaluation of potential, performance appraisal, succession planning, professional development and identification of training needs. Final decision is to be taken. It may be used for one or more objectives also. The jobs in assessment centre are to be performed by keeping objectives in mind. The objectives and approach of assessment centre are undergoing changes with emerging need of the organization in stiff competitive situation. Before finalizing the objectives a careful study of business environment is to be carried out with the help of internal experts and consultants.

(b) Assessees

Assessees will participate in the assessment centre. Their performance is to be assessed by multiple assessors. Decision should be taken regarding who would participate. It is to be finalized regarding level, jobs, numbers, criteria and procedure for selection. The required number of participants can be made available for performance appraisal as decided.

(c) Assessors

The assessors are required at the assessment centre for assessment of performance of the participants. The requirement of multiple assessors is there for this job. Planning is to be done before assessment work starts regarding number, age, sex, job, qualification, training, experience, levels, areas of expertise, selection criteria and procedure of assessors. The requirements of assessment work should be fulfilled by the assessor at proper time.

(d) The Performance Appraisal Data

These are recorded, reported, restrictions on access to data, keeping and control of data, feedback procedure, time duration for storage of data are to be finalized. Particularly for a selection application, it is recommended that the data after the expiry of the specified time the data should not be used because these become outdated and become useless also.

(e) Qualifications of Consultant or Assessment Centre Developer

These people are responsible for the development of the center or of the exercises/simulations for the centre should be identified and their selection criteria like qualifications, commission, experience, area of expertise, training, past achievements etc., should be specified in advance before taking their service in designing and development of assessment centre.

(f) Techniques for Appraisal

At assessment centre different types of exercises are to be used. The different participants take part in assessment centre belonging to different levels, areas and jobs. For their assessment work the exercises should be specified in advance. As per requirement these are to be selected. Proper selection of assessment exercises meet requirements of assessment. There are a number of exercises available but out of them the suitable for assessment work are to be specified.

(g) Procedure for Assessment

During performance appraisal the candidates are given different tests or exercises. They perform these and their performances are assessed by the multiple assessors. The method of assessment work is to be specified. The sequence of activities step by step is to be mentioned clearly. Right from starting to completion point all steps are to be highlighted properly. This maintained the uniform performance and confusions are avoided. If not specified then everyone who are involved in assessment work will not have clarity about their jobs.

(h) Facilities at Assessment Centre

At assessment centre the participants perform given exercises. For conducting these exercises the certain facilities are required. These facilities include like a big hall, rooms, office, workstation arrangements, recording facilities, office automation, personal computers, simulation workstation, questionnaires, video-audio recording and playing facilities, timekeeping, stationeries, management games, case studies etc. These facilities are to be specified and made available before the assessment work starts. Without these the work may hamper to a good extent. Planning should be done in time with proper care.

(i) Assessment Ratings

The performances of assessees are assessed by the multiple assessors. The repeated observations are taken by them. Finally their reports are prepared. In data integration they prepare a feedback by considering the reports of various assessors. The performances are to be rated. In planning work the assessment ratings and the procedure for using these ratings are to be decided. This will make the things easier for the assessors. The objective of assessment may be served in a better way.

(j) Legal Requirements

The planning is to be done as per the existing laws of the home country and where the assessment centre conducts programmes. In different countries the different provisions are there relating to immigrants, racial groups, social, religious, age, sex etc. These are to be taken into account. The provisions of law should not be attracted. The planning and policies should be prepared in such a way that the planning comply with the legal requirements.

11. JOB ANALYSIS

Job analysis should be planned in advance in the planning stage itself. It gives the clear guidelines to the assessors what they are going to assess. Without this the dimensions to be observed may not be clear or may miss to observe. This makes the work of assessor systematic and easier. It is the study of job description and job specification. It should have two parts one for assessors and other for assessees. The selection of both parties is to be done as per job analysis. Right participants and right assessors are to be selected at assessment centre. The knowledge of these two elements will given the knowledge about the jobs to be performed and determine the requirement of knowledge, skills, attitude, aptitude, qualities, ability, capability, motivation level, initiatives etc., that are required for effective working on the job and give good performance. These are to be evaluated in the performance appraisal as demonstrated by employees during job performance. Without job analysis the assessors will not be in position to do the justice in appraisal work. The job analysis vary from job to job and it is bit difficult to study. It may be complex and different from the previous jobs studied. If the data pertaining to old and new jobs are available then the comparative study of these jobs becomes easier. If the future anticipated job is not available then analysis can be done on the basis of projected tasks and skills.

12. COMMUNICATION TO PARTICIPANTS

After planning and preparation of job analysis the next step is communication to the participants regarding objectives of assessment, methods of selection, choices for participation, exercises , schedule for assessment, procedure of assessment, staff general information, results, feedback, reassessment, contact persons etc. The information should be passed to the participants to make them to understand and perform properly. The following information to be communicated to the participants:

(a) Objective

The objective of the program and the purpose of the assessment center for which it has been established should be communicated. The objective of the participants available at assessment centre is to be informed them clearly.

(b) Selection of Participants

The method or procedure for selection of the participants should be explained to them in advance. It should be clear in their mind. The criteria for selection also may be highlighted to them if required.

(c) Choices of Participation

If there is any options the individual has regarding the choice of participating for fresh employment, advancement, development in the assessment centre as a condition should be communicated in advance to make the things very clear.

(d) Exercises

The briefing is to be given regarding the exercises the participants are going to perform. The detailed information regarding type of exercise, method of performing the exercise and sequence of activities to be performed are to be given to them. During performance of exercises the participants may not have doubts about the exercises.

(e) Staff General Information

The general information regarding the administrative staff, dealing persons and the assessors, their roles, training, experience, area of expertise etc., are to be passed on to the participants before the assessment starts.

(f) Timing of Assessment

The performance assessment is to be carried out during a definite period of time. It is to be communicated. The dates and timing for everyday are to be informed. So, the necessary arrangements can be made by them if required. They should be mentally prepared for the schedule and confusions might be avoided.

(g) Materials

The information are to be passed to them regarding the materials to be used during performance of exercises, assessment work, to be collected from assessment centre, return of materials to the centre and maintained by the centre.

(h) Procedure of Performance

The participants are to be informed regarding the exercises are to be performed, the activities are to be performed step by step, the use of technology if applicable etc., are to be highlighted. If not mentioned then these are going to create doubts for participants.

(i) Performance Results

The assessors take the repeated observations while the tasks are performed by the participants. The information regarding the procedure for preparing the results, uses of results, validity of results and documentation of results are to be informed to them. All issues relating to the result should be made clear to them in advance.

(j) Feedback on Performance

The feedback on performance is prepared by the assessors. The information regarding the feedback preparation, type of feedback, method of giving feedback and time of giving the feedback should be communicated to the participants

(k) Alignment of Result

It is to be mentioned in advance that how the assessment center results will be aligned with organizational objectives, strategy and culture. Further how it will be used in human resource management system in future. These aspects should be clarified.

(l) Procedure for Reassessment

If any candidate is not satisfied with performance feedback then they may apply for reassessment of the result. The procedure is to be explained how it can be done and when, where and which participants should apply for reassessment.

(m) Access to Records

It is to be informed that if anyone is interested to access the records or reports of assessment centre then who can access and what are the conditions under which a participant can apply.

13. PERFORMANCE ASSESSMENT

The fourth stage in assessment centre is performance assessment. The participants and assessors both make them available at the specified time for their task performance. They have received all relevant communication from the management and assessment centre. Now the actual tasks are to be executed. It includes the following tasks:

(a) Tasks Assigned

For performance assessment purpose, as per the jobs of the candidates the different tasks are assigned as per the schedule prepared. Timings are specified for every activity is to be performed on a particular day. Every aspect of the exercise is made clear to the participants and they are asked to perform.

(b) Exercise Performance

The participants take their assignments and start their jobs. They use all their competencies to perform the given jobs. As per the instructions passed to the candidates the jobs are performed and if situation demands the guidance are also taken from the assessors.

(c) Observations

Simultaneously the assessors are also briefed regarding their duty for assessment and the procedure for assessment. The assessors are more in number. They take the observations repeatedly on each activity. At least two observations are taken by each assessor. The assessment work continues for the specified period. The observations are recorded, notes prepared, audio-video recording and check lists are marked. It is very difficult to remember every point of observation so documentation is necessary for assessors. The involvement of assessors to a good extent is required to observe the performances properly.

(d) Schedules Followed

Before starting, both parties are briefed regarding the schedule to be followed. Both are available at the specified time and the work starts. Breaks also take place as per the schedule. The candidates remain present for the duration specified. It may vary from job to job. Generally it takes 3-5 days for assessment work at assessment centre.

(e) Report Preparation

On the basis of observations recorded by assessors, they prepare reports on the assessment of participants. This report is required at the time of integration of data meeting. It gives clear picture to the assessors at the time of discussion in final assessment meeting. It gives clear details of every exercise performance.

(f) Data Integration

The observations made by different assessors are discussed in meeting. Every aspect of the reports of every assessor are taken into account. Finally through mutual discussion or using statistical methods the final result is prepared. To reach to the final decision is bit difficult because consensus over the issues may not be there early. It can be said it is a time consuming meeting.

(g) Performance Feedback

As per communication made to the participants in the beginning of performance assessment, the feedback to the participants is to be given. The time, method of communication and conditions are to be followed for giving feedback to the candidates. The strengths, weaknesses, difficulties faced and areas need to be improved are to be communicated under feedback. It is an important activity in performance appraisal at assessment centre.

14. PERFORMANCE REVIEW

After preparation of final result and feedback the final stage of assessment centre process is performance review. In this activity, every aspect of assessment centre is to be reviewed to find out whether the establishment of assessment centre is useful or not. If it is useful then to which extent and if not then what can be the reasons so that the remedial actions can be initiated for improvement. In review the assessment centre aspects like objectives, participants, assessors, duties performed by them, assessment exercises used, facilities provided at assessment centre, procedures for assessment, utility of assessment centre and finally the effectiveness of assessment centre for all concerned. Wherever the discrepancies are found, then causes of these are to be found out. On the basis of causes of discrepancies the suggestions are to be made to the management. These suggestions are to be considered in planning for future.

15. ASSESSORS' TRAINING

Assessors are trained, qualified and experience persons. When they are appointed or selected for the job of assessor at assessment centre they may not have the experience of performance appraisal at assessment centre. Some time the new methods, techniques, technology and procedures are introduced in assessment centre and the assessors are not familiar to these. The need for training is strongly felt. Training gives knowledge and skills and in turn these give confidence to the candidates. Further confidence contributes in giving good performance and satisfaction of performance at job. These are the ultimate objectives of training and organization. So the assessors also should go for training. Assessor training is an integral part of the assessment center program. Assessor training should have clearly stated training objectives, contents of training, training methods, types of training, training programmes, training evaluation, performance guidelines, and quality standards. These can fulfil the requirement of assessors at assessment centre. These are explained below:

(a) Objectives of Assessors' Training

The objectives of assessor' training are to be clearly explained. It should give clear idea for designing and conducting the training for them. The objectives of their training may be to obtain reliable and accurate assessor judgements. It is difficult to have the trained assessor who can give reliable and accurate judgements. If the judgements are not proper then they may misguide the management over the performance appraisal issue. The training is to be conducted to achieve this objective.

(b) Contents of Training

Training for assessor is bit difficult to plan. But deciding the contents of training for assessors the following items are to be included:

(i) The Behavioural dimensions such as competencies, attitude, aptitude, motivation, leadership, team spirit, willingness to shoulder responsibilities, initiatives for problem solution etc.

(ii) Job analysis, types of participants, jobs, level and competencies needed for performance.

(iii) Performance techniques or exercises required for assessment of performance, nature, methods for carrying out exercises and their applications.

(iv) The performance observation, recording, preparation of notes, check list required, classification, report preparation, participation in meetings for final result preparation and feedback on performance.

(v) Rating scales and methods, their application and rating errors and avoidance of rating errors.

(vi) Behaviour at work place required for assessor, like, dislike, action, reaction, support, opposing, mutual discussion, cooperation and team spirit, leadership and initiative for problem solution.

(vi) Knowledge of professionalism, knowledge of the organization, jobs, objectives of assessments, knowledge of the target job, the ability to give accurate oral or written feedback and consistency in role playing.

(c) Training Methods

For imparting training, the training methods are to be selected. For selection of training methods the consultants, internal experts should be consulted. These people are having better knowledge for assessment centre jobs. For training of assessors' the training methods may include a variety of training methods. These include lectures, group discussion, conferences or seminars, observation of practicing candidates, observations of other assessors, video demonstrations etc. There may be other methods also. Those can be selected as the need arises.

(d) Types of Training

For training of assessors a variety of trainings are to be conducted. The purposes of assessors cannot be fulfilled by one type of training. These may include the following types of training:

(i) Competency familiarization: To perform any job, a set of competencies are needed. Without competencies the jobs cannot be performed. It is the duty of assessors to observe the performance and competencies and related behaviour of participants. The training pertaining to familiarization of competencies should be imparted. This makes the jobs of assessors' easier. The judgements regarding competency observations can be reliable and correct.

(ii) Interview training: At assessment centre interview is also used for performance assessment. The evidences of performance are collected through interview method. The assessor should know how to conduct interview and what types of questions should be asked to the performers. The training is to be given on how to prepare for interview, conducting interview, behaviour during interview and closing of interview. The questioning and listening skills of assessors' are developed through this type of training. SOAR technique is used for this purpose:

S - Situation is explained when, where, what and who are involved in it.

O - Objective – what objective the participant wants to achieve in the situation.

A - Action taken by the individual to achieve the objective should be understood.

R - Result given by the individual, level of effectiveness of action should be known to assessors.

(iii) Group observation and recording training: The assessors should be trained regarding observations of individuals in group. The different group-exercises are used at assessment centre so during these exercises the assessors should be in position to watch them carefully, understand the behaviour of participants, recording the observations and finally the report is to be prepared. This skill is to be developed in assessors. This is very important part of assessors' job.

(e) Training Programmes

Whatever has been planned to be implemented. The planning of training is to be executed. The training programmes are to be conducted as per planning. The arrangement of facilities is to be made at the location finalized. The selection of assessors should be made as per planning and they should be detailed for training. The trainers are to be selected from inside or outside of the company. The schedule is to be prepared and training is to start as per the schedule. Time period for training is decided by the management and training is conducted as per planning. Finally to know the effectiveness of assessors' training evaluation is to be carried out.

As per the points discussed in training of assessors the work is done then the training of assessors is definitely going to be effective. The very objective of training to get reliable and accurate judgements on performance assessment would be accomplished. The result is going to be fruitful and very effective and efficient. It might contribute in identification of potentials, development, career planning, recruitment and selection of employees.

16. TECHNIQUES USED IN ASSESSMENT CENTRES

An *assessment centre* has been established with the objectives to find out the potentials of the participants for new jobs in future or higher jobs. Therefore, it involves the use of different methods like events, tests and exercises, assignments being given to a group of participants to assess their competencies to take higher responsibilities in the future. Generally, they are given the tasks similar to the job they would be expected to perform if promoted or new jobs expected to performed in future. The methods/tools/techniques used in most of the centres are explained in the table below:

Table 11.1: Techniques Used in Assessment Centre

Techniques	Description	Required competencies
Case Study	Practical situation faced by an organization is given to the candidates to read and answer the questions relating the situation given.	Reading, understanding, and analytical skills, gathering and prioritization of information, time-management, working in simulated situation under pressure
Interview	Face to face interaction between participants and assessors to find out more from information from them relating to personal, attitude, behaviour etc.	General awareness, knowledge of jobs, analytical skills, etiquettes, communication, dressing sense, body gestures, interpersonal skills, listening perception, capacity, personal attributes, teamwork.
Fact-finding Exercise	Study to find out the facts relating to the problems faced through collecting information from respondents with interview or questionnaire.	Knowledge of research procedure, conducting interviews, Communication, knowledge of language presentation, professional and interaction skills.
Group discussion	It is a one type of interview where the participants are more in num-	Knowledge of topics, Personal assertiveness, communication skills, group beh-

	bers. Used to test the knowledge, and behaviour of participants.	aviour, teamwork, Interpersonal skills, leadership quality, motivation of others and drive for result
In-tray Test	Documents preparation, storage, maintenance of records, prioritizing documents, drafting letters, replies to letters, mailing and delegating	Knowledge of documents, recording keeping and storage skills, Time-management, analytical skills, business acumen and communication. important tasks
Problem Solving Task	Task is given to complete with limited resources and time.	Positive attitude, initiative for problem solution, analytical skills, creativity, lateral thinking, resourcefulness
Presentation	Presentation of ideas on a pre-decided topic for a limited time with or without technology help.	Knowledge of language, technology uses, presentation delivery, working under pressure and dressing sense.
Psychometric/ Personality/ Aptitude test	Includes a personality questionnaire and/or numerical, verbal, and diagrammatic reasoning tests.	Knowledge of language, mathematics, behavioral interaction, reasoning ability, general awareness, conscientiousness, personal traits and teamwork.
Role Play Exercise	A role is assigned with the objectives to find out the potentials of relating to the actual jobs.	Knowledge of jobs, working procedure of jobs, patience, willingness to accept new responsibility and motivation.
Written Exercise	Expression of ideas or give summary of the ideas on the given topic in written relating to the business jobs.	Language knowledge, writing ability, analytical skills, summarization, written communication and time management.
Simulation	Working situation similar to actual job is created and asked participants to perform the tasks at assessment centre with objective to assess the potentials of participants.	Thorough knowledge of jobs, tasks to be performed to complete jobs, likely problems faced during jobs, training, experience, acceptance of instructions, initiatives for problem solving and willingness to perform.

17. CONCLUSION

Assessment centre is a modern method of performance appraisal. It is an improvement over other traditional methods. In assessment centre a comprehensive and standard procedure is used. For evaluation purpose different techniques have been used. These include job simulation, business games, situational exercises, group discussion, presentation, reports, role plays, case analysis etc. These techniques are applied for candidates for their performance appraisal to find out the potential for selection, special training, and promotion and development activities. Assessment centre is a separate unit or section within the organization that has been established with the objectives for performance appraisal and mainly to identify the potential of employees for future requirements. Generally it is centrally located in the organization or at the corporate or divisional office.

The performance feedback is communicated to the candidates as per planning of assessment centre. The assessment centre can be used for potential appraisal as well and for development purpose also. The potential of employees are identified for future new or higher jobs. On the basis of appraisal the deficiencies in competencies are identified and the programmes for development are conducted. It serves the requirement of appraisal and development both.

Assessment centre has been defined by various experts, practitioners, consultants and academicians as follows:

(a) An assessment centre is a comprehensive standardized procedure in which multiple assessment techniques such as situational exercises and job simulation (business games, discussions, reports & presentations) are used to evaluate individual employee for variety of manpower decisions. - Udai Parikh & TV Rao

(b) Assessment centres are means of helping an organization to identify the strengths and potential development areas of its staff in relation to a particular job or role. - Beacon consultants, 'Assessment centers'

There are different methods of performance appraisal like traditional and modern methods. Out of modern methods assessment centre is one of them. The appraisal method can claim the status of assessment centre if it includes the multiple features. These features are: multiple competencies, multiple objectives, multiple observers, multiple participants for assessment, multiple techniques for assessment, multiple simulations, and multiple observations. The establishment of a centre for assessment of performance of employees is called as assessment centre. The functions of assessment centre may not be performed as required if the essential requirements are not fulfilled. For its effective working the certain essential elements must be there so that it can be considered as assessment centre. These elements are: job analysis, predefine competencies, behavioral classification, assessment techniques, simulations, repeated observations, multiple observers, trained assessors, systematic recording system, reports preparation, and, data pooling

Purely we cannot find any centre is working for assessment or development functions. The both functions are being performed by assessment centres. Some are in more assessment work and less in development whereas some are more in assessment and less in development functions. The present assessment centres work between the two extremes of assessment and development. In nutshell it can be said the present assessment centre works as a development centre also. The certain objectives of assessment and development are fulfilled by the assessment centre. These are: selection, career development, identification of potentials, motivation plans, succession planning, allocation of challenging assignments, management development, identification of training needs, and identification of a global pool of talented managers. From the study of above functioned performed by assessment centre it can be said the present assessment centre are less as a assessment centre but more as a development centre. The objectives, functions and approach of the assessment centre have undergone drastic changes as per the emerging need of the organization. Further in future it would be affected more and more. The future role of assessment centre in stiff competitive situation would be more significant. The future of assessment centre method would be bright definitely.

Assessment centre is one of the modern methods for performance appraisal. It overcomes the mistakes of traditional methods. But is a bit difficult and complicated to plan and implement. For this purpose trained persons are needed. Assessment centre designing, developing and managing process includes a set of activities. Designing and running an assessment centre is a complex project. It consists of a set of interlinked activities. For this purpose a lot of external factors are to be considered otherwise the design of the assessment centre may not be proper. The first step in this process is planning for assessment centre. Before going for planning of assessment centre the study of environment is to be carried out. After considering all the factors the planning work for assessment centre can be undertaken.

For planning purpose the management should take the line managers into confidence regarding the present situation, difficulties faced and the objectives for which they want to establish assessment centre. The meetings are to be arranged when the participants agree to attend and contribute for planning purpose. The planning for assessment centre would be done for objectives of organization, assessees for assessment, assessors who would assess the performance, data recording pertaining to assessment, qualification of consultants or assessment centre developer, methods of appraisal, procedure for assessment, facilities required for assessment, assessment rating and legal requirements for assessment centre establishment.

Second stage involved in the process is job analysis. Job analysis should be planned in advance in the planning stage itself. It gives the clear guidelines to the assessors what they are going to assess. Without this the dimensions to be observed may not be clear or may miss to observe. This makes the work of assessor systematic and easier. Right participants and right assessors are to be selected at assessment centre. Without job analysis the assessors will not be in position to do the justice in appraisal work. The job analysis vary job to job and it is bit difficult to study. After planning and preparation of job analysis the next step is communication to the participants regarding objectives of assessment, methods of selection, choices for participation, exercises, schedule for assessment, procedure of assessment, staff general information, results, feedback, reassessment, contact persons etc. The information should be passed to the participants to make things to understand and perform properly.

The fourth stage in assessment centre is performance assessment. The participants and assessors both make them available at the specified time for their task performance. They have received all relevant communication from the management and assessment centre. Now the actual tasks are to be executed. It includes the tasks job assigned, exercise performance, observations, schedule for assessment, report preparation, data integration and performance feedback. An assessment centre has been established with the objectives to find out the potentials of the participants for new jobs in future or higher jobs. Therefore, it involves the use of different methods like events, tests and exercises, assignments being given to a group of participants to assess their competencies to take higher responsibilities in the future.

After preparation of final result and feedback the final stage of assessment centre process is performance review. In this activity, every aspect of assessment centre is to be reviewed to find out whether the establishment of assessment centre is useful or not. If it is useful then to which extent and if not then what can be the reasons so that the remedial actions can be initiated for improvement. In review the assessment centre aspects like objectives, participants, assessors, duties performed by them, assessment exercises used, facilities provided at assessment centre, procedures for assessment, utility of assessment centre and finally the effectiveness of assessment centre for all concerned. Wherever the discrepancies are found then causes of these are to be found out. On the basis of causes of discrepancies the suggestions are to be made to the management. These suggestions are to be considered in planning for future.

18. QUESTIONS FOR REVIEW

1. What do you know about assessment centre? Discuss the objectives for establishment of assessment centre.
2. Discuss the evolution of assessment centre abroad and in India.
3. Define assessment centre and explain salient features of it in detail.
4. Critically evaluate the role of assessment centre as an appraisal method.
5. What cannot claim the status of assessment centre? Describe.
6. What are the essential elements of an assessment centre for its effective working? Explain.
7. Critically evaluate the importance and role of assessment centre as a development centre.
8. What are the objectives fulfilled by assessment centre through performance appraisal? Highlight them.
9. Write short notes on the following:
   (a) Job analysis.
   (b) Assessment techniques used in a centre.
   (c) Multiple observations and observers.
   (d) Data pooling.
   (e) Identification of potential.
   (f) Succession planning.
10. For designing an assessment centre what are the topics to be considered in planning.Explain

11. Do you feel the communication to participants regarding objectives, methods of selection, exercises, schedule for assessment, procedure for assessment etc. necessary? Comments
12. Do you feel training for assessors are necessary for assessment in an assessment centre? Explain.
13. What should be the contents of training programme for assessor's training? Discuss.
14. For planning of assessor training which topics should focused to make it more effective. Elaborate.
15. Discuss the techniques being used at assessment centre for appraisal of participants in detail.
16. How do you evaluate the role of assessment centre for appraisal in future? Comment.
17. Write short notes on the following;
    (a) Simulation
    (b) Psychometric or aptitude test
    (c) Group discussion
    (d) Types of training for assessor
    (e) Training methods
    (f) Performance review
    (g) Procedure of performance
    (h) Legal requirements for formation of an assessment centre.

19. OBJECTIVE QUESTIONS

1. Assessment centre is a traditional method of performance appraisal. In assessment centre a comprehensive and standard procedure is used evaluation of employees. Do you agree?
    (a) Fully agreed
    (b) Partially agreed
    (c) Not agreed
    (d) Not applicable
    (e) Cannot say anything
2. 360 degree performance appraisal is done by assessors.
    (a) Successors
    (b) Predecessor
    (c) Assessors
    (d) All concerned parties with the employees
    (e) None of the above

3. Assessment centres are means of helping an organization to identify the strengths and potential development areas of its staff in relation to a particular job or role. – is stated by:
   (a) Iain Ballantyne and Nigel Povah
   (b) Richard J. Jefferies
   (c) Ernest E. Cooke
   (d) Beacon consultants
   (e) None of the above

4. This __________ may include educational qualification, skills, knowledge, attitude, aptitude, ability, capability, leadership quality, initiatives for problem solving and team spirit.
   (a) Multiple competencies
   (b) Multiple simulations
   (c) Multiple objectives
   (d) Multiple observations
   (e) All the above

5. It is an exercise designed to create the artificial work like conditions similar to the actual jobs. What is it?
   (a) Job analysis
   (b) Simulation
   (c) Assessment techniques
   (d) Predefined competencies
   (e) None of the above

6. For recruitment and selection purpose the candidates apply to the:
   (a) Organization
   (b) HR Department
   (c) Respective departments
   (d) Assessment centers
   (e) All the above

7. The existing manpower is to be replaced in future so for that purpose the planning is necessary. Which process is being talked about here?
   (a) Recruitment
   (b) Succession planning
   (c) Induction
   (d) Replacement planning

8. In a country the assessment centres were developed in peacetime in which the civil service and other parts of the public sector were included. Name the country:
   (a) United Kingdom
   (b) USA
   (c) Japan
   (d) France
   (e) Italy

9. Arrange the process of designing, developing and managing assessment center:
   1. Performance assessment
   2. Planning
   3. Performance review
   4. Job analysis
   5. Communication to participate

(a) 1, 2, 3, 4, 5 (b) 2, 3, 4, 1, 5
(c) 2, 4, 5, 1, 3 (d) 2, 1, 3, 5, 4

10. Training for assessor is bit difficult to plan. But deciding the contents of training for assessors certain items to be included. Identify the items:

(a) Behavioural dimensions (b) Performance techniques
(c) Rating scales and methods (d) All the above
(e) None of the above

Answer Keys:

Question No.	Answer	Question No.	Answer
1	b	6	d
2	d	7	b
3	d	8	a
4	a	9	c
5	b	10	d

Chapter

12

360 Degree Performance Appraisal Method

1. INTRODUCTION

Today is the time of globalization in every world markets. The worldwide national economies have been liberalized. There are free movements of manpower, machines, materials and money from one country to another with no restriction or limited restrictions. Most of the markets are covered by domestic and multinational corporations. There is high degree of competition in the markets from local, national and outsiders in every market. The global business environment is very sensitive. It is changing every moment. It is rapidly changing and it can be said it is turbulent at present. It is very difficult to say what environmental factor is going to change in near future. Social, cultural, legal, economic, political, technology and competition factors are undergoing changes. The situation becomes very uncertain and risky. It is very difficult to take proper decision.

To improve effectiveness in the business everyone is trying but not in position to achieve the success. Some of them are in position to do the things better due to their talented and motivated manpower. The management has realized worldwide that the manpower is a very valuable resource. It should be well selected, trained, developed and motivated so that the desired results can be achieved. For this objective different functions have been performed by human resource management. On of these functions is performance appraisal. The need for proper performance appraisal has been felt. The efforts are put to find out the good and poor performers so that they can be corrected, trained, developed and motivated to give the proper performance standards. Without out finding out it is not possible to target the corrective and motivational plan for development and motivation of employees. The requirement of proper performance appraisal has arisen.

There are many performance appraisal methods. Some of them are not in position to serve the objectives of performance appraisal. Therefore, on the basis of characteristics of 360 degree appraisal method, it is found that this method is in position to give proper appraisal without much error. Appraisal in this method is done by different persons who are in touch with the person relating to his jobs. From different angles, parties and different times the feedback are taken. The information summarized and then average of that is taken as appraisal of person. Due to the average many appraisal errors can be overcome. It might be fair, correct and without any appraiser bias. It is generally accepted that the opinions of two or more persons or parties are always better than one. This is in position to meet the requirement of appraisal and management for fulfilling the pre-decided objectives. Further it depends upon implementation of the appraisal method. This may contribute for development and motivation of employees. Further, the expected standards of performance may be fulfilled. The objectives of the organization may be served in a better way.

The experts have given the opinion regarding new method of performance appraisal. But there is no guarantee that it will work in all organizational culture. It may be suitable or may not be. For implementation purpose special care is to be taken otherwise it may not give the required result. For calculating the score of performance of employees a higher degree of skills is required and it is time consuming also. For this purpose the appraiser should be trained. Without proper training the appraisal again may be improper. The whole purpose of this method might be defeated. Before going for this method comprehensive discussion is need whether to go for this or not. It may be opposed by employees and their trade unions too.

2. MEANING OF 360 DEGREE APPRAISAL METHOD

The maximum measurement of an angle is 360 degree. It is the measurement of all directions. This measurement is applied to performance appraisal means the performance of employees is appraised by all concerned persons relating to his jobs. 360-degree is a measurement of a full circle angle and feedback is obtained from all who are in contact with employees. It includes seniors, juniors, peers, customers, suppliers, self and others. Everyone whoever is connected to his job all parties are important for business purpose. They directly or indirectly give business to the company. It is the duty of the persons to perform the job as per the expectation of the management. Therefore, their performances are also assessed by concerned parties. That is why this method is called 360 degree appraisal method. The appraisal is from all directions, by all concerned parties on everyday basis round the year. None of the job element is left uncovered. It gives very wide coverage in the performance appraisal of the employees.

360 degree feedback is given by the persons who come in contact with employees on job. This is known as 'multi-rater feedback because it is given by number of persons. It is the most comprehensive appraisal where the feedback about the employees' performance comes from all the different sources directly or indirectly in touch with the person performing the job. The respondents for an employee can be from 360 degree directions and can include peers, managers, subordinates, team members, customers, suppliers/vendors - anyone who comes in touch with him relating to the work of employee. The performance feedback is given about employee on the job. The 360^0 Appraisal method helps the HR Department to have better understanding of the competitive advantages and disadvantages of the current human resources and channelize their efforts towards performance excellence and higher productivity.

3. MAIN APPRAISERS IN PERFORMANCE APPRAISAL

In 360 degree performance appraisal the performance feedback is given by everyone whoever is having concerned business with the employees' job. These may include customers, clients, seniors, juniors, peers, vendors or suppliers, bankers and creditors. These parties are very important and management is interested to maintain good relations with them. Simultaneously on the basis of good relations they want to evaluate the performance of the employees to whom he is dealing. This 360 degree appraisal method is like a sword with two edges. The importance of these parties is explained below:

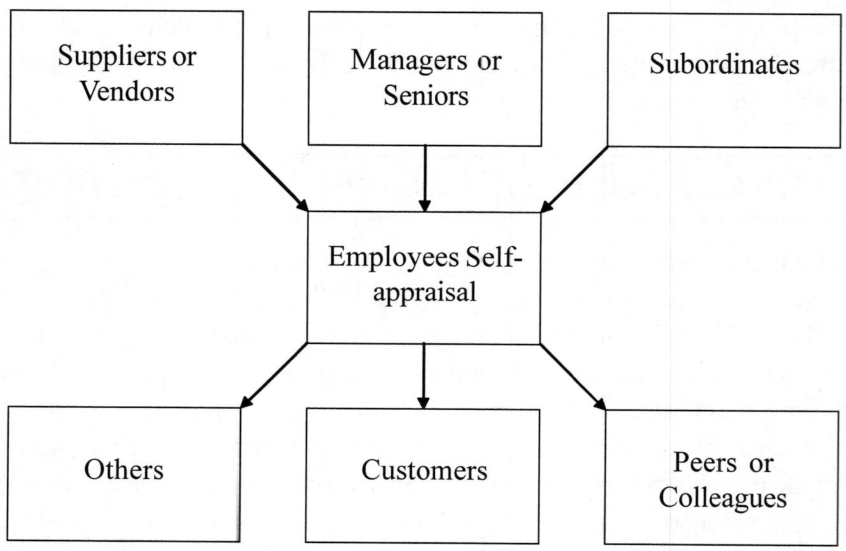

Diagram 12.1: 360 Degree Performance Appraisal

(a) Employees

The concepts of human resource, personnel, employees, labour force and manpower are interchangeable. We frequently use these terms one in place of the others. The term employee is most widely used and it has been defined by different authors and laws. A *person* who is hired to provide *services* to a *company* on a regular basis in *exchange* for compensation and who does not provide these services as part of an independent *business.* The employees are a live and most important resource in an organization. In performance management these people discuss and agree on objectives, performance standards, competencies required etc. In performance appraisal also under 360 degree appraisal method their role is very important. They perform the tasks, fulfil responsibility, achieve performance standard with available competencies and have experienced the difficulties while doing the jobs. They know their strengths and weaknesses better than others and they can suggest the areas where they need help, coaching and training. Keeping these points in mind, management takes feedback from employees also under this appraisal method. This serve the purpose as expected. That is the reason the feedback from employee is also taken into account in appraisal of performance.

(b) Customers

Customer is an important party for the company. It is the party that receives or buys or consumes the goods or services in exchange of money and having the ability to choose between different products from different suppliers or manufacturers. Further the customers can be explained that the party that is having business dealing with the organization directly. The customers give business to the company. Every company is looking forward for the customers. The customers give opportunity to serve them by goods or services. Customers make the business or break the business. Companies are trying their level best to create awareness among customers, reminding them of their products through advertisement, persuade them to buy their goods or services and further put their best efforts to retain them. They only give the business to the company.

Customers understand the value of their money and buy the products where their money is worth paid. None of the companies can take chance to miss the customers. It is difficult to get a customer and further it is more difficult to retain the customers. From management point of view the customer is a very important party and it cannot afford to miss them. Management wants to know how the customers are dealt by the customers. So the feedback is taken from them also. They can find out the persons who are not serving the customers properly. The remedial or motivational actions can be initiated for concerned employees. That is the reason the performance feedback regarding employee is taken from the customers.

(c) Vendors or Suppliers

A vendor word is from French language (*vendre*), meaning to sell. Vendor as a party may be a person or company that sells goods or services to other party in the economic production chain. He is called a vendor or supplier. He supplies different types of items to a person, retailer, wholesaler, manufacturer or any other concerned party. The items may be stationery, raw- materials, components, spareparts, semi-finished goods, machines, fuels etc. Retailers and wholesalers are vendors of products to consumers. Anyone who supplies goods and services to any other person is called supplier or vendor. Suppliers form a very important link in the business. They provide the supply of required items in required quantity, quality and time. That helps to maintain the continuity of the business. If it is not maintained the supply chain will be disturbed and business or company will suffer losses.

Suppliers are very essential for the success of an organisation. Raw-materials and components are needed to complete the finished product of the organisation. Suppliers do have power. They become more powerful if they are the only supplier or one of the limited number of suppliers, no substitute of their products supplied or high cost involved in changing over suppliers. For selection of a supplier the criteria like price, location, stability, reliability and competencies of supplier are considered. Good relations with suppliers matter lot for the business. If good relations are not maintained then it may affect the business adversely. Suppliers receive the orders and supply the items as per the need. The supply should not be disturbed. The person dealing with suppliers should take care of these things. Management cannot afford to lose a good supplier. It is to be maintained because it is a very important party for business. The dealing of persons who are in contact with them is very important. That is why the management is interested to know the performance of concerned employee. The feedback is taken from suppliers or vendors if applicable to the job or employees.

(d) Seniors or Managers

Different people are working at different levels in every organization. The levels of management are top, middle and lower level. Generally the performance appraisal is done by head of the departments. These are the people in hierarchy working at middle level. The managers are responsible for planning and directing the work of employees working under them, monitoring their work, and taking corrective action when necessary. They plan for the work, give directions, instructions, guide, coach and help in problem solution on the job itself. By utilizing the available resources they get the work done from their subordinates. The performance of employees is also appraised by them. They know every information pertaining the employees involvement, performance standards, behaviour at work, competencies, difficulties faced, initiatives taken for problem solution and leadership quality. All these affect the performance of employees. To get the exact information about employees' performance, feedback is taken from seniors or managers. This helps a lot for the management for planning of corrective, compensation and development functions. Therefore, the feedback is sought from managers also.

(e) Subordinates

Subordinates are a group of people who are at the lower level in chain of authority. Employees at lower level are subject to the authority of the one on the next level above. In most of the organizational structure hierarchy there are a larger number of people at the lower level than at the top. These employees work under direct supervision of managers or other experienced persons. They receive orders, instructions guidance, coaching and counseling from them and perform the tasks assigned to them. They are looking for help to their seniors whenever they face any difficulty. They are responsible for doing the work as per the instructions given by their seniors. They form very important part in accomplishment of the objectives. Management is interested to know the opinion of these persons also when they are instructed, guided and motivated by the supervisor or not. The performance feedback from this group forms a very important link for performance appraisal of seniors. Due to this they are also included in appraisal of performance.

(f) Peers or Colleagues

In a large organization many people are working at different levels and jobs. Some seniors and some are juniors. The people those who are working of same rank, position, ability etc., are called peer. The employees who have equal standing with another in rank, position, jobs qualification, ability etc are called peers. In brief the persons working at the same level and position are called peers. For example one manager production is working with another manager–quality control, both are of manager rank and both are in-charges of their work. People at horizontal level working are called peers. In performance appraisal the feedback from colleagues are also required. When one person works then he comes in contact with other persons of same level in their day to day work, the performance feedback is required. The information regarding the behaviour, dealing, success, failure, attitude, approach towards work, competencies etc., of employees are needed for appraisal purpose. This will provide proper insight from colleagues' point of view. That is why management likes to take feedback from peers also.

(g) Others

There are other parties also other than mentioned earlier who are in contact with the company for their business purpose. They may include bankers, creditors, consultants, research experts, recruitment agencies, sales tax agencies etc., Their feedbacks are also taken regarding the employees with whom they are in contact in their routine business. The employees contact them, take their service, react, suggest, follow-up the things with these parties. To know the performance of employees they are asked to give feedback. The information may be received regarding the good or bad experience, satisfaction or dissatisfaction, achievements or failure for input to the final performance appraisal by managers. This will provide very vital information on performance to the management.

4. ESSENTIAL CONDITIONS FOR EFFECTIVE 360 DEGREE APPRAISAL

No doubt 360 degree performance appraisal is a modern method of performance appraisal. The traditional methods exist with some limitations. These limitations can be overcome very easily. Mainly the subjectivity of managers in performance appraisal can be overcome by getting performance feedback from others. Further it may find out the point which was not noticed by the managers. The feedbacks are taken from different angles and persons so the coverage is very wide. To make it more effective the following conditions are necessary:

(a) Top management support is essential to get involved everyone in appraisal. Without support of top management it cannot be done properly.

(b) Confidence of employees must be developed regarding the present appraisal process. If it is implemented properly then confidence would develop. This will get everyone involved willingly.

(c) Objectives should be brought in the appraisal. The subjectivity should be avoided. This way the errors and biases can be avoided.

(d) A comprehensive plan for preparation and implantation should be prepared. Further it should be communicated to everyone timely. Collaboration between superior and subordinates takes place.

(e) Clear cut appraisal policy should be designed in advance with positive thinking. Training or guidance of the persons who are giving the performance feedback should be there, if possible.

(f) Proper time should be given to the parties giving information regarding performance feedback to the management.

5. ADVANTAGES OF 360 DEGREE FEEDBACK

There are many advantages of this method. Some of them are mentioned below:

(a) It provides feedback to the management on the basis of performance recognized by other parties. It provides the base for self-evaluation also.

(b) It overcomes error and bias of manager by collecting feedback from others. The average of the available information will be taken. The performance appraisal errors are overcome by this method. The appraisal is fair and correct.

(c) On the basis of information regarding success, failure and difficulties faced, the need for training and career development is identified. Then work can be done on this so that timely requirements of skills and knowledge can be fulfilled.

(d) Provides basis for corrective actions like promotion, demotion, transfer, wage cuts or rise etc., rewards, recognitions and compensation plans are decided on the basis of feedback received.

(e) Get everyone involved whoever is attached with the organization and team spirit and cooperation develop. It creates healthy work environment of mutual understanding, trust, openness and help of each other whenever required.

(f) Contributes in bringing the changes in attitude of employees, job commitments and customer satisfaction.

(g) Helps the organization to focus on developmental efforts of individual and organization as a whole. In present business environment where the success of the organisation depends on continuous development, that is possible through organizational development. It facilitates in aligning individual capabilities and behaviors with organizational strategies.

(h) Adds value to the organization by providing understanding of performance, development needs, competencies and roles, improves, morale of good performers, decrease training cost by identifying development needs, increase team ability, ensures better interpersonal relationship, provide road map for development planning, better communication and achievement of objectives.

From the study of this topic it can be said the advantages of 360 degree performance appraisal are multidimensional. Only care should be taken that it should be implemented in good organizational culture by taking everyone into confidence. Otherwise it is going to misfire.

6. SELF-APPRAISAL METHOD

In 360 performance appraisal, one of the parties who do the appraisal is employee himself. The performance feedbacks are taken from all directions from all concerned persons on regular basis. When the feedback is given by employee is called self-appraisal. Self-appraisal is a method of performance appraisal in which the employee evaluates his own performance and then discusses feedback with his managers or supervisors. This method is the very beginning of performance appraisal process. Employees are considered by management as important link for performance appraisal. It provides opportunity say something about own performance with logical reasons. It encourages employees to take responsibility for their own performance by appraising their own strengths, weaknesses, difficulties, achievements or failures and promoting self-management of development goals.

It is a good preparation for performance appraisal and the things become easier for managers in performance appraisal. But this should not be taken as substitute of appraisal done by manager or supervisor. This creates a sense of self-participation, motivation and voluntarily disclosing the deficiencies to managers so that timely action can be taken for improvement. Generally it is done by employees with the help of self-appraisal format where he rates himself by identifying the difficulties faced, achievements, failure, strengths, weaknesses and problems faced during performance of jobs. It is very difficult for the immediate assessing manager to remember all details of achievements and failures of his subordinates. It may be very helpful for manager and employee to give the proper evaluation of employees. The appraisal is done by the employees after getting guidelines from managers. The employees fill up the appraisal form and the feedback is discussed with managers. After discussion only the appraisal will be considered. In most of the organisation the self-appraisal is a part of performance appraisal. It helps in guiding the manager to understand the performance of his subordinates, timely and properly. It is a new approach towards the appraisal of employees away from traditional approach.

(a) Does Self-appraisal Make a Difference?

It is considered as important part of performance appraisal. It is open secret that people never see themselves and others have perception about them. It is doubtful whether the self-appraisal is going to make the difference in performance appraisal. If the self-appraisal is in line with the perception of others it might be considered. If not then it may be inflated or irrational and managers may not consider it logical and proper. Some of the employees raise questions on validity of self-appraisal system. A self-appraisal does not lead to a fruitful result unless it is accepted by the manager. It is important to know the impression or perception of manager and the final results. Self-appraisal generally provides one side of data to the managers.

The experts from the field opined that it does not influence the managers but provides a lot of information. In most of the cases the self-performance appraisal is highly inflated and irrelevant. The self-appraisal is a very good method of appraisal but the following problems are faced in it;

(i) The objective of appraisal is not clear to employees.

(ii) Employees are trained and qualified for self-performance appraisal. They face a lot of difficulties in filling the appraisal form.

(iii) Performance feedback not done properly. The appraisal is inflated.

(iv) Performance appraisal is considered as unwanted and creating overburden for many managers.

(v) Appraisal is considered for rewards, incentives and corrective action but not for development purpose.

(vi) HR managers work on the basis of rules and regulation and work more as an administrator than a facilitator

(vii) Appraisal if more on perception base and not on basis of documentation.

These are the main problems faced but there might be some more problems faced in performance appraisal of lesser importance.

(b) Guidelines for Effective Self-appraisal

The appraisal is done by the individual and there are chances of favour or bias. But to give proper self-appraisal the following guidelines should be followed:

(i) The appraisal should be done honestly and fairly. The employees must take his appraisal as appraisal is being done of other person/colleague.

(ii) Employees must do homework before he is doing his performance appraisal. He must collect his data relating of achievements, failures and difficulties faced during the year.

(iii) Bring objectivity in appraisal system. The subjectivity should not be there. If person being neutral does the appraisal the efforts will be proper and unbiased.

(iv) Employee shoulder work on self-appraisal with positive attitude. With positive attitude only the responsibility can be taken for appraisal.

(v) Proper coverage in appraisal should be there. All aspects like responsibility, Performance standards, strengths, weaknesses, difficulties faced, failure and achievements should be covered properly.

(vi) Willingness to shoulder more responsibility should be there among employees going for self-appraisal. They should do the work willingly and discuss with managers for further improvement.

(viii) Proper guidance and motivation from managers should be there before filling up the appraisal form. If these things are there the self-appraisal will be proper.

7. CONCLUSION

There are many performance appraisal methods. Some of them are not in position to serve the objectives of performance appraisal. Therefore, on the basis of characteristics of 360 degree appraisal method, it is found that this method is in position to give proper appraisal without much error. Appraisal in this method is done by different persons who are in touch with the person relating to his jobs. From different angles, parties and different times the feedbacks are taken. The information summarized and then average of that is taken as appraisal of person. Due to its average may appraisal errors can be overcome. It might be fair, correct and without any appraiser bias. It is generally accepted that the opinions of two or more persons or parties are always better than one. This is in position to meet the requirement of appraisal and management for fulfilling the pre-decided objectives.

The maximum measurement of an angle is 360 degree. It is the measurement of all directions. This measurement is applied to performance appraisal means the performance of employees is appraised by all concerned persons relating to his jobs. 360-degree is a measurement of a full circle angle and feedback is obtained from all who are in contact with employees. It includes seniors, juniors, peers, customers, suppliers, self and others. Everyone whoever is connected to his job, all parties are important for business purpose. They directly or indirectly give business to the company. That is why their feedback is taken and it is called 360 degree appraisal method. 360 degree feedback is given by the persons who come in contact with employees on job. This is known as 'multi-rater feedback because it is given by number of persons. It is the most comprehensive appraisal where the feedback about the employees' performance comes from all the different sources directly or indirectly in touch with the person performing the job

No doubt 360 degree performance appraisal is a modern method of performance appraisal. The traditional methods exist with some limitations. These limitations can be overcome very easily. To make it more effective the following conditions are necessary: top management support, confidence of employees, objectives should be brought in the appraisal, a comprehensive plan, clear cut appraisal policy, proper time should be given to the parties giving information. If these conditions are fulfilled then the appraisal through this method would be very effective. There are many advantages of this method. Some of the advantages contributes in performance appraisal, it overcomes error and bias of assessing employee development, provides basis for corrective actions, organizational climate study, contributes in bringing the changes in attitude, helps the organization to focus on developmental efforts, adds value to the organization.

From the study of this topic it can be said the advantages of 360 degree performance appraisal are multidimensional. Only care should be taken that it should be implemented in good organizational culture by taking everyone into confidence. Otherwise it is going to misfire.

8. QUESTIONS FOR REVIEW

1. 360 degree performance appraisal is a new method of appraisal; its looks more attractive. Do you agree with this?
2. Define 360 degree appraisal method and why it is called 360 degree only. Explain
3. What are the parties involved in 360 degree performance appraisal method? Explain the roles.
4. Why the feedback is taken from all the persons who are in contact with the employee performing the tasks relating to business of the company? Explain
5. Explain the essential conditions for effective working of 360 degree appraisal method in detail.
6. Highlight the advantages and disadvantages of 360 degree appraisal method being used in organisations.
7. Define self-appraisal method. Does self-appraisal method make a difference in appraisal?
8. Write short notes on the following:
   (a) Guidelines for effective self-appraisal.
   (b) Role of peers.
   (c) Self-feedback from employees.
   (d) Need for 360 degree appraisal method.
   (e) Suppliers' feedback.
   (f) Role of customers.

9. OBJECTIVE QUESTIONS

1. Appraisal in this method is done by different persons who are in touch with the person relating to his jobs. Which method is being talked about here?
   (a) Rating scale
   (b) Field review method
   (c) 360 degree performance appraisal
   (d) Critical incident method
   (e) All the above
2. 360 degree performance appraisal method is also known as:
   (a) Multi-rater feedback
   (b) Multi-rater scale
   (c) Both a and b
   (d) Cannot say anything
   (e) None of the above

3. In 360 degree performance appraisal the performance feedback is given by everyone whoever is having concerned business with the employees' job. These may include customers, clients, seniors, juniors, peers, vendors or suppliers, bankers and creditors. Do you agree?

   (a) Fully agreed
   (b) Partially agreed
   (c) Partially disagree
   (d) Not agreed
   (e) Not applicable

4. It is difficult to get a customer but it is not difficult to retain the customers.

   (a) Fully agreed
   (b) Partially agreed
   (c) Not agreed
   (d) Not applicable
   (e) Cannot say anything

5. What all parties are consulted for 360 degree performance appraisal of an employee?

   (a) Supervisors and subordinates
   (b) Senior managers
   (c) Venders and customers
   (d) All of the above
   (e) None of the above

6. State True/False of the following statements:

   1. Top management support is not essential to get involved everyone in appraisal. Without support of top management it can be done properly.
   2. Proper time should be given to the parties giving information regarding performance feedback to the management.
   3. Objectives should be brought in the appraisal. The subjectivity should be avoided. This way the errors and biases can be avoided.
   4. Confidence of employees must be developed regarding the present appraisal process.

   (a) T/T/T/T
   (b) F/F/F/F
   (c) F/T/T/F
   (d) F/T/T/T
   (e) T/T/T/T

7. Performance appraisal helps the organization to focus on developmental efforts of individual and organization as a whole. It facilitates in aligning individual capabilities and behaviors with organizational strategies. Do you agree?

   (a) Don't agree
   (b) Partially agree
   (c) Fully agree
   (d) Not applicable
   (e) Cannot say anything

8. State True/False of the following statements:

   1. Appraisal if more on perception base and not on basis of documentation.
   2. Performance appraisal is considered as wanted and does not create overburden.

3. HR managers do not work on the basis of rules and regulation and work more as an administrator than a facilitator.
4. Bring objectivity in appraisal system. The subjectivity should not be there.

(a) T/F/T/F *(b)* T/F/F/T
(c) F/T/T/F *(d)* T/F/F/F
(e) F/F/F/F

9. The main advantage of 360 degree appraisal methods are;
   (a) It provides feedback to the management on the basis of performance recognized by other parties. It provides the base for self evaluation also.
   (b) On the basis of information regarding success, failure and difficulties faced the need for training and career development is identified.
   (c) Provides basis for corrective actions like promotion, demotion, transfer, wages cuts or rise etc., rewards, recognitions and compensation plans are decided on the basis of feedback received.
   (d) Contributes in bringing the changes in attitude of employees, job commitments and customer satisfaction.
   (e) All the above

10. It is a method of performance appraisal in which the employee evaluates his own performance. It encourages employees to take responsibility for their own performance by appraising their own strengths, weaknesses, difficulties, achievements or failures and promoting self-management of development goals. This is known as:
   (a) Self-appraisal method *(b)* Management by objectives
   (c) Assessment centre *(d)* Forced choice method
   (e) None of the above

Answer Keys:

Question No.	Answer	Question No.	Answer
1	c	6	d
2	a	7	c
3	a	8	b
4	b	9	e
5	d	10	a

Chapter

HRD Audit

1. INTRODUCTION

Today in the competitive situation the role of employees is very important. The business environment is changing rapidly and becoming more competitive. Multinational corporations have realized that in the present situation it is very difficult to carry out the business effectively and efficiently. The questions of growth, stability, and to excel in the performance arise. The technology, legal systems, needs of customers and expectations are also changing drastically. It has become very difficult to meet the two ends. So in the global market the importance of talented and motivated human resource is felt strongly. For accomplishment of the objectives of the organization there should be proper co-ordination between HR functions and objectives or goals of the organization. HR functions should be properly aligned with short and long-term goals. Keeping this in mind a number of corporations have established separate HRD departments. They have established HRD systems and made structural changes in the organizations and integrated them with HR functions. Many top executives have established HRD departments with the hope that they will be getting solutions to their problems, issues and challenges. Human resource is a very critical resource and it needs a lot of time from management to keep it talented, young and motivated. HR functions are people intensive and cannot be ignored. Talented and motivated manpower is capable to give competitive advantage to the company. Therefore, it is the need of the hour to develop human resource. The need for HRD is realized at all levels in the organizations. There are examples of corporations where HRD functions are playing significant role in improving goodwill of the corporations and giving competitive advantages.

To ensure HRD functions are performed properly as per planning and effectively, HRD audit is required. It is an attempt to evaluate these alignments and ensure that they are taking place as per the planning. HRD audit is an examination and verification of development functions, strategies, HRD department structure, systems, styles, skills of the people at work and link of HRD with human resource planning, policies and total quality management. Having established a separate HRD cell or department does not give guarantee of good human resource development. Essential conditions for a good HRD are:

(a) Recognition of strategic importance of human resource by top level management in the organization.

(b) Identification of role of HRD.

(c) Top level management understands its role in HRD.

(d) Suitable climate of mutual understanding, openness, trust and team spirit for learning to develop competencies.

(e) Supporting HR policies are formulated and implemented.

(f) A competent manager is appointed to manage HRD functions.

(g) As per the need and strategies of the organization the HRD systems are planned and implemented.

(h) Business objectives and HRD systems are reviewed periodically and aligned to fulfill the tasks.

(i) Top management approach and support required too promote a good learning culture.

(j) HRD functions and their implementations are reviewed periodically and realigned and modified to meet objectives.

To fulfill the objectives of HRD functions, it is necessary to check and verify whether the functions are performed according to the planning of HRD. For this reason the HRD audit has come into existence. Human resource planning, strategies, HRD systems, department structure, competencies, styles are evaluated in the context of short and long-term objectives of the organization. If any discrepancy is found the remedial actions are taken to align and modify them as per the need of the hour.

2. REASONS FOR HRD AUDIT

To make the show successful and increase the effectiveness of the organization, management found the solution in competent manpower. Human resource development functions should be performed as per the planning and expected results. To ensure and not to take chance the Organizations undertake HRD audit due to following reasons:

(a) To make HR functions and processes relevant to the goals, HRD audit is needed. To improve the effectiveness of human resource at work HRD functions are performed. To ensure these functions are meeting the requirement to achieve organizational goal, HRD audit is needed.

(b) To face the challenges thrown by liberalization and globalization, organizations find themselves in an awkward position to maintain their lead in the markets. There is a gap created between existing and required level of competencies. It ensures that the HRD functions for development of competencies are performed and fulfilling objectives.

(c) To bring professionalism in employees. HRD activities are performed. The required competencies of employees in different areas are improved through this. The efforts are there to make employees, real professionals at work. Efforts are put through audit to ensure that the efforts are put in the right direction to make employees professionals.

(d) To improve productivity and lower production costs, high level of skills, positive attitude, motivation, level of commitment and team spirit are needed. These are improved through development activities. To ensure further that the development activities are really contributing in improving the talents of manpower.

(e) For expansion and diversification, in new areas a large number of employees are required in different markets. The workforce under this situation becomes diversified. To train, motivate, educate, and get commitment from such workforce, HRD programmes are to be planned and implemented. To make it sure that these programmes are helpful in their objectives achievement, HRD audit is strongly needed.

(f) To make HRD Manager more effective at work, HRD audit is carried out. It ensures the manager that the efforts put in improving the effectiveness of manpower are proper and contributing in accomplishment of the objectives.

(g) To develop excellence in performance and give competitive advantages to the organization, HRD activities are carried out. To make it doubly sure that efforts are put in the right direction for improving performance of employees, organization and image as a whole in the markets.

For the above mentioned reasons the need for HRD was felt and various multinational corporations have established a separate HRD departments or an independent cell under Human Resource Management. Today HRD and HRM words are synonymous and interchangeable and used in different corporations.

3. HRD AUDIT

Human resource is a key factor in performance of business activities and its success. This has been realized in many organizations but not in all. The HRD functions are not performed as per expectations and in some cases management is not supporting HRD functions. Therefore, it forced to go for thorough evaluation of the HRD functions to improve effectiveness of the organization as a whole. The thorough evaluation and examination of existing HRD systems, planning, structures, styles, culture and competencies finds the appropriateness and adequacy for the organization. If not aligned properly then human resource becomes a liability of the organization. This is called HRD audit. It is an evaluation of an organization, structure, systems, process, project or product to check the accuracy and correction of accounts, records or action.

An audit is defined as "a formal examination of an individual or organization's accounting records, financial situation, or compliance with some other set of standards" (Black's Law Dictionary, 7th Edition, 1999). Black's further outlines other types of audits:

(a) **Independent audit:** an audit conducted by an outside person or firm not connected with the person or organization being audited.

(b) **Internal audit:** an audit performed by an organization's personnel to ensure that internal procedures, operations, and accounting practices are in proper order.

(c) **Compliance audit:** an audit conducted by a regulatory agency, an organization or a third party to assess compliance with one or more sets of laws and regulations.

A company hires an independent audit firm, sets date for audit and as per the schedule the auditor performs a physical examination of financial documents, and receives an opinion either confirming or denying management's statement of conditions. Independent auditors conduct the audit at unique, verifiable point in time. Any audit not conducted with the required time frame may not serve the purpose and it will become invalid.

HRD audit is a comprehensive evaluation of the current human resource development planning, objectives, strategies, structure, systems, styles and skills in the context of the short and long-term business objectives of the corporation. HRD audit assesses the current activities and finds out the future HRD needs. HRD audit starts with an understanding of the future business plans and corporate strategies. HRD audit can be done in a better way in organizations where long-term plans are formulated. It may be carried in other organizations also where long-term planning are not formulated but it may not be successful. HRD audit conducted effectively may be in a position to answer the following questions:

(a) What are the goals to be achieved by the organization in short medium and long terms?

(b) What are the HRD system being used for development of competency of employees for present, immediate future and long-term?

(c) What is the level of effectiveness of the present existing HRD systems?

(d) Is the structure of HRD department suitable for requirement of the organization?

(e) Does management contribute in creating favourable climate for learning in organization?

HRD audit starts with defining the objectives of audit. It examines and evaluates structure of HRD department, HRD systems, effectiveness, strategies for HRD, management style, competencies of human resource in line with the objectives of the organization. It compares with the planning and finds out the deviations in the actual practices prevailing in the company. Remedial actions are taken to align these with the need of the organization so that HRD functions' effectiveness can be improved.

4. HRD AUDIT PROCESS

In the past, the audit was conducted to examine the practices of finance and accounting to ensure that the accounting principles were followed and problems were identified for smooth accounting function. It was made compulsory for every organization and on the basis of successful working of this audit; it was applied in human resource development activities also. It is checking and verification of HRD practices to measure the health of human resource development functions. There are various reasons for conducting HRD audit. The HRD process is a complicated process and in it a number of activities or steps are taken in sequence. It is time consuming process. The steps involved in HRD audit are interrelated. Each step is logically depending upon its preceding steps so that the organization gets a clear view of the health of HR development functions. The steps involved in HRD process are as following:

(a) Framing of Policy

First of all, HRD policy is to be prepared by HRD managers. For development of human resource the functions to perform are to be decided in discussion with other managers, responsibility for HRD, fixing job responsibility and accountability, expected standard of performance, competencies needed, duration for performing such functions, costs involved are to be decided in the policy. It would provide the guidelines for conducting HRD audit.

Secondly, HRD audit policy is to be prepared for conducting audit. It would be in line with the HRD policy. In this, areas of HRD audit, selection of auditors, schedule for conducting audit, responsibility for conducting HRD audit, procedure for conducting audit, and costs involved in audit are to be decided for the smooth functioning of audit work.

Thirdly, preparation for audit is to be carried out. The auditors are to be selected as per the policy guidelines. The audit schedule for the whole year is to be finalized and communicated to all concerned. The responsibility for conducting audit is fixed and budget is made available for auditors, expenses. This includes all homework activities for conducting HRD audit.

(b) Pre-audit Preparation

The auditors appointed for conducting HRD audit prepare themselves for conducting audit. They go through the published work of the company such as HR manuals, reports, handbooks, training records, forms, and otherss for collecting relevant information. The HRD manager should supply these records and reports to the auditors. If not done so then a pre-audit information request is to be forwarded to the client who is responsible for audit in the company. Any client can be asked to carry out a self-assessment of the HRD functions by the auditors. number of questions can be asked to the client pertaining to HRD policy and practices. This would help the auditors to identify the key areas of HRD for audit focus.

(c) Conducting HRD Audit

According to the schedule prepared, the auditors visits the different locations in the company to get ideas regarding various aspects related to human resource development. The auditors may be internal team or outsiders. The necessary arrangement is to be made for their lodging, boarding and transportation of the auditors. The auditors checks various records, reports, conducts interview of employees and managers who are connected with the particular activities. Records and reports related to selection, training opportunities offered, promotion, transfers, rewards and recognitions, compensation packages, grievances related to these topics are checked and verified. The auditors are experts in finding the faults with the existing systems. They interact with employees to know the behaviour of employees on different jobs. The duration may be for a couple of days or weeks. The different methods for conducting audit can be used as per the need of the situation. This audit is conducted with the objectives to remove difficulties and improve HRD practices and their effectiveness in future.

(d) Preparation of Audit Report

After conducting audit with the help of interviews, records checking, questionnaires, referring to various published works of the company, workshops and observations, the auditors prepare a audit report. The team of auditors discusses every issue they have come across and final report is submitted to the client. During the audit visit whatever the discrepancies observed are recorded in the report. The activity, department, and person responsible for that is highlighted in the report. The report suggests the remedial steps to remove the discrepancies and report to the auditor in charge regarding corrective action.

(e) Follow up Action

After submission of the auditor's report, the client is asked to take the corrective action so that the difficulties can be removed in time. The objective is to bring improvement in HRD functions and policy. A time limit is given to the concerned manager. On expiry of the specified period, the auditors expect the response from the clients. If not received, the corrective response are again sent to the client. If no attention is paid to the report then head of the company can be contacted. Till the corrective action is not taken to the satisfaction of the auditors the audit process is not complete.

5. HRD AUDIT AND BUSINESS DEVELOPMENT

Every business unit has been established with the objective to grow, stabilize and excel in the business. It wants to develop in products, services, markets, technology and earn profit. As per the planning, organizations prepare their plans, establish different departments, hire talented and motivated manpower. The work continues till it is checked. It is the principle of nature to exercise control over all activities. If control is not exercised then there are chances that the work may not be performed as per the plan or expectations. The irregularities are likely to take place. The deviation from plans may be there minor or major. To keeps the efforts in line with the plans and expectations it is necessary to exercise control. HRD audit is one type of control exercise for human resource development activities. Further HRD functions are performed to meet the needs of the business. But the functions are not performed as per expectation, so HRD functions need to be reviewed periodically. Through HRD audit the weaknesses and irregularities are identified and remedial actions are taken. This helps to improve the efficiency of the HRD area. HRD audit plays important role in development of business in the following areas:

(a) Convinces management to rethink in line with long-term business strategies and plans.
(b) Brings changes in the style of top management.
(c) Clarifies the role of line managers and HRD managers.
(d) Reviews and modifies the existing HRD mechanisms.
(e) Attracts attention of management towards HRD.
(f) Gives direction for recruitment and selection processes.
(g) Helps to fix the responsibility and accountability of employees.
(h) Reviews and modifies the existing practices of management.
(i) Identifies the linkage between HRD and quality system.
(j) Helps to make HRD activities cost effective and adds value to HRD.

Through HRD audit the weaknesses in planning, strategies, style, competencies, structures, and learning climates are found. The timely actions are taken to remove the problems. The periodical review of HRD functions helps realign and modify them as per need so that the expectation for which HRD functions are performed, are fulfilled. This helps the employees to improve their competencies and contribute in giving better performance. The better performance of employees ultimately contributes in increasing performance of the organization. This way the organization performs better than its competitor and gets competitive advantage over other competitors. Ultimately all these develop the goodwill of the organization in the market.

6. METHODOLOGY OF HRD AUDIT

A team of specialized auditors is formed and asked to conduct audit as per the schedule fixed by the management. During audit the team of auditors uses different tools to assess the appropriateness and adequacy of HRD planning, systems, structure of HRD department, competencies of human resource, organizational culture for HRD and support and style of top level management and other concerned parties. There are many methods of conducting HRD audit. They may be used alone or in combination. Following are the methods for HRD audit:

(a) Interviews

It is a face to face communication with the management and employees. Auditors get in touch with the respondent, ask questions and record the answer obtained. The answers can be recorded during or after interview but this is the responsibility of auditor and must be recorded clearly and correctly. During interview the questions can be asked as desired by the auditors. If auditors prepare a questionnaire in a pre-arranged order and give a definite structure. It is called structured interview. When no structure of questionnaire is prepared and interview is conducted without pre-arranged order then it is called unstructured interview. It entirely depends upon the requirements and desire of the auditors. Interviews can be conducted on telephone or through mail. There is no strict rule regarding the type of interview to be used by auditors.

(b) Questionnaire

Second method of collecting data from employees is questionnaire. The auditors who are interested for conducting HRD audit, prepare a questionnaire relating to various aspects of human resource development activities. The questions can be asked relating to HRD activities undertaken, process followed, mechanisms used in HRD process, responsibility of HRD functions, involvement of concerned parties, HRD climate, identification of HRD needs, preparation of HRD programmes, implementation and execution of HRD programmes, effectiveness of HRD programmes, impacts of HRD programmes on attitude, skills, motivation, performance and effectiveness of the organization as a whole, the problems faced during HRD programme etc. The questions can be close or open ended questions. This would help in collecting the relevant data from the employees of the unit.

(c) Workshop

This method for conducting HRD audit is different from individual and group interviews. In the workshop the auditors conduct a workshop and participants vary from twenty to hundreds according to objectives of the audit. The auditors conduct audit on different subsystems of HRD. The presentation can be made by the participants. In subsystems, the activities can be included like process, mechanisms, structure, responsibility, performance appraisal, career planning and development, management development programmes, counseling, rewards and recognitions etc. In this method the participation must encouraged so that there should be free flow of information. It would be helpful as a diagnostic tool by providing relevant information to top level of management for designing and reviewing HRD interventions further. It is to be carried out very carefully by trained auditors only.

(d) Observation

Observation method for collecting the information is used by the experts on the bases of their knowledge and experience. It cannot be used by the new researchers, if it is done so there is possibility of committing the mistakes. During the audit visits the auditors visits various places where employees are related in a company. Such places may be residence, play grounds, hospitals, hostels, training classes, workshops, working sheds, canteen, restrooms etc. During their visits the auditors collect data on the basis of their observation during the visit. They observe the working and living environment, attitude, team spirit, sense of cooperation and commitment, interest in jobs etc. The auditors know that these things are having direct impact on the working and attitude of the employees. It is difficult to remember every point during observation so a check list can be prepared by the auditors for recording the data during audit visits.

(e) Analysis of Secondary Data

When a company plans, prepare programmes, conducts HRD programmes, and conducts review of those programmes, a lot of data are recorded by the responsible managers, The data can be recorded relating to the participants age, experience, type of training programme attended, number of times undergoing training, technical skills possessing or not, interest in developing personal skills and benefits of training and development programmes. The auditors ask the responsible managers for such data and analysis can be carried out. This analysis can give insight into various HRD aspects. On the basis of this analysis the management can take remedial actions for further improvement so that the effectiveness of HRD programmes goes high. Only thing required in this method is that there should proper documentation of data.

(f) Analysis of Published Works

Time to time a company publishes its reports, manuals, various records, newsletters and other Literatures relating to various activities of the company. If any report is relevant to human resource development activities, the analysis can be carried out by the auditors to find out whether the HRD programmes was carried out as per the plan or not. Auditors carried out then what are effects of them on accomplishment of the objectives of the organization. If the auditors find weakness or problems in HRD efforts the remedial actions can be suggested for further improvement. The analysis would help to find the exact position of HRD efforts in that organization. This method can be used as per the requirement of the auditors.

7. LIMITATIONS OF HRD AUDIT

HRD audit is the examination and verification of HRD aspects. It is a very useful process. There are many advantages of HRD audit but its limitations are following:

(a) Lack of Proper Response from Employees

During audit process, the employees think that this is a unnecessary activity and it may go against them so they hesitate to share the information with auditors. Some give half response or sometime avoid giving information. As a result there is no output from the audit. Auditors are not in position to carry out proper audit. To get proper response from employees the management must convince employees that it is in interest of employees and organization and not going to affect them adversely. They should be motivated to give proper information to auditors.

(b) Special Care is Needed to Conduct HRD Audit

When conducting HRD audit, special care should be taken regarding selection of auditors, activities for audit selection and timing for audit. The trained auditors should be selected on the basis of their experience and proven past records. The activities and timing for audits are to be decided so that it should not affect the audit as well as routine work of the organization. Proper involvement of HRD managers, auditors and top level of management is necessary. This audit should be taken as a positive process for checking the irregularities in HRD activities. If proper care is taken then there is possibility of good result from audit conducted. In present time it is difficult for the leading multinational companies to ignore planning and implementation of HRD audit. Special care is taken by them.

(c) Shortage of Time

When audit is conducted, the auditors are given very less time to audit a lot of HRD related activities. The auditors do not find sufficient time to study all activities and collect data. They carry out the work hurriedly and they are likely to given half or wrong report sometime. They are under pressure of targets always. Proper time should be given for conducting audit in the organization.

(d) High Cost of Conducting Audit

During audit process a lot of arrangements are to be made for the auditors. For them lodging, boarding, transportation, entertainment and fee arrangements are to be made. The total cost for conduct audit for a fortnight period, a large amount is involved. It adds to the costs of the organization and profitability goes down. The cost should be reduced reasonably by appointing internal auditors if possible.

(e) Evaluation of Units and Systems not of Individuals.

In HRD audit the activities or subsystems involved are evaluated. The efforts are put to find out the gap between planning and actual work carried. The comparison of these two finds the deviation in activities. But efforts are not put to evaluate the caliber required and possessed by the individual employees. In this line also efforts should be put by the auditors.

Despite its limitations, HRD audit is very useful. It provides information to assess all aspects of HRD. It helps to improve the overall effectiveness of the organization. On the basis of audit reports management can take the remedial action to improve the effectiveness of HRD programmes, employees and organization as a whole.

8. HRD SCORECARD

To measure the effectiveness of HRD functions during HRD audit, HRD scorecard was introduced by TVS RAO in 1999. This scorecard helps to know the strengths and weaknesses of HRD activities being carried out in the company. The exact position of human resource development activities in an organization is made clear to the management with the help of scorecard. nIn this scorecard Rao has taken four dimensions only and it is felt that it needs other areas to be covered like strategies, commitment of top level management, role of other parties and desire for learning. He has used letter grades to assess the maturity of dimension. The letter grades do not make the picture very clear. Therefore, point grades are suggested to make the assessment more effective and instant. In this scorecard total eight dimensions are assessed as shown below. A format of HRD scorecard is appended below:

Table 13.1: HRD Scorecard: A Dummy Company

Serial No.	HRD Dimension	Score	Remarks If Any
1.	Systems	5	
2.	Strategies	4	
3.	Structures	4	
4.	Manager competencies	4	
5.	Climate	3	
6.	Objective orientation	2	
7.	Management commitment	4	
8.	Contribution of other parties	2	
9.	Desire for learning	4	
10.	Implementation of program.	3	
11.	Total score	35 out of 70	50%.Result is Average. Needs focus on Serial No. 5, 6, 8 and 10 mainly.

Points: Very poor-1, Poor-2, Fair-3, Average-4, Good-5, Very good-6, and Excellent-7.

9. HRD AUDIT AND OD

With rapidly changing environment mainly technology, economy, competition and customer demands and expectations it had become compulsory to improve internal strength of the company. Out of resources being used in business units' manpower is the most important. Therefore, special focus is being given for improvement of knowledge, skills, competencies of employees, and maintain them motivated. This is the main objective of HRD functions. To ensure whether HRD functions are being performed properly or not HRD audit is carried out. HRD audit helps to assess all relevant areas of HRD pinpoints the weak areas where special attention can be given and effectiveness can be improved. This contributes in overall development of the organization. It will not be wrong if it is said HRD audit is an OD intervention. It gives many insights in improvement of performance of people and organization as a whole. HRD audit helped in developing clear cut policies for employees regarding various aspects, favourable environment, systems and procedures, performance appraisal, training programmes, career planning, morale and motivation. It contributed to find out weakness and suggested ways to improve the situation. In many organizations this has been accepted and conducted. It resulted in improvement of performance, profit earning, customer satisfaction and goodwill of the company. Finally it can be said HRD audit contribute in giving competitive edge to the company over its competitors. The success of it as OD intervention depends upon post audit implementation.

10. ROLE OF HRD AUDIT

Human resource development audit is very important functions in HRD department. It ensures that all efforts put by HRD managers and staffs are proper or not. If there is problem any where then these can be corrected so that effectiveness of HRD functions improves. It affects the manpower, performance, roles, accountability, and image of the organization, HR policies and practices and overall quality of services. The role played is very important and provides a lot of benefits. These are explained in detail under the following heads:

(a) Improvements in Effectiveness of Human Resource and HRD Systems

HRD audit checks and verifies the different functions performed for development of human resource to ensure that they proper and helpful for development of competencies of manpower. The HRD audit also checks various HRD systems used by the management for development of human resource. If during this verification if anything is found out of order then remedial actions are suggested. It ensures that the functions performed, subsystems used and level of competencies developed are as per planning. HRD systems used mainly are recruitment and selection, training, orientation, performance management, career planning and development, counseling, coaching and communication. The functions and systems can be redesigned for improving effectiveness of manpower and organization as a whole. It contributes in improving the overall effectiveness also.

(b) Increasing Importance of Talented and Motivated Human Resource

Human resource development activities are performed mainly for human resource. The importance of this resource has been realized. It is now considered as the most important resource in the organization. It is a live resource and utilizes other resources for further generation. Without human resource other resources are useless. In present time, further need for talented and motivated human resources are felt. For development of employees various types of functions are performed. The main focus is on human resource. HRD audit is interested for improving knowledge, attitudes and skills required by the employees in the organization according the plans. It checks the irregularities to make the HRD functions more effective. The focus of all concerned is on human resources and their talent improvement

(c) Positive Changes in Attitude of Management

Under changing global competitive environment, it has become difficult for the management to take care of the business alone. They need the support of human resource and that too talented and motivated one. They have realized that the competencies level is to be improved. They have started considering that human resource is a very valuable resource and they consider them as an important party in the organization. HRD functions have been undertaken with the objective to create environment for a learning organization. A learning culture has been created with the support of the top level of management in some of the organization but some of the managers are still not in favour of this. HRD audit has contributed in bringing positive changes in working style of the management by pointing out the deviations in HRD functions and systems for developing and improving the employees. It provides a lot of information for bringing new changes to meet the organizational development and change process.

(d) Improves Overall Effectiveness of Training

In present global era, there is need for higher skills of manpower. The existing manpower is not in position to meet the requirements. The training needs are identified. As per planning the needs of different types of training are identified, programmes are designed, study materials prepared, schedules of training are prepared and training programmes as per planning are conducted. In the last the training effectiveness are evaluated. All these activities are audited in HRD audit. During whole process of training careful analysis is carried out to ensure that the training is conducted properly with optimal costs. Through this the unwanted activities and costs are checked. This helps in contributing in development of knowledge and skills of the trainees. The overall effectiveness of the training improves. The role played by HRD audits is very important and it cannot be ignored in mainly medium and larger organizations.

(e) Better Recruitment & Selection Policy and Procedure

An HRD audit points out the weaknesses in management practices relating to human resource development. The management is willingly to take remedial action for improvement also. This creates a good environment in the organization. Over and above the competence level for entry in the organization is decided in audit functions. All these ensure the more and better employees would be attracted by the organization. The recruitment and selection policies should be prepared accordingly. The situation is made very clear to the aspirants and selection authority for selection of the candidates. This would definitely improve recruitment and selection policy and procedure to a good extent.

(f) Improvements in Management Practices

For development of human resource a lot of functions are performed by the management. These functions include manpower planning, recruitment and selection, orientation, training, management development, compensation, performance appraisal, promotion and transfer, welfare and wellness of employees, leadership, coaching, counseling and communication. These functions are responsible for development of human resource. During audit these functions or practices are checked and verified whether these are performed as per the planning or not. During this verification if any irregularity is found is reported to the management for improvement. This improvement in practices would be helpful in future for improving the effectiveness of the organization.

(g) Contributes in Role Clarification

In performance management planning the roles of all concerned parties are clarified through mutual discussion. The roles of employees, supervisors, managers, trainers etc. are clearly defined and communicated. In their routine functions, everyone is asked to perform his functions to give the standard performance. During HRD audit the functions of all concerned are evaluated. If any discrepancy is found there is reported to top management for remedial action. Under fear of audit report, everyone is scared to perform the jobs as agreed. The required standard performance is given by everyone. The confusion in roles of various parties involved is avoided. The efforts are properly utilized for achieving the goals.

(h) Fixes Performance Accountability

In performance management functions in a joint meeting the roles of all employees are decided. There is no confusion is this and it is clearly communicated. The responsibility and accountability of everyone is fixed and asked to play their role. In audit the jobs performed, steps taken for performing the tasks, results achieved, and contribution in achieving overall objectives of the organization are assessed. If any discrepancy is found then the concerned person is held responsible. No one can escape from their accountability. The only way is to improve or quit the job. This compels the employees to take interest in their jobs and their own development. Finally, it contributes in improvement in performance of the organization as a whole.

(i) Supports Long-term Strategy in Business

Now doubt the HRD audit has been accepted by the management under compulsion. Due to high level of competition the need for talented people is felt. To meet this requirement HRD functions were initiated. Further, to ensure return on HRD functions the audit was introduced. The HRD audit was accepted as a long-term strategy for improving and maintaining effectiveness of manpower and organization both. It forces the management to get involvement of employees in most of the activities, they must be involved in various plans so that their level of commitment can improve. If involvement is high then sharing of information would be good and audit result would be better. Due to this in long run all concerned are going to get benefits. This has been realized by the management and now investment in HRD related activities is considered as investment which pays in the long-term.

(j) Improvement in Total Quality

In the planning in beginning the job responsibility, jobs to be performed, standard of performance expected are decided. The same are communicated to all employees. They work accordingly and put their efforts to meet the requirements. As when they face difficulties they are guided by the supervisors. They are supported by the management by providing good work environment. Over and above in audit the weaknesses are identified and remedial actions are taken. The good performers are motivated further. This improves the level of motivation, commitment, team spirit and sense of cooperation. All these improve the overall quality of performance, products, services and performance of the organization. The overall quality in the organization improves due to all these efforts.

11. CONCLUSION

Today in the competitive situation the role of employees is very important. The business environment is changing rapidly and becoming more competitive. Multinational corporations have realized that in the present situation it is very difficult to carry out the business effectively and efficiently. To ensure HRD functions are performed properly as per planning and effectively, HRD audit is required. It is an attempt to evaluate these alignments and ensure that they are taking place as per the planning. HRD audit is an examination and verification of development functions, strategies, HRD department structure, systems, styles, skills of the people at work and link of HRD with human resource planning, policies and total quality management. To ensure and not to take chance the organizations undertake HRD audit due to many reasons to make HR functions and processes relevant to the goals, face the challenges thrown by liberalization and globalization, bring professionalism in employees, improve productivity and lower production costs, expansion and diversification, in new areas, and make HRD manager more effective.

To develop excellence in performance and give competitive advantages to HRD audit the weaknesses in planning, strategies, style, competencies, structures, and learning climate are found. The timely actions are taken to remove the problems. The periodical review of HRD functions helps realign and modify them as per need so that the expectation for which HRD functions are performed are fulfilled. This helps the employees to improve their competencies and contribute in giving better performance. The better performance of employees ultimately contributes in increasing performance of the organization. This way the organization performs better than its competitor and gets competitive advantage over other competitors. Ultimately all these develop the goodwill of the organization in the market.

A team of specialized auditors is formed and asked to conduct audit as per the schedule fixed by the management. During audit the team of auditors uses different tools to assess the appropriateness and adequacy of HRD planning, systems, structure of HRD department, competencies of human resource, organizational culture for HRD and support and style of top level management and other concerned parties. There are many methods of conducting HRD audit such as questionnaire, interview, workshop, observation and secondary data. They may be used alone or in combination. In many organizations this has been accepted and conducted. It resulted in improvement of performance, profit earning, customer satisfaction and goodwill of the company. Finally it can be said HRD audit contribute in giving competitive edge to the company over its competitors. The success of HRD audit as OD intervention depends upon post audit is implementation. If audit report implemented strongly it is likely to give expected result otherwise not.

12. QUESTIONS FOR REVIEW

1. What are the essential conditions for effective HRD?
2. Everyone is talking of corporate sector for HRD and HRD audit. Discuss the reason for HRD audit undertaken in companies.

3. Define HRD audit and explain its features in detail.
4. What questions can be answered when HRD audit is conducted properly? Explain.
5. Discuss the role of HRD audit in business development of a company.
6. Highlight the areas where HRD audit plays an important role in develop of business in an organization.
7. Explain HRD audit methodology in detail.
8. Short notes:
   (a) HRD and OD
   (b) HRD Scorecard
   (c) Limitation of HRD audit
   (d) Types of audit
9. What do you know about HRD process and discuss the main steps involved in it?
10. Critically evaluate the role played by HRD audit in different areas of a company in present competitive situation.
11. How do you evaluate the future of human resource development audit in Indian companies involved in multinational markets in business?

13. OBJECTIVE QUESTIONS

1. To fulfill the objectives of HRD functions it is necessary to ....whether the functions are performed according planning of HRD.

   (a) Check and verify
   (b) Create and verify
   (c) Check and communicate
   (d) Create and communicate
   (e) All the above

2. An audit conducted by an outside person or firm not connected with the person or organization being audited is called

   (a) Outside audit.
   (b) Independent audit
   (c) Internal audit
   (d) Compliance audit
   (e) None of the above

3. HRD audit is conducted by the organization to ensure that the HRD functions are performed as per planning. It starts with defining the:

   (a) Objectives
   (b) Goal
   (c) Problems
   (d) SWOT analysis
   (e) Appraisal

4. The steps involved in HRD process are arranged in sequence as:

   1. Framing of Policy
   2. Pre-audit Preparation
   3. Conducting HRD Audit
   4. Preparation of Audit Report
   5. Follow up Action

   (a) 1,3,4
   (b) 1,2,3,4
   (c) 1,3,4,5
   (d) 1,2,3,4,5
   (e) None of the above

5. The periodical review of HRD functions helps realign and .... them as per need so that the expectation for which HRD functions are performed, are fulfilled.

   (a) Distributing
   (b) Perform
   (c) Modify
   (d) Re-prepare
   (e) None of them

6 . Observation method cannot be used by the new researchers because it is on the basis of experience of the auditor. New researchers are likely to commit more mistakes. It is:

   (a) True
   (b) False
   (c) Some time true, some time false
   (d) Can't say
   (e) None of the above

7. HRD audit is conducted to check and verity the HRD functions so that these can be aligned with the planning and need of the organization. A lot of related activities are to be audited. For conducting HRD audit it should be given:

   (a) Proper authority
   (b) Proper time
   (c) Proper person
   (d) All the above
   (e) None of the above

8. HRD audit contributes in overall development of the organization. It gives many insights in improvement of performance of people and organization as a whole. HRD audit is an OD intervention if it is said it would:

   (a) Not be wrong
   (b) Be wrong
   (c) Not be right
   (d) Be difficult
   (e) No idea

9. The HRD audit was accepted for improving and maintaining effectiveness of manpower and organization both. It is considered as a:

   (a) Short-term strategy
   (b) Long-term strategy
   (c) Short-term process
   (d) Long-term process
   (e) None of the above

10. HRD audit affects the manpower, performance, roles, accountability, and image of the organization, HR policies and practices and overall quality of services. The role played is very important and provides a lot of benefits. These are:
    (a) Improvements in effectiveness of human resource and HRD systems
    (b) Positive changes in attitude of management and overall effectiveness of training
    (c) Improvements in management practices, policies and procedures, role clarity and fixed performance accountability
    (d) Supports long-term strategy in business and improvement in total quality
    (e) All the above

11. HRD audit is the examination and verification of HRD aspects. It is a very useful process. There are many advantages of HRD audit but its limitations are:
    (a) Lack of proper response from employees
    (b) Special care is needed to conduct HRD audit
    (c) Shortage of time and high cost of conducting audit
    (d) Evaluation of units and systems not of individuals.
    (e) All the above

12. To measure the effectiveness of HRD functions during HRD audit, HRD scorecard was introduced. This scorecard helps to know the strengths and weaknesses of HRD activities being carried out in the company. It was introduced by:
    (a) TVS Rao (b) Abraham
    (c) Ishwar Dayal and KK Verma (d) Khandelwal
    (e) None of the above

Answer Keys:

Question No.	Answer	Question No.	Answer
1	a	7	b
2	b	8	a
3	a	9	b
4	d	10	e
5	c	11	e
6	a	12	a

Chapter

Training

1. INTRODUCTION

It is not possible for an industry to recruit all the trained personnel for carrying out its productive functions. Even when persons are appointed with some previous training, this may not be sufficient and wholly suited for the jobs they are expected to do. Moreover, the natures of jobs in the industry are fast changing. New methods and processes are being discovered everyday and the old techniques are becoming obsolete. Howso ever competent and capable a person may be he cannot do his best at his job unless he is systematically trained in the correct methods of doing the job. Thus training becomes necessary not only for the new entrants to work effectively, but also to teach new methods to the present employees. It is because of this reason that most of the big enterprises spend quite a lot of money on education and training programs for its staff personnel.

2. MEANING AND DEFINITIONS OF TRAINING

Training is defined as "the act of increasing the knowledge and skills of an employee for doing a particular job." Training implies activities that teach employees how to perform their present jobs better. It is the training that prepares people to perform their present jobs more efficiently. Training teaches employees required skills, knowledge or attitudes and helps them in improving their performance by improving new skills, new techniques of doing the work and by improving their work habits. Training is thus aimed at improving the performance of personnel in their present positions or jobs. There can be many objectives in designing a training programme such as to enable new appointees to reach required standards of performance as quickly as possible; to reduce wastage of time or cost; to introduce correct methods and innovations; to achieve, maintain or improve quality standards. Some of the leading management experts have defined the concept of training as under:

(a) "Training is the systematic modification of behavior through learning which occurs as a result of education, instruction, development and planned experience." (Micheal Armstrong)

(b) "Training consists of planned programme designed to improve performance at the individual groups, and organizational levels. Improved performance, intern, and implies that there have been measurable changes in knowledge, skills, attitudes and social behavior. (Wange F. Cascio)

(c) "Training is a short term process utilizing a systematic and organized procedure by which no managerial personnel learn technical knowledge and skills for a definite purpose" (L. L. Stenmetz)

(d) "Training refers only to instruction in technical and mechanical operations. Specifically stated training is the organized procedure by which people learn knowledge and skill for a definite purpose." (J. P. Campbell)

(e) "Process of developing an understanding of some organized body of facts, rules and methods. This information concerns largely the operative phases of an applied knowledge." (R. C. Davis)

3. TRAINING AND DEVELOPMENT

Development of employees refers to those activities that prepare them for future jobs or positions. Development represents all those activities or programs of teaching skills, knowledge or attitudes that increase employee's potential and prepare them for future positions. The distinction between training and development is very thin. Whereas training prepares employees for performing present jobs, development prepares employees for future assignments. The difference between training and development is primarily one of the intent and can be made on two counts, namely contents and the level of employees for which they are directed. Training is generally linked with the operational tasks and goals of organization. Training programs are confined to improve job related skills so as to enable employees to perform their present jobs in a better way. These programs help in preparing them for a particular job. Their need for training is limited to knowledge, skills and technology needed for the present jobs. Development programs are linked with the future needs of the organization needed for future managerial positions. Training is a short-term process utilizing a systematic and organized procedure by which non-managerial personnel acquire technical knowledge and skills for a definite purpose. It refers to instructions in technical and mechanical operations like operation of some machine. It is designed primarily for non-managers. It is for a short duration, and is for a specific job related purpose. Training is a short-term process utilizing a systematic and organized procedure by which non-managerial personnel acquire technical knowledge and skills for a definite purpose. In other words it refers not to technical knowledge or skills in operation, but to philosophical and theoretical educational concepts. It involves broader education and its purpose is long-term development.

Both training and development programmes are necessary for any organization. But not all organizations show awareness of the need for development. This is perhaps due to the fact that the fruits of training programmes are more apparent and can be obtained more quickly.

Table 14.1: Training and Development

Area	Training	Development
(i) Topics	(i) Technical, skills & Knowledge	(i) Managerial and Behavioral Skills and Knowledge
(ii) Aim	(ii) Specific job related	(ii) Conceptual and General Knowledge
(iii) Period	(iii) Short-term	(iii) Long term
(iv) Training	(iv) Mostly Technical and Non-technical managerial	(iv) Mostly for managerial
(v) Group	(v) Personnel	(v) Personnel

4. NEED OR IMPORTANCE OF TRAINING

Training is a vital and necessary activity in all organizations. It plays a large part in determining the effectiveness and efficiency of the establishment. The need of or importance of training to a business firm or industry may be explained as follows:

(a) Heightens Morale

Possession of needed skills helps to meet such basic human needs as security and ego satisfaction. Elaborate personnel and human relations programme can make a contribution towards morale, but hollow shells if there is no solid core of meaningful work done with knowledge, skill and pride.

(b) Reduces Supervision

The trained employee is one who can supervise himself. Both employee and supervisor want less supervision. But greater independence is not possible unless the employee is adequately trained.

(c) Reduce Labour Problem

Employees are so well trained that they can experience the direct satisfaction associated with a sense of achievement and knowledge that they are developing their inherent capabilities at work.

(d) Minimum Accident and Wastage

An important advantage of training is that accident, spoilt work and damage to machinery and equipment can be kept to minimum by well trained employees. The improved skills helps in performing tasks easily and better performance. It avoids accidents and wastes.

(e) Increases Productivity

Increased productivity is possible only when there is an increase in quantity of output. Training programmes, by increasing skill, aptitude and abilities of workers result in increased productivity.

(f) Increases Organizational Stability and Flexibility

Stability, the ability of an organization to sustain its effectiveness despite the loss of key personnel can be developed only through creation of a reservoir of trained replacement. Flexibility, the ability to adjust to short run variation in the volume of work, requires personnel with multiple skills to enable their transfer to jobs, where the demand is highest. There is no great organizational asset than that of trained motivated personnel.

(g) Fulfills to Manpower Needs

When the skills are required by a company, it often finds it most practical to select and train from within the organization rather than seek the skilled personnel from the outside labour market.

(h) Benefits to Employees

As employees acquire new knowledge and jobs skills, they increase their market value and earning power. The possession of useful skills changes their value to their employer and thereby increases their job security. Training may also qualify them for promotion to more responsible jobs. This, of course, increases their pay and status.

(i) Obsolescence Prevention

Training and development programme foster the indicative and creativity of employees and help to prevent manpower obsolescence which may be due to age, temperament or lack of motivation or the inability of a person to adapt him to technological changes.

(j) Learning Time Reduction

A well-knit training programme reduces learning time to reach the level of acceptable performance. The trainer explains every concept, steps involved and procedure for performing he job. The trainee finds himself in good position and confidence develops. He can take chance to learn the new things.

5. OBJECTIVES OF TRAINING

Broadly speaking the objectives of education and training programme contribute to.

(a) Greater organizational effectiveness; and

(b) Accomplishment of the employee's personal objectives.

No doubt these objectives cannot be claimed to be primary objectives. They are definitely the secondary objectives of any desirable changes in the organizational behavior.

Let as now spell out briefly the objectives of education and training programmes.

(a) Greater organizational attributes from the development of certain organizational attributes that can be improved.

(i) Effective executive leadership.

(ii) A complement of people who are competent to perform their assigned tasks effectively.

(iii) The organizational attributes of stability, flexibly and capacity for growth.

(iv) Good organizational morale.

(b) Accomplishment of the personal objectives by the employees are obtained because the training programme helps the individual employees in their personal growth and efficiency and provides mental job satisfaction.

6. TRAINING NEED ASSESSMENT

Regardless of the specific methods used to evaluate needs, any thorough assessment effort must address their key areas — the organization, the job task and the individual

(a) Organization Analysis

It looks at the proposed training within the context of the rest of the organization. A prime consideration is whether or not the proposed training will be compatible with the organization strategy, goals and culture, and whether employees are likely to transfer the skills they learn in training to their actual jobs. If training is to be provided to a large number of employees throughout the organization, analysis should know which units should receive. The training first answers which units need it most. Alternatively, one may decide to begin with units known to be especially receptive to training in order to develop a record of success and a positive image for the training program among others in the organization.

The organization's future plans must also be considered. For instance a training specialist would not want to plan a massive training effort for a product process that top management plans to discontinue in a year or two. Finally, the availability of trainer's facilities, financial resources and the priorities of competing training programs must be considered as part of the organizational analysis.

(b) Task Analysis

The duties and responsibilities of the job, together with the knowledge, skills and abilities needed to perform them, are the focus of the second stage of needs analysis called task analysis. The purpose of this step is to verify that task is important and employees should be trained for the same and also to develop in depth information about the task knowledge and procedures that should be taught. The trainer will need to call on subject matter experts such as superiors and high performing employees to generate this information.

(c) Individual Analysis

The final level of analysis looks at the individual to be trained. The individual analysis attempts to determine which employees should receive training and what their current levels of skill and knowledge are. The trainer may single out individuals on the basis of their past performance or select an entire work group or all incumbents with a specific job title. Then the trainer assesses, or it least estimates, the skill and knowledge levels of the chosen trainees, so that the training is neither too simple nor too complex.

7. LEVELS OF TRAINING

Just as there is the distribution of administration in different levels for the efficient management, the training programme may also have its own levels for effective results. The following are some of the import levels of training of the employees:

(a) Unskilled Workers

They require training in improved methods of handing their work to reduce the cost of production and do the job in the most economical way. Such employees are given training on the job itself and the training is imparted either by their immediate superior officers or sardars or foremen.

(b) Training of Semi-skilled Workers

This category of employees needs training to meet with the requirements of the industrial establishments. It is necessitated because of introduction of mechanization and rationalization. Normally such training is given by more proficient workers. It may continue for a few hours of weeks, the duration being dependent upon the number of operations in the manufacturing process as also the speed and accuracy required. The training is imparted by giving instructions in various semi-skilled operations.

(c) Training to Skilled Workers

Skilled workers are provided training through the apprenticeship system varying in length up to period of five years. Crafts training are imparted through training centers and the industry itself. The technology is changing very fast so with this the skills of the skilled workers are to be updated. The training is to be conducted positively.

(d) Training to Other Staff

Besides the above categories of unskilled, semi skilled and skilled workers, other employees are also required to be trained. They are computer operators, typists, stenographers, accountants, clerks etc. They need training in their respective fields but normally such training is not provided. Salesmen are also given training about the nature of the products; routine associated with finalization of the order and the salesmanship art together with the latest knowledge of the products being developed in the organization.

(e) Training to Senior and Supervisory Staff

Since the supervisors form a very vital link in the chain of administration, they need most and up to date training and orientation at frequent intervals. The training programmes for the supervisory staff must be specific and tailor-made to fulfill the need of the enterprise.

8. PRINCIPLES OF TRAINING

Training is a process. It is continuously. It has a long time and cost involved with it for training purpose, a good training policy is to be prepared. Employees and organization both must be benefited by the training policy. Proper training policy should check irregularities in training. Irregularities such as over-training, imitation of training programme of other firm's inadequate tools and equipments misuse of testing techniques, can take place. So for effective training, following principles must be followed:

(a) When trainees feel the need of training, they will be more responsive.

(b) Rewards and punishment make training more fruitful.

(c) If trainee is encouraged during training, the result will be better.

(d) Feedback system must be used in training.

(e) Through training, behavior of the trainees can be changed.

(f) Rate of learning decreases when complex skills are involved.

(g) Training must be goal oriented.

(h) Study materials must be made meaningful and must be provided in time.

9. TRAINING METHODS

There is no one best technique of training that can be used in every situation. More than one Technique may be applied in imparting instructions. Techniques of training that are generally used to impart training are categorized as (a) on the job techniques (b) off the job techniques. These are explained in detail:

(a) On the Job Training

Numerous training methods can be used while the man is engaged in the process of productive work. On the job training methods are suitable for all personnel. Various methods of on the job training are as follows:

(b) On Specific Job

The most common and formal on the job training programme is training for a specific job. Current practice in the job training has been strongly influenced by the war time training within industry (TWI) which was first designed to improve the job performance through job instruction training. TWI also included training for supervisors to improve job performance. There are following methods of training on specific job:

(i) Experience: This is the method of on the job training. Learning by experience cannot and should not be eliminated as a method of development though as a sole approach, it is wasteful, time consuming, and inefficient. In some cases this method has proved to be very efficient though it should be followed by other training methods to make it more meaningful.

(ii) Coaching: On the job coaching by the superior is an important and potentially effective approach if superior, is properly trained and oriented. The technique involves direct personnel instruction and guidance, usually with extensive demonstration and continuous critical evaluation and correction. The advantage is increased motivation for the trainee and the minimization of the problem of learning transfer from theory to practice. The danger in this method lies in the possible neglect to ccaching by superior.

(iii) Understudy: The understudy method makes the trainee an assistant to the current job holder. The trainee learns by experience, observations and limitation. If decisions are discussed with the understudy, he can be informed on the policies and theories involved. The advantage of this method is that training is conducted in practical and realistic situation. However disadvantages are many. The method takes care of mistakes and deficiencies of existing managerial practice. Moreover, the understudies are frequently neglected by those they assist.

(iv) Job rotation: It is another on the job training method in which worker is imparted training in a variety of jobs and is shifted from job to job for this purpose. This method helps the worker to be versatile in many jobs. This type of training very useful for the organization as it can utilize the services of various workers on other jobs as well in the time of need in case of absences, leaves, departures or exists. It also gives the workers a sort of flexibility and helps in breaking monotony of work.

(v) Apprenticeship: A major part of training time is spent on the job productive work. Each apprentice is given a programme of assignments according to a predetermined schedule which provides for efficient training in trade skills. This method is appropriate for training in crafts, trades and technical areas, especially when proficiency in a job is the result of relatively long training or apprenticeship period, e.g., job of a craftsman, a machinist, a printer, a tool maker, a pattern designer, a mechanic etc.

(vi) Job instruction: Training is an on the job and the trainee learns how to perform his work while working on his present job. It is a way learning by doing. The training is imparted by a trainer, supervisor or senior and experienced co-worker the very work situation.

(vii) Training centre training: It involves classroom training imparted with the help of equipment and machines identical to those in use at the place of work. Theoretical training is given in the classroom, while practical work is conducted on the production line. It is often used to train clerks, bank tellers, inspectors, machine operator, typists etc.

(viii) Vestibule training: Under this method the trainee is trained under similar conditions of work, in a kind of miniature factory, of work ship or pilot plant. After this training he is exposed to real life situation in the factory. It is often considered as preliminary to the job training. This enables the trainee to overcome nervousness and get the best out of the training. He becomes mentally prepared to handle the job.

(ix) Simulation: It is extension of vestibule training. The trainee works in closely 'duplicate' real job condition. This is essential in cases in which actual on the job practice is expensive, might result in serious injury, a costly error or the destruction of valuable material or resource, e.g., in aeronautical industry.

(x) Internship training: This training is usefully meant for such person and such jobs where advanced theoretical knowledge is to be backed by practical experience on the job. It is with reference to joint programmes of technical and professional institution and the industry or big business houses that usually employ such technicians and professionals. The students of engineering colleges are sent for this type of training to the big industries, and the medical student to big hospitals. Similarly, management's students or students undergoing company secretary course are sent to big and advanced corporate organizations. The aim of such training is to bring about a balance between theory and practical of the knowledge.

(c) Off the Job or Classroom Methods

Training on the job is not a part of everyday activity under these methods. Location of this training may be a company classroom or outside place owned by the organization, an educational institution or association, which is not a part of the company. These methods are:

(i) Lectures: These are formally orgiastic talks by an instructor on specific. Topics this method is useful when philosophy, concepts, attitudes, theories and problem solving have to be discussed. The lectures can be used for a very group to be trained in a short time. These are essential when technical or special information of a complex nature is to be imparted. The lectures are supplemented with discussions, film shows, case studies, role playing etc. This is also known as implant or in-house training.

(ii) Case study: This method helps the trainee to learn how other tracked the problems or situations as and when they arms. In this form of training, a trainee undertakes a case study and' learns how decisions were arrived at and taken. Usually, a trainee studies a case which is related to his job. Case studies help in developing decision making skills. Case study method of training is a technique. Cases are discussed in group. Each member is asked to present his analysis.

(iii) Seminar or team discussion: The group learns through discussion of a paper on a selected subject. The paper is written by one or more trainees. Discussion may be on a statement made by the person in charge of the seminar or on a document prepared by an expert. The material to be analyzed is distributed in advance in the form of required reading.

(iv) Brainstorming: This is the method of stimulating trainees to creative thinking. This approach developed by Alex Osborn seeks to reduce inhibiting forces by providing for a maximum of poses and ideas are invited. Quantity rather than quality is the primary objective. Ideas are encouraged and criticism of any idea is discouraged. Chain reaction from idea often develops. Later, these ideas are critically examined. There is no trainer in barnstorming.

(v) Role playing: Here trainees act out a given role as they would do in a stage play. Two or more trainees are assuaged roles in a given situation, which is explained to the group. There are no written lines to be said and naturally, no rehearsals. The role players have to quickly respond to the situation that is ever changing and to react to it is they would in the real one. It is a method of human interaction which involves realistic behavior in an imaginary or hypothetical situation

(vi) Self-study: This technique is very useful when the trainee is distantly placed or the instruction to be imported does not need personal interaction. Instruction is imparted through carefully planned materials which are sent in the form of manuals, videotapes or recorded castes etc. Self-study is the best method for self-development. However, principles of learning are not taken care of in this technique.

(vii) Sensitivity training: Sensitivity training is the most controversial laboratory training method. Many of its advocates have an almost religious zeal in their enhancement with the training group experience. Some of its critics match this favor in their attacks on the technique. As a result of criticism and experience, a somewhat revised approach often described as team development training has appeared. It was first used by National Training Laboratories at Bethel, U.S.A. The training groups themselves were called 'T Group'. Since then its use has been extended to other organizations, universities and institutes.

(viii) Programmed instruction: In recent years this method has become popular. The subject matter to be learned is presented in a series of carefully planned sequential units. These units are arranged from simple to more complex levels of instruction. The trainee goes through these units by answering questions and filling the blanks. This method is expensive and time consuming.

10. TYPES OF TRAINING

The training programmes are always organized with different and specific purpose in view. Accordingly the type of the training programme will depend on purposes of such programmes.

Following are the usual types:

(a) Induction Training

The purpose is to familiarize the new entrants to the organization, its objective, rules and working conditions.

(b) Job Training

In case of new entrants the purpose is to acquaint them with the jobs they are expected to perform and to train them to handle the equipment and raw materials correctly and perform the job operations efficiently. For the old employees the purposes is acquaint them with the latest methods of executing the jobs and improve further their efficiency.

(c) Training for Promotion

Promotions provide encouragement to employees and in many organizations; senior posts are filed by promotions. Promotion carries with it new responsibilities for which the incumbent must be prepared. The purpose of this type of training is to meet this demand.

(d) Refresher Process

With the passing of time, employees are likely to forget some of the instructions and methods, which they might have learned earlier. This type of training is supposed to revive the earlier learning's in the minds of the employees through short term refresher courses.

11. TRAINING PROCESS

The objective of training is to achieve a change in the behavior of those trained. In the industrial situation this means that the trainee shall acquire new techniques, skills, problem-solving abilities and develop work attitude. It is expected that the employees apply their newly acquired knowledge on the job in such a way that it can help them in the achievement of the organizational goals. Training should be provided according to the objectives and strategy of the organization so that their skill can be improved to perform the job and contribute to the achievement of the organizational goals. The training process includes the following steps:

(a) Corporate Objectives.

(b) Training Strategy.

(c) Identification of Training needs.

(d) Fixing Training Goals.

(e) Designing Programme for Training.

(f) Conducting Training Programme.

(g) Evaluation of Training Programme.

12. DESIGNING PROGRAMME FOR TRAINING

Training programmes are costly and time consuming. Therefore, they need to be drafted very carefully. Usually in the organization of training programmes, the following steps are considered necessary:

(a) Decision about Trainees.

(b) Decision Regarding Trainers.

(c) Selection of Training Methods.

(d) Levels of Training.

(e) Finalizing Training Syllabus.

(f) Decision Regarding Place for Training.

13. CONDUCTING TRAINING PROGRAMME

After designing training programme the next step is to conduct programme. For conducting the training many difficulties are to be faced such as availability of trainers, training schedules and record keeping. Following steps should be taken to conduct the training programme:

(a) Organizing Training Facilities.

(b) Preparation of Training Schedules.

(c) Operation of Training Programmes.

(d) Evaluation of Trainee's Performance.

14. EVALUATION OF TRAINING PROGRAMME

Evaluation of training is necessary, to ascertain the usefulness of worthlessness of the training, and to find out whether it has been relevant to the identified training needs, whether money and time spent on it has been worthwhile and should be continued or whether there is need for modifying the training programmes in terms to period, content, method or faculty.

Thus the process of evaluation involves the following step:

(a) Devising evaluation criteria before training begins.

(b) Pretest to know the level of knowledge of worker before training.

(c) Post tests are the test after the training to know the level of knowledge after training and improvement if any made as a result of training.

(d) Assessment of performance at the job to know how far the learning as a result of training has been transferred to job and has resulted in improved performance.

(e) Follow up studies to find out whether training has brought about specific behavioral changes in the trainees and how well they have retained the learning.

Besides assessing the usefulness of a training programme, evaluation also helps, in finding out the deficiencies of the programme and in devising better programmes in future. Any evaluation begins with the criteria which depend on the objectives. Some of the criteria could be:

(a) Reaction of Trainees, i.e., whether the participants liked or disliked the programme.

(b) Learning, i.e., whether the concepts, ideas and principles of the training were intellectually assimilated by the participants.

(c) Behavioral Changes, i.e., whether the training caused people to alter their behavior on job.

(d) Impact on Organization Effectiveness, i.e., whether the modified behavior caused positive result, such as an increased output, improved quality and lower costs.

These criteria can be viewed as either subjective or objective.

Subjective Criteria call for opinions of participants who are asked about their impressions of training effectiveness. This can be done during training at its close or at some period after the training has ended. Similar evaluation may be made by trainees and management.

Objective Criteria relate to effects of training by measuring specific outcomes. For example, review is made of performance appraisal of trainees following the training programme.

After the evaluation is made, the situation should be analyzed to find the probable causes for a difference between expected outcome and actual outcome. Consequently necessary precautions should be taken for designing and implementing future programme to avoid these.

15. RESPONSIBILITY FOR TRAINING

In an organization the responsibility of training lies on top management, personnel department and training supervisors. Top management is responsible for training policy, its review and training budget. Personnel department is responsible for arrangement, conducting and evaluation of training programme. Supervisors are responsible for giving training to trainees. The supervisors should be assigned the tasks those who are having perfect knowledge of the jobs. All supervisors should not be assigned this task otherwise it may leads to problems or improper training. For fixing the responsibility of training and development the special care is to be taken so that the objectives of training and development should not be defeated.

16. CONCLUSION

Training is defined as "the act of increasing the knowledge and skills of an employee for doing a particular job." Training implies activities that teach employees how to perform their present jobs better. It is the training that prepares people to perform their present jobs more efficiently. Training teaches employees required skills, knowledge or attitudes and helps them in improving their performance by improving new skills, new techniques of doing the work and by improving their work habits. Training is thus aimed at improving the performance of personnel in their present positions or jobs. Training consists of planned programme designed to improve performance at the individual groups, and organizational levels. Improved performance, intern, and implies that there have been measurable changes in knowledge, skills, attitudes and social behavior. Development of employees refers to those activities that prepare them for future jobs or positions. Development represents all those activities or programs of teaching skills, knowledge or attitudes that increase employee's potential and prepare them for future positions. The distinction between training and development is very thin. Whereas training prepares employees for performing present jobs, development prepares employees for future assignments. The difference between training and development is primarily one of the intent and can be made on two counts, namely contents and the level of employees for which they are directed. Training is generally linked with the operational tasks and goals of the organization. Training programs are confined to improve job related skills so as to enable employees to perform their present jobs in a better way. These programs help in preparing them for a particular job. Their need for training is limited to knowledge, skills and technology needed for the present jobs. Development programs are linked with the future needs of the organization needed for future managerial positions.

Training is a short-term process utilizing a systematic and organized procedure by which non-managerial personnel acquire technical knowledge and skills for a definite purpose. Training is a short term process utilizing a systematic and organized procedure by which non-managerial personnel acquire technical knowledge and skills for a definite purpose. The need for training and development has been felt to improve the effectiveness of human resource in the organization so the competitive advantages can be achieved. The different methods have been used for this purpose and these are used in different organizations. In an organization the responsibility of training lies on top management, personnel department and training supervisors. Top management is responsible for training policy, its review and training budget. Personnel department is responsible for arrangement, conducting and evaluation of training programme. Supervisors are responsible for giving training to trainees. The future for training and development will be very bright because the products, services and expectations of the customers and clients are increasing day by day. The company with competent human resource only can handle the situation in the market and enjoy the leadership in the field.

17. QUESTIONS FOR REVIEW

1. Define training and compare it with development.
2. Discuss importance of training. How would you assess training needs?
3. Explain objectives and principles of training.
4. Highlight on the job training methods in detail.
5. Describe off the job training methods used by many organizations.
6. Mention the steps involved in training process.
7. Short notes on:
   (a) Types of training
   (b) Levels of training
   (c) Responsibility for training
   (d) Classroom lectures
   (e) Role playing
   (f) Workshops and seminars
   (g) Case study method

8. Discuss importance to training evaluation to make training more effective.
9. Training gives knowledge; knowledge gives confidence and better performance. Dissus.
10. Short notes on:
    (a) Simulation
    (b) Vestibule method
    (c) Apprenticeship
    (d) Internship.

18. OBJECTIVE QUESTIONS

1. "The act of increasing the knowledge and skills of an employee for doing a particular job" is known as:
    (a) Recruitment
    (b) Training
    (c) Promotion
    (d) Increment
    (e) Transfer
2. Training is a short-term process utilizing a systematic and organized procedure by which non-managerial personnel acquire knowledge and skills for a definite purpose. This is:
    (a) Technical
    (b) Theoretical
    (c) Practical
    (d) b and c
    (e) None of the above
3. Broadly speaking the objectives of education and training programme contribute to.
    1. Greater organizational effectiveness
    2. Accomplishment of the employee's personal objectives
    3. Promotion of individual
    (a) Only 1
    (b) Only 2
    (c) 1 & 2 both
    (d) All the above
    (e) None of this
4. The duties and responsibilities of the job, together with the knowledge, skills and abilities needed to perform them are the focus of the second stage of needs analysis called:
    (a) Job analysis
    (b) Job duties
    (c) Need analysis
    (d) Task analysis
    (e) None of the above

5. The attempts to determine which employees should receive training and what their current levels of skill and knowledge are known as:
   (a) Organizational analysis
   (b) Workers analysis
   (c) Individual analysis
   (d) Group analysis
   (e) All the above

6. The employees are provided training through the apprenticeship system varying in length up to period of five years. They are:
   (a) Skilled Workers
   (b) Unskilled Workers
   (c) Semi-skilled Workers
   (d) Senior and Supervisory Staffs
   (e) None of the above

7. Techniques of training that are generally used to impart training are categorized as
   1. On the job techniques
   2. Off the job techniques.
   3. Classroom techniques
   (a) Only 1
   (b) Only 2
   (c) Both 1 & 2
   (d) All the three
   (e) None of this

8. The method makes the trainee an assistant to the current job holder. The trainee learns by experience, observations and limitation. This method is known as:
   (a) Understudy
   (b) Coaching
   (c) Apprenticeship
   (d) Simulation
   (e) Case study

9. This is the method of stimulating trainees to creative thinking. This approach developed by Alex Osborn seeks to reduce inhibiting forces by providing for a maximum of posers and ideas are invited
   (a) Brainstorming
   (b) Sensitivity Training
   (c) Self-study
   (d) Programmed Instruction
   (e) Simulation

10. The training process includes these steps:
    (a) Corporate objectives and training strategy.
    (b) Identification of training needs and fixing training goals.
    (c) Designing and conducting training programme.
    (d) Evaluation of training programme.
    (e) All the above

11. The process of evaluation of training programme involves these steps:
    1. Devising evaluation criteria before training begins.
    2. Pretest to know the level of knowledge of worker before training.
    3. Post tests are the test after the training to know the level of knowledge after training and improvement if any made as a result of training

    (a) 1 & 2 (b) 2 & 3
    (c) 1 & 3 (d) 1, 2 & 3
    (e) None of the above

Answer Keys:

Question No.	Answer	Question No.	Answer
1	b	7	c
2	a	8	a
3	c	9	a
4	d	10	e
5	c	11	d
6	a		

Chapter

15 Management Development

1. INTRODUCTION

Under the era of globalization and liberalization, the business environment is undergoing changes drastically. All external environmental factors are undergoing changes and in this situation nothing is certain except changes. There are uncertainty and risks in the business. Now multinational companies have entered in markets of different countries with high degree of technology and with rich resources. Tough competition is being faced in domestic as well as international markets. It has become very difficult to grow, stabilize and excel in the business activities. To understand and work in this uncertain situation is a great challenge. Further, it is needed to perform better and before other competitors. The need for higher degree of skills and knowledge is strongly felt in this situation. Talented and motivated human resource is needed at present. Sincere efforts must be put to develop human resource of the organization at all levels. The development activities for workers, supervisors, managers, and board members are needed. Through talented manpower competitive advantage can be achieved over other competitors. Human resource development is a systematic and planned activities designed by an organization to provide its members with the opportunities and facilities to learn necessary skills and develop competencies to perform the current jobs and prepare them for further jobs also. Human resource development process is facilitated by mechanisms or subsystems like role analysis, performance appraisal, training, organizational development, potential development, job rotation, welfare and reward. People are helped to acquire new competencies through the various systems continuously. This has been realized and accepted at macro, micro and individual levels.

2. MANAGEMENT

We needed **management** in past and today also to get the desired result effectively and efficiently. The nature of **management** practices have varied area to area and jobs to jobs. At present there is need of **management** in each and every aspect of our lives including different activities in an organization. The management practices are used in our personal life, family, social, economic, political and professional areas. Where we consider the activity is less important then less time and focus is given on that activity. Management is a group of persons that is having control over business activities in an organization. The main functions performed by management of the company are planning, organizing, controlling, directing, motivating people and budgeting for activities. These functions take place in every organization and are highly integrated with each other directly or indirectly.

It can be said the management is the art of getting the work done from others by utilizing the available resources effectively and efficiently to achieve the predetermined goals. The different types of activities are being performed in an organization such as production, marketing, financial, human resource, logistic, research and development, storage etc., These jobs are performed by different persons because all jobs cannot be performed by one person or a team due to limitations of an individual. That each team is called a branch of management. In management also the people are working at lower, middle and top levels. Top level of management is mainly involved in planning and controlling activities, Middle level of management is involved in direction and controlling more and less in planning work. The lower level of management is involved in execution of plans and involved in performing the tasks and getting work done from their subordinates.

In the present situation to perform a variety of functions a high degree of managerial skills is needed. It is to be developed timely so that the work is not affected adversely. The management enjoys the higher authority in an organization and they delegate the authority to their subordinate as per requirement to get the jobs performed. The team of management is responsible for achieving the objectives of the organization. They put their best efforts to get the work done from subordinates. During this they guide, instruct, counsel and motivate the people to get their high level of commitments towards accomplishment of the targets. The resources are being used as per the need of the business activities, these resources are used very effectively and efficiently. The role of management in an organization is very important. So there is strong need for development of the management team so that their efficiency can be improved in the competitive global markets and organization gets the advantage along with the managerial staff also.

In a business organizations the co-ordination and direction of the efforts of others is a major part of the management job. The manager has to deal not only with the staff but also with others outside his own group, and has a decided influence on the organization. In any organization, each supervisor, foreman, executive is a manager in the area of his responsibility. In the past, the emphasis has been on the technical or functional aspects of management. Early writers on classical management such as Fayol described management in largely systematic, functional terms. Management is concerned with achieving organizational goals through: Forecasting, Planning, Organizing, Motivating, Co-ordinating, Controlling, Directing. People who developed these technical skills and were delegated the authority to use them, became the 'elite' group in organizations known as management. Modern theories of management highlight the multidimensional role in different areas as under:

(a) Dealing competently with organizational policies.

(b) Successful managing change.

(c) Confronting ethical issues and dilemmas.

(d) Ensuring personal 'survival' and career success in organizations.

(e) Safeguarding personal health in a stressful environment.

3. DEVELOPMENT

Development is necessary to bring interest in the activities and without any development, interest is lost. Development means improvement over the existing position. It can be applied to any area of our life. Development of employees refers to those activities that prepare them for future jobs or positions. Development represents all those activities or programmes of teaching skills, knowledge or attitude that increase employee's potential and prepare them for future positions. The environment is uncertain and changes are taking place rapidly. With the high level of competition and advance technology a gap between existing and required competencies exists. The tasks cannot be performed as per the changing needs of the organisation for lack of high level of competencies. These are to be improved and prepared the human resource for performing the present jobs and preparing them for future assignment. Due to development activities the requirement of competencies will be always in line with the organizational requirement. It would be well to tune to time and requirement. The distinction between training and development is very thin. Whereas training prepares employees for performing present jobs, development prepares employees for future assignment. In training the knowledge and skills are improved pertaining to the current jobs. The employees are put on job or off job training and they are taught about the system, working procedure, difficulties faced and solutions of the difficulties faced during current jobs. The current jobs can be performed effectively. The objective of development activities is to keep the effectiveness of the organization high even in future also.

4. MANAGEMENT DEVELOPMENT

In present scenario, the global business environment is changing rapidly. The effectiveness of the organization as a whole is under threat to sustain further. Organizations are putting best efforts to keep pace with the changing environment and keep them fit the competitive situation by improving overall performance. It has been realized that it is only manpower that plays very vital role in improving effectiveness of the organization. The need for organization development has been strongly felt. One of the important OD intervention is management development through which the managerial staff is selected, trained, motivated, and equipped for future assignments. Whenever vacancies arise, they are given opportunity for promotion from within the organization. They avoid appointing trained managers from outside. This helps in satisfying the development needs of the existing managers and provides satisfaction and motivation. Ultimately it develops loyalty to organization.

In future the organization would be position to maintain good relations, working environment and high reputation to attract talented managers in the organization. The organization gets multidimensional benefits from management development process. This practice has been accepted worldwide and even in developing countries also. It is the sponsored programme by the organization for education, training, improving skills, providing opportunities and position in future so that the changes are managed properly. Since last three decades management development has become more popular due to its contribution in economic success of the organization. The attitude of management has been shifted to human resource and considered that human resource is the most important resource of the organization that utilizes other resources and generated them further in the interest of the organization. The organization with talented and motivated workforce can survive and grow in stiff competitive situation even with shortage of other resources.

The manager is the dynamic life-giving element in a business. The caliber and performance of managers will largely determine the success of a business. If the business wants to improve the quality of its managers, it must expend money and effort and introduce imaginative and systematic development schemes for them in which as managers they play a crucial role. All enterprises need to devote great attention to the continuous supply of their future managers — both functional and general. The management development process ensures that the enterprise has the effective managers it needs to accomplish its present and future requirements. It seeks to improve the performance of existing managers providing them relevant opportunities to grow and develop. It also ensures that management succession within the organization is provided for. Thus, it increases the organization's business strategies.

Management Development is a process in which managers working at different levels learn and improve their ability, capability, knowledge and skills for improving the performance of individual as well as the organization. The effectiveness of managers at work contributes a lot to the success of every organization. The new approach of human resource management is that money used in development of employees and managers is considered as an investment and not as a cost. Along with their jobs the managerial staff is provided opportunities to learn and improve their competencies. This whole process is known as management development. The managerial staff is prepared to improve their performance on present jobs and preparing them for further assignments also. Management development is a systematic process of training and growth by which managerial personnel gain and supply skills, knowledge, attitudes and insights to manage the work in their organizations effectively and efficiently. Management development program includes the activities short courses, leadership courses, management education and training programs, coaching, guiding and mentoring. These programmes can be conducted in-house or outside by consultants or experts.

5. DEFINITIONS OF MANAGEMENT DEVELOPMENT

Management development is defined by the leading management experts as follows:

(a) "A conscious and systematic process to control the development of managerial resources in the organization for the achievement of goals and strategies." (Molauder, 1986)

(b) "An attempt to improve managerial effectiveness through a planned and deliberate learning process."

(c) "It is a programme of training and planned personal development purporting to prepare and aid managers in their present and future jobs." (Yoder)

(d) "Management development is a business led process. The business determines what kind of managers it requires to accomplish its strategic goals as well as how to obtain and develop such managers. Although there is stress of self-development, the business must indicate the directions towards which self-development should occur?" (Armstrong)

(e) That function which from deep understanding of business goals and organizational requirements, undertakes are:

   (i) To forecast need, skill mixes and profiles for many positions and level.

   (ii) To design and recommend the professional, career and personal development to ensure competence.

   (iii) To move from the concept of management to the concept of 'managing'.

(f) The process of ensuring that an organization has the appropriate management skills and competencies to meet its developing needs. Existing skills and abilities are assessed and actual or potential shortfalls are identified with the aim of ameliorating them. Various programmes and interventions may be used for this purpose, including training, *mentoring,* or role-play and *team building* exercises. - *A Dictionary of Business and Management*

(g) "The process of developing knowledge, skills, ability, and capability called competences of managerial and potential managerial staff of the organization. It is a planned process to manage the changes by talented and motivated managers for improving overall effectiveness of the organization"

From the study of various definitions of management development it is said that it is an intervention for development of the organization. This is the approach of the management to deal with the planned changes in the organization. Keeping in view the changing needs of the environment the managerial staff is educated, trained and equipped with the competencies so that as and when the need arises can be managed effectively. The objective of management development process is to improve the effectiveness of the organization through effectiveness of managers and potential managers in future. Through this the organization improves internal strength of manpower. The approach is focusing present as well as future.

6. NEED FOR MANAGEMENT DEVELOPMENT

A business organization has to develop the potential of all those who are in management positions or who are fresh from management positions or who are fresh from management institutions and have the potential for development. This development is necessary because of the following reasons:

(a) The competition for talented people who are capable of development is increasing. They are less in supply as per the demand. The need for their development in organization is felt. The talented persons can give better performance for improving effectiveness of the organization.

(b) Society is facing a rapid rate of technological and social change. Under changing business environment the changes are to be managed so that technology can be operated properly and products and services can be modified as per needs of the customers in the society.

(c) Business and industrial leaders are increasingly recognizing their social and public responsibilities which call for a much broader outlook on the part of management. The social responsibility is to be fulfilled to stay in high image of the public.

(d) Managers have to be developed for handling problems arising out of increasing size and complexity of organizations. Due to entry in a large number of markets with more number of products the size is increasing and organization is becoming more complex. To deal with this situation the skilled managers are needed.

(e) There is need to improve performance despite these complicated environmental factors. The efforts are needed in business to improve its product, lower its cost and extend its use will continue to be a major aim of managers. The high competency managers are needed for this purpose.

(f) Management labour relations are becoming increasingly complex. Due to diversity in organization the relationship between different parties becomes a major issue. The trained and experienced managers can deal this situation properly for developing healthy work environment.

(g) To understand and adjust to changes in socio-economic forces including changes in public policy and concepts of social justice and industrial democracy problems of ecology.

But it was also pointed out that if the human resource is to become a critical success factor; organizations must be prepared to develop individual managers and management teams that are not only flexible, adaptable and innovative in technical, financial and business issues, but skilled in HRM as well. To achieve this, organizations must be prepared to establish as a strategic imperative, greater investment in continuous management education and development.

Organizations which take sincere efforts and invest in management development process for development of the managers and potential managers, gets benefits in the following activities:

(a) Exploit future opportunities and potential.

(b) Adapt successfully in the face of major change.

(c) Develop new markets and products.

(d) Retain and motivate employees.

(e) Create and sustain an effective management team.

(f) Survive and prosper.

From the study of the above mentioned points it is said that the management development is the need of the changing global business environment. The change agents take it as an OD intervention for educating, training and motivating the managers to shoulder the challenging responsibility. This contributes in improving the performance of managers, employees and organization with healthy working relationship. The organization gets multidimensional benefits out of this. Due to these reasons management development is needed in the present competitive situation.

7. MANAGEMENT DEVELOPMENT PROCESS

Management development programme must be conducted effectively. In this process, many steps are to be taken by the management. The following interrelated steps are involved in MD process:

(a) Organization Planning

This step is concerned with ascertaining development needs that calls for organizational planning and forecast of its needs for present and future growth. This is generally based upon a comprehensive program of job description, job specification and job analysis. The management should ascertain well in advance the future course of organizational development, the kind of executives needed and kind of education, experience, training, special knowledge, skill, personal traits, etc., required for each work. Most companies train their own executives except when they experience a critical shortage of specialized high level talent. In the latter case, executives are hired from outside.

(b) Assessment of Present Management Talent

It is made with a view to determine qualitatively the type of personnel that is available within an organization itself. The performance of a management individual is compared with the standard expected of him. His personal traits are also analyzed so that a value judgment may be made of his potential for advancement.

(c) Preparation of Management Manpower Inventory

It is prepared for the purpose of getting complete information about each management individual's bio-data and educational qualifications, the result of tests and performance appraisal. The information is generally maintained on cards, one for each individual. It may also be maintained on replacement tables or charts. From these, it can be known that several capable executives are available for training for higher positions.

(d) MD Programme Planning

It is undertaken to meet the needs of different individuals keeping in view the differences in their attitudes and behavior and in their physical, intellectual and emotional qualities. The weak and strong points of an individual are known from his performance appraisal reports and on the basis of these tailor-made programmes are framed and launched. Such programmes give due attention to the interests and goals of the subordinates as well as the training and development opportunities which exist within an organization.

(e) Implementation of Development Programme

This job is done by the personnel department. A comprehensive and well conceived programme is generally prepared containing concentrated brief courses. Such courses may be in the field of human relations, time and motion study, creative thinking, memory training, decisionmaking, leadership courses and courses in profession and the time and the cost involved.

(f) Evaluation of Development Programme

The evaluation of training has been defined by Hamblin as "any attempt to obtain information on the effects of training programme and to assess the value of training in the light of that information." According to him, the objectives of evaluation training are: assessing the reactions of trainees, job behavior, improvement in performance, contribution to organizational objectives etc. The means of evaluating development programmes may include: observation ratings, surveys, interviews etc.

If these steps are followed meticulously, the objective of MD programme will be accomplished effectively. The managers and organization both would be benefitted by management development programme.

8. OBJECTIVES OF MD PROGRAMME

Managerial development is very significant in the context of industrial and organizational management. Among the five factors of production, management is the most important. It acts as a leader; it takes work from the other factors. Without management any factor cannot work. Hence, more efficient and economical production and industrial development is based on the efficient management only.

Management can collect good and right factors and can establish effective coordination among them. To create good relations between factors and departments of organization and establishment of good relations between labour and capital is possible through the efficient management only. Hence with the maximum production at minimum cost, one can withstand competition in the market easily and establish the credit in the market. At present, specialization of of scientific management and mechanization are given more stress. This has developed the importance of management. All those jobs of the industry could be done only through the efficient management and the efficient management can be made through the main objectives of management development programme which are:

(a) To assure right number of managers of required skills.

(b) To improve skills of managers.

(b) To improve performance of managers.

(d) To improve leadership quality of managers.

(e) To improve relations and cooperation between departments.

(f) To encourage managers to grow and accept responsibility at higher level.

(g) To maintain good performance of managers throughout their employment.

(h) To improve the efficiency of managers as well as organization.

9. METHODS OF MANAGEMENT DEVELOPMENT

(a) On the Job Methods

When an executive is thoroughly committed to the need for developing his subordinates and is qualified and willing to give time for development, possibly, on the job method is the best method. It is the most common and formal method of executive development. The following methods are important in this connection:

(i) **Coaching:** When a manager takes an active role in guiding another manager, we refer to this activity as coaching. Just as track coaches observe, analyze and attempt to improve the performance of their athletes, "coaches" on the job can do the same. The effective coach, whether on the track or in the corporate hierarchy, gives guidance through direction, advice, criticism and suggestion in an attempt to aid the growth of employee.

(ii) **Understudy assignments:** The summer methods in organization are characterized by a particular phenomenon: a rapid rise in the usage of understudy assignment, as development technique to replace vacationing managers. By understudy assignments, we mean potential managers are given an opportunity to relieve an experienced manager of his or her job, and act as his or her substitute during the period. This label also describes permanent "assistant to" positions as well as temporary opportunities to assist managers in completing their jobs.

(iii) **Position rotation:** The next method of executive development is position rotation. The major objective of job rotation training is the broadening of the background of trainee in the organization. If an executive is rotated periodically from one job to another job, he acquires a general background. The main advantages are: it provides a general background in all functional area of the business. Training takes place in actual situation. Competition can be stimulated among the rotating trainees. However due to rapid specialization this technique has become less effective and less useful.

(iv) **Committee assignments:** Assignment to a committee can provide an opportunity for the employee to share in managerial decision making to learn by watching others, and to investigate specific organizational problems. When committees are of an *'ad hoc'* or temporary nature, they often take on task force activities designed to level into particular problem, ascertain alternative solution and make a recommendation for implementing a solution. These temporary assignments can be both interesting and rewarding to the employees' growth. Appointment to permanent committees increases the employee's exposure to other members of the organization, broadens his or her understanding and provides an opportunity to grow and make recommendations under the scrutiny of other committee members.

(v) **Special project:** This is a very flexible method. Under this method an executive may be assigned a project that is closely related to the objectives of his department. For instance, a trainee may be assigned to develop a system of cost control in the execution of an order. The trainee will study the problem and make recommendations upon it. This project would also help in educating the trainee, the importance of cost and understand the organizational relationships with the accounting and other departments. Thus, the trainee acquires the knowledge of allied subjects also.

(vi) **Committees and junior boards of management:** These are composed of middle level managers selected on the basis of merit rating who meet regularly and act as idea men. Their proposals are considered by responsible general executive and may be referred to the Board of Directors if found suitable. This broadens the perspective of the members and instills in them a sense of responsibility.

(b) Off the Job Methods

In these methods, the executives have to leave their work place/office and devote their entire time to the development objective. The following methods come under this category:

(i) **Lecture courses:** Formal lecture courses offer an opportunity for managers or potential managers to acquire knowledge and develop their conceptual and analytical abilities. In large organizations, these lecture courses may be offered in-house "by the organization itself and supported by outside college course work. Small organizations can utilize courses offered in development programs at universities and colleges and through consulting organizations. Often, college and university faculties are willing to provide the unique needs of an organization.

(ii) **Role playing:** Role playing technique is used for human relations and leadership training. Its purpose is to give trainees an opportunity to learn human relations skills through practice and it develops insight into one's own behavior and its effect upon others. Thus its objective is very narrow, i.e., to increase the trainee's skill in dealing with others. It can be used in human relations training and sales training because both these involve dealing with other people.

(iii) **Sensitivity training:** Sensitivity training or 'T-group' training means the development awareness and sensitivity to behavioral patterns of oneself and others. It is an experience in interpersonal relationships, which result in a change in feeling and attitudes towards oneself and others. T-groups are helpful in unlearning and learning certain things. They help the participants to understand how groups actually work and give them a chance to discover how they are interpreted by others. It also aims at increasing tolerance power of the individual and his ability to understand others. The sensitivity training programmes are generally conducted under controlled laboratory conditions.

(iv) **In basket exercise:** This is a variant of simulation. The trainee is provided with a desk and a variety of immediate problems in his basket. His reactions and decisions become the basis for critical evaluation and discussion.

(v) **Transactional analysis:** In this practice it is assumed that people have three basic states of being — parent, child and adult. These states or traits are manifest in their transactions as a regulator and evaluator of others. Person influenced by the child trait tend to feel inferior and dominated. Those with the adult trait view life as it is experienced in reality. One figures it out by oneself not as one was taught or how one wished or fancied it to be. Two persons with the adult trait will conduct a transaction with thoughts and mutual recognition with T. A. training can lead to modified behavior by providing personal insights.

(vi) **Management games:** Games, which are frequently played on an electronic computer that has been programmed for the particular game, provide opportunities for individuals to make decisions and to consider the implications of a decision on the other segments of the organization with no adverse effect, should the decision be a poor one.

(vii) **Conference methods:** They permit trainees to think about problems, express themselves, assess the opinion of others, understand teamwork and develop leadership conferences — include human relations, supervision, general economic understanding, personnel administration, labour relations and allied numerous problems.

10. MANAGEMENT EDUCATION

The demand for management education has increased in the last two decades. Due to liberalization the challenges and opportunities for aspirants for managerial posts have been increased. To meet the requirement of managerial staff the governments across the globe have taken initiatives. In India now the government permitted the management and technical education institutions in private sector. At present there are nearly 5000 management and technical institutions providing education at graduation and postgraduation levels. The students are educated and trained in their respective field in the institutes. These students are absorbed by the industries across the country. There is a need to match the curriculum and structure of education to the growing needs of the industry. These institutes started providing short-term and regular programmes for fresher as well as working executives. Some time the candidates in jobs are sponsored by the companies. The objective of sponsoring the working staff is to educate, train and motivate the employees for new assignments in future.

In last two years the government authority has given liberal permission for more number of such institutions. Due to this the quality of education for technical and managerial staff has been affected. In present time it has been reported by the industry people that the competencies of fresh candidates is not up to requirement of the industry. They lack in communication, analytical technical and decision making skills. It has become necessary to evaluate the quality of education provided by these institutions in private sector. Government has taken steps in this direction to maintain quality of education in field of technical and management. Government has taken step and has introduced accreditation in universities and institutes under control of governments. Accreditation is the end process Quality Assurance. NAAC has been made responsible for assessing the quality of course structures, methods of teaching, infrastructure, selection and appointment of staff and faculty members, development of faculty members, students counseling and supports etc. The accreditation certificate awarded to the institute ensures its standard of education and reputation. Parliament passed an act for establishment of All Indian Council of Technical Education (AICTE) with the objective of promoting, regulating and developing management and technical education in India.

It is responsible for defining the basic framework for maintaining quality of the business education, granting permission for starting new institutes and expansion of existing institutes. But still there are many problems faced and due to that the effectiveness of management education has gone down. Despite a number of weaknesses the body is working with focus on course curriculum, quality assurance, selection and appointment of faculty members, infrastructure facilities, role of management institutions, periodic inspections, value and ethics involved in administration etc., the main functions of this body are developing management education and scientific method, exercising supervisions over management institutions, organizing seminars, workshops and conferences, carrying out research and publication activities. The existing system of Management Education is still affected due to profit interests of owners to a good extent. There is a gap between the subjects and the objectives of management education and this cannot achieve goals of management development, creating spiritual, ethical, moral values in business etc., It is assumed that if AICTE performs its functions properly then the quality of management and technical education would definitely improve.

11. ENVIRONMENT FOR MANAGEMENT DEVELOPMENT

Environment means the surrounding or atmosphere in which the employees are working in a particular organization. Environment is affected by attitude of management, relationship between managers and employees, rules, regulations, authority, delegation of authority, autonomy, accountability, responsibility, working conditions, welfare and compensation system. All these factors are controllable factors and management can adjust these factors to create healthy working environment. If the healthy working environment is created, management development programme is possible. Otherwise question of MD programme does not arise. Further to plan, implement and review MD programme, support of top management is essential.

Initiative should be taken by the top management in this regard. The general awareness regarding globalization and challenges created by this should be very high. The management should analyse the situation very carefully and timely. The emerging trends are to be indentified and their impacts are to be assessed. The gap between the existing and required talents should be found with the help of experts or consultants. There should be open discussion with the experts in this regard. For development of the organization the different interventions are to be decided. The management development is one of them. The proper focus should be given on this because the business activities are planned and managed by the managers. Proper support, allocation of budget and favourable change in attitude of top management towards manpower would create healthy environment. That is highly suitable for management development programme in the progressive organization.

12. CONCLUSION

Now multinational companies have entered in markets of different countries with high degree of technology and with rich resources. Tough competition is being faced in domestic as well as international markets. It has become very difficult to grow, stabilize and excel in the business activities. To understand and work in this uncertain situation is a great challenge. Further, it is needed to perform better and before other competitors. The need for higher degree of skills and knowledge is strongly felt in this situation. Talented and motivated human resource is needed at present. Sincere efforts must be put to develop human resource of the organization at all levels. The development activities for workers, supervisors, managers, and board members are needed. Through talented manpower competitive advantage can be achieved over other competitors.

Management is a group of persons that is having control over business activities in an organization. The main functions performed by management of the company are planning, organizing, controlling, directing, motivating people and budgeting for activities. These functions take place in every organization and are highly integrated with each other directly or indirectly. The management enjoys the higher authority in an organization and they delegate the authority to their subordinate as per requirement to get the jobs performed. The team of management is responsible for achieving the objectives of the organization.. The role of management in an organization is very important. So there is strong need for development of the management team so that their efficiency can be improved in the competitive global markets and organization gets the advantage along with the managerial staff also. Management Development is a process in which managers working at different levels learn and improve their ability, capability, knowledge and skills for improving the performance of individual as well as organization. The effectiveness of managers at work contributes a lot to the success of every organization.

From the study of various definitions of management development it is said that it is an intervention for development of the organization. This is the approach of the management to deal with the planned changes in the organization. Keeping in view the changing needs of the environment the managerial staff is educated, trained and equipped with the competencies so that as and when the need arises can be managed effectively. The objective of management development process is to improve the effectiveness of the organization through effectiveness of managers and potential managers in future. Organizations which take sincere efforts and invest in management development process for development of the managers and potential managers, it gets benefits to exploit future opportunities and potential, adapt successfully in the face of major changes, develop new markets and products, retain and motivate employees, create and sustain an effective management team, and survive and prosper. The interrelated steps involved in MD process are organization planning, assessment of present management talent, preparation of management manpower inventory, MD programme planning, implementation and evaluation of development programme

The demand for management education has increased in the last two decades. Due to liberalization the challenges and opportunities for aspirants for managerial posts have been increased. To meet the requirement of managerial staff the governments across the globe have taken initiatives. In last two years the government authority has given liberal permission for more number of such institutions. Due this the quality of education for technical and managerial staff has been affected. In present time it has been reported by the industry people that the competencies of fresh candidates is not up to requirement of the industry. They lack in communication, analytical technical and decision making skills. It has become necessary to evaluate the quality of education provided by these institutions in private sector. The existing system of Management Education is still affected due to profit interests of owners to a good extent. There is a gap between the subjects and the objectives of management education and this cannot achieve goals of management development, creating spiritual, ethical, moral values in business etc. For any sort of development activity a healthy work environment is necessary. If the healthy working environment is created, management development programme is possible. Otherwise question of MD programme does not arise. Further to plan, implement and review MD programme, support of top management is essential.

13. QUESTIONS FOR REVIEW

1. Define management development and discuss the need for management development.
2. What are the functions performed by managers/executives in present time?
3. Highlight the main steps involved in management development process.
4. Explain the essential elements of a MD programme.
5. Describe the objectives of MD programme in detail.
6. Which methods would you suggest for management development?
7. Short notes on:
   (a) Environment for management development.
   (b) Sensitivity training method
   (c) Identification to MD needs.
   (d) Development programme planning.
   (e) Review to MD Programme.
   (f) Management education

14. OBJECTIVE QUESTIONS

1. It described management in largely systematic, functional terms. Management is concerned with achieving organizational goals through: forecasting, planning, organizing, motivating, coordinating, controlling, and directing. This has been defined by:
   (a) Rao and Abraham (b) Fayol
   (c) Ishwar Dayal (d) All the above
   (e) None of the Above
2. It is management development, through which the managerial staff is selected, trained, motivated, and equipped them for future assignments. Whenever vacancies arise, they are given opportunity for promotion from within the organization. They avoid appointing trained managers from outside. This helps in satisfying the development needs of the existing managers and provides satisfaction and motivation. Ultimately it develops loyalty to organization. It is known as:
   (a) Management development (b) OD intervention
   (c) Organization development (d) All the above
   (e) None of the above
3. It is a process in which managers working at different levels learn and improve their ability, capability, knowledge and skills for improving the performance of individual as well as organization. The effectiveness of managers at work contributes a lot to the success of every organization. It is known as:
   (a) Human resource development
   (b) Management development process
   (c) Management development
   (d) Career development
   (d) None of them
4. It is a systematic process of training and growth by which managerial personnel gain and supply skills, knowledge, attitudes and insights to manage the work in their organizations effectively and efficiently. Management development program includes the activities short courses, leadership courses, management education and training programs, coaching, guiding and mentoring. These programmes can be conducted in-house or outside by consultants or experts. It is known as:
   (a) Management development
   (b) Management development program
   (c) Management development process
   (d) Organization development process
   (e) All of the above

5. "Management development is a business led process. The business determines what kind of managers it requires to accomplish its strategic goals as well as how to obtain and develop such managers. Although there is stress of self-development, the business must indicate the directions towards which self-development should occur?"It has been defined by:
   (a) Molauder
   (b) Yoder
   (c) Armstrong
   (d) A Dictionary of Business and Management
   (e) None of them

6. Management development programmed must be conducted effectively. In this process, many steps are to be taken by the management. Which one is not inter related steps involved in MD process:
   (a) Organization planning
   (b) Assessment of present management talent
   (c) Preparation of management manpower inventory
   (d) Organization development planning
   (e) Implementation of development programme

7. When committees are of an *'ad hoc'* or temporary nature, they often take on task force activities designed to level into particular problem, ascertain alternative solution and make a recommendation for implementing a solution. These temporary assignments can be both interesting and rewarding to the employees' growth. Appointment to permanent committees increases the employee's exposure to other members of the organization, broadens his or her understanding and provides an opportunity to grow and make recommendations under the scrutiny of other committee members. It is known as:
   (a) Understudy assignments
   (b) Committee assignments
   (c) Position rotation
   (d) Coaching
   (e) All the above

8. T-groups are helpful in unlearning and learning certain things. They help the participants to understand how groups actually work and give them a chance to discover how they are interpreted by others. It also aims at increasing tolerance power of the individual and his ability to understand others. T-group training also known as:
   (a) Sensitivity training
   (b) Role playing
   (c) Lecture courses
   (d) Off the job method
   (e) None of them

9. In this practice it is assumed that people have three basic states of being — parent, child and adult. These states or traits are manifest in their transactions as a regulator and evaluator of others. Person influenced by the child trait tend to feel inferior and dominated. Those with the adult trait view life as it is experienced in reality. One figures it out by oneself not as one was taught or how one wished or fancied it to be. It is known as:
   (a) Transactional analysis
   (b) In basket exercise
   (c) Management games
   (d) Off the Job Methods
   (e) All the above

10. It is affected by attitude of management, relationship between managers and employees, rules, regulations, authority, delegation of authority, autonomy, accountability, responsibility, working conditions, welfare and compensation system.
   (a) Organization Environment
   (b) Environment
   (c) Working environment
   (d) Culture
   (e) None of the above

Answer Keys:

Question No.	Answer	Question No.	Answer
1	b	6	d
2	b	7	b
3	c	8	a
4	a	9	a
5	c	10	b

Chapter

Career Planning and Development

1. INTRODUCTION

The strong need for higher productivity and performance has been felt in every organization across the world because the situation is very competitive and critical. It has become very difficult to increase production or sales due to tough competition. The company is interested to increase the production volume and it can increase also but the demand of the products may not be there so strong in the market that the whole quantity would be consumed. The stock would be pilling up. This would lead to losses for the company. Every competitor is trying to increase its sales but cannot. The customers are divided among competitors. Further, the profitability can be increased by increasing price of the products. The increased price might give the deterrent effect on the sales. The management is in fix what to do and what not, to increase the profitability of the company. The way to solve this problem is through cost reduction by giving higher productivity and performance. The operation cost would go down and it would contribute definitely in increasing the production quantity, quality and profitability of the company.

The HR management is keenly interested for proper utilization of manpower so the performance can be increased and sustain in future also to keep on achieving targets. This can be done through different approach. For this purpose managing performance of employees as a whole is very important. Performance management takes care of this function. Performance management maintains, develops and motivates the people at work to give better results. In the present competitive situation the organization that gives better results can survive, stabilize, grow and excel in the performance. It helps a lot in achieving the objectives of HRM. Performance management includes activities to ensure that goals are consistently being met in an effective and efficient manner. Performance management can focus on performance of the organization, a department, processes to build a product or service, employees, etc. The performance management is mainly concern with the performance of the people, systems and organization. To achieve this objective performance management performs a variety of functions. These functions are summarized below:

(a) Create healthy work environment

(b) Develop performance plans

(c) Selection of appropriate people

(d) Decision regarding performance standard

(e) Plans for development of employees

(f) Measurement of performance

(g) Conducts performance feedback

(h) Design compensation, recognition and reward system

(i) Contributes in developing good will

To get the talented and experienced persons is very difficult and further it is more difficult to satisfy and motivate them and maintains so continuously. The different tools have been used by the performance management like proper recruitment and selection, placement, training and development, promotion, compensation, welfare, job security, rewards and recognition, career planning and development. Career planning and development is one of the tools of the management to improve the performance and maintain it consistently by satisfying their expectations and motivating them. Performance management in leading organizations is paying more attention on the career and its development of employees. The importance of this tool is increasing day by day and in future it would be contributing to achieve the objectives of performance management.

2. CAREER DEFINITIONS

In ancient time this awareness regarding career was not there before modernism, many workers would often inherit or take up a single lifelong position generally followed by their parents. The need for career selection was not felt at all. With the spread during the enlightenment of the idea of progress and of the habits of individualist self-betterment the need for career was felt. In present time the environment is very competitive and highly technology oriented. It has become for every individual to meet the two ends in life. For survival and grow everyone is compelled to choose the area to start and develop his career. Without proper career in life a lot of difficulties are to be faced. The progress would be stopped or hampered. For this it is the demand of every one to select, start and follow the career. Due to fast developing technology and education there is a wide range of choices of career and became possible to plan career. This situation has further created the opportunities for career counselors and career advisors to guide the people in selection and development of their career.

The word career covers all types of employment ranging from semi-skilled through skilled, and semi-professional to professional. The term *careers* have often been restricted to suggest an employment commitment to a single trade skill, profession or business firm for the entire working life of a person. In recent years, however, *career* now refers to changes or modifications in employment during the foreseeable future. The career concept is increasing importance in present time and it has been defined by experts as follows:

The initiative taken, tasks performed and progress done by a person throughout a lifetime, especially related to that individual job or profession. The concept of career generally includes the *jobs held, titles* achieved and *work/*targets achieved over a long *period* of time, rather than just referring to one *position.* The employees may stay with one job throughout their life of get their jobs change very frequently by analyzing the prevailing situation. For example a lawyer performs one job throughout his life with different clients whereas one person changes jobs from one sector to another and jobs also. One person working in government department as a clerk developed his educational qualification and resigned. He gets a new job in Industry as a manager as an accountant. After some years he changes the jobs and become customer relationship manager in a bank. These both cases are example of a career.

(a) The etymology of the term comes from the Latin word *carrera,* which means race as in "*rat_race*", a career is a course of successive situations that make up some activity, the series of jobs or positions a person held over a period of time by which one earns one's bread.

(b) Career is defined by the *Oxford English Dictionary* as an individual's "course or progress through life (or a distinct portion of life)". It is usually considered to pertain to remunerative work (and sometimes also formal *education*).

(c) The traditional concept of career has been concerned with progression up an ordered hierarchy within an organisation or profession. Career refers to an individual's *works* and life roles over their lifespan. This version of a career makes it clear that people can progress through their career horizontally as well as vertically.

(d) Career is a lifestyle concept that involves a sequence of work or leisure activities in which one engages throughout a lifetime. Careers are unique to each person and are dynamic, unfolding throughout life.

(e) A career is a sequence of positions/jobs held by a person during the course of his working life. According to Edwin B. Flippo, "Career is a sequence of separate but related work activities that provides continuity, order and meaning to a person's life".

(f) Broadly, the concept of career is used to refer to entire work life of an individual. It can be defined in a narrow sense, to be the succession of jobs and/or ranks held by a person in a particular organisation. An individual's career begins with placement in a job and ends with departure from the organisation which may be through retirement, resignation or death. In between, the career progression consists of changing tasks, tenure in various jobs, temporary or permanent promotions, transfers etc.

Career of an employee represents various jobs performed by him at different levels in an organisation during the course of his working life. This is show as career path. In the case of an ordinary worker, the career path includes the following job positions: Trainee – Probationer – Lower divisional clerk – Assistant upper divisional clerk- Upper divisional clerk – Assistant section officer- Section officer. In case of an executive in a marketing department of a company the career path might include the following position: Marketing executives – Senior executive – Assistant manager – Deputy manager – Manager – Senior manager – Asst General manager –Deputy General manager – General manager – Asst. Vice President – Vice President – Senior Vice President – President.

A career is the sum total of all of your work-related contributions to society in a lifetime. This includes time and effort spent to provide goods, services, or benefit to others. A career includes paid, un-paid, volunteer, part-time, and full-time positions. Your career includes many life roles you may not think of: student, homemaker, babysitter, office worker, doctor, lawyer, etc. A career encompasses all the roles you play and duties you perform. You may have many jobs or positions that make up your career, but you only have one overall career. There are various career options in the modern world of work: Self-Employed, Organization Employed, or Project-Employed.

No one is interested to work at one position in an organization throughout his life. Employees (of all categories) want to progress in their careers. This provides them higher level of salary, higher status and opportunity and to fulfil higher level of responsibility by using their knowledge, education and skills effectively. An individual with potentials joins a firm not for job but for career development in the long run. It becomes the responsibility of the organization to provide them with the better opportunities for their career development and get the best service for the organization. This improves the morale of the employees, leads to proper utilization of manpower; improve performance and productivity of employees as well as of organization.

3. CHARACTERISTICS OF CAREER

From the study of various definitions given by experts the characteristics of career are summarized and these are following:

(a) Everyone selects goals and objectives of his career in his life.

(b) The strategies are developed to achieve the goals and objectives.

(c) Every employee holds various positions/ jobs during the working life.

(d) Specific rules, policies or procedures are developed to implement the career strategy,

(e) Systematic evaluation of the career progress towards achievement of goals and objectives.

(f) Modification strategy to match the achievements of objectives and goals.

(g) Due to development of technology, education, social and commercial activities the need for career has been felt by everyone.

(h) Employees earn their bread and butter by selecting and developing their career.

(i) The scope for career counsellors and career advisors services has developed.

4. CLASSIFICATION/TYPES OF CAREER

For easy understanding of career, it can be classified as follows:

(a) Specific Job Career

It is identified with pursuance of career in one institution or department. The organization or department has not changed throughout the career.

(b) Cadre Career

Cadre career is one where a cluster or a group of posts are arranged vertically, i.e., hierarchically from lower to higher with different levels of responsibilities. Here, any member belonging to that cadre can be deployed to any of the posts, within the cadre-jurisdiction according to seniority, qualification, experience and pay scale.

(c) Inter Governmental Careers

These are identified with more than a single governmental jurisdiction. An example of this is All India Services, where members belonging to this service move from Centre to the States to occupy administrative positions. In India Indian Administrative Services officers work under central and state governments as per the jobs assigned to them. This pattern is followed in USA also.

There can also be two other concepts of career, namely, closed career and open career, depending on the limitations on entrance or the norm of recruitment.

(d) Closed Career System

The classification is done on the basis of entrance or norms of recruitment and selection of candidates. This can explained as one time entrance system, which means that once, at a young age, usually pre-determined, one enters the 'Monastery' or a specific cadre order, one has to spend an entire life time in that jurisdiction with no chance of coming out of it.

(e) The Open-Type Career System

This system can be described that the person is permitted to entree at any or all grade-levels, the entry is governed by certain conditions like qualification requirements, age and experience etc. The conditions are prescribed well in advance for a group of posts by the authority. The candidates are allowed on the basis of merit or conditioned fulfilled. This open career system is welcomed by the young blood because it gives opportunities for them to enter at all levels.

5. CAREER STAGES

From beginning of career to discharge from jobs the individuals passes through a number of stages. These stages are interrelated logically and in sequence. The requirements of persons vary from stage to stage. It is the responsibility of management to take special care of those requirements.

This would make the situation more comfortable for the employees of the organization. Individuals have different career development needs at different stages in their careers are explained below:

(a) Induction Stage

When an employee is recruited for a post in any cadre for long time, the candidate does know much about the organization. He is having a lot of confusions and anxiety about his job, rules and regulation, relationship with different persons and working pattern. The employer should take the charge of the situation and care for career of the candidate from that time itself. He is the beginner in the career and needs a lot of support. This is the stage for establishing identity in the organization. The management of the organization should take care of the candidate and help him in establishing his identity. The management should conduct the induction programme, familiarization of job and person, rule and regulation and job training on or off the job as per the need of the jobs. This helps a lot to the new candidate as it clears most of doubts, develops relationship with seniors, and provides supports in establishment in the organization. Due to these efforts of the management the new entrants are very comfortable in their jobs and starts their career in a happy mood.

(b) Establishment and Development Stage

The second stage is the establishment and developmental stage. The candidate in this stage of the career is well established and puts best efforts in the job to give higher performance and productivity that ultimately contribute in profitability and goodwill of the organization. This stage is also known as blooming stage of the career. This involves growing and getting established in a career: During this stage the candidate is at junior level. They should be oriented in such a way that they feel they are working in a good working environment and get lot of learning opportunities. They should develop positive attitude of the candidate towards the organisation. They should be assigned the challenging tasks with motivation of employees. Further, the management of the organization should develop the strategy to motivate them and get the best service from them for the organization. Time to time development opportunities are to be provided so that they can sharpen their skill. The candidates those who are lacking in competencies are to be identified and efforts should be there to arrange for training or retraining to develop their competencies so their effectiveness at jobs can be improved. It would give them the job satisfaction.

(c) Middle Level Stage

At this stage the employee has experience of working in a particular company of nearly 10 to 15 years. A person in job is having the knowledge of his job, working procedure, rules and regulation, company position and his career in future in present company. To get the best of such employees, proper dealing is needed. They should be taken into confidence while discussing HR polices or their interests should be considered. They should feel well secured in job. Further, there should be proper communication from management regarding their development and promotion opportunities. Their involvement in decision making should be increased to a good extent. This would provide them a high level of satisfaction. Finally, they would be committed to their job and the organisation. This would help to get the best efforts from them that is required by the management.

(d) Senior Level Stage

At this stage the employees are at the senior level. They have experience of a number of years. This is called full booming stage. Candidates are at senior position of management, enjoy higher status, assigned responsibility of higher level and get higher pay scale. They are involved in planning and policy formulation activities in the organization. To get the best performance from them the strategy of the organization should be to provide them better opportunities for exposure, adjusting them in different roles in their career, The top level management is career-oriented and providing them the opportunities for self-actualization, developing leadership quality, developing positive attitude towards the organization. All these would develop a high level of commitment of senior managers and provided them a high level of satisfaction. Finally, higher involvement in jobs would improve the performance, productivity and profitability of the organization. This is ultimate objective of performance management and that can be achieved very effectively.

(e) Retirement Stage

When a person reaches to the age of superannuation or resign or dies is called retirement stage. The persons have given their services to the organization for a long time. They have been with the company and best of the life has been given for the company. These persons should be treated with respect. At the age of retirement or death whatever the benefits they are supposed to get should be given without any problem. When there are leaving the organization they should be seen off with proper respect. After retirement, if any query or problem is there then it also should be dealt properly with respect. When they go out they should speak about the management of the company in positive sense. This would help the company in attracting talented and better employees in future.

6. CAREER MANAGEMENT

Career Management is a part of human resource management that takes care of career. For management of career of employees the major activities involved are planning and development related to career. The responsible manager in this first plans for the career of employees. The planning is related to each job in its department. It plans regarding the type of job, job description, job specification, movement of employees from one to another level and up to the top position, condition for movement etc., Further, for each level the competencies required, gap between the existing and required levels of competencies, need for development of knowledge and skills, selection of candidate for training and development etc are also to be planned. The plan is ready then is implemented by the career management. The requirement of training and development facilities are to be planned and arranged. So it can be said planning and development of activities relating to career are all part of career management. These two concepts of career planning and development are studies under two different headings. But it is said definitely there is urgent need for career planning and development in the present time in most of the organizations. The responsibility of career planning and development is fixed so that it can be planned, implemented and monitored properly so that the objectives of the organization can be fulfilled as per expectation of the management.

7. CAREER PLANNING

Planning is the process of deciding the future course of action to be followed in advance before starting the action. Generally, it is wise to think before doing any job. The phrases go true. Think before you speak or look before you leap. It gives the idea to have thoughts before doing anything in our life. The planning *process*

1. identifies the goals or objectives to be achieved,
2. formulates strategies to achieve them,
3. arranges or creates the means required, and
4. implements, directs, and monitors all steps in their proper sequence. It is applicable for all activities without any exception. Without planning the clear direction would not be there regarding what to do, when to do, how to do, where to do and who would do. If planning is done then there would not be any confusion at all regarding these things. The work would be done as per plan and the result would be achieved properly. Planning is like a lighthouse that shows the path to the performers. In planning, relating to a particular activity number of options is to be generated, options are evaluated, and finally the best option is selected and implemented. Planning may be for short, medium or long-term depending upon the duration of the planning. The concept of planning also can be applied to career of individual then is called career planning.

The type of career planning depends upon the target group for whom this has been done. The target groups are young students and existing employees already in job. The term career planning is frequently used both for youth studying in colleges as well for the employees in jobs in an organization. Students by considering the education, qualities, aptitude decide what they want to be in future in their life after their education. They have to plan their career in the beginning itself. In such career planning, counselors, career advisers, teachers, senior friends, parents and family members offer helping hand and guide them in selection of the career. It would enable them to use their abilities, talents and qualities to full extent so that they can make their life happy. The term career planning and development is also used for employees who are already in jobs in organizations. It is advocated that if the organizations are interested to get the best service of employees then they should plan for training and development programme for their employees more effectively. This would be beneficial for both employees and organization as a whole. The developed competencies would be available with the organization to get the best output. This type of career planning is called organizational career planning.

Career Planning is defined by various authors as follows:

(a) **Career planning** is the process of establishing career objectives and determining appropriate educational and developmental programs to further develop the skills required to achieve short- or long-term career objectives.

(b) The continuous process of evaluating your current lifestyle, likes/dislikes, passions, skills, personality, dream job, and current job and career path and making corrections and improvements to better prepare for future steps in your career, as needed, or to make a career change.

(c) Career planning is the process by which one selects career goals and the path to these goals. Career development is those personal improvements one undertakes to achieve a personal career plan. Career and management is the process of designing implementing goals, plans and strategies to enable the organization to satisfy employee needs while allowing individuals to achieve their career goals. So, due to this career planning and development is necessary to each and every employee in an organization. The need of career planning and development is felt in each and every organization of today's global world.

(d) Career planning refers to the formal programmes that organizations implement to increase the effectiveness and efficiency of the human resources available. Career planning and development is the responsibility of the HR department of the organization. As already noted, every person joining an organization has a desire to make career as per his potentiality, ability, skills and so on.

Career planning is one important aspect of human resource planning and development. Every individual who joins an organization desires to make a good career for himself within the organization. He joins the organization with a desire to have a bright career in terms of status, compensation payment and future promotions. From the point of view of an organization, career planning and development have become crucial in management process. An organization has to provide facilities/ opportunities for the career development of individual employees. If the organizations want to get the best out of their employees, they must plan regularly the career development programmes in their organizations.

8. COMPONENTS OF CAREER PLANNING

The career planning is very crucial for human resource management in an organization to meet the needs of the changing time. To improve the effectiveness of the organization at work place, in society and in market, special focus is to be given. In past, this was neglected to a very good extent. The focus of HR manager should be there on the following components of career planning:

(a) Career Planning Formulation

HR plans are relating to different functions of the department. These are to be prepared well in the beginning in discussion will top level management and employees. This would contribute in getting the support of all parties concerned. HR plans can be prepared regarding HR planning, recruitment and selection, training and retraining, career, promotion, wages and incentives, rewards and recognition, development activities etc. The plans would make the job of managers very easy to convince employees well in time. Every employee would have clarity regarding HR activities and related aspects. These plans are to be prepared according to the corporate plan. There should be proper matching so the objectives of corporate planning could be achieved within target time.

(b) Career Path

Career path is the route that is to be followed by individual from lower to higher level of jobs. Management now plans job sequences for transfers and promotions of their employees. This makes transfers and promotions systematically with advance information to employees. Career path creates suitable mental makeup of employees for self-development. This route is to be decided by HR manager in consultation with the top level management, consultants and employees. The path shows from one position to other position how much time is taken and what role or tasks are to be performed so that the person can move from one to other position. Career path is to be decided for different jobs under various departments. Further, it shows how much time is taken from lower to the last position in total. It is to be communicated to all concerned employees on different jobs. It gives clear picture to every employee regarding his career positions, roles, and time required to get that position. The confusions are avoided and employees knowing every aspect related to career put efforts or play roles for further movement. The involvement, commitment and performance level of employees improve a lot. That is the ultimate goal of management of the organization.

(c) Performance/ Potential Appraisal

Performance/potential appraisal are part of career planning. This component has been attached with the career planning. The objectives and standards of performance to achieve the objectives are decided in advance. These are communicated to every employee. They are assigned the job to perform. Round the year their performance standards, quality of work, difficulties faced, competencies shown during work and initiative to shoulder the responsibility for problem solving and leadership are appraised. The current performance and potential for further assignment both are assessed. Those are giving performance as per the standards and having potential for future assignments are considered for development opportunities or promotion.

(d) Promotion Policy

Everyone is interested for advancement or development of career. No one is interested to work at one position throughout his career. He is looking forward for promotion. When a person is promoted he gets higher salary, status and higher level of responsibility is to be fulfilled. This contributes a lot in development of motivation of employees. It is only motivation that creates interest to shoulder the responsibility willingly. The involvement of employees increase and finally it leads to higher productivity and performance. This is only the final goal of management. So the promotion policy should be decided by the management and it should be linked with the career planning. To get a promotion or movement from lower to higher position the criteria like time, qualification, experience, achievements, behavior at work and discipline are decided. The promotion policy is to be communicated to all concerned in time. Further, it should be implemented fairly. This will make the position of the career of individual in job and contributes to retain the good and talented employees.

(e) Development/ Rewards or Incentives

After performance appraisal the appraisal of employees should be reviewed. It is a function of performance management. During review efforts should be there to find out the contribution of employees towards achievement of objectives in terms of performance standards achieved. Quality of work, discipline, behaviour at work and initiative for problem solution, difficulties faced during job performance and deficiencies in competencies. This would give the clear picture about contribution from employees and finds out the potential for future assignment. On the basis of this review the development activities are to be planned. Those who are lacking in competencies they should be given training.

Those who are performing well having high degree of competencies and face no difficulty during work should be given opportunities for the new and better assignment. The consistent good performers' cases should be considered for further performance also. The good performers should be given higher level of salary increments, incentives. Their cases should be considered for rewards and recognition. This would contribute a lot in satisfying the career needs of the individual and provide them the job satisfaction. Such people would take the interest in the job and would not like to change job. The retention of employees would be very easy for the management. It should not be ignored and linked with the career development. It saves time, efforts and money of the organization and makes the employees available continuously without any interruption.

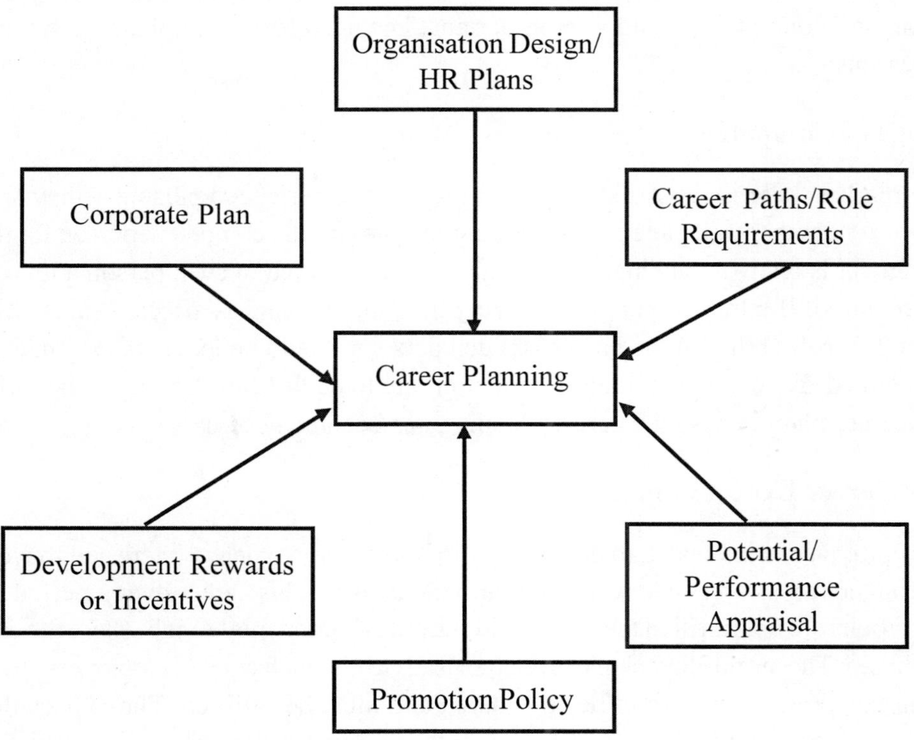

Diagram 16.1: Components of Career Planning

(f) Preparation of Corporation Plan

The business environment is very risky and uncertain so it is to be scanned at regular interval. It is not done then the efforts may not be put in the right direction. Time to time the corporate plans is to be reviewed or prepared. The new trends in the markets must be considered so that the effectiveness of the company should be maintained high. The objectives or targets should be reviewed and adjusted with the changing needs. For achievement of objectives what jobs are to be performed should be decided. The job description and job specification are to be developed; the expected standards of performance from employees should be planned well in time. This would make the things clear for middle level of management. According to corporation plan the career planning is to be adjusted for future action.

9. NEED FOR CAREER PLANNING

Career planning is very important in the present time for every organization. In past there was no much focus on career planning. The level of competition was very less and job opportunities were limited. There was no shortage of working force. With fast changing business environment, high level of competition and fluctuating demand of products or services the need for talented and motivated manpower was felt strongly. The talented and motivated persons can be procured, developed and retained by the organization. There are a number of techniques for this purpose. Career planning is one of them and very important. The need for career planning was felt due to following reasons:

(a) Shortage of Competent Employee

In the market there is a short supply of skilled and experienced persons. They are in short supply and every company management is looking forward for the competent person for their work. The management is ready to pay higher package even. For search of such person a lot of time and efforts are required. If a trained person is leaving the job, the work is affected substantially. That might affect the profitability of the business. Such persons should no leave the organization. They should be retained. To retain them their expectations are to be fulfilled. These can be fulfilled with the help of career planning. So the career planning has become necessary.

(b) Higher Career Expectation

Every employee is interested to do progress in his career. No one is interested to work on one position throughout his career. He wants to climb the ladder in his career over a period of time. If these expectations are not fulfilled then he would start looking for another job where the expectation would be fulfilled. The un-fulfillment of expectation leads to dissatisfaction of employees. To overcome this problem the expectations are to be considered and must be fulfilled. The expectation can be fulfilled to a good extent through career planning. If the person is getting promotion or higher level of jobs over a period of time then that person would be highly satisfied. He would develop positive attitude towards the organization. The retention of employees would be very easy for the management.

(c) Lack of Interest in Jobs

When employees are assigned the jobs in the beginning they perform the tasks very sincerely. Over a period of time they start losing interest in jobs due various reasons like hard work, poor working condition, poor welfare facility, lack of job security, unfavourable working environment and attitude of management, poor or inadequate salary and inadequate development opportunities. The level of commitment in job is reduced. The productivity and performance level of employees both go down. Finally, the organization is the sufferer. There are different techniques that can solve the problem. Out of these, career planning can solve the problems related to career development and opportunities in job. If the interest in job is back due to better career planning then the organization would be benefitted. That is why the need for career planning has been felt.

(d) Wastage of Resources

The management is not in position to make the show successful despite availability of all required resources. He is not getting the support from employees, supervisors or managers, when there is no mutual understanding, sense of cooperation and team spirit the friendly environment cannot be created. In this situation the machines would be running without work, the time would be wasted or production waste would increase. The productivity per person or system would go down. The production cost would go high and in result the profitability of the whole organization would go down. That is not accepted by the management. The management is interested for optimum utilization of all resources. It is only possible when cooperation and team spirit is there among employees. Career planning could be one of the methods for creating good working environment of cooperation and team spirit. The management feels in present time it is need of the hour and cannot be ignored.

(e) Wrong Job Placement

In the beginning when a new employees is selected and placed on a job the placement may not be correct or as per his aptitude and skill. While performing the tasks he might not take interest in the job. If it is so then all efforts put in this direction are fruitless. To overcome this problem when the performance appraisal review is there the potentials of the persons are identified. According to the potential the future assignments are allocated to the persons. Through career planning this can be solved. Person having hope that his talent would be recognized by the management and proper placement would be there in future, he continues in the job. That is why again the need for career planning has been felt.

(f) High Level of Employees Turnover

Whenever a person is satisfied with the prevailing situation he is not going to quit that situation. When he is not happy then only he would be thinking for another operation. This is applicable in every sphere of our life. In job when a person is not happy with the job due to various reasons he would definitely think to change the job. Nowadays the young people are changing the jobs very fast every after six month. If they are not happy over a small one issue the job is changed. It has become very difficult to retain the trained and experienced persons. There is great challenge to maintain the satisfied working force. The major issues for changing the jobs are unhealthy working environment, lack of job security, low pay package and inadequate promotion opportunities. Out of these the promotion or development opportunity, cause of turnover can be minimized by career planning. So it is important for the organization to accept career planning.

(g) Low Level of Motivation

Motivation is the desire to do the work and that comes from the deepest corner of the heart. It gives a trigger to accept the responsibility and do the job. It creates interest to do the work, creates attachment and develops sense of duty. With interest the work would not be there even years may pass. At work place the motivation level is to be maintained high. When level of motivation is high the persons would be performing the tasks even without asking. They taken initiatives of their own and shoulder the responsibility. This thing is missing then the production quantity, quality and productivity all are badly affected. There might be many reasons for low level of motivation. The situation is to be studied and if the de-motivation is due to career development and opportunity for promotion then it can be overcome through career planning definitely.

10. OBJECTIVES OF CAREER PLANNING

In past the importance of employees was very low. The management use to exploit them as per their requirements. They were asked to work for longer working hours and were paid very less salary. The workers were helpless because they did not have the other option to earn their livelihood. With the development in education, technology, competition the situation has changed drastically. Now there a large number of trained and educated persons to work and job opportunities have also changed. If a person is not satisfied with one job then frequently they are changing. Over and above the competition in the market has created very tough situation for the management to do the business. The demand of the products of the company that provides the products or services at lower price, better quality and better service to the customers is increasing. It is very difficult to meet the two ends at this crucial juncture. It is only possible with better performance and productivity of employees and machines. This work can be done by trained, experienced and motivated manpower. This only makes the difference in the market.

The company with talented and motivated manpower is only bringing the products or services at lower price and before others because due to their higher productivity and performance the production or operation costs go down. The need for talented and satisfied workforce is strongly felt by the management. Career planning is now one of the most important elements of human resource management but still it is also among the most neglected and least developed in many companies. Management of the organizations is trying to do so by using different techniques. The objective is to make them satisfied, develop and retain them for longer period. One of the techniques used for this purpose is career planning. The objectives of career planning are following:

(a) To attract, develop and retain the competent manpower in the organization.

(b) To provide adequate development and promotional opportunities.

(c) To develop the potential of employees for future assignments.

(d) To utilize the manpower and other resources more effectively in the organization.

(e) To provide proper job placement to employees.

(f) To improve the level of job satisfaction of employees at work place.

(g) To reduce the labour problems and turnover to minimum level.

(h) To improve motivation and morale of employees.

(i) To enhance the level of commitment and attachment towards the organization.

(j) To create healthy working environment in the organization.

(k) To improve performance, productivity, profitability and goodwill of the organization.

These above mentioned objectives can be fulfilled to a very good extent provided the management takes sincere interest in career planning and its implementation. This has proved successful in motivating and retaining high potential individuals whose future appears to lie within the organization. Having a clear idea of the rules of the development and promotion in career, they will be prepared to invest their efforts to meet the requirements of the company and move up in career ladder. There are examples in industry like Tata Group, IBM, HUL etc., could be achieved by these objectives to a very good extent. The management had paid special interests on career planning in their companies. Further, it has created a very healthy working environment of mutual understanding, openness, trust, cooperation and team spirit. This is very helpful for better working and progress of the organization. The future of career planning seems to be very bright in these companies. That is why every employee is interested to join these companies if he gets the chance in future.

11. SCOPE OF ORGANIZATIONAL CAREER PLANNING

Career planning is not limited to one activity relating to career. A number of activities are to be performed by human resource manager at different time. The scope of career planning is very wide. The scope is further widened when it is related to corporate plan and promotion policy. It starts with human resource planning. Job analysis, types of jobs, different levels of job, positions, roles to move from one position to other position, opportunities for training, development and promotion, counseling, career information, career route or path, skills assessment and time frame for all these activities. The scope of career planning covers the following activities and explained in detail below:

(a) Human Resource Forecasting and Planning

According to corporate plan the activities are to be performed. The activities may be related to route work, opening of new factory or offices, entry into new markets, and increasing the existing capacity of the company. To perform these activities there would be need for the manpower. As per the plan the requirement of manpower is to be identified. It would identify the number, type, location and time of requirement of manpower. It would be decided how many new persons are to be selected and method of recruitment and selection to meet the requirement of manpower in time so that the objectives can be fulfilled.

(b) Communication of Career Information

The requirement of manpower has been finalized then it becomes necessary to communicate to the employees through proper method so that the clarity should be rather regarding the type, number, location and time of the jobs. The opportunities for training, development and promotion for the existing employees should be timely communicated so that they can avail the opportunities properly. Timely communication of this information would get proper response and support from the employees. Otherwise the expected result may not be there and employees may oppose it also. Here, information relating to career opportunities (promotions, training for self-development, etc.) will be supplied to employees. Supplying career information/opportunities has special significance as this motivates employees to grow and reach to higher position.

(c) Career Counselling

Whenever new vacancies or opportunities are there in the job it should be communicated. After communication the employees would have some idea in mind but the idea may not be clear to go for it or not. They need career counseling. The arrangement is to be made for career counseling by experts or senior managers related to the field. This career counseling would provide proper guidance to the aspirants. It would help them to move in the right direction and right decision can be taken. Without counseling there may not be proper response from the candidates. It should be provided through periodic discussions with their subordinates. Such career guidance encourages subordinate employees to take interest in certain areas where suitable opportunities of career development are available. It is impossible through internal guidance and motivation of employees for the selection of possible career paths. Such counseling is required when employees are interested plan their own careers and develop themselves for better career and good progress in their life.

(d) Career Path

The next activity is to decide career path in the organization for the employees to climb the ladder. It is called career path. Career path is the the route to be followed while moving from one position to another. Management plans job sequences for transfers and promotions of their employees. This makes transfers and promotions systematically with advance information to employees. Career path creates suitable mental makeup of employees for self-development. Predefined career path gives clear picture to employees regarding their position, next position to get, time duration and efforts required to achieve. The employees can have idea regarding total time duration to reach to the top position. The confusions are avoided and it helps employees in their career planning. This is a very important activity of career planning.

(e) Training for Career Planning and Development

For proper implementation of career planning and development the persons are to be trained. In case of trained persons it can be implemented. It should be conducted along with job analysis, jobs and manpower requirement. It would develop the back group for proper career planning and development activities. It is to be performed by HR managers well in time. Training would give knowledge of the job, confidence and better performance during job. This finally would improve the efficiency of the person performing the tasks of career planning and development.

(f) Identification of Competencies for Movement

The next job of career planning and development is identification of competencies for movement from one job/position. The competencies or criteria may be education qualification, training, experience, sex, performance in recent past, performance standards achieved, initiative for problem solving, leadership quality and behaviour at work and potential for future assignments. This would help in identification of the employees for promotion and development activities. The clarity would be maintained in decision making. The confusion of employees on other hand would be avoided.

12. ADVANTAGES OF CAREER PLANNING

In the last decade the importance of career planning has been increased due to liberalization of economies across the world. The competition level increased to a great extent from multinational companies. The requirement of higher productivity, performance and quality of work can be fulfilled if the company is maintained talented and motivated manpower. If not it should be do done. For this purpose career planning helps a lot to meet the requirement for satisfying and retaining employees. There are multidimensional benefits of career planning to performance, employees, organization and finally to the society. The major advantages of career planning are explained below:

(a) For Individuals

Advantages for individuals are following:

(i) Gives knowledge of various career development and promotion to employees.

(ii) Encourages employees to avail training and development facilities for skill development.

(iii) Provides help in making career decision according to his lifestyles, traits, preferences, family environment, scope for self-development and aptitude etc.

(iv) Helps in identification of employees for promotion from within the organization.

(v) Contributes in motivating, satisfying and providing job satisfaction through promotion and development activities.

(vi) Increases sense of responsibility, commitment and attachment to the job and organization.

(vii) Employee will await his turn of promotion rather than changing to another organization. This will lower employee turnover.

(viii) Increase productivity and performance on job from employees.

(ix) It satisfies employee esteem needs and develop positive attitude towards organisation.

(b) For Organizations

A long-term focus of career planning and development would solve many employees related problems and effectiveness of manpower and utilization of different resources will be proper. There are many advantages of career planning and development to the organization as a whole and these are explained below:

(i) Helps in attracting and retaining talented manpower in the organization.

(ii) Satisfies the employee expectations and minimizes employee labour problems

(iii) Makes easier for management to get support and cooperation of employees.

(iv) By attracting and retaining the people from different cultures, enhances cultural diversity.

(v) The employees' turnover reduced and help in retaining the employees for long time.

(vi) To create healthy working environment in the organization.

(vii) Improves performance, productivity and profitability.

(viii) Provides a fairly reliable guide for manpower forecasting.

(ix) Career planning facilitates expansion and growth of the enterprise.

(x) Finally, the goodwill of the company improves in the market.

13. DISADVANTAGES/LIMITATIONS OF CAREER PLANNING

The career planning and development process is very useful in normal time. Further it is very useful when company is interested in increasing its production capacity, expansion, entries in new world markets and establishing new factor or opening new branch offices. But it is not effective always. It is not useful in certain cases. The main problems in career planning are as follows:

(a) Career planning can become unsuitable or smaller organization. It can be suitable for medium and larger size of organization when fresh candidates are to be taken at higher level.

(b) In a developing country like India with fast changing business environment it becomes ineffective in the long run. May not be suitable for over a period of ten years or so. It is to be reviewed time to time otherwise the effectiveness would go down.

(c) Career planning is not an effective technique for low profile employees who are unskilled and illiterate. For them the career planning does not have any meaning. It becomes ineffective.

(d) In family business houses in India, family members are interested for fast development than other professional. They do not follow the career planning and career path. The whole process is disturbed and it remains on paper only for them.

(e) Systematically career planning becomes difficult due to impartial implementation. When opportunities are going on the basis of personal favour, nepotism in promotions, political intervention in recruitment and selection of reserve category candidates'

(f) When both wife and husband are working in the same organization, if one is getting the opportunity for development then as per the transfer policy the case of other also to be considered. The process again becomes ineffective.

(g) When it becomes necessary to downsize the manpower, the career planning and development process becomes useless. The question of further development does not arise at all.

(h) When career opportunities are declining due to technological changes, the question of career development does not arise. The solution of the problem is not with the career development but it lies with career shift only.

14. ROLES IN CAREER PLANNING AND DEVELOPMENT

Career planning and development is mainly the responsibility of HR management because the management is interested for proper utilization of manpower currently and retain them for future so that consistency in performance and productivity can be maintained. It becomes very effective when employees, managers and employers all together are involved in career planning and development activities. The efforts would be very fruitful in this situation. The roles of these parties are explained below:

(a) Role of Individual

For the individual employee, career planning means matching individual strengths and weaknesses with occupational opportunities and threats. In other words, an employee wants to purse the career where the opportunities are available according to his qualification, interest, aptitude and skills in which he can have progress as per the expectation. For this purpose one has to perform the following tasks:

(i) Accept responsibility willingly for planning and development: This is only when a person is interested. Without interest no one can compel employee to go for extra efforts for planning and development. He should be happy at work place and take initiative for self-development efforts.

(ii) Self-assessment: With proper interest the employees should assess their strengths and weakness. This would include interest, ability, capability, knowledge and skills, aptitude, qualification, physical health, initiative for handling new job, desire for future development and experience at job and values of his work in organization and outside in the industry. When this analysis is done the clear picture would be in mind of employees. They would have clear ideas regarding their potentials and capacity. On the basis of this the employees should think further for career development.

(iii) Find out career opportunities: After self-assessment the employees should find out the career opportunities inside and outside of his organization. If the career opportunities are available within then details of that opportunities to be known. If outside of the organization the opportunities are available then what level, where and what criteria needed for getting those opportunities. The comparison should be carried out so that the relative worth of opportunities would be available for taking further step.

(iv) Establish goals and career plans: The employees should establish their career goals. The goals may be for short, medium or long-terms. To achieve these goals the career plan should be prepared. This would take the employees in the right direction. Sincere efforts are to be put in this direction for materializing the career benefits.

(v) Avail development opportunities: After deciding the career goals and plans the employees should take interest for self-development. Whatever the development facilities are provided by the employers should be availed. For this purpose the employees should shoulder the responsibility for availing career development facilities. Lack of interest in this is not going to give the proper result. Wholehearted efforts should be there in this direction.

(vi) Consult with seniors: If an employee is interested for career development and availing opportunities within the company he should discuss with his seniors, because the senior persons are having proper knowledge regarding career development. For this purpose good relations are to be maintained with seniors and should work on their advice.

(vii) Follow up action on career plans: Whatever has been planned by the employees should be implemented strongly. As per goal and planning the efforts should be put for availing opportunities, developing potentials and competencies and appearing for test, examination etc., to avail the opportunities. Proper implementation would give timely result.

(b) Role of Managers as a Mentor

(i) Performance feedback: The support of managers is highly needed for planning and development of employee's career. When as a part of career planning and development the performance appraisal is done then timely and correct performance feedback is needed. They should be guided and counseled on job without any hesitation. Without their help the employees cannot improve their competencies and performance. This would solve many problems of employees and make them satisfied at work.

(ii) Provide development opportunity and support: When the opportunity for development arises the timely information and chance should be given to employees. During that period the total support of managers should be there. This would make the situation very comfortable for employees to learn and develop their competencies for further development. The employee would feel at home during this development assignment.

(iii) Participate in career counseling: When the employees are interested to establish their career goals and plan they need the support of experts. They do not have proper knowledge and information regarding this. They look forward to the seniors. The managers or seniors must counsel them regarding their career development. They can show them the right path to move and develop their career in further within and outside of the organization.

(iv) Support in development plans: The manager should give their support to the employees whenever they are interested to go for their career development plan. They should guide them regarding the development opportunities available, availing conditions and efforts needed to avail development opportunities. With proper guidance only the career development plans can be prepared in right way.

(c) Role of Employer

(i) Proper communication: The role of employer is very important in career planning and development. The corporate planning is only the base for further planning. Career planning and development is also aligned with the corporate planning. The mission, objectives, policies and procedures should be timely communicated to all employees and managers. It would give the clear picture regarding career planning and development. The efforts would be put in the right direction otherwise not.

(ii) Arrangement for training and development opportunities: It is the responsibility of employers to make necessary arrangement for training and development facilities and the opportunities should be provided for employees. As per the requirement of various jobs the training and development facilities are to be arranged within or outside of the organization. The different methods can be used for this purpose such as classroom lectures, vestibule method, workshop, seminars, conferences, role playing, case study and others.

(iii) Providing information: The management is providing the information to the employees at all levels regarding career and career programmes arranged for development. If timely information is given the efforts would be put in right direction timely. The requirements of the company for increasing capacity or expansion can be met without any difficulty.

(iv) Offers career paths for employees: In the beginning itself, the employers must prepare the career path for employees that they are going to follow in their career if they continue to stay in the same company. With the idea of getting further position through career path the employees would put their sincere efforts to achieve their targets. The employer would be in position to retain them for long period. So the offer for career path for employees should be there timely from employer.

(v) Provides final career oriented performance feedback: The performance appraisal is carried out by supervisors, managers and head of department. The final appraisal report that is to be considered for further training, development and promotion should be communicated to the concerned by the employees. The final performance feedback would avoid confusions and make the position clear in mind of employees. If some improvement is needed that can be done by the employees in time for future opportunity. It should be provided by the employer.

(vi) Provides mentoring opportunities: The employer should make necessary arrangement for providing the mentoring service to the subordinate to support in the growth and self direction. The responsibility should be fixed by the employer for this also. It would help to guide many needy employees and the healthy environment in organization would develop for further career development.

(vii) Support in individual development plans: The employer should go one step ahead that it should provide the support or plans for employees' development. In the beginning this is to be provided to the employees. It should be felt by the employees that the management is interested for their development also.

(viii) Provides support programmes: For development of the academic qualification, skills and knowledge the employers should provide with such programmes. In some of the leading organization where management attitude is very favourable for all round development of employees providing such programmes.

Finally it can be said if employees, managers and employers all are interested in career planning and development activities then the result of it would be very useful for all parties concerned. It would first of all create a healthy work environment and later on all related benefits would go to employees, managers, employers, organization and to the society. Only thing is that the sincere and willing efforts should be there in this direction.

15. CAREER PLANNING AND DEVELOPMENT PROCESS

Career planning is one important activity of human resource planning and development. Every individual while entering an organization desires to make a better career during his stay in it. Everyone joins the organization with strong interest to have a bright career in terms of status, salary packages, and future promotions. From the point of view of an organization, career planning and development have become crucial in management process. An organization has to provide facilities/opportunities for the career development of individual employees. If the organizations want to get the best utilization of all resources, must plan regularly the career development programmes in their organizations. In brief, career planning can be called the formal programmes that organization undertakes to increase the effectiveness and efficiency of the human resources available. Career planning and development is the responsibility of a cell under HR department or HR department itself. To make the best use of ability, potentials and interest a number of activities are to be performed. It is ongoing and continuous process over a period of time. The steps involved in career planning and development process the following steps are involved:

(a) Analysis of Employees

The first step involve in this process is analysis of employees. It is the preparation part for going career and development process. The target group is employees. Their analysis is to be carried out to find out the details relating to employees for introduction of this process. This is to be carried out before career planning. The information collected from analysis would provide the platform to the planners to make projections for the planning period and to help in the evaluation of plans. The analysis would be carried out to collect the information about regarding the following:

(i) Total number of employees, sex, age distribution, qualifications, experience, positions, area of specializations, etc.

(ii) Job structure related information such as level of job, job profile, level of responsibility, qualification academic and technical, experience for each category.

(iii) Needs of employees in the organization relating to different categories at work, inside and outside of organization, social, security, financial, welfare, etc.

(iv) Span of control available within the organization suitable or not, meeting the requirement or not, reactions of supervisors and employees etc.

(v) Staff members employed at corporate office, branches and fields.

(vi) Facilitates provided for training and development by the company inside, help taken from outside agencies in India and abroad.

From the analysis the required information for beginning career planning would be made available. This information are for the target group. The information collected on above mention points serves as the base for the preparation of career development plan for the future period.

(b)Analysis of Situation

After analysis of employees' information the next step is to analysis the situation of the company. The corporate plans are to be studied to find out the situation prevailing in the organization. The plans may be for adding capacity to the production plant, entering in new markets, expansion of the existing one or opening a new factory or branch offices in India or outside of India. The situation should be clear then only the further stop can be taken. The detailed information are to be taken for further planning and development activities. Without information the efforts may not be in right direction.

(c) Identifying of Career Needs

In this third step of career planning and development process efforts should be put to find out the type of employees, number of persons, area of specialization and locations wise. The need for future development are to be found out on the basis of information collected regarding qualification, experience, knowledge and skills, performance appraisal report and potentials. The exact needs are to be identified so that timely action can be taken for career development of the employees.

(d) Selection of Priorities

For selection of candidates for further placement and developement the criteria of selection are to be decided. It would make the things very clear for the management for shortlisting the candidates for providing development opportunities as it is not possible to provide opportunities to everyone at a time. Management should take timely decision considering the strengths and weaknesses of employees and requirements of the organization for different purposes. It should be decided by the management in discussion with managers, supervisors and if required the consultants or experts of specific areas. This may lead to a good decision.

(e) Development of Career Plan

This is the most important step in the whole process. The plan should include the objectives to be achieved, The performance standards to be given, time frame for target achievement, required competencies the employees should possess, type of behaviour required at work, leadership quality and level of initiative for handling challenging tasks, the section or division for implementing the plan and time are to be decided for developing plan. Such plan must describe the following in concrete form/forms:

In order to execute the career development plan, the organization should prepare and introduce policies and programmes for training and career development for all categories of employees to improve their competencies and confidence so that they can shoulder the higher and challenging responsibility. The efforts should be there to encourage them for career development within or outside of the organization. The preference should be given on promotion or transfer basis within the organization. The cases of fresh recruitment also should be highlighted in the development plan. The promotion criteria of merit cum seniority should be considered and unwanted barrier should be removed for effective promotion policy. Finally, a plan is to be finalized in black and white. It should contain all detailed information whatever has been discussed above.

(f) Implementation and Monitoring

Once the career plan has been prepared it is required to implement in the respective department or division. It should be timely communicated to managers, supervisors and employees all at a time. There should be clarity in mind of everyone regarding every aspect of planning and development of the career. The responsibility for implementation is to be fixed so that the things would be done otherwise no one is going to take the responsibility seriously. Periodical reports are to be submitted to HOD human resource department. The tasks are to be completed within the stipulated time. Further it should be monitored by HOD human resource department or director in charge. The reports should be perused and if any irregularity is there then the remedial action to be taken. This strong implementation and monitoring would be in position to meet the requirements of the corporate plans for expansion or opening of new locations etc.

(g) Review of Career Planning and Development

Whatever planned for the career developed during implementation a lot of difficulties are faced. It might give the good result also. It should not be taken as guaranteed that it would give perfect result always. It should be review periodically at least once in a year. This review would find out the difficulties, deficiencies, mistaken done and any other problems faced. This would find out the gap between the target and performance actually achieved. This would measure the effectiveness of the process. The exact position of effectiveness of the career planning and development process would be known after review only. For conducting review the help of experts should be taken and it should be reviewed impartially.

(h) Development of Future Plan

This is the final step of this process. From review whatever weak points have been noticed in current plan work should be done on those so that the weaknesses can be removed. On the basis of current plan performance the career needs for future period can be identified. To meet the future needs the current plans are to be modified and adjusting it so that the effectiveness of career plan improves. On the basis of this the next plan can be prepared. For next plan the training and development facilities can be arranged further, new priorities can be added, responsibility of implementation or procedure can be changed. It would be aligned with corporate plan and objectives of the organization.

16. ESSENTIAL CONDITIONS FOR EFFECTIVE CAREER PLANNING AND DEVELOPMENT

Once the career planning and development activities have been started it should meet the requirement of employees' career and organization as a whole. The employees should get the training and development opportunities, transfer and promotion in their career. Further, the requirements of organization such as expansion of business, entry into new markets, opening of new factory or offices etc., should be fulfilled. If it is not done so the effectiveness of the career planning and development process is low. To make it more effective the following conditions should be fulfilled:

(a) Joint Discussion for Formulation of Planning

In the beginning for formulation of plan a joint discussion should be there among management, supervisors and employees. The help should be taken from external consultants or experts if required. Before discussion a healthy environment should be created so the meeting can be arranged. The every aspects relating to career opportunities, criteria for availing the opportunities, training and development facilities required, responsibility and procedure for implementation of the plan, time frame required, and others should be discussed openly in friendly atmosphere and points from different parties should be considered if approved by majority. This would be in position to give a good plan and opposition employees would be avoided.

(b) Prompt Communication

After formulation of career planning, it is the responsibility of the manager in charge to communicate clearly and timely to all concerned. There should be clear ideas regarding every aspect of career planning and development. It should give guidelines to the employees those who are interested for their career development. If timely and proper communication is not there then there are chances of confusions and opposition from employees and their unions. To get the support of all and achieve the objectives of the plan the timely and proper communication is necessary. The effectiveness of career planning and development would definitely improve.

(c) Proper Implementation

After communication of the plan the next condition required is its proper implementation. For implementation the responsibility for implementation, time, procedure and reporting etc., should be fixed. These would make sure that everything is understood and everyone is doing the work as per the plan. If lapses are there in implementation the work would not be done in time, the objectives would not be fulfilled and would further create frustration among concerned parties. Attention should be given on monitoring also.

(d) Periodical Review

To claim the plan is very effective it should be reconsidered. The current plan might be good but with the changing time it may not be in position to meet the requirements of employees and organization. To adjust with the requirement of all concerned it should be reviewed at least once in a year. If not done so over a period of time the effectiveness of the plan would be very low and it would become useless. Top level management should take the responsibility with manager in charge without fail.

(e) Link with Corporate Plan

The career planning and development should be linked with corporate plan. After scanning of business environment the corporate plan is prepared. In this the major objectives are decided. What company wants to do and where it wants to reach in near future. To achieve these objectives efforts are to be put. The performance standards are to be achieved. For this purpose the skills, knowledge, ability, capability, aptitude and interest are required. If the employees are not having these competencies then there is need for training and development. The opportunities for development are to be given to employees on the basis of certain criteria so that the targets of performance can be achieved. The career planning and development should be linked with the corporate plan. If it is done then clear direction are there for its planning and implementation. If not done so the working of it would not be effective.

(f) Relate Career Plan with Promotion

For planning and development of career it is needed that it should be related to promotion policy of the company. In career everyone is interested to move forward. The opportunities for development are to be given then the conditions for development or promotion are to be decided. When it is related to promotion policy the confusion in planning and development of career related activities would be done in a better way. Promotion policy should be part of career planning and development or should be related to this.

17. CONCLUSION

The strong need for higher productivity and performance has been felt in every organization across the world because the situation is very competitive and critical. It has become very difficult to increase production or sales due to tough competition. The management is in fix what to do and what not to increase the profitability of the company. The way to solve this problem is through cost reduction by giving higher productivity and performance. The operation cost would go down and it would contribute definitely in increasing the production quantity, quality and profitability of the company. The HR management is keenly interested for proper utilization of manpower so the performance can be increased and sustained in future also to keep on achieving targets. This can be done through different approach. For this purpose managing performance of employees as a whole is very important. Performance management takes care of this function. To get the talented and experienced persons is very difficult and further it is more difficult to satisfy and motivated them and maintains so continuously. The different tools have been used by the performance management. Performance management in leading organizations is paying more attention on the career and its development of employees. The importance of this tool is increasing day by day and in future it would be contributing to achieve the objectives of performance management.

In ancient time this awareness regarding career was not there before modernism, many workers would often inherit or take up a single lifelong position generally followed by their parents. The need for career selection was not felt at all. With the spread during the enlightenment of the idea of progress and of the habits of individualist self-betterment the need for career was felt. Broadly, the concept of career is used to refer to entire work life of an individual. It can be defined in a narrow sense, to be the succession of jobs and/or ranks held by a person in a particular organization. An individual's career begins with placement in a job and ends with departure from the organization which may be through retirement, resignation or death. In between, the career progression consists of changing tasks, tenure in various jobs, temporary or permanent promotions, transfers etc. From beginning of career to discharge from jobs the individuals passes through a number of stages. These stages are interrelated logically and in sequence. The requirements of persons vary from stage to stage. It is the responsibility of management to take special care of those requirements. This would make the situation more comfortable for the employees of the organization. Individuals have different career development needs at different stages in their careers.

The term career planning and development is also used for employees who are already in jobs in organizations. It is advocated that if the organizations are interested to get the best service of employees then they should plan for training and development programme for their employees more effectively. This would be beneficial for both employees and organization as a whole. The developed competencies would be available with the organization to get the best output. This type of career planning is called organizational career planning. Career planning is the process by which one selects career goals and the path to these goals. Career development is those personal improvements one undertakes to achieve a personal career plan. Career and management is the process of designing implementing goals, plans and strategies to enable the organization to satisfy employee needs while allowing individuals to achieve their career goals. So, due to this career planning and development is necessary to each and every employee in an organization. The need of career planning and development is felt in each and every organization of today's global world. The need for career planning was felt due to shortage of competent employee, high level of dissatisfaction, higher labour turnover, tough competition, increasing operating costs etc.

From the point of view of an organization, career planning and development have become crucial in management process. An organization has to provide facilities/opportunities for the career development of individual employees. The steps involve in career planning and development process are analysis of employees analysis of situation, identifying career needs, selection of priorities, development of career plan, implementation and monitoring of plan, review and development of future plan. Once the career planning and development activities have been started it should meet the requirement of employees' career and organization as a whole. The employees should get the training and development opportunities, transfer and promotion in their career. Further, the requirements of organization such as expansion of business, entry into new markets, opening of new factory or offices etc should be fulfilled. If it is not done so the effectiveness of the career planning and development process is low. To make it more effective the following conditions should be fulfilled:

18. QUESTIONS FOR REVIEW

1. Define career and explain characteristics of it in detail.
2. Discuss classification of career with suitable examples.
3. What are the stages involved in career of the employees in an organization? Discuss.
4. What do you mean by career development and do you feel it is necessary for company in present time?
5. Define career planning and discuss its characteristics.
6. Discuss the need for career planning for a medium and large size of organisations.
7. Explain advantages and disadvantages of career planning and development.
8. What are the steps involved in career planning and development process? Discuss them.
9. Describe the roles of employees, managers and employees in career planning and development.
10. Discuss the essential conditions for effective career planning and development.
11. Write short notes:
    (a) Self-assessment
    (b) Analysis of career opportunities
    (c) Career planning for students
    (d) Career counseling
    (e) Succession planning
    (f) Career planning linked with promotion policy

(g) Scope of career planning
(h) Responsibility of career development
(i) Future of career planning and development

19. OBJECTIVE QUESTIONS

1. Career is as "course or progress through life (or a distinct portion of life)". It is usually considered to pertain to remunerative work (and sometimes also formal education). It is defined by:

(a) Edwin B. Flippo
(b) Oxford English Dictionary
(c) Peter Luther
(d) All the above
(e) None of the above

2. At what stage the employee has the experience of working in particular company of nearly 10 to 15 yrs?

(a) Senior level stage.
(b) Establishment & development stage.
(c) Middle level stage.
(d) Induction stage.
(e) None of the above

3. Where the need for career planning is not supported from employees, management or supervisors?

(a) Wrong job placement.
(b) Lack of interest in job.
(c) Low level of motivation.
(d) Wastage of resources.
(e) None of the above

4. In which step the scope of organizational career planning gives clear picture to employee regarding their position in the organization?

(a) Career path.
(b) Career Counseling.
(c) Communication of career Information.
(d) Human resource forecasting & planning.
(e) All the above

5. What are the multidimensional benefits of career planning?

(a) Lifestyle, traits & preferences.
(b) Performance, employees & organization and society.
(c) Improves productivity, performance & profitability
(d) All the above
(e) None of these.

6. In which step the employer uses classroom lectures, vestibule method, workshop, seminar, conference and case study?
   (a) Proper communication.
   (b) Providing information.
   (c) Arrangement for training & development opportunities.
   (d) Providing mentoring opportunities.
   (e) All the above
7. What is the next step after joint discussion for formulation of planning?
   (a) Periodical review.
   (b) Link with corporation plan.
   (c) Proper implementation.
   (d) Prompt communication.
   (e) None of the above
8. Career planning is called:
   (a) Organization career planning.
   (b) Performance career planning.
   (c) Development career planning.
   (d) Management career planning.
   (e) None of the above
9. The objectives of career planning are:
   (a) To attract, develop and retain the competent manpower in the organization.
   (b) To provide adequate development and promotional opportunities.
   (c) To develop the potential of employees for future assignments.
   (d) To utilize the manpower and other resources more effectively in the organization.
   (e) All the above
10. Cadre career means:
   (a) Single governmental jurisdictions.
   (b) One institution or department.
   (c) Basis of entrance or norms.
   (d) Cluster or a group of post are arranged vertically
   (e) All the above

Answer Keys:

Question No.	Answer	Question No.	Answer
1	b	6	c
2	c	7	d
3	d	8	a
4	a	9	e
5	b	10	d

Chapter

17 Performance Management

1. INTRODUCTION

Every organization performs its task with the help of resources as men, machine, materials and money. Except manpower other resources are non-living but manpower is a live and generating resource. Manpower utilizes other resources and gives output. If manpower is not available then other resources are useless and cannot produce anything. Out of all the factors of production manpower has the highest priority and is the most significant factor of production and plays a pivotal role in areas of productivity and quality. In case, lack of attention to the other factors those are non-living may result in reduction of profitability to some extent. But ignoring the human resource can prove to be disastrous. In a country where human resource is abundant, it is a pity that they remain under-utilized. In wording of Oliver Sheldon "No industry can be rendered efficient so long as the basic fact remains unrecognized that is human." The people at work comprise a large number of individuals of different sex, age, socio-religious group and different educational or literacy standards. These individuals in the work place exhibit not only similar behaviour patterns and characteristics to a certain degree but also they show much dissimilarity. Technology alone, however, cannot bring about desired change in economic performance of the country unless human potential is fully utilized for production. The management must therefore be aware not only of the organization but also employees and their needs.

The principal component of an organisation is its human resources or 'People at work'. Human resources have been defined from the national point of view as, "the knowledge, skills, creative abilities, talents and aptitudes obtained in the population: whereas from the view point of the individual enterprise, they represent the total of the inherent abilities, acquired knowledge and skills as exemplified in the talents and aptitudes of its employees". Jucius calls these resources 'human factors' which refer to "a whole consisting of interrelated, interdependent and interacting physiological, psychological and ethical components. The human resource is critical and difficult to manage. It is because human behaviour is highly unpredictable. It differs not only from individual to individual but often on the part of same individual at different points of time. In spite of biological and cultural similarities, human beings not only differ in their appearance but also in their capabilities based on their background, training and experience. Human resource or a person at work is the most important component of the undertaking. Management cannot afford to ignore human resource at any cost. In simple sense, human resource management means employing people, developing them, utilizing, compensating and maintaining their services in tune with the job and organizational requirements.

It is this human resource which is of paramount importance in the success of any organisation because most of the problems in organisational settings are human and social rather than physical, technical or economic. Failure to recognise this fact causes immense loss to the nation, enterprise and to the individual. In the words of Olivery Sheldon, "No industry can be rendered efficient so long as the basic fact remains unrecognized that it is principally human. It is not a mass of machines and technical processes but a body of men. It is not a complex of matter, but a complex of humanity. It fulfills its function not by virtue of some impersonal force, but by human energy." The concepts of human resource, personnel, employees, labour force and manpower are interchangeable. We frequently use these terms one in place of the others. The term employee is most widely used and it has been defined by different authors and laws as follows:

2. EMPLOYEE PERFORMANCE

Every organization has been established with certain objectives to achieve. These objectives can be achieved by utilizing the resources like men, machines, materials and money. All these resources are important but out of these the manpower is the most important. It plays an important role in performing tasks for accomplishing the goals. The question arises that how these resources are utilizes by manpower. Further, the business environment is changing drastically. The environmental factors are uncontrollable. These are beyond control of management of the firms. One has to adjust with the external factors to do the business in the market. Every environmental factor like social, cultural, legal, political, economic, technology and competition gets changed very fast. For effective working the knowledge of these factors is must otherwise the plan will misfire. In present situation it is difficult to predict about anything. It is uncertain to say that what will happen tomorrow. Again the need for highly skilled and dedicated manpower is felt who can give the best output. Nowadays the markets are also very competitive and there is cut-throat competition. For every organization it is difficult to start, survive, stabilize and excel in the business. The firm that gets the advantage over other competitors through their talented and dedicated manpower can take the lead in the market. The contribution of employees on job is the most important factor for development and excellence in business. The performance of employees on different jobs in close coordination is needed for success of the unit.

Employees are performing different jobs in an organization depending upon the nature of the organization. They mainly perform tasks like production, storage, manufacturing, transportation, marketing, purchasing, distribution, promotion of business, finance and accounting, human resource, research and public relations. All these activities are interrelated to achieve the targets. These are to be performed by the employees properly so they can give their best output at the job. This will have great impact on the total production, sales, profit, progress and market position of the company in the market. Various factors like skills, training, motivation, dedication, welfare, management policies, fringe benefits, salary and packages, promotion, communication etc., are responsible to encourage the people to work sincerely and give their best output. The importance of employees' performance must be understood by the management and sincere efforts must be put in that direction. The management of the company taking timely steps in that direction will be in position to develop and motivate the people to do so. Finally the company may take the lead in the market and grab the opportunities available in the market.

3. ADVANTAGES OF HIGHER EMPLOYEES' PERFORMANCE

Following are advantages of higher performance to the individuals, organization, society and nation as a whole:

(a) The productivity of individual on job increases.

(b) Employee gets job satisfaction at job.

(c) Psychological problems of employees come to low level.

(d) Involvement of employees in their jobs increases.

(e) A sense of commitment and loyalty among employees develop.

(f) Employees get higher salaries and incentives on production basis.

(g) Quality and quantity of the total production increase.

(h) Sales and market shares of the company in the market improves.

(i) Profit improves and that leads to progress of the business.

(j) Goodwill of the organization goes high.

(k) All these contribute in the development of national economy and living standard of the society as a whole.

4. PERFORMANCE MANAGEMENT

The main objective of human resources management is to utilize the human resources in a most optimal manner so that targets can be achieved very effectively and efficiently. For this purpose managing performance of employees as a whole is very important. Performance management takes care of this function. Performance management maintains, develops and motivates the people at work to give better results. In the present competitive situation the organisation that gives better results can survive, stabilize, grow and excel in the performance. It helps a lot in achieving the objectives of HRM. Performance management includes activities to ensure that goals are consistently being met in an effective and efficient manner. Performance management can focus on performance of the organization, a department, processes to build a product or service, employees, etc. This concept has been defined by various authors as follows:

(a) Performance management is the process of creating a work environment or setting in which people are enabled to perform to the best of their abilities. Performance management is a whole work system that begins when a job is defined as needed. It ends when an employee leaves your organization. Many writers and consultants are using the term "performance management" as a substitution for the traditional appraisal system. A performance management system includes the following actions:

   (i) Develop clear job descriptions.

   (ii) Select appropriate people with an appropriate selection process.

   (iii) Negotiate requirements and accomplishment-based performance standards, outcomes, and measures.

   (iv) Provide effective orientation, education, and training.

   (v) Provide on-going coaching and feedback.

   (vi) Conduct quarterly performance development discussions.

   (vii) Design effective compensation and recognition systems that reward people for their contributions.

   (viii) Provide promotional/career development opportunities for staff.

   (ix) Assist with exit interviews to understand WHY valued employees leave the organization.

(b) Performance management is the larger process of defining what employees should be doing, ongoing communication during the year, linking of individual performance to organization needs, and the evaluating or appraising of performance.

(c) Performance management involves enabling people to perform their work to the best of their ability, meeting and perhaps exceeding targets and standards. For successful performance management, a culture of collective and individual responsibility for the continuing improvement of business processes needs to be established, and individual skills and contributions need to be encouraged and nurtured. Where organizations are concerned, performance management is usually known as company performance and is monitored through business appraisal.

(d) Performance management: A framework that identifies opportunities for performance improvement through use of performance measures such as standards and indicators.

(e) Performance measurement: A process of assessing the achievement of pre-determined goals and objectives through the measurement of the following types of indicators: inputs, processes of delivery of activities and services outputs, and outcomes.

(f) Performance management: Using a set of tools and approaches to measure, improve, monitor and sustain the key indicators of a business.

(g) Performance management: The process of quantifying, measuring, correcting and reporting system service levels.

(h) Performance management: An empirically based approach to evaluating operational, clinical and financial segments of a provider. It is a program evaluation methodology to measuring results by *benchmarking* internal statistics against those of empirically based standards

(i) Performance management system (PMS) is the heart of any "people management " process in organization. Organizations exist to perform. If people do not perform organizations don't survive. If people perform at their peak level organization can compete and create waves. -TVS Rao

(j) Armstrong and Baron (1998) defined it as "A strategic and integrated approach to increasing the effectiveness of organizations by improving the performance of the people who work in them and by developing the capabilities of teams and individual contributors"

(k) Performance management is: 'The development of individuals with competence and commitment, working towards the achievement of shared meaningful objectives within an organisation which supports and encourages their achievement' (Lockett).

(l) 'Performance management is managing the business' (Mohrman and Mohrman,).

(m) Performance management is the process of 'Directing and supporting employees to work as effectively and efficiently as possible in line with the needs of the organisation' (Walters,).

(n) Performance management is the process of creating a work environment or setting in which people are enabled to perform to the best of their abilities. Performance management is a whole work system that begins when a job is defined as needed. It ends when an employee leaves your organization.

The PM approach is used most often in the workplace but applies wherever people interact—schools, churches, community meetings, sports teams, health setting, governmental agencies, and even political settings. PM principles are needed wherever in the world people interact with their environments to produce desired effects. Cultures are different but the laws of behavior are the same worldwide.

5. FUNCTIONS OF PERFORMANCE MANAGEMENT

The performance management is mainly concern with the performance of the people, systems and organization. To achieve this objective performance management performs a variety of functions. These functions are summarized below:

(a) Create Healthy Work Environment

HR or performance manager works with the people. Their objective is to create an environment of openness, trust, mutual understanding, team spirit and cooperation. In this environment only the manpower can be utilize more effectively to contribute to organizational goals. They create environment with the help of HR policies, day to day dealing, rules and regulations regarding leaves, welfare, promotion, discipline, incentives, training etc. It creates confidence in persons to work without worry.

(b) Develop Performance Plans

Management goes for planning of the job, competencies required for performing the jobs and standards required for performance of the jobs. It includes job description, job specification and fixation of job performance standard. Through these plans only the type of person required can be ascertained.

(c) Selection of Appropriate People

To carry out the various types of jobs in the organization manpower is needed. The required type and number of people are to be selected from the aspirants. So they may be made available at right place in right time for accomplishment of the tasks at required time. This is possible through proper recruitment and selection of employees.

(d) Decision Regarding Performance Standard

Performance management as a function of human resource management, The management takes decision regarding the required standards of the performance in consultation with top level management, head of departments and experts or consultants. They consider the lowest, highest and average performance of the people at work. After detailed discussion the most realistic standards are fixed by the management.

(e) Plans for Development of Employees

Performance management is interested for development of both employees and organization. With the development of one is the development of both. He conducts orientation of the persons, provides education, and finds out the need for training and conduct training programme for development of skills, knowledge and competencies. This can contribute in improvement of the performance of persons and company.

(f) Measurement of Performance

After planning and development activities the next task of performance management is to measure the performance of the people at work. For measurement of performance the different criteria has been fixed such as output per hour/shift quality of work, behaviour, discipline, level of commitment etc. This helps to find out the poor and good performers out of the lot. On the basis of it further remedial action can be taken.

(g) Conducts Performance Feedback

After measurement of performance of all employees the management finds the slow moving persons. The objective of performance management is to find out the reasons for slow going. They conduct coaching session for such people and give feedback to them. They suggest ways to improve their performance also. This clarifies many doubts of the employees. It helps a lot the persons to understand their caliber and difficulties. Through the coaching and counseling session the attitude of the employees is changed positive.

(h) Design Compensation, Recognition and Reward System

Through performance appraisal system the slow and fast working persons are identified. As per the output the management designs the compensation, recognition and reward system. For good performers the incentives are designed as per the output. They are given better incentives whereas slow working persons may be given less incentives or may be denied. Good performers' tasks are recognized by giving appreciation letter, prizes or rewards. Sometime they may be considered for further promotion also. This keeps on motivating the people whether a slow or fast working person.

(i) Contributes in Developing Goodwill

By performing the functions like creating good working environment, planning for performance, measuring performance, providing performance feedback, designing suitable compensation, recognition and reward system the management helps in improvement of the performance as a whole. The work related employees problems are sorted out. It gives a sense of confidence and motivation among persons. These persons create publicity by word of mouth inside and in the public outside. It contributes a lot in creating high goodwill of the company. Provide promotional/career development opportunities for staff.

According to TVS Rao the performance management system includes the following actions:

(i) Identifying the parameters of performance and stating them very clear.

(ii) Setting performance standards

(iii) Planning in participative ways where appropriate, performance of all constituents

(iv) Identifying competencies and competency gaps that contribute/hinder to performance

(v) Planning performance development activities

(vi) Creating ownership

(vii) Recognizing and promoting performance culture

6. CONCERNS OF PERFORMANCE MANAGEMENT

Performance management is an important function of human resource management. HRM is mainly interested for proper utilization of manpower and contribute to a good extent in achieving the objectives of the organization. In nutshell, it can be said that through better performance it is to make the organization more effective in the present competitive situation. The following are the main concerns of performance management:

(a) Concern with Productivity

It is first of all concerned with the output per person/system/machine/group. It is concerned with the results achieved, the performance of activities, competencies needed to perform these activities from every individual, group or department and organization as a whole. In present uncontrollably, risky and rapidly changing environment it is difficult for every one to survive, stabilize, grow and excel in their performance. Those who are in position to give excellent performance are leader in the market. They are only grabbing maximum opportunities. Performance management is mainly concerned for better result through processes, input and required competencies. It is possible through planning, developing, measuring and review of the performance of everyone. Performance management plays an important role for effective working of HR management.

(b) Concern With Planning of Performance

Performance management is concerned with planning of the performance of people at work for better result in future. This means defining expectations expressed as objectives and in business plans. It plans the roles of everyone, standards of performance to be given in advance so that the actual performance can be compared with these standards. The performance of individual or group is aligned with the goals of the organization.

(c) Concern With Performance Measurement and Review

The next concerned of it is to measure the output of individuals and systems periodically. Further it is to compare with the standards already fixed. This shows the position of the performance whether the result is in the required direction or not. If the result is as per the planning then it is to be maintained otherwise it needs the remedial action for improvement. This position must be reviewed further for better result also Though this concern many irregularities will be removed and there may be better and smooth performance of everyone concerned in achieving the objective of the organization.

(d) Interest in Continuous Improvement

Performance management philosophy is based on innovation in every area of the organization. Concern with continuous improvement is based on the belief that continually striving to reach higher and higher standards in every part of the organization will provide better performance and will be in position to give competitive advantage to the organization over its competitors This means clarifying what organizational, team and individual effectiveness look like and taking steps to ensure that those defined levels of effectiveness are achieved. As Armstrong and Murlis said that helps in establishing a culture in which managers, individuals and groups take responsibility for the continuous improvement of business processes and of their own skills, competencies and contribution.'

(e) Concern With Continuous Development

It follows the Japanese concept of Kaizen. Performance management is concerned with creating a culture in which organizational and individual learning and development is a continuous process. HR managers are putting their efforts for creating a healthy working environment for everyone. That is very helpful for learning and work. People learn from success and face the challenges in their routine functioning.

7. BENEFITS OF PERFORMANCE MANAGEMENT

Performance management is a very important part of human resource management. The focus of it is on development aspects of individual and organisation performance. The approach of performance management is positive. In present highly competitive environment, a high degree of skill and commitment is needed to understand the environment and perform accordingly. Everybody is benefited by actions of performance management. It is bit difficult to summarise the benefits of it in detail. It is possible to get all employees to reconcile personal goals with organizational goals. One can increase productivity and profitability for any organization and that leads to progress of the organisation. It can be applied by organisations or a single department or section inside an organisation as well as an individual person. The process is a natural, self-inspired performance process and appropriately named the self-propelled performance process (SPPP). It is claimed that the self-propelled performance management system is:

(a) The fastest known method for career promotion;

(b) The quickest way for career advancement;

(c) The surest way for career progress;

(d) The best ingredient in career path planning;

(e) The only true and lasting virtue for career success;

(f) The most neglected part in teachings about management and leadership principles;

(g) The most complete and sophisticated application of performance management;

(h) The best integration of human behaviour research findings, with the latest management, leadership and organisational development principles;

(i) The best automated method for organisational change, development, growth, performance and profit;

(j) The quickest way for career building, career development and moving up on the stepping stones of the corporate career ladder;

(k) The surest and fastest way for increased motivation, productivity, growth, performance and profitability for both the individual and the organisation;

(l) The best career builder and career booster for any career; and inspirational, as it gets people moving, makes them self-starters in utilising own talents and initiative, automatically like magic.

It helps in creating good working environment of openness, mutual trust, cooperation and team spirit. People work with their high degree of motivation and without work stress. In healthy working environment people work in team and that leads to multidimensional benefits to individuals, teams, departments, sections, divisions and organisation as a whole. The benefits of it are numerous and these are financial and non-financial both. Managing employee or system performance facilitates the effective delivery of strategic and operational goals. Following are the gains from performance management:

(a) Financial Gains

Financial gains from performance management are following:

(i) Improve productivity and production of the company.

(ii) Reduce costs due to sincere and skilled manpower.

(iii) Complete the projects well in time because everyone is giving his best performance at work.

(iv) Aligns the organizational and individuals goals and that avoids all delays in performance.

(v) Through proper and timely communication the objectives are clarified and desired action can be achieved from employees as management wants.

(b) Non-financial Gains

Following are non-financial gains from performance management:

(i) Healthy working environment avoids work stress of the employees,

(ii) Optimizes incentive plans to specific goals for overachievement, not just business as usual

(iii) Employees feel satisfied when the working environment is friendly.

(iv) Employees get chance for further career development, training and promotion etc.

(v) A sense of belongingness, attachment and commitment develops among employees.

(vi) It leads to a high degree of motivation in employees and further creates a sense of loyalty towards the organisation.

(vii) Persons understand the importance of their roles and get engaged in contributing to the organisational goals.

(viii) Create transparency in approach and dealing among employees.

(ix) High confidence in organisation and its processes like salary, bonus, promotion etc.

(c) Effective Management Control

(i) Approach of person is flexible, responsive to management needs and performing the tasks.

(ii) Displays better data relationships.

(iii) Helps to comply in inspection, audit and other legalities.

(iv) Simplifies communication of strategic goals and gets involvement of lower level employees too.

8. PERFORMANCE MANAGEMENT AND PERFORMANCE APPRAISAL

Performance is often defined simply in output term that is needed for achievement of pre-decided goals. Performance is concerned what job is done, how it is done and what has been achieved. The concept of performance has been expressed by Brumbach as follows: 'Performance means both behaviour and results. Behaviours are the product of mental and physical efforts applied to tasks and that can be observed apart from the result from the job. This definition of performance concludes that when managing performance both inputs (behaviour) and outputs (results) need to be considered. In present turbulent and highly competitive business environment the question of survive and grow matters a lot. Management is under pressure to increase the productivity of everyone so that competitive advantage over competitors can be achieved. This is the main objective of performance management. Performance management is a process for establishing a shared understanding about what is to be achieved and an approach to managing people that increases the probability of achieving success (Weiss & Hartle).

It is about the everyday actions and behaviors people use to improve performance in themselves and others. It cannot be divorced from the management processes that pervade the organization. Performance management is the process of creating a work environment or setting in which people are enabled to perform to the best of their abilities. Performance management is a whole work system that begins when a job is defined as needed. It ends when an employee leaves your organization. The overall goal of performance management is to ensure that the organization and all of its subsystems (processes, departments, teams, employees, etc.) are working together in an optimum fashion to achieve the results desired by the organization. Performance management strives to optimize results of everyone and results of the organization.

Any focus of performance management within the organization (whether on department, process, employees, etc.) should ultimately affect overall organizational performance management as well. Achieving the overall goal requires several ongoing activities, including identification and prioritization of desired results, established means to measure progress toward those results, setting standards for assessing how well results are achieved, tracking and measuring progress toward results, exchanging ongoing feedback among those participants working to achieve results, periodically reviewing progress, reinforcing activities that achieve results and interviewing are also measures. Organisation is established to achieve certain objectives. Achievement of goals or targets depends upon the performance of individual employees. Hence it is quite necessary to understand as to what extent employees have been successful at their jobs for achievement of their goals. Thus performance appraisal forms an important part of HRM. This necessitates the study of this topic.

"It is the evaluation or appraisal of the relative worth to the company of a man's services on his job." (Alford and Beatty)

Performance appraisal is a systematic periodic and impartial rating of employee's excellence in matters pertaining to his present job and to his potentialities for a better job." (Flippo)

Performance appraisal is mainly used three purposes. (i) As a basis of reward allocation such as salary increments, promotion and other rewards etc. (ii) Performance appraisal will point the weaknesses of employees and will spot the areas where development efforts are needed. Performance appraisal a tool identification of deficiencies. (iii) It can be used the selection and development programme. It will differentiate satisfactory performers from unsatisfactory ones. It will help the management to perform functions relating to selection, development, salary, promotion, penalties, layoff and retrenchment.

It is sometimes assumed that performance appraisal is the same thing as performance management. But there are significant differences. Performance appraisal can be defined as the formal and periodical assessment and rating or ranking of individuals by their managers or immediate supervisors at, usually, an annual review meeting. Whereas performance management is a continuous, broader, more comprehensive and natural process of management that clarifies mutual expectations, emphasizes the support role of managers who are expected to act as coaches rather than judges and focuses on the future. Performance appraisal has been criticized by people because here approach is like bureaucratic and top-down under the control of human resource managers. It was often backward looking, concentrating on what had gone wrong, rather than looking forward to future development needs.

Performance appraisal schemes existed in isolation. There was little or no link between them and the needs of the business. Line managers have frequently rejected performance appraisal schemes as being time consuming and irrelevant. Employees have resented the superficial nature with which appraisals have been conducted by managers who lack the skills required, tend to be biased and are simply going through the motions. As Armstrong and Murlis assert, performance appraisal too often degenerated into 'a dishonest annual ritual'. The differences between them as summed up by Armstrong and Baron are set out in Table 17.1.

Table 17.1: Performance Appraisal & Performance Management

Performance appraisal	Performance management
(a) Top-down assessment	Joint process through dialogue
(b) Annual appraisal meeting	Continuous review with one or more formal reviews
(c) It is a part of performance	It is a wider concept than appraisal management process
(d) Use of ratings and ranking	Ratings less common
(e) Monolithic system	Flexible process
(f) Focus on quantified objectives	Focus on values, behaviour as well as objectives.
(g) Looks back to find out what has gone wrong in performance.	Looks forward for further development.
(h) Often linked to pay	Less likely to be a direct link to pay.

(i) Bureaucratic paperwork	Documentation kept to a minimum.
(j) It is carried out by immediate supervisors	Line managers are involved and in discussion with experts and consultants

9. PRINCIPLES OF PERFORMANCE MANAGEMENT PLAN

For effective working of performance management, management must keep certain guidelines in mind. These guidelines may help in proper working and avoid much confusion during work. Experts have suggested the following principles:

(a) Continuous Coaching, Feedback and Communication

Performance management is considered a continuous process, not an event. For its proper and effective working the principles of continuous coaching and feedback are integral to success. These will definitely coordinate the related activities properly.

(b) Effective Communication

The Performance Management Plan involves line managers, supervisors, experts and consultants. To coordinate between them a proper timely and effective communication is needed. If it is not there the objective of the plan will be defeated. It will ensure mutual understanding of work responsibilities, priorities, and performance standards and measurements.

(c) Discussion and Evaluation

Discussion and evaluation of specific job should be there. The discussion and evaluation should be regarding nature of jobs, tasks, competencies needed to perform these jobs, major duties and responsibilities and the performance standards. These must be specifically defined and communicated as the first step in the process.

(d) Performance Standards

Performance standards for each major duty/responsibility must be defined and communicated to all concerned. These standards are to be decided in mutual discussion with line managers, manager in charge of the job, persons performing the jobs, in-house experts and consultants. Through detailed discussion the lowest, highest and average performance of the performers are to be taken in to account before finalizing the performance standard. These must be feasible to achieve by an average performer.

(e) Employee Involvement and Development

The performance management revolves around the manpower. The management must kept in mind that they must be involved the it and efforts must be there for their development and improvement of performance at work They must be motivated to develop their competencies, involve in the jobs and give best output to contribute in achievement of the organizational goals. Without proper involvement and development of employees it is not at all effective.

(f) Fair Performance Evaluation

The evaluation of the performance of people at work should be carried out timely. It should be fair without favour and fear. If it is done so then the exact position of the performance given by the employees will be clear. Otherwise misguiding result will be there. The very objective of the performance measurement will not be served. The performance evaluation should not be frequent but at least annually it should be carried out because it is time and efforts consuming.

(g) Proper Documentation

The principle of proper documentation should be considered an important principle for effective working of the plan. The plan should be drawn and documents should be prepared. It should be communicated for all concerned who have been identified. The development, recognition, compensation and reward plan should be in black and white. Proper records are to be maintained. Further, proper documents of performance appraisal are needed for further remedial action. If these are not prepared then whenever confusion is there the documentary evidence cannot be given and management has nothing to refer in case of doubts arise regarding past decisions taken

(h) Performance Evaluation for Everyone

The performance appraisal of all employees should be carried out. It is not only applicable to lower and middle levels. It should be applied to the top level also. The senior level performs must be evaluation on the basis of the successful administration of the plan and ongoing performance management responsibilities

(i) Training For Managers, Supervisors and Employees

The training should be made available for everyone in the organization. It should be encouraged. It will keep the knowledge of the persons up to date. With changing technology, working procedures and new methods the present competencies becomes outdated. This has the effect on the performance. Special importance must be given for training of all levels of people.

(j) Consistent Performance Management Plan

The plan should be consistent. It should not be changed frequently. Further, should be consistent with federal and state laws. If proper attention is not given to this principle then confusion can be created among people those who are involved in performance management directly or indirectly.

10. PERFORMANCE MANAGEMENT PROCESS

Process can be explained as a set of activities and these activities are arranged in a logical sequence of occurring and these cannot be changed The activities in performance management are similar to the other process in organisation like planning, organising, controlling and management by objectives. In it a set of activities are involved. To perform the functions of performance management these activities are to be carried out in their required sequence. The performance management process requires many ongoing activities in the organization. This includes identifying and prioritizing goals, defining what constitutes progress towards goals, setting standards for measuring results, and monitoring performance, counseling, coaching, communication, motivation and feedback of performance to employees, review of performance, development plans, implementing effective goal-oriented activities, and intervening to create improvements when needed.

The performance management process focuses on overall performance of the unit. Great importance is given to the activities mentioned above for effective accomplishment of the goals of the organization on the methods. In most of the orgnisations these activities are performed but it is not hard and fast for every organization. The steps in the performance management process may vary from one organization to another organization. But special focus will be given to the activities of higher priority. Most programs include certain core activities working from the highest level of the organization down to the smaller components. The performance management process can be explained the diagram shown below:

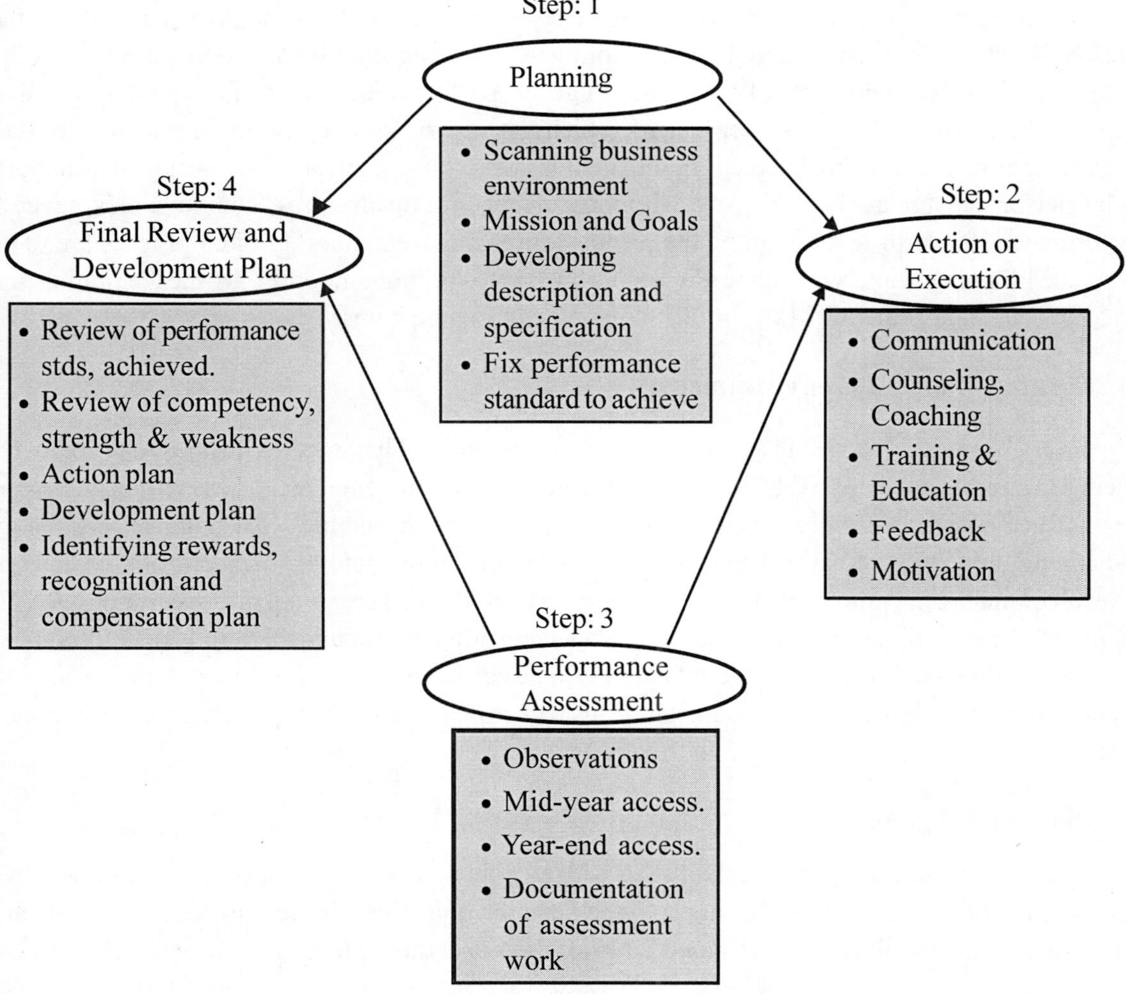

Diagram 17.1: Performance Management Process

11. STEPS IN PERFORMANCE MANAGEMENT PROCESS

After depth study of various organisations, it is found that in every organisation different steps have been taken and there is no similarity in steps in performance management process. It entirely depends upon the requirement of the organisation and the management working pattern. Some organisations take help form the consultants and some are having their own internal experts for scanning the business the business environment, identifying and prioritizing the goals, fixing responsibility and accountability, expected performance standards and many more work related aspects. In large organisation mostly the below mentioned steps are followed but in small and further smaller organisations some of the steps may be or may not be followed. It is summarised that the following steps have been involved in different organisations in general but exactly not similar in all:

(a) Step 1: Planning

Planning is the process in which the future course of actions has been decided in advance. This helps in giving the direction while performing the tasks. Without planning the objective of doing the work will not be clear. There may be many confusions such as what is to be done, how it is to be done, when it is to be done etc. That is why to go for performance management process the first step will be planning. The first step during which the supervisor and employee accomplish will discuss regarding current business environment, mission of the organization, present goals, and jobs to be performed for achieving goals. Methods of performing the jobs, competencies needed, performance standards and assigning the responsibility and accountability of employees are to be planned. Planning stage will make the whole process working smoothly. In the beginning the performance management will go for planning of the following items:

(i) Scanning of business environment:

Every business is carried in an atmosphere or surrounding. That is called business environment. There are internal and external factors of it. The internal environmental factors are within control of the management whereas the external factors like social, cultural, economic, legal, political, technology and competition etc., are beyond control of management. These factors are uncontrollable and out of reach of management to control. They change very rapidly and create a lot of uncertainty. A high degree of risk is involved in the business. For proper and effective planning the study of environment becomes inevitable. The study of these factors is to be carried out and try to find out the threats and opportunities for the business of the company. This will provide inputs to the planning for performance management.

(ii) Mission and goals:

Every organisation has been established with an objective in the business. The mission shows the objective of existence in the business. To achieve the objectives the certain goals or targets are to be fulfilled. The goals are to be decided for everyone concerned. The goals can be for individuals, team, section, department and organisation as a whole. The managers, supervisors, and employees through discussion will agree for the goals to be achieved. The special care should be taken that the goals should be realistic and feasible to achieve. These should not be beyond capacity to achieve.

(iii) Developing job description and job specification:

To fulfil the goal requirement the certain tasks are to be decided. What jobs are to be performed and how these will be performed. First of all the jobs profile is to be prepared. The work, jobs and tasks are to ascertained. The decision is to be taken regarding the major work, its components, level of responsibility, reporting system, location of the jobs and sub-jobs etc. Next, the procedure or method of doing the jobs is to be finalized. In method the involvement of manpower, machines, equipment and steps for performance of jobs are to be decided. After finalizing jobs and methods of doing the jobs, the job specification is to be finalized. For performing the skills, knowledge, educational qualification, work experience, attitude, ability, capability, the level of risk involved etc., are to be discussed and finalized. If the required competencies are available then it is alright. Otherwise efforts should be there to find out how the required competencies can be acquired and developed. Finally in this the job responsibility and accountability of everyone is to be agreed and fixed. This will give the clear guidelines regarding the jobs to be performed, method of performing the job, competencies required for performing the jobs, responsibility and accountability of the jobs.

(iv) Fixing performance standard:

For accomplishment of the goals the jobs are to be performed. Now, what level of performance is expected from the employees is to be discussed. For fixing the performance standard the comprehensive discussion should be there among managers, supervisors, employees, in-house experts and consultants. The performance standard should be feasible to achieve. These should not be very low or high. The performance of slow, fast performer may not be suitable for everyone. That is why the average performance should be taken into account. Standards are the statements that specify what constitutes good work. The all concerned persons involved in fixing performance standards develop the list of specific job tasks, and then they write statements that specify how the quality of the work will be determined. The performance standards should be specific, measurable, attainable and time-based. The performance standards should be decided regarding the quality of work, quantity of output, with reference to the time taken, manners of work performed, method of doing the tasks, behaviour and costs involved in performing the jobs. These will give a clear idea to the supervisors and performers regarding what are expected from them on job.

(b) Step 2: Action or Execution of Plan

After planning of performance management the next step is action or execution of the plan. If the plan is good and not implemented properly the result will be poor and poor plan implemented strongly then many irregularities can be overcome. This stage is very important. In execution stage, the actions are to be taken simultaneously with work. The action regarding communication of performance plan, coaching, training and education, motivation and feedback of the performance should be taken by the managers or supervisors responsible for the jobs. Whatever has been planned by the authority, must be communicated to all concerned regarding objectives, jobs, methods or procedures, competencies, goals, responsibility and accountability and performance standards expected from the performers. This will help a lot in understanding the requirements and confusions will be avoided. This will help to get the support of everyone concerned. The objective of the planning will be made easier to achieve if proper, purposeful and timely communication has taken place. When the need for training and education has been identified, the sincere efforts should be put to train and educate the people on and off the jobs. This will help to develop knowledge, skills and competencies of the employees. The trained people will get confidence in the jobs, confidence will give better performance and it will give further the job satisfaction to the job performer.

During the work there may be many difficulties faced by the employees. The manager or supervisor must coach and guide the persons if any problem is faced. The problems are to be solved on the spot. The proper coaching must be carried out regarding the system, its parts, performance procedure, and most likely difficulties faced on the jobs. This will avoid confusion on the spot and performance will improve. This finally will give job confidence and satisfaction to the performers. Another important action during the work is motivation of the employees. They employees must be motivated by the managers and supervisors by giving timely support, proper behavior of supervisors showing interest in jobs of juniors, rules and regulation are implemented with human touch. The motivational aspects will create a desire to work strongly on the job. It will contribute to improve the performance standard related to quality and quantity of output, time, cost and manners. This is the ultimate goal of the performance management process.

Talented and motivated workforce can create a wonder for the organization. This may give the multidimensional benefits to the organization. Finally the image of the unit may be created and developed further. When the persons are assigned the jobs and they start performing, they themselves do not know how they are performing. Time to time they must be informed by the supervisors regarding what they are doing and how they are doing. Getting feedback the confusions can be clarified. If any problem is faced or confusion is there then action can be taken by them during the work. This problem will not prolong. People will work without any work stress. If the managers and supervisors are taking these actions in time, the ultimate goal of improving the performance will be achieved undoubtedly.

(c) Step 3: Performance Assessment

The next phase will be performance assessment or appraisal. After planning and execution of the plan it becomes necessary to see whether the job is performed as per the planning and guidelines. The performance is to be reviewed. If it is not done then the employees and managers will not take interest in the whole process of performance management. The performance will be assessed during the work, mid of the year and finally at the end of the year. It is a difficult work to be done properly. The following jobs are to be done in the assessment of performance:

(i) Observation:

Under planning the works have been assigned to the employees. The employees have been communicated, guided, motivated and feedback taken time to time from them. Further, it is to be seen whether they are doing the work as per expectation and goals set. The managers and supervisors will observe the working on day to day basis. Whenever they visit to the work, discuss the issues with the employees or interacting, they must observe the attitude, interest, manner, approach, involvement and output given on shift or daily basis. When employees interact with their peers, supervisors, managers, vendors, clients and other staff members, the information should be gathered on day to day basis regarding their behaviour and performance. This will help in assessing the performance of the employees.

(ii) Mid-year assessment:

The performance review takes place twice during the year. During the mid-year review, performance is reviewed almost after six months. It is to be done without writing down the comments in the assessment report. At this stage no documentation is required formally. During the review the work done by the person, difficulties faced during the work, competencies shown, discipline, type of behaviour expressed and level of commitment give should be recorded. Through observation the information gathered will help the supervisor to prepare the midyear assessment report. After report a review meeting is to be conducted. For this it should be communicated to all concerned. Through mutual discussion the date and time for the review meeting will be decided. It should be communicated to all concerned. At the specified date, time and venue the review meeting will be conducted. The focus of the review meeting will be on overall performance and interruption will not be allowed during discussion. The supervisor should explain the purpose of conducting the meeting, present overall assessment of employees. During discussion if any doubt is there then it should be clarified. At the end of the meeting the supervisor should assure the employees for help regarding the assessment problems and must thank to all participants for their participation. After the meeting the final performance review form is to be filled up and the responses and comments from supervisors and employees should be summarized. The members should be encouraged to give if they have any other comments. Finally, the complete report is to be signed by the supervisor and members. The proper file is to be maintained for further reference.

(iii) Year-end assessment:

On completion of the year the performance assessment is to be carried out. In every organization the appraisal practice is adopted. This brings the success, failure and obstacles faced during the year to the knowledge of managers and employees. All work related aspects are considered for evaluation of the performance. The performance appraisal is generally done by supervisors, self, peers, juniors and all who are directly or indirectly attached to the employees relating to the work. The major difference between the two reviews is that that no results or ratings are put on the paper in midyear review. The supervisor should tell the employee that the mid-year review explains the present result and it is the preparation for the final assessment.

For yearend assessment the supervisor should collect the information and motivate the members to get involved actively so that the better result can be achieved. They can raise questions regarding new ideas for development of performance, career development and examples for achievements. The employees should explain the situations beyond control of the employees and these should not be considered for appraisal. For final appraisal different criteria like job proficiency, attitude, discipline, behaviour with other persons, competencies on job, leadership, team-spirit etc. are generally considered. These may vary from organization to organization. Supervisor must motivate the persons for self-appraisal. The appraisal form will be filled by the supervisor. He must take proper time to study the work of everyone before giving result or rating. Proper care should be taken to give fair and impartial assessment.

Generally the **following errors** are likely to take place in assessment:

- **General bias errors:** It depends upon the attitude of the assessor. Some may be very strict and other may be very liberal during the assessment work. They may not consider the actual performance of the employees for assessment work. It affects everyone in general.
- **Halo effect:** During assessment when the assessor considers or gives importance to one of the criteria of the assessment and ignoring the other factor, the error is likely to take place. This is called halo effect. It gives wrong assessment of the employees.
- **Relation rating error:** When one task is related to another task then the assessor gives importance to that logical relationship more. It creates the error in the assessment.
- **Contrast and similarity errors:** The assessors assess the other employees based on their own assessment. The assessment may be similar or contrast to assessment of the employees.
- **Central tendency errors:** When the evaluator does not take the extreme steps for evaluation. He avoids the extreme two ends. He follows the central path and gives and average rating for the performance. The range of assessment is very narrow. It dissatisfies the excellent performers but protect the poor performers also.
- **Proximity errors:** When raters assess one high side then he assesses others also high side this is called proximity error. He wants to do justice with every one but in the beginning he has done the assessment on wrong side and that affects the whole assessment.
- **Rating inflation:** When supervisor's rating goes very high without any reason is called inflated rating. The supervisor should make that the ratings are on fact based and not based on emotions or feeling of individuals.

There is no hard and fast rule that these errors will take place with every assessor. But these are like to affect the assessment work of the assessors. The assessors should keep these points in mind and review the rating errors on regular basis. If the proper care is taken then the assessment work will be adequate. Accountability can be rated as, does not meet standards, improvement, or standards. On each rating the assessor is supposed to give clear comments on the appraisal form. For example if the person exceeds standard them comment should be," very good, keep it up in future also". Similarly the other criteria like behaviour, leadership, quantity and quality of output, discipline, commitment to the work, level of competencies etc., are to be rated. Finally the overall performance of the employees is to be rated. It should be followed by the comments from the assessor. The assessor is to sign the assessment form and submit to the concerned cell in HR department.

(iv) Documentation of assessment:

In performance assessment stage the final activity is to be performed is documentation. This activity is very important. In this the assessors have to fill up the assessment form. It should be signed and if needed should be sealed. The rating of the performance is to be kept confidential. Proper care should be taken so that the documents should not be tampered or altered by anybody. This document will be reference for review meeting for development plan preparation. The remedial or development action will be taken on the basis of the assessment report. The assessment report should be in black and white. The oral assessment report is not going to serve the purpose. The person who is experienced in maintaining the documents must be consulted. Further, the storage of the documents also should be taken care of. If proper care is taken in preparation, signature, communication and storage of documents the further planning work will become very easy.

(d) Step 4: Final Review and Development Plan

After performance assessment at the end of year the management go for final review of the performance They review of responsibility and accountability, performance standard achieved, the competencies the employees possess, leadership quality shown, discipline during work, teamwork, level of commitment and comments from supervisors and employees will be studied in detail. The efforts should be put by the management to find out the weak point in the process and work on that so that for future there should not be any problem. The very objectives of the performance management should be achieved. Timely and prompt action can be initiated to control the problem in the beginning itself. The management should have the proactive approach regarding the performance management process. The final review and development stage must involve the following activities:

(i) Review of performance standard achieved:

In the performance assessment the appraisal has been done. That performance will be reviewed. There may be better performance standard the employees have achieved but management is having innovative approach to look forward and find out how the performance can be achieved better over the present performance standard. The jobs have been assigned to the employees to perform. There accountability has been fixed to perform and they are answerable to the management. How far they have achieved or fulfilled the responsibility. The standards of the performance in terms of quality, quantity, discipline, leadership, initiative in problem solving, costs etc., will be reviewed. The comparative study will be carried out to find out the deficiencies in these criteria. The management will suggest the points to improve further if any deficiency is found in the assessment. Further the management will review the consequences of the present performance in future in highly competitive situation in the markets. Management is not interested to take any chance of failure in the efforts.

(ii) Review of competency strengths and weakness:

The different types of jobs are being done in an organization as per nature and size of the organization. To perform these jobs a set of competencies is required. In competency we may include skills, knowledge of job, ability, capability, attitude, behaviour etc. Management will see that the people selected for the jobs to perform are right type of people. They are having these competencies or not. If they are having then they expressed these during the work or not. The difficulties faced by the employees during the year while performing the jobs will be reviewed. They will find out why the difficulty has been faced and who faced on which job. Further, the areas where the employees have shown their required competencies and did not face the problems will be reviewed. From these review the management will pinpoint the areas where the development is needed. The suitable steps will be taken or suggested for improvement.

(iii) Action plan:

On the basis of performance assessment the review committee will have the input relating to the performance standard, competencies, difficulties, behaviour, discipline, commitment, initiative etc. On the review of these where the deficiencies are found out the action plan will be prepared. If the performance standard has not been achieved the jobs and performs will be under the action plan for improvement. The plan will be prepared for improvement in standard on the job and of individuals. If any person is not having good behaviour, discipline or initiative in the work then the corrective action will be suggested against those persons. If the competencies are not shown by the persons then steps will be initiated against them to correct them. If there is no problem with the manpower but problem is found out with the machines then the corrective steps will be suggested to improve the availability of the machines for use through proper maintenance of the machines. The action plans will be prepared to remove the problems with the machines, materials, manpower, and working procedures.

(iv) Development plan:

From the review of the performance assessment or appraisal the review committee gets the input for development plan. The experts are having the prevailing knowledge of the prevailing market conditions and business environment. They get the updated knowledge about environmental factors like social, legal, economic, political, cultural, technology and competition. They are informed regarding the threats and opportunities for the company business in the national and international markets. To survive in new business, grow and stabilize in the existing business and further where the company is doing well to excel in performance, the development plans are prepared by the review committee.

The committee can prepare development plans for training, education of employees, arranging refresher courses for existing employees, changing of working procedure, on replacement of technology totally fresh training programme, leadership development programme, customer orientation programme and many more programmes can be included in the development plan as per the need of the time. The main objective of development plan is to keep the organization young and more effective to do the business effectively and efficiently in the present cut-throat competitive market situation.

(v) Identifying rewards, recognition and compensation plan :

During the work assessment some of the employees have achieved the standard more than expectation. They must be identified and plan for their rewards and recognition should be prepared. Their efforts should not go unnoticed. Their efforts should be recognized and accordingly they should be appreciated. Further the compensation plan also should be prepared. The company is getting better results, sales and profits. Out of these the employees should be paid. The payment can be made in different forms. It depends on the compensation plan of the review committee. This will contribute to improve the morale and motivation of the people. This will enable them to create interest to do the work. The many labour problems can be avoided. Further it will make the things easier for the management to achieve the standard of performance. Ultimately it will contribute a lot in accomplishment of goals of the organization decided. The objective of the organization will be fulfilled.

12. CHARACTERISTICS OF PERFORMANCE MANAGEMENT PROCESS

From the study of performance management definitions and steps involved in performance management process the following characteristics have been found:

(a) Continuous Process

The performance management is a continuous process. It involves communication from top to bottom and feedback from bottom to top. It takes place round the year. The process cannot be completed within a short period. When one year performance process is completed then it starts for the next year. It is a never ending process. There are continuous dialogues between supervisors, managers and employees regarding communication, coaching, counseling, motivation and feedback. The objective behind these dialogues is to make the people to understand and perform as per the expectation so that the goals can be achieved.

(b) Use of Ranking and Ratings

In this process for evaluation purpose repeatedly and ranking and ratings have been used for different factors. The ranking and ratings are used for communication, coaching, performance standards, behaviour, discipline, level of commitment to achieve the tasks, leadership quality shown, initiatives taken for problem solving etc. There are different ratings and rankings required for completion of the assessment work. For example meets standards/ does not meet standards/ exceeds standards or first, second, third, fourth ranking in the lot.

(c) Focus on Behaviors

The tasks have been assigned to the employees and their accountability has been fixed. While performing the tasks the employees express their actions and reaction relating to the work. It is called the behaviour of the persons at work. It is very important aspect and management give special focus on it, During work employees shows different aspects of behaviour such as happy, unhappy, like, does not like, arguments, no arguments, obey, disobey, support, does not support, cooperate, does not cooperate, initiatives, no initiatives, discipline, indiscipline, commitment, no commitment etc. There are many aspects like this. Here some of them are mentioned. For evaluation purpose different agencies have developed different performance appraisal system. The employees are rated on the basis of these factors.

(d) Cooperative Approach

The performance management process involves a cooperative approach between managers, supervisors employee, focusing on regular discussions about responsibility, accountabilities, performance standards expectations, performance appraisal, review of action, development and compensation plans. They begin the year with an extensive discussion regarding these points time to time. All concerned persons take initiatives for giving expected performance standards and better behaviours during the work. The approach among them is very cooperative and contributes in accomplishment of the targets fixed.

(e) Training for All Concerned

Training provides knowledge, skills and contributes in development of overall competencies of the persons. The training is needed for all persons working at different levels. For managers they should be trained in planning process and communication. The supervisor will be required to go through a training program for conselling, coaching, motivation and performance appraisals. They should be trained regarding these points so that he can do the needful to help the employees whenever they need the help. It will solve many problems and employees can be guided and motivated to do the work so the expected results can be easily achieved.

(f) Scope for Performance Improvement

In performance management process the efforts have been put to find out the strengths and weakness of all concerned so that the action and development plans can be prepared. This will help in overcoming the problems and strengths will be further strengthened. Ultimately the performance of everyone will improve. Further, the companies are facing tough competition in the markets. The company which gives better performance will take the competitive advantages over their competitors. So the focus is to improve the performance with better teamwork. Management is looking forward for further improvement repeatedly.

13. ROLES OF SUPERVISORS, EMPLOYEES AND REVIEWERS

Several people share the responsibility in performance management process activities like planning, communication, coaching, feedback, training and education, motivation, assessment of performance, review of plans etc. The detailed descriptions of the roles played by the people in this process are explained below:

(a) Roles of Manager and Supervisor

Coaching:

- Conduct conselling and provide coaching whenever required to the employees whose performances are below standards.
- Identify and suggest ways to the employee for improvement in performance. Accept suggestions from employees for motivation and active roles for further planning of development plans.
- Timely communicate to employees regarding betteropport unities and improved procedure for improving the work create confidence among employees for suggestions for further improvement in performance
- Make proper observations regarding the performance of the employees and the gathered information that help them in mid year, final assessment at the end of the year and other planning work
- Keep records of achievements and complaints got from customers regarding employees work.

Review:

- Maintain the records about the employee's performance and on the basis of that final assessment of performance is done.
- Ask the employee for feedback regarding their good and poor performances, and problems faced that may affect their working efficiency.
- Complete appraisal form and discuss ratings and comments with the employee.

(b) Role of employees

Planning:

- Meeting and discussion with their managers and supervisors in the beginning regarding accountability, performance standards and behaviour. Further, give suggestions for better performance to the managers.

- Discussion with managers about expectation from them relating to accountability, performance standards and behaviours.
- Clarification of doubts if exist from managers and supervisors about accountability, performance standards and behaviour at work.
- For better performance they discuss with their managers and supervisors
- Regarding managers' and customers' expectations, job priorities and budget etc.

Coaching:

- Accept their responsibilities for continuous improvement, development, accountability, performance standards, behaviour etc.
- Considering the periodical feedback from seniors as suggestion for further improvement in performance and not to take it in negative way. It should be taken as opportunity to learn more and improve skills
- Discuss with them regarding their progress at work and difficulties faced during the work for getting coaching from supervisors for improvement in performance
- Inform managers when they perform their work properly and fulfil the required standards. It should be known to them regarding their achievements.
- As and when required, they ask for meeting with supervisors for problem solution and suggestions for further improvements.
- Remember the points discussed in planning meeting regarding the accountability, performance standards and behaviour time to time.

Review:

- Monitor their performance, ask others and keep records of their progress
- Prepare for review discussion with the support of their on performance.
- Participation in the review meeting and highlight their accomplishments and suggestions made by them to the supervisors in appraisal form.

(c) Role of Reviewers

Planning:

- Discuss with the managers and supervisors regarding how their planning meeting was planned and conducted.

- Check the ratings for the accountability and performance standards whether these are feasible to achieve or not.
- Make sure that the planning points discussed in the meeting have been communicated to the employees or not and find out the point of disagreement also during planning meeting.

Coaching:

- Cross check with the managers and supervisors whether the counselling and coaching sessions have been conducted or not
- Discuss with supervisors regarding the progress of various employees, their involvement and helping the weak performers

Review:

- Discuss with supervisors regarding review meeting and type of feedback they are going to give.
- After every planning and review meeting, they should sign the minutes of the meetings and ask the supervisors also to do the same thing properly.
- Check the filled up appraisal form, the entries made by supervisors and employees, rating and results given by the supervisors. Ask the supervisor how the appraisal process was conducted and suggestion for improvement for future.
- Make sure supervisor has discussed with employees each rating and rankings with written comments wherever applicable in the result part of the form.
- Check the consistency of supervisors and managers in performance appraisal, use of appraisal system, appraisal of number of employees, explanation of ratings to employee
- Discuss with the supervisor regarding the type of feedback given to the employees regarding their performance. It may be oral or written.
- Remind them to praise the performers if not done because it may encourage the employees to do better in future.

14. CONCLUSION

Present business environment is very uncertain and risky. It is very difficult to understand and predict about future. Mistakes are likely to take place. A high degree of skill is needed to understand the situation and take decision. If slight mistake is there then it may lead to the business in great problem. Over and above the highly competitive situation compels every organization to wake up and do the business. It is not possible to do the business the way organization wants. A high degree of competency is needed at levels of management and employees. The need for highly talented and motivated human resource is felt. If the employees are highly talented and motivated then they would be in position to give better performance and higher level of productivity. The companies having talented and motivated manpower are bringing better products/ services for customers and capturing the opportunities in the market and others are not in position to do so. So the importance of talented and motivated manpower or human resources has been realized at management level. They are interested to hire, train and maintain the manpower in such a way that they are in position to achieve the performance standards and objectives of the organization properly.

Human resource management is focusing on performance management of employees so that they can maintain their position in the market and further sustain in the business. The human resource is critical and difficult to manage. It is because human behaviour is highly unpredictable. It differs not only from individual to individual but often on the part of same individual at different points of time. In spite of biological and cultural similarities, human beings not only differ in their appearance but also in their capabilities based on their background, training and experience. Human resource or a person at work is the most important component of the undertaking. Management cannot afford to ignore human resource at any cost. The firm that gets the advantage over other competitors through their talented and dedicated manpower can take the lead in the market. The contribution of employees on job is the most important factor for development and excellence in business. The performance of employees on different jobs in close coordination is needed for success of the unit.

Performance management maintains, develop and motivate the people at work to give better results. In the present competitive situation the organisation that gives better results can survive, stabilize, grow and excel in the performance. It helps a lot in achieving the objectives of HRM. Performance management includes activities to ensure that goals are consistently being met in an effective and efficient manner. Performance management can focus on performance of the organization, a department, processes to build a product or service, employees, etc. Performance management is the process of creating a work environment or setting in which people are enabled to perform to the best of their abilities. Performance management is a whole work system that begins when a job is defined as needed. It ends when an employee leaves your organization. It helps in creating good working environment of openness, mutual trust, cooperation and team spirit. People work with their high degree of motivation and without work stress. In healthy working environment people work in team and that leads to multidimensional benefits to individuals, teams, departments, sections, divisions and organisation as a whole.

The benefits of it are numerous and these are financial and non-financial both. Managing employee or system performance facilitates the effective delivery of strategic and operational goals. Major gains from performance management are financial and non-financial. The Functions of performance management include creating healthy work environment, develop performance plans, selection of appropriate people, decision regarding performance standard, plans for development of employees, measurement of performance, conducts performance feedback, design compensation, recognition and reward system, contributes in developing goodwill. By performing these functions the management helps in improvement of the performance as a whole. The work related employees problems are sorted out. It gives a sense of confidence and motivation among persons. These persons create publicity by word of mouth inside and in the public outside. It contributes a lot in creating high goodwill of the company

The activities in performance management are similar to the other process in organisation like planning, organising, controlling and management by objectives. In it a set of activities are involved. To perform the functions of performance management these activities are to be carried out in their required sequence. The performance management process requires many ongoing activities in the organization. This includes identifying and prioritizing goals, defining what constitutes progress towards goals, setting standards for measuring results, and monitoring performance, counseling, coaching, communication, motivation and feedback of performance to employees, review of performance, development plans, implementing effective goal-oriented activities, and intervening to create improvements when needed. For effective working of this process, business *performance management software* is mainly used in organizations.

From the study of performance management definitions and steps involved in performance management process the following characteristics have been found:

(a) Continuous process

(b) Use of ranking and ratings

(c) Focus on Behaviours

(d) Cooperative approach

(e) Training for all concerned

(f) Scope for performance improvement

Several people share the responsibility in performance management process activities like planning, communication, coaching, feedback, training and education, motivation, feedback, assessment of performance, review of plans etc. The major contribution in this process is of employees, supervisors, managers and experts relating to planning, coaching and review of performance of employees.

15. QUESTIONS FOR REVIEW

1. Define employee / human resource of the organisation and discuss its importance.
2. Human resource is the most important resource in a company. It utilizes the other resources for production and further generation of resources. Discuss.
3. Define manpower or employees and explain the salient feature of employees.
4. Discuss the concept of employees' performance and impact of it on business of the company.
5. Higher employees' performance is the concern of management of the company in present global competitive environment. Elaborate.

6. Define performance management and explain the characteristics of it in detail.
7. To maintain the performance of employees in an organization, explain the main functions performed by performance management.
8. Elaborate the concerns of performance management of the company in present situation.
9. Describe the benefits of performance management to the company in detail.
10. What are the different types of gain of performance management to various parties? Discuss.
11. Define performance management and performance appraisal and differentiate between them also.
12. For effective working of performance management which principles or guidelines would you keep in mind or follow? Explain.
13. How do you evaluate the future of performance management in highly competitive global situation?
14. Write short notes on the following:
    (a) Consistent performance management plan
    (b) Proper documentation of appraisal
    (c) Performance standard and behaviour
    (d) Financial and non-financial gains
    (e) Effective management control
    (f) Interest in continuous improvement and development
    (g) Concern with higher productivity
    (h) Contribution in development of goodwill by performance management
    (i) Relation of better performance and profitability in a company.
15. Define performance management process and explain its main characteristics of it.
16. Discuss the main steps involved in performance management process with the help of diagram in detail.
17. What are the activities involved in planning stage? Discuss them.
18. Communication, coaching, and training and feedback are very important in performance management process. Explain.
19. Discuss performance assessment and elaborate the activities involved in global competitive environment in detail.
20. What types of errors take place in assessment process? Explain.
21. Highlight the roles played by supervisors, managers, experts and employees in performance management process.

22. Write short notes on the following:
    (a) Execution plan
    (b) Planning for performance.
    (c) Performance assessment

16. OBJECTIVE QUESTIONS

1. What are the principal components of the organization?
   (a) Human factors.
   (b) People at work.
   (c) Knowledge & skills of human being.
   (d) All the above
   (e) None of these.
2. Performance management is the process of creating a work environment or setting in which people are enabled to perform to the best of their abilities. Many writers and consultants are using the term "performance management" as a substitution for:
   (a) Effective orientation.
   (b) Design effective compensation.
   (c) Traditional appraisal.
   (d) Provide promotional development.
   (e) All the above
3. Author " Mohrman & Mohrman" states:
   (a) Performance management is managing the business .
   (b) Strategic & integrated approach.
   (c) Directing & supporting employee.
   (d) Creating a work environment.
   (e) All the above.
4. It helps to find out the poor and good performers out of the lot. On the basis of the this assessment further remedial action can be taken. It is known as:
   (a) Conducts performance feedback.
   (b) Measurement of performance.
   (c) Contributes in developing goodwill.
   (d) Selecting of appropriate people.
   (e) None of the above.
5. Full form of SPPP?
   (a) Self-performance performance process.
   (b) Self-proprietor performance process.
   (c) Self-propelled performance process.
   (d) Self-prepared production process.
   (e) None of these.

6. A strategic and integrated approach to increasing the effectiveness of organizations by improving the performance of the people who work in them and by developing the capabilities of teams and individual contributors. It is defined by

   (a) TV RAO
   (b) Armstrong and Baron
   (c) Khandelwal
   (d) Heartly
   (e) None of the above

7. What is the 4th and final step of performance management process?

   (a) Planning.
   (b) Action or execution.
   (c) Performance assessment.
   (d) Review & development plan.
   (e) None of the above

8. The performance management process involves a approach between managers, supervisors employee, focusing on regular discussions about responsibility, accountabilities, performance standards expectations, performance appraisal, review of action, development and compensation plans. This approach is known as:

   (a) Training for all concerned approach.
   (b) Use of ranking & rating approach.
   (c) Cooperative approach.
   (d) Continuous process approach.
   (e) None of the above

9. What is the role of employees in the following activities?

   (a) Coaching & Review.
   (b) Planning. Coaching & Review
   (c) Performance feedback
   (d) None of the above
   (e) All the above

10. From the study of performance management definitions and steps involved in performance management process the characteristics of is:

    (a) Continuous process
    (b) Use of ranking and ratings
    (c) Focus on Behaviors
    (d) Cooperative approach
    (e) All the above

Answer Keys:

Question No.	Answer	Question No.	Answer
1	b	6	d
2	d	7	b
3	d	8	a
4	a	9	c
5	b	10	d

Chapter

Workforce Diversity and Human Resource Development

1. INTRODUCTION TO CULTURE DIVERSITY

When business activities are carried out in different countries, the companies come across different economies, political systems, cultures, markets, customers and employees. The differences are noticed in these and it is called diversity in cultures and markets. Diversity is a very wide term and bit difficult to define it. It includes main elements are like sex, age, race, religion, region, work style, experience, education, values, physical and technical competencies, trust, beliefs, traditions and customs, mental caliber, personality, experiences, affiliation, economic development, per capita income, marital status, knowledge, preference and tastes for products, area of specialization etc. In Workforce America Managing Employee Diversity as a Vital Resource, diversity is defined as "otherness or those human qualities that are different from our own and outside the groups, to which we belong, yet present in other individuals and groups".

The various factors of culture created diversity in different areas. The different categories of diversity are following:

(a) Diversity in workforce

(b) Diversity in the markets

(c) Stakeholder diversity

In the India and abroad workforce diversity is the most dominating category of diversity. Employees of Indian companies are becoming increasingly heterogeneous in nature. Since globalization in last two decades, diversity of workforce has become an important issue for HR managers. There are a number of reasons for this diversity such as large percentage of working women due to increasing education of female, younger age employees, national and international mobility of manpower increasing job opportunities across the world, and experience at international assignments etc. Other elements of culture in most of the countries are contributing to diversity. Especially in India employees are coming from different cultures, caste, creed, religion, region, language, sex and economic backgrounds. These elements are making the things difficult to understand the differences among employees. Managements find it difficult to communicate and manage these people properly.

Further, due to globalization the Indian companies are hiring foreign employees from different countries. Over and above due to mergers and acquisitions that took place in recent past and added to workforce diversity further. The diversified feature of workforce are creating difficult situation for management. Management of diversity in workforce is a great challenge for the management of the organization.

There is diversity in markets also. India is a big country with many states and union territories. In most of the states there are different cultures and languages spoken. When Indian companies are carrying out its business activities, they have to use different marketing techniques to communicate, persuade and retain the customers. They find it difficult to develop and maintain good customers' relations. Since globalization Indian companies are doing business in foreign markets and focusing customers of different cultures are diversified. There are different expectations regarding product, price, quality and customers' service. It is difficult to understand the market diversity for effective marketing in Indian and foreign markets. The need for knowledge of diversified markets is felt. This situation can be handled by a global manager only.

There are different stakeholders of the company in the global era. The main stakeholders are owners, shareholders, customers, clients, bankers, consultants and government etc. They are having different interests with the organization. There is diversity in interests of stakeholders. These stakeholders are very sensitive and expect better performance from the company. Further in foreign markets due to foreign clients the diversity is increased. The management of the company finds difficult to manage the diversified interests of various stakeholders. In this situation a manager with national and international experience are needed. If ignored then there may be different problems from the stakeholders.

2. ROLE OF CULTURE

In different cultures the needs for the products exist but the tastes and preferences of consumers in different countries vary slightly for the similar products. Products that are marketed across the world are not in position to serve customers of different culture in better way. These need little adoption in products according to expectations of customers across national markets; thus, global integration is facilitated. The role of culture plays an important role in understanding customers and matching products for them. The products, features are to be modified for successful marketing. Each country is unique because it has different roots in economic, history, physical conditions, culture, language, caste, creed, religion. These differences in customers and markets complicate any international business activities for the organization. It becomes very difficult to carry out the business without cross culture knowledge. Managers who ignore culture role put their organizations in a great problem in global markets. Because each culture has its own norms, customs, and expectations for behavior and that affect the people as customers. The success of an organization depends on management ability to understand the cross-cultural issues especially related to customers and manpower working in that organization.

Modern organization management constantly is facing challenges in dealing with different situations due to diversity in organizations. Almost all big organizations across the world are facing the challenges of diversity. Indian organizations are no exception to this. In India, and foreign countries majority of mergers and acquisitions, foreign direct investments, joint ventures etc., that have taken place involving multinational companies. In developed and developing countries there is drastic growth in percentage of working women. Further, cultural elements like language, religion, age, education also have added to the diversity in organizations worldwide. It is important for management to understand how these elements or dimensions affect thinking, attitude, performance, motivation, commitment, success and interactions with others. The organizational barriers faced in this way should be examined, found and remedial action should be initiated promptly.

3. MANAGING DIVERSITY

Workforce diversity is a reality at multinational companies across the world. Even in India after globalization the same situation is being faced. It cannot be ignored at the cost of business. The diversity is to be managed at organization level. Managing diversity is defined as "planning and implementing organizational systems and practices to manage people so that the potential advantages of diversity are maximized while its potential disadvantages are minimized," according to Taylor Cox in "Cultural Diversity in Organizations." Managing diversity means accepting the differences of employees and considers these differences in a positive way as a valuable asset for the organization. It would enhance healthy management practices for developing better understanding, relations and cooperation without any discrimination at individual level. The support of workforce would help the management to achieve the objectives effectively. It is not possible for management to do so alone in any organization.

It would provide a distinct advantage in an era over arch rivals in the markets in stiff competitive situation. Workforce heterogeneity feature should be taken as a positive point to promote creativity and heterogeneous groups have shown better results and salutation of the problems. This can be a vital asset at a time when the organisation is undergoing tremendous change and development for better suggestions and ways for effective working. The organization can develop a good reputation as a good employer with well managed diversity. It would help to attract better and talented manpower and save times, efforts and costs. Managing diversity means managing the employees differences and focusing on maximizing the capability so that they can contribute in accomplishment of organizational objectives. Affirmative action focuses on specific groups for attaining a particular task. The scope of diversity management is wider than a particular affirmative action.

High reputation of the company would help to develop diverse customers' base for business. The ultimate goal of the organization of high reputation is achieved through managing diversity. It becomes a long-term asset of the organization. Diversity management cannot be ignored and if done so then it is at the cost of the organization. The losses of time, efforts, money and efficiency take place. It may lead to group differences, grievances, lower level of commitment, low productivity and quality of the products. The reputation of the company would be affected and in future more customers and better employees may not be attracted. It affects adversely in the long run. For this management should take special care in the present competitive situation.

In the diversified environment it has become necessary to manage the diversity issue effectively. There is no one solution of this problem but sincere efforts are needed in this direction. The following strategies are to be adopted for diversity management:

(a) Modification in Policies

To address diversity issues, the existing policies, procedures, rules, and regulations are to be modified. These should be made to meet the needs of a diverse workforce, motivate and maximize the potential of all workers, so that the organisation can be well positioned in the competitive situation for better performance for carrying out business activities. Management should take timely care for necessary modification though comprehensive discussion over diverse features of workforce.

(b) Cultural Training of Diversified Workforce

For managing diversity in India and abroad a plan is to be prepared for training the people so that they can meet the needs of diversity management. Cultural training should be conducted because the workforce is highly diversified. This training is needed for all managers and employees. The cultural training should focus on developing one organizational culture irrespective of different cultures of employees. They should like to start liking in new organization culture. This would avoid cultural differences. The workforce itself is diversified and in this case the employees should know the features of workforce. They should know each element of it and impact of it on working of the organization. Skills are to be developed so that the worker should understand and accept the diversity concepts, management involvement in it, self-awareness, in terms of understanding own culture, identity, biases, prejudices, and willingness to challenge and change current practices that present barriers to different groups in workforce. They should start respecting other cultural values also. With these skills the employees would be in position to support management in managing diversity.

(c) Clarification of Job Requirements

For procurement of the employees, in the beginning itself the job requirements are to be clarified properly. The need for skills to perform the jobs effectively in a diverse environment should be specified. in the job, for example, job requirements like qualification, training, experience, achievements etc., to be highlighted in advance to avoid confusions. When hiring an employee then explain the job responsibilities and expectations clearly. In selection of the candidates these should be considered also without any deviation.

(d) Sound Recruitment and Selection

For recruitment and selection proper care is to be taken so that the problems from different groups of workers should not arise. First of the vacancies are to be highlighted in different language newspapers. The procedure for receiving applications, selection and appointment should be followed meticulously without any deviation due to personal bias. According to the information given tests and interviews are to be conducted. In interview panel the members should be appointed from diverse groups from workforce so that the question of bias should not arise among employees.

Ensure that the selection committee members are selected on the basis of jobs, departments, length of service, and variety of life experiences. Efforts should be there to select the suitable candidates without any discrimination and favour. On the basis of merits the candidates should be finally appointed. This would become very helpful in managing diversity and developing good image of the company in markets for attracting talented employees in future.

(e) Proper Communication

Management should pay proper attention towards communication when communicating to diverse segment of employees. It should be to the point and objectives should be clearly specified. It should be in one common language and no preference to some to of the languages known to the diversified workforce. It is suggested that different languages should be ignored and it should be in English or national language of that country. The communication should not be biased or in favour or against any group of workforce. It should be with the objective to communicate to the target group without any other intention. It should be in position that the meaning is understood and gets feedback. It should hold the people together for achieving objectives of the organization.

(f) Equal Treatment

Fair treatment means "treating everyone with one approach." In a diversified workforce of organization the employees represent different segments of the population. They all should be treated as one group as a whole. There should not be any discrimination on the basis of caste, creed, language, religion, sex, region, relations etc. The facilities, opportunities and benefits should be made available for everyone on the basis of eligibility criteria and not on cultural backgrounds. Training, promotion, career development welfare, rewards, recognitions, incentives, welfare facilities, wage increments or cuts etc., should be made available those to who meet the qualifying criteria only. Employees should be dealt with one standard only. Different standards for different segments of workforce should not be used. The treatment should claim fairness in approach. This would avoid differences among employees and grievances at individual or group level should be prevented. Such efforts on the part of supervisors and managers would be definitely appreciated by employees and clear transparency in dealing would develop. This in the long run develops confidence among people working in that organization.

(g) Broader Approach for Living in Diversity

At present in global environment the organization are having diversified workforce. It should be taken in positive way and should be considered as part and parcel of working in an organization. Accept it as a reality and let diversity be there. We should start living in diversity itself. Nowadays even some of families are also diversified. All should start living in diversity. It means the whole world should be taken as one market and creates a cultural and social environment in which all employees and managers are living. In it all are included and considered important for achieving the objectives of an organization. All employees should forget their local identity and consider them as world citizen. As due to job opportunities they move from one country to another the old approach is not going to give fruit to employees. Now they do not have local boundaries. This broad approach would help everyone to manage diversity. The managers as change agents should explain the challenges and opportunities of diversity worldwide. They should be trained and advised for mutual trust, respect and support. The products and services are to be modified with proper research work to meet the demands and expectations of customers in different markets across the world. This approach definitely would be very fruitful and magical.

4. MANAGERS' ROLE IN DIVERSITY MANAGEMENT

Managers are providing very important link in management of the organization. They are having control over all the activities of the organization. Their role in normal situation is also very important and further in diversified situation it becomes more important. The manager's role in managing diversity is explained below:

(a) Conducts survey and collect data for regular audit, review, and assess the progress of individuals, departments and organization as a whole.

(b) Motivate workforce for consultation, discussion, suggestions, involvement so that their commitment level improves in managing diversity.

(c) Aligns HR interventions with diversity objectives for proper management of diversity.

(d) Participate and motivate shared leaning by developing network with managers of the company and outside for update of management of diversity.

(e) Develops healthy working environment of openness, mutual respect, trust, understanding, cooperation and team spirit through proper communication to inform employees regarding diverse policies and practices and consult them for better suggestions and ideas.

(f) Develop culture and social ambience of proper behaviour among employees with respect, dignity, standards and values. This is developed with the support of top level management. The developed behaviour is to be followed in routine working so commitment of employees improves.

(g) Review and take remedial actions to correct the unsuitable or unfair practices, procedures and perceptions that hinder managing diversity.

(h) Designs training, development and team building programmes according to the objectives of diversity management so that desired performance can be achieved by managing diversified interests, views and perceptions.

(i) Through market research the trends in diversified needs of customers / clients are identified and then products or services are adjusted to match their requirement for better performance in business.

(j) Managers should focus on fairness in dealing with diversified workforce and support business goal achievements by giving suggestions, options and choices.

(k) Managers should take decisions regarding recruitment, training and development, and assigning responsibility on the basis of merit, competence and potential without any subjectivity.

5. DIVERSITY TRAINING

Under liberalization of economies the companies entered business in various countries. The global economies integrated, migration rules liberalized, and search for best talents for performing tasks across the world contributed in creating diversity of workforce. The people from different cultures are having different cultural elements and all these are affecting the behaviour of people and business also. It varies not only company to company, industry to industry, region to region, country to country, but varies across the world. When employees of vivid experiences, cultural values, and personal lifestyles work together in an organization, come together, they interact with others and share cultural values and experience of others. It provides a lot of opportunities and challenges.

It is up to the management to deal with this diversity. If diversity is not managed or managed poorly, it can lead to confusion, misunderstanding, inefficiency, and conflict and disengagement. Where managed properly, it is a positive resource and provides multi-dimensional benefits for society as well as organisations. It creates healthy work environment of trust, mutual understanding, cooperation, team spirit and openness. The people interact more and share cultural values, education and experience of others working with them. The people get opportunity to compare their potentials with others, take interests for their development and leads to creativity. This creativity is applied in different areas for performance of tasks. The end results would lead to improvement in behaviour, commitment, quality, quantity and profitability of the company. Finally the image of the company develops in global markets. It can be said if diversity is managed properly it contributes to achievements of objectives otherwise it may lead to total failure also. It is up to the management whether it recognizes the cultural differences of employees or not. The issue is very critical.

In diversity, training the main areas are attitudes/awareness, knowledge, and skills. It is expected the trainers should have the competencies to provide high performance diversity training and consultation. Attitude/awareness means to know how personal attitude/ awareness, moral positions, and individual differences affect the workforce. The trainer should train the people on this issue. Knowledge relating to the job concepts is to be improved through training. Skills refer to the ability to perform the tasks effectively. These areas are to be improved through diversity training of diversified workforce. The performance after diversity training is to be evaluated periodically to keep the actual performance in line with standards decided. To impart diversity training the trainer should have high level of competency so that the desired objectives are achieved.

(a) Approaches of Manager When Leading Diverse Teams

According to Michael Bird opinion when a project manager takes the responsibility to manage the project in different culture with diversified workforce, in the beginning the efficiency and effectiveness of the manager is low. It is due to that the manager is not having knowledge regarding diversified workforce and their cultures etc. He is not in a position to motivate, guide and satisfy them through communication. The productivity goes down in this case despite sincere efforts of the manager. In this case the manager should improve knowledge of diversified workforce and their behaviour, management practices and methods to improve overall performance of the project team. This is possible through diversity training of the management team. Through diversity training the manager gets awareness regarding diversified workforce and working for managing the project effectively, he should take the following approach:

(i) Recognize that diversity brings a lot of opportunities and challenges for individuals and organization.

(ii) Respect for all cultures and create awareness of employees also regarding different culture and cultural values.

(iii) Promptly work to create interests, participation, sharing of cultural values, skills and knowledge, and experience among them and developing healthy working environment.

(iv) Improve the overall mutual understanding, cooperation, team spirit, motivation, satisfaction, retention of employees and reducing conflicts.

(v) Encourage participation, suggestions, creativity, flexibility, innovative ideas among the team members so that the best use of available talents becomes possible

Bird further remarket that if the managers are effectively managing diversity provides good chances for improvement in cooperation, skills and knowledge, relations, performance, profitability and image of the company. It should be taken by the manager in such situation for effective management of assignments in cross-border countries.

Diversity training and role of trainers are becoming more popular in present time due to changing demographics and workplace diversity, increasing interpersonal conflicts and challenges, increasing presence in global community of companies, increasing tough competition in domestic and international markets, and increasing number of lawsuits of employees. Where there is diversified workforce there is need for the diversity trainer to deal with the situation more effectively. Even the companies where no diversity effects exists, are also prepared to hire the diversity trainers or take their help to prepare them for the future challenges. It can be said the role of diversity trainer in future is going to be more important undoubtedly.

(b) Hiring of Diversity Trainers

The organizations hire diversity trainers as per the requirements of the organization. Nowadays, even people hire diversity trainers as a personal coach in present diversified situation and competition to maintain their effectiveness in their works by improving intellectual skills. The trainers provide training and consultation like other trainers. Diversity trainers provide their services in a variety of ways. They provide training and consultation through lectures, workshops, interview, and group discussion suitable to the situation in demand.

The trainers are helpful in case when they are competent. They should have competencies to understand attitude, awareness, knowledge and skills of workforce properly. If they are competent then only would they be in a position to guide, motivate and participate in different activities of training. He should be in a position to create training environment for willing participation and interest to learn more. If they lack in competencies then proper diversity training and consultation cannot be conducted. They would not be in a position to solve any of the problems and they themselves would become problem for the organization. A special care is to be taken in selection of diversity trainers. Diversity trainers are to be engaged as per the jobs and needs of the organization. The duration should not be very short or long. The effectiveness of diversity training should not go down. Regarding this there are no strict guidelines available. Generally, the duration of 3-4 hours workshop is most suitable. The trainers are to be paid as per programme conducted or hours or day basis. The fee is to be decided on the basis of qualification, experience and proven records of the trainers.

6. CROSS-CULTURAL EDUCATION AND TRAINING

In present situation we are living in era of globalization. The world markets are shrinking into a village market due to liberalization of policies, faster means of communication and transportation facilities. This situation provides a lot of opportunities and challenges for the corporation and manpower. The multinational organizations started their businesses across the world without any limitations. This has created a lot of diversity in manpower, markets and customers. In fact, big companies carrying out business in different countries having different cultures, the cross culture issues affect most of areas of business. It has become difficult to perform the tasks more effectively. Manufacturing is done in one country, assembling in second and marketing is done in third, fourth and so on. To do so the communication and international business decisions become very complex for carrying out business in global markets. Leading companies are facing tough situation to deal with it. Under this diverse situation the difficulties of corporations are increasing day by day. Even the people got job opportunities across their nations are finding difficult to adjust with other cultures if they are not trained properly. Expatriates become failure in this situation due to a number of reasons that may include cultural adjustment, poor management and productivity, difficulties in coping with stress and relational capabilities. Bhaskar-Shrinivas pointed out that lack of cultural adjustment is the strongest determinant of disengagement and withdrawal decisions. To deal with this situation more effectively the efforts should be there to improve cultural adjustment so that the desired objectives are fulfilled. In this situation the need for cross-cultural training and education has been felt.

Cross-cultural training is another way of managing diversity in an organization. It has been the main method used for facilitating effective cross-cultural communication and interaction. Cross-cultural training was defined as a procedure or practice used to increase an individual's ability to cope with cross-cultures and perform well in a new cultural environment. Zakaria said that cross-cultural training helps in transition from a home-based management local mode to a new suitable cultural mode. Cross-cultural training contributes in increasing the ability of employees to understand culture, values and ethos of another culture. It develops the interest to understand employees own background and cultural heritage. They should feel good about own culture and similar way the employees should accept and appreciate culture of other employees. For example, employees of Indian culture should know and appreciate own culture and further in same way accept and appreciate culture of English and American also. This helps a lot in adjustment with the people of other cultures and many related problems can be avoided.

Keeping in view the advantages of cross culture training, many companies have established cross-cultural training programs continue to struggle with understanding the business value and to get benefits of these programs. But still many of them have to start cross-cultural training programme in the near future. In absence of this they have adopted the practice of outsourcing their main activities also. Despite its importance, it has been criticized by some of the experts on the grounds that it is insufficient and incomplete so far. It is a waste of time, efforts and money. Keeping both its advantages and criticisms in mind it is concluded that it is fruitful in present time and would be more beneficial in near future.

When people from diverse and conflicting cultures meet and work together, they are provided cross-cultural training. They start respecting their own culture as well as of others. They work together for achievement of the objectives of the organization for which they are working. This develops a healthy work environment and that is beneficial for all concerned. The importance of cross-cultural training is increasing day by day and it helps in the following:

(a) Working in different culture countries.

(b) Collaboration for working on one project with teams from other countries of different cultures.

(c) Working of divisions or departments of the company in different countries.

(d) Suppliers from other countries for outsourcing activities.

(e) Customers located in different countries of different cultures.

(f) When partners and alliances with parties from diversified cultures.

7. CROSS-CULTURAL EDUCATION AND TRAINING PROCESS

Cross-cultural education and training process is a complex process. In it a set of activities are arranged in a logical sequence and the stages or activities involved in are creating cross culture awareness, providing cross-cultural education, and providing coaching or consultation. These are explained below:

(a) Creating Cross-cultural Awareness

The first step in this process is to create cross-cultural awareness. When employees are working with people of different cultures do not know elements of own culture and of others. They should be educated regarding own cultural factors which affect their own trust, belief, attitude, perception and understanding. Simultaneously they should know the cultures of others also. They should be in a position of compare and contrast between the different cultures. This would develop knowledge base of different cultures of employees. It would be helpful to understand the people and their cultures. It would develop broader view of employees. They would start liking their own culture and take pride in that. Similarly they like and appreciate the cultures of other employees. This helps a lot in developing new organizational culture out of the diversity. This is the need of the hour in globalization era. This affects on perception, attitude, teamwork, cooperation and performance. If proper care is taken in creating awareness the organization would be benefited in a number of ways. For creating awareness properly the managers should have thorough knowledge of different cultures. Cross culture education is very well helpful for developing better relationship and even for business partnership and alliances.

(b) Providing Cross-cultural Education

For diversified workforce the employees are provided education in the field of management in different countries. The objective of this education is to provide knowledge to the employees relating to management of the companies in different countries. It helps to create awareness regarding companies in various countries and cultures manage their employees and projects and business. It provides knowledge about different strategies, methods and management processes used by various companies in different countries. It provides knowledge about the culture affects on business and people behaviour. It highlights the differences in different countries in these activities. On the basis of knowledge the comparison is possible and of these areas the best practices, methods, and strategies can be identified and used to affect the business and behaviour of the clients, customers and public as a whole. This becomes very helpful the company which carry out the business across the borders in international markets.

(c) Providing Cross-cultural Coaching

When company is performing its business in different countries of diverse culture, facing may cultural issues to solve. The knowledge of managers is not sufficient to handle it effectively. They need coaching or consultation from experts of that country. If the coaching or consultation is provided then it would bring changes in thinking, attitude, and problem-solving *vis-à-vis* cross-cultural issues. If that is not timely available then it may become a bottleneck in cross-border mergers, acquisitions, FDI, and other business activities. For example, Indian companies involved in oil exploration business in African country, the employees are not familiar with African culture and they face a lot of difficulties over cultural issues. They need help from experts from that country so that the cultural issues can be handled effectively. Different methods for this purpose can be used as per need of the situation. The methods of providing coaching or consultation vary from culture to culture.

8. TYPES OF CROSS-CULTURAL TRAINING

Under the broad umbrella of cross-cultural awareness, education, and coaching fall several minor, but distinct types of training. Each type of cross-cultural training has a single objective to inculcate demonstrable levels of cultural awareness in employees where a common cross-cultural reference point is not present or doesn't exist at any significant level. Different types of cross-cultural training are there to fulfil the objectives. These can be used individually or in parallel. These are following:

(a) Training for Dealing Cross-cultural Challenges

Diversity of cultures is creating a lot of challenges and opportunities. The difficult situation is to deal with the challenges and to be become more effective in job performance. The training imparted is with the objective to deal the challenges without any difficulty or less difficulty. In this type of training the methods, techniques, strategies and practices used in different countries workplace are highlighted. The workforce is made aware regarding those things and in turn can be applied in future working. It explains the challenges arose due to cultural diversity, suggests ways to deal with such challenges and provides possible solution to those challenges so that the effectiveness of cross cultural teams can be improved. This would be in position to create awareness, develop trust and confidence so that the team spirit is developed among them. This ultimate would contribute to cooperation, smooth working and effective communication.

(b) Training for Diversified Workforce

Due to globalization in business activities, a lot of job opportunities are made available across the world. The multinational companies during their business have employed talented employees from different countries. The workforce due to this has become highly diversified. The management faces an uphill task to deal with this diversified manpower. For that purpose the management is provided training to develop awareness regarding cultural elements, values and behaviour. Human resource management team deals with the people and this training is especially useful for them. With proper knowledge of employees and their cultural background the HR manager finds himself in the position to deal with people from various cultural backgrounds. This helps a lot in understanding people and contributes in maintaining good relationship at work place. The peaceful working definitely improves the quantity and quality of the performance.

(c) Training on Specific Country

This depends on the situation of the business. When a company is having business in a particular country, there is need to know the culture of that country only. Training should be conducted to create awareness of culture of that country only. The training should be provided regarding geographical location, climate, culture, economy, behaviour of people of that countries, consumption pattern, social and moral values etc. This would create awareness of managers and help in dealing with the customers, clients, partners, employees and consultants. If the knowledge regarding the specific country background is good, then difficulties would not be faced by dealing managers. Their effectiveness on jobs would definitely improve. If proper care is not taken regarding this then at every step a lot of difficulties are to be faced and may lead to failure in that country. This training is mainly for the managers working in that specific country or visiting to that country. This is specially designed for teams and personnel who need to visit overseas countries and interact with clients or teams from foreign cultures. This training covers, in detail the particular values, ethos, morals, behavior and business practices and customs of a particular country or an ethnic group.

(d) Training in Management Practices

Training is provided to the managerial staff for managing the business activities across the world in diversified cultures and manpower. The different practices, methods, techniques, strategies and philosophy used by management team in different countries are highlighted. There awareness is created so that these can be applied in managing projects across the world. It enables the management to understand business management activities across the global markets and manage, guide and supervise the cross-cultural teams. This would help in performing the tasks smoothly without any difficulty. The effectiveness of management team over cross-cultural projects would improve definitely.

(e) Training for Conducting Negotiations

During business activities performed across the world market, the management takes a lot of decisions. For finalizing a deal relating to business they are involved in negotiation. For example, deciding partners, mergers, acquisition, joint ventures, dealers, vendors and employees the negotiation process is involved. It is very difficult to deal with negotiation with parties of diversified culture. In this type of training awareness is created regarding cultural backgrounds and negotiation skills developed to deal with cross-cultural parties. This training is of a special type and helps to equip with negotiation skills relating to specific culture, negotiating team, clients, customers, employees. Due to developed negotiation skills the deals can be finalized effectively or settlement can be made by negotiating on terms and conditions applicable to the deals. Without proper negotiation skills the agreements, settlements and deals cannot be finalized properly. Finally these affect the business performance.

9. CROSS-CULTURAL EDUCATION AND TRAINING EFFECTIVENESS

The effectiveness of the cross cultural education and training programme depends on many factors. If proper care is taken by the management in designing, implementation and review of the programme then the effectiveness is going to be high without any doubt. If there are lapses in these activities then definitely there are chances that the effectiveness would go down. It can be said the deeper the well, cooler the water. It is directly related to care and involvement of management responsible for cross-cultural education and training programme. The effectiveness can be maintained if following points are considered and managed properly and further due to proper management the effectiveness can be improved with timely adjustment in existing practices. The factors affecting the effectiveness are following:

(a) Structure of the Programme

Structure of cross-cultural education and training programme is to be designed to meet the requirement of business in different countries. The contents of the programmes should be according to the objectives, target group, skills needed, duration, position, responsibility and locations. These points are to be kept in mind to match the requirements. The programme can be designed for executives, senior managers and top executives located in different countries. The programme can be of foundation, technical, team building etc. The duration of course should vary with objectives and target group for whom the programme has been designed. Contents and timing and duration of courses should be as per the requirements of the target groups. If proper care is not taken then it may lead to mismatch and objectives of the programme would be defeated. Special care should be taken in future. Through review, the programmes can be modified so the effectiveness can improve further.

(b) Continuity of the Programme

The cross-cultural education and training programmes should be conducted till the objectives are fulfilled. These should not be stopped in-between without achieving the objectives. Further one programme should be connected with the other programme in course curriculum itself. The employees should know which course they are undergoing for a particular duration. The programme should be completed properly and on completion of the course the candidates should be evaluated and certification should be done. This would improve morale of the employees. If not done so the effectiveness of the whole programme would go down and there would be wastage of time, efforts and money. It should not be taken lightly.

(c) Quality of Programme

Quality means the pre decided standards of performance are met properly and give satisfaction to the concerned parties. It can be said quality is defined as fitness for use. When the programme is designed, implemented, evaluated and completed should be as per the pre decided standards. There should not be any deviation anywhere. If any deviation is there then immediately the remedial actions are to be taken. The effectiveness of the system should not go down. Quality should be maintained in course structure, course pre-work, content, delivery, evaluation of performance according to standard of excellence. Special efforts should be put to complete the programme without any irregularities. Further, if responsible manager is not satisfied with any area of programme then immediate remedial action should be taken so that in future the effectiveness of the programme can be improved.

(d) Consistency of Performance

When conducting cross-cultural education and training programme the delivery should be proper. From one course to another course the standards of performance should be maintained. The quality is to be maintained. If quality is not maintained properly and regularly then the result would not be achieved. It would not be in position to develop confidence in candidates. The objectives of the programme would be defeated if consistency in performance and quality are not maintained, Proper care should be taken for future so that effectiveness can be improved. If lapses are there in this the candidates would not take interest in such programmes.

(e) Properly Justified Programme

The cross cultural education and training programme can be designed and implemented for creating awareness among employees regarding different cultures, motivating their participation and developing good working environment. The programme should be justified properly. The justification whether it is required or not, design and implementation for the target group is proper, course contents, training methods, involvement of technology, assessment methods, costs involved, time and efforts needed for completion of the programme. If the answer regarding these points is positive then it should be conducted otherwise not. There should be proper justification and should not face opposition in later stages.

(f) Suitable for Target Groups and Easy to Measure

The structure of the programme should be designed in such a way that it is meeting the objectives of the programme. It may be for different parties such as managers, employees both in different locations. The contents, schedule, methods of conducting training programme, duration etc., should be such that it becomes suitable to the target group to fulfil the objectives of the training programme. Time to time it should be adjusted as per the requirements of concerned parties. It should not mismatch to the requirements. It should be designed as tailor-made programme. Further, the impact of it on knowledge, awareness and performance should be measureable. If it is so then only the effectiveness of the programme can be measured and can say whether it is good or poor. These two things are possible on the basis of feedback from the participants. After getting feedback the programme can be further tailored and the effectiveness and results of programme can be measured.

If the management takes proper care regarding the above mentioned points then the effectiveness of the programme would be good. If any deviation is found in feedback then efforts can be put to improve the conditions. The effectiveness in future also can further improve.

10. RELATION BETWEEN CROSS-CULTURAL PROGRAMMES AND BUSINESS RESULTS

The cross-cultural education and training programme are conducted with the objectives to create awareness regarding diverse culture, develop interests to participate, mutual understanding, team spirit, cooperation, trust, openness and healthy work environment. It is to be measured that how much the objectives are fulfilled. There is close relation between the programme and results. The behaviour of employees and managers can be assessed whether the desired changes has been made or not. The behaviour of employees and all levels is to be assessed. If the programme designed and conducted properly the impact would be positive and if not then the result would go negative. The direct link exists between the programme and impact on behaviour of concerned employees. Proper care of responsible management team would contribute in developing interests and participation in activities. These in turn would develop cooperation and team spirit in a healthy working environment. The team building becomes easy in healthy work environment. In environment of openness and trust the free communication takes place. This helps a lot to coordinate the activities for smooth working.

On the basis of proper communication and team spirit the employees take active interest in activities and decision making. The decisions become easy and proper decisions can be taken. The decision may be very fruitful for the organization, employees and business. During decision making open discussion would be there on every possible alternative and best would be selected. All these are going to effect behaviour, motivation, satisfaction, commitment, and willingness to shoulder the responsibility. These things would give positive impact on the performance of individual, department, division, company, profits, and image of the company. The company would get competitive advantage over its arch rivals in the global business. Now it can be said if the approach of the management in cross-cultural education and training programme is proper then it would give positive impact on all aspects of the business discussed here. If not then the impact would be in negative way and may lead to failure. There is direct relation between programme and business results and it depends upon management of the programme itself.

11. DIVERSITY TRAINING AND CROSS-CULTURAL TRAINING

The focus of multicultural training is on educating people to understand and appreciate cultural differences of own and respect for other cultures. Other side the focus of diversity training is on building one community rather than pointing out how different cultures and people are different. Acceptance and appreciation of differences in cultures is important but not to be considered on the highest priority. The abilities to make others comfortable and included are most important, no matter how much you know about their culture. Cross-cultural training having focuses on educating people to know and manage them first in their own country with diversified cultures and in other countries so that they become successful in their profession. In diversity training the objective is to create a new organizational culture suitable to the demanding situation.

12. HRD PROGRAMME FOR DIVERSIFIED WORKFORCE

The principal component of an organization is its human resources or 'People at work'.

It is this human resource which is of paramount importance in the success of any organization because most of the problems in organizational settings are human and social rather than physical, technical or economic. Failure to recognize this fact causes immense loss to the nation, enterprise and to the individual. People at work comprise a large number of individuals of different sex, age, education, experience, socio-religious group and with different expectations. These individuals in the work place exhibit not only similar behavior patterns and characteristics to a certain degree but they also show much dissimilarity. The management of manpower is challenging task because of the dynamic nature of the people. No two persons are similar in mental abilities, traditions, sentiments and behavior. They differ widely also as groups and are subject to many and varied influences. People are responsive. They feel, think and act; therefore they cannot be operated like a machine or shifted and altered like a template in a room layout. They therefore need a tactful handling by management personnel. If manpower is properly utilized, it may prove a dynamic motive force for running an enterprise at its optimum results and also work for maximum individual and group satisfaction in relation to the work performed. The management must, therefore, be aware not only of the organizational but also of the employee and self-needs. None of these can be ignored. Further, under globalization the workforce has been further diversified. It has become very difficult for management to understand these people, their behaviour, expectations and need. The need for their high level of commitment has been strongly felt across the world.

13. SOCIALIZATION THROUGH ORIENTATION

When an employee joins an organization he is new to it. He does not know about management, objectives, mission, products, services, clients, customers, technology used, rules, regulations, policies, nature of job and responsibility etc. He does not have clear ideas about these and he is having a lot of anxiety and expectation relating to the job and organisation. Having new persons employed the next step that HR manager is to make use of the employed person as early as possible. Utilization, motivation, job satisfaction and retaining newcomers pose a challenge to HR manager. If it is not done properly then there are chances the turnover occurs during the first few months on the job itself. The organizations having employed the new persons have little opportunity to get return on investment in new entrants who leave the jobs. The newcomers' turnover is problematic issue and about this management and researchers are worried about it. They are interested and focus on this issue to meet the objectives through organizational socialization. It has been used with the objective to familiarize new employees with new jobs, new roles for adjusting in organization so that they are retained for longer period.

To make his position comfortable and reduce the anxiety that new employee is going to experience, sincere efforts should be made to adjust the person into the informal organization, working culture and jobs. The initial HRD effort designed in this direction for employees' socialization. It guides the employee and help in adjusting him in the job, group and the organization as a whole. Socialization is defined as "a process in which an individual acquires the attitudes, behaviors and knowledge needed to successfully participate as an organizational member." Socialization cannot be completed within a limited period because it is an ongoing process that sometimes may take and longer period also. It is a sense-making process that helps new entrants to adapt in organizational situation and make his place in the organization.

Socialization formats in each company are different but the objectives are almost similar.

However, the purpose is to create awareness of the new employees regarding the employment terms and conditions, job, department, management of the company, company policies, rules and regulations, compensation rates and benefits, organisation culture, team membership, training and development, career development opportunities, performance appraisal, discipline, welfare and wellness facilities, and post retirement benefits etc. The basic objective is to make the employee more familiar with the above mentioned areas in the beginning itself so that he can become more productive and give required standard of performance and return on the investment made on him by hiring him. The socialization process would make the person more comfortable at job and in organization so that his performance would improve and stay in organization would be longer.

14. SOCIALIZATION PROCESS

Socialization process of employees regarding organization is a continuous process. It starts before an employee joins the organization and continues during his employment also. It may take longer time also. The stages involved in this process are explained below:

(a) Before Joining

It is expected that every candidate comes with certain set of information regarding organization, image, values and expectations from the organization. It has been accepted in the first stage. Without getting familiar with the organization and related areas no one is going to even think to join. This stage explicitly recognizes that each individual arrives with a set of organizational values, attitudes, and expectations. New entrants are socialized regarding skilled and managerial jobs in their schools, colleges and institutes. Pre-employment socialization is beyond the specific job. In an advertisement relating to vacancies in an organization, the information are given relating to organization and other related areas. In selection process the right type of employees in required number are selected to ensure that they fit in the organization properly. The candidates present themselves to the selection committee in such way that they meet the expectations of the selection process. This creates awareness regarding organization as a whole and this is called pre-employment socialization.

(b) At the Time of Joining

This stage is known as encounter stage also. Upon entry into the organization, new employees are entering with certain expectations. Here the employees find differences between expectations and actual position regarding their jobs, colleagues, supervisors, managers, packages, facilities and the organization in general. If expectations are nearly equal to the reality then it supports the perceptions of the employees generated before joining. If they find the differences then they need the socialization regarding standards of the organization and replace the previous assumptions. If proper socialization has not taken place then there are chances that the new entrants may detach from the organization by leaving the job itself. If the dissatisfaction level is high then there are chances that they may leave early. The chances of leaving the jobs can be reduced if proper care is taken in the selection process before joining the organisaiton.

(c) Adjustment Stage

After joining the job the employees encounter some problems due to differences. It becomes difficult for them to work smoothly. They work out to find out the solution of the problems. They make necessary changes of their own or with the help of supervisors or managers. They adjust themselves with the prevailing situation in the organization and feel comfortable with the work. With this the persons become satisfied at their workplace and develop attachment with the organization. It may contribute to retain the employees for longer period and sense of belongingness or attachment further develops. This stage is called metamorphosis also. Metamorphosis stage of socialization process is complete when new employees have become comfortable with the organization and their work teams. The employees find themselves in relaxed position, develop good relations and understanding with their colleagues, supervisors, managers, better understanding, mutual support and trust, environment of openness and team spirit develops. All these leads to develop healthy work environment. It is essential in the organization to motivate and get high level of commitment from them towards achievement of objectives of the organization. The commitment, performance, productivity, profitability and image of the organization as a whole improve. The chances of leaving the organization are very rare except the unavoidable situation like death, sickness and retirement.

15. PERSONS INVOLVED IN SOCIALIZATION PROCESS

New employees' socialization or orientation covers the activities involved in introducing a new employee to the organization and to his or her work unit. The responsibility of conducting orientation programme is to be fixed on shoulder of some parties. This can be done by the supervisor, the HR Department, Peers, CEO, or combination of any of these.

(a) HR Department

HR department can conduct the orientation in order to socialize the newly hired employees with the working environment of the organization. HRM plays a major role in new employee orientation-the role of coordination, which ensures that the appropriate components are in place. In addition HRM also serves as a participant in program. As job offers are made and accepted, HRM should instruct the new employee when to report to work. However, before the employee formally arrives, HRM must be prepared to handle some of the more routine needs of these individuals.

(b) Supervisor

Immediate supervisor of particular department can also be the source of informing the employees about the culture, rules, procedures and policies of the organization. Mostly in smaller organizations, orientation may mean the new member reports to supervisor, who then assigns the new member to other employee who will introduce the new member to other coworkers. This may be followed by a quick tour to show the different parts and departments of the organization.

(c) Peers

Peers is group of employees working at same level of new entrants but these are the employees employed earlier and have not left the organization because they adjusted with the organization and comfortable with their job and in organization. They have experience and knowledge all related issues regarding orientation of the new employees. During their introduction and in routine work they get involved in discussion regarding job and organization related topics. They inform the new entrants regarding their expectation and requirements of the organization. During this a lot of queries are answered by the colleague and help them in adjusting in the new job. They listen the difficulties of the new entrants and give then proper time to solve their difficulties. They provide them proper company and the new entrants do not feel isolated and frustrated at their job. They contribute a lot in orientation of the new entrants not only in the beginning but also at later stages.

(d) Organizational culture

Organizational culture is a pattern of living and working in an organization. The culture of each organization varies from market to market. The organization culture is created by management philosophy, mission, objectives, rules and regulation, policies, communication language, behaviour pattern with senior, juniors and peers, and practices during work. It expresses the dos and don'ts of any organization are to followed by members. When an person joins an organization, he is exposed to all these and get himself adjusted to meet the requirement of the organization. He behaves as per the behaviour standards, adjust with the situation, The organization culture plays vital role in orientation of the new employees. Through it the practical experience is made by the new entrants.

(e) Chief Executive Officer

Up to mid were twentieth century the attitude of the management was not favourable towards the employees. They were not considered as an important party. Due to development in technology and competition they were compelled to change their approach. Since last few decades they changed their approach and consider that employees are a very important resource for progress of the organization. They started taking interest in employees and their related activities. They have become more approachable to the employees. During orientation they get involved. They take the responsibility to welcome new employees in domestic and abroad assignments and discuss the jobs they have selected. He discusses with new entrants regarding their jobs and their roles at work towards organization. He is involved in motivation of the new entrants and takes part in socialization of them. It gives a positive message regarding approach of the top management towards employees and their career.

16. CONTENTS OF ORIENTATION PROGRAM

There is no clear cut guidelines regarding contents of orientation programme of new entrants However, the list of contents vary from organization to organization. Generally agreed topics involved in orientation programme are following:

(a) Introduction

It involved the topics related to introduction of organization, history of organization, managers, head of department, immediate supervisors, trainers, training programme, colleagues, technology, and work systems.

(b) Job Profile

Job profile provides job related information such as nature of job, job contents, procedure for performing job, job responsibility, importance of the job, job location machines and tools used in performing job, job documentation, safety measures, Job tasks, Job safety requirements, overview of job, job objectives, relationship to other jobs.

(c) Organization Related Issues

This covers the information related to organization mission, objectives, management philosophy, organization structure, products and services of the organization, employers details, board of directors, organizations of employer, name & titles of board members, employee's designation and departments, location and layout of plants and facilities, probationary period of new entrants, production process and systems, company policies and rules, disciplinary regulations, career development opportunities, performance management, promotion and transfer, communication channel, change process, bargaining and negotiation process, grievance handling process, and other related issues.

(d) Employee Benefits

List of employees' benefits includes the information regarding the benefits provided to the employees. It includes pay scale, increments, dearness allowances, transportation and housing allowances, bonus, leave with pay, privilege leave, weekly off, training and educational benefits, insurance, facilities for family, medical facilities, provident fund, gratuity, maternity benefits, loan or advance payments, canteen, clothing and safety aprons, cultural celebration and other related benefits.

17. TRAINING ON SEXUAL AND OTHER HARASSMENTS

In diversified workforce the employees are of different cultures, values, behaviour standards and moral values. At workplace, when they meet with others and interact due to job relations or in informal way they share their cultural values, behaviour standards and experience. They work as a team for achieving their desired performance. During this sometimes, unwanted activities take place like sexual, colour, race, religion, caste, language harassments. The concerned parties feel harassed and they do not find themselves in comfortable position. This is a disadvantage of diversified workforce under globalization. The number of women workers and workers from minority are increasing day by day. The management cannot stop appointing employees from different sex and cultural background. It is accepted that the diversified workforce is the result of globalization and it is to be continued with the organization. It has been realized by the management that the harassments are taking place at work place and it is undesireable for smooth working. Further it has been recognized by governments of different countries and steps have been taken to prevent and solve the harassment related problems.

Harassment training programme has been accepted by USA, UK, and other developing countries including India. Such training programmes have been accepted by the industries also worldwide. The best way to prevent sexual harassment is to adopt a comprehensive sexual harassment policy. The aim is to ensure that sexual harassment does not occur and, where it does occur, to ensure that adequate procedures are readily available to deal with the problem and prevent its recurrence. Policies and procedures should be adopted after consultation or negotiation with employee representatives. Experience suggests that strategies to create and maintain a working environment in which the dignity of employees is respected are most likely to be effective where they are jointly agreed. The sexual harassment training should be conducted for workers, supervisors and managers so that the awareness can be created, and consequences should be known to all employees.

The harassment policy and training programme are to be to be designed. These should highlight the nature of harassment, types of harassment, situation of harassments, acts of harassment, effects of harassment, identify the aggrieved party, procedure of reporting harassment, procedure for dealing with harassments, and responsibility for harassment dealing. The policy is to be communicated to the employees at the time of orientation and during their stay in organization time to time. It should be communicated through circulars, notices, meetings, and discussion clearly. The responsibility of communication of the policy should be fixed in beginning itself. For redressal of harassment related grievances a committee is to be appointed as per laws of the country. The committee members must be representation of the minority and women workers. Sincere efforts should be put in by the committee members so that the harassments are dealt properly. If it is done so then a sense of security among minority employees develop. They would find themselves in a comfortable position. It would contribute in developing and healthy working environment. This is needed to retain the existing customers and attract better employees from different cultures, sex and countries. The image of the company in the markets would improve positively.

(a) Sexual Harassment Law in India

Sexual and other harassments laws have been framed by some of the countries and some have made suitable adjustment with the constitutional laws to combat harassments. In India, it has been accepted in the recent decade by The Supreme Court as human rights violation when discrimination that affects Women's Right to Life and Livelihood. The definition of the sexual harassment has been clearly defined and employers are given guidelines to prevent sexual harassments at work places. Apex Court of India has issued guidelines, named as Vishaka Guidelines, for prevention and solution of sexual harassment. Under it the employers are made responsible for providing safe working environment for women. Vishaka guidelines applicable to all working women in different capacity such as part time, fulltime, on contract, honourary in public, private organized and unorganized sectors in India.

The guidelines are issued for prevention of the harassments and necessary steps to be taken for prevention of sexual harassment at work place. For this purpose a policy is to be prepared, communicated, and a committee is to be appointed for dealing with this issue. According to the definition of The Supreme Court, the sexual harassment is any unwelcome sexually determined behaviour, such as physical contact, a demand or request for sexual favours, sexuall remarks, showing pornography, any other physical, verbal or non-verbal conduct of a sexual nature. In return of benefits, promotion, and facilities etc., if a supervisor requests for sexual favour is a sexual harassment. Further, if the work environment is made more hostile for women worker such as physical touching, brushing, pushing women are not condition of employment.

18. CAREER PLANNING AND DEVELOPMENT PROGRAMME

In present global scenario, most of the MNCs are having diversified workforce. It is due to the companies are operating their business across the world and the requirement of manpower cannot be fulfilled from one country or culture. Manpower for different locations are picked up as per the needs of their business. The diversified workforce is the need of the hour and it cannot be avoid. For motivation, retention and commitment of employees it is necessary that career planning is to be done and development programme is to be conducted without any further delay. The career planning and development programme would make the situation clear to the workforce regarding their career opportunities, efforts of management for their career development. This helps ultimately to keep the people motivated, confident and retain them for longer period. Due to this company, managers, employees and clients all are benefited.

Now, next thing is that the existing planning and programme may not be suitable for the diversified workforce. It might be suitable for one location or culture but not suitable for different locations in different culture based countries. The necessary modifications are to be done keeping in view managing the diversity of workforce in the organization. The traditional approach for working women and minority employees cannot work in the present global competitive situation. Special provisions should be made for selection of candidates, conducting programmes for males and females separately if required, discrimination free implementation of career planning and development programmes. These should be related to promotion, incentives, increments, rewards and recognitions. It would help the employees, management and organization as a whole to get competitive advantages in competitive markets over its arch rivals

19. PROMOTION OF DIVERSITY

Under globalization the organizations are operating in various countries. To manage the activities across the countries, manpower is needed. It is not possible to get required manpower from one country for jobs in another country. The manpower is procured from many countries as per the need of the organization. Further, with development of women education, the number of women workers in the workforce is increasing. The multinational companies are now having diversified workforce. Due to this it is a challenging task to manage the diversified workforce. Over and above, the diversified is very useful for the organization because the talented persons are acquired; knowledge and experience are shared in the interest of the organization. No doubts due to cross-cultural workforce a number of problems are faced. Women workers are treated discriminately. They are not treated equally. Males are not ready to give equal opportunities to female workers and mainly at higher level. They are not appointed to the higher posts generally.

Further, the workers from minority are harassed on the ground of race, colour, caste, creed, religion etc. Women sexual harassment further makes the situation more difficult for the management. All these affect the development of working environment. To deal with the situation, and with the objective to develop a healthy working environment, the diversity should be motivated. The leader should take lead in this situation to motivate appointment of women and minority workers at different levels. The policies are to be prepared and implemented in this regard. The interest of the leaders in this area would develop confidence in employees belonging to minority. The talented employees from different minorities would be attracted by the organization. This would in return give healthy relationship and peaceful work environment. The organization would be benefitted from different angles. The role of top and middle level management is very important in motivation of diversity and get best of the situation.

20. CONCLUSION

Due to globalization the various factors of culture created diversity in different areas. The different categories of diversity are Diversity in workforce, Diversity in the markets, and Stakeholder diversity. Since globalization in last two decades, diversity of workforce has become an important issue for HR managers. Management of diversity in workforce is a great challenge for the management of the organization. There is diversity in markets also. India is a big country with many states and union territories. In most of the states there are different cultures and languages spoken. It is difficult to understand the market diversity for effective marketing in Indian and foreign markets. There are different stakeholders of the company in the global era. The main stakeholders are owners, shareholders, customers, clients, bankers, consultants and government etc. They are having different interests with the organization. There is diversity in interests of stakeholders. The role of culture plays an important role in understanding customers and matching products for them. The products features are to be modified for successful marketing. Managers who ignore culture role put their organizations in a great problem in global markets. The ultimate goal of the organization of high reputation is achieved through managing diversity. It becomes a long tern asset of the organization. Diversity management cannot be ignored and if done so then it is at the cost of the organization. In the diversified environment it has become necessity to manage the diversity issue effectively. There is no one solution of this problem but sincere efforts are needed in this direction. The strategies adopted for diversity management are modification in policies, cultural training of diversified workforce, clarification of job requirements, sound recruitment and selection, proper communication, equal treatment, and broader approach for living in diversity.

Now it is the need of the time to manage the workforce diversity. One of the methods to deal with diversity is diversity training. Diversity training is **training** for diversified workforce with the objectives to increase cultural awareness, interest, participation, sharing of values, knowledge, and skills, and finally healthy work environment. Cross-cultural training is another way of managing diversity in an organization. It develops the interest to understand employees own background and cultural heritage and should accept and appreciate culture of other employees. Different types of cross cultural training are there to fulfil the objectives. The factors affecting the effectiveness are structure of the programme, continuity of the programme, quality of programme, properly justified programme, suitable for target groups and easy to measure. In present competitive situation, it has become very difficult for each organization to perform its jobs effectively. Now it is question of survival, growth, stabilize and excel in the performance. The need for talented manpower with self motivation has been felt to work with latest technology and in competitive situation. The uphill task with the human resource management is to select, train, motivate, get commitment, and contribute in achievement of the objectives. The diversified manpower is to be developed and motivated and for that purpose management should design HRD programme to achieve the objectives effectively and efficiently. The HRD programme should include the sub programmes like socialization through orientation, career planning and development, training on sexual harassment, and motivation of diversity.

The initial HRD effort designed in this direction for employees is socialization. It guides the employee and help in adjusting him in the job, group and the organization as a whole. It is a sense-making process that helps new entrants to adapt in organizational situation and make his place in the organization. It starts before an employee joins the organization and continues during his employment also. It may take longer time also. The stages involved in this process are before joining, at the time of joining, and adjustment stage. This can be done by the supervisor, the people in HR Department, Peers, CEO, or combination of any of these. The best way to prevent sexual harassment is to adopt a comprehensive sexual harassment policy. The aim is to ensure that sexual harassment does not occur and, where it does occur, to ensure that adequate procedures are readily available to deal with the problem and prevent its recurrence.

The career planning and development programme would make the situation clear to the workforce regarding their career opportunities, efforts of management for their career development. This helps ultimately to keep the people motivated, confident and retain them for longer period. Due to this company, managers, employees and clients all are benefited. Now, next thing is that the existing planning and programme may not be suitable for the diversified workforce. The necessary modifications are to be done keeping in view managing the diversity of workforce in the organization. Special provisions should be made for selection of candidates, conducting programmes for males and females separately if required, discrimination free implementation of career planning and development programmes. These should be related to promotion, incentives, increments, rewards and recognitions. It would help the employees, management and organization as a whole to get competitive advantages in competitive markets over its arch rivals

The multinational companies are now having diversified workforce. Due to this it is a challenging task to manage the diversified workforce. Over and above, the diversified is very useful for the organization because the talented persons are acquired; knowledge and experience are shared in the interest of the organization. No doubts due to cross-cultural workforce a number of problems are faced. Women workers are treated discriminately. They are not treated equally. They are not appointed to the higher posts generally. Further, the workers from minority are harassed on the ground of race, colour, caste, creed, religion etc. Women sexual harassment further makes the situation more difficult for the management. To deal with the situation, and with the objective to develop a healthy working environment, the diversity should be motivated. The leader should take lead in this situation to motivate appointment of women and minority workers at different levels. It would be in the interests of employees, organization and society as a whole.

21. QUESTIONS FOR REVIEW

1. Define culture diversity and explain various categories of it in detail.
2. How do you evaluate the role of culture for managers to adjust products and services as per expectations of people from different cultures?
3. "Managing diversity is planning and implementing organizational systems and practices to manage people to get optimum advantages of diversity." Discuss
4. Diversity provides a lot of opportunities and challenges for the organization in present global environment. Do you agree with statement or not? Discuss
5. There is no one solutions for diversity. What strategies would you adopt for managing diversity if you are appointed as a manager in the company to deal with? Explain
6. Critically evaluate the role of a manager in diversity management in detail.
7. Do you feel diversity training is suitable strategy for managing diversity in an organization? Discuss.
8. Explain the objectives and areas of diversity training used by management in present time.
9. Highlight the approaches of manager leading diverse team in international assignments.
10. The need for diversity training and trainers is strongly felt by organization having diversified workforce. Discuss
11. Discuss selection, hiring, costs and benefits of hiring diversity trainer.
12. Compare and contrast between diversity training and cross-cultural training in brief.
13. Define cross-cultural education and training and discuss the importance of it in present scenario.
14. Discuss the main steps involved in cross-cultural education and training process in detail.

15. Explain different types of cross-cultural training used for diversified workforce in MNCs.
16. Highlight the factors effecting effectiveness of cross-cultural education and training in detail
17. Critically evaluate the relationship between cross-cultural programmes and business results.
18. Write short notes on the following:
    (a) Properly justified cross-cultural education and training programme
    (b) Consistency of performance of programme
    (c) Training for conducting negotiation
    (d) Training in management practices
    (e) Cross-cultural coaching
    (f) Creating-cross cultural awareness
    (g) Clarification for job requirements
19. Discuss the broader approach for living in diversity in present time.
20. Being an HRD manager of an MNC what would you include in HRD programme for diversified workforce of the corporation?
21. What do you know about socialization through orientation? Explain
22. Discuss the main steps involved in socialization process in detail.
23. Explain the training on sexual and other harassments and laws relating to these in India.
24. Short notes on the following:
    (a) Persons involved in socialization
    (b) Contents of orientation programme
    (c) Motivation of diversity
    (d) Career planning and development programme for diversified workforce.

22. OBJECTIVE QUESTIONS

1. Diversity as a Vital Resource, diversity is defined as "otherness or those human qualities that are different from our own and outside the groups, to which we belong, yet present in other individuals and groups".

    (a) Fully agree *(b)* Partially agree
    (c) Partially disagree *(d)* Fully disagree
    (e) Cannot say anything

2. The companies are doing their business in different markets and fields. There are different stakeholders of the company in the global era. The main stakeholders are:
   (a) Owners, shareholders,
   (b) Customers, clients,
   (c) Bankers, consultants
   (d) Government etc.
   (e) All the above

3. The various factors of culture created diversity in different areas. The different categories of diversity are:
   (a) Diversity in workforce
   (b) Diversity in the markets
   (c) Stakeholder diversity
   (d) All the above
   (e) None of the above

4. The success of an organization depends on management ability to understand the cross-culture issues especially related to concerned parties working in that organization are:
   (a) Customers
   (b) Manpower
   (c) Both (a) and (b)
   (d) None of the above
   (e) All the above

5. Workforce diversity is a reality at multinational companies across the world. Even in India after globalization the same situation is being faced. Do you agree with this statement?
   (a) Fully agree
   (b) Partially agree
   (c) Partially disagree
   (d) Fully disagree
   (e) Cannot say anything

6. The manager's role in managing diversity is to:
   (a) Conducts survey and collect data for regular audit, review, and assess the progress of individuals, departments and organization as a whole.
   (b) Motivate workforce for consultation, discussion, suggestions, involvement so that their commitment level improves in managing diversity.
   (c) Aligns HR interventions with diversity objectives for proper management of diversity.
   (d) Participate and motivate shared leaning by developing network with managers.
   (e) All the above

7. For managing workforce diversity the strategy of fair treatment means
   (a) Treating everyone with one approach
   (b) Treating everyone with different approach.
   (c) Treating should not be biased.
   (d) None of the above.
   (e) All the above

8. In diversify training the main area of training are
   (a) Attitude
   (b) Knowledge
   (c) Skills
   (d) All the above
   (e) None of the above

9. The first step of cross culture education training process is
   (a) Providing cross-culture education
   (b) Providing cross-culture coaching
   (c) Creating cross-culture awareness.
   (d) All the above
   (e) None of the above.

10. Socialization process of employees regarding organization starts before an employee joins the organization and continues during his employment also. It may take longer time also. It is a:
   (a) Customized process
   (b) Non-randomized process
   (c) Continuous process.
   (d) All the above
   (e) None of the above.

11. Person involved in socialization process in an organization are:
   (a) HR department
   (b) Peers
   (c) CEO
   (d) all of the above
   (e) None of the above

Answer Keys:

Question No.	Answer	Question No.	Answer
1	a	7	d
2	e	8	c
3	d	9	c
4	c	10	c
5	a	11	d
6	e		

Chapter

19 Organization Development and Human Resource Development

1. INTRODUCTION

Change is a natural phenomenon. It is likely to take place. It may be at different paces. Some time the changes taken place fast and sometime slow depending upon the prevalent situation. It is likely to take place in every sphere of our life and there is no exception. In this world nothing is permanent except change. It is sure the changes would take place. It can be said in this world nothing is permanent. Due to changes the situation is uncertain and risky. The business environment is also changing rapidly. The factors affecting the business are social, cultural, economic, legal, political, technological and competition. These have gone under rapid changes. To carry the business effectively it was required by the organization to work according to the changing environment or surrender to the changes. Those who have changed the strategy to do the business as per the changes have achieved success in the business and are leader in the business and earning a huge profit every year. In the present situation social set up, economy and its development, government policies, technology, education of the people and level of competition have undergone drastic changes. It is needed to match the internal factors with the changing external factors so business can be carried effectively and efficiently.

An organization is a human grouping in which the jobs are preformed for attainment of specific objectives. Every organization has its objectives to be fulfilled. Organizations may be of different types and with different objectives. An organization may be a manufacturing firm, insurance company, a governmental agency, hospital, university and a religious trust.

It may be small or large, simple or complex, objectives of the organization differ from organization to organization but remain relatively constant. These are likely to be modified over a period of time with the changing environment. Organizational goals may be more than one and organization tries to achieve these goals. In order to achieve these goals effectively and efficiently a set of rules and regulations is required. These rules and regulations will assist its members in accomplishment of the organizational goal. Large organizations in public and private sectors are operating their business from different locations scattered in different parts of the country and performing different types of activities. In the corporate sector for attainment of objectives varieties of functions are performed by utilizing the available resources. We include men, machines, money and materials. These words are starting with letter M so these are called 4Ms. These resources are being used by the management in the organization. Out of these, human resource is the most important resource because through the combined efforts of men, other resources are utilized for accomplishment of the goals. Without human being other resources will be unproductive. Hence, human resource is the most important resource that is to be managed properly.

The human resource is given increasing significance in modern organization. Obviously, a majority of the problems in organizational setting are human and social rather than physical, technical and economic. The failure to recognize this fact causes great loss to the nation, enterprise and the individual. People at work comprise a large number of individuals of different sex, age, education standards and groups. These people at work exhibit not only similar behaviour patterns and characteristics to a certain degree, but they also show many dissimilarities. Each individual who works has his own set of needs, drives, goals and experiences. Management, therefore, must be aware not only of the organizational needs but also needs and goals of employees.

The human resources assume importance from an economic standpoint at national, enterprise and individual levels of analysis. Ginzberg pointed out, human resource is the key to economic development. However, they are being wasted through unemployment, disguised unemployment, outdated skills, lack of job opportunities, poor personnel policies and practices and problems of adjusting to changes. There exists a wide scope to increase productivity through their proper development. The physical resources will not give output unless the human resources are applied to them. At enterprise level, there is also an urgent need for effective utilization of the human resource to attain organizational goals. This can be done by understanding their nature, potentials and limitations of human resource, developing and utilizing it to the optimal ability, maintaining its quality and coordinating it with other resources. From individual point of view, development of employees will get them a source of economic advantage, improves the economic status and living standards.

Further, to improve the effectiveness of the organization there is need to bring improvements The jobs, job designs, working procedures, technology, structure, competencies of human resource, relationships, products, services etc. If the improvements or changes are made in these areas the organization as a whole would develop. The effectiveness of the organization in the market would definitely improve. The organization would be in a position to achieve the predetermined targets in time effectively and efficiently. The organization would do the thing better and before its competitors. It can be said that there is direct relationship between HRD and OD. The sales, profitability and market share of the company would improve. The company would enjoy the leadership position in the markets. The image of the company would definitely improve. So it is concluded that the organization development as whole is the need of the time in the stiff competitive situation in present global era.

2. ORGANISATION CHANGE

When an organization works in the prevalent environment, the working of the organization is affected by the external factors. None of the organizations can work in isolation. The business environment is drastically changing and so the impact on working is also in similar way. The external factors are uncontrollable and no one is having control over them. The external factors are social, political, cultural, economic, technology, competition, legal etc. These are undergoing changes. Some time the changes are minor and sometimes major. These changes cannot be ignored. To do work in an organization effectively the internal factors are to be changed. If changed as per the need of the situation the work would not be affected. Otherwise the work would be affected and the effectiveness of the company would go down. The competitive advantage to the company would be missing. The management must focus on the changes in environment because the changes are constant and sure. They are likely to take place. They are closely related to all spheres of our lives. There is no exception to the changes. It is likely to take place to everyone and everywhere.

In this world the situation has become more complex and increasingly interrelated, changes have affected us a lot. Thus, change may sometimes appear sooner or later frequently and randomly. They changes may be sometimes wanted or unwanted. We are slowly becoming aware of the changes and consequences of them. Organizations must take these changes as a challenge and should not be ignored. It is a matter of survival, growth and excellence in their performance. Timely steps are to be taken so that the effectiveness can be maintained or improved to face the challenges. The change is a very paramount factor in present time. The organization changes create imbalance between existing and new required skills, knowledge, technology and process. An adjustment is to be done in jobs, working conditions, procedures, technology, competencies, structure etc. The adjustments are not accepted by the human being and changes are resisted. The ability to handle the changes effectively is to be developed for effective working and efficiency of individual, teams and organization as a whole. The organizations which learn and adjust with the changes excel in their business and those who don't are not in a position to cope up with changes struggle for survival. This term has been defined by many experts as follows:

3. NATURE OF CHANGE

Organisation change is a dynamic process through which an organization can move from the existing to the new improved position. It is very essential for the organization for survival, stabilize, grow and excel in its performance. The main **characteristics** of change are:

(a) Change is the law of nature. It definitely takes place sooner or later.

(b) It is a continuous process affected by external factors in environment.

(c) It is vital for survival, stabilize, grow and excel in performance of its activities.

(d) The pace of change cannot be predicted. It may be fast, medium or slow.

(e) The changes may be planned or unplanned, natural or adaptive as per situation.

(f) The changes are uncontrollable and organizations have no control over them.

(g) The changes are to be managed effectively so competitive advantage can be achieved or maintained by the organization.

(h) The importance of change management in future competitive situation would be more.

When company, management and employees interact then organization culture is created. The features, values, brief, traditions, customs, religion, celebration of festivals, worships, language, dresses etc. affect everyone. A new pattern of living is developed. The change management while performing its functions should consider the following elements:

(a) Evolution of the Company

There is definitely good effect of evolution of the company on perception of change. These factors affect the acceptance of the changes or not. Evolution related factor like social background, political influence, history of management, financial position etc., give good influence on change acceptance or not. The following points to be taken into account for planning of changes by change management:

(i) Origin of the company, values associated with the company, Objectives, customers' perception, management approach towards changes etc.

(ii) Sources of employees, experience of employees regarding previously implemented changes, and resistance from different levels of employees to changes.

(iii) Traditions, conventions, practices, policies, norms relating to these the people in organization are accustomed, and any threat to existing one of these.

(iii) Interpersonal relationship, power delegation, with people responsible for change management.

(iv) Impact of changes on power sharing and its balance, looser and gainer due to changes in position, status, and grade related to pay scale.

(b) Management and Organisation

Changes affect everyone in the organization without any exception. The effects may be more at one level and less at other level. The changes affect skills, knowledge, structure, procedures, systems, technology etc. The roles of the management and others also change.

4. LEVELS OF CHANGES

When management is interested to make the improvements or changes in the existing pattern, the changes can be brought in and at various levels. These changes are made at different levels as per need of the situation. There is no hard and fast rule that the change would take place at one level at a time. It may take place at random or planned way. The situation demanding the change is very powerful. The changes can be made at individual, group or organizational levels. These are explained below in the given paragraphs.

(a) Individual Level

The changes are made to the activities related to individual. At micro level the changes are made and that affects the individual or each employees. The examples of individual are transfer, promotion, training and development programmes, shifts in job assignments etc. These changes are made for individuals and these are affecting the working, competencies, motivation, relationship, satisfaction level commitments etc. These are not going to affect the organization much when made individually. The impact of such changes is very less. These changes may have impact on the group and in turn the groups may have effect on the organisatioin in long run. When we take a number of changes together they may have repercussions beyond them on group and organization as a whole.

(b) Group Level Changes

Group is collection of persons closely related to each other. The group is having the common objectives. The group affects the behavior of its members to a good extent. Examples of groups are team, section, department, division, location etc. The group is assigned the jobs to perform. The group is very powerful. The dynamics of group should be understood by the management The organizational changes can be implemented for a group such as job assignment, replacement of technology, working procedure, communication pattern, welfare facilities, motivation, leadership, training and development etc. These changes may have strong influence on the behaviour of group members. The members may support or resist the changes as per their perception and convenience. If the changes are opposed by the groups then it becomes difficult for the management to implement. It is very difficult to convince the group and overcome the resistance. When the changes are proposed or suggested by the group, implementation of changes becomes very easy due to their cooperation. The effectiveness of the efforts for improvement goes high. The group dynamics should be understood by change management for better implementation. The group level changes definitely have significant effect on the organization as a whole.

(c) Organisation Level Changes

For implementing changes at organization level then all parties are involved. All individuals, groups, teams, departments etc. are involved. The organization as a whole is affected by the changes. The decisions regarding these changes are taken by the top level management. The decisions are not taken or implemented by one or two managers. The changes at organizational level can be made in planning, objectives, organization structure, ownership, remuneration and incentive systems, technology replacement etc. For planning and implementation of organization changes a lot of time and efforts are needed. These changes are having their impact on the whole organization. Everyone is affected by these changes. The support of employees, managers and unions is must for proper implementation of changes. If opposed the desired result of the changes would not be there. The changes at organization level for bringing improvement are referred as organisation development.

These three levels of changes are interrelated. The changes at one level are affecting the other level more or less. For example the changes at individual level would have effects on group more and at less at organizational level. The changes at group level would affect the organizational level more and less at individual level.

5. IMPORTANCE OF CHANGE

Change is the law of nature. It takes place in every sphere of our life without any exception. Change is inevitable. It is to take place and no one is having control over change. Only thing is that some time change takes place slow and some time fast in environment. The law of change states that one should not be constant over the time. It is necessary to keep pace with the changing time. If not done so that party would suffer and be laggard in performance of its activities. For many people these changes are inconvenient, as they require adaptation. A lot of efforts are needed to adapt to the changes. With the existing systems or position we find more convenience so we resist changes. We only accept the changes willingly when we find that the change brings convenience reduced costs, comfort and saving time. The changes demand adaptation if we want to perform our work properly. This is applicable to the organizations also. For development and growth, all organizations must adapt to the demands of their business environment timely. The changes are to be made in processes, systems, quality, products, services, management and manpower as demanded by the situation. The organizations adapting the changing get advantages in their performance, satisfaction, sales, profits, market shares and reputation. Due to adaptation to changes the business health of the organization improves a lot. The changes are important due to following reasons:

(a) Provides Place of Growth

When the company is interested to grow and expand, it takes on more projects, clients, production and work. The existing structure is sufficient to keep operations going, growth can force a company to make structural changes in different areas to accommodate the new workload. For example, more employees are to be selected for performing these tasks, more number of managers and supervisors are needed. Without changes like these, an organization cannot complete projects or activities and would become ineffective in its business performance. So for growth changes is strongly needed.

(b) Provided Solution of Problem

In the continuously changing business environment the organization finds difficult in operating some of its activities. Due to sincere efforts also the problem is not solved. Then changes are needed in that area so the problems can be solved. For example the operating machine is old but well maintained. It is not in position to produce more and products of better quality in comparison with product of competitors. It is needed that the machine must be changed with the new technology machine so that that problem can be addressed.

(c) Keep Up to Date to Demand

The motivation factor for change in an organization which is interested for progress in business may feel the need to keep up to date its processes, systems, manpower, structure, and market trends. Keeping pace with the changing time brings better performance in products, services and give higher profitability. With this motivation the changes are accepted by the management of the organization. Due to timely changes the company is in position to accept the new challenges in the turbulent business environment.

(d) Marketing of Organisation

The company that is interested to produce more and sell its products in the markets needs a good number of employees. It is bit difficult to attack talented people in good number. It is only possible when the management of the company makes necessary changes in pay, incentives, career development opportunities etc. These changes attack better employees so the need of the organization for development can be fulfilled. The changes are important in this area.

(e) New Income Streams

A company takes a risk every time when it introduces a new product, service projects, entering new markets in domestic as well as foreign markets. However, these changes are going to give the new sources of business and income. Through these efforts the business is diversified and chances of risks are also reduced. It opens the avenues for revenue generation. There are many leading organizations in the market earning a lot of revenue through these changes. The changes have opened new arena for new sources of income.

6. RESISTANCE TO CHANGE

When the new ideas or action are introduced in our life, we generally do not accept it. It may be even useful for us. Most people prefer predictability and stability without disturbance in both their personal and professional lives. People generally avoid changes that upset order, threaten their status, self-interests, comfort, increase stress or involve risk. When changes are brought people that do not or like, feel good then resist the changes. Sometimes these are not supported or opposed. When they do so it is called resistance. Resistance to change is the action taken by the people when they think that the change in ideas or action as a change is going to create a threat for them. The threat may be small or big for them and accordingly the opposition is faced. Resistance may be active or passive, from individual or group, aggressive or gentle. The resistance is likely to take place in our social, family, friend circle and in organization also. The resistance continues and, sometimes increases, until people are able to recognize the benefits of change and understand the benefits are worth more than the risk or threats to their self-interests. Our resistance can block change unless we take interest in it and learn from it. Resistance provides source of information which can help change to move forward in a positive direction.

Resistance to change is normal and natural phenomenon and always happens. We are naturally resistant to changes. The term of resistance is defined in the field of electronics. According to dictionary definition, "Resistance is the opposition made when the current is passed through a conductor it converts electrical energy into heat or another form of energy." The heat and the energy both are desired and useful but if not taken care of can create problems also. This definition can be applied to human being also. For human being the resistance to change is the opposition of the human being to change, generate energy that can be useful to transform or hamper the progress. When changes are brought to the organization in processes, systems, structure, job designs and employees are opposed by the people at different levels. The people may oppose these changes due to various reasons. Workers may resist due to their point of view and management may oppose from their angle. Workers may not have the idea of the changes, feel threat to their jobs, find difficult to perform new jobs easily etc. Managers may oppose that they have not taken into confidence, threat to the status, unwillingness to shoulder new responsibility etc. There are different sources of resistance to change in an organization. The resistance source may be organizational forces, sub-unit forces, group forces, and individual forces. These are explained the following paragraphs:

(a) Resistance from Organisation

When changes are introduced in an organization, these are opposed by the organization itself. The internal organization factors make the things difficult to implement according to the need of the changing environment. The objectives of changes cannot be fulfilled. The organizational factors that resist the change are following:

(i) Organisation culture:

At the work place many persons work together in an organisation. A pattern of working develops there and this is called organization culture. It covers traditions, belief, conventions, practices, norms, value and interpersonal relationship. When the changes are introduced the cultural factors are affected. The roles of employees, their norms, values, status, earnings etc. are affected. They have joined the organization with certain expectations from the organization. If the expectations are threatened by changes then they are likely to oppose the changes. It can be said that the changes are not as per the cultural factors then resistance undoubtedly takes place. This situation is to be taken care of properly.

(ii) Organisation strategy

For accomplishment to its activities the organization adopts certain strategies. For its effective working the strategy is needed. The strategy is the game plan or course of action that has been decided by the management in organization to achieve objectives in advance. In present competitive situation the need for strategy is strongly felt. But sometimes the organization strategy becomes obstacle for changes. In the present strategy the managers become accustomed and stick to it for performing their routine tasks. If the change disturbs the present working strategy the resistance is likely to take place due to present working strategy from managers.

(iii) Structure of organization

Structure shows the relationship between different people working at different levels, their working relationship, sharing of power, authority and responsibility. It shows who reports to whom and how many persons report to him. When organization structure is prepared it shows the tasks relationship that affects the work and behaviour of people. With the change in people the work relationship is not affected and it remains unchanged. The employees become used to this pattern and when changes are introduced, they oppose the changes because their working pattern gets affected.

(iv) Established pattern

In an organization certain procedures and systems are followed to get the performance from employees. They are acquired, oriented, trained, guided, compensated, rewarded, punished and motivated to perform the assigned tasks. A good number of procedures and systems are involved. This established a pattern of working in the organization. The same performance can be achieved with less number of procedures and systems if changes are introduced. Due to the established pattern the resistance is likely to take place.

(b) Resistance from Departmental Forces

When changes are made in a section/ department/ division the resistance is felt at this level. It can be named as sectional, divisional or departmental forces resisting changes. These are following:

(i) Difference in approach towards change

This is the major source of resistance to changes. When changes are introduced in and organization or departments, in section/ division/ department these are viewed from different angle as per their point of view. The approach of functional/ divisional/ departmental heads differs. They may take the changes differently according to their own interests and benefits. The changes are explained to employees in different ways. Therefore, the resistance would be there from different units on different points as explained to the employees. For example if the performance of the business goes down and management is interested bringing changes. The resistance from different units would be different. Production manager may demand for better technology for higher production quantity and quality, HR manager may demand facilities for training and development facilities, Research and development division may focus on research facility and higher budget for this. Finance manager may demand cost reduction so the performance of the business as a whole can be improved. The approaches of various departmental heads are different and resist the changes.

(ii) Resource allocation

Another source of resistance at unit level is allocation of resources. Every unit performs its function with the help of manpower, machines, money and materials. When these resources are allocated to them may create problems for changes. If a department is allocated less then requirements, the managers would not be happy and likely to oppose the changes in future. If a unit is over allocated then the manager may take it guaranteed for future that his department would be allocated more in future also. It may oppose changes in future.

(iii) Task relationship

In an organization different types of jobs are being performed. These jobs are not performed independently. These are interdependent and being performed by different persons, departments and under different facilities. Close coordination is need for good performance. When change is made at one level then changes are need at other levels also. The change process becomes very difficult. Due to the inconvenience caused the persons working in different units or within unit resist the changes. For example, For production, funds are provided by finance manager, manpower by HR manager, market information by marketing manager and materials from store manager. When demand in the market goes high the change in production volume is needed. The changes are to be made at all departmental levels. This may be opposed in some of the departments because it needs a lot of effort to meet the change requirements.

(iv) Power, politics and conflicts

When changes are made in the department for betterment. It may benefit some of them and not all. The benefits may be at the cost of others. This definitely would not be liked by the sufferers. It may affect the position, packages and other facilities of individual. The differences in opinions, liking, disliking and approach cause conflict among them. Then power struggle and politics would take place in the department. Some of them may be in favour or changes and some not. The changes cannot be implemented properly. The required support would be missing. For example, in competitive situation the top level management is interested to cut down the production cost. The change proposed is to buy the raw materials at lower cost. This is likely to affect the quality of raw materials but may benefit to cut the production cost. Due to this the quality of the products may go down and would affect the position of production and marketing managers. The products would not be preferred by the customers with lower quality. This definitely would get opposition from production and marketing managers.

(c) Resistance from Employees

At employees level resistance is likely to take place. When an employee joins an organization with certain expectations. He performs his duty in routine and works according to instructions and procedures. A working pattern develops and he gets accustomed to that situation. He is used to this situation. If any change is introduced in this he is likely to oppose the changes because he and his position is disturbed. The reasons for resistance are following:

(i) Biased attitude

When mind of the employee is already biased regarding changes, he is likely to oppose the changes. He would not be ready to accept anything regarding changes. His mind is already occupied by bias and that is not a good thing. Self-ego, defence, commitment, expectations affect the attitude. This adversely affects the perception of individuals and they interpret the situation from their personal benefits point of view.

(ii) Anxiety for personal losses

When changes are made then they affect the employees at all level. They may have fear and worries regarding their personal losses like losing jobs, earning, position, status, comfort and freedom. They are not ready to accept the changes until they are convinced regarding changes and their benefits to employees.

(iii) Uncertainty and risks

Due to uncertainty and risks also employees resist changes. When the employees are not sure what is the nature of change, how it would be introduced and what would be the impact of change, there would be uncertainty in their mind. They may visualize the risks in implementation of changes.

(iv) Non-involvement of employees

Non-involvement of employees creates psychological problems. They may take is as a matter of ego, status, reputation etc. When changes are planned and implemented the managers and employees are not taken into confidence. They are not involved by the top management in planning and implementation of the changes. They may feel bad and level of commitment would go down. There would be no positive support from them.

(v) Individual perception

Individual perception affects the behaviour of employees. When changes are introduced; employees have their perception regarding type of change, need for change, method of implementation, success and failure of change, capacity of organization to implement etc. Perception regarding these would affect the attitude of employees significantly. It may create problem and resistance to change is likely to take place.

(vi) Established habits of employees

During their routine work, they follow certain instructions, procedures and rule. A pattern or working develops and they get accustomed to that situation. The employees develop their habits and it continues further for a long time. They feel comfortable with the established habits. When changes are introduced then they are disturbed. Due to the disturbance, inconvenience and extra efforts required for change implementation they feel highly disturbed. So they may oppose the changes.

(vii) Other reasons

In addition to above reasons there are other reasons also. On the grounds these employees may resist the changes. These reasons may be justified also. These reasons may be competency needed to handle changes, time required for adjustment, cost for implementation of changes, capability of organization etc. There may be more reasons of this type due to that they may resist the changes.

These reasons can be overcome by the management if the employees are taken into confidence before planning and implementation of changes. They must be involved in this whole process from top to lower level of employees. If they are convinced regarding effects and benefits of changes then cooperation from them can be expected.

(d) Resistance from Groups

Group is a collection of people that has been formed with an objective to achieve. They work together to achieve that objective. There may be different types of groups in an organization. These may be formal and informal. Most of the works are performed by groups in the organization. When changes are introduced they are resisted by the features of groups. These are explained below:

(i) Group cohesiveness

Group cohesiveness is the power or strength that keeps the group member together. Higher the degree of cohesiveness more is the attachment among people in group. When change is introduced it might be opposed by the groups. The group together takes the interest of it more important than that of organization interest and resistance is likely to take place. Group may be interested to maintain its existing position. Management must keep this thing in mind so the opposition may not be there.

(ii) Group norms of behaviour

When the people work in a group certain norms or standard of behaviour are developed. While working in day to day routine work most of the people follow these standards. A pattern or working behaviour develops by this. If change is introduced and affecting the working patterns then the members oppose the changes. They are not used to the new changes. Therefore, there is opposition due to norms of group behaviour.

(iii) Group ideology

Group ideology is the thinking or philosophy of the group. This affects the routine work of the group. The thinking may be positive or negative, cooperative or non cooperative, progressive or non progressive. Due to this ideology the group members behave. If introduced changes affect the ideology then there are chances of resistance to changes from groups.

While introducing changes management must have proper knowledge of groups existing in the organization. The group dynamics should be taken into account for bringing changes. The group members should be taken into confidence and their participation should be insured before changes. The results would be more effective.

7. DEFINITIONS OF OD

With the turbulent business environment there is uncertainty and risk in business. It has become very difficult to keep pace with the changing time. It has become necessary to adjust the internal factors so that the objectives can be achieved effectively and efficiently. This has become very difficult to do so. With this situation the nature and needs of organizations are changing dramatically. To meet the needs of organization proper steps are to be taken so that the effectiveness of it can be improved. The ability to manage the changes must be developed. It would be important assets for the organization. If not done so then there is great risk in its business. Correspondingly, the profession of organization development (OD) has been changing to meet the changing needs of organizations. Experts have expressed their views regarding approach of organization development. No doubt with the time the approach of organization development has undergone drastic changes. The approaches of past and present are not similar. Therefore, it may be most useful to consider more than one definitions of organization development. Some of the definitions given by experts are explained below

"Organization Development is an effort planned, organization-wide, and managed from the top, to increase organization effectiveness and health through planned interventions in the organization's 'processes,' using behavioral-science knowledge." — Beckhard,

According to Schmuck and Miles, "Organization development is a planned and sustained effort to apply behavioural science for system improvement, using reflexive, self-analysis methods."

According to Warren Bennis, organization development (OD) is a complex strategy intended to change the beliefs, attitudes, values, and structure of organizations so that they can better adapt to new technologies, markets, and challenges.

Warner Burke emphasizes that OD is not just "anything done to better an organization"; it is a particular kind of change process designed to bring about a particular kind of end result. OD involves organizational reflection, system improvement, planning, and self-analysis.

The term "Organization Development" is often used interchangeably with organizational effectiveness, especially when used as the name of a department or a part of the Human Resources function within an organization.

"Organization Development is the attempt to influence the members of an organization to expand their candidness with each other about their views of the organization and their experience in it, and to take greater responsibility for their own actions as organization members. The assumption behind OD is that when people pursue both of these objectives simultaneously, they are likely to discover new ways of working together that they experience as more effective for achieving their own and their shared (organizational) goals. And when this does not happen, such activity helps them to understand why and to make meaningful choices about what to do in light of this understanding." Neilsen,

"Organization development is a system-wide application of behavioral science knowledge to the planned development and reinforcement of organizational strategies, structures, and processes for improving an organization's effectiveness." Cummings and Worley. "Organisation development is a set of behavioural science based theories, values, strategies, and techniques, aimed at the planned change of the organizational work setting for the purpose of enhancing individual development and improving organizational performance through the alteration of organizational members' on the job behaviour", Porras and Robertson.

"Organization Development is a body of knowledge and practice that enhances organizational performance and individual development, viewing the organization as a complex system of systems that exist within a larger system, each of which has its own attributes and degrees of alignment. OD interventions in these systems are inclusive methodologies and approaches to strategic planning, organization design, leadership development, change management, performance management, coaching, diversity, and work/life balance," Matt Minahan.

Organization Development: "Collaborating with organizational leaders and their groups to create systemic change on behalf of root-cause problem-solving toward improving productivity and employee satisfaction through strengthening the human processes through which they get their work done" Michael Broom.

Burke has defined, "Organisation development is a planned process of change in an organisational culture through the utilization of behavioural science, technologies, research and theories."

Alderfer CP defined, "Organization development is a process used to enhance both the effectiveness of an organization and the well-being of its members through planned interventions." Notice three keys points here. First, OD enhances the effectiveness of the organization. Effectiveness in this context is defined as achieving organizational goal and objectives. Second, OD enhances the well-being of organization members. Well-being refers to the perceived overall satisfaction each organization member feels toward his or her job and work environment. Generally speaking, having challenging and meaningful work leads to high work satisfaction and if rewarded by the organization to higher satisfaction with rewards as well. Thus OD is intended to enhance both personal and work satisfaction. Third, OD is used to enhance the effectiveness of organisation and individual well-being through planned interventions. Planned interventions refers to sets of structured activities in which selected organizational units targets groups or individuals engage with a task or sequence of tasks where the task goals are related directly or indirectly to organizational improvement. Thus, planned interventions or interventions strategies are the primary means through which organizational improvement and changes take place.

Organisation development is not simple approach. It is a planned and system process of organization change. The changes are to the management to improve effectiveness of systems, individual and orgnisation as a whole. The **main characteristics of OD** are following:

(a) It is a planned approach for changes to manage.

(b) The objective is to bring improvement through change management.

(c) The goal is to make whole organization more effective in its business performance.

(d) OD process involves the whole organization for change.

(e) The focus is on individual, groups and organization.

(f) For long-term changes it takes time for implementation.

(g) Guidance of the outsider expert as a change agent is needed.

(h) Active participation of the change agent in OD interventions is needed

(i) Favourable organization culture is good for it.

(j) Research is needed for identification of problem, data collection analysis and action for problem solution

Effectiveness of people and organization can be improved by:

(a) Establishing relationships with key personnel in the organization for entering and contracting with the organization

(b) Researching and evaluating systems in the organization to understand dysfunctions and/ or goals of the systems in the organization

(c) Identifying techniques/interventions to improve effectiveness of the organization and its people;

(d) Applying approaches to improve effectiveness in the organization.

(e) Evaluating the effectiveness of the applied techniques and their results.

Organization Development (OD) is an effort to increase an organization's ability to improve itself as a humane and effective system. **Elements of OD** may include:

(a) Finding ways to adapt to the changing situation to meet organisational requirements.

(b) Establishing changes in structures, processes and climate that allow it to effectively manage its important business

(c) Increasing the ability to manage functions like organization culture, training and development, attracting new talents, interpersonal relationship and physical conditions.

(d) Increasing its ability to adapt to new conditions, and managing changes effectively.

It is concluded that the organization development is a planned effort organization-wide and managed from the top level of management to improve health and effectiveness of the organization through planned techniques using knowledge of different disciplines.

8. IMPORTANCE OF ORGANISATION DEVELOPMENT

With the changing and turbulent environment the risks and uncertainly prevails. It has become very risky for the organization to carry out its business and achieve the objectives effectively and efficiently. In business a huge capital is involved. There is no certainty that the organization would stay in competition and business in future. With the changing time the requirements and existing competencies are different. A gap is created between these two. It has become necessary to bridge this gap by bringing suitable changes at individual, group and orgnisation level in processes, systems, management, products, services and competencies of manpower. The organization where management has paid proper attention to the changing requirements could bring suitable changes in time. The performance of the organization as a whole has improved. They are doing the things better and before others and maintaining their position in the markets. The importance of OD can be judged from the following advantages:

(a) It is need to bridge the gap between the existing and required abilities.

(b) It improves the processes, systems, people and management capabilities.

(c) Performance of the organization as a whole improves,

(d) The quality and quantity of products improves as per demand of the customers.

(e) The sales and revenue of its products and services go high.

(f) The profitability of the company goes high.

(g) The financial position of the company improves.

(h) The market share of the company improves.

(i) The company gets competitive advantage over their arch rivals in markets.

(j) The reputation of the company as a whole improves.

Due to above explained advantages it can be said that the OD very necessary with the present uncertain environment. It cannot be ignored and if done so there are chances the company may lose its business in the markets. It is matter of survival, growth, stability and to excel in performance. These requirements can be fulfilled through OD efforts. It is concluded that in the present time the need for OD is strongly felt. It is very important for every organization to be fighting tough in competition.

9. ESSENTIAL CONDITIONS FOR EFFECTIVE OD

Every organization is interested for its overall development. A lot of sincere efforts are needed for designing, planning and implementation of OD programme. The effects of OD programmes are not immediate. It is a very comprehensive process, time consuming and impact is delayed. A lot of patience and resources are needed for this process. Over and above if it satisfies the favourable conditions then only the required changes can be brought in different areas of organization. If not the expected result would be missing. The possibility of success can be improved if the following conditions or prerequisites are fulfilled:

(a) Effective leadership

The organization development is a complex process. It is very difficult to understand the emerging trends, needs to deal with changes and interventions for development. Only the trained and experienced person can take the lead as a change manager. He must be well motivated, trained, and having proven track record for such OD activities. The leader of this caliber only can take the organization in the right direction. Resistance is normally faced from most of the employees. He must in position to convince the people about changes, benefits of changes and future of employees and organisation.

(b) Services of Change Agent/ Consultant

It is not possible for every organization to have internal expert for development of organization as a change manager due to various limitations. In this situation the services of external change agent or consultants should be available in vicinity or markets. The services can be availed as and when required. This reduced the implementation of costs of OD programme and requirements of the programmes can be fulfilled. If the external change agents are not available then a full time change manager is to be appointed. In absence of these two the OD programme planning and implementation is not possible.

(c) Top Management Support

In an organization, for every activity whether small of big, the approval of top management is needed. When top management is not interested then nothing can be done or half-hearted efforts would be there. In case of organization development the resources required are more. These are to be procured in time and required quantity. The top level management should take the initiative in this case. If not done so then a lot of difficulties would be faced. Middle and lower levels managers alone cannot bring the desired results.

(d) Healthy Working Environment

In an organization the working atmosphere develops while working there. A lot of factors are responsible for developing this environment. The factors affecting the working environment are management attitude, policies, compensation and incentives rates, health, safety and welfare of all persons, working conditions etc. These are to be managed by the management properly for improvement. Environment of mutual understanding, trust, cooperation, team spirit should prevail. The people should feel relaxed, free from all worries and work happily. This gives happiness and satisfaction to the people concerned in organization. This is very favourable for OD programme.

(e) High Level of Commitment

In organization development programme efforts are required from all concerned employees. They should take the responsibility and accountability willingly for their own development, performance of their duties, giving standard performance to contribute in goal achievement of individual and organization as a whole. Without willingness of employees the OD programmes cannot be successful. A lot of opposition would be faced by the change manager from employees working at different level. They should be explained the need for change and benefits of bringing planned changes. They should be taken together for further movement. Without commitment of employees implementing organization development programme is just like to bell a tiger.

(f) Availability of Internal Resources

The areas under OD are human resource, structure, strategy, work design, technology, products and services. To bring the desired changes a lot of efforts are needed along with resources like men, machine, materials and money. These are to be updated and sufficient to meet the requirements of planned changes. Shortage of resources would make all efforts fruitless or less effective. These are to be arranged before planning and implementation of OD programmes. For example to replace the technology the requirement of capital and trained manpower is there. If these resources are not available or insufficient to buy technology or incapable to operate the new technology, the objective of OD is defeated. Therefore, rich and sufficient resources are needed for effective OD activities.

(g) Proper Planning and Implementation of Interventions

In OD programme, before starting the activities, designing, planning and implementation of OD intervention is very important. The environment should be carefully analysed and emerging trends are to be identified. As per the trends the needs are to be identified. The interventions as per the analysis are to be designed. The selection of interventions out of available options is to be carried out. As per schedule it is to be implemented and for implementation the responsibility is to be fixed. It is should be reviewed periodically. All these jobs are to be performed promptly otherwise the OD development programme may deviate from its objectives. The desired changes may not be made for improving effectiveness of the organization. Special care should taken by the change manager.

(h) Complete Knowledge of OD Interventions

The interventions selected for organization development programme are very important for achieving the objective of it. Before planning and implementation of intervention the change manager should have proper knowledge of these interventions. If proper knowledge is there then they would be in position to plan and implement these. Without knowledge they would not be in a position to plan, implement the intervention. They would not be in a position make suitable adjustment from time to time during implementation. The intervention may not suit the requirement. Without or insufficient knowledge would create many problems and situation would become more difficult. The effectiveness improvement cannot take place definitely.

(i) Need for Collaboration

Managers and employees are dissatisfied with the industrial policies which are based on laws and management attitude. The conflict of interests between parties develops and this spoils the working atmosphere in the organization. This affects the progress of the business. Further, technological and environmental changes makes the things difficult to carry out the business under environment of conflicts, misunderstanding, and distrust. All concerned parties including unions are forced to review their relations in the interest of the business. They should adopt collaborative approach to solve the problem. This would bring all concerned parties to move around the objectives of the programme and results can be achieved. Therefore, collaborative approach is recommended for effective working of OD programme.

There are many favourable conditions for effective working of organization development. There is a big list of these but the above mentioned are the main essential conditions for this purpose. If management takes special care of these conditions to maintain to required standard the result of OD programme would be highly satisfactory. The organization would be in position to improve its effectiveness in all areas.

10. ORGANIZATION DEVELOPMENT INTERVENTIONS

Organization development is a planned change process using various techniques/ methods/ interventions such as behavioural, structural and technical interventions targeting individual, groups and organization by using to bring planned changes for improving effectiveness of the organization in the competitive environment. The readers should not get confused with interventions as it is new term used in place of methods or techniques. Organization Development (OD) interventions or techniques are the methods created by OD professionals and consultants these are more in number. Interventions are principal learning processes in the "action" stage organization development. OD interventions are planned activities or programs designed to effect change in some facet of an organization. Many interventions have been developed over the years to deal with different problems faced by the organizations. However, they all are geared up for attaining desired improvement in the entire organization through change. Organizations interested to bring more and drastic changes using various interventions, targeting individuals, groups and organization for bringing changes processes, behaviour, attitudes and skills, and strategies. Cummings and Worley stated that these interventions "link the internal functioning of the organization to the larger environment; transforming the organization to keep pace with changing conditions"

OD interventions are generally initiated or supported at the top and require employee participation and commitment, therefore, visionary leaders as change agents, developing a vision, and providing continuous guidelines are most important. Kanter, Stein & Jick considered that OD interventions require a strong leader role. "An organization should not undertake something as challenging as large-scale change without a leader to guide, drive and inspire it. These change advocates, play a critical role in creating a company vision, motivating company employees to embrace that vision, and crafting an organizational structure that consistently rewards those who strive toward the realization of the vision." The interventions may be introduced by a change agent as part of an improvement program, or they may be used by the client itself under a programme or collectively to introduce desired changes in selected areas. It is not possible for one organization or consultant to use all the interventions. These are used as per the need of the time for different targets to bring the planned changes. The use of interventions at different levels and targets takes a long time. There is no hard and fast rule that a particular intervention is to be used for bringing changes in individual process, groups, structure and strategy.

As and when the environment is changing the external forces compels to adjust as per the change so that the effectiveness in performance can be maintained. To improve the effectiveness at that time in particular area the interventions are to be used. Even in a very large organization all interventions developed by the professionals are not in use but it is necessary for the managers to have knowledge of various interventions to face the emerging challenges. When the needs arise in the organization the manager can use these interventions. The use of organization development interventions was less in past because of the business environment was not changing very fast. It was stable and predictable. So with the time it became uncertain and risky. More challenges are being faced in present time. It has become difficult to face the challenges effectively. To come up to the level of expectation of challenges the improvements are needed. The improvements in processes, structure, technical area and strategy are needed.

11. DESIGNING INTERVENTION STRATEGY

The starting point of any organization development programmed is defining the intervention strategy. In present competitive business situation it is very difficult to avail the opportunity in the markets Every organization tries its level best but due to tough competition the results are not achieved. The need for game plan is strongly felt to improve the capability of the organization as a whole. The organizations coming with game plans are in position to do the thing better and before others and availing the opportunity in the markets. Therefore the strategy is needed for implementing OD interventions. Organisation development intervention strategy is a game plan for integrating different activities to bring desired improvement for improving effectiveness of the organization as a whole. This strategy is a game plan for change by using behavioural, technical and structural methods.

In designing intervention strategy the change manager, change agents, HRD professional and others play important roles. They must work in close coordination for effective results. Designing intervention strategy process involves the steps are: analysis of environment, development and implementation of action plan and evaluation of the strategy. These are explained below:

(a) Analysis of Environment

Every organization operates its business in an environment. The organization cannot work in isolation. The external environmental factors affect the internal factors of organizations. The external factors are mainly social, cultural, legal, political, economic, technology, competition, and governmental policies. These factors undergo changes time to time and affect the internal factors such as management ideology, rules and regulations; skills of manpower, technology used, working internal atmosphere, the critical study of this environment is to be carried so there should be proper alignment of internal and external factors to improve the effectiveness of the organizations in the economy or markets. The study should cover the emerging trends, causes or forces of changes, competition level in the market, current position of the organization, changes proposed to meet the requirements, nature of working atmosphere, support of management, supervisors and union, resistance to change, time and cost involved in implementing the changes. The industry and company analyses are to be carried out. The analysis should give the clear picture to the change manager and change agent for further action.

(b) Development and Selection of Intervention

After identification of the problem area in the environment the plan for strategy is to be prepared. There may be many options with the change manager to decide about handling the problems. The pros and cons of every alternative options are to be considered. The available options of various interventions are to be evaluated on the basis of cost, time, support, output, feasibility, resistance, move of competitors and skills requirements. After open comprehensive discussion with change agent, managers, union leaders and employees then plan for intervention strategy to be finalized. The selection of strategy would be proper if the above factors are taken into account.

(c) Implementation of Intervention

After development of the plan the next step is to implement the intervention. The plan should include the purpose of the activity, timing for implementation, involvement of employees, responsibility for implementation and costs needed. The plan should be communicated to all concerned persons in the organization. It should be put on track to bring the required changes so that the objectives can be fulfilled as per plan. The implementation is to be watched carefully by the change manager and agent so that timely corrective actions can be initiated. It should be ensured by the change manager and agent that energy, cooperation and commitment of employees should be there for proper implementation of intervention. Ongoing review is to carried out to get feedback so that required adjustment in implementation can be carried out to maintain effectiveness of intervention.

(d) Review of Intervention

After a definite period of time the intervention results are to be reviewed. The review is needed to find out whether the intervention is working as per the plan or not, the results are as per the standards fixed or not. In review results, difficulties faced, resistance to change faced, time and cost involved, attitude of the involved persons, skills of employees for performing jobs etc., are to be considered. In this evaluation the main objective is to find out the effectiveness of the intervention in bringing the desired change. By considering all the factors if it is found the effectiveness is high then it should be implemented further with more energy and commitment level. If anywhere related to implementation the problems are identified, immediate action is to be suggested so that the intervention brings results as per the plan. The purpose of conducting review is to keep the intervention tuned to the requirements of time and improve effectiveness further.

12. TYPES OF OD INTERVENTIONS

For improving the effectiveness of organizations the OD professionals and consultants have worked in the past and they have developed many OD methods. These were not developed at a time but have taken a long time. The focus on OD in past was not much. It has increased in last few decades. Similarly the number of OD interventions also increased with the time. In 1960s focus of techniques was on human being for improving relationship interpersonal, intergroup and intra-group.

The other areas in organizations were not touched. In 1970s the focus shifted to bring improvements in job designs, workers' relationship, production cost reduction, workflow, production methods and technology. The objective was to improve efficiency and satisfaction of workforce in the organizations. Later on the focus shifted to work flow, target achievement and performance management through quality circle, total quality management, self-directed team, reengineering etc.

In the last two decades the focus again shifted to improve mission, objectives, culture and strategy. All the above focuses at different times were to improve effectiveness of the organization by getting high level of commitment from employees. Various techniques have been used by the experts and on the basis of feedback from different organizations applied the techniques, a list has been prepared and classified that is appended below;

(a) Human Process Interventions

These interventions are directed at human resource of the organization that is the most important resource in it. The objective of them is to improve the attitude, behaviour and interpersonal relationship. Employees' performs the tasks in groups so they must improve their relationship in groups also. The positive attitude is the key to accept responsibility and accountability for higher performance. Interpersonal skills are to be improved. Major problems in the organizations are human related. When they are working in group they are likely to face problems. With improved skills the intergroup problems should be solved properly. Most popularly used techniques are following:

(i) Feedback survey:

In this technique a survey of employees is conducted to collect data from them relating to their routine work. The information are collected to know their feelings and reaction. The objective is to find out the problematic areas where the remedial actions can be initiated timely. This is the proactive approach of OD manager. The intervention provides information on selection procedure, orientation, policies, training facilities, salary and incentives, rewards and recognition, career opportunities, management approach, welfare facilities and structure, hours of work, working conditions, handling, and relations are collected and the reports are supplied to the top management. On the basis of analysis the data, the problems are identified and remedial actions are suggested to solve the problems. For collection of data, teams are formed at all levels so that proper data can be collected. The survey can be conducted properly when the employees are accepting and supporting this technique. For this, the employees should be taken into confidence by convincing the objective of it to them.

(ii) Team building

Team building is a process in which attachment among group members is developed. The attachment further develops commitment and responsibility towards the group members. The team building is possible in healthy work environment. The change manager and agent should take the members into confidence by communicating the objectives of changes. Team building is an effort to help the work group to identify, analyse and solve its own problems. Working procedure, interpersonal relationship and effectiveness at work can be improved. There are different groups in an organization working on different jobs. These groups are taken as team under organizational development efforts. These groups are helpful in introducing changes in the organization. The team may include jobs related group, committees, task forces etc. In a team members may be change agent or advisor, groups leader or in charge, and other members. In this the members of the team meet regularly, discuss the difficulties faced during the work, and find out the solution for better working. The focus of team building is to improve the effectiveness and interpersonal relations in the organization through teams.

(iii) Sensitivity training

Group Sensitivity training means the training is given to a selected group of employees to provide them greater sensitivity to the behaviour of others and improve understanding of group and group processes. It is also known as T-Group training. T stands for training and it means training for the selected group. This is an old technique of OD and still it is used in organizations. The main objectives of this technique are to increase awareness of own behaviour, behaviour of others, sensitivity to others behaviour and understanding of group activities. The selected employees are brought in experimental laboratory circumstances where workers will be brought together to do something together.

The environment is open and free and away from the work. The members discuss freely without any formal agenda and supported by a facilitator. Facilitator is to provide an opportunity to the participants to express their attitude, feeling, ideas and beliefs. The focus of this training is on individual behaviour, group interaction and relationship. It helps in understanding people, develop appreciation for others, develop specific behavioral skills and improve interpersonal relationship in group. It is like a brainwashing process to enable special knowledge and development regarding behaviour and relationship. The expected results from sensitivity training are improved ability to empathize with other group members, better listening skills, higher tolerance, conflict solution skills and broad-mindedness. This technique has used in the past by many organizations. But it has been criticized also that it is less effective and if not provided with a trained facilitator it can be dangerous also.

(iv) Managerial grid training

The managerial grid was developed by Blake and Mouton as a theory of leadership. The managerial grid training as an OD intervention is an extension to the managerial grid theory. The objective of this intervention is to improve the effectiveness of managers or leaders pertaining to work and people so that overall effectiveness of the organization can be improved. On the basis of a structured questionnaire the data are collected from managers. The managers are to be motivated to participate in this process willingly. The two important dimensions in this are management concern for production and people. This determines the position of managers where they stand. The analysis decides the manager or leader style. After determining the manager's position in the grid, training for managers starts to improve concerns for production and people. The focus is on production planning and interpersonal communication. The training would help the managers to interact with others and remove conflicts. The efforts put to bring improvement in leaders style up to team management style. By improving the leaders style the effectiveness of the organization as a whole would definitely improve. This intervention got acceptance from many organizations in present time.

(b) Techno-structural Interventions

Techno-structural OD interventions became popular in late 1970s due to improvement in technology competition. The organizations felt burnt due these factors. It became difficult to stay in complition and survive. The OD interventions were use to improve effectiveness of organizations. The objectives were to improve production volume, quality, reduce production costs and improve group relationships. The necessary changes were made in technical and structure areas like department or organization structure, productions methods, job-designs, product quality and quality of working life. The techno-structural interventions are developed on the basis of research and their focus is to improve productivity, quality and overall efficiency of groups and organizations. A variety of organizational development interventions are used or suggested in various organizations in present time. Some of them are explained below:

(i) Job enlargement

Job enlargement is one type of job design. The jobs are redesigned to meet the requirement of work in organization in particular situation. The objective of this intervention is to increase the responsibility of the employees by adding variety of jobs to his jobs. It is the other technique of job redesign. In this more activities are added with the original job and provide greater variety and require more efforts and skills. It reduces monotony caused by doing the same job repeatedly. Job enlargement is a horizontal expansion of a job with an addition of more tasks. The job becomes more challenging and employees become better prepared for other similar assignment. It leads to higher wages and improves worker satisfaction. It provides satisfaction to the employees and creates willingness to learn and improve their skills. As an OD intervention it is helpful in getting commitment of employees for effective working.

(ii) Job enrichment

Job enrichment is also like job enlargement a technique of job redesign. This is also used as an OD intervention in many organizations. The objectives of this intervention are to increase the competencies of employees and their performance by making jobs more interesting. Job enrichment means addition of more responsibilities, autonomy and control of the job. It increases the responsibility of the employees vertically. The employees are asked to perform the task of next higher level with freedom of action. It motivates the employees and affects the performance. It provides opportunities for advancement growth and development. This satisfies the need of higher level. It creates interest in employees to learn more and more. This helps to increase the competencies of employees and their performance too. The job redesign techniques are used by the management in public and private sectors both these make the jobs more interesting and improve the competencies of the employee. These techniques can be used individually or in combination as per the requirement.

(iii) Structure redesign

Structure redesign is another intervention of OD. The objective of this technique is to bring changes in structure of the organization and its departments as per the need of the changing time to suit to the requirements. When the present structure is found unsuitable to achieve the objectives the structural changes are done. The changes may be done on the basis of jobs, area of specialization, area or markets and products or in combination of these factors. The leading companies in the markets are following this technique for making the organisation more effective in accomplishment of its targets. The involvement of top level and middle level of management is must. This technique takes less time and efforts to implement it. For example the marketing division of a leading company is structured on the basis of products and areas.

(iv) Flexible working schedule

Flexible working hours is also used as an OD technique. The objectives of this intervention are to meet the requirements of work of organization and employees. This is in position to handle the situation arises time to time. In this the working hours in offices and factories are adjusted as per the demand in the markets. If the demand of the products increases then the management changes the working hours in two or three shifts to meet requirements and make organization more effective. Without changing the working schedule the production demand targets can be not achieved. If the demands go down then again change is made to adjust. Simultaneously, some of the employees are having problems at a particular point of time in working hours then they can be adjusted in another shift. It is possible without any much difficulty. It only needs to convince the employees and take them into confidence.

(v) Quality of work life

Quality of work life is a technique used for organization development. This has been used by the leading organizations across the world. The objective of this technique is to improve physical and motivational factors at the work place so the working life improves. Modern management has been aware of the fact that human factor is the most important factor of production. The effectiveness of the organization will be doubled if the management can tap the unrealized potential in their human resource. The management should have the basic knowledge about human behaviour and human interrelationship. For development of the workers and organization good wages, incentives and better service conditions contribute. But the environment in which workers are working is also equally important. The environment mainly includes temperature, light, safety, welfare, behaviour, trust, mutual understanding and attitude of different parties. Management is interested to improve the quality of working at the work place through concept of quality of work life.

The focus of quality of work life is to improve the working life by paying attention on physical and motivational factors like flexibility in working hours, autonomy in job performance. This will help to improve the atmosphere of work. The environment of initiative, trust, mutual understanding, and teamspirit will enable the management to motivate the employees to learn more and utilize the human resource in the best way. But in this direction a little progress has been done. The slow progress is due to lack of understanding and inadequate support from management. Bharat Heavy Electrical Ltd. (BHEL) has taken initiative in this direction in the past. BHEL improved the environment through Job-redesign and very encouraging results were obtained. Due to this teamspirit, self-esteem, job satisfaction and individual skills developed. It creates support and commitment from employees' side for OD.

(vi) Quality circles

Quality Circles is another technique of organization development used by the management in various organizations. This is a Japanese concept and ha been accepted worldwide due to its importance. Quality circle is a team that has been formed with the objectives to maintain quality in the organization. It is a semi-autonomous work groups involving circle leader, steering committee and key managers and staff members. It has been formed for implementing the quality control processes, and maintains quality in organization. The quality circle members are trained on their jobs for performing their duty. During their routine they observe the processes, products and services whether their quality is maintained or not. Whenever the team finds out any irregularity, a report is submitted to the management with causes, effects and recommendation for problem solution. Further, quality circle is used by HRD managers to get involved in the organizational matters to improve the quality by solving the problems. This mechanism has been coined in Japan. It gave very good result and more psychological satisfaction. With the efforts of this team the quality is maintained and it contributes in improving in image of the organization in the markets. It is very useful for development of organization and its business.

(vii) Total quality management

Total quality management is the contemporary technique for OD. The present business environment situation is highly changing and competitive. In this situation the organizations find difficulty in maintaining its profits, sales and overall effectiveness. Management realized that the situation can be faced by maintaining quality in the organization. It is a very critical factor to deal with competition. Total quality management is a set of tools or techniques focusing all areas of organization like employees, products, services, process, structure, and strategy. It is the philosophy of the management moving around quality. Management is interested to maintain quality in actions, thinking, behaviour, products, and services. Quality is like a flood for them that brings water everywhere. Everyone is committed to the concept of quality. The performance standards are fixed, performance measured, evaluated and remedial actions are taken for maintaining quality. Everyone is involved maintaining and improving the quality right from top to lower level people.

Functioning is possible in healthy work environment. To maintain healthy working environment a lot of efforts are needed from management side. The environment of better understanding, mutual trust, team spirit, cooperation, and commitment should be developed and maintained. This situation helps to get full cooperation from employees. They would be ready to take responsibility and accountability for quality maintaining and improvement. In this process the quality is maintained and further improved. The improvement is incremental and not sudden or drastic. It has been used by the leading corporations in India and abroad. The future of TQM as an organization development intervention is bright. For this purpose special care should be taken by the management that the long-term gains should not be sacrificed for short-term gains. Its popularity in organizations is increasing day by day due to its good outcomes.

(viii) Business process re-engineering

Business process re-engineering as a technique for organization development is more technical in nature. Michael Hammer, the management expert who initiated the re-engineering to achieve dramatic improvement in critical contemporary measures of performance such as cost, quality, service and speed. The concept of re-engineering has been around for nearly two decades and was implemented in a piecemeal fashion in organization. The production organizations have undertaken re-engineering by implementing concurrent engineering and pull type production system. The main objective of this re-engineering process is to achieve a significant improvement in processes so the customer requirements of quality, speed, innovation customization and services are met. Michael Hammer has proposed seven following principles are: Organize around outcomes and not tasks, work should be carried out where it makes the most sense to do it, people who collect information should be made responsible for processing of the information also to minimize the need of another for processing, treat geographically dispersed resources as though they were centralized — by using information technology, link parallel activities instead of integrating their results, decision making should be made part of the work performed and build control into the process, and capture information once at the source where it was created to avoid wrong entries and entry costs.

The re-engineering process involved the following steps: State a case/explain the need for re-engineering, identify the process for re-engineering, evaluate enablers/supporting factors of re-engineering-IT and human capabilities, understand the current process, create a new process design, and implement the re-engineered process. For re-engineering the certain points are to be kept in mind such as suggested for implementation. These are codification of re-engineering provides guidance and directions for consistent and efficient implementation, clear goal and consistent feedback and higher level involvement in re-engineering changes. This process brings drastic changes that affect the performance of the organization to a good extent. This technique contributes in improving the effectiveness of the organization. The only difficulty is that this must be tried by the expert managers only, otherwise the result is likely to be adverse.

BPR and TQM are differentiated by many persons. The difference between these two is clarified here in the few lines given. Re-engineering is often compared to TQM. Some people say these are same but others say not. Michael hammer said these are compatible and actually complement to one another. Both are centered on a customer focus. Main contributions from quality management are: Quality management influences company culture and values by exposing it to changes. The basic differences between them are: Quality management emphasized continuous and incremental improvement of processes that are in control whereas reengineering is about radical discontinuous change through process innovation. The given process is enhanced by TQM until it has useful lifetime. Reengineering improves the process by radical change and the entire cycle of the process starts again.

(c) Human Resource Interventions/ Practices

The practices used by human resource management are many, to perform certain functions. If we prepare a list of them then the number would be more. The HRM practice used in organizations are used as OD intervention with the objectives to feel comfortable during work so that they are satisfied. With satisfaction the commitment, willingness to shoulder the responsibility, motivation, commitment, attachment, performance and productivity of employees improve. The HRM practices used to mould the behaviour and attitude of employees are acquiring, training, performance appraisal, rewards and recognitions, career planning and development, goal setting, employees' wellness etc. The OD managers must get involved in action research and help the management to bring suitable changes in HRM practices to meet the emerging needs in organisation pertaining to human resource development. The HRM practices used as OD interventions in various organizations across the world are following;

(i) Management by objectives (MBO)

Management by objectives is a concept developed by Peter Druker in past. Now it is used as an OD intervention. It involves the process of educating the concerned persons about this method, fixed objectives and agreement for achieving clear cut quantifiable objectives, evaluation of objectives and feedback for deviation and remedial actions. It is a technique for goal setting as per goals of the organization. The goals are communicated of everyone and asked to perform to achieve them. If in performance any deviation is found then prompt remedial actions are taken by the management. The deviation in individual and organizational goals are checked and both are kept well aligned This intervention would be in position to develop and maintain unity in the organization, All managerial level are involved in goal setting. The efforts under this intervention are properly streamlined in one direction. This improves the effectiveness of the organization as a whole by reducing time, efforts and costs in performing the tasks. Implementation of MBO would be more effective if implemented properly with willing support of top level management. The role of MBO is likely to be more in future due to competitive situations in worldwide markets.

(ii) Training

Training is one of the important mechanisms for development of executives and employees and finally organisation. The focus of training should be on development of competencies. This will include job skills, interpersonal skills, team building skills, problem solving skills and self-management skills. Routine training programme can upgrade only technical competencies but cannot contribute much in overall growth and personality development. This system is frequently used as HRD sub-system. In some of the companies HRD was equated with training. Even today also the training centre has been designated as HRD centre or training department as HRD department. The main objectives of training intervention are: on the continuous basis the competencies of employees (technical, managerial, human and conceptual) are ensure to be developed so that employees and executives perform their tasks effectively, provide inputs to all concerned in scientific and cost effective manner to develop competencies, and to develop a culture of learning.

Training is a vital and necessary activity in all organizations. It plays a major role in determining the efficiency and effectiveness of the establishment. Different methods of training are being used to impart training to managers and employees. The main methods of training are coaching, understudy, job rotation, apprenticeship, vestibule training, simulation, lectures, case study, seminar brain storming, role playing and sensitive training. Training is mainly used in large and medium size of organizations. This has been used to develop the attitude, knowledge and skills of employees in both public and private sectors. Due to this mechanism the improvement achieved are improved behaviour of employees, feeling of attachment developed, tendency of hiding own mistakes and highlighting the mistakes of others reduced, avoid deliberate confrontation and interest in suggestion scheme etc., more interest in family affairs, awareness of needs of wife and children increased and industrial relations improved. Technical training develops technical skills and behaviour training develops attitude, interpersonal skills, sense of attachment and interest. Many Indian companies like SBI, Petrofils (Baroda), L&T are providing both types of training to their people. They have improved the organizational effectiveness and enjoying high reputation.

(iii) Performance and potential appraisals

Performance and potential appraisals are used as OD intervention. The focus of this method is on human resource of the organization to bring required changes in their performance and attitude. Appraisal system is an important mechanism of HRD. Under appraisal system we can have two types of appraisal. These are performance appraisal and potential appraisal. Performance appraisal is the process of evaluating the performance of employees quantitatively relating to the job for which he is employed. Performance evaluation will point out the weaknesses and strengths of the employees. This will spot the areas where employees are weak and development efforts are needed. Performance appraisal is a tool for identification of deficiencies. It will differentiate between satisfactory and unsatisfactory performances of employees. The performance appraisal helps the management to perform functions relating to selection, development, salary administration, lay-off and retrenchment. It provides guidelines for training and development of individuals. It encourages the employees at all levels to work hard since they are aware that their performance is being appraised and it can result into a reward also. It is also helpful for the development of organization, as objectives of company and development programmes can be matched with competencies of employees.

Potential appraisal is also used for development of workers, supervisors and executives. Organizations where HRD is in practice, appraise the employees, potentials periodically in order to find out their suitability to the changing requirement of the present job and future placement. Potential appraisal is important for the continuous development of the organization, diversification, entering into new markets, technological changes etc. So to take up the changing situations it becomes necessary for the organizations to develop the employees on continuous basis. The basic objective of potential appraisal is to find out the ability of employees and to discuss with them the ways and means through which he can realize his full capacity and continue to grow in the organization. It helps by providing the information for human resource planning and development programmes for employees. Further, it is very important to manage the high potential managers and it is possible through potential appraisal system. Surveys have been conducted by experts regarding potential appraisal. Rao (1982) and Rao & Abraham (1986) have conducted the surveys and remarked that potential appraisal has not been conducted systematically in Indian organizations.

(iv) Career planning and development

Career planning and development is used as an OD intervention in leading organizations. It has been used to motivate the employees to learn and move further in career. A person joins an organization with certain expectations and aspirations. These aspirations and expectations are the motivating factors for individuals. In turn organization provides the support to employees through healthy environment for their growth. In the favourable environment, the major thrust of HRD is to bring shift in the organization culture. The main areas will be honesty, openness, personal development, career and growth aspirations of all members. These are matters of considerable interest to employees at all levels and will tend to become more openly talked about. Interaction between organization and individuals develops and this develops or builds the sense of commitment to the organization.

Pareek and Rao (1998) say "Career development means the development of the general technical and managerial career in the organization. Career planning implies planning of specific career paths of the employees in the future in the organization with the help of reporting officer. As such planning flows from manpower planning and potential appraisal. Career planning gets closely linked with these components of human resource system."

Career planning and development is a slow and participative process. Both individuals and organization take part in this process. Career Planning involves the activities are: preparing of manpower inventory, finding out the manpower requirement at different levels for future through human resource planning, designing career path for different types of employees, preparing plans for training and development of employees of different categories at different levels, plan for promotion of employees, review of the planning and to measure effectiveness of the plans.

Career development will include the following activities: Supporting the employees to assess their career needs in the organization, seminars, simulation, workshop, assessment centres, tests and interviews, publishing the career path in the organization, matching the career opportunities in the organization with needs, expectations and capabilities of employees through job rotation, job enlargement, coaching etc. The career planning and development mechanism has been followed by a number of organizations. Many of them have designed the career path and it is liked with the promotion of employees. This way it has become a motivating factor for employees. In the present time career planning and development is considered as a part of the career system and is linked with manpower planning, recruitment and potential appraisal. This intervention is helpful in development of organization through motivation and development of human resource in organization.

(v) Welfare and wellness of employees

Welfare and wellness of employees is also one of the interventions used for OD. The objective of using the method is to take care of well-being of employees to improve level of commitment to their jobs and organization. Employees' welfare is the effort of employer to establish within the existing working, living and cultural conditions of the employees beyond what is required by law, the customs of the industry and conditions of the market. ILO report speaks of "Welfare of employees as such services facilities and amenities which may be established outside or in the vicinity of undertakings, to enable the persons employed therein to perform their work in healthy and congenial surroundings and to provide them with amenities conducive to good health and high morale." ILO Asian Regional Conference Report – II, 1947.

In the highly inflationary economy like ours the salaries paid to the employees are not adequate to meet day to day requirements. At this crucial juncture it is required to support the employees by providing them various facilities like health, medical, education, transportation and house accommodation. Over and above safety and security of employees should be properly cared. This would make the employees available and fit for duty. This welfare programme shall create a sense of attachment to the organization. The organization will be benefited in the long run. The welfare measures started by employers can be divided in to two parts like:

- Statutory Welfare measures like drinking water, shelter or lunchroom, canteen, medical, safety measures, and storing under Factories Act, 1948.
- Voluntary welfare measures like transport, housing, education, medical, credit, entertainment and uniform facilities.

These facilities will help the employees indirectly and their different needs will be satisfied. A satisfied group of employees will have a greater sense of belongingness to the organization. This will change the behaviour of the employees in the desirable manner. Tata group companies like TELCO and TISCO started providing welfare facilities to their employees much before the laws came into existence.

(vi) Recognition and rewards

Recognition and reward is also used by the management as a tool for human resource development and organization development. Any HRD effort that wants to improve the performance of employees must consider the proper reward system. Better performance given by the employees must not go unnoticed. It must be recognized and rewarded by the management. Both employees and executives are having needs and motives. Further, attention should be paid for individual and team rewards. Proper reward system motivates the people and to utilize the existing skills. Further, it creates the interest to acquire new competencies. For reward system following can be considered: Appreciation letter, additional annual increments in salary, reward for good work, praising employees in functions orally, cash rewards, and incentives. Proper reward system will give a drive to the employees to perform well. And well performers are given better opportunities. This would help in the utilization and development of human resource. This intervention has been very fruitful for organization development in most of the leading companies in worldwide markets. The contribution of it would be more in future also.

(vii) Counselling

Counselling as a technique used by management to bring desired changes in behaviour of employees for organization development. Counselling means listening problems of employees and suggesting them the steps to be taken for problem solution. Counselling is an important mechanism to provide them guidance and solve their problems. For guidance and problem solution counselling session must be conducted at regular intervals. It will be better if an organization is having the trained counsellors. If not, then counsellors must be trained on their job. Further, immediate supervisors must be given the responsibility of counselling. The concerned employees facing the problem can approach to the counsellor and present their problems. At the earliest, counsellor must suggest the solution. This will help to solve the problems and will keep them free form tension and satisfied with the job. It is suggested that counselling sessions should be conducted more frequently at senior and junior levels. This counselling can help to avoid many conflicts and help the workers both in their jobs and personal life. In private sector companies like L&T and Voltas have taken initiatives in this direction. The counselling service can be extended to personal and family life of workers. Voltas conducted counselling session in its Thane Plant for drunkard employees to solve their problems. This achieved the success up to a good extent. Through counselling management can provide adequate guidance to workers and help them to learn more and more and even from their own mistakes. Ultimately, it contributes in improvement of performance of employees and organization for improving overall effectiveness.

(viii) Participation

In present time due to awareness of management towards workers, unions, society and others, the importance of their participation in decision making has been realized. That is why participation is being used as an OD intervention. The objective of this technique is to develop sense of belongingness, attachment and commitment among workers and union leaders towards organization and their jobs. Government, businessmen, administrators and social workers all are interested to improve the functioning of industrial units. They wanted to bring the concept of democracy to the industry. Industrial democracy means management of a unit by the people and for the people. Here people mean all those concerned with a unit, i.e., owners, managers, workers, state and society. The purpose of industrial democracy is to give the workers a sense of belongingness to the organization and the sense of commitment to various decisions taken. In absence of it they will consider themselves just employees having no commitment to the objectives, policies and plans of the organization. Ultimately this will hinder the effective working of the organization. Industrial democracy is an ideal, an ultimate goal and should be approached for the benefit of employees, the industry and the society as a whole.

Whereas workers participation is a process through which efforts are being put to reach to the goal. This has helped in introducing planned changes in organization because it overcomes resistance from all concerned parties. This is very useful for organizing development activities. Workers' participation is an essential step in the direction of industrial democracy. It is a vehicle with the help of it we can reach to the destination of industrial democracy. Workers' participation in management increases productivity, efficiency, brings harmony and better relations. In this workers' participates in decision making and take the decision jointly. It can only be described as a communication and consultation, either formal or informal, by which employees are kept informed regarding affairs of the organization and they are asked to express their opinion and contribute to decision making. Workers' participation in management is a very important mechanism for all round growth of employees and organization. There are different forms of participation. These are works committee, joint management council and board presentation. Steps taken by the government in this direction were considered as coercion from government.

Research findings report that the worker director scheme in banks failed to create favourable climate in industrial relations. Some of the firms have experimented but in a limited manner. Steel Tubes of India, a small-scale company had made significant progress in this direction. It started the scheme through two participative institutions of joint committee and Jansabha, Free access and responsiveness developed through democratic institutions. This has helped in introducing planned changes in organization because it overcomes resistance from all concerned parties. This is very useful for organization development activities. With favourable changed attitude of owners or management the future role of this intervention in OD would be more important.

(ix) Building Effective Task Force

Another mechanism of HRD is building of an effective task force. It is the responsibility of the HR manager to build effective team of employees. Strong task force influences the individual employees also. The strength of the work team and its culture can be improved by the concerned manager in different situations. The manager can set up a team for solutions of the problem instead of solving the problem himself. This type of task forces is very effective in dealing with special issues. Task forces are given the particular time to complete the task within the given time period. The concept of task force is used for urgent task to deal with the task on war footing. The task force working contributes to collaboration. If the organization is interested to develop the quality of service or products, it can do with the help of the task force.

For effective building of task force, management can use recognition of the task force and reward system. The most productive team must be rewarded. Competition must be introduced for selecting the most productive team or best task force. It should be on the basis of contribution more in target achievements, cost reduction and quality improvement. Criteria of team selection and areas of competition are to be planned carefully. Some of the rewards may be of high prestige and of use to the group. The main objective of task force building is to confront the issues openly, developing system of proper and frank feedback to each other and to generate alternative solutions of the problems collectively. The team can be guided by the concerned manager and can improve the areas where needed. The building of task force contributes to the favourable environment to learn and put the best efforts. This results in development of employees and good performance. The mechanism of building task force is used mainly in ONGC, military, police and many other organizations in India. Ultimately, it is very useful HRD and OD as a whole.

(x) Role analysis

Role analysis is a technique that analyse the role of everyone in the organization to find out the effectiveness of individuals on their jobs. The focus is on proper utilization of human resource so that overall effectiveness of the organization can improve. With the development of business and economy activities of organizations are becoming complex and more. At different levels different activities are being performed. In a corporate unit activities are performed at top, middle and lower levels. These activities include production, storage, logistics, marketing, operation, finance and accounting, human resource, research and development, communication, transportation, public relations etc. As per area of specialisation these activities are assigned to employees. To know the contribution of employees to the objectives of the organisation it is required to analyse the function being performed. This process is called role analysis. It is a function of HRM to understand these jobs. Detailed study of jobs is needed not only for planning, recruitment and selection, training, performance appraisal but also for development of people. Some of the leading companies in the markets are using this as an OD intervention.

(d) Strategic/ Organisation Transformation Interventions

The present environment is drastically changing and it creates uncertainty and competition. The competition level in worldwide markets is increasing due to liberalization of economies. The companies are facing tough competition from MNCs and domestic competition. The expectations and demands of customers are changing fast. The companies are facing difficulties to meet the requirements of the changing time. In foreign markets they face more difficulties and effectiveness in their performance is not very high. The risks involved in business are increasing more and more. To handle this situation more effectively, different strategies are adopted by the management. Some of the strategies used by the companies are following:

(i) Joint venture

Joint venture is a method or strategic intervention to deal with the situation more effectively. Under this strategy, the companies are performing their business jointly because they are not capable to work alone in a better way. That is why they join hands under an agreement. When they work jointly, their internal strength improves and they get advantage of their unity. Effectiveness in the operation in markets improves. This has been used by leading companies in Indian and foreign markets. Maruti an Indian organisation joined hand with Suzuki from Japan. Suzuki very sound in automobile technology but no knowledge of Indian customers and markets. Maruti was with sound knowledge of customers and Indian market but not perfect in technology. Under joint venture their strength improved and now they are leader in car manufacturing in Indian market. The joint venture strategy has handled the situation very effectively. The overall business of both the companies' improved a lot. It has the successful story in markets worldwide.

(ii) Mergers and acquisitions

Merger and acquisition strategy has been used as an OD intervention by leading corporate. In present situation, the companies are facing tough competition and due to this they are not in position to achieve their targets of increased sales, profits and market shares. When they are with sound financial condition and manpower they adopt the strategy of merger and acquisition. The company merges with other or takes over the other companies. This strategy has been in use worldwide. In India Tata Motors acquired Jaguar and Rovers. Tata Steel acquired Corus from foreign market. Due to this the companies have become leader worldwide. Their effectiveness and business both developed at high rate. This strategy is more popular in corporate sector. There are many examples in all markets.

(iii) Diversification

Diversification is another strategic intervention for OD. In uncertain business environment and changing demand and expectation of customers the level of risks involved is very high. To neutralize the risks in business, the companies have adopted this strategy in the long-term interest of the organization. The business is diversified for different customers, in different markets, products and services. They do not like to keep all eggs in one basket at a time. Example of Godrej, Reliance, and Tata are there in the markets. They have diversified their business and enjoys high position in markets.

(iv) Integration

Integration is a strategy in which the present activities of business of the company are integrated with backward and forward activities. The objective of this intervention is to get synergetic effect to the business. For example, production activity is related to raw materials backward and to marketing forward. The company gets benefits of cheaper raw materials and marketing profits from its own outlets. Tata Steel integrated with mines for iron ore/coal raw materials. The production of steel and cars are supplied to the customer through its own distribution network. The business is affected by these two integrations. It is used by many leading companies in India and abroad. Only thing is that while deciding the integration, special care is to be taken for success.

(v) Diversified organization culture

Diversified organization culture is another intervention for transformation of the organization. In an organization, people are from different age, sex, caste, culture, creed, region, language, state and countries. During their work they interact with other and share their cultural value. They should not retain their original cultural value but the new organizational culture should be developed. They should feel comfortable with the new organization culture. The existing thinking of people should be replaced by new one. It should create healthy atmosphere for work. People should feel relief in the new culture so that they work willingly. The commitment of employees should be developed. HR practices should be managed in such a way the people interact more and share the values of others.

(vi) Learning organization

Learning organization is a technique for organization development. In turbulent and risky environment the high degree of skills are required to understand the situation and perform the tasks better and before competitors. The new competencies are to be learnt. In learning organization, everyone is willingly engaged by identifying own problems, skills required, and finding the solution of the problems. The efforts are there for continuous improvement of the organization. The healthy working environment can contribute in developing learning organization. The learning organization becomes more effective in dealing stiff competitive situation and get competitive edge over other rivals. Essential conditions for successful learning organization are suitable structure, favourable HR practices, proper communication, healthy working environment and culture, support of top management, and able leadership. The change manager should focus on learning organization activities.

13. ROLES IN ORGANISATION DEVELOPMENT

Organisation development process is very comprehensive and it involves jobs, work design, structure, individuals, groups, strategy, processes, procedures, technology and culture of the organization. It takes a long time to get the desired results. For improving the effectiveness of the organization through OD the involvement of all concerned persons is needed. Right from top level to bottom levels all are attached with organization development. Change manager, change agent, managers, workers and unions play their role in their own capacity. It is expected that everyone must give the desired contribution for organization development. The roles of different parties are explained below:

(a) Role of Change Manager

Change manager is the person responsible for bringing development in various areas of the organization. He starts his role from identification of needs for change, situation analysis, deciding intervention for development, implementation and review of the intervention. In some of the organization the organization development responsibility is assigned to one person independently whereas in other organizations the role is played by the manager along with routine functions. The change manager may find difficulty in planning and implementation of strategy because of resistance from functional managers. When additional job of OD is given to the functional manager then he may not give proper attention to the development activities. The task of OD should be given to the person at higher level so that he can create the situation suitable for organization development. The change manager should be an expert of his field and must have knowledge regarding manpower, processes, procedures, technology, structure and strategy for effective working. The training should be given to the executives to play role of change manager. The role of change manager is very important in organization development because he provides proper planning and guidance for bringing desired changes in organization.

(b) Role of Change Agent

Change agent is a person outside of organization and be may be called as consultant. When the company is not involved in much development activities, it may take service of the experts from the markets. In case of regular development jobs the company employs a full time change manager or jobs may be assigned to one internal manager who is expert in that job. The change agent is having knowledge of the particular field. Right from study of internal and external environment, industry and company analysis, designing, developing, selection and implementation of intervention he is involved and provides support to the managers. He works for his consultation fees or commission. As per the requirements he provides his services.

For selection of the change agent the management should take proper care. On the basis of his proven track record the consultant should be finalized. The feedback should be taken from the companies where he has already worked as a change agent successfully or from markets. The available information should be verified properly otherwise the decision may be wrong. The change agent explains the changes, their types of changes and benefits expected from such changes to the employees. He convinces all concerned persons to get them into confidence and get their support. If it is done so successfully, the resistance from employees would not be there. The role of above mentioned activities is very important. The expertise and involvement of change agent in OD activities would affect the success of OD. He may lead the OD programme successfully if level of commitment on his part is high.

(c) Role of HRD Manager

Organisation development and human resource development are having the common objectives of development. Human resource is one the areas of OD. For achieving objectives an HRD Manager plays an important role. Designing, planning and implementation of intervention for OD and HRD are the main functions of HRD manager. Through development of human resource the organization development is possible. The main purpose of concerned department is to create the favourable climate for learning and development. In the favourable environment the employees learn from the learning facilities provided in an organization and from their own experience also. The employees should be motivated by the department to utilize their potential. Due to continuous learning the employees will acquire new competencies (skills, knowledge, capability and attitude). The main objective of HRD department is to develop the competencies of the employees to meet the changing needs of the organization. To achieve this objective the concerned department should perform the following major functions in HRM intervention for OD:

(i) Formulate the human resource policy in the organization and open support of top management.

(ii) Create a constant desire to learn and develop by inspiring employees by line managers.

(iii) Canalize all HRD efforts in one direction to achieve the goals of the organization.

(iv) For creating and developing suitable climate, planning and designing of new systems and methods.

(v) Monitoring of implementation and performance of various human resource development mechanisms.

(vi) Close contact with associations and unions and their inspiration.

(vii) Conducting research periodically relating to various human aspects.

(viii) Supply relevant information to the top management.

(ix) Influencing formulation of personnel policies due to staff expertise

To perform the above-mentioned functions, it is required that HRD manager staff of the concerned department, must be well qualified and experienced. Otherwise these activities cannot be performed effectively. Keeping in view the functions performed by HRD manager for development of human resource and organization, it is concluded that the role played is very important and essential for successful effort for achieving high level of effectiveness of organization as a whole.

(d) Role of Trade Union

Management are not having positive attitude towards trade unions. Trade unions are considered opponents of the management. These are mainly confined to issues like wages, bonus and working conditions. But they had paid no attention towards the development of workers in past. In the recent past initiatives have been taken by the management for development of human resource and organisation. Trade unions have not supported the initiative taken by the management due to various reasons. Now it is time for management to deal with the fears and doubts of trade union. Management should have continuous interaction with the trade unions regarding OD activities. Trade unions must be taken into confidence and they must be involved. Working climate of trust and understanding must be developed. These efforts will develop involvement of unions in development programmes. Trade unions should play the positive roles in development of employees.

The role of trade union for development of organization is important. The trade union can play the following roles:

(i) When the initiative for development of organisation comes from management, trade unions must cooperate. If no initiative from management side then trade unions must initiate for development of workers. The improved communication between management, union and employees can strengthen the role of trade unions.

(ii) Trade unions should provide counselling service to workers regarding excessive drinking, smoking, drug addiction, gambling etc. In absence of counselling the employees get involved in evils.

(iii) Trade union must help the employees to acquire knowledge and skills regarding work and human processes like team spirit, empathy, helping and attitude.

(iv) Trade union must put continuous efforts to improve employees' welfare programme for overall development.

(v) Trade unions should sponsor appropriate research projects to collect relevant data regarding various dimensions of workers needs, aspirations, development needs etc. They can seek involvement of experts, academicians by participating in research problems relevant to the trade unions.

For better and effective role in HRD and OD, trade union should be professional. This means HRD within union. Trade unions had ignored development of union leadership. Trade unions must develop union leadership. The new developmental role will acquire new skills in the union leadership and the unions will play their roles more effectively.

14. POSITION OF ORGANISATION DEVELOPMENT

It was difficult to find out in which direction organization development was moving. In past the focus of organization development was more on employees, well-being of employees and human approach. The focus in past was more on development of skills, knowledge and competencies through HRD mechanisms. With the rapid changes the focus of organization development has shifted from human resources to structure, processes, strategy and technology. The approach of organization development has become wider in present time. The approach of OD manager is stronger for bringing required changes in various areas so that the effectiveness of the organization can be increased. This helped in getting competitive advantage to the organization in present situation. In last two decades the efforts are put to align HRD and OD practices in line with the strategic objectives of the organization. However, experts opined that for development in various areas the management should not shift its focus from wellness of the employees because manpower is the most important party in OD. The focus should be there on individual and organizational issues. The focus should be as per the need of the situation and should be fruitful. It should not lose its importance in organization. In future the focus is to be on review time to time.

15. IMPLICATIONS FOR OD MANAGER

The emerging trends in environment are making the situation very awkward for everyone. The changes are uncertain, fast and many in numbers. It is very difficult to understand them and their effects. Many environmental factors are undergoing changes. It becomes difficult for the managers how and what to do for keeping the position intact. Over and above the rival competitors are also trying to make them more effective in their business efforts. In this situation the managers find themselves in very difficult position. For development of organization many interventions are designed and implemented to improve organizational effectiveness. The following implications are there for OD manager and others:

(a) Rapidly changing environment that is difficult to understand. It becomes very difficult to deal with this situation more effectively and before their competitors.

(b) Advance technology with short product life cycle creates gap for required skills and knowledge for its operation by employees.

(c) Changes create uncertainty and risks. Due to this the changes are resisted by managers, employees and unions. It becomes very difficult to convince all to take them together.

(d) Poor relationship between change agent and target groups not in position to create confidence. The cooperation of these parties is missing.

(e) Managers themselves are sticking to old practices and not ready to accept the new changes due to fear of loss of position, power, earning and jobs. The managers are not in a position to take the lead in changes.

(f) A lot of difficulties in designing and implementing organizational development intervention. At every step difficulty and resistance are faced.

(g) For bringing changes in organization for improving effectiveness of the organization, areas covered are very wide. A lot of efforts are needed for this purpose.

(h) Organisation development is a time consuming and slow process. It is very difficult to bring the change immediately and measuring its effect is very difficult.

Due to the above mentioned difficulties or implication by OD managers the situation becomes very difficult for changes. Sincere efforts with a lot of patience are needed on part of OD managers to deal with the situation effectively. Only this approach can help the manager to bring changes, improve effectiveness of the organization and claim success.

16. RELATIONSHIP BETWEEN HRD AND OD

HRD is a process for development of human resource in the organization. Human resource is developed by developing their competencies like ability, capabilities, attitude, knowledge and skills. Its emphasis is on motivational aspects of human being and organizational culture which help in development of competencies. Human resource development is needed to develop competencies for growth and vitality of an organization. Organization development attempts to help the organization development in different ways using a variety of intervention including human processes, structural changes, technological changes, and strategic changes, human process changes etc. The focus of both is on development only their areas differ. Areas of OD are human resource, structure, products, services, quality, strategy, and work design. It means it includes the whole organization for development whereas HRD has focus only on human resource in the organization. It is interested to develop the competencies of the human resource so that they can perform their jobs in a better way to achieve the desired performance. The HRD/ OD assumptions are: Psychology and organization behaviour are the bases, collaborative approach for problem solution, focus on internal factors to manage changes, high commitment from employees needed, conflicts are natural but should be managed properly, healthy working environment suitable, developed competencies of human resource required for improving effectiveness of human resource and organization as a whole.

Both processes keep their employees in the forefront in preparation of their plan and their implementation. Focus of HRD is on employee's development and focus of organization development is on development of organization as a whole. Industrial relations are mainly concerned to maintain good relations between parties and to protect the interests of workers and management both in a balanced way. For HRD the focus and scope are narrow that is only individual, for OD the focus and scope are wider and that is on team and organization as a whole. For industrial relations the focus is on management, workers and their unions. Of the three concepts the focal point differs due to philosophy and purpose of the functions. But the dynamics of human processes are similar. HRD and OD can contribute a lot in the field of industrial relations. It is concluded that in OD, HRD is a part only. But no doubt it is the most important part of OD. Without HRD the question of OD does not arise. The collaborative approach is needed between HRD, OD and industrial relations for effective results in future.

17. CONCLUSION

In turbulent business environment the situation is uncertain and risky. The business environment is also changing rapidly. The factors affecting the business are social, cultural, economic, legal, political, technological and competition. These have gone under rapid changes. To carry the business effectively it was required by the organization to work according to the changing environment or surrender to the changes. Those who have changed the strategy to do the business as per the changes have achieved success in the business and are leader in the business and earning a huge profit every year. It is needed to match the internal factors with the changing external factors so business can be carried effectively and efficiently. The human resources assume importance from an economic standpoint at national, enterprise and individual levels of analysis. Ginzberg pointed out, human resource is the key to economic development. Further, to improve the effectiveness of the organization there is need to bring improvements The jobs, job designs, working procedures, technology, structure, competencies of human resource, relationships, products, services etc., are undergoing changes. If the improvements or changes are made in these areas the organization as a whole would develop. The effectiveness of the organization in the market would definitely improve. The organization would be in a position to achieve the predetermined targets in time, effectively and efficiently.

Organisation change is a dynamic process through which an organization can move from the existing to the new improved position. It is very essential for the organization for survival, stability, growth and to excel in its performance. When management is interested to make the improvements or changes in the existing pattern, the changes can be brought in and at various levels. The situation demanding the change is very powerful. The changes can be made at individual, group or organizational levels. The changes are important due to various reasons like provides place of growth, provides solution of problems, keep up to date to demand, marketing of organisation, new income streams etc. To make OD more effective certain conditions are to be fulfilled. There are effective leadership, services of change agent/ consultant, top management support, healthy working environment, high level of commitment, availability of internal resources, proper planning and implementation of interventions, complete knowledge of OD interventions, and need for collaboration.

Organization development is a planned change process using various techniques/ methods/ interventions such as behavioural, structural and technical interventions targeting individual, groups and organization by using to bring planned changes for improving effectiveness of the organization in the competitive environment. Strategy is a game plan for change by using behavioural, technical and structural methods. In designing intervention strategy the change manager, change agents, HRD professional and others play important roles. They must work in close coordination for effective results. Designing intervention strategy process involves the steps are: Analysis of environment, development and implementation of action plan and evaluation of the strategy. The focuses at different times were to improve effectiveness of the organization by getting high level of commitment from employees. Various techniques have been used by the experts and on the basis of feedback from different organizations applied the techniques. For development of organization many interventions are designed and implemented to improve organizational effectiveness. It is concluded that in OD, HRD is a part only. But no doubt it is the most important part of OD. Without HRD the question of OD does not arise. The collaborative approach is needed between HRD, OD and industrial relations for effective results in future.

18. QUESTIONS FOR REVIEW

1. Critically evaluate the current position of business environment in global markets.
2. Define organisation change and explain its nature in detail.
3. Which elements or points should be kept in mind while performing its functions by change management?
4. Organisation changes take place at different levels. Explain levels of changes.
5. Discuss the reasons for which the changes are important in our life and in an organisation.

6. When changes are introduced in an organisation, they are opposed. Discuss.
7. What are the forces of resistance to change in an organisation? Explain.
8. Define organisation development and discuss its main characteristics on the basis of various definitions.
9. How effectiveness of employees and organisation can be improved? Describe.
10. Elaborate the signification of organisation development to an organisation.
11. Discuss the essential conditions for making OD programme more effective.
12. Prepare a detailed list of organisational development interventions being used in leading organization on the basis of your knowledge.
13. What do you know about OD intervention and strategy for it? Discuss.
14. What do you know about designing intervention strategy process? Discuss main steps involved in it.
15. How would you categorize OD interventions? Elaborate.
16. How many various types of OD interventions are being used in leading organisation in industries?
17. Explain human process interventions and prepare a list of them and discuss in brief.
18. Briefly explain various techno–structural interventions used for OD in companies.
19. Define total quality management and business process reengineering and differentiate between them.
20. What do you know about HR interventions? Explain their roles also.
21. Discuss in brief strategic interventions used by organisations for transformation purpose.
22. Highlight the roles of different parties involved in organisation development.
23. Elaborate major implications for organisation development manager.
24. Critically evaluate the relationship between HRD, OD and industrial relations.
25. Short notes on the following :
    (a) Changes at individual level.
    (b) Resistance from employees.
    (c) Unfavourable attitude of employees towards changes.
    (d) Group cohesiveness as a force of resistance.
    (e) Elements of OD.
    (f) Advantages of OD.
    (g) Healthy working environment for OD.
    (h) Implementation of intervention.

26. Briefly explain the following topics:
    (a) Team building.
    (b) Job enrichment.
    (c) Quality Circle.
    (d) Career planning and development.
    (e) Mergers and acquisitions.
    (f) Whither organisation development.
    (g) Role analysis.
    (h) Role of trade union in OD.

19. OBJECTIVE QUESTIONS

1. Human resource is the key to economic development. However, they are being wasted through unemployment, disguised unemployment, outdated skills, lack of job opportunities, poor personnel policies and practices, and problems of adjusting to changes.
   (a) Ginzberg   *(b)* Elton Mayo
   (c) JS Mill   *(d)* Udai Parikh
   (e) None of the above

2. The organization changes create imbalance between existing and new required skill, knowledge, technology and process. An adjustment is to be done in jobs, working conditions, procedures, technology, competencies, structure etc., for improving effectiveness. Do you agree with the statement?
   (a) Fully agree   *(b)* Partially agree
   (c) Partially disagree   *(d)* Fully disagree
   (e) Cannot say anything

3. Organisation change is a dynamic process through which an organization can move from the existing to the new improved position. The main characteristics of change are:
   (a) Change is the law of nature. And it is a continuous process.
   (b) The pace of change cannot be predicted. It may be fast, medium and slow.
   (c) The changes are uncontrollable and organizations have no control over them.
   (d) The changes are to be managed effectively so competitive advantage can be achieved or maintained by the organization.
   (e) All the above

4. The organizations adapting the changes get advantages in their performance, satisfaction, sales, profits, market shares and reputation. Due to adaptation to changes the business health of the organization improves a lot. The changes are important due to:

(a) Provides place of growth
(b) Provided solution of problem
(c) Keep up to date to demand
(d) Marketing of organisation and new income streams
(e) All the above

5. When changes are brought to the organization in processes, systems, structure, job designs and employees are opposed by the people and there are different sources of resistance to change in an organization. The sources of changes are:
   (a) Organizational forces, (b) Sub-unit forces, group forces,
   (c) And individual forces. (d) All the above
   (e) None of the above

6. If the favourable conditions are satisfied then only the required changes can be brought in different areas of organization. If not the expected result would be missing. The essential conditions for effective organization development are:
   (a) Effective leadership and top management support
   (b) Services of change agent/ consultant, complete knowledge of OD interventions and need for collaboration
   (c) Healthy working environment with high level of commitment
   (d) Availability of internal resources with proper planning and implementation
   (e) All the above

7. "Organization development is a system-wide application of behavioral science knowledge to the planned development and reinforcement of organizational strategies, structures, and processes for improving an organization's effectiveness." This was advocated by:
   (a) Cummings and Worley. (b) Matt Minahan.
   (c) Alderfer CP (d) Porras and Robertson
   (e) Beckhard,

8. It is to "link the internal functioning of the organization to the larger environment; transforming the organization to keep pace with changing conditions" It is known as:
   (a) OD interventio (b) HRD
   (c) Industrial relations (d) Human resource planning
   (e) None of the above

9. In the last two decades the focus again shifted to improve mission, objectives, culture and strategy. Various techniques have been used by the experts and on the basis of feedback from different organizations applied the techniques. These techniques are:

(a) Human process interventions
(b) Techno-structural interventions
(c) Human resource interventions/ practices
(d) Strategic organisation transformation interventions
(e) All the above

10. Organisation development process is very comprehensive and it involves jobs, work design, structure, individuals, groups, strategy, processes, procedures, technology and culture of the organization. The major roles played by various parties are:

(a) Change manager and change agent
(b) HRD Managers,
(c) Workers and unions
(d) All the above
(e) None of the above

Answer Keys:

Question No.	Answer	Question No.	Answer
1	a	6	e
2	a	7	a
3	e	8	a
4	e	9	e
5	d	10	d

Chapter

20 Knowledge Management and HRD

1. INTRODUCTION

The business environment is changing rapidly. The factors affecting the business are social, cultural, economic, legal, political, technological and competition. These have gone under rapid changes. To carry the business effectively it was required by the organization to work according to the changing environment or surrender to the changes. Those who have changed the strategy to do the business as per the changes have achieved success in the business and are leader in the business and earning a huge profit every year. In the present situation social set up, economy and its development, government policies, technology, education of the people and level of competition have undergone drastic changes. It is needed to match the internal factors with the changing external factors so business can be carried effectively and efficiently.

Till recently the basic factors of production were land labour and capital and knowledge was inferior to capital. However today, knowledge is considered as a value creator and knowledge management is a competitive tool. Before, industrialization knowledge management was not an important area of management. There was a little need to bring changes for practical knowledge management. With the industrialization the ability to produce large volume at lower cost was possible. In the competitive situation, it is needed to make the organization more effective. The need for theoretical and practical knowledge was strongly felt. To do the business effectively, serve the customers in a better way and produce large quantity and maintain higher quality of products the need for knowledge management was felt.

2. KNOWLEDGE

Knowledge in the workplace is the ability of the people and organization to understand and act effectively It has been managed by managers workers and proactive individuals, Those responsible for survival in competitive environments always have worked to build the best possible knowledge. Knowledge forms the fundamental resources for effective functioning and provide valuable assets for sale or exchange. From business point of view explicit and systematic knowledge management has not been of general concern until recently. Knowledge has two elements explicit and tacit knowledge. Explicit knowledge includes assets such as patents, trademarks, copyrights, business plans, market research and lists of customers. Explicit knowledge is documented and stored for future use. Tacit knowledge is the know-how contained in the mind of the human resource that is difficult to grasp and be documented. It is difficult to recognize, generate, share and manage. Knowledge further is classified as theoretical and practical knowledge. Theoretical knowledge is acquired through reading study materials such as newspapers, books, reports, and manuals and practical knowledge is acquired through working on the jobs.

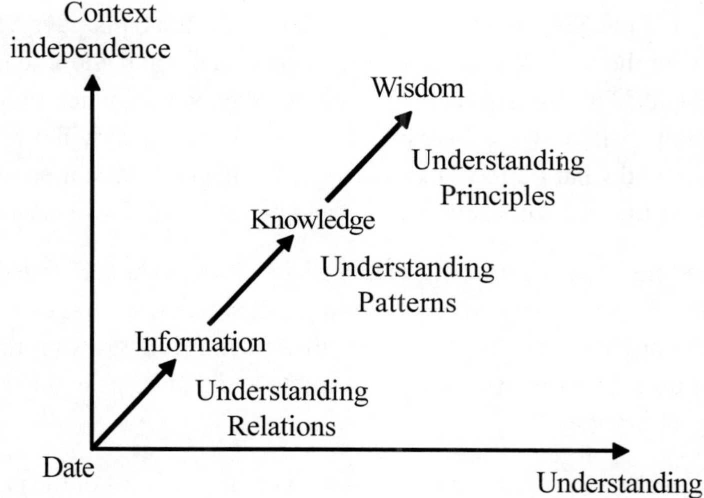

Diagram 20.1: Data Information and Knowledge

There is close relationship between data, information, knowledge and wisdom. Data means facts regarding processes, procedures, manufacturing formulae, business plans and customers. These data are collected as per the requirement and analyzed. The analysis of data gives information or messages regarding description, concepts and definitions. The information creates awareness and develops knowledge regarding understanding patterns. Wisdom is created by the knowledge and that helps to take decision, the situation to carry out the business effectively. Wisdom embodies principles moral and insight and these helps in the formulation of plans policies and strategy. All these four points work in combination and to the context otherwise these are of no use.

3. KNOWLEDGE MANAGEMENT

An Example

This example uses a bank savings account to show how data, information, knowledge, and wisdom relate to principal, interest rate, and interest.

Data: The numbers 100 or 5%, completely out of context, are just pieces of data. Interest, principal and interest rate, out of context, are not much more than data as each has multiple meanings which are context dependent.

Information: If I establish a bank savings account as the basis for context, then interest, principal, and interest rate become meaningful in that context with specific interpretations.

Principal is the amount of money, ₹ 100, in the savings account.

Interest rate, 5%, is the factor used by the bank to compute interest on the principal.

Knowledge: If I put $100 in my savings account, and the bank pays 5% interest yearly, then at the end of one year the bank will compute the interest of ₹ 5 and add it to my principal and I will have ₹ 105 in the bank. This pattern represents knowledge, which, when I understand it, allows me to understand how the pattern will evolve over time and the results it will produce. In understanding the pattern, I know, and what I know is knowledge. If I deposit more money in my account, I will earn more interest, while if I withdraw money from my account, I will earn less interest.

Wisdom: Getting wisdom out of this is a bit tricky and is, in fact, founded in systems principles. The principle is that any action which produces a result which encourages more of the same action produces an emergent characteristic called growth. And, nothing grows forever for sooner or later growth runs into limits.The principles creates wisdom and that helps in making right decision to do the business more effectively.

In past land, labour and capital were considered main resources of the production. But with the changing environment it is not working out today. To create value and improve the effectiveness of the people, systems and organization the need for knowledge and knowledge management is felt strongly. Knowledge is considered as a value creator and knowledge management is a competitive tool. Knowledge management has become the latest tool in the management circle. Management experts have defined the concept of knowledge management as follows:

"Knowledge management is about obsolete what you know before others obsolete it profit by creating the challenges and opportunities others have not even thought about." **–More**

Knowledge management caters to the critical issues of organizational adaptation, survival and excellence in competitive environment. Essentially it embodies organizational process to seek synergistic effect by combining information, technology, creative and innovative capacity of human beings. Goal of knowledge management is to sustain individual and business performance through learning and adaptation process, Knowledge management is too help not only to survive but also to thrive.

"Knowledge management is an emerging set of processes, organizational structures, applications and technologies that air to leverage the ability of capable, responsible and autonomous individuals to act quickly and effectively." **—Gartner**

In knowledge management process three stages are involved. These are:Unfortunately, there's no universal definition of knowledge management (KM), just as there's no agreement as to what constitutes knowledge in the first place. For this reason, it's best to think of KM in the broadest context. Succinctly put, KM is the process through which organizations generate value from their intellectual and knowledge-based assets. Most often, generating value from such assets involves codifying what employees, partners and customers know and sharing that information among employees, departments and even with other companies in an effort to devise best practices. It's important to note that the definition says nothing about technology; while KM is often facilitated by IT, technology by itself is not KM.

(a) Knowledge Generation: It includes all activities knowledge creation, knowledge acquisition synthesis, transmission of knowledge and knowledge adaptation. One of the interesting features is for these activities is the need for intensive and responsible communication and culture that is accepting of new ideas and is prepared to support exploration. It brings to light knowledge that is "new" to the individual, to the group, and to the organization.

(b) Knowledge Codification: It provides representation of knowledge so that it can be "reused" either by an individual or organization with the help of rules. For different types of knowledge rules are prepared. In future if predicated rules are followed that particular knowledge can be used otherwise not. It can be codified with help of charts, diagrams and symbols.

(c) Knowledge Transfer: "Movement of knowledge from one location to another" is called knowledge transfer. It can be transferred from one person to another person or from one job to the other through interaction. Knowledge can be transmitted through communication channels by accessing the site of the different experts. Transfer of knowledge does not denote a full replication of the knowledge in the receiving unit. Indeed, knowledge is often modified in the receiving unit.

4. FACTORS AFFECTING KNOWLEDGE MANAGEMENT DEVELOPMENT

With the fast development in the environment it was difficult to carry out the business effectively. It was a matter of survival and growth for the organization. So the need for knowledge and knowledge management was felt. Need to manage knowledge was not a luxury but it was a necessity. It was driven by forces of competition, marketplace demand was, new operating and management practices and introduction of information technology. These factors are classified in three groups. These are:

(a) External Factors: These factors are of the external environment and these are not with in the control of the management of the organization. These cannot be managed by the organization. These factors are globalization, international competition, sophisticated customers, high caliber competitors and suppliers. These factors compelled the management to adjust with the changing needs and do the business.

(b) Internal Factors: With the fast developing economy there were a lot of challenges and opportunities. To avail the opportunities it was need to develop the internal resources. So important changes took place in the organization. These sources are such as problems in production, increased technological capability and understanding human behaviour and practices.

Organizations faced a lot of difficulty to do the business properly. It was felt to match the internal factors with the external factors. To do so the requirement of knowledge and knowledge management was strongly felt. It can be said in nutshell that all these factors more or less in combination were the driving forces for development of knowledge management.

5. BENEFITS OF KNOWLEDGE MANAGEMENT

Today in the information driven economy, the firms try to explore the best opportunity and derive the best value of the physical and intellectual assets. Management accepts that knowledge must be generated, stored, updated and shared to serve as the foundation for collaboration. Following are the main benefits of knowledge management to the firms:

(a) Fosters the innovation by encouraging the sharing of knowledge among employees and managers.

(b) Contributes in development of knowledge and confidence of the employees.

(c) Enhances the performance of human resource and machines.

(d) Contributes the quantity and quality of output.

(e) Boosts revenues by introducing products and services faster in the markets.

(f) Enhances job satisfaction of the employees and improves retention of human resources.

(g) Provides basis for incentive and reward for employees.

(h) Reduces operation costs and eliminating redundant or unnecessary processes.

(i) Improves overall effectiveness of the organization to get competitive advantages.

6. CHALLENGES OF KNOWLEDGE MANAGEMENT

Development of knowledge management was not an easy task. Lot of difficulties were faced by the management to develop knowledge. The following challenges were faced:

(a)Ignorance of People and Cultural Issues: It was difficult for the management to take the people together because they were not treated properly. They were not motivated to surrender the knowledge and experience. Incentive programmes were not used.

(b) Technology: Technology was to support the management to develop knowledge but technology started dictating terms in functioning of management. Therefore, knowledge management found difficult to work and develop.

(c) Knowledge Management is not Static: Knowledge is not static like the physical assets. The knowledge diminishes with the time so it should be generated, stored, shared and upgraded with the time. If not so it will be outdated and useless. So management found it difficult to work.

(d) Lack of Expertise: Knowledge management people were not expert in their job in the beginning. They themselves were not sure what to do and what to develop. This was the problem in the beginning. These difficulties made the situation unfavourable for the development of knowledge and knowledge management. But it was a necessity for the organization to survive and grow in the competitive situation. It could overcome the difficulties and developed further. At present the situation of knowledge management is highly satisfactory.

7. HUMAN RESOURCE DEVELOPMENT (HRD)

Out of production resources human resource is a live and generating resource. It is required to be developed with the development of technology. For effective working it is needed to develop their competencies to improve overall effectiveness of the organization. In the modern times, management has grown very complex and it has acquired new dimensions. So to tackle the new challenges management has recognized the development of competency of people, coordination between people at different levels, minimizing production cost and improving productivity. The priority in personnel management has changed vastly. Now the tasks of framing rules, regulations and standing orders have been changed to promote the motivation generating factors and minimize the de-motivating factors for maximum capacity utilization.

HRD is the process of helping people to acquire competencies. In an organizational context, HRD is a process by which the employees of an organization are helped in a continuous and systematic way to:

(a) Acquire or develop capabilities required to perform various functions relating to their present and future roles.

(b) Improve their general capabilities as individuals, discover and exploit their available potential for their own and organizational development purpose.

(c) Improve supervisor–subordinate relationship, teamwork and collaboration among different departments in an organizational culture and to contribute to the welfare, motivation and pride of employees. Human resource development therefore is defined as the total knowledge, skills, creative abilities, talents and aptitudes of an organization's workforce as well as the values, attitudes and beliefs of the individuals involved.

Human resource development process is facilitated by mechanisms or subsystems like performance appraisal, training, organizational development, potential development, job rotation, welfare and reward. People are helped to acquire new competencies through the various systems continuously. Personnel management has to deal with the interactive policies, techniques and procedures that together can help to develop the human resource of an organization. Line managers and staff personnel can cooperate to make sure that all these activities are planned and administered with the aim in mind. Since every achievement in every activity is related to human resource, it is important that a department is created within the organization to serve continuously the areas of human resource development.

8. NEED FOR HUMAN RESOURCE DEVELOPMENT

Employees feel the need of knowledge, skills attitudes and values to perform the task efficiently. We call these competencies. Higher degree of competencies is required for higher degree and quality of job performance. Hence to achieve the goals in the changing situation, it is necessary to develop competencies continuously in an organization. In the present competitive situation to survive, grow and excel, the competent and motivated employees are essential. To maintain the growth level over a period of time, competencies of employees need to be sharpened or developed as organization operates in the changing environment. The organizations are interested to develop their business though products or services. They want to bring effectiveness in the organization through cost reduction, delay reduction, better customer satisfaction, service promptness and better quality. Hence for these, the organization needs to develop its human resource competencies to perform better.

For example, a university, bank, hospital, profit making company etc., are interested to improve their services and want to give better satisfaction to customers, HRD activities may be needed to be undertaken to equip the employees with better competencies. Thus the need for HRD is felt by every organization that is interested in the following objectives to be achieved:

(a) To stabilize itself
(b) To grow
(c) To diversify the products or services
(d) To renew itself to become more effective
(e) To improve its systems, products and services
(f) To change and become more dynamic
(g) To play the role of a leader.

9. HUMAN RESOURCE DEVELOPMENT CLIMATE

HRD climate plays an important role in developing competencies of employees, motivation and teamwork. The climate can be created by the top management support and style by using the different HRD mechanisms. HRD climate helps to achieve the end and it is an end itself. Climate means the atmosphere in which different tasks are performed in an organization. Both the informal and formal structures of an organization contribute to create the organization culture.

Climate is the atmosphere in which persons work, support, decide, reward, restrict and find out about others. The term "Climate" represents internal environment that conditions the quality of cooperation, team spirit, dedication and commitment of employees to the job. It affects the efficiency with which the objectives are converted into goals. Climate influences the morale and attitudes of the people towards work and the organization as a whole. Organization climate became popular in the last quarter of 20th century and this concept has been reviewed repeatedly. Climate has been defined as follows:

Hellriegel and Slocum (1974) defined organizational climate as a "set of attributes which can be perceived about a particular organization and/or its sub-systems, and that may be induced in the way that organization and/or its sub-systems deal with their members and environment".

"Organization climate is a relatively enduring quality of the internal environment that is experienced by the members influences their behaviour and can be described in terms of values of a particular set of characteristics of the organization." **Renato Tagiuri**.

"Organization climate is the set of characteristics that describes an organization and distinguishes one organization from other organizations, are relatively enduring overtime and influences the behaviour of the people in the organization", **Forehand & Gilmer**.

From the above-mentioned definitions it can be said that if the organization climate is good and favourable then development of human resource is easy and effective. When climate is not favourable then HRD activities will be hampered. The main elements of HRD climate are openness, confrontation, trust, autonomy, understanding and team spirits.

10. HRD CLIMATE AND ORGANIZATIONAL CLIMATE

Human resource development climate is a part of climate of an organization. HRD climate means the perception of the employees regarding atmosphere or environment for development of human resource in an organization. Following are the features of HRD climate:

(a) Treating the people as the most valuable resource at all levels in an organization.
(b) Developing the competencies of employees is the job of everyone in an organization.
(c) Employees are capable to change and acquire the competencies at any stage of life.
(d) Timely communication and free discussion rather than secretive.
(e) Inspiring to take initiative and risks.
(f) Top management support to employees to know their plus and minus points
(g) Climate of trust.
(h) Cooperation and team spirit.
(i) No favour and no fear tendency.
(j) Favourable personnel policies
(k) Healthy human resource development practices.

All organizations are not having the above-mentioned tendencies. HRD climate helps to develop individual competencies, team spirit and efficiency of the entire organization. For measurement of HRD climate, a questionnaire can be prepared relating to above-mentioned features and information can be collected and analyzed. Factor contributing to HRD climate may include philosophy and style of top management, personnel policies, HRD mechanisms, attitude of personnel staff and commitment of line managers.

11. KNOWLEDGE MANAGEMENT AND HRD

With fast changing economic conditions, Competition, technologies, legal systems, methods and procedures the need for development of human resource is needed. The requirement of higher level of competencies, ability, capability, skill, attitude and aptitude was strongly accepted. The question arises that how can these be developed. Therefore, the concept of knowledge management was developed. In knowledge management the systematic stages involved are generation or acquiring, codification, transferring and sharing, and application of knowledge. Generation of knowledge takes place through research and development activities. The experts work on this and develop innovative products and services. In acquiring of knowledge the employees of required talents are recruited and selected from outsiders and sometimes the trained and experienced persons of the other competitors. Further in codification of knowledge the rules are made regarding knowledge and it is protected. When it is required it is used as per the rules and guideline and protected from leakage to the other parties. Knowledge management takes care of the transmission and sharing of knowledge among other employees through printed materials, workshops, seminars, and on-job training

This is possible in good environment of mutual understanding, trust, collaboration, team spirit and belongingness. HRD managers are also interested for the development of competencies of the employees with knowledge management. Goals of both KM and HRD manager are similar, i.e., development of knowledge of human resources. Both branches of management try to develop a favourable environment for aforesaid purpose through proper recruitment and selection, proper compensation methods, favourable attitude of management, welfare facilities for employees and chances for development in career. All these factor will create a desire among employees to surrender their knowledge and experience and learn further to be more suitable for the job in future. Therefore it can be said in nutshell that knowledge management contribute in the development of human resource through generating or acquiring, codification of, transmission and sharing of knowledge among other employees. This ultimately contributes in development of capability, effectiveness of the people and organization as a whole.

12. FINDINGS

From the study of knowledge management, the findings are following:

(a) Business environment is changing rapidly so it has become compulsion for the organization to keep pace with changing environment for doing business effectively.

(b) Knowledge is the awareness and understanding of the work place regarding processes, methods, procedures, manufacturing formulae, research and development activities, and lists of customers.

(c) Knowledge helps to improve capability of individuals, systems and organization as a whole to perform better and improve effectiveness of the organization. This provides competitive advantage over others.

(d) Knowledge management is that branch of management that takes care of generation or acquiring, codification, transmission and sharing of knowledge with other employees.

(e) External environmental factors that affected the development of knowledge management are globalization, international competition, high level of customer awareness, development of technology, and changes in social, cultural and economic factors.

(f) Internal factors that affected development of knowledge management are increasing number of production problems, cost reduction, higher competency of employees and awareness of management regarding human behaviour and practices.

(g) Knowledge management acquire knowledge through recruitment and selection, generate knowledge through research and development, transmit knowledge through communication channels and study materials, and share the information through lectures, seminars, workshops and training methods.

(h) Main difficulties faced by knowledge management are lack of knowledge regarding behaviour and culture, lack of knowledge regarding changing technology, and dynamic nature of knowledge and its handling.

(i) For development of the competencies of people it is necessary to create favourable organizational environment so that people can take interest to learn more.

(j) The objective of HRM and knowledge management is same to develop ability and capability of human resources to improve overall effectiveness of the organization. Both branches of management are working at present to contribute to achieve their objective.

(k) Efforts of knowledge management and HRM contribute in development of competencies i. e, skills, knowledge, attitude and aptitudes of employees. This has provided higher degree of capability and improved overall effectiveness of the human resources and organization. Due to this organization are enjoying competitive advantages over others in the international market and enjoying leading position.

13. SUGGESTIONS

(a) Knowledge management should not be overloaded with the jobs other than managing knowledge-based assets. Otherwise the efficiency of it goes down.

(b) Favourable working environment should be created so that people can surrender their knowledge and experience by introducing incentive programmes.

(c) Counselling session must be conducted to deal with behaviour of the employees and creating awareness regarding importance of knowledge in this competitiveness.

(d) Knowledge management programmes should be continuously updated, modified and evaluated as per the requirement to keep the knowledge afresh.

(e) Efforts should be put to share the personal knowledge because it is very difficult.

(f) People should be motivated and made to realize that individual interest is inferior to organizational interest. They should not think by sharing their knowledge and experience their importance will go down.

(g) Use of communication technology should be more so communication can take place well in time and gap can be avoided.

(h) Knowledge managers should be trained on communication technology, human behavior and practices in the organization so functions can be performed properly.

(i) A knowledge network should be established in which managers of other organization can become member and share their knowledge with others through meetings, discussion, seminars and workshops.

(j) Knowledge managers should work in collaboration with human resource managers for development of capability of employees because the goal of both is common.

(k) Finally the emphasis should be on using interdisciplinary teams with a focus on the best mix of competencies and understanding to be applied to the work at hand.

14. CONCLUSION

In present time the business units are finding very difficult to carry out the business effectively and efficiently due to fast changing environment. Changes are taking place very rapidly. It becomes necessary for everybody to keep pace with the changes so effectiveness in the work does not go down. For business organization it is a matter of survival, growth, stabilization and excellence in business. Various internal and external factors forced the development of knowledge and knowledge management. It is knowledge through which the capability of human resources and organization as a whole can be improved to get competitive advantages. Knowledge management performs the activities of acquiring or generating, codification, transmission and sharing of knowledge among others.

Contribution of knowledge management in improving overall effectiveness of the organization is strongly accepted. In performing these tasks management faced a lot of difficulties such as changing nature of knowledge, cultural factors, human behaviour and practices. But through sincere and dedicated efforts these difficulties have been overcome. Knowledge managementn's main goal is to develop knowledge and capability of employees and organization and it has achieved it also to a very good extent. Along with human resources in close collaboration it develops favourable environment for development of competencies of the people. This interdisciplinary approach helped a lot in development of human resources, capability and effectiveness of all parties. Finally it can be said that the future of knowledge management is very bright in the era of information technology.

This is possible in good environment of mutual understanding, trust, collaboration, team spirit and belongingness. HRD managers are also interested for the development of competencies of the employees with knowledge management. Goals of both KM and HRD manager are similar, i.e., development of knowledge of human resources. Both branches of management try to develop the favourbale environment for aforesaid purpose. Therefore it can be said in nutshell that knowledge management contribute in the development of human resource through generating or acquiring, codification of, transmission and sharing of knowledge among other employees. This ultimately contributes in development of capability, effectiveness of the people and organization as a whole.

15. QUESTIONS FOR REVIEW

1. Do you feel this is requirement of knowledge in present rapidly changing environment or not? Discuss.
2. "Knowledge impress the capabilities of human resource and overall effectiveness of the organization." Explain.
3. How would you explain the relationship between data, information, knowledge and wisdom?
4. Define knowledge management and explain its main features.
5. Discuss knowledge management development definitions and functions in detail.
6. Highlight the factors responsible for development of knowledge management development.
7. Elaborate the challenges faced by knowledge management in present time.
8. Elaborate the relationship between knowledge management and HRD.
9. What are the benefits of knowledge management? Explain.
10. Short notes on the following:
    (a) Explain and implicit components of knowledge
    (b) Findings on KM
    (c) Suggestion for improvement
    (d) HRD climate
    (e) Need for HRD

16. OBJECTIVE QUESTIONS

1. The ability of the people and organization to understand and act effectively in the workplace which has been managed by managers, workers and proactive individuals is called:
   (a) Knowledge (b) Skills
   (c) Competency (d) Attitude
   (e) All the above

2. Movement of knowledge from one location to another from one person to another person or from one job to the other through interaction is called:
   (a) Knowledge Migration (b) Knowledge Transfer
   (c) Brain Drain (d) Knowledge Flow
   (e) None of the above

3. Knowledge creation, knowledge acquisition synthesis, transmission of knowledge and knowledge adaptation is together known as:
   (a) Knowledge Generation (b) Knowledge Acquisition
   (c) Knowledge Development (d) Knowledge Gathering
   (e) None of the above

4. Employees feel the need of knowledge, skills attitudes and values to perform the task efficiently. This is called:
   (a) Self-awareness (b) Dissatisfaction
   (c) Motivation (d) Competencies
   (e) Accountability

5. It is the atmosphere in which persons work, support, decide, reward, restrict and find out about others and it represents internal environment that conditions the quality of cooperation, team spirit, dedication and commitment of employees to the job. It is called
   (a) HRD Climate (b) Work Place
   (c) Work Space (d) Work Climate
   (e) OD climate

6. The awareness and understanding of the work place regarding processes, methods, procedures, manufacturing formulae, research and development activities, and lists of customers is called:
   (a) Knowledge (b) General awareness
   (c) Competency (d) Process
   (e) Information

7. The branch of management that takes care of generation or acquiring, codification, transmission and sharing of knowledge with other employees is called:
   (a) Research & development
   (b) Knowledge management
   (c) Knowledge acquisition
   (d) Knowledge recording
   (e) Knowledge sharing

8. Treating the people as the most valuable resource at all levels in an organization is a feature of:
   (a) Big organisation
   (b) Excellent marketing
   (c) HRD climate
   (d) Organisational culture
   (e) None of the above

9. Mechanisms or subsystems like performance appraisal, training, organizational development, potential development, job rotation, welfare and reward facilitates:
   (a) Human resource development process
   (b) Research & development Process
   (c) Poaching Process
   (d) Recruitment Process
   (e) None of the above

10. The interactive policies, techniques and procedures that together can help to develop the human resource of an organization are dealt by
   (a) Senior Management
   (b) Personnel management
   (c) Union Officer
   (d) Supervisor
   (e) All the above

Answer Keys:

Question No.	Answer	Question No.	Answer
1	a	6	a
2	b	7	b
3	a	8	c
4	d	9	a
5	a	10	b

Chapter

Employees Counselling and Well-being

1. INTRODUCTION

The present time is very uncertain and it is very difficult to perform the task as per the requirements in different sphere of life. Personal life is full of struggle and a lot of efforts are put to meet the day to day need of individual and life. Job opportunities are not much, inflation is very high, needs and expectations are increasing, and tough competition is being faced. The situation becomes very difficult for everyone in present time. Counselling is very old in our society and with the present situation it has become necessary in different areas. In every-day life parents counsel their children, doctors counsel their patients, teachers counsel their students and supervisors counsel their subordinates for better working. Everyone is interested to solve the problems and live happily, perform better and get good results so that the life becomes prosperous.

For some of the jobs an individual is in position to perform and meet the need of the self and dependants. Some of the needs are not fulfilled because the individual is not in a position to understand or perform due to lack of ability. He is under pressure due to various reasons. This situation continues and leads to stress and finally it adversely affects the individual psychology, health, performance and personal life. Similarly, the situation prevails in an organization and industry. The situation is very competitive due to globalization and entry of multinational companies in various markets. It is matter of survival, growth and excellence in the business activities. Every organization is trying its best to give better products, services and performances so that it can enjoy better position in the business. Most of the leading organizations have realized the importance of attracting, training, motivating and retailing highly skilled and committed employees to get competitive advantage in the markets over their rivals. Employees, counselling add another feather in the cap of the organization to do so. The importance of counselling due to this is going high day by day.

Every organization is interested to perform better and before other organization to avail better opportunities. The strategies are prepared to achieve the objectives more effectively and efficiently. For that purpose every employee is given the task to perform for achieving the pre–decided targets. They try to do their best and despite this they are not in position to achieve the targets. Most of the time on their job they are under pressure due to unrealistic targets or work-load, constant pressure to meet the deadlines, career-related problems, responsibility and accountability, interpersonal conflicts with their peers, superiors and subordinates, problems in adjusting to the organizational culture, number of customers to increase and maintain, difficulties faced with new jobs and technology, fear of poor performance and loosing the jobs etc. They are under pressure due to workload and not in a position to give proper time to their personal and family commitments. The individual comes under pressure and stress is created. This stress affects individual health, psychology, performance, family relations etc. The adverse effects of the stress are many on employees in their organizations. Finally the performance of employees, organization, quality of products and services, profits etc., goes down. It is not acceptable by the management in the present highly competitive situation.

This situation of employee is very critical and going to give multi-dimensional adverse effects. The management should not take chance to ignore this situation. If done so the organization is to suffer. Organization cannot not afford this. The approach of the management should be proactive towards its employees. The interest of the management should be there to recruit, train, motivate and maintain the satisfied workforce. For this purpose the problems of the employees should be looked into. The efforts should be there to find out the causes of the problems of employees and steps should be there for providing help. It can be done with the help of employees counseling to a good extent if timely actions are taken by the management. Counselling is one of the mechanisms used by the management for human resource development. In prevailing situation, the importance of employees' counselling is increasing. The future role of counselling would be more important too.

2. MEANING AND DEFINITIONS OF COUNSELLING

Counselling is a process and it is described as it provides help and support to the persons who who find themselves in problems and they are not in position to solve the problem of their own. The problems may be faced in any area of life such as personal, family, society, business, health and jobs. When the problems are faced any area of life then it starts affecting adversely psychology, health, relationship, performance. It creates a lot of stress and which is difficult to digest for a longer period. The need of help of somebody is required who can listen, guide, support and show the path to solve the problems. This is called counselling. So it can be said the counselling is the process of listening, guiding, supporting, consoling, advising and showing the path to solve the problems of persons who are facing these problems. Anyone can face the problems relating to his life, health, career, performance and jobs. Counselling concept has been defined by experts as follows:

Wren is of the opinion that the "counselling is a personal and dynamic relationship between two individuals—an older, more experienced and wiser (counsellor) and a younger, less wise (counsellee). The latter has a problem for which he seeks the help of the former. The two work together so that the problem may be more clearly defined and the counsellee may be helped to a self-determined solution".

Webster's Dictionary defines counselling as "consultation, mutual interchange of opinion, deliberating together".

Robinson said that "the term counselling covers all types of two .person situations in which one person, the client is helped to adjust more effectively to himself and his environment"

Strong defined counselling as "face to face relationship in which growth takes place the counsellor as well as the counsellee".

At a work place the employees are interacting with different people from diversified background. It takes a lot of painstaking efforts to adjust with other and work effectively. The employees are exposed to the different situations in an organization and performing various types of jobs at different times. They are asked to follow certain rules, regulations, instructions, procedure while performing their duties. These may be favourable to them or not but they have to follow during their jobs. The employees are given various types of jobs to perform at different times as per the situation. They may have the skills to perform the jobs or not. They cannot deny the work but face difficulties. Over and above they are to perform as per the performance standards, targets, customers, expectations and cost reduction. All these situations are creating pressure on employees. They are under stress and it affects their mental, physical conditions, performance, relationship, personal and family life. Other side some of the employees not working hard and avoid the work and do not follow the rules of conducts are not acceptable in the organization. The hardworking employees are not in position to solve their problems of their own and hardly working employees willingly avoid the work or create problems. They need the help of experienced person who can help, support and guide them to solve problem. In this the supervisor or manager listen them sympathetically, try to find out the causes of difficulties, suggest and guide them to solve the problem. This process is called employee,s counselling. Time to time this technique has been used by HRD manager to solve the problems of employees so that their performance and skills are improved. For diversified working force it is becoming more and more popular because it helps a lot of the employees to solve the problems and adjust with the people of different cultures.

The concept of employees counselling has been defined by various experts as follows;

Employee counselling is a psychological technique and that is used in various forms. The main objective of it is to support the employees by providing them advice, guidance, suggestions to solve the prevailing problems and improve physical and mental conditions, performance and which can take many forms. It is conducted with problem solving approach by supervisors, managers or consultants.

Employee counselling is defined as a process which is initiated by the responsible manager or counsellor for providing assistance to employees facing problems. It is conducted to listen, understand problems and provide guidance, advices and suggest ways to solve them. It is mainly to provide job related, personal and confidential help to those who are facing the problems. If not done so then it might affect working, increasing difficulties, loss of job interest, accidents, absenteeism, poor performance and productivity and poor relationship.

Employee counselling is a vehicle of communication to provide assistance in a practical and effective way to the problem affected employees. Through this efforts are put to get employees relived from difficulties and motivate them to utilize their potential for contributing in accomplishment of individual performance and objectives of the organization in interests of all concerned.

3. CHARACTERISTICS OF EMPLOYEES COUNSELLING

In the past the success of a company was attributed to traditional factors and these are becoming less important in present time. The most important factor of success in present time is selection and management of high quality workforce and it is very critical. In present time, HR consultants and practitioners are busy in designing and developing new, better and innovative techniques to attract, motivate and retain talented and high quality workforce. One of the new techniques is employees counselling and it is gaining popularity. On the basis of the study of various definitions and thought of various experts, the main characteristics of employee counseling are following:

(a) Service offered to employees.

(b) Service is conducted in organization.

(c) Focus is on problems faced by employees.

(d) Objective of counselling is problem solution.

(e) Employee counselling serves all concerned.

(f) Employee counselling is a continuous process.

(g) Role of counsellor is important in counselling.

(h) Half-knowledge is a dangerous thing, is completed through counselling.

4. OBJECTIVES OF EMPLOYEE COUNSELLING

The objectives of employee counselling are multidimensional and all concerned parties are benefitted due to employees, counselling. The parties involved in benefits from employee counselling are employee, family member, peers, subordinates, seniors, organization and society as a whole. Due to this the popularity of employee counselling is increasing day by day in corporate section and mainly in medium and large sizes of organizations. The role of employee counselling in future will be more important.

It has been used by the managers in most of the leading organization with the objectives to understand the problems of employees,

(a) To advise, guide and suggest ways to solve the problems of employees so that they are relieved from the problems they are facing at their workplace.

(b) To improve satisfaction level of employees, motivation, level of commitment, performance and contribution towards accomplishment of organizational objectives.

(c) To manage the employees more effectively so that attraction and retention of talented and motivated workforce becomes easier for the management in future.

(d) To maintain satisfied, talented and motivated workforce so that the desired performance can be given to meet market expectations to get competitive edge in business.

(e) To improve productivity, performance of the organization as a whole, profits, organizational effectively, and image in the markets.

5. PROBLEMS DISCUSSED IN EMPLOYEE COUNSELLING

When an employee is working in organization he comes through different activities, interact with different persons and face situations. These are having various types of impression on employees. This may be favourable or nonfavourable. If the impression is favourable then it is willingly accepted by us. If not favourable then it creates problem for the employees and going to give adverse effects. When unfavourable impression is there, it creates difficulties and situation becomes awkward for working in the organization. The employees faces a number of problems from different areas such as personal, family, society, job, performance, working environment, interpersonal relationship and career development. These are explained below:

(a) Job Related Problems: When an employee is facing problems related to his performance and due to that he gives poor performance. In this type of problems we can include lack of training, poor coaching, behaviour of peers and supervisors, difficult working procedure, poor working conditions, lack of cooperation from team members, lack of competencies, newly purchased technology, poor maintenance of the machines operating, lack of recognition to the work performed, lack of career development opportunities, poor salary structures, improper welfare and social security measures, improper retirement benefits, target pressure and higher expectations of employer etc.

(b) Personal and Family Problems: Another type of problems of employees is relating his personal life. This can include such as poor educational level, low caliber to understand work, drinking, smoking, gambling, short temperament, poor financial condition, marital relationship, family disputes, poor health due to diabetes, hypertension, away from family for a longer period, leave not granted as and when required, poor health of family members etc. All these are related to the employees personally and give a cause of stress and adversely affect the working, health and mind of employees because the employee carries these personal problems at work place also.

(c) Other Problems: Other problems can range from working environment, interpersonal relationship and working conditions. These may include unfavourable attitude of management, unfavourable rules, policies, poor career opportunities, poor working conditions, lack of trust, confidence, mutual understanding, team spirit and cooperation, power struggle, politics, lack of proper leadership, unfair approach of seniors, disputes, poor support from unions, poor work life quality, and other problems not directly related to employees.

These are some of the problems faced by the employees and there may be more problems related to different jobs. But these are the main problems generally faced by employees found from the study of the documents referred to those maintained in various organization for conducting employee counselling.

6. EMPLOYEE COUNSELLING PROGRAMME

Most of the leading organizations are interested in conducting counselling of employees because it is manpower that contributes in success of the organization. It is not possible to afford to work with workforce under stress and lower motivation. It is needed to take proper care of employees so that they are free from problems, work properly and maintain good relationship in the organization. It contributes finally in the progress of all concerned parties. It is the need of the hour to attract and retain the skilled manpower. HR consultants and practitioners are focusing in designing more useful and innovative tools for attracting and managing better employees. Due to this, popularity of employees counselling is getting momentum day by day. The organization are designing and providing employees counselling programme for their employees with the help of internal experts if they are having. If not then help of external experts or consultant is taken for conducting employees counselling programme.

(a) Components of Programme

In employees counselling programme the different types of activities are involved as per the need of the employees. Due to this the major components or activities involved are different as mentioned below:

(i) Identification of problems: The first component of employee counselling programme is identification of problems of the employees. The problems may be faced in different areas which are not yet identified. Different techniques have been used for identification of problems such as questionnaire, laboratory tests and training of employees. For instance, while conducting tests the problems of diabetes, hypertension, cholesterol etc., can be identified. It helps to take the remedial action as early as possible. If the problems not identified timely then the adverse effect will be more harmful for employees.

(ii) Educating employees: There are certain areas where the employees are involved in bad habits and the consequences are not known to them. For example, the employees are involved in drinking and smoking activities regularly. The counsellor educates them regarding the bad effects on health, mind, financial conditions and family relationship. It is provided with the help of lectures, videos and pictures. The objective is to educate them and motivate them to take preventive steps in future.

(iii) Counselling of employees: In this the manager or consultant gets involved with employee who faces the problems. They interact face to face and discuss the problems of employee. He tries to listen, understand and provides advice or suggestions to solve the problems. It may be related to work performance, health, personal and marital of employees. Through counseling service the employee is relieved from the problems and condition of employee improves.

(iv) Direction for assistance: In this programme when counsellor finds that it is not possible to solve the problem on his own then it becomes necessary to refer or direct the employees to other experts or sources for assistance. For instance, if an employee is facing hypertension problem and counsellor is not in position to solve this, the employee is directed to take help of medical expert so that the problem can be solved at the earliest. There may be many other such cases when help of other experts is sought for problem solution.

(v) Execution of techniques: In this activity the manager gets involved in implementation of the techniques or interventions so that the problems can be solved or prevented so that in future it can be prevented. For instance, conducting medical check-up, eye testing camps, nutrition programme, cleaning campaign, cooking of healthy food in canteen or cafeteria of the organization etc., are execution of the activities. Such programmes are to be conducted by the managers in the organization itself.

7. ESSENTIAL CONDITIONS FOR EFFECTIVE EMPLOYEE COUNSELLING PROGRAMME

During routine work the employees face difficulties or problems due to unseen reasons and these are affecting their morale, performance, relationship and productivity. If it is not taken care of timely, the effects would be more harmful. Through employee counselling the problems can be listened and advice, suggestions and guidance can be given to the employees. If sincere efforts are put the problems would be solved to a great extent. If not so then the problem may continue despite of counselling also. The most of the times the employees are having low morale to perform the jobs due to lack of skills, excessive workload, excessive pressure for meeting targets, career expectations, personal and marital problems. The effective way of dealing with the problems of employees is that the counselling should be conducted properly and at right time. To conduct employee counselling more effectively then certain conditions are to be fulfilled. These are following:

(a) Top Management Support: For conducting employee counselling the support of top management is necessary. Without support of top management the activities cannot be planned and implemented. The employees must be considered by management as a very valuable resource of the organization and it should be managed effectively. If the support and commitment are proper then the counselling definitely would be more effective.

(b) Proper Formulation and Communication of Policy for Employee Counselling: With the approval of the top management a policy for conducting employee counselling should be prepared well in advance. It should be prepared with discussion with other managers and consultants so that all elements of counselling are taken care of properly. Procedure, situation, responsibility and time duration etc., are to be decided in the policy. It should be in position to guide all concerned. Further, it should be timely and properly communicated to all managers and employees to create awareness regarding this.

(c) Listen and Show Confidence: During counselling process the manager or consultant should give proper time to listen the problems of employee. Confidence should be shown to the employee that the problem would be solved definitely. The problem should not be ignored at any cost because it is going to affect badly in long run. The abilities of employees must be respected and must be told that every employee is important and organization having high expectations from them. The healthy work environment would develop confidence and trust in employees. It finally motivates the employees to take initiative to solve the problem and perform better.

(d) Focus on Major Issue of Problems and Not Individual: The focus of the manger or counsellor should be there on the problems. It is problem that is the main culprits due that bad effect are taking place. The problem may be major or minor it should not be ignored and must be dealt with proper focus. Efforts should be there to understand the problems and their causes and not the individual employees. That would help to conduct counselling more effectively.

(e) Give Suggestions, Advice for Solutions: After understanding the problem, the efforts should be there to find out the causes of the problems. On the basis of analysis, certain advice, guidance and suggestions are to be given to the employees so that timely the problems are solved. In this process the employee should be involved and confidence should be developed so that he can take active part in problem solution. Without giving any suggestion or advice the listening of problem become useless. These should be given timely and not delayed.

(f) Preparation of Action Plan: The manager should prepare an action plan for problem solution. For a particular type of problem certain tasks are to be performed over a period of time for problem solution. It should be in position to guide the counsellor and the employees. For this purpose, the manager should get involved very actively so that the other team members are performing their tasks very cooperatively.

(g) Documentation of Counselling Programme: When the employee counselling programmes are conducted related to different areas, the records should be maintained properly. This would help the managers and others to take future actions and planning. On the basis of records the related decision and actions can be taken very effectively. It should not be ignored and the responsibility for keeping related records should be fixed in advance itself.

(h) Follow up: The last step in the counselling programme is follow up and it should be done properly. It should be done at regular interval to see the effectiveness of the counselling programme. It would help to find out the success and drawbacks of the programme. On the basis of this the remedial actions can be taken to make it more effective. Irregularities can be checked on the part of employees whether they have taken proper steps to solve the problems or not.

If the counselling is done properly by keeping in view the above mentioned conditions then it can be expected that it would give wonderful result in improving morale, performance, productivity and level of commitment of employees towards the organization and their family. It is going to develop a healthy working environment and that is essential for all development activities. If genuine intention is there to solve the problem through counselling then it is going to give better results.

8. COUNSELLING AND PSYCHOLOGICAL COUNSELLING

Employee counselling and psychological counselling are two separate concepts and different from each other. Employee counselling is the counselling conducted for only working employees of an organization in the form of advising, consoling and sharing what happens in all spheres of life, suggesting for problem solution and it does not need a specialized counsellor. The employee counselling is conducted related to job and personal problems. It is a continuous process in an organization and conducted for employees working at various levels. It is a friendly problem solving approach in a good working environment. The employee counselling is a concern of everyone whoever is connected with the employees facing difficulties. In an organization the managers or experts are not charging any fee from the employees for conducting counselling. This is arranged by the organization only.

Other side the psychological counselling is a process that is conducted for individual and not for an employee. It cannot be conducted in informal way and it emphasizes a formal relationship between the individual and the counsellor. The focus this counselling is to solve the problems faced by the individual and it is not general in nature. It is more specific. It helps in solving the problems as disclosed by the clients. The assistance offered in psychological counselling is limited and it is confined to specific times and duration for the clients. It comes to end when the objectives are fulfilled. The relationship between counsellor and counseling comes to an end. There is need for specialized counsellor trained by the institutes in the particular field. The candidates of psychology are trained for counseling in different areas by various institutes. They are well trained and they provide the services with consultation fees. They maintain the confidentiality, objectivity during their counselling sessions. The counselling is conducted by the experts at their own costs.

9. EMPLOYEE ASSISTANCE PROGRAMMME

Employee is considered the most important resource in an organization because it is the live resource and it utilizes the other resources to generate them further. So the need for talented and motivated human resource is strongly felt. For that purpose, the interventions are used for human resource development. One of these is employee counseling. Under employee counselling the assistance is provided to the employees to resolve their problems through employees assistance programme. The employees are provided confidential individual assistance and support service to employees to help them in solution of their problems of personal and performance areas. These problems affect the health, life, behaviour, relationship and performance. Through EAP programme these problems are taken care of and employees are assisted, this program is helpful in drinking, smoking, drug addictions, financial and legal difficulties, substance abuse and marital problems.

Employee assistance programe has been defined by the experts as follows:"Services offered by employers to their employees to help them overcome problems that may negatively affect job satisfaction or productivity. Services may be provided on-site or contracted through outside providers. They include counselling for alcohol dependence and drug dependence, marital therapy or family therapy, career counseling, and referrals for dependent care services. See also *Industrial Social*

Work," Barker. "An employment-based health service program designed to assist in the identification and resolution of a broad range of employee personal concerns that may affect job performance. These programs deal with situations such as substance abuse, marital problems, family troubles, stress and domestic violence, as well as health education and disease prevention. The assistance may be provided within the organization or by referral to outside resources." (International Foundation of Employee Benefit Plans, 2005). "A confidential personal counselling service funded by an employer. EAPs provide professional counsellors with whom individuals can discuss their work- and non-work-related problems, which may be emotional, financial, or legal or related to alcohol or drug misuse." (Dictionary of Human Resource Management)." While the EAP started out as a way to help employees with alcohol and drug addiction, EAP professionals today say they need to be well rounded to address an array of problems. Issues that may affect job performance that are brought up by employees as often as any traditional addiction include personal relationships, depression, and anxiety, experts say." (Pace, 2006). "Strategic analysis, recommendations and consultation throughout an organiitazation to enhance its performance, culture and business success. These enhancements are accomplished by professionally trained behavioral and/or psychological experts who apply the principles of human behavior with management, employees and their families, as well as workplace situations to optimize the organization's human capital," Rothermel. "An employment-based health service program designed to assist in the identification and resolution of a broad range of employee personal concerns that may affect job performance. These programs deal with situations such as substance abuse, marital problems, family troubles, stress and domestic violence, as well as health education and disease prevention. The assistance may be provided within the organization or by referral to outside resources."

An Employee Assistance Programme is an arrangement for employee benefit provide counselling, referrals, advice and suggestion to solve the stressful issues and cost is borne by the organization. The services are provided free of costs or partly. These may include the problems of personal, health, family, marital relationship, and substance abuse. The services are usually provided by a third-party if experts are not available from employees of the organization. When it is conducted by third party, the company receives only information regarding the services offered by the experts and personal details and services given kept confidential.

An employee assistance program (EAP) is voluntary efforts made by the organization for assistance of employees with the help of expert agencies that provides a variety of support programs for the employees. EAPs are aimed mainly at work-related, personal and problems originated those affect the morale and job performance in an organization. In present time the leading organizations are taking interest in EAPs due to high level of competition under globalization. At workplace the employees were facing problems of drinking, drugs, smoking and such others. So to solve these problems the concept of the EAP originated in later first half of twentieth century and it picked up momentum in second half of twentieth century mainly in seventies. Since then, EAPs have evolved and many organizations adopted this to deal with a variety of problems such as hypertension, drugs, alcoholic, poor health, marital problems, works stress, financial and legal difficulties, and family disputes.

The Employee Assistance program (EAP) is both an educational and presentational program. It is also a **confidential** counselling and referral service available as a benefit to employees and their dependants. EAPs are plans that help in identifying and resolving issues faced by employees through short-term counselling, referrals to specialized experts outsider or internal experts of the organizations, and follow-up services. In an ideal situation, the employees are expected to come to workplace with unoccupied mind, and work at their best capacity to meet the performance standards. But it is fact that they are facing a lot of problems at their home in their families relating different issues. Their minds are preoccupied with those problems and they are bound to bring them at workplace. This situation affects the workers, performance, organization and reputation in the long run. It is impossible to prevent the employees' problems to zero level but with the help of EAP the employees are provided help or assistance so that these can be controlled or prevented to a good extent.

With this intention, many organizations started with this programme and many are interested in future to start for their employees. They have trained their managers and supervisors so that the behavioural problems can be taken care of properly to avoid adverse effects on health, performance and productivity. With the changing scenario the modern EAP systems are designed to provide services not only for personal and health problems but for other problems such as marriage counselling, crisis planning, extra marital relationship, depression, stress, financial difficulties, illness among family or co-workers, children education and their career and pre-retirement planning. Some of them have gone one step ahead and include the problems of eldercare issues, AIDS and HIV, natural disasters, and workers education, and workplace violence. In future the scope of EAP is definitely going to expand with the increasing complexity of life.

The main feature of an EAP is that it is a fee free service to employees and their immediate dependants, either offered through experts of the company or a third party, that helps employees maintain a balance between work and life. The focus for employees is on their physical, mental, emotional health and well-being. EAPs focus on helping employees when they experience problems in their lives and interested to avail service of counsellors. The major problems for which the assistance is being provided in India and abroad by leading organization in public and private sectors are many. EAPs offer services to employees through face to face interaction between employees and counsellors individually at the appointed time, telephonically if the meeting is not possible due to distant locations, on line, supply of study materials etc. Any of the methods can be selected by the employees for assistance. EAPs are required to maintain confidential data as per the policy in accordance with privacy laws and professional ethics. A manager finds that there is need to refer to the experts for assistance then he may refer an employee to the EAP counsellor. Availing EAP assistance service may be used by employees to maintain the proper balance of work and personal life.

10. ADVANTAGES OF EAP

Employee assistance programme was launched by some of the organization with the interest to solve the problems of employees related to work and personal. The management was interested to manage the workforce more effectively so that the overall effectiveness of the organization can improve in the stiff competitive situation in the market. A lot of efforts are put by the management in this direction for arranging counsellors, counselling sessions and other related facilities. In the beginning it was started with the work related and personal problems. But with the demanding time, the scope of employee counselling programme extended beyond these problems. From this programme there are many benefits to the employees, family members, society, organization etc. The main advantages of EAP are explained below:

For Employees

The main advantages from EAP to employees are following:

(a) Employees get relived from the problems through this.
(b) All depression, distress and psychological problems are solved.
(c) Employees feel relaxed and get satisfaction at work place and in life.
(d) The employees get trigger for motivation towards work, organization and life.
(e) Level of commitment and performance of employees improve.
(f) Quality of performance and productivity of employees go high.
(g) Ultimately these may contribute in incentives, development, increments and promotion of employees.

For organization

The main advantages of EAP to organization are following:

(a) Lower medical costs on employees for their wellness.
(b) Easily maintain satisfied manpower in the organization.
(c) Helps managers to concentrate on their main activities and not on counselling alone.
(d) High level of commitment of employees towards their jobs and organization.
(e) Reduced absenteeism, labour turnover and other related problems in organization.
(f) Healthy working environment is created.
(g) High quality of performance and productivity of employees.
(h) Profitability of the organization goes high.
(i) It is a cost management tool.
(j) Helps to attract better employees and retain them easily.
(k) Overall effectiveness of the organization improves in the business and markets.
(l) Finally the reputation goes high in the industry.

11. SUBSTANCE ABUSE IN THE WORKPLACE

Substance abuse, also known as drug abuse or alcohol abuse, refers to a maladaptive pattern of use of a substance that is not considered dependent and useful for health in nonmedical contexts. Some of the drugs most often associated with this term include alcohol, amphetamines, cocaine, heroin, marijuana, or nicotine. Addiction is the same irrespective of the drugs used. Alcohol or drugs abusers are those who use these regularly despite of recurrent social, interpersonal, and legal problems as a result of alcohol/drug use. Harmful use causes either physical or mental damage. The user becomes addict of alcohol or drugs. They find comfortable with the drugs and become dependent on them. Dependence is at such a point that stopping is very difficult and causes severe physical and mental reactions from withdrawal.

The employees come from different backgrounds from various parts of the country and even now from different countries also. The environment where they live affects a lot on the habits of people. Some of the people get these habits in early age and become habitual to use intoxicant substances which are not useful for health. They learn from their family members, friends and relatives to use these items. The uses of such items vary from area to area. Mainly alcohol is used by the worker because it is cheaper than other drugs and easily available in locality. In western countries the use of alcohol and drugs is more comparatively. The occasional use of drugs is not going to affect much but here concern is for regular use and in more quantity. The use of such items in present complex situation is increasing day by day and it affects all concerned badly.

The problems created due to drugs abuses may include many diseases such as:

Abdominal pain, amnesia, anesthetic, anxiety, blood pressure, botulism, breathing, cancer, chest pain, coma, cough, delirium, depression diarrhea, discharge, dizziness, heart disease, heart rate, hepatitis, weight loss, jaundice, trauma etc. The disease affects the mind and body of the workers. They come under depression or stress. When they come to work place then all stresses are brought at the work place also. The workers under stress are not in position to perform due to their physical and mental positions. They are not in position to give attention to the work due to sickness and like to commit mistakes. It may lead to accidents and even fatal accidents. The quality of performance and total output go down. Unnecessary the production or operation costs increase drastically. At work place the workers behaviour becomes intolerable. They get involved in quarrels, disputes, arguments, indiscipline as these are undesirable things at work place. Finally the work, environment, and relationship all are adversely affected.

Due to loss of work, health and life everybody is worried to get rid of abuses of drugs. Individual, family members, relatives, employers and government are interested to check the uses of drugs so that people can work in healthy environment. Efforts are being but in this direction but nothing could be achieved substantially. The leading organizations are conducting EPA programmes through which they want to provide assistance to the employees, educate those regarding abuses and helping them to leave the habits of drug consumption. The uses drugs at workplace has been banned and disciplinary actions were taken against the defaulters. In most of the countries such acts have been enacted to check the abuses. If implemented properly and proper assistance are provided then the workers would be saved from abuses of drugs definitely.

12. MENTAL HEALTH PROBLEMS

The employees are facing different types of problems such as personal, family, health and performance and substance abuse. These problems are having impact on the body and mind of the employees. Over and above they are under pressure due to responsibility, accountability, meeting targets. Due to all these things the workers get disturbed mentally and physically. They are under depression and stress. It causes the mental illness. Mental health problems can range from relatively minor worry relating do different issues to serious mental breakdowns in which the individual concerned appears to lose total control on thinking and action. The different types of mental illness are there faced by workers in medical terms. It is a very disturbing situation to the workers and employers. It does not mean the employee is suffering due to illness but social stigma is also added to that in the society. It cannot be tolerated in the long run because the impact is very heavy on all concerned. The mental illness affects the body and mind and due to that he is not in position to do the work properly. It leads to lack of interest in jobs, lack of control over body and decision making, poor performance, absenteeism, accidents, death, loss of work, increasing operation costs, and overall lower profitability. Personally the employees get early retirement, financial and social difficulties, family relationships etc., are badly affected.

Mental health problems have become one of the leading problems for all concerned including individual, family, society, employers and the nation. Everybody is concerned for solution of this problem. It has become necessary to maintain good mental health at the workplace so that the adverse effects to business, society and employees can be controlled or avoided further. The poor mental health should be tackled at workplace with sincere efforts. With the present complex situation at workplace the number of persons suffering from mental health problems is increasing day by day across the world. It is a source of anxiety and panic at workplace. There is no exception that the number is increasing in only one country. It is adding to the burden of our society and national economy. It is to be taken care of properly and timely. All these are adding up to a need for incorporating a well informed programme for providing assistance to the employee so that they can get rid of such problems to a good extent.

Through employee assistance programme the employees have been referred to counsellors and experts for help or treatment. They have noticed that the mentally ill employees faced the following problems:

(a) Lack of control over mind and body.

(b) Involved in indecent acts such as crime, rape and incest.

(c) Lack of sexual fitness and poor marital relationship and divorce.

(d) Depression, quarrelling and suicide.

(e) Harassment of family members or children.
(f) Sexual harassment at workplace.
(g) Poor relationship at work, in family and society.
(h) Difficulty in adjustment with others.
(i) Financial and legal problems.

In India a high percentage of employees are coming from rural areas with agriculture background. The financial condition of their family is not good so they face a lot of difficulties in life. It may become one of the major factors for depression and stress. When they face mental illness then they often turn to temples and shrines, tantriks and not to doctors. Some social workers are trying to change this by focusing their efforts on the society relating to such problems. Government is also interested to check this problem but so far nothing concrete has been done.

Treatment and support for mentally ill employees is being provided in *psychiatric hospitals, clinics* or other *community mental health services.* In many countries services it is being provided on the basis of individual problems, independence and choice to regain his meaningful life. The problems of mental health are treated through psychotherapy, medication, counselling. Here the concerned topic is related to employees' assistance and to tackle this situation the efforts have been put by the leading organization though employee assistance programme through which the employees are facing mental health problems are referred by their managers to the counsellors or medical experts for treatment. They are also authorized to approach personally so that time and efforts are saved. The experts provide their services to deal with the problems of the employees through discussion, tests and treatments. Over and above the governments in different countries also have taken initiatives to deal with the situations promptly. American with Disabilities Act of 1990, and Mental Health Parity act of 1996 have been passed by USA government in this line to deal with the situation. In developed and developing countries the governments are interested to bring such laws which can deal with the problems of mental health at work place in future.

13. APPROACH TOWARDS EMPLOYEE PROBLEM SOLUTION

The problems of employees are accepted as unnecessary and unavoidable thing and these affects the personal mind, body, thinking, performance, relationship, personal life etc. It is to be dealt very carefully because the problems are giving very harmful effects to the employees, their family and organization. The proper approach towards problem solution can handle the situation and can prevent or control and bad effects of employees problems. For problem solution the EAPs approach should keep the following guidelines in mind:

(a) Human Resource as a Very Valuable Resource: The employees are very valuable for the organization. Without happy and motivated manpower nothing can be done as desired. It cannot be overlooked. The interest of employees should be considered on top priority and it should be considered that any favour in this direction for employees' problem solution is done would have positive impact on the overall performance of the organization.

(b) Personal Problems are Defined as Performance Problems: No doubt, the personal problems affect the performance of the employees and organization. When it is to be defined it should be defined as operational problems and not as personal problem specifically. It is going to affect the employee psychologically. The supervisor should monitor the performance of employees and where it is required to assist them in performance. The employee would accept it willingly and work would not be affected.

(c) Proper Referral of Employees: When the problems are identified with the specific employee, then he should be referred to the experts for counselling, treatment etc. The case can be referred by the managers, supervisors, union representatives and self. There should not be restriction that only the manager can refer the case. The trade union representatives also should be motivated to come forward for help in find out the problems for early solution. The main objective is solution of the problems and not procedure to follow.

(d) Providing Mental Health Insurance: The employees and their family should be provided mental health benefits so that the problem is dealt properly. It should be provided with the employee benefit packages where the facilities for treatment and referral are not available with the small and medium size of companies. The financial burden on employee is taken care of through this help.

(e) Avoid Hiring Problematic Employees: The management should take proper care in recruitment and selection that the employees should be selected without any chronic disease or problem. Proper psychological and medical tests are to be conducted to avoid the problematic employees. It would help to prevent the problems of employees and save time of the management.

(f) Proactive Approach of the Management: The employees facing the problems may be due to personal or job related reasons. The management should not consider it a burden on the organization. They should not take action only when the problems have taken place. But the approach should be proactive and efforts should be there to prevent such problems for future.

These are some of the points the management should follow in EAP programme. There may be more point also. If these are taken care of the approach would be proper. EAP would be more effective to deliver the goods for which it has been launched.

14. EMPLOYEE HEALTH PROMOTION OR WELL-BEING

Health is wealth. It means according to the Concise Oxford English Dictionary, 11th edition, health means no illness or injury; the ability to cope with everyday activities; and a good mental and physical condition. Health as a state of completes physical, mental and social well-being and does not only consist of the absence of diseases and infirmities. - The World Health Organization (WHO) On the other hand, wealth is defined as availability of various types of assets in possession. It means the health is considered as wealth in our life due to state of complete physical, mental and social well-being of persons. The healthy persons enjoy joy and happiness in their life with all rich resources. Without wealth the life is full of difficulties, worries, sickness and stress.

It is summarized from this statement that if a person can maintain himself healthy then he can earn wealth and live happily otherwise not. The health is to be maintained by preventing problems, diseases, and accidents. It goes true that prevention is better than cure. It has been realized in our society and workplace also. At work the people are working and that is considered the most important resource to utilize other resources like machine, money, materials etc., to generate wealth further. In the present situation it has been accepted that it is manpower if maintained healthy, happy and motivated the desired results can be achieved otherwise the question does not arise. A lot of research has been done in this field for maintaining and promoting health of the employees. Governments also enacted various laws across the world to cure, prevent and educate employees regarding their health. In India there are provisions regarding health, safety, insurance, compensation, medical facilities etc., to maintain the workforce healthy and support them by providing various facilities in this line.

The health of employees affects their body, mind, personal life, work performance, relationship and level of commitment towards the organization. Finally it contributes in good performance, profits and reputation of the unit. It has been reported by business units that after health promotion programmes the productivity has increased up to 5 % which is a very good impact. Worldwide leading corporate units have started taking initiatives for this and started various activities for curing, preventing problems and promoting employees health. Some of the experts suggested and leading organizations took initiatives to provide facilities for employees, On the basis of that the main activities for promoting employees health are exercise and physical fitness, nutrition and weight control, regular medical check-up, substance abuse programme, communicable disease etc. These are explained below:

(a) Exercise and Physical Fitness

The management has taken initiative in many organizations worldwide for exercise and physical fitness of the employees. They focus on exercises that keep the employees physical fit. A physically fit employee finds himself in good condition to perform to his best capacity. Due to exercise many lifestyle problems can be controlled. Physical exercise is defined as a bodily activity that enhances or maintains *physical fitness* and overall *health* and well-being of a person. The different types of exercises are performed for various reasons stretching, pushups, yoga, cycling, running, jogging, swimming, skipping, playing various games, weightlifting etc. Frequent and regular physical exercise helps in improving the condition by controlling blood pressure, sugar level, heart attacks, obesity, indigestion problems, depression etc. It also improves mental and physical health, positive attitude, self-esteem, physical figure and sex appeal. Finally, it brings happiness to the individual going for regular exercises. For exercise and maintaining physical fitness the following steps are to be taken:

(i) Creating awareness regarding importance of physical fitness and exercises: The management of the company should take initiative for creating awareness regarding importance of physical fitness and role of exercises through lectures conducted by physical trainers, experts internal or external at regular intervals. It should remind them the important of it. The benefits of it should be highlighted so that they can enjoy in future.

(ii) Motivation of employees: The employees should be motivated to attend regular classes of physical fitness and avail the facilities provided by employers. They should be provided with participation certificate, physical fitness competition and prizes on annual basis and may be considered in their assessment under heading of physical fitness. It would definitely induce them to taken interest in it.

(iii) Providing facilities for physical exercises: The employers are providing and if not then they should provide the facilities for physical exercises for their employees within premises if possible. If not within compass then at the nearest place arrangement should be there or should tie up with the community resources in the locality. The facilities like gymnasium, table tennis and lawn tennis courts, play grounds, health club membership, availability of sports kits and equipment, appointed trainers and supporting staff. These facilities can be made available to the employees when they are not on work. All necessary arrangements should be made for this purpose. Timely the sports events should be conducted within the company and should participate in outside competitions.

(b) Nutrition and Weight Control

Nutrients are very essential and important in our lives. Our body performs many activities and for that purpose energy is needed. For that the food that gives required calories is needed. Without energy the activities cannot be performed properly. The balance of energy in calorie is to be maintained. According to the research, the calories required for male per day is approximately 2400 and for female 2000 respectively. We eat different types of food items those give different level of calories to our body. The food items like bread, cereal, rice, and grams etc., which give us nutrients such as vitamin B, vitamin E, fiber, and iron are more preferred items by dieticians. Fruits and vegetables consist of complex and simple carbohydrates. Other food items like meat, fish, butter, ice-creams, sweets, cakes, chocolates, processed cheese, potato chips provide more calories some of them are rich in fats and add to cholesterol and sugar. Fats and sugar are not nutrients and they are harmful in the long run definitely. The dieticians advise to avoid such food stuffs in large quantity. It affects the functioning of our body. **Nutrition** explains the relationship between physiological function and the food items we eat.

Eating habits affects a lot to our body. Eating types of foods should be known to everyone because these help us to live a healthy life. We should take balanced food with full of nutrients helps to prevent having diseases and keeps us healthy. Food items lower and increase the risks to life and it depends on the type of food items we take. Eating habits of taking less or more quantity also affects our body calorie balance. In addition to that the food we take nowadays is more of junk food. Working people, school children and others consume more quantity of junk foods such as burger, sandwich, samosa, chips, pakodas, dosa, idlis, vadas, dosas, upma, pongal, bonda, bajjis, pakoras, thalis, chicken, mutton, rajma wraps & rolls, milkshakes, doner kebab, dum biryani, pao bhaji, stuffed parath, as noodles, pizzas etc.

The junk food is full of taste, salt, sugar, fats. It is readily available in the markets and working places. These are more convenient for use and use often. With the time we become addicted to the junk food. The junk food does not provide us calories and it is not nutrients. It does not give any energy to our body and in the long run we gain unnecessary weight. Our body is badly affected by tiredness, anxiety, blood pressure, diabetes, heart attacks, depression and indigestion. Nowadays there are chances of heart attacks, hypertensions and diabetes in young age also. The situation is very critical. It is to be tackled very soon because it is poisoning our body system. Keeping in view the experts suggested to the management of the companies to take proper steps regarding proper nutrition of employees and control over their weight. The following suggestions have been advocated in this direction:

(i) Creating awareness regarding nutrition and obesity: The efforts should be put by the management of the company to create awareness regarding nutrition and obesity. The information is to be given regarding food items, their impact and contribution in our balanced food, each group of food items. Further, the dieting habits and their effects are to be explained. The effects of food items taken, number of times food taken in a day, quantity taken in our body is to be properly explained. The obesity, causes of obesity, and steps to check the obesity should be explained with proper care. It should be explained by the dieticians and medical experts regularly in classrooms with the help of videos.

(ii) Nutrient balanced food to be provided: At workplace in medium and large size of the companies, canteens and cafeterias are made available for employees for their meals and refreshments. At this point the management should make sure that the food items are of required nutrients of low calories is to be provided. As a preventive measure it should be tried. Junk food is to be prohibited strictly in the premises. Proper care should be taken by the in-charge so that proper meal is served and in time only. This would check the unnecessary food items, eating habits and timing also. Further, if the management is interested then the employees should not be allowed to bring their packed lunch or to bring from outside. This definitely would check the food and eating habits.

(c) Regular Medical Checkup of Employees

In this the approach of the management is reactive and proactive both. The efforts are put to provide facilities for regular medical checkup of all employees so that the condition of all parts of the body becomes clear. If any problems are diagnosed then remedial action can be taken. Generally, we do not go to expert or doctor for treatment if the situation is not critical. We do not know even our problems also. In regular checkups such unknown problems can be identified and existing problems can be controlled through medication or treatment. It is well understood by the corporate sector that medical facilities like regular medical checkup of employees in present complex stressful situation do not go unrewarded. It impacts positively in maintaining a healthy working force. It has been suggested by the government and other governing bodies to take care of health though various measures and one of them is medical checkup.

The big organizations with more number of employees are mainly involved in providing such facilities like Indian railway, defence services, ONGC, Tata group companies. They are having their clinics, laboratories and hospitals to provide all type of medical facilities. Medium size of organizations are having tie up with outsider agencies to provide medical checkup, treatment and hospital facilities. The need for regular check up is strongly felt in the stressful life. According to ASSOCHAM report suggested that employee health care should be promoted as its introduction can improve chronic and lifestyle diseases of India Inc. Employees leading healthy lifestyles tend to take lower sick leaves with improved work performance and increased productivity that reduces overall costs of the organization. It suggests government to provided direct and indirect support in form of subsidies; tax breaks etc., to those companies that are offering preventative healthcare facilities to their employees by offering in different methods. For providing regular medical facilities the following steps are suggested:

(i) Formulation of regular medical checkup policy: The HR manager should take initiative to prepare regular medical checkup policy in consultation with medical experts and other managers. The policy should include need for regular medical checkup, timing for checkup, types of checkups as per the nature of jobs, procedure for checkup, referral procedure for treatment and prevention of problems, types of facilities available at centre location, responsibility for implementation and follow up of medical checkups. The special care should be taken on every aspect of the policy which would help in proper implementation.

(ii) Types of regular medical checkups: To keep the employees fit in the working environment the types of checkups are to be decided. It can be decided by the medical experts internal or external. The types of tests include a number of tests for eye, blood, sugar level, hypertension, heart, liver, kidney, urine, stool, brain, stomach, pregnancy etc. The tests would help to find out whether the functions of the body are proper or not. On the basis of test report the preventive or corrective treatments can be given to the employees. If not done then the problems would continue for the longer period and going to add to more harm to the health of the employees.

(iii) Implementation of medical checkup policy: The policy formulated for check should be implemented properly. For this the responsibility of medical expert or medical assistant should be fixed. The laboratory facilities are to be arranged internally or externally. The policy should be communicated properly to all concerned. The tests are to be carried out regularly and on the basis of suggestions, referral or treatments ar to be provided. The effects of tests on health are to be reviewed time to time to ensure that the programme is more effective.

(d) Creating Awareness Regarding Substance Abuse

To keep the employees healthy and get their contribution in achievement of objectives, it is necessary to save them from abuses of substances which are harmful to the human body. The employees get habit of consuming harmful items and slowly they become use to those. It becomes very difficult for them to get rid of such substances. The harmful substances when used regularly affect the health of the employees. Such substances are biddi, cigarettes, tobacco, gutkha, khaini, liquor, ganja, opium, charas, brown sugar, heroin, cocaine, marijuana, or nicotine. These substances affect working of heart, kidney, liver, brain, veins, fertility and sex of employees. These become the causes of many diseases such as cancer, heart attack, depression, mental disorder, digestion, tiredness, anxiety, hypertension etc. The health of employees is badly affected. It is not acceptable in the organizations. They are not in position to give their output at their full capacity and add to costs of the organizations. It is to be taken care of by the management. Regarding this the employees should be made aware that the substances, harms our body and due to them our whole life. For this purpose the help of experts should be taken to create awareness regarding abuses of substances. The efforts should be there to help employees in stopping consumption of such items through lectures, seminars, videos. Sincere and regular efforts only can help employees to leave uses of these items and improve health.

(e) Creating Awareness Regarding Communicable Diseases

Communicable diseases are those diseases which can be communicated from one person or animal to another. Communicable diseases are also known as infectious diseases. The communicable disease takes place when one healthy person comes in contact with a patient. A disease is said to be communicable if it spreads from one person to another. A disease is said to be non-communicable if it does not spread from one person to another. The communicable diseases can spread through food, air, water and contact from one to another person. These diseases are caused due to transmission of viruses, bacteria, fungi, protozoa and parasites. There are three main categories of communicable diseases; gastrointestinal, sexual, and respiratory. Communicable gastrointestinal diseases, for example are cholera (an intestinal disease caused by a parasite), attack the organs of the digestive system. Gastrointestinal diseases are usually the result of consuming contaminated food or water.

The diseases transmitted through sexual contact are called sexually transmitted diseases (STDs), sexually transmitted infection (STIs), or venereal disease (VD). They are also transmitted through blood donation, using infected needles etc. The disease transmitted through air and water is not preventable whereas through contact the diseases are preventable. The diseases become fatal if timely action is not taken for detection and treatment. The most common *communicable diseases* worldwide are cholera, yellow fever, anthrax, H1NI, plague, aid, botulism, brucellosis, diphtheria, q-fever, malaria, rabies, chancroid, pertussis, smallpox, leprosy, syphilis, poliomyelitis, influenza legionellosis, rubella, hepatitis, invasive meningococcal disease, tuberculosis, tularemia, avian influenza (bird flu), hydatid disease, yersinosis, tetanus, rickettsial diseases, hepatitis c, typhoid, paratyphoid, mumps, cryptosporidiosis etc.

In our routine work the employees come in contact with other persons directly or indirectly. It may transmit the germs or virus of communicable disease. This affects the health very badly. For this purpose the management should discuss with the medical experts for prevention and cure of communicable disease. They should be made aware regarding use of items of patients and effects of it. They should be educated regarding sexual contact with a number of partners and bad effects of that. They should be informed regarding safe methods to have sex. Time to time the lectures, seminars and videos should be used to educate the employees regarding communicable diseases, causes, effects of diseases and prevention methods. The awareness regarding this would definitely prevent employee to get communicable disease and help them to maintain their healthy body.

15. CONCLUSION

Employee counselling is a psychological health care intervention which can take many forms. Its aim is to assist both the employer and employee by intervening with an active problem-solving approach to tackling the problems at hand. Due to a number of problems faced by employee their health, mind, performance and relationship are affected adversely. The final result is poor productivity. These costs increase substantially when lost productivity resulting from inefficiency and low level of involvement of employees in jobs. The need for counselling has been felt to solve the problems of employees through discussion so that their effectiveness at workplace can be increased. Few organizations can now afford to ignore the consequences associated with employees' psychological health. It gives an opportunity to employees to discuss their problems for solution in a strictly confidential and supportive atmosphere. In counselling the employees gets help in the form of information, guidance, coaching and suggestions for problems solution.

The employees are facing different types of problems at workplace and the situation of employee is very critical and going to give multi-dimensional adverse effects. It management should not take chance to ignore this situation. If done so the organization is to suffer. Organization cannot not afford for this. The approach of the management should be proactive and reactive both towards its employees. The interest of the management should be there to recruit, train, motivate and maintain the satisfied workforce. For this purpose the problems of the employees should be looked into. The efforts should be there to find out the causes of the problems of employees and steps should be there for providing help. It can be done with the help of employees counseling to a good extent if timely actions are taken by the management. Counselling is one of the mechanisms used by the management for human resource development. In prevailing situation, the importance of employees' counselling is increasing. The future role of counselling would be more important. On the basis of the study of various definitions and thoughts of various experts, the main characteristics of employee counselling are following:

(a) Service offered to employees.

(b) Service is conducted in organization.

(c) Focus is on problems faced by employees.

(d) Objective of counselling is problem solution.

(e) Employee counselling serves all concerned.

(f) Employee counselling is a continuous process.

(g) Role of counsellor is important in counselling.

(h) Half-knowledge is a dangerous thing, is completed through counselling.

The employees faces a number of problems from different areas such as personal, family, society, job, performance, working environment, interpersonal relationship and career development. These problems are creating hardships for employees at workplace. Experts suggest the use of counselling for this purpose. It has been used by the managers in most of the leading organizations with the objectives to understand the problems of employees, to advise, guide and suggest ways to solve the problems of employees, to improve satisfaction level of employees, motivation, level of commitment, to manage the employees more effectively, to maintain satisfied, talented and motivated workforce, and to improve productivity, performance of the organization as a whole, profits effectively, and image in the markets. In counselling process the support, service, help, advice, referral, medical treatment etc., have been provided through employee assistance programme, health care programme and wellness.

An Employee Assistance Programme is an arrangement for employee benefit provide counselling, referrals, advice and suggestion to solve the stressful issues and cost is borne by the organization. The services are provided free of costs or partly. These may include the problems of personal, health, family, marital relationship, and substance abuse. The services are usually provided by a third-party if experts are not available from employees of the organization. When it is conducted by third party, the company receives only information regarding the services offered by the experts and personal details and services given kept confidential. Employees' mental health and substance abuse are mainly taken care of in assistance programme. From this programme there are many benefits to the employees, family members, society, organization etc. The approach of employees assessment programme is both proactive and reactive as demanded by the situation.

The health of employees affects their body, mind, personal life, work performance, relationship and level of commitment towards the organization. Finally it contributes in good performance, profits and reputation of the unit. It has been reported by business units that after health promotion programmes the productivity has increased up to 5 % which is a very good impact. Worldwide leading corporate units have started taking initiatives for this and started various activities for curing, preventing problems and promoting employees health. Some of the experts suggested and leading organization took initiatives to provide facilities for employees, On the basis of that the main activities for promoting employees health are exercise and physical fitness, nutrition and weight control, regular medical check-up, substance abuse programme, communicable disease etc.

16. QUESTIONS FOR REVIEW

1. Define employee counselling and explain its main characteristics.
2. Highlight the objectives of employee counselling in detail.
3. Employee counselling is considered as an HRD intervention. Discuss.
4. Discuss the types of problems faced by employees and prepare a list of those problems.
5. What do you know about employee counselling programme and discuss the need for it?
6. Explain the main components or activities of employee counselling programme in detail.
7. Discuss essential conditions for conducting employee counselling programme in detail.
8. What is employee assistance programme? Explain the need for it in organizations.
9. Highlight the main advantages of EAPs for employees and organizations.
10. What are the substances that affect the health of employees and diseases are acquired when these are used regularly? Discuss
11. Define the mental health of employees and its effects of working on them. Discuss the problems faced by mentally ill employees during their work.
12. What should be the approach of management towards problems solution under EAP and what points should be kept in mind in their approach?
13. For promotion of employee health the main focus of the programme should be on activities like exercise and physical fitness, nutrition and weight control, regular medical check-up, substance abuse programme, communicable disease etc. Do you agree with this statement?
14. For regular medical check of employees for maintain good health what steps would you suggest as an expert to the management? Explain
15. Is it necessary to create awareness of employees regarding harmful substances and their abuses, communicable disease under health promotion programme of employees?
16. Short notes on the following:
    (a) Substance abuse at workplace
    (b) Mental health problems
    (c) Counselling and psychological counselling
    (d) Documentation of counselling programme
    (e) Education employees regarding problems faced
    (f) Job related problems
    (g) Role of a counselor
    (h) Focus on problem solution and not person
    (i) Communicable diseases and their impacts on health

(j) Blood pressure and sugar level checkup
(k) Exercise and physical fitness.
(l) Facilities for sports and exercises.
(m) Referral of employees to experts by various parties

17. OBJECTIVE QUESTIONS

1. Counselling is one of the mechanisms used by the management for human resource development. In prevailing situation, the importance of employees' counselling is increasing. The future role of counselling would be more important too. Do you agree with this statement?

   (a) Fully agree (b) Partially agree
   (c) Partially disagree (d) Fully disagree
   (e) Cannot say anything

2. "The term counsellling covers all types of two person situations in which one person, the client is helped to adjust more effectively to himself and his environment" Who defined this?

   (a) Webster Dictionary (b) Strong
   (c) Wellington (d) Robinson
   (e) None of them

3. Employee counselling is a vehicle of communication to provide assistance in a practical and effective way to the problem affected employees. Through this efforts are put to get employees relived from difficulties and motivate them to utilize their potential for contributing in accomplishment of individual performance and objectives of the organization in interests of all concerned. Do you agree with this statement?

   (a) Fully agree (b) Partially agree
   (c) Partially disagree (d) Fully disagree
   (e) Cannot say anything

4. On the basis of the study of various definitions and thoughs of various experts, the main characteristics of employee counselling are following:

   (a) Service offered to employees.
   (b) Service is conducted in organization.
   (c) Focus is on problems faced by employees.
   (d) Objective of counselling is problem solution.
   (e) All the above

5. Employee counselling has been used by the managers is most of the leading organization with the objectives:
   (a) To understand the problems of employees,
   (b) To advise, guide and suggest ways to solve the problems of employees,
   (c) To improve satisfaction level of employees, motivation, level of commitment,
   (d) All the above
   (e) None of the above
6. In counselling process the support, service, help, advice, referral, medical treatment etc, have been provided through:
   (a) Employee assistance programme,
   (b) Health care programme and wellness
   (c) Both (a) and (b)
   (d) Social security
   (e) Training
7. The employees face a number of problems which creates hardship for employees at workplace are from different areas such as:
   (a) Personal, family, society,
   (b) Job and job performance,
   (c) Working environment,
   (d) Interpersonal relationship and career development.
   (e) All the above
8. Some of the experts suggested and leading organizations took initiatives to provide facilities for employees, On the basis of that the main activities for promoting employees health are:
   (a) Exercise and physical fitness
   (b) Nutrition and weight control
   (c) Regular medical check-up
   (d) Substance abuse programme, communicable disease
   (e) All the above
9. The organization are designing and providing employees counseling programme for their employees with the help of experts and main components of the programme are:
   (a) Identification of Problems
   (b) Educating and counselling of employees
   (c) Direction for assistance and execution of techniques

(d) All the above
(e) None of the above

10. "Strategic analysis, recommendations and consultations throughout an organization to enhance its performance, culture and business success. These enhancements are accomplished by professionally trained behavioral and/or psychological experts who apply the principles of human behavior with management, employees and their families, as well as workplace situations to optimize the organization's human capital." It was advocated by:

(a) Rothermel
(b) Dictionary of HRM
(c) Pace
(d) Willian Armstrong
(e) None of the above

11. Substance abuse, also known as drug abuse or alcohol abuse, refers to a maladaptive pattern of use of a substance that is not considered dependent and useful for health in nonmedical contexts. Some of the drugs most often associated with this term includes:

(a) Alcohol, amphetamines,
(b) Cocaine, heroin, marijuana, or nicotine.
(c) Ganja, charas, opium
(d) All the above
(e) None of the above

12. The mental illness affects the body and mind and due to that he is not in position to do the work properly. It leads to:

(a) Lack of interest in jobs, lack of control over body and decision making,
(b) Poor performance, absenteeism, accidents, death, loss of work,
(c) Increasing operation costs, and overall lower profitability.
(d) Personally the employees get early retirement, financial and social difficulties
(e) All the above

Answer Keys:

Question No.	Answer	Question No.	Answer
1	a	7	e
2	d	8	e
3	a	9	d
4	e	10	a
5	d	11	d
6	c	12	e

PART — 4
HRD CASES

Chapter

Case Study

1. PERFORMANCE MANAGEMENT AT TATA STEEL

The Tata Group of Companies has always believed strongly in the concept of collaborative growth, and this vision has seen it emerge as one of India's and the world's most respected and successful business conglomerates. The Tata Group has traced a route of growth that spans through six continents and embraces diverse cultures. The total revenue of Tata companies, taken together, was $70.8 billion (around ₹ 3,25,334 crore) in 2008-09, with 64.8 per cent of this coming from business outside India. In the face of trying economic challenges in recent times, the Tata Group has steered India's ascent in the global map through its unwavering focus on sustainable development. Over 363,039 people worldwide are currently employed in the seven business sectors in which the Tata Group Companies operate. It is the largest employer in India in the Private Sector. The Tata Group of Companies has business operations (114 companies and subsidiaries) in seven defined sectors – Materials, Engineering, Information Technology and Communications, Energy, Services, Consumer Products and Chemicals. Tata Steel with its acquisition of Corus has secured a place among the top ten steel manufacturers in the world and it is the Tata Group's flagship Company. Other Group Companies in the different sectors are – Tata Motors, Tata Consultancy Services (TCS), Tata Communications, Tata Power, Indian Hotels, Tata Tea and Tata Chemicals.

The Tata Steel Group has always believed that mutual benefit of countries, corporations and communities is the most effective route to growth. Tata Steel has built an imposing presence around the globe. With the acquisition of Corus in 2007 leading to commencement of Tata Steel's European operations, the Company today is the tenth largest steel producer in the world with employees' strength of above 81,000 across five continents. During the financial year 2009-10, the Group recorded deliveries of 24 million tonnes against 28 million tonnes in the previous year, the decline being a reflection of the global economic slowdown mainly in the UK and European operations. The Group recorded a turnover of ₹ 1,02,393 crores in 2009 - 2010. The Company has always had significant impact on the economic development in India and now seeks to strengthen its position of pre-eminence in international domain by continuing to lead by example of responsibility and trust.

Tata Steel's overseas ventures and investments in global companies have helped the Company create a manufacturing and marketing network in Europe, South East Asia and the Pacific-rim countries. The Group's South East Asian operations comprise Tata Steel Thailand, and Nat Steel Holdings, which is one of the largest steel producers in the Asia Pacific with presence across seven countries. Corus is Europe's second largest steel producer. With main steelmaking operations in the UK and the Netherlands, Corus supplies steel and related services to the construction, automotive, packaging, mechanical engineering and other markets worldwide. Corus comprises three operating Divisions, Strip Products, Long Products and Distribution & Building Systems and has a global network of sales offices and service centres, employing around 37,000 people worldwide. Headquartered in Bangkok, Tata Steel Thailand is a major steel producer in Thailand and is the largest producer of long steel products with a manufacturing capacity of 1.7 mtpa. NatSteel Holdings is headquartered in Singapore and is a leading supplier of premium steel products for the construction industry. It became a 100% subsidiary of Tata Steel in February 2004. NSH produces about 2 MT of steel products annually across its regional operations.

Management of the company believes in collaborative growth and it has become most successful and respected business conglomerates. The company is having business across the world and at present it is facing tough competitions from other MNCs. Though, the business is governed by business ethics. The company has used a large portion of equity in philanthropic trusts for the welfare of the society. The Tata brand is one of the favourite brands across the world and it has been ranked 25th most innovative company in the world. It operates its business with mutual benefits of company, community and countries. In India most of the people know Tata Group. The reputation of the groups is very high. In present scenario the competition is faced and it is of very high level. The management is aware of the importance of human resource and it was in the past also.

Since 2008 the business environment in India and abroad has undergone drastically changes. Mainly completion level, technology and economics have changed a lot. Due to low demand and slow down of economy, many companies have become bankrupt. It became a matter of survival. Everyone felt the pinch of financial crisis. Here management felt the need to identity the good and slow performers. Management decided to continue with good performers and motivates the slow performance for VRS. To reduce the production volume, the plants were shutdown for some days of week. The importance of talented, motivated and good performing employees was strongly realized. HR, Head was specially instructed regarding this. No further appointments were made. Efforts were put to improve the effectiveness of manpower and organization as a whole so that the competitive edge can be maintained in the markets across the world in future also.

The responsibility of HR management has been assigned to mange performance consistently. To do so management performed the functions of planning of objectives, fixed performance standards to achieve objectives, communication of objectives and performance standards, counseling, guiding, training and development of needed employees motivation and feedback on performance created healthy work environment, measurement of performance, designed compensation recognition and rewarded system and contributed in production volume, quality, profit and goodwill of the company was mainly concerned with productivity and performance, planning of performance, measurement of performance interest in consistent performance and development. Due to these efforts the company could face the recession period without much difficulty. It got support of employees, working environment of openers, mutual trust, cooperation and team spirit was created. It could improve, productivity, production, performance of employees reduced operation cost, objectives were fulfilled and could maintain the high reputation of the company across the world. That steel consolidated profit in year 2008-2009 and 2009-2010 improved beyond expectation. It created a solid attachment among employee's management and the company as a whole.

Questions

1. Critically analyse the business environment of Tata steel in year 2008 and 2009?
2. Were the concerns of performance management of Tata steel in prevailing financial crisis proper? Discuss
3. Do you think the functions performed by performance management to sustain productivity and performance were adequate? Comment.
4. If you are appointed as a consultant in that situation what you would have suggested to face the slow down situation, Explain.

2. 360° PERFORMANCE APPRAISALS AT WIPRO

At present Wipro is one of the leaders in information technology industry. It is having business in India and outside of India also. It is nearly 60 years old company. Wipro started as a edible oil producer in 1947 from an old mill founded by Azim Premjis' father under the name Western India Vegetable Products. Its Chairman is Azim H Premji. In 1977 it entered the IT segment and today it has become a multinational company with business in European, American and African countries. From business volume point of view it is the third largest IT services companying India.

Management of Wipro realized the importance of human resource its talents and motivation. That is why it is the first people capability maturity model (pcmm) level company and also first Indian company to adopt six- sigma. It has been ranked third best HR Management Company in India and total strength of employees is nearly one lakh as on today. Management of Wipro is very professional and has framed hr policies for various hr functions.hr polices prepared and implemented at Wipro are manpower planning, internal and external recruitment, intensive training and development, performance appraisal, promotion, transfer, and demotion, job rotation, administration section, grievance handling, kaizen activities, welfare activities, Wipro employee stock option plan (wesop) allows employees to share in the company's success

In present situation Wipro is facing tough competition in national and international markets. It has become for most of the company to take the lead in the market. Management realized the importance of human resource, competencies, motivation, labour productivity and performance of employees. To maintain these things high the management is interested to find out the good and poor performers. For that reason the performance appraisal policy has been adopted. In past the traditional methods for individuals and group appraisals were used. But in present situation the need for proper appraisal is need so that the company can take competitive advantage over its competitors. The performance appraisal policy has been implemented with the objectives like aims of a performance appraisal at Wipro, give feedback on performance to employees., identity employee training needs, document criteria used to allocate organizational rewards, from a basis for personnel decisions: salary increases, promotions, disciplinary actions, etc., provide the opportunity for organizational diagnosis and development, facilitate communication between employee and administrator, and validate selection techniques and human resource policies to meet federal equal employment opportunity requirements.

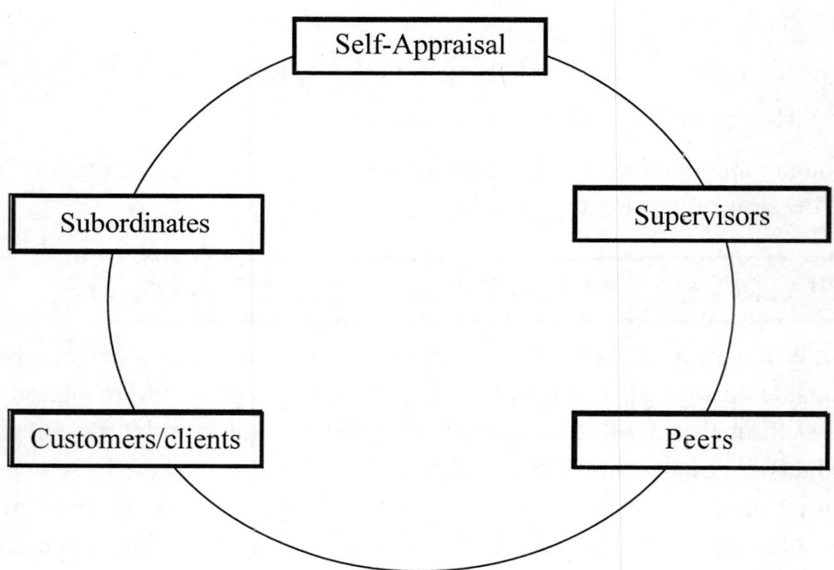

Diagram 22.1: The appraisers in performance appraisal

The focus of the performance appraisal is on measuring and improving the actual performance of the employee and also the future potential of the employee. Its aim is to evaluate what an employee does. Keeping in view the weaknesses of old traditional methods of performance appraisal the management introduced 360 degree performance appraisal methods. Top HR professionals of the company feel that for effective working of this method the essential conditions are: The mission and the objective of the feedback must be clear, employees must be involved early, resources must be dedicated to the process, including top managements time, confidentiality must be assured, and The organization, especially top management, must be committed to the program. It would be very advantageous for the individual employee, team and the whole organization.

To carry out the performance appraisal the responsibility has been assigned to the supervisors and head of the departments. They are instructed to perform the tasks as per the laid down procedure meticulously at specified time. For appraisal purpose in present method the feedbacks are taken from self, subordinates, supervisors, peers, clients and customers. The feedbacks are taken frequently from all these parties. For appraisal purpose it has been decided to appraise the performance yearly basis. Importance is equal to all the feedbacks received from various parties. The appraisal review is carried out in the last for planning, development and training, promotion/demotion, incentives, increments/ wage cuts etc.

The main objectives of this appraisal are to keep the performance of employees in line with the requirement of target accomplishment time to time so that the company can sustain the performance and market share in the market. This way it contributed to get the competitive advantages over arch competitors in markets. Finally, top management feels that 360 degree method of appraisal is in position to meet the objectives of appraisal policy at present and in future too it would be fruitful with required changes.

Questions

1. Do you feel the approach of top level management is proper towards the importance of employees and their performances?
2. Are you satisfied with the objectives of performance appraisal carried out in the company?
3. Critically evaluate the performance appraisal carried out through 360 degree appraisal method at Wipro.
4. Do you feel the current appraisal method would be in position to appraise employees properly and provide competitive benefits to the company in future also? Comment.

3. ASSESSMENT CENTRE

Dolphin International Ltd. is a multinational company having its corporate office in Brazil. Brazil is one of fast developing countries across the world. It is one of the countries of BIRCs group. The economy growth is very good. There are a lot of business and job opportunities in Brazil. It is expected in near future it would be one of the leading economies across the world. DIL was established in a town by an entrepreneur who was an engineer by profession. He worked in some of the leading companies in Brazil for nearly 15 years and later on started his own business. Finally he established DIL. It is nearly 60 years old company. It started its business in the chemical sector. It started doing business very well and slowing it added other units in the same sector. It became of the leading chemical company of the country. The top level management could visualize the opportunities in Brazil and thought for diversification of the business for availing business opportunities and minimizing business risks. Management took help from the leading consultants of the country and made the mind to start new businesses in automobiles, information technology, readymade garments and agro products. The first unit of the new business was established in automobiles industry because the demand of vehicles in very fast developing economy of Brazil started increasing. To avail this opportunity this sector was selected first of all. The company could maintain the consistent performance and profitability of the group.

With sound financial position the company did not face any difficulty and continued with the second, third, fourth and further for expansion. It covered nearly four new sectors with the new business. The locations of their plants were across the country. Within a period of 20 years of new business, the company entered into international business. It opened its branches and located plants in European, African, Latin American and Asian countries. There was a great demand for the trained, talented and experienced manpower across the world. It was very difficult for the management to procure the required type and quality of manpower. To sustain the good and consistent performance management, it was finalized to establish assessment centers for selection and identification of new candidates for different types of jobs in DIL group.

The performance management and appraisal policy were prepared so that these can contribute in higher performance, productivity and profitability of the group. The appraisal objectives are to find out the contribution of employees towards their objectives, behavior during work, strength and weakness of employees, deficiencies in competencies. Further to find out the potentials for future assignments. In brief it is said the appraisal policy is for appraisal of current performance and appraisal of potentials for future development. Keeping in view the objectives, assessment centre has been used for appraisal as modern method. Management has planned and established an assessment centre. Suitable infrastructure facilities like rooms for assessors, administrative office, training or classrooms, facilities assessment techniques arrangement, office automation facilities have been arranged. The assessors have been selected on the basis of their expertise in particular field. From every area one expert has been appointed. Required administrative staff has been place in the assessment centre.

In the beginning of financial year 2009, the MD of the company was worried to fight the slow growth of the sales and business. He called meeting of all directors and discussed the issue to improve performance of employees and selection of talented persons to fill up the vacant positions HR Director was directed to get assessment centre in picking up suitable candidates. GM In charge of assessment centre was called in corporate office and the planning and objectives of the meeting were clearly communicated to him. Next day, GM of assessment centre called the meeting of Head of Department of assessment centre. The issue was discussed for procurement of suitable candidates for various jobs. Everyone was instructed to implement the plan. Administrative manger contracted various Head of Department to find out the number of vacancies. Advertisement were published in leading in leading newspapers to invite applications while deciding the job specifications administrative manager did not discuss with HODs and as per his perception, job specification was published.

According to the plan, a large number of candidates applied. Next month the applicants were instructed to prepare and appear to selection process. On arrival of the applicants they were instructed regarding rules, regulation, types of exercises, time duration and assessment procedure. The communication part was perfect without any doubt. The selection was planned for three days so far lodging, boarding and transportation the suitable arrangements were done. One first day the general and aptitude tests were conducted. Nearly half of the applicants were rejected. Second day psychometric and group discussions were conducted. The psychologist responsible for the test did not report for the duty without informing the GM. The psychometric test could not be conducted. Third day for technical and specialisation area, the test were conducted. One of the technical experts was not informed regarding the programme. He took it in a personal way and felt his ego was hurt. He did not attend the examination duty and went to the medical centre for check up, complaining breathing problem

The test could not be conducted in time. After waiting for one hour, the expert but from different area of specialisation was detailed. During assessment process, the expert could not examine the candidates in their area of specialisation. The candidates had many confusions and arguments with the expert. They made a complaint with GM also. In technical area of instrumentation, the candidates were not available with suitable qualification and experience. The applicants were not examined and in return they also lodge a complaint to GM, assessment centre. In last, out of three days programme only a few candidates were selected. In nutshell, the objectives of the programme could not be achieved. This matter was reported to HR Director. It made him very angry and asked GM to give written explanation of malfunctioning.

Questions

1. MD of the company visualized the business environment and felt the need for better talented people and their performance in present time. Do you agree with him? Comment
2. The GM of assessment centre explained the planning and its objective to HOD of assessment centre. Was he right in his approach?
3. Find out the problems in this case and the persons who were responsible for creating the problems.
4. What were the causes for failure of assessment exercise? Discuss in detail.
5. Being in the position of GM, assessment cen the, what steps you would have taken to have effective assessment of candidates at assessment centre?

4. SELF-PERFORMANCE APPRAISAL AT IBMR BUSINESS SCHOOL

With liberalization of Indian economy many MNCs entered in Indian market from various continents in different industries. The MNCs were from most of the developed countries. Their positions in technology, manpower, finance, manpower and products were very strong. This situation created cut throat competition in the market. The situation for Indian companies was very critical due to tough competition from strong competitiors. It was very difficult to do the business very effectively. It was a matter of survival, grow and excel in the existing businesses. Management of most of the companies felt the need for better productivity and performance of employees. So the requirement of talented and motivated people was strongly felt who can give higher productivity and better performance to get competitive edge over their rivals. It was felt at the government level also. Government took initiatives, universities and Institutions were allowed to go for professional courses so that the competencies of people can be improved to handle the situation very effectively.

With the same objective management of Institute of Business Management planned in this direction to impart professional education in the field of management, computer and mass communication the first unit of Institute of Business Management and Research was founded in 1999 at Hubli, an industrial city of North Karnataka state., Institute of Business Management and Research (IBMR) was envisioned as an Institute, dedicated to benefit careers by developing and delivering study programmes of University that extend beyond the traditional limitation of classroom and emphasizes the broader approach that has a truly global relevance. It started its working with limited programmes from Hubli centre and opened its institutions at Ahmedabad, Bangalore and Gurgaon up to 2009. The faculty and staff members were totally selected on the basis of merit. They were further trained and motivated for their self-development also further through research, publication and participation in different conferences, seminars and workshops. They were provided transportation, lodging, boarding and with registration fees with leave to appear in seminars, conferences and present their research papers.

The institutes provided wonderful facilities for study, placement and research to students and faculty members. The environment created in institutes contributes a good extent to provide platform for their education can career development. It could achieve the objectives very effectively with the team of talented and dedicated persons. The management of institute was further interested to motivate and retain the good performers so that the effectiveness of the organization can be sustained. In this line the self appraisal system was introduced along with assessment of supervisors. The interest of this type of appraisal was that the talents of employees should not go unnoticed. If it is not noticed by the supervisor it can be reported by the employees. At the end of the every academic year assessment of employees have been carried out every year. The self-appraisal report of year 2009 from employees' side is given below:

Table 22.1: IBMR - Self-performance Appraisal (Year 2008-09)

Sl No		Appraisal Criteria Total 100 Marks					
		Perform. Achieved (20 Marks)	Behaviour (20 Marks)	Competency (20 Marks)	Leadership (20 Marks)	Initiatives (20 marks)	Marks Obtained
	Academic Deptt.						
1	Mrs V. Dahiya	18	18	19	18	19	92
2	Mrs Monika G	20	19	19	19	19	96

3	Mrs.Priyanka Gohil	19	20	18	19	18	94
4	Ms Poonam A	18	19	18	18	20	93
5	Ms.Karishma Singh	19	19	19	19	20	96
6	Mrs.Rajlakshmi	19	20	18	20	18	95
7	Mrs. Pragna K	18	19	18	18	18	91
8	Mrs. Kavita Sharma	18	19	19	18	18	92
	Marketing Deptt.						
9	Mr Kiran R K	18	18	19	17	19	91
10	Mr Gaurav Gandhi	19	18	19	19	19	94
11	Mr Ram Bhushan Yadav	19	19	19	19	19	95
12	Ms Jaya Ludhani	19	19	19	19	19	95
13	Mrs. Usha. Chettiar	19	20	19	19	20	97
	Admin Deptt.						
14	Mrs. B. Vidhani	18	19	18	20	19	94
15	Mr. S. Shah	20	19	20	20	19	98
16	Mr. N. Vaishyak	19	19	20	19	20	97
18	Mr. L. Raval	20	19	19	19	20	97
19	Mr.R. Chauhan	18	19	18	18	17	90
20	Mr. Ashok	15	13	15	16	12	71
21	Mr. Bhadresh	19	19	19	19	20	96
22	Mr. Jagat Singh	19	18	19	19	20	95
23	Mr. Deepak	18	19	19	19	19	94
24	Mr. N. Parmar	19	19	20	20	20	98
25	Mr. R. Bhati	19	19	19	19	20	96
26	Mr. N. Bhati	16	18	15	15	16	80
27	Mr. Arvind Bhai	18	18	19	19	19	93
28	Mr Baccharam	19	19	19	19	19	95

Date: Signature of the Appraiser

Place:

When the self appraisal report was prepared and presented to the senior level of management it was not appreciated because the appraisal done by supervisors and self employees were not matching. There was a lot of difference between these two. In some of the cases the differences in scores were from 25 to 30 percents. It was remarked that the appraisal is highly exaggerated and confusing also. The top level management took the rational approach and instructed the manager to go with supervisors' appraisal only. The self-appraisal method took a lot of time in communication, guidance and finally the result was not feasible to implement. Therefore, the effectiveness of self appraisal method of appraisal was very low.

Questions

1. Critically analyse the situation of the case and find out whether assessment done by employees' was on very higher side.
2. The performance appraisal methods accepted by the management were proper or not. Give your comments on this issue.
3. Being an employees of the institute, what do you say whether remarks given by top level management in the last was proper?
4. You are appointed as a consultant to improve the performance appraisal system of the institute, what would you suggest?

5. TEAM BUILDING AND EMPOWERMENT FOR EFFECTIVE PERFORMANCE

Apex Pharmaceutical Company was established in 1955 by a chemist, Mr SK Prajapati. It is located in outskirts of Ahmedabad city, a metro and commercial city of Gujarat state. The major products of the company are drugs and drugs related chemicals. It is having distribution network mainly in western India. It is a very fast developing company with innovative approach. During their routine work it was observed that the lower-level of staff members were not providing cooperation for completion of their tasks. This complaint was made to the managers repeatedly. This way the work was affected. HR manager was interested to improve the performance and effectiveness of the manpower so that the objectives of the organization can be achieved.

The company provided extensive training in HRM to executives, managers, supervisors and office staff. Some of the managers and officers were not happy with work of subordinates, clerks, peons, drivers, sweepers etc. According to them total efficiency cannot be achieved without support from all angles. As part of HRM training programme, few training sessions were conducted for peons and drivers of the company. During the course of training questions pertaining to role, status, functions, duties and responsibility of every person in the company were tackled. It was found that in the context of job role ambiguity, role playing, job stress etc., were the major problems which were affecting the work culture and performance .

According to peons and some drivers it hardly makes any difference at lower level of job as to whether one is serving in a big company or a small one. For big bosses it is a question of higher status, power, money etc., as their jobs, offer them perks and power. They can take important decisions. While encouraging peons for participation, some important suggestion pertaining to time management, came out from peons' angle-allocation of work, perception of their own role and extended responsibilities. They came out with suggestions that every department sends peons for postal services to one and the same courier at different time, but the courier office dispatches all letters after 4-30 p.m. on the same day or the other day. In this situation if only one peon collects letters from different departments and visits the courier office at a specified time, other peons' service can be utilized for more important task. Some peons came out with a suggestion that if they are given mobile telephone number of their own boss, they can convey important message to their boss, when he is out for company's work. Both the suggestions were implemented immediately and during the course of a seminar one peon contacted his boss on mobile telephone and retained a very big and important order of sales. This could be interpreted as an extension of the role of a peon's job.

While discussing about how image and status of the company matters for an employee, it came out with an analysis of very significant event in the life of a peon. A peon's son was kidnapped by terrorist. Relatives and friends consoled him and the family. They also asked him to forget about his son as is beyond the reach of a small man to tackle such a situation or solve such important problems. He contacted Human Resources Manager who along with his team of the Department of Human Resources, filed complaint and did all the legal, social and psychological compliances and assured him that his son will be back within a week. Even though his son was taken away to Punjab border he was back within five days. When police brought peon's son back by a jeep, police superintendent remarked "You need not worry about any calamity for your son again as you are serving in a company which enjoys esteem and status in the society."

While dealing with a drivers' team, a number of suggestions came out during group discussion regarding timely repairing of cars, checking of petrol, oil, water etc. Some of the drivers realised that their own timeliness and punctuality would make their boss more efficient. It matters more when their bosses have to attend important meetings and conference, They also realised that an executive's personal assistant, secretary, clerk and driver or peon enjoys hidden powers and status and high responsibility also, which can be interpreted as role extension. Similarly driver also realised that when they take manager or this family member to a doctor, a driver also establishes repo with the doctor, which work in emergency when he or his family members fall sick. In the context of the above case discussion and counselling session, it could be seen that important principle of (1) participative management (2) teamwork (3) principle of specific objectives (4) decision making (5) establishing interpersonnel relations, (6) building up organisational culture and climate are applied.

Questions

1. Which principles of team building are implemented in this case situation?
2. To what extent workers should be empowered to take decisions?

3. How does worker's attitude change regarding perception of their own role and responsibilities towards industry?
4. Do you feel this work culture can contribute to motivate lower level of employees to understand, shoulder the responsibility, and improve the performance at work? Comment.

6. PERFORMANCE APPRAISAL

Sukun Electronics Company Ltd. has been in telecom sector since 1980. It was established at Gurgaon industrial area phase I. It was established by one telecom engineer who worked for twenty years in Department of Telecom in Delhi. It was providing telecom services in different circles of DoT. The services provided by the company are basic telephones, multi-access rural radio system, optical fiber and mobile services. It recently has diversified its operations in Television and Computer manufacturing. The management was interested to recruit the suitable candidates on the basis of merit, work performance and high performance appraisal. The policy was prepared and communicated to the HR manager.

The recruitment for different levels started. In the beginning, for the new separate divisions, company employed the employees at lower and middle levels. Many applications were received for the post of senior commercial manager for computer division. But the management did not consider any candidate suitable for the position. One candidate was more qualified than required. He was appointed as Joint General Manager. Mr. Ram joined the company viewing that he would be considered for General Manager's post on the basis of his performance. Mr. Shyam, DGM in the company and one of the candidates for the post of General Manager did not like this. He expressed his grievances to the management. To handle this issue, Mr. Kapoor, General Manager of Telcom Division was made General Manager in-charge of computer division also for some time until a new manager was appointed. Mr. Kapoor was also interested in computer division because of prospects and prestige among top management. He considered this as an opportunity to prove his performance.

In this company different types of performance appraisal are being used. Performance of superiors is appraised by their subordinates. Keeping this in view, Mr. Shyam and Kapoor both wanted to down performance of Ram. Both were working in collaboration to pull down Mr. Ram. They wanted to win support of subordinates. Hence they promised better facilities and higher wages to subordinates. They played politics in the organisation and created many groups such as pro-Shyam, pro-Kapoor and anti-Ram. But Mr. Ram is very sincere, hard working and quite away from politics. Mr. Ram was keeping management well informed regarding this development. At the end of the year, the subordinates completed performance appraisal of superiors. They considered the factors like educational qualifications, behaviour, discipline, creativity and job attachment. In this performance appraisal, they assigned the following scores out of 100: Ram - 86, Shyam - 40, and Kapoor - 58

Questions

1. Is the performance appraisal done by subordinates correct? Argue.
2. What do you suggest to keep politics away from performance appraisal?
3. Is the approach of top management regarding the selection on the basis of this type of appraisal system genuine?
4. Being consultants of the company for selection of the right candidates for the different posts what would you suggest to the management to maintain better work environment in the company.

7. APPRAISAL AS A TECHNIQUE OF MOTIVATION

Seven Stars was a Hotel in Manali, Himachal Pradesh in north part of India. It is located in the outskirts of the city on state highway. The location of the hotel is very near to the tourist spots. Every day a large number of tourists were attracted every day. Especially during summer it was very difficult to manage them because there used to be a good rush. The management paid special attention to the requirements of the visitors. The feedback of the visitors was excellent in the past. To sustain the same performance in future the management planned to maintain the motivation of employees high so that they can give their best. Under performance management planning it was finalized to provide them incentives and promotion if higher performance is maintained consistently. The responsibility of performance assessment was given to Mr. Kapoor. He was a compensation manager of the hotel. He was a sincere and hardworking employee of the hotel He was to give the ratings out of 10 to each employee of the hotel so that they can be shifted to the higher cadre. An employee who scores more than 8 out 10 are eligible for these benefits.

Mr. Mehra who was the general mamager of the hotel, was not in a good mood as his relative Mr. Khanna was not rated more than 8 out 10. So he called upon a meeting of the head of the departments of the firm. Mr. Tandon (Front office manager), Mr. Patel (F&B manager), Mr. Singh (Housekeeping manager) together discussed the problem of Mr. Khanna, Mr. Tandon also raised a point to rate Mrs. Radhika (receptionist, who was with Human Resource Management of the hotel since last 7 year) higher in the firm and to raise her position as the supervisor of the Front office depertment. Mr. Mehra also agreed to this point. The head of the departments started interfering in appraisal system for their close employees. This created frustration among them to a good extent.

When actually the meeting started and Mr. Kapoor started giving the rates of the employees, Mr.Mehra interrupted him and raised the two points which Head of depertments discussed in their meeting. To this Mr. Kapoor said that the job evaluation should be on the basis of the performance of an employee and not on the basis of their relation with the head of department or the number of years of their association with the hotel. Mr. Mehra and Mr. Tandon felt insulted and they left the meeting. The other managers did not appreciate the move of these two persons. The matter was reported to Managing Director of the company. He called an urgent meeting of the all head of the departments and scolded them furiously. He was very much interested in maintaining the performance of the employees of the hotel. Without wasting a single day he ordered not to interfere in the appraisal done by Mr. Kapoor in future.

Questions

1. What is the problem of the case? Is it the genuine problem or not? Discuss.
2. Comment on the appraisal method of the employees done by manager in charge critically.
3. Was Mr. Mehra right in giving the rating? What action would you suggest against him if he is wrong in his approach?
4. If you would be in place of Mr. Kapoor how you would have handled the problem?

8. PROMOTION OF EMPLOYEES AND WORKING ENVIRONMENT

Eastern Telecom Ltd has been providing telecommunication service in eastern sector of India Head office of ETL is located in Shillong, Capital of Meghalaya state. This was established by Mr Saurav Chatterjee. It started with 10 employees and at present it has total 1250 employees on roll. Mr Chatterjee is very innovative in approach. He had discussion with a good number of consultants. He wanted to manage his company professionally. The company was facing very tough competition. Further the employees started preferring other competitors because the promotion given to the employees were very late. It was not giving motivation to the employees. Finally, the performance of employees and company was affected a lot. There was a trend in the market to hire talented, motivated and trained people for the jobs. The management highly recognized the importance of performance and productivity in profitability of the company.

Considering all the factors of the prevailing situation, a consulting firm providing consultation service in human resource area was hired to manage human resources of the company effectively and efficiently in 1999. The consulting firm conducted research study in the company. Data were collected from employees from different levels and records of the company. The research report was prepared and submitted to ETL. The consulting firm suggested a promotion policy for employees working at different levels in various departments. Main features of suggested promotion policy are:

(a) Every employee is entitled for promotion.

(b) Duration from one level to next higher level promotion is fixed, i. e., 3 years minimum.

(c) Criteria for promotion are merit, experience and annual confidential reports of last 3 years.

(d) Policy is to be communicated to everybody in advance.

(e) Promotion policy to be implemented without any favour or fear.

The recommended promotion policy was communicated to all employees. Within a period of two months, the first promotion list was prepared. 20 persons from different department were promoted. This action was objected by the employees. They lodged their complaints to the management. General Manager (HR) conducted counselling of these five persons. General Manager informed that the other persons were not considered due to their poor performance. They were suggested to improve their report in future so that their case might me considered in future. Since 2000, the company maintained good industrial relations and its net profit also increased rapidly. A very healthy working environment was prevailing in the company.

Questions

1. What do you say the approach of Mr. Chatterjee was proper? Discuss.
2. Do you find any loopholes in the promotion policy suggested by consulting firm?
3. How do you evaluate the impact of present policy for future of the company?
4. Mr. Chatterjee visualized the prevailing situation of the business and realized the importance of employees, performance and productivity for profitability of the company. Critically analyze this approach.

9. PROMOTION POLICY

E-Value serve limited is a Bangalore based software company which markets the IT products with a capacity of 1000 employees. The company follows a strict employee recruitment policy. The employee selected will be trainees with the company and after completion of their training they will be absorbed at the entry level managerial position. The company also follows the procedure that only the entry level recruitment would be done externally and while the high level position will be occupied by the internal employees through promotion and transfers. So the employees working with the company always had a chance to get promoted. All the employees have a mentioned stipulated period when the promotions are done. Only in case of urgency the company invited application externally for the high level positions.

In the year 2000, they needed an assistant manager (marketing) due to termination of the present one. So the company invited applications for the following position through newspapers and references of the present employees. There were 3 employers who were just promoted as assistant managers because of their performance. The job specification was that the candidate should have at least 1 years experience in marketing and preference will be given to the candidate who have marketed IT products with any organization. Mr. Robin Thomas who had just completed 2 years service in retail applied for the following position and got selected. He agreed with the job profile and joined the organization in 2000. Now as the company declared the promotion dates for the employees, he will be promoted as marketing manager in the year 2005 and the other 3 employees will be promoted in the same year but earlier than Mr. Robin.

Now in the year 2003 there came an urgency of the marketing manager due to sudden resignation. And the company decided to give advertisement in the newspaper to invite direct recruitment. The Job specification was mentioned as the candidate should have at least 5 years of experience in marketing. Mr. Robin also met the specification and also applied for the job. But he was not called out of the other applicants. As he had 2 years of experience earlier and he already completed 3 years with the company so he should be considered for the position. Looking to the following situation he applied through the proper channel. But his application was not accepted. He could not understand the logic behind that and he resigned from the job.

Questions

1. What is the problem in this case?
2. Is it right on the part of the company not to call Mr. Robin for the interview?
3. Is Robin's grievance genuine? If it was genuine then what can be the impacts on performance of employees in future?
4. As the Vice President (HR), how would you have handled this situation?

10. PROMOTION ADVERSELY AFFECTED BEHAVIOUR

Om Shanti Televenture ltd. is a call centre service providing company. Mr. Aushotosh is a B.Com., graduate from Gujarat University and had been working in the company for three years. Mr. Ashutosh was working quite well as a customer care executive. He was considered as a hardworking employee because of his good record as a customer care executive. This company was widely recognized for its reputation as the industry leader is providing good customer care service as a call center. Om Shanti Co., had a tie up with Tata Indicom for providing information to its customers. Mr. Ashutosh is respected not only in his department but also in company because of his nature. He is quite good in his work because of technical knowledge of companies of prepaid vouchers scheme. Because of his two years record company has decided to promote him as a floor manager.

After becoming the floor manger he thought that all the employees must have the knowledge of all companies scheme, and then he thought that he was superior to others. Sometimes, in past when there was any problem which couldn't be solved by the customer care executive, they asked Mr. Ashutosh. He didn't like it and shouted at them. So they did not like to ask him again. Mr. Ashutosh did not like even when he was asked by the new employee who does not know much about the company and his job. He even did not care about his employees break time means he did not give recess. This was not liked by the other employees and because of this some of them started to give up the job.

Because of this prevailing environment company started losing its trained employees. This increased the employee turnover. This created frustration among juniors and they lost interest in jobs. The level commitment from subordinates was very low. The objectives and required standards of the performance, quality of work and behaviour at work all were affected badly. At the end of the year it was disclosed that the profit of the company has gone down drastically. Due to this the Board of Directors was worried. It became very difficult to maintain good position in the market. A meeting was called to discuss how to handle the situation and come on the right track so that earlier position in the market can be achieved. A leading consultant was hired to look into this situation and suggest certain points for improvement.

Questions

1. Was the decision of promoting Mr. Ashutosh as floor manger right? Give reasons.
2. What advice would you like to give to Mr. Ashutosh in order to improve his behavior?
3. Should the Company terminate Mr. Ashutosh? Justify your Answer
4. In this case you are appointed consultant to handle the situation. Give suggestions to the management for improving the conditions.

11. HEALTHY WORKING ENVIRONMENT AND HIGHER PERFORMANCE

Deluxe Electrical Engineering Company started it operation in 1968 in vicinity of Bangalore city. It was manufacturing electric goods for homes and industry purposes. It collaborated with a company from western country. It was doing well in the beginning but slowly the problem started with the people due to HR orientation of the management. A new HR director was appointed and he made major changes in the policies. Some of the changes were not accepted by the managers and employees. Slowly the frustration took place among employees. They were not coming openly to express their frustration. It continued for a time and affected the attitude of people, interest in the work, productivity, and performance of the company and finally the profitability of the company as a whole.

Human Resource Planning and Recruitment procedure was such that people were selected from heterogeneous group. Managers, officers, technicians and engineers belonged to different religious and cultural background. Practically no two individuals belonged to one and the same city having common language, religion or culture. Ideology of the company was such that under such circumstances it would be difficult for the workers and staff members to form a union. They may not be able to discuss with each other anything pertaining to company's policy. Same ideology worked well in maintaining good industrial relations but it came in the way of building up a positive work culture. Workers could not share their feelings with each other. Managers and staff members were indifferent to each other. A group of engineers had problems with personal secretaries, stenographers, clerk and technicians. Major questions were pertaining to allocation of duties, distribution of work load, timing, shift system etc. By continued persuasion, interaction among members could take place.

The employees suggested that a meeting of all should be called so that the issues can be discussed in open atmosphere. Common meetings were arranged during tea time. People who could not meet each other were able to make friendship. They started inquiring about each other's personal well being. Problems of adjustment with work schedules were sorted out and discussed. Supervisors, technicians, middle management people and workers jointly distributed work load. Time schedule were fixed. Three hours group sessions were conducted every week for about one and a half years. During two years' time, counseling session were conducted on HRM practices of decision making, management of conflict, change of attitude, accommodating each other's view point etc. Small group were formed for discussing and sorting out problems pertaining to improving the quality of work and productive efficiency. Number of individuals (cases) and groups were identified for building up a work culture, organisational climate and meeting objectives of the organisation.

Absenteeism and turnover rate which was highest during 1994 to 1997 came down gradually in the years 1999 to 2000. Team building and positive work culture were brought slowly and gradually. Entire counseling process of HRM leads to establishing good interpersonal relationships through group interaction. Continuous counseling, calling meetings, celebrating social and religious festivals together, providing incentives in the form of birthday wishes, giving cards and gifts, wishes for marriage anniversaries and counseling on shocking and tragic events brought managers and others nearer to each other. A sense of belongingness, warm mutual trust and acceptance was created. Free medical checkup of staff members along with dependants was introduced by the company based on values and ethos of Indian environment, formal and in formal meetings were arranged with staff members, managers and workers. It was like quality circle of Japan colored with Indian social values.

During the course of third year end or so, tremendous changes were found in the attitude of managers and others. They started thinking positive regarding their job, responsibility and company. They started discussing every issue with openness, mutual understanding and interest, and with cooperation. Major disputes and grievances were resolved in the premises of the company. In this environment employees were having very good time with the managers and peers. Absenteeism and turnover rates were minimized continuously. It led to increased productivity. Committed and dedicated work force developed. Human Resource Management brought changes in the attitude of executives, managers, staff and workers. Company's objectives were realized slowly and gradually to a very good extend to the satisfaction of every one.

Questions

1. Critically analyse the situation of the case and which approach is better first or second to maintain healthy work environment from improving performance and productivity of employees and company as a whole. Discuss.
2. Discuss important factors for building good interpersonal skills have been used by the managers and employees of this company.
3. Was the approach of management for recruitment of employees so that the unionism should not take place proper? Argue.

4. It was opined by one of the leading consultant when he was contacted by the management that the steps taken by the employees are proper and need of the hour. It should be maintained. Do you agree with his opinion?

12. WORKERS INCENTIVES FOR INCREASING PERFORMANCE

Perfect Consumers Ltd a medium size of a manufacturing company in consumer goods. It is located at GIDC area Vapi, Gujarat. The owner selected this site due to various favorable factors such as availability of labours, raw material, climatic conditions, governmental supports and concessions. It started manufacturing in 1983 and first year sales turnover was only ₹ 5 lacs. Mr. Chetan Desai, the owner of the company was an entrepreneur with proper vision. He purchased new machines, searched for better row materials, improved relations with government machinery and other parties related to the business directly or indirectly. His sincere efforts paid him in return. Within a period of five years the sales turnover touched to ₹ 5 crore. From 1989 to 1997 the sales turnover increased marginally. It touched to ₹ 8 crore in 1997. Mr. Chetan Desai Was putting his sincere efforts but the production volume could not increase as per his exportation.

In April 1998, Mr. Desai and his son were invited by his relative in a function of the company of his relative. They attended the function and they were impressed by the way employees participated in the function and performed. Apex Consumers Ltd, company of their relative was also operating in consumers goods since 1988. In 1997 its sales turnover touched to ₹ 75 crore. The progress of the company clicked in mind of Junior Desai and he requested his father to visit Apex Company and see the working. At the plant they found that in absence of managers and supervisors the workers were working without wasting a single minute. Their involvement and interest in work wear of high degree. They were impressed by this. The issue was discussed by Mr. Desai with his brother-in-law with the objective to find out the reasons of commitment and cooperation of workers. Apex company management explained the reason of good performance. They pay salary plus incentives to those who give more than the target output. Mr. Desai too discussed with his son and implemented it in their company. It clicked and within one year the sales turnover reached to ₹ 20 crore.

Questions

1. How do you evaluate the approach of Mr. Chetan Desai before 1997? Discuss.
2. Comments on the approach of Apex company management in detail.
3. Do you feel the steps taken by Mr. Desai after visit to Apex was proper? Discuss.
4. Being consultant of the company what would you suggest to manage the performance of employees in future.

Chapter

Bibliography

1. Agarwal M.K., *Human Resource Development in Public Sector Undertakings,* Sarup & Sons, New Delhi, 1995.
2. Aguinis Herman, *Performance Management,* 2nd Edition, 2009 Pearson Edu, New Delhi.
3. Amarchand D. and Jayaraj B.J., *Corporate Culture and Organizational Effectiveness,* Business Press, 1992.
4. Arya P.P. and Gupta R.P., *Human Resource Management and Accounting,* Deep and Deep Publication Private Ltd., New Delhi, 1999.
5. Arya P.P. and Tandon B B., *Human Resource Development,* Third Edition, Deep & Deep Publication, New Delhi, 1998. -Human Resource Development pp 31-45.
6. Ashwathappa K., *Human Resource and Personnel Management, Text and Cases,* Second Edition, Tata McGraw-Hill Publishing Company Ltd., New Delhi, 1999.
7. Ashwathappa K, *Human Resource Management & Personnel Management,* IIIrd edition 2003, TMH, New Delhi.
8. Athalai B.N. : HRD : The state of the art in Indian Telephone Industries Ltd., *Indian Jr. of Training & Development,* 17(1),1987, P. 23-28.
9. Athreya. M.B, Rao., T.V., et al *"Integrated HRD Systems-Intervention Strategies",* (1988).
10. Aziz A., *Performance Appraisal: Accounting and Quantitative Approaches,* 1993, Pointer.
11. Basu Mihir K, *Managerial Performance Appraisal in India,* Vision Books Pvt. Ltd.
12. Bernardin H.J, Beatty R.W, *Performance Appraisal: Assessing Human Behavior at Work,* 1984, Kent Pub., Boston.
13. Bhatia S.K. and Nirmal Singh, *Principles and Techniques of Personnel Management/ Human Resource Management,* Second Edition, Deep & Deep Publication Private Ltd., New Delhi, 2000.

14. Bhatia S.K, *Performance Management: Concepts, Practices and Strategies for Organization Success,* 2007, Deep & Deep, New Delhi.
15. Bhattacharya D.K., *Human Resource Management,* Excel Books, New Delhi, 2002.
16. Billimoria R.P. & Singh N.K., *Human Resource Development, Vikas Publishing House Pvt.Ltd, New Delhi, 1985.*
17. Birkinshaw, J. (2000), *Entrepreneurship in the Global Firm,* London: Sage Publications,London.
18. *Boisot, M.H., Knowledge Assets,* Oxford University Press, New York, 1998.
19. Brian Towers, *Handbook of Human Resource Management,* Beacon Books, New Delhi, 1998.
20. *Brinkerhoff, R.O. (1987). Achieving Results From Training.* San Francisco: Jossey-Bass.
21. Brooking A., *Intellectual Capital, Core Assets for the Third Millennium Enterprise,* International Thompson Business Press, 1996.
22. Bukowitz and William, *The Knowledge Management Field Book,* Pearson Education, London.
23. Cardy, R.L. & Dobbins, *G.H. (1994) Performance Appraisal. Alternative Perspectives.* Cincinnati, OH: South-Western.
24. Cardy R.L., *Performance Management: Concepts, Skills and Exercises,* 1st Edition, 2008, PHI, New Delhi.
25. Carnevale, A.P., Gainer, L.J., & Villet, J. (1991). *Training in America: The organization and strategic role of training.* San Francisco: Jossey-Bass.
26. Cartin Thomas J., *Principles and Practices of Organizational Performance Excellence,* 1st Edition, 2004, PHI, New Delhi.
27. Charles Despres and Daniele Caubel, *Knowledge Horizon, Year 2001,* Butterworth Heinemann, New Delhi.
28. Chaturvedi Abha, (1987), *Achieving Harmonious Industrial Relations,* The Times Research Foundation, Pune.
29. Christopher B. and Graeme S., *Strategic Human Resource Management,* Beacon Books, New Delhi, 1998.
30. Cole G.A., *Personnel and Human Resource Management,* Fifth Edition, Book Power, London, 2002.
31. Dale Neef, *Knowledge Management and Organization Design,* Butterworth Heinemann Business Books.
32. Das Ratan, *Gandhi in Twenty-first Century,* New Delhi, Sarup, 2002.

33. David A.D. and Stephen P.R., *Personnel/Human Resource Management,* Third Edition, Prentice Hall of India, New Delhi.

34. Dayal Ishwar and others: *Successful Applications of HRD Case Studies of Indian Organizations,* New Concepts, New Delhi, 1996.

35. Dayal. I and Dayal. A.K. *(1983). Organizing for Management Concept,* New Delhi.

36. Derek Biddle and Robin Evenden, *Human Aspect of Management,* Jaico Publishing House, Mumbai, 2002.

37. Dasgupta P., The Welfare Economics of Knowledge Production, *Oxford Review of Economic Policy, 1998.*

38. Donald Cooper and Pamela Schindler, *Business Research Methods,* Sixth edition, Tata McGraw- Hill Publishing Company Limited, New Delhi, 1999.

39. Drucker P.F. *The Practice of Management,* 1954, Harper, New York.

40. Dudeja V.D., *Human Resource Management and Development in the New Millennium,* Commonwealth Publishers, New Delhi, 2000.

41. Dwivedi R.S., *Managing Human Resources: Personnel Management in Indian Enterprises,* Galgotia Publishing Co., New Delhi, 1997.

42. Dwivedi R S, *Managing Human Resource & Industrial Relations,* Reprint 2002, Galgotia Publishing Company, New Delhi.

43. Edwards, M.R., & Ewen, A.J. (1996). 360 degree feedback, New York, *American Management Association.*

44. Ferner, A. (1997), Country Of Origin Effect And Human Resource Management In Multi-national Companies, *Human Resource Management Journal, 1997.*

45. Fisher, Schoenfeldt and Shaw, *Human Resource Management,* Ist Edition 1997, All India Publishers and Distibutors, Chennai.

46. Fisher Martin, *Performance Appraisal,* 1995, Kogan Page.

47. Fleming Neil, *Coping With a Revolution: Will the Internet Change Learning,* Lincoln University, Centerbury, New Zealand.

48. Vroom V.H, *Work and Motivation,* 1964, Wiley, New York.

49. Gael, S. *(1988). The job analysis handbook for business, industry and government (Vol. 1 & 2)* New York: Wiley: Gatewood.

50. Gangadhara Rao, Surya Prakash Rao and Suba Rao, *Human Resource Management in Public Sector,* Himalaya Publishing House, Mumbai, 1991.

51. Gangal S.C, Gangal Anurg, *Contemporary Global Problems: A Gandhian Perspective,* Jammu, Vinod, 1995.

52. Gary Dessler, *Human Resource Management,* Prentice-Hall of India Pvt. Ltd., New Delhi, 2003.

53. Ghosh Biswanath, *Human Resources Development & Management,* Vikas.

54. Gilley, J.W., & Eggland, S.A. (1989). *Principles of human resource development.* Reading, MA: Addison-Wesley.

55. Goel Dewkar, *Performance Appraisal and Compensation Management: A Modern Approach,* 2nd Edition, 2008, PHI, New Delhi.

56. Grove, D.A., & Ostroff C., *Program evaluation.* In K.N. Wexley (ed.), Developing human resources. Washington, DC: BNA Books, (1991).

57. Glacier Project Papers. London: Hlenemann. Davts. L.E. and Cherns. A.B. (eds) (1975). *The Quality of Working Life (Vol. 1).* New York: Free Press.

58. Guest D. E. (1996), *Human Resource Management, Trade Unions and Industrial Relations,* International Thomson Press London.

59. Hartley, D.E. (1999) *Job analysis at the speed of reality.* Amherst, Mass: HRD Press.

60. Hartley, D.E. (2000). *On-demand learning: Traning in the new millennium.* Amherst, MAHRD Press.

61. Henderson Richard I, *Practical Guide to Performance Appraisal,* Reston Publishing Co. INC, USA.

62. Ian Beardwell and Len Holden, *Human Resource Management: A Contemporary perspective,* MacMillan India Ltd., 1998.

63. Jackson S.E, Schuler R.S, *Managing Human Resource Through Strategic Partnership,* 2003, Quebec, South Western.

64. Jacobs, R.L., & Jones, M.J. (1995). *Structured on-the-job training.* San Francisco. Berrett-Koehler, 19.

65. John Ivancevich, *Human Resource Management,* IIIrd Edition, TMH, New Delhi.

66. John Werner and David Harris, *Human Resources Development,* III edition, Thomson Southwestern Publication.

67. *Journal for Quality and Participation, Asian Strategy Leadership Institute Review,* Hewlett-Packard Executive Intelligence.

68. Kandula Srinavas, *Performance Management: Strategies, Interventions, Drivers,* 3rd Edition, 2009, Phi, New Delhi.

69. Kandula Srinivas R., *Human Resource Management & Organization Development,* ICFAI.

70. Kapoor S.K. and Punia B.K., *Organization Behaviour and Management,* SK Publisher, New Delhi, 1998.

71. Khandelwal A.K. (1988), *Human Resource Development in banks,* Oxford and IBH Publishing co., New Delhi.

72. Khandelwal A.K. (1985), Development Approach to Industrial Relations, *Business India* July1985.

73. Kumar G.V.V. *Performance Appraisals: A Comparative Study,* 1990, Discovery Pub. House.

74. Kuruvilla, S., (1996), *Economic Development and Industrial Relations: The Case of South and South-East Asia,* Industrial Relations Journal.

75. Landy Frank J, Farr James L, *The Measurement of work Performance Methods Theory and Applications,* Academic Press INC Ltd., London.

76. Lloyd L. Byars and Leslie W.R., *Human Resource Management,* Fifth Edition, Irwin Publication, Chicago, 1999.

77. Luis, David B. Balkin and Robert L. Cardy, *Managing Human Resource,* Prentice-Hall of India, New Delhi, 2002.

78. McGregor. D. *(1966). Leadership and Motivation.* Cambridge, Ma~ MIT Press.

79. Mager R.F., *HRD Training & Development,* Volume 5, Jaico Publishing House, Mumbai, 1999.

80. Mager R.F, Pipe P, *Analyzing Performance Problems,* 1984, Belmont, CA: lake.

81. Maheshwari & T.V. Rao: *Eds. Excellence through Human Resource Development: improving productivity and competitiveness.* Tata McGraw Hill Publishing Company Ltd., New Delhi, 1990.

82. Malhotra R.K., Nachhattar Singh and Sharma S.D., *Encyclopedia of Modern Management Series: Personnel Management,* Anmol Publications Pvt. Ltd., New Delhi, 1997.

83. Mamoria C.B. and Gankar S.V., *Personnel Management: Text & Cases,* 21st Edition, Himalaya Publishing House, Mumbai, 2001.

84. Mangaraj Sujata, *Human Resource Development Practices,* Himalaya Publishing House, Mumbai, 1999.

85. Margerison Charies, Macann Dick, *Team Management: Practical New Approaches,* 992,Viva Books.

86. McLagan, P. (1989). *Models of excellence: The conclusions and ecommendations of the ASTD training and development competency study.* Alexandria, Va: ASTD.

87. Mejia, Balkin and Cardy, *Managing Human Resources,* IIIrd Edition 2004, PHI,

88. Michael V.P., *Human Resource Management and Human Relations,* Himalaya Publishing House, Mumbai, 1996.

89. Mishra Anil Dutta, Singh Renu Kumari and Tiwari Sajeev Kumar, *Gandhian Alternatives to Contemporary Problems, Delhi, Abhijeet, 2004.*

90. Modi Bhupendra Kumar, *Performance: A Manager's Challenge,* 1996, TMH, New Delhi.

91. Monappa A. and Saiyuddin M.S., *Personnel Management,* Third Edition, Tata McGraw-Hill Publishing Company, New Delhi, 1996.

92. Murphy, K.R., & Cleveland, J.N., (1991). *Performance appraisal:* Allwyn and Bacon.

93. Nadler (Leonard) & Wiggs (Garland), *Managing Human Resource Development: A Practical Guide.* Jossey -Bass Publishers, San.

94. Nadler, L., & Nadler, Z. (1994). *Designing training programs: The critical events model* (2nd Ed.) Houston: Gulf Publishing.

95. Neale Frances, *Handbook of Performance,* 1995, Jaico.

96. Nair M.R.R. & Rao T.V., (Eds): *Excellence through Human Resource Development, Improving Productivity and Competitiveness, New Delhi,* Tata McGraw Hill publishing Company Ltd.

97. National HRD Network (1989). *"Towards Organizational Effectiveness."* Conference Papers.

98. Nirmal Singh and Bhatia S.K., *Industrial Relations and Collective Bargaining,* Deep and Deep publications Pvt. Ltd., New Delhi.

99. Pareek Udai and Sisodia V., *HRD in the New Millennium,* Tata McGraw-Hill Publishing Company Limited, New Delhi, 1999.

100. Pareek Udai, *Motivating Organization Roles (1987),* Rawat publication, Jaipur.

101. Pareek Udai, *Role effectiveness Exercise* (1974), Learning systems, New Delhi. 102. Pareek Udai, *Task Analysis for Human Resource Development, (1988),* California University Associated.

103. Parikh Udai and Rao T.V., *Designing and Managing Human Resource System,* III edition, Oxford and IBH Publication.

104. Parker Glenn, Kropp Richard P., *Team Building: A Sourcebook of Activities for Trainers,* 1999, Viva Books.

105. Pattanayak Biswajeet, *Human Resource Management,* Prentice Hall of India, New Delhi, 2002.

106. Pattanayak Biswajeet, *Human Resource Training,* Wheeler Publishing, New Delhi, 1998.

107. Peter Dowling, Denice Welch and Randall Schuler, *International Human Resource Management: Managing People in Multinational Context,* Southwestern Thomson Learning.

108. Phillips, J.J (1996). *Accountability in human resource management":* Houston: Gulf Publishing.

109. Pfeiffer William, *The Encyclopedia of Team Building: Activities,* 1996, Ben Johnston Pub.Co.

110. R.D. & Field, H. S. (2001). *Human resource selection* (5th edition). Fort Worth, TX: Harcout College Publishers.

111. Ramaswamy E. A., & Schiphorst F. B., (2000), Human Resource Management, Trade Unions and Empowerment: Two Cases from India, *International Journal of Human Resource Management.*

112. Rao, Chawla, *360 Degree Feedback & Assessment & Development Centres,* Excel Books.

113. Rao TV and Abraham, (1986), *HRD Climate in Indian organizations,* Oxford & IBH publishing company, New Delhi.

114. Rao T.V, *Appraising & Developing Managerial Performance,* 2nd Edition, 1999, Excel Books, New Delhi.

115. Rao V.S.P., *Human Resource Management Text and Cases,* Excel Books, New Delhi, 2000.

116. Rao T.V., HRD Audit: *Evaluating The Human Resource Functions For Business Improvement,* Response Books, New Delhi, 1999.

117. Rao T.V, *Performance Appraisal: Theory and Practice,* Vikas, Delhi.

118. Rao TV, *(1990) The HRD Missionary, The role and functions of HRD managers and HRD departments,* Oxford and IBH Publishing company New Delhi.

119. Rao TV, (1985), *Integrated Human Resource Development,* University Associate annual.

120. Rao T.V., Kuldeep Singh and Baburaj V. Nair, *Selected Readings in HRD,* Tata McGraw-Hill Publishing Co., New Delhi, 1996.

121. Rao T.V, K.K. Verma, A.K. Khandelwal and S.J. Abraham: *Alternative Approaches and Strategies of Human Resource Development,* Rawat Publication 1988, Jaipur.

122. Rao T.V. & D.F. Pereira, *Recent Experiences in Human Resources Development,* Oxford & IBH Publishing Company, New Delhi 1986.

123. Rao T.V, Parrek Udai, *Redesigning Performance Appraisal Systems,* 1996, TMH, New Delhi.

124. Ratnaja Gogula, *Knowledge Management A New Dawn, Year 2002,* ICFAI, Hyderabad.

125. Rawat. Brown. W. and Jaques. E., *Alternative Approaches and Strategies of Human Resources Management,* Jaipur. (1965).

126. Reddy W. Brendan, Jamison Kaleel, *Team Building: Blueprint for Productivity and Satisfaction,* 995, S.Chand, New Delhi.

127. Reddy B. Rathan, *Effective Human Resource Training and Development Strategy,* Himalaya Pub.

128. Reddy Sumati, *Training and Development,* ICFAI.

129. Robert Mager and Peter Pipe, *HRD Training & Development,* Jaico Publishing House, 1999.

130. Robert Cross and Sam Israelit, *Strategic Learning in a Knowledge Economy,* Butterworth Heinemann Business Books.

131. Rothwell, W.J., & Kazanas, H.C., *(1992). Mastering the instructional design process.* San Francisco: Jossey-Bass.

132. Rudrabasavaraj M.N., *Executive Development, (India and Abroad),* First Edition, Himalaya Publishing House, 2001.

133. Rudrabasavaraj M.N., *Dynamics of Personnel Administration,* Himalaya Publishing House, Bombay, 1998.

134. Rudrabasavaraj M.N., *Global Human Growth Model,* Millennium Edition, Himalaya Publishing House, Mumbai, 2000.

135. S.K. Goel, *Gandhian Perspective on Industrial Relations (A study of Textile Labour Association, Ahmedabad, 1918-48),* Delhi, Shipra, 2002.

136. Sahu R.K., *Performance Management System,* 1st Edition, 2007, Excel Books, New Delhi.

137. Sahu R.K., *Training for Development,* Excel Books.

138. Sarma A.M, *Performance Management System,* 1st Edition, 2008, Himalaya Pub, Mumbai.

139. Sivananthiran. A, Venkataratnum C. S., *Globalization and Labour Management Relations in South Asia, South Asian Multidisciplinary Advisory Team,* International Labour Organization, New Delhi, 1999.

140. Sharma A. M., *Personnel and Human Resource Managing,* Himalaya Publishing House, Mumbai, 1998.

141. Sharma V.K., *Human Resource Management,* Vikas Books Private Limited, New Delhi, 2002.

142. Shaikh A.M, *Human Resource Development and Management,* S.Chand

143. Shriram Nikam, *Destiny of Untouchables in India: Divergent Approaches and Strategies of Mahatma Gandhi and Dr. B. R. Ambedkar, 1998.*

144. Silvera D.M, *Human Resource Development: The Indian Experience* (2nd Ed), New Delhi, News India Publications, 1990.

145. Singh (AK) & Sen (AK): HRD Culture - A Model, *Mol Management Journal,* Vo1.5, 1st January, 1992, New Delhi. p. 113.

146. Sinha, Sinha and Shekhar, *Industrial Relations, Trade Unions and Labour Legislation,* PHI, New Delhi.

147. Sodhi, J. S. (1999), *Industrial Relations and Human Resource Management in Transition.* New Delhi: Shri Ram Centre for Industrial Relations and Human Resources.

148. Srivastava S.,(2003), What is the true level of FDI flows to India? *Economic and Political Weekly,* February 15.

149. Srivastava Dinesh K., *Strategies for Performance Management,* 1st Edition, 2005, Excel Books, New Delhi.

150. Suba Rao P., *Essentials of Human Resource Management and Industrial Relations (Text, Cases and Games),* Second Edition, Himalaya Publishing House, 1999.

151. Suri Ratanam & Gupta, *Performance Measurement and Management,* 1st Edition, 2004, Excel Books, New Delhi.

152. Terence Jackson, *International Human Resource Management a Cross Cultural Approach,* Sage Publication.

153. Tesoro, F, Tootson, J., (1978). *Training needs analysis: Review and critique.* Academy of Management Review.

154. Tesoro, F., & Tootson, J. (2000). *Implementing global performance measurement systems: A cookbook approach.* San Grancisco: Jossey-Bass/Pfeiffer.

155. Thomaskutty C.S., *Management Training and Development,* Himalaya Publishing House.

156. Towers B., *Human Resource Management: A manual,* Infinity Books, New Delhi, 2000.

157. Varghese Susan, *HRD Experience at Crompton Greaves (1986),* Oxford & IBH Publishing Company, New Delhi.

158. Venkat Ratnam and Srivastava B.K., *Personnel Management and Human Resource,* Tata McGraw-Hill Publishing Company, New Delhi, 1997.

159. Wayne Cascio, *Managing Human Resource,* Sixth Edition 2003, TMH, New Delhi.

160. Werner John and David Harris, *Human Resources Development,* III edition, Thomson Southwestern Publication.

161. Weiss Tracey B, Hartle Frankin, *Reengineering Performance Management,* 1998, St. Lucie Press.

162. Welboume T.M, Mejia Gomez L.R, *Optimizing Team Based Incentives,* 2000 MacGraw Hill, New York.

163. West Michael A., *Effective Teamwork,* 1996, Excel Books, New Delhi.